INTRODUCTION TO

# LAW AND LEGAL REASONING

(College Edition to Legal Methods, 2nd Edition)

*by*

JANE C. GINSBURG
Morton L. Janklow Professor
of Literary and Artistic Property Law
Columbia University

Illustrations by
Adine Kernberg Varah, Esq.

FOUNDATION PRESS

NEW YORK, NEW YORK

2003

THOMSON

WEST

COPYRIGHT © 2003 By FOUNDATION PRESS

        395 Hudson Street
        New York, NY 10014
        Phone Toll Free 1–877–888–1330
        Fax (212) 367–6799
        fdpress.com

Printed in the United States of America

**ISBN** 1–58778–562–5

 *TEXT IS PRINTED ON 10% POST CONSUMER RECYCLED PAPER*

. . . I was much troubled in spirit, in my first years upon the bench, to find how trackless was the ocean on which I had embarked. I sought for certainty. I was oppressed and disheartened when I found that the quest for it was futile. I was trying to reach land, the solid land of fixed and settled rules, the paradise of a justice that would declare itself by tokens plainer and more commanding than its pale and glimmering reflections in my own vacillating mind and conscience. I found ". . . that the real heaven was always beyond." As the years have gone by, I have become reconciled to the uncertainty, because I have grown to see that the process in its highest reaches is not discovery, but creation; and that the doubts and misgivings, the hopes and fears, are part of the travail of mind, the pangs of death and the pangs of birth, in which principles that have served their day expire, and new principles are born.

Benjamin Nathan Cardozo, *The Nature of the Judicial Process* 166 (1921)

To George
and Paul and Clara

*

# PREFACE

This course book serves an undergraduate course in introduction to law and legal reasoning. It is designed to initiate students in the legal methods of case law analysis and statutory interpretation. In a course of this kind, students should acquire or refine the techniques of close reading, analogizing, distinguishing, positing related fact patterns, and criticizing judicial and legislative exposition and logic. All of this is fairly standard to the first year, indeed, the first semester, of law school. I hope that college students learn from a course in legal methods not only familiarity with these new techniques, but sufficient mastery of them to avoid losing sight of the practical consequences of their implementation, especially should they later begin law studies in professional school.

This course book seeks to prompt students to take a critical distance from the wielding of the methods. In this way, one hopes, students should learn that "thinking like a lawyer" does not mean letting oneself be seduced by the artifice of enunciating and manipulating categories. Nor does it mean diligently and complacently working one's way through a text without stepping back to inquire whether the resulting interpretation makes any common sense.

This course book includes a comparative law dimension. In addition to materials on civil law, this book affords a glimpse of the variations among common law jurisdictions, including the U.K. and other Commonwealth countries. Just as common lawyers and civilians' methodologies often diverge, so the formulation of precept and argument by English judges can seem rather alien to Americans, despite our shared common law orientation. Americans should learn, from the outset, that our legal methods are neither the only, nor necessarily the best, ones. This text does not purport to provide systematic instruction in foreign law, however. Its aspiration is more modest, yet also more fundamental: by offering an occasional comparative law perspective, to challenge the insularity that too often characterizes American legal thought and practice. An appreciation of other common law approaches as well as of civil law systems is likely to become increasingly important to tomorrow's lawyers; the start of legal studies is as good a place as any to begin to promote that understanding.

A course and a text like these should constantly prompt the student to ask whether an analysis leads to outcomes the student would have approved before starting an introductory law course. One goal of a Legal Methods course is to push the student to go beyond stating a conclusion, to articulate and evaluate the steps and arguments leading to that conclusion. But if "thinking like a lawyer" may require students to think differently than before because it demands that they spell out their reasoning and justify their responses, it by no means demands that they believe in different goals or principles than before. Rather, they should be all the better equipped to advance the positions to which they subscribe.

Finally, the illustrations of Adine Kernberg Varah, Esq. enliven this book. Ms. Varah's unique depictions encapsulate a variety of concepts in legal methods with humor and striking acumen. I trust that readers will agree that her contributions have made this book both more thought provoking and more fun.

JANE C. GINSBURG

June 2003

# ACKNOWLEDGMENTS

As with the 1996 First Edition of this casebook, I continue to owe a great deal to the work of my Columbia Law School colleagues John M. Kernochan, Arthur Murphy, and the late Harry Jones, whose Legal Method:Cases and Text Materials, Copyright © 1980, The Foundation Press, Inc., liberally informs this casebook. I hope that they would find that this book respects and continues in their spirit.

The illustrations of Adine Kernberg Varah, Esq. (Columbia Law School JD '95) that enlivened the First Edition reappear in this edition, along with additional illustrations newly created for this edition. Ms. Varah's unique depictions encapsulate a variety of concepts in legal methods with humor and striking acumen. I trust that readers will agree that her contributions have made this book both more thought-provoking and more fun.

Olivia Radin and Cathleen Ellis, both Columbia Law School JD Class of 2004, made substantial and invaluable contributions to the Second Edition. I am also indebted for new or revised text notes to Professor Gary Bell of the National University of Singapore, and to Daniel Kalderimis (LLM Columbia 2004), Associate in Law, Columbia University.

Other Associates with whom I have worked over the years, and whose suggestions have consistently improved this book, deserve renewed thanks as well: Judith Smith (Columbia LLM 2003), Professor Jo Mossop of Victoria University, Wellington, N.Z.; Professor Andrew Perlman, Suffolk Law School; Professor Camille Nelson, St. Louis University; Professor Brad Wendell, Washington & Lee Law School; Professor Adele Blackett, McGill University, Montréal Canada; William Ryan, Esq. (Columbia JD '92, LLM 1997); Professor Donna Young, Albany Law School; Professor Lorne Sossin, Osgoode Hall Law School, Toronto Canada; Professor Celia Taylor, University of Denver College of Law.

I would also like to thank Prof. William Eskridge for instructive and amusing discussions of the new textualism.

From the First Edition, thanks also to my Columbia colleagues Richard Briffault, David Leebron and Peter Strauss, as well as to past research assistants: Judith Church, Esq. (Columbia JD '92); Ashima Dayal, Esq. (Columbia JD '96); Justine Harris, Esq. (Columbia JD '96); Suk Kim, Esq. (Columbia JD '94); Cristine Mesch-Sapers, Esq. (Columbia JD '95); Alison Wang, Esq. (Columbia JD '97); and David Zlotchew, Esq. (Columbia JD '96).

Special thanks for administrative support to Nick Giannou.

*

# SUMMARY OF CONTENTS

# TABLE OF CONTENTS

# TABLE OF CASES

Principal cases are in bold type. Non-principal cases are in roman type. References are to Pages.

*

INTRODUCTION TO

# LAW AND LEGAL REASONING

PART I

# GENERAL BACKGROUND[1]

**1.** Portions of this casebook are revised and adapted from Harry Jones, Arthur Murphy & John M. Kernochan, Legal Method: Cases and Text Materials (Foundation Press, 1980), used with permission of the authors and Foundation Press.

## A. CASE LAW

The common law does not work from pre-established truths of universal and inflexible validity to conclusions derived from them deductively. Its method is inductive, and it draws its generalizations from particulars.

Benjamin Nathan Cardozo, The Nature of the Judicial Process 22–23 (Yale Univ. Press. 1921).

## 1. ORIGINS, NATURE AND AUTHORITY

### a. HOW CASES MAKE LAW

The decisions of judges, or of other officials empowered by the constitution or laws of a political entity to hear and decide controversies, create case law. As the name "case law" suggests, a particular decision, or a collection of particular decisions, generate law—that is, rules of general application. How is it that a court's determination of the rights and obligations of the particular parties before it can apply to the disputes of persons who were not before the court? From the point of view of the parties to a lawsuit or other contested controversy, what matters is the immediate outcome, the result the tribunal reaches in their case. Suppose that A has sued B for damages for asserted breach of contract, and that the court has reached a decision in their case. For A and B, the decision has immediate, and specific, significance: B either will or will not have to pay a determined amount of damages to A. In the view of judges, lawyers, and law students, however, the decision takes on broader perspective. The decision becomes a possible source of generally applicable case law. In other words, the decision in A v. B becomes authority for determining subsequent controversies. Just as the court in A v. B will have sought guidance from prior, similar, decisions, so later judges and advocates will look to A v. B for a rule by which to measure later parties' conduct.

The wider authority of prior decisions in individual cases may not seem self-evident at first, but consider the opposite proposition. Suppose a society in which every disputed claim is heard and decided on its own individual merits, and with no regard whatever for consistency of the results from case to case. This society offers the means of settling disputes, but the society has no "case law." Each decision presents a result unto itself. Each decision is therefore unpredictable. Unpredictability in adjudication may provoke both instability in social relations, and the fear that little more than personal whim controls the judges' decisions. There is in fact, in most societies, a strong urge to make general law from particular decisions.

How are we to account for this widespread inclination to make general law from particular decisions? Karl N. Llewellyn, the leading spokesman for the group of legal philosophers known as the American Legal Realists, offered the following explanation:

> Case law in some form and to some extent is found wherever there is law. A mere series of decisions of individual cases does not of course in itself constitute a system of law. But in any judicial system rules of law arise sooner or later out of such decisions of cases, as rules of action arise out of the solution of practical problems, whether or not such formulations are desired, intended or consciously recognized. These generalizations contained in, or built upon, past decisions, when taken as normative for future disputes, create a legal system of precedent. Precedent, however, is operative before it is recognized. Toward its operation drive all those phases of human make-up which build habit in the individual and institutions in the group: laziness as to the reworking of a problem once solved; the time and energy saved by routine, especially under any pressure of business; the values of routine as a curb on arbitrariness and as a prop of weakness, inexperience and instability; the social values of predictability; the power of whatever exists to produce expectations and the power of expectations to become normative. The force of precedent in the law is heightened by an additional factor: that curious, almost universal, sense of justice which urges that all men are properly to be treated alike in like circumstances. As the social system varies we meet infinite variations as to what men or treatments or circumstances are to be classed as "like"; but the pressure to accept the views of the time and place remains.[2]

Students will become aware, as their study of law proceeds, that adherence to precedent has its other side. A court that follows precedents mechanically or too strictly will at times perpetuate legal rules and concepts that have outlived their usefulness. The continuing problem in a legal system that recognizes past decisions as authoritative sources of law for future cases is how to maintain an acceptable accommodation of the competing values of stability in the law, served by adherence to precedent, and responsiveness to social change, which may call for the abandonment of an outworn legal doctrine. This problem of stability *versus* change will be a recurring theme in this casebook.

b.  THE DISTINCT CONCEPTS OF LAW AND EQUITY

Historically in Anglo–American law, law and equity operated as distinct legal systems with separate procedures, causes, and remedies.[3] This system originated in the historical distribution of powers found in the King's Council after the Norman Conquest of England in 1066.[4] As one commentator recently summarized the history:

**2.** "Case Law," 3 Encyclopedia of the Social Sciences 249 (1930).

**3.** George L. Clark, Equity § 1 (New York ed. 1921).

**4.** 1 John Norton Pomeroy, A Treatise on Equity Jurisprudence §§ 31–36 (5th ed. 1941); see also, William F. Walsh, A Treatise on Equity § 2 (1930).

In the first hundred years after the conquest, central government in England was essentially the King in Council, and the Council embodied all of the functions of government: executive, legislative, and judicial. ...The King's Chancellor was probably the most important member of the Council, with a multitude of functions. ...The common law courts gradually emerged out of the Council and became fixed institutions sitting at Westminster. However, in those more fluid times, the Council and the King himself continued to receive petitions seeking justice. The Chancery Court [responsible for equity] had its beginnings in the practice of royal disposition of humble petitions for justice.[5]

The common law system was writ-based: Writs were issued and sealed by the Court of Chancery and directed the local sheriff to empanel a jury to find facts and deliver a verdict when the royal justices took the case.[6] Eventually, writs became limited in number and formulaic.[7] If the subject of the litigation did not fit an existing writ, it could not be brought before the royal courts. In such cases, litigants could petition the King and Council to intervene on behalf of justice.[8] The Chancellor acted as part of the Council in this process and eventually became sole recipient of such petitions.[9] The Chancellor assumed judicial powers during the fourteenth century[10] and acted under the direction of the Council until approximately the late fifteenth century, at which point equity jurisdiction became exclusively his.[11]

The Chancellor was originally an ecclesiastic figure who applied the law in accordance with good conscience, leading to the concept of equity as a discretionary tailoring of the law to reach equitable or just results.[12] "Equity," however, has come to be a term of art in law which has a meaning distinct from its colloquial meaning of fairness or fair share:[13]

> The term "equity" is an illustration of [the] proposition that some words have a legal meaning very unlike their ordinary one. In ordinary language "equity" means natural justice; but the beginner must get that idea out of his head when dealing with the system that the lawyers call equity. Originally, indeed, this system was inspired by ideas of natural justice, and that is why it acquired its name; but nowadays equity is no more (and no less) natural justice than the common law, and it is in fact nothing else than a particular branch of

---

**5.** Morton Gitelman, The Separation of Law and Equity and the Arkansas Chancery Courts: Historical Anomalies and Political Realities, 17 U. Ark. Little Rock L.J. 215, 216 (1995).

**6.** See, e.g., Walsh, supra note 4, at § 2; Gitelman, supra note 5, at 220.

**7.** Henry L. McClintock, Handbook of the Principles of Equity § 1 (2d ed. 1948); Walsh, supra note 4, at § 2.

**8.** McClintock, supra note 7, at § 1; Pomeroy, supra note 4, at §§ 11–12a.

**9.** Walsh, supra note 4, at §§ 2–3;

**10.** Id. at § 2.

**11.** McClintock, surpa note 7, at § 2; Gitelman, supra note 5, at 221.

**12.** See Clark, supra note 3, at § 1; Walsh, supra note 4, at § 3.

**13.** See McClintock, supra note 7, at § 25; 1 Joseph Story, Commentaries on Equity Jurisprudence § 3 (14th ed. 1918).

the law of England. Equity, therefore, is law. The student should not allow himself to be confused by the lawyer's habit of contrasting "law" and "equity," for in this context "law" is simply an abbreviation for the common law. Equity is law in the sense that it is part of the law of England; it is not law only in the sense that it is not part of the common law.[14]

Even given this meaning, equity is distinguished by its flexibility and is often referred to as discretionary.[15] As discussed above, however, a judge sitting in equity does not have unfettered power but applies equitable concepts within a well-defined system of such remedies.[16] According to one commentator:

> In Anglo–American law equity means the system of distinctive concepts, doctrines, rules, and remedies developed and applied by the court of Chancery in England and by American courts sitting in equity. In short, "equity" and "equitable" refer to the whole body of equitable precedent and practice.... [E]quitable relief was, and is, considered a matter of judicial discretion, not a matter of right. Thus, a party who sought equitable relief could not demand it as a matter of right simply upon a showing of specific facts that would fit the case into one for equitable relief. This is what commentators mean when they say that granting or denying equitable relief is within the discretion of the court. They do not mean that the court has the power to grant equitable relief in every type of case presented as the spirit moves the judge; rather, what they mean is that parties who have placed their case within the category of cases traditionally qualifying for equitable relief were not automatically entitled to it.... [P]arties who successfully made a case for equitable relief—showed that theirs was the type of case where equitable relief had been granted in past cases—still had to invoke the discretion of the court to grant such relief.[17]

Today, law and equity are merged in most jurisdictions in the United States, which means that judges can apply both legal and equitable remedies to controversies given the controlling case and statutory law.[18] Legal remedies involve damages for past wrongs.[19] Equitable remedies include preventive injunctive relief and other non-compensatory forms of relief such as specific performance (where the defendant is ordered to perform her obligations under a contract rather than pay monetary damages for her default).[20] Restitutional remedies form a second category of equitable

---

**14.** Glanville Williams, Learning the Law 25–26 (11th ed. 1982), reproduced in Black's Law Dictionary (Bryan A. Garner ed., 7th ed. 1999).

**15.** See Story, supra note 13, at § 28.

**16.** See C. C. Langdell, A Brief Survey of Equity Jurisdiction 1 (1908) ("Equity jurisdiction is a branch of the law of remedies[.]").

**17.** Kevin C. Kennedy, Equitable Remedies and Principled Discretion: The Michigan Experience, 74 U. Det. Mercy L. Rev 609, 610, 613–14 (1997).

**18.** Only Arkansas, Delaware, Mississippi, and Tennessee maintain separate courts of law and equity. Gitelman, supra note5, at 244.

**19.** Story, supra note 13, at § 30.

**20.** Id.

remedies. Courts order restitution to prevent unjust enrichment by causing the defendant to return to the plaintiff items or amounts unjustly taken.

Furthermore, "legal" claims (formerly called "actions at law") carry with them the right to a jury trial whereas "equitable" claims (formerly called "bills in equity") do not. As one judge has written: "In civil matters before the district court...the distinction between law and equity is now limited to the type of remedy imposed and the parties' right to a jury trial."[21]

As you read cases that refer to "equity," keep in mind the historical basis for the distinction between law and equity, the types of remedies that law and equity afford, and the constraints on judicial discretion that apply.

## c.  THE COMMON LAW DOCTRINE OF PRECEDENT

Professor Llewellyn was undoubtedly right in his contention that case law can be found "in some form and to some extent" in every legal system. But case law is uniquely authoritative and influential in a "common law country," which the United States is by inheritance from England. The Anglo–American legal system, unlike the "civil law" system which prevails with variations in most of the other non-Commonwealth countries of the world, explicitly recognizes the doctrine of precedent, known also as the principle of *stare decisis*. It is the distinctive policy of a "common law" legal system that past judicial decisions are formally and "generally binding"[22] for the disposition of factually similar present controversies. This basic principle, firmly established centuries ago in the royal courts of England, was naturalized as American by the "reception" of the common law in the United States.

When, and for what future cases, will a judicial decision or group of decisions operate as precedent? The term "precedent" is a crucially important term of art in the vocabulary of our law. Let us note, first, a kind of territorial limitation: a judicial decision is a precedent in the full sense of the word only within the same judicial system or "jurisdiction." Thus a decision of the Supreme Court of California is a precedent and so generally binding in future "like" cases in that court and in "lower" California courts, but it is not a full-fledged precedent for future cases arising in the courts of Ohio or Vermont or some other state. Even a decision of the Supreme Court of the United States is not a binding precedent in a state court, say the Court of Appeals of New York, unless the legal issue decided

---

**21.**  Leandra Lederman, Equity and the Article I Court: Is the Tax Court's Exercise of Equitable Powers Constitutional?, 5 Fl. Tx. Rev. 357, 373 (2001) (quoting The Honorable Marcia S. Krieger, "The Bankruptcy Court is a Court of Equity": What Does That Mean? 50 S.C. L. Rev. 275, 281 (1999)).

**22.**  "Generally" binding is an imprecise but unavoidable way of saying that a court will follow precedent almost all the time, and

except when it is persuaded, in unusual and quite undefinable circumstances, that the precedent is too unsound or socially unjust to be adhered to. For a long time in England, precedents were taken to be absolutely binding, but that rigid notion never caught on in American courts and, since 1966, has been on the way out in England. See Part II.B.2 "Overruling," infra.

by the Supreme Court decision was a federal question, that is, one involving the interpretation or effect of a federal statute or regulation or of the Constitution of the United States. The possible influence of a judicial decision on future cases arising in other jurisdictions will be considered in Part II; it is sufficient to note now that a decision has the full status and effect of precedent only on the deciding court's home grounds.

A second restriction on what is and is not "precedent" in the full and technical sense has already been suggested, perhaps, by our discussion so far. Even within the same jurisdiction, a decision is precedent only for "like," that is, factually similar, future cases. To put the matter more precisely, a judicial decision is a precedent, and so generally binding, only in future cases involving the *same material facts*. As the first-year law student will soon discover, this limitation is far easier to state in general terms than to apply in concrete situations. No two disputes will ever be identical in every factual particular. How is one to determine, or argue, that a factual difference between a past decided case and a case now presented for decision is, or is not, a difference in *material* facts? Case law processes require careful analysis, matching and distinguishing of the facts of cases. This is one of the distinctive arts of the common or case lawyer and will be explored in depth in Part II of this casebook. By the end of the first semester, the beginning law student will find that case matching and comparison has become a matter of second nature.

Even when the jurisdiction is the same and the pending new case is found to possess the same material facts, some judicial decisions will have greater weight as precedent than others. Thus, for example, the weight or influence of a precedent is greatly affected by the place of the court that decided it in the judicial hierarchy of its jurisdiction, that is, by whether it was a "higher court" decision or a "lower court" decision. Three tiers of courts exist in the federal judicial structure and in the more populous states: (1) trial courts, (2) intermediate appellate courts, and (3) a highest appellate court or "court of last resort," called in most jurisdictions the Supreme Court. Less populous states are likely to have only two tiers in their judicial structures: trial courts and an appellate court of last resort. The American state court systems and federal court system are described in some detail at pages 11–20 of this casebook. One should not assign the same force as precedent to the decision of a state intermediate appellate court as to a decision of that state's court of last resort, and should not expect a decision of a United States Court of Appeals to have the same precedent force as a decision of the Supreme Court of the United States. As to the decisions of the trial courts, particularly State trial courts, where most of law's day-to-day business is done, these are rarely published and, even when published, are not likely to have much force as precedent except in future cases in the same trial court. As a result, the overwhelming majority of the cases included in this and most other law school casebooks are decisions of appellate courts.

As you will see later in the course, the definition of precedent remains open to debate and has engendered a fierce controversy within the federal bench and among commentators and public advocacy groups. See section II.A.3 for further discussion.

## d. "RES JUDICATA" AND "STARE DECISIS"; "REVERSAL" AND "OVERRULING"

Every final decision of an appellate court has a dual impact or effect: (1) as an authoritative settlement of the particular controversy then before the court; and (2) as a precedent, or potential precedent, for future cases. A lawyers' Latin expression denominates each of these effects: *stare decisis,* as we have seen, for the impact of the decision as precedent; *res judicata* for its effect as a resolution of the immediate controversy. Do not confuse these Latin terms and the concepts they symbolize. The latter addresses a decision's impact in the individual case; the former, its impact on the legal norm of conduct.

The following example should illuminate the difference. Suppose that P (plaintiff) sues D (defendant) advertiser in State X, for using P's photograph without his permission in an advertisement for breakfast cereal. The trial court decides in D's favor, on the ground that in State X, there is no claim against the non consensual use of private citizens' photographs for purposes of trade, nor have the courts there recognized a "right of privacy." The Supreme Court of X, the court of last resort in that state, affirms the judgment. This decision is a final and conclusive settlement of the controversy between P and D: The case is now *res judicata,* and the losing party, P, cannot bring this claim again.

Now, to make plain the difference between *res judicata* and *stare decisis* as legal terms of art, suppose further that the Supreme Court of X, ten years later, and in another case involving the non consensual use of a private citizen's photograph for purposes of trade, is persuaded that its refusal to recognize a right of privacy in this context is not a sound legal doctrine for present-day conditions, and so "overrules" P v. D, thus finding against the advertiser in the new case. Although this overruling decision is a deviation from the norm of *stare decisis,* U.S. courts of last resort have never regarded precedents as absolutely binding—only as "generally" binding—and have reserved to themselves a largely undefined authority to overrule even clear precedents when considerations of public policy require a change in the case law. (The problem of overruling is the subject of a subsequent section of this casebook, see Part II.B.2, infra.)

What, however, of the particular claim of P v D? Now that the Supreme Court of X has changed the law, and "overruled" the decision reached in P's case ten years earlier, should not P be able to bring his suit again, and prevail in his claim? The answer is clear, and adverse to P. His particular claim has been finally and conclusively settled against him; the doctrine of *res judicata* bars P from ever suing on that claim again.[23] As a

---

**23.** By "that claim," it is important to understand, "on those facts, when they occurred." The Supreme Court of X's overrul- ing of P v. D would entitle P to bring a new claim against D in the event that, *after* the Supreme Court's decision, D were again to

result, the final decision of a court of last resort can be more conclusive and permanent in its aspect as a settlement of a particular case (*res judicata*) than it may be in its aspect as general law for the future (*stare decisis*).

It is important here to underscore one other distinction in legal terminology: between "overruling" and "reversal." In the later privacy case, the Supreme Court of X "overruled" its decision in P v. D. The Supreme Court of X did *not* "reverse" P v. D. The two notions are distinct, and carry different consequences. They are not interchangeable. The highest court of the jurisdiction "overrules" its own precedent. The prior decision continues to bind the parties to it, but the overruled decision is no longer authoritative as to subsequent controversies. By contrast, a higher court "reverses" the decision of a lower court. When a higher court "reverses" a decision, it reviews the lower court's judgment, and concludes that the lower court has reached an erroneous result (on the facts or on the law) in that case. As a result, the lower court's judgment is set aside and is no longer effective as to the parties to that controversy.

### e.  A NOTE ON RESTATEMENTS

As the common law of the various U.S. States became increasingly complex, its "rules" were becoming more uncertain and thus harder to discern. Many believed that orderly "restatements" of the law were necessary to improve and clarify the work of legislators, judges, lawyers and academics. One effort to systematize or organize the law in a variety of common law subjects—such as Agency, Conflict of Laws, Contracts, Judgments, Property, Restitution, Security, Torts, and Trusts—has taken the form of Restatements of the law published by the American Law Institute (ALI). ALI was organized in 1923 following a study by a group of prominent law professors, practicing attorneys and judges known as "The Committee on the Establishment of a Permanent Organization for the Improvement of the Law." The Committee had reported that the two chief defects in American law, its uncertainty and its complexity, had produced a "general dissatisfaction with the administration of justice."[24] William Draper Lewis outlined the Restatement's original objectives in 1937:

> The object of the [American Law] Institute in preparing the Restatement is to present an orderly statement of the general common law of the United States. . . . The object of the Institute is accomplished in so far as the legal profession accepts the restatement as *prima facie* a correct statement of the general law of the United States.

Introduction to *Restatement of Restitution* at ix. (1937).

The incorporators of ALI included Chief Justice and former President William Howard Taft, future Chief Justice Charles Evans Hughes, and former Secretary of State Elihu Root. Judges Benjamin N. Cardozo and

---

use P's photograph in an advertisement without P's permission.

**24.** Am. Law Inst., About the American Law Institute, *available at* www.ali.org/ali/thisali.htm.

Learned Hand were among its early leaders.[25] While not intended to be enacted as a statute by legislatures, Restatements do assist state and federal courts in determining patterns of prior judicial decisions in the common law. In this way, they have been largely successful in addressing the uncertainty and complexity of the common law. As one judge recently noted, "[ALI's] monumental first Restatements, pronouncing on the fundamental principles of the common law, have greatly influenced the advancement and unification of legal principles in this country. Revisions of the initial Restatements have permitted the Institute to reassess stated principles and to recognize developing concepts."[26] It is important to note, however, that a particular Restatement provision does not have the force of law until it is adopted as an authoritative statement by courts deciding cases.

## E. Allen Farnsworth and William F. Young, Selections For Contracts: Statutes, Restatement Second, Forms, 93–95 (1992) (excerpt).

As originally conceived, the first Restatement was to be accompanied by treatises citing and discussing case authority, but experience proved that group production of such volumes was not feasible. As they stand, the Restatements consist of sections stating rules or principles (the so-called black letter), each followed by one or more comments with illustrations, and in the Restatement Second also by Reporters' Notes in which supporting authorities are collected.... An eminent critic of the Restatement of Contracts immediately questioned the value of "black-letter Principles" not supported by discussion and analysis. "The Institute," he wrote, "seems constantly to be seeking the force of a statute without statutory enactment." Clark, The Restatement of the Law of Contracts, 42 Yale L.J. 643, 654 (1933).... As courts and scholars began to deploy the rules, they gained in concreteness and resonance. The process of supplementation has been gradual, and will doubtless continue to be so.... On occasion a legislature has given statutory backing to one or more provision of the Restatement. For example, in dealing with a problem of tort law (products liability), the Oregon legislature referred to certain comments in the Restatement Second of that subject, and declared: "It is the intent of the Legislative Assembly that the rule stated in [part of the statute] shall be construed in accordance with" those comments. But the directive force of Restatement language is generally not so great. To what measure of authority is the Restatement entitled, then, in the courts?

This general question can have only a general answer. The Supreme Court of Oregon has emphasized the difference between statutory and Restatement texts:

**25.** Ibid.

**26.** Herbert P. Wilkins, Foreword, *Symposium on the American Law Institute:* *Process, Partisanship, and the Restatements of Law*, 26 Hofstra L. Rev. 567 (1998).

Although this court frequently quotes sections of the Restatements of the American Law Institute, it does not literally "adopt" them in the manner of a legislature enacting, for instance, a draft prepared by the Commissioners on Uniform State laws, such as the Residential Landlord and Tenant Act. In the nature of common law, such quotations in opinions are no more than shorthand expressions of the court's view that the analysis summarized in the Restatement corresponds to Oregon law applicable to the facts of the case before the court. They do not enact the exact phrasing of the Restatement rule, complete with comments, illustrations, and caveats. Such quotations should not be relied on in briefs as if they committed this court or lower courts to track every detail of the Restatement analysis in other cases. The Restatements themselves purport to be just that, "restatements" of law found in other sources, although at times they candidly report that the law is in flux and offer a formula preferred on policy grounds.

Brewer v. Erwin, 600 P.2d 398, 410 n. 12 (Or.1979).

## 2.   THE JUDICIAL HIERARCHY

As discussed above, precedent operates to bind subordinate courts within the superior court's jurisdiction. Thus a decision by the court of last resort in one state is binding on all courts within that state but not binding on any court in any other state. (The reasoning of a court regarding a new issue, however, may be useful for courts in other jurisdictions when they are considering the same issue for the first time and is called "persuasive authority.") A decision by the Supreme Court of the United States is binding on all other courts as to constitutional and other federal questions. A State's highest court (and not the U.S. Supreme Court) has the last word on issues of that state's law.

Because of the important influence of outstate decisions as persuasive authority in American law, law school casebooks, other than those on Constitutional Law and other federal law subjects, usually include cases drawn from many jurisdictions. You will find that American appellate courts exhibit a marked degree of mutual respect for each other's decisions. Some decisions will have greater influence than others on the thinking of judges in other states. The prestige of the court that rendered the decision, or the prestige of the particular judge (e.g., Cardozo) who wrote the opinion of the court, may also affect the persuasiveness of the decision to the courts of other jurisdictions.

Thus, the hierarchical structure of the U.S. court system, set out below, has fundamental implications for the degree of authority that precedent commands. To appreciate the scope of a prior decision's authority, it is therefore very important to understand the placement of a court within the judicial hierarchy. The interaction between Federal and State courts will be discussed in greater detail in other courses you take. For the purposes of this discussion, it suffices to note briefly that principles of federalism (which you will study in your Constitutional Law, Civil Procedure, and other courses) determine the domains of these interacting legal systems.

## a.  THE FEDERAL COURTS

There was no regular federal judiciary under the Articles of Confederation. In the 22nd Federalist, Alexander Hamilton described this "want of a judiciary power" as "a circumstance which crowns the defects of the confederation," for, he continued, "Laws are a dead letter without courts to expound them and define their true meaning and operation."

Hamilton's views on this issue are an accurate report of the consensus arrived at, with surprisingly little debate or discussion, when the delegates to the Constitutional Convention had assembled in Philadelphia in May, 1785. Max Farrand, author of the classic study of the Convention, concluded simply: "That there should be a national judiciary was readily accepted by all." As the Convention proceeded, there were lively disagreements over methods for the selection of federal judges and over the categories of cases to which the federal judicial power was to extend, but the necessity of a federal judiciary—at least of a national Supreme Court as ultimate arbiter of foreseen disputes between states or between a state and the new national government—was universally recognized.

Article III of the Constitution reflects this consensus:

Article III. Section 1. The judicial Power of the United States shall be vested in one supreme Court and in such inferior Courts as the Congress may from time to time ordain and establish.

The Supreme Court is the only federal court directly created by the Constitution itself. The other courts in the federal judicial system are created by Acts of Congress enacted pursuant to Article III. The landmark statute in the evolution of the federal judicial system was passed by the first Congress as one of its early orders of business and became law on September 24, 1789. This statute, entitled "An Act to establish the Judicial Courts of the United States," embodied the first Congress's decision on the issue that the Constitution itself had not resolved: whether there should be federal *trial* courts as well as a Supreme Court or whether the interpretation and enforcement of federal law should be left entirely to the existing state trial and appellate courts, subject to review by the Supreme Court of the United States. The organization of the federal judiciary has greatly changed over the years since 1789, but the decision of the first Congress to establish a federal judicial system, of trial as well as appellate courts, set the course for the national judicial future.

The basic federal court system as it now exists is a three-tier hierarchy: (1) trial courts of general jurisdiction, known as the *District Courts;* (2) intermediate appellate courts, called the *Courts of Appeals;* and (3) the *Supreme Court,* specifically provided for by Article III of the Constitution and operating as the court of last resort for the federal judicial system and, in matters of federal law, for the state judicial systems as well. There are also a few specialized federal courts (e.g., the Claims Court, the Bankruptcy

Court, or the Tax Court), which operate more or less like District Courts in their specialized jurisdiction, as well as the Court of Appeals for the Federal Circuit, whose jurisdiction includes exclusive authority over patent appeals.

### The Thirteen Federal Judicial Circuits

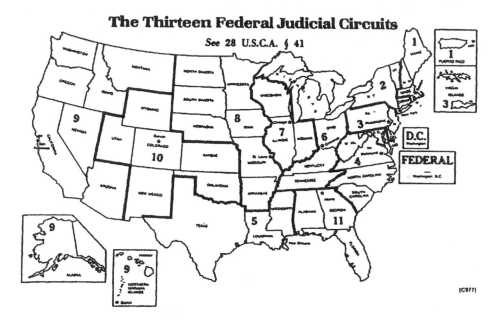

See 28 U.S.C.A. § 41

#### i. The District Courts of the United States

By existing Congressional legislation, the United States is divided into 91 federal judicial districts,[27] each with its District Court. Every state has at least one District Court; about half the states have only one, e.g., the United States District Court for Nevada. There is one District Court for the District of Columbia and one for Puerto Rico.

The more populous states have been divided into two, three or four districts. In New York, for example, there are four United States District Courts, one each for the Southern, the Northern, the Eastern and the Western District. There are now about 665 federal district judges, distributed more or less according to the differing volume of judicial business in the 91 districts. Thus, there are now 62 judges for the Southern District of New York (including 14 magistrate judges[28]) and 52 for the Central District of

---

**27.** This includes the District of Columbia and Puerto Rico, but does not include the District Courts of the Virgin Islands, Guam, and the Northern Mariana Islands, which for some purposes are treated as District Courts of the United States.

**28.** A United States Magistrate Judge is a federal trial judge appointed to serve in a United States district court for a term of eight years. He or she is appointed by the life-tenured federal judges of a district court, District Judges, who supervise the activities of the Magistrate Judges by assigning civil cases for jury or non-jury trial upon consent of the parties and for pre-trial matters. Similarly criminal cases are assigned to Magistrate Judges on the consent of the parties, except for the trial of felony cases. In 2002, there were 471 full-time Magistrate Judge positions authorized, enabling the courts to

California (including 19 magistrate judges), as against 4 for the Western District of Wisconsin (including 2 magistrate judges) and 10 for the District of Wyoming (including 7 magistrate judges).[29] Trials in a District Court are normally presided over by a single judge, although there are a few situations, such as cases challenging the constitutionality of the apportionment of congressional districts or statewide legislative bodies or when injunctions are sought on federal constitutional grounds against the enforcement of state or federal statutes, in which a three-judge panel must be convened.[30]

Although they correspond in essential function to the state trial courts of general jurisdiction, there is a sense in which the jurisdiction of the District Courts of the United States is a limited one: They, like other federal courts, cannot entertain cases that fall outside the "judicial power of the United States" as defined in the Constitution. Article III, Section 2 of the Constitution is the controlling text and sets the outer bounds beyond which the federal courts cannot exercise, or be vested by Congress with, jurisdiction. Article III, Section 2 provides, in pertinent part, as follows:

> The judicial power [of the United States] shall extend to all cases, in law and equity, arising under this Constitution, the laws of the United States, and treaties made, or which shall be made, under their authority;—to all cases affecting ambassadors, other public ministers and consuls;—to all cases of admiralty and maritime jurisdiction;—to controversies to which the United States shall be a party;—to controversies between two or more States;—between a State and citizens of another State;—between citizens of different States,—between citizens of the same State claiming lands under grants of different States, and between a State, or the citizens thereof, and foreign States, citizens or subjects.

As a result, the jurisdiction of a District Court of the United States must be based either on the *character of the controversy* (for example, that it is a case "arising under this Constitution [or] the laws of the United States") or on the *character of the parties to the controversy* (for example, that it is a controversy "to which the United States shall be a party" or one "between citizens of different States").

Most of the cases which make up the workload of the District Courts are within one or another of three categories: (1) cases to which the United States is a party, which includes both civil cases in which the United States is plaintiff or defendant and all prosecutions for violation of federal criminal statutes; (2) cases involving a "federal question," which means a question involving the interpretation or effect of a provision of the Constitution or of a federal statute or regulation; and (3) cases involving "diversity of citizenship," that is, suits between citizens of different states of the

---

manage increasing caseloads with limited resources. http://www.fedjudge.org.

**29.** Catherine A. Kitchell, *BNA's Directory of State and Federal Courts, Judges and Clerks* (2003 edition).

**30.** See 28 U.S.C. 2284.

United States. For the purposes of this "diversity" jurisdiction, a corporation is deemed to be a "citizen" both of the state in which it is incorporated and of the state in which it has its principal place of business.

Existing federal legislation imposes a further limitation on District Court jurisdiction in some "federal question" and all "diversity of citizenship" cases: The "matter in controversy must exceed $75,000." A case within federal jurisdiction—for example, a controversy between citizens of different states and involving more than $75,000—may, as a matter of "venue," be brought in a district in which either the plaintiff or the defendant resides. If the plaintiff in such a case chooses, as he may, to file his suit not in a federal District Court but in a state trial court, the defendant may in certain circumstances have the case "removed" to the federal court for the same district, where it will then be heard and decided. Note, however, that a "diversity of citizenship" case cannot be removed by the defendant if brought in a state court of the state in which the defendant himself resides, but a "federal question" claim can be removed regardless of the parties' citizenship. The historical origins of "diversity of citizenship" jurisdiction derive from a concern of former times that a citizen of one state might not be fairly treated in the courts of the state of his adversary's residence, and even this old concern is inapplicable when the defendant is, so to speak, sued on his own home grounds.

Whenever you encounter a federal court decision in this Legal Methods casebook, or for that matter in any casebook or case reporter, ask yourself why this case is within federal court jurisdiction; i.e., is it based on the nature of the parties, a "diversity of citizenship" case, or does it "arise under" federal law?

Procedure in the District Courts is uniform throughout the United States and takes no account of the differences in court procedures that exist from state to state. In 1934, Congress empowered the Supreme Court to prescribe uniform Rules of Civil Procedure applicable both to "actions at law" and "cases in equity" in District Courts throughout the country. The uniform rules, commonly referred to as the "Federal Rules" were promulgated by the Supreme Court and have been in effect, albeit occasionally amended, since 1938. The most recent amendments to the rules were effective as of December of 2002.

## *ii. Courts of Appeals of the United States*

Existing federal legislation further divides the United States into judicial circuits, each with its own Court of Appeals[31]Appeals lie as a matter of right to each Court of Appeals from the District Courts located within the geographical area comprised by its circuit. There are now thirteen judicial circuits. One of the additions—the eleventh circuit—was created by splitting off Alabama, Florida and Georgia from the old fifth circuit. The

---

**31.** In older case reports, the student will find the federal intermediate appellate courts referred to as the "Circuit Courts of Appeals." The accurate usage now is simply "Courts of Appeals"; e.g., United States Court Appeals, Second Circuit.

other relatively new circuit, the Federal Circuit, differs from the others in that its jurisdiction is defined in terms of subject matter rather than geography. It was created in 1982 and inherited the appellate jurisdiction of the old Court of Claims and the Court of Customs and Patent Appeals. The number of circuit judges for each Court of Appeals varies similarly—and, in fact, corresponds considerably more closely than existing circuit boundaries do to contemporary Court of Appeals workloads. Thus there are presently 28 Circuit Judges for the vast Ninth Circuit, and only 6 for the First Circuit. See 28 U.S.C. 44(a).

Federal appeals in both civil and criminal cases are heard by panels of three judges, although, on very rare occasions, the full complement of circuit judges may sit "en banc" to hear and decide a case of particular difficulty or importance. Normally the three judges who participate in a federal appeal are all circuit judges, but Congressional legislation authorizes the summoning of district judges to sit temporarily "by designation" in the Courts of Appeals when pressure of appellate business requires. In recent years, as the volume of federal appellate litigation continues to mount, it has become quite common to have federal appeals heard and decided by a Court of Appeals consisting of two circuit judges and one district judge.

### iii.   The Supreme Court of the United States

The most important point to grasp and remember about the functioning of the Supreme Court as the court of last resort of the federal system is that only a small fraction of the controversies in which Supreme Court review is sought is ever accepted by the Supreme Court for hearing and decision "on the merits." In recent Terms, the Supreme Court has heard fewer than one hundred cases a year. By contrast, in 2001 the U.S. Court of Appeals for the Second Circuit decided almost 4,000 appeals. A disappointed litigant cannot secure Supreme Court review merely by contending, however persuasively, that the decision handed down against her was wrong; she must first persuade the Supreme Court that the issues presented by her case are important enough, as issues of general federal law, to justify Supreme Court consideration. In almost all cases, review by the Supreme Court of federal and state appellate court judgments can be secured only by a "petition for a writ of certiorari," which the Supreme Court, in the exercise of the broad discretion conferred upon it by Acts of Congress, may grant or deny. As a matter of Supreme Court practice, if four or more of the nine justices vote to take the case, that is, to hear and decide it on its merits, the Court will "grant certiorari." If the petition for certiorari is denied, as the overwhelming majority of them are, the judgment of the Court of Appeals or state appellate court stands as the authoritative last word in the particular controversy.

It is important to understand that Supreme Court denial of a petition for certiorari does not necessarily imply Supreme Court approval of the theory or result reached by the Court of Appeals or other court from which the review was sought. Denial of certiorari may mean no more than that the justices do not believe the issues involved in the case important enough, in terms of the sound development of *federal law,* for full-dress Supreme Court attention. A sound policy basis underlies the discretionary nature of Supreme Court appellate jurisdiction: if appeal to the Supreme Court were available in all cases, the Court would be overwhelmed with ordinary appeals and unable to give full and deliberate consideration to the great cases it must decide with finality as umpire of the federal system, authoritative guardian of constitutional liberties and final overseer of the consistency and substantial justice of the general law administered in the courts of the United States. Thus, the Court is most likely to take a case if the federal courts of appeals have come out differently on the same question of interpretation of federal law. (This is known as a "Circuit split.") The records for a recent year demonstrate the extent to which the Supreme Court exercises its discretion under the certiorari procedure to keep its adjudicative workload within manageable bounds: during the October 2001 Term, the Supreme Court reviewed 2,210 for certiorari, but granted only 82 (less than 4%).[32]

## b. THE STATE COURTS

Each of the fifty states of the United States has its own system of courts. Court structures and court nomenclature differ greatly from state to state, but all the state court systems exhibit what may be called a hierarchical structure, that is, a pattern of organization in which the decisions of "lower" courts may be taken for review to a higher ranking tribunal. Ninety percent or more of the state "cases" a law student reads in casebooks are appellate decisions, but all these appellate cases will have passed through a "trial" stage and perhaps an intermediate appellate stage before reaching the state's "court of last resort."

The following sketch of the tiers in a typical state court hierarchy is unavoidably very much generalized—for example, some states with relatively small populations do not have an intermediate appellate court—but should be sufficient for present purposes. A first year law student will find it interesting and worthwhile to become familiar with the pattern of court organization that exists in the state in which he expects to practice and with the names by which the various courts in her state are known.

### i. Trial Courts of "Inferior" Jurisdiction

Every state has its "inferior" or "petty" trial courts with jurisdiction limited to civil suits involving relatively small amounts of money and to minor violations of the criminal law. In many rural areas, these courts still go by the ancient name, Justice of the Peace (or "J.P.") Courts; in the cities, they are more often called Municipal Courts or City Courts. The civil

---

**32.** See 71 U.S.L.W. 3 at 3080. Petitions for certiorari *in forma pauperis* (chiefly petitions by indigent persons convicted of crime) are excluded from this calculation as unrepresentative of the ordinary operation of the certiorari procedure. During the October 2001 Term, the Court reviewed 6,958 petitions for certiorari *in forma pauperis,* and granted only six (less than .1%).

jurisdiction of an "inferior" or "petty" trial court is usually defined in terms of the amount of money in dispute; thus the jurisdiction of the Justice of the Peace Court may be limited to claims not exceeding $100, while a metropolitan Municipal Court may be empowered to decide claims up to $1,000. Similarly, the jurisdiction of an "inferior" criminal court is likely to be defined in terms of the maximum jail sentence, commonly six months, or maximum fine that may be imposed if the defendant is found guilty of the particular offense charged.

### ii. Trial Courts of General Jurisdiction

If a civil claim or criminal prosecution involves an amount of money, or a potential criminal sentence, beyond the jurisdiction of an "inferior" trial court, it must be filed and heard in a "trial court of general jurisdiction," that is, a court empowered to try all kinds of cases, without monetary or subject matter limitation. Practically all the appellate cases in law school casebooks will have been tried originally (or re-tried, on appeal by the losing party, after earlier judgment in an "inferior" court) in a trial court of general jurisdiction.

Every state has a set of trial courts of general jurisdiction, but there are differences in nomenclature from state to state. In some states, the trial court of general jurisdiction is known as the Superior Court ("superior," presumably, to the "petty" courts described above), in other states as the District Court or Circuit Court, names reflecting the typical division of the states into judicial districts or circuits. A few states retain old common law names, e.g., Court of Common Pleas. New York, to the great confusion of out-of-state lawyers and frequent bewilderment of its own electorate, calls its trial court of general jurisdiction the Supreme Court, with the incidental consequence that New York trial judges of general jurisdiction are "justices," whereas the members of the State's distinguished court of last resort are mere "judges."

In every state, trial courts of general jurisdiction are distributed geographically throughout the state, so that litigants can have access to them without journeying to the state capital. Thus each state is divided into a number of judicial districts or circuits and a court established for each district or circuit, with at least one district or circuit judge for each of these geographical units. In metropolitan districts and other areas of large population, there will be many judges for each district; the Superior Court of Los Angeles, for example, has 441 judges.[33] Although their principal function is the trial and initial (final, if unappealed) determination of important civil and criminal controversies, state trial courts of general jurisdiction typically act also as appellate tribunals to decide appeals from the judgments of "inferior" trial courts and to review the actions of certain state administrative agencies, such as workers' compensation boards, licensing authorities, and public utility commissions.

---

**33.** Catherine A. Kitchell, *BNA's Directory of State and Federal Courts, Judges and Clerks* (2003 edition).

A complete inventory of any state's trial courts will have to take account, also, of the specialized trial courts that are found in almost every state: Family Courts, Probate Courts, and the like. Some states have separate courts, with specially appointed or elected judges, for probate, divorce or criminal matters. In other states, only the one multi-judge trial court of general jurisdiction exists in each district but specialization is achieved by assigning one or more judges of that court to a particular task (e.g., the Family Court) at the beginning of each judicial term. During the first half of the 20th-century, a number of states still had a set of courts for "common law" actions and another set for "equity" cases, but procedural reforms, specifically the so-called "merger of law and equity," have brought about a virtual disappearance of this terminological survival of days past.

### iii.  Appellate Courts

Every state has its "court of last resort," the appellate court at the top of the judicial hierarchy and the one which determines with finality (subject to occasional review on "federal questions" by the Supreme Court of the United States) what the particular state's law is and should be. In most states, this highest court in the hierarchy is called the Supreme Court of the state, but other names are in use here and there: Supreme Judicial Court, Supreme Court of Appeals and, as in New York, Court of Appeals. "Whatever the name, its function is the same: to review the action of the lower judicial tribunals of the state. This is the exercise of appellate jurisdiction. The scope of judicial review which the court exercises in such cases is relatively narrow; it does not retry the case on the merits, and it does not substitute its idea of justice for those of the trial court; what it does is to review the record of the proceedings to determine whether or not the lower court committed error in its procedure or in applying the substantive law to the facts of the case." Green, "The Business of the Trial Courts," in Jones (ed.), The Courts, the Public and the Law Explosion 7, 16 (1965).

The contemporary idea that one's "day in court" includes the right to appellate review of every adverse trial court judgment is a quite recent development. Appeal was a "matter of grace," not a "matter of right," at English common law and even during the first century or so of American legal history. Under existing statutes in every state, the party who loses at the trial court stage of a litigated controversy has a right to have the trial court judgment reviewed at least once by a court other than the one that originally entered it. One inevitable result of this recognition of appeal as a matter of right was, of course, a vast increase in appellate litigation which, particularly in the more populous states, soon led to hopeless congestion of the dockets of the state courts of last resort.

In response, most States have created intermediate appellate courts, empowered to strain out and finally dispose of the bulk of appellate litigation—cases, for example, that raise no new or difficult issue of law—so that the court of last resort can give its full attention to novel and socially important controversies. The prevailing contemporary policy is to give the court of last resort very wide discretion over the granting or denial of applications for its appellate review. If appeals from a state's intermediate appellate court to its court of last resort were granted too freely, the intermediate appellate court would not be performing the vital "screening out" function for which it was created. As the volume of litigation continues to grow in almost every state, the intermediate appellate courts become increasingly the final tribunal for authoritative disposition of far more cases than will ever reach the state's court of last resort.

The following chart illustrates the variety, and complexity, of the court system of one state—New York.

**NEW YORK COURTS OF CIVIL JURISDICTION**

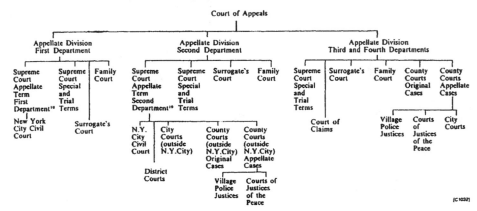

## 3.   THE COURT SYSTEM IN PRACTICE: THE STRUCTURE OF A LAWSUIT

Professor Karl Llewellyn described substantive law as follows:[34]

[C]ertain bodies of law, which we call substantive—the substance of the law—deal with what ought to be, with whether contracts ought to be enforced at law, and when; with what formalities are necessary to make a last will stick; with how to form a corporation and how to issue its stock, and how to keep investors from having any say in it; and what words are necessary to make an effective lease or deed of land; and so on. Procedure[35] constitutes the mechanism through which rules

---

**34.**   Karl Llewellyn, The Bramble Bush 16 (1930). [Hereafter cited as The Bramble Bush.]

**35.**   Professor Llewellyn had the following to say concerning the distinction between substantive law and procedure:

But from another angle this distinction tends to disappear. For if you whistle your soup you may be looked at queerly, you may be laughed at; you may even fail to be invited out again, another time.

But if you slip in your legal etiquette it is not a question of queer looks or laughter or of what may happen later; it is likely to cost you your case right here and now; your case, and your client's case. The lawyer's slip in etiquette is the client's ruin. From this angle I say procedural regulations are the door, and the only door, to making real what is laid down by substantive law. Procedural regulations enter into and condition all substantive law's becoming actual when

of substantive law have effect. Procedure controls all aspects of the manner through which rules of substantive law are applied; whether a particular person has standing to bring a particular suit; the forum in which the suit may be brought; the manner in which her claim must be asserted; the ground rules of proof of his claim; the remedy which is afforded; the manner in which the judgment is enforced. In the words of one scholar, "the road to court-made justice is paved with good procedures."[36]

You will learn about various aspects of procedure in other courses, such as Civil Procedure, Evidence, Administrative Law, Federal Courts and Conflicts of Law. But even at this stage you need to know something about procedure. The first third of the course is devoted to a study of case law. In reading cases we are seeking to determine what the case decides as to the substantive law, or, to phrase it somewhat differently, what proposition of substantive law a case may be said to stand for. This depends upon the exact question the court had before it for decision, which in turn depends on the procedure to date in the case.

At first, the profusion of procedural steps encountered in a lawsuit may prove bewildering. To clarify the subject and put it in perspective, consider the following outline of a lawsuit.

## a.  THE PLEADING STAGE

The "client," when he first comes to the lawyer, does not have a case; he has a problem. The lawyer's first task is to ascertain "the facts." This task is crucial, and it is not as easy as it sounds, even in uncomplicated situations. Clients are no less—sometimes they are more—prone to misunderstanding, misimpression, and faulty recollection as the next person.

there is a dispute. Again this is no reason for not marking off procedure and evidence and trial practice as fields for special and peculiar study apart from substantive law. They should be so marked off. They should be marked off for the most intensive study. But they should be so marked off not because they are really separate, but because they are of such transcendent importance as to need special emphasis. They should be marked off not to be kept apart and distinct but solely in order that they may be more firmly learned, more firmly ingrained into the student *as conditioning the existence of any substantive law at all*. Everything that you know of procedure you must carry into *every* substantive course. You must read each substantive course, so to speak, through the spectacles of that procedure. For what substantive law says should be means nothing except in terms of what procedure says that you can make real.

The Bramble Bush 17–18.

**36.**  Maurice Rosenberg, *Devising Procedures that are Civil to Promote Justice that is Civilized*, 69 Mich.L.Rev. 797 (1971). Professor Rosenberg also observed (at 797):

In a democracy, process is king to a very large extent, and this is especially so in the judicial branch. Even though substantive laws command attention, procedural rules ensure respect. Why is this true? One powerful reason is that when people end up in court, their case typically is not a matter of right against wrong, but of right against right. Decent process makes the painful task of deciding which party will prevail bearable and helps make the decision itself acceptable.

Sometimes clients lie, and even when they aim at the truth, they often miss—for all of the reasons encountered in non-legal contexts.

Assume that you are the lawyer, and that your client (X) tells you the following: He received a series of increasingly taunting postcards sent by F, his former fiancée during the course of her honeymoon with her new husband. As a result, X claims to have suffered severe emotional distress, resulting in neurological disturbances (personal injury). Moreover, overcome by a bout of depression while driving, he drove his car into a tree, destroying the front end (property damage).[37]

For the purposes of this discussion (but not in real practice), assume further that you are satisfied that the facts correspond to your client's assertions, and that they can be proved in court.[38] Next, you will need to determine if these facts state a claim under the applicable law. In many instances, the existence of a legal violation (if the facts alleged are proved) will be clear. For example, if your client alleged that the other party reneged on a written agreement to sell him her house, your client would have stated a claim for breach of contract. In other cases, however, it may be less clear that the defendant has violated a legal norm. For example, if your client claims to suffer humiliation because a newspaper published a true account of his divorce or of his filing for personal bankruptcy, but neither the common law in your jurisdiction, nor local legislative authorities have recognized a claim for this kind of invasion of privacy, then the newspaper will have committed no legal violation. Even if you determine that your client does have a legal claim, you should expect the defendant to dispute your client's case both on the facts and on the law, as we shall see.

If you are satisfied that the facts your client alleges can be proved, and that they make out a legal violation, you will now have to determine in what court you will "bring your action." This will depend on what courts "have jurisdiction" of the type of action, which may turn on such factors as the amount of money involved and the states of residence of the parties. Assuming that the court has "subject matter jurisdiction," the person sued (the "defendant") must be subject to the jurisdiction of the court. Without personal jurisdiction no valid judgment can be rendered against the defendant. A defendant who lives in the state where the court is located (the "forum"), or who has committed the wrongful act there, will usually be amenable to suit in that forum.

Ordinarily, personal jurisdiction is acquired by the service of process on the defendant. The forms vary in different jurisdictions but in most you will initiate the lawsuit by "serving" a "summons" and "complaint" on the defendant. Service of process is a story in itself which is best left to the course in Civil Procedure.

---

**37.** This hypothetical is inspired by a real case, Halio v. Lurie, 15 A.D.2d 62 (2d Dept.1961), discussed in Flamm v. Van Nierop, infra, part B.1.d.

**38.** The rules governing what can be proved in court and how to prove it are covered in the course in Evidence.

The complaint is the "pleading" in which the person suing (the "plaintiff") states the facts that in his view entitle him to a judgment against the "defendant," F in our case. The complaint must set forth a statement of the allegations clear enough to enable the defendant to prepare his defense, and allege facts sufficient to "constitute a cause of action," that is, facts which under the controlling law entitle him to judgment.

Once the complaint has been served, the next move is up to the defendant and her lawyer. There are four courses of action open to you (now as defendant's lawyer):

1. *Do nothing,* in which event, the court, after a proper interval, will enter a *"default "*judgment against your client, which the plaintiff will be able to collect against your client's property. For obvious reasons this is not often the recommended response.

2. *Serve (and/or file in court) a motion to dismiss for failure to state a claim.* (Older cases refer to this motion as a "demurrer.") By this pleading you would say, in effect, "even if the alleged facts are true, there is no rule of law that permits X to recover against F on those facts." The demurrer is the pleading involved in the *Roberson* and *Garrison* cases, infra pp. 85 and 170. Since the motion to dismiss, or demurrer, admits, temporarily, the truth of the facts alleged by the plaintiff, it raises a pure issue of substantive law.

3. *Serve (and/or file) an answer.* An *answer* denies all (or some) of the facts alleged in the complaint. It thus raises an issue of *fact* between the parties, not an issue of *law.* (Usually, in U.S. pleading, all facts stated in the complaint and not denied by the defendant are taken as true.)

4. *Serve (and/or file) an affirmative defense.* (What the old cases call a plea by way of confession and avoidance.) By this pleading, you admit (again, as in the case of the motion to dismiss, temporarily) the truth of the facts alleged and (unlike the motion to dismiss) that those facts standing alone would win for plaintiff, but allege new facts which require a different result. In our supposed case, the pleading might be in effect, "Yes, your statement of facts is true, but the acts you complain of happened more than three years ago and your claim is barred by the statute of limitations."

As noted above, the motion to dismiss for failure to state a claim raises a pure question of substantive law. It is as though the defendant said: I concede (for the sake of argument) that the facts alleged are true, but the law does not provide for a recovery against me on the basis of those facts. For example, suppose that in our case, F said "I admit (for purposes of this motion) that I sent you the postcards intending to hurt your feelings and to cause you emotional harm, but the law in this jurisdiction does not recognize the tort of intentional infliction of emotional distress."

Assuming that the defendant moves to dismiss for failure to state a claim, the motion will be argued before the court and either granted or denied. If it is granted, usually the plaintiff will be given an opportunity to "replead," i.e., to allege additional facts, if they exist, sufficient to state a claim. If he is unable to do so, he may appeal. If the motion to dismiss is denied, and the defendant has, in addition to moving to dismiss, controverted the plaintiffs' allegations of fact, the case will go to trial (or in some jurisdictions the defendant may appeal immediately).[39] If she does not dispute the facts, there is no need for a trial. The case proceeds directly to judgment, on the law, which may be reviewed on appeal.

Up to now, we have been talking about the defendant's motion to dismiss. Precisely the same kind of issue (i.e., an issue of substantive law) may arise when defendant raises an affirmative defense that plaintiff controverts. For example, suppose that F admitted the allegations of the complaint, but asserted that X was negligent in driving a car when he was emotionally unfit to drive. X could challenge the legal sufficiency of F's affirmative defense. X could admit that he drove while suffering from emotional distress, but could deny that driving under those conditions was negligent. Alternatively, X could challenge the facts F alleged. X could contend that he did not know, and should not have known, that his emotional distress would impair his ability to drive.

### b.   THE TRIAL STAGE

Although it may not appear so from case books, the overwhelming majority of cases do not raise issues of substantive law. In most cases, the parties do not dispute the law, but only the facts.

Let us assume that an issue of fact has been raised by the pleadings, that is, that your client, at the pleading stage, filed an answer denying some or all of the facts stated in the plaintiff's complaint. Thus an issue of fact is raised between the parties, which will require trial,[40] before a jury or (if a jury is waived by the parties) trial before a judge sitting as a jury— "bench trial."

What are the principal procedural events that occur, or can occur, at the trial stage?[41] We begin with the presentation of the plaintiff's case:

1.   Plaintiff's opening statement to the jury, "I expect to prove...."
In some states (e.g., New York) this may be followed immediately by defendant's opening statement (if defendant chooses to make one) as to what defendant expects to prove. In other states, defendant's opening statement comes later, at the start of defendant's case.

---

**39.** In those jurisdictions where an appeal does not "lie" immediately, the denial may be appealed at the end of the trial.

**40.** It is, of course, possible that although the pleadings may raise an issue, there may be "no *genuine* issue of fact" between the parties, i.e., that there is no evidence to support the claim or demand in the pleadings. Such cases may be disposed of without trial by "summary judgment."

**41.** This outline omits the very important procedural devices by which the parties obtain information in advance of trial, such as examinations before trial, requests for admission, document discovery and interrogatories. Nor does it discuss the important and interesting process of jury selection. These issues form part of the course in Civil Procedure.

2. Next come the direct and cross-examinations of plaintiff's witnesses—the witnesses called by plaintiff's counsel testify and are cross-examined by defendant's counsel. Here you may have "objections" to the introduction of evidence, for example, on the ground that the evidence is inadmissible as hearsay. If the court, after defendant's objection, lets the evidence in, defendant will "except" to the ruling and so preserve her right to challenge the ruling on appeal if the jury verdict goes against her.

3. At the end of plaintiff's evidence, defendant may ask the trial court for a "directed verdict" or, in the federal courts, for a "judgment as a matter of law" (F.R.Civ.P. 50). By making one of these motions, defendant is saying, in effect, that plaintiff has not proved enough—i.e., has not offered adequate evidence in support of his allegations of fact—to enable any reasonable jury to bring in a verdict for him. You will note that these motions attack the sufficiency of plaintiff's proof of facts and, ordinarily, do not raise a question of substantive law.

4. Assuming that defendant's motions have been made but denied by the court, defendant presents her evidence, i.e., calls witnesses to prove her version of the facts. Thus again, we will have the direct testimony and cross-examination of witnesses and may have objections to evidence (this time from counsel for plaintiff) and exceptions to the court's rulings thereon.

5. At the end of defendant's evidence, plaintiff may move for a directed verdict (rarely granted, however, to the party with the "burden of proof") or the defendant may again move for a directed verdict on the ground that she has now shown so clearly that plaintiff's asserted version of the facts is not true that no reasonable jury could do otherwise than find for defendant.

6. If all these motions are denied, plaintiff and defendant sum up before the jury, plaintiff having the right, usually, to make the closing argument.

7. The next, and crucial, stage of the trial is the "charge to the jury." The judge gives her instructions to the jury as to the applicable law of the case. Thus, for example, in our hypothetical case, the judge might advise the jury about as follows: "If you the jury find that the defendant sent the postcards, with the intention of causing the plaintiff emotional distress, and that the cards did cause the plaintiff to suffer emotional distress, you will bring in a verdict in the amount of his medical expenses and personal suffering. If you find that a reasonable person in plaintiff's position would not or should not have been aware that his emotional distress would impair his ability to drive, then you will also bring in a verdict for the amount of his property damage." The instruction stage is one of the most important for our immediate purposes, and you should know something about its realities:

    a. In actual practice, few instructions are ever drawn up by the trial judge as a matter of her own literary initiative. What usually happens is that each side draws up draft instructions and submits them to the judge. The judge then looks at the draft instructions submitted by both sides and decides which ones to give to the jury (she will probably revise the words). Either side in the litigation may:

> (i) except, i.e., record objections, to any instruction or part thereof, which he believes is an erroneous statement of the law; or

> (ii) except to the refusal of the judge to give his *instruction*.

b.  Since the instruction is, in substance, a statement to the jury of the substantive law applicable to the facts of the case, it is at the instruction stage that you are quite likely to have a sharp issue of law between the parties, decided by the trial judge and specified by the losing party as the ground for his appeal. This is particularly true in tort actions, where a very large percentage of appeals in modern cases come up on, or involve, an appeal from the instructions given to the jury.

8.  After the judge delivers her instructions, the jury retires for deliberation and, ultimately, brings in its "verdict." Most jury verdicts are general, a statement of result in some such form as "We, the jury, find for the plaintiff in the sum of $50,000." So-called "special" verdicts, by which the jury answers specific questions of fact submitted to it by the judge, are becoming more frequent.[42] However, a general verdict with interrogatories (by which the court instructs the jury to reach a general verdict, but requests answers to one or more questions so that the basis for the verdict is disclosed) is less controversial and often preferred by judges over the special verdict.[43]

## c.  MOTIONS IN THE TRIAL COURT AFTER VERDICT

After the jury has returned its verdict, but before the trial court has entered "judgment"[44] in the action, the party who lost before the jury can make one or more of several motions. Many appeals come up to the appellate courts from the action of trial courts granting or denying one of these motions, so you should get a general idea now as to the kind of question each motion raises. Terminology and practice will differ considerably from state to state, but it should be possible to get a general understanding without too much difficulty.

Most sweeping of the motions after verdict is the motion for judgment notwithstanding the verdict which is also referred to by the "law-Latin" name "judgment non obstante veredicto" (or, familiarly, judgment n.o.v. or j.n.o.v.), in which the party against whom the verdict is pronounced goes so far as to ask that judgment be given for him or her in spite of the jury

---

**42.**  See, e.g., Mark S. Brodin, *Accuracy, Efficiency and Accountability in the Litigation Process—the Case for the Fact Verdict*, 59 U.Cin.L.Rev. 15 (1990).

**43.**  Jack H. Friedenthal et al, CIVIL PROCEDURE 551–552 (West Group, 1999).

**44.**  Note and remember the difference between "verdict" and "judgment."

findings. In the federal courts, this motion is a "motion for a judgment as a matter of law."[45]

More common is the motion to set aside the verdict as against the weight of the evidence and grant a new trial. Both this motion and the modern motion for judgment n.o.v. are attacks on the sufficiency of the evidence to support the verdict. You may well ask at this point what gives the judge (to whom all motions are addressed) the right to disregard a verdict of a jury which in our system is the cherished and time-honored instrument for finding the facts. The answer is that we require *as a matter of law* a minimum amount of evidence to support the jury verdict.[46] This amount, variously phrased as "more than a scintilla," or such that "reasonable persons may not differ," is obviously an imprecise standard and susceptible to abuse. In practice, however, most judges will only rarely displace a jury verdict, and when they do, will ordinarily not grant judgment n.o.v., but instead set aside the verdict and grant a new trial.

The losing party may also move for a new trial on a number of other grounds such as an error by the judge in ruling on evidence, an error in the instructions, misconduct by the jurors, or excessive damages. The usual rule is that a losing party cannot appeal any errors of the trial court which

**45.** "The standards for granting a motion for a directed verdict and for granting a motion for judgment notwithstanding the verdict are identical.... We will take the issue from the jury 'only if all the evidence favors the movant and is susceptible of no reasonable inferences sustaining the position of the non-moving party.'" Ruwitch v. William Penn Life Assur. Co., 966 F.2d 1234 (8th Cir.1992) (citations omitted).

**46.** The following definition of the test for the correctness of the grant of a motion for a directed verdict is from Combs v. Meadowcraft, Inc., 106 F.3d 1519, 1526 (11th Cir. 1997), cert. denied 522 U.S. 1045 (1998):

In conducting our review: "[W]e consider all the evidence, and the inferences drawn therefrom, in the light most favorable to the nonmoving party. If the facts and inferences point overwhelmingly in favor of one party, such that reasonable people could not arrive at a contrary verdict, then the motion was properly granted. Conversely, if there is substantial evidence opposed to the motion such that reasonable people, in the exercise of impartial judgment, might reach differing conclusions, then such a motion was due to be denied and the case was properly submitted to the jury". Carter v. City of Miami, 870 F.2d 578, 581 (11th

Cir.1989). Under the foregoing standard, the nonmoving party must provide more than a mere scintilla of evidence to survive a motion for judgment as a matter of law: "[T]here must be a substantial conflict in evidence to support a jury question." Id. To summarize, we must consider all the evidence in the light most favorable to [the plaintiff] and determine "whether or not reasonable jurors could have concluded as this jury did based on the evidence presented." Quick v. Peoples Bank, 993 F.2d 793, 797 (11th Cir.1993) (citation and internal quotation marks omitted).

The test for the granting of a judgment notwithstanding the verdict is substantially the same: "A ... court may enter a judgment notwithstanding the verdict when, viewing the evidence in the light most favorable to the non-moving party, (1) there is such a complete absence of evidence supporting the verdict that the jury's findings could only have been the result of sheer surmise and conjecture, or (2) there is such an overwhelming amount of evidence in favor of the movant that reasonable and fair minded men could not arrive at a verdict against him. Haskell v. Kaman Corp., 743 F.2d 113, 120 (2d Cir.1984), quoting Mattivi v. South African Marine Corp., 618 F.2d 163, 168 (2d Cir.1980)."

he did not call to the trial court's attention by filing a motion for a new trial.

If all motions after verdict are denied, the trial court formally enters judgment for the party to whom the jury awarded the verdict. This judgment is *res judicata* of the controversy between the parties unless notice of appeal is given by the losing party within a required number of days.

### d.   EXECUTION OF THE JUDGMENT

If the plaintiff has obtained a judgment against the defendant and the defendant does not pay or otherwise satisfy the judgment, the plaintiff is entitled to execution. In the case of a judgment for money, (the usual case in our system) the plaintiff obtains a writ from the court directing the sheriff (or similar official) to seize property of the defendant, sell it, and with the proceeds pay to the plaintiff the amount of his judgment.

Execution, like service of process, is a story by itself. Just as it can be very difficult to serve process on a reluctant defendant, it can be very difficult to collect from a determined, unscrupulous, judgment debtor. The securing of a judgment can be only the beginning of a long trail to compensation. Execution is of great importance to the client. Inability to enforce a judgment because of the insolvency or intransigence of the defendant may make meaningless all that has gone before. As a result, before initiating an action it is important to assess whether the defendant has the resources, and the compliance, to satisfy a judgment.

### e.   THE APPEAL STAGE

Most cases you will read in law school are appeal cases and you need to have some background on the appellate process if you are fully to understand them.

First of all, in the U.S. system, the appellate court does not retry the case on its merits or take additional evidence. The focus of the appellate court's scrutiny is on the correctness of the rulings of the trial court. The documents at which the appellate court will look in its review include the record—the pleadings, the transcript of the testimony at the trial or an edited portion, the exhibits entered into evidence, the trial court's rulings—and the "briefs" of counsel, i.e., statements (usually printed) of the arguments supporting each side's position in the litigation. No additional testimony is taken, nor is new evidence submitted. Most law libraries have many copies of briefs and records and you should look at a few.

After the briefs and the record are filed, the case is set up for oral argument and argued before the appellate court. After oral argument and study of the briefs and the trial record, the judges of the appellate court meet in conference, discuss the case, and assign the writing of the opinion of the court to one of its members. The opinions are more than individual essays of the judge. When written by the assigned judge, the draft opinion will be circulated for initialing, and when approved by all the members of the panel, or a majority, the opinion is filed as the opinion of the court. There may also be concurring opinions (the concurring judges agreeing with the result but differing in some way from the majority opinion) and dissenting opinions.

One last point should be emphasized. A lawsuit is a complicated and long drawn out proceeding. Many points of dispute will come up. Few, if any, trial judges can avoid error in every ruling in a complicated case. This is particularly true of rulings from the bench during the course of trial. Unlike appellate judges, who enjoy the leisure of hindsight on the trial court's determinations, and time to research and reflect on their own rulings, the trial court frequently must make snap decisions. Sometimes these are wrong. Should all such errors warrant reversal by the appellate court? Many times, the errors are "cured" by subsequent events, or the questions on which erroneous rulings are made turn out to be unimportant. As a result, an error in the trial court will not provoke a reversal unless it is "prejudicial," i.e., unless it did—or might have—prejudicially influenced the outcome of the case.

## B.   LEGISLATION

### 1.   ATTRIBUTES AND TYPES

#### a.   THE GENERALITY OF LEGISLATION

In section A, we saw how case law generates rules inferred from prior decisions. Rules of general application derive from an accumulation and synthesis of the results and reasoning in particular controversies. The common lawyer is accustomed to reasoning from the particular to the general. Specific examples play an important role in the common lawyer's approach, as do the facts of individual cases.

But case law is not the only source of law, even in a common law system. Legislation supplies another principal, and increasingly important, source of law. The drafting and interpretation of legislation call on skills and analyses different from those honed in the adjudicative process. While case law begins with particular controversies, legislation imposes a general rule. Where case law analysis calls on the lawyer to move upward from specific facts to a general principle to discern how the solution in one case can guide the resolution of another, the interpretation of legislation requires reasoning from the general to the specific, to determine whether and how a rule claiming wide application in fact governs an individual controversy.

Moreover, legislation does not simply declare rules; it expresses them in specific language. With legislation, every word (indeed, every punctuation mark) counts. As the late Edwin W. Patterson wrote in the first Legal Methods casebook, Neal Thomas Dowling, Edwin Wilhite Patterson and Richard R.B. Powell, Materials for Legal Method (1946):

A proposition of case law may be correctly stated in several different ways, each of which is equally "official." A statute (proposition of legislation) is stated as an exclusive official wording of the rule. Case law is flexible; legislation is (textually) rigid.

Statutory interpretation requires working with the words of the statute. Their meaning may be uncertain, but their presence is not. Interpreting the text should not mean rewriting or paraphrasing it. Courts inevitably have great latitude in determining the meaning and application of statutory language in concrete situations, but only the legislature is authorized to change a statute's wording by the process of amendment. (As you work through the materials in Part III of this casebook, consider to what extent the judicial interpretation of statutes in fact follows these precepts.)

To some extent, the methods of case analysis and statutory interpretation converge. Judges interpret statutes, and their accumulated interpretations become, in effect, the case law of the statutes. Once a court has given a statute a particular interpretation, the principle of *stare decisis* applies to that interpretation: Lower courts in that jurisdiction are as bound by the interpretation as they would be had the rendering court resolved an issue of common law. Of course, the legislator is not bound by the court's interpretation: It is free to amend the statute to impart a different meaning to the text. (On legislative reaction to prior decisions interpreting a statute, see Part III.D.3 of the casebook, infra.)

## b.   TYPES OF LEGISLATION

Legislative precepts are prescribed general rules expressed in authoritative verbal form. The statutes enacted by Congress and the legislatures of the states are legislation of the classic and most familiar kind. In the present section, however, the term "legislation" will denote not only federal and state statutes but also the other types of general legal rules that are prescribed in administrative regulations, municipal ordinances and the like. Even the Constitution of the United States or a state constitution is "legislation" in this broad sense (although of higher political and legal obligation than "ordinary" legislation), because a constitution, too, is a rule-prescribing instrument, one which expresses in authoritative form the general rules, or principles, that govern the exercise of political power in an organized society and safeguard individual interests from unwarranted governmental intrusion.

Because of the wide dispersion of law-making power in the United States—the constitutional division of legislative authority between the national government and the states and the delegation of subordinate legislative power to administrative agencies and, in the states, to city councils and other municipal bodies—American legislation is an aggregate of precepts from many sources. Conflicting directions are frequently encountered in this mix; a state statute, for example, may be or seem in conflict with existing federal legislation or a state administrative regulation with a municipal ordinance on the same subject. Individuals and corporations, and so the lawyers advising them, are often faced with the problem of what to do when one law-maker has commanded certain behavior and another law-maker has ordered a quite different course of action. In determining which of two competing legislative commands is the one to be obeyed, or to be given controlling force by a court in a litigated case, the manifest first step is to consider the degree of authority with which each of the two law-makers spoke to the subject at hand. The types of legislation briefly sketched in the following paragraphs therefore follow our legal system's hierarchy of legislative norms, from most to least authoritative.

### i.   The Constitution of the United States

The Constitution sets out the norms that govern the distribution of political powers in our society and the ways in which—and purposes for which—these powers are to be exercised. In our legal order the Constitution is "law," and law of the highest authoritativeness and obligation. Even a deliberately enacted federal statute can be challenged in the courts as beyond the legislative power delegated to the Congress by the Constitution or as violative of some provision of the Bill of Rights or other constitutional guarantee of individual interests against impairment by government action. Similarly, the Constitution of the United States, as "supreme Law of the Land," is the ultimate authority to which reference must be made to determine the validity of state and municipal legislation. The Constitution, in its inception, related almost entirely to the structure and operations of the national (or "federal") government, but since the adoption of the 13th, 14th and 15th Amendments in the years following the Civil War, the prohibitions of the Constitution have been of equal importance in relation to state legislation and to action taken by state and local officials.

### ii.   Federal Statutes

Article I, Section 1 of the Constitution of the United States provides that "all legislative Powers herein granted shall be vested in a Congress of the United States." The powers so granted to Congress are enumerated in considerable detail in Article I, Section 8, which concludes with a broadly worded grant of authority to "make all Laws which shall be necessary and proper for carrying into Execution the foregoing Powers." What are the constitutional and legal consequences when Congress, as it has done quite often in recent years, enacts a statute which, although clearly within the scope of its law-making authority under Article I, Section 8, conflicts directly with existing state legislation or state constitutional provisions? The "supremacy clause" (Article VI, paragraph 2) of the Constitution supplies the answer.

The supremacy clause, one of the key provisions of the Constitution, provides in full as follows:

> This Constitution, and the Laws of the United States which shall be made in Pursuance thereof; and all Treaties made, or which shall be made, under the Authority of the United States, shall be the supreme Law of the Land; and the Judges in every State shall be bound thereby,

any Thing in the Constitution or Laws of any State to the Contrary notwithstanding.

The words are carefully chosen and their meaning and effect clear. A federal statute "made in pursuance" of the Constitution is a part of "the supreme Law of the Land" and so of superior authoritativeness to any state constitutional provision, state statute or other type of state legislation.

### iii.   Treaties

Article II, Section 2 of the Constitution provides that the President

shall have power, by and with the Advice and Consent of the Senate, to make Treaties, provided two-thirds of the Senators present concur.

A treaty in its essence is a diplomatic instrument, a compact between nations, and it may seem strange to see treaties included in an inventory of the types of legislation. Nonetheless, there are a few circumstances in which a treaty made by the President with the advice and consent of the Senate has much the same legal effect as a federal statute. Suppose, for example, that a treaty between the United States and some other nation provides that the citizens of each country shall be fully entitled to inherit property or to engage in all kinds of business in the other country. By the explicit terms of the supremacy clause of the Constitution of the United States, just considered in its relation to federal statutes, this treaty is a part of the "supreme law of the land" and so is superior in legal authoritativeness to any type of state legislation. The citizens of the nation with whom the supposed treaty was made are thus entitled to inherit property or to engage in any kind of business in State X, even if State X has a statute or state constitutional provision restricting the inheritance of property or the carrying on of designated kinds of business to American citizens. The place of treaties and the treaty power in our constitutional system raises many complex questions, some of them of lively contemporary importance, but these questions must be left to later courses in International Law and Constitutional Law. It is sufficient now to note the possibility that a treaty may have an incidental side-effect as federal legislation.

### iv.   State Constitutions

State constitutions existed before the drafting of the Constitution of the United States. Almost all of the thirteen original states adopted constitutions in 1776 or 1777. These first state constitutions and those adopted early in the 19th century were much like the Constitution of the United States in content and style, that is, they were largely confined to essential matters like basic governmental structure and the definition and distribution of political powers and, except in their bills of individual rights, expressed in terms of broad principles or standards as distinguished from narrowly stated rules.

Every state has its constitution, and the typical state constitution of today is a far bulkier document and is likely to deal at length and in very specific terms with subjects like school and police administration, lotteries, state and municipal budgeting, the tenure of civil service employees, and the powers to be exercised by irrigation and sewer districts. Such explicit and detailed provisions are written into a state constitution for the manifest purpose of making it impossible for a subsequent state legislature to change the law on the subject by simple statutory enactment. It is far harder politically to amend a state constitution than to repeal or amend a statute; a two-thirds majority in each house of the state legislature is commonly required to propose a state constitutional amendment, and an amendment so proposed must typically be approved by popular referendum which may, in its turn, require more than a simple-majority vote of the electorate.

State statutes are, of course, subject to challenge in the courts on federal constitutional grounds, but, because of the great specificity of most state constitutions, the state constitutional barrier may be the more difficult one to overcome. A state statute that would unquestionably pass Supreme Court scrutiny as consistent with the Constitution of the United States can nonetheless be held invalid by a state court of last resort as a violation of some provision of the local state constitution. And that will be a final and conclusive determination because the Supreme Court of the United States is not superior in authority to state courts on questions of local state law.

## v.  State Statutes

It is sometimes said that state statutes are less important in the day-to-day work of lawyers than they once were, because federal regulatory activity has vastly expanded. To say this is to overlook two other developments during approximately the same time: (1) the extension and intensification of state controls, imposed by or based on statutes, in such areas as consumer protection, environmental management and equal employment opportunity; and (2) the increasing tendency of state legislatures to intervene in traditional private law fields by replacing old case law rules with new and presumably more up-to-date legislative norms.

The effectiveness of a state statutory provision as an authoritative rule may be challenged in court, as we have seen, on one or more of several grounds: that it violates some more or less explicit prohibition in the Constitution of the United States, that it contravenes some provision of the local state constitution or that it conflicts with some more authoritative federal statute, treaty or administrative regulation. But it is misleading to concentrate too much on the possible vulnerability of state statutes to constitutional challenge. Ninety percent or more of the statutes enacted by a busy state legislature at one of its sessions will raise no serious question of federal or state constitutional law. The lawyer's work in dealing with state statutes is chiefly a work of interpretation, of determining the meaning and effect of enacted statutory language for specific cases and counseling situations. Part III of this casebook (pages 255–554) is designed to develop the insights and skills that are necessary in the interpretation of statutes, both state and federal.

### vi.  *Municipal Ordinances*

The rules enacted by the legislative branch of a local or "municipal" unit of government are authoritative precepts of legislation within the unit's territorial limits. These prescribed rules of local legislative origin are commonly called "ordinances" (to distinguish them from the "statutes" enacted by Congress and the state legislatures), and that is what we shall call them here, even though they sometimes bear another name (e.g., "by-law"). A municipal ordinance is, of course, legally ineffective if inconsistent with a higher norm of federal law or with a provision of the state constitution and is usually, but not always, inferior in authoritativeness to a conflicting state statute—"not always" because many state constitutions contain so-called "home rule" provisions which, to one or another extent, may empower cities and other municipal units to enact ordinances, on a few designated subjects, that are not vulnerable to disapproval or modification by the state legislature. Insofar as the law-making power of the municipal unit comes to it by statutory delegation from the state legislature, however, the rule prescribed by a municipal ordinance must yield to the conflicting direction of a state statute and may, like an administrative regulation, be repealed or modified by subsequent action of the legislature.

### c.  NOTE ON UNIFORM CODES

One way to systematize the law and make it uniform across state jurisdictions is to reduce the common law to statutory form and seek adoption by state legislators. The Uniform Commercial Code (UCC), developed and monitored by the American Law Institute (ALI) in collaboration with the National Conference of Commissioners on Uniform State Laws (NCCUSL), represents the most successful of such efforts.[1] The UCC is a comprehensive code aimed at simplifying and standardizing (rather than restating) most aspects of commercial law. You are likely to study sections of the UCC closely in your contracts class. Helping to promote commerce between states by making it simpler to pursue transactions in various jurisdictions, the Code covers the sales of goods, commercial paper, bank deposits and collections, letters of credit, investment securities, and secured transactions. The UCC which took ten years to complete and another 14 years before it was enacted across the country[2] is generally viewed as one of the most important developments in American law. It has been enacted (with some local variations) in 49 states and in the District of Columbia and the Virgin Islands, as well as partially in Louisiana.[3]

**1.**  Other ALI proposals for law reform include model statutory formulations such as the Model Code of Evidence, the Model Penal Code, a Model Code of Pre–Arraignment Procedure, a Model Land Development Code, and a proposed Federal Securities Code.

**2.**  See http://www.nccusl.org.

**3.**  See Am. Law Inst., About the American Law Institute, at www.ali.org/ali/thisa-li.htm.

In addition to collaborating with the ALI on the UCC, the NCCUSL has drafted more than 200 uniform laws on numerous subjects and in various fields of law since its organization in 1892. The conference comprises more than 300 lawyers, judges and law professors, appointed by the states as well as the District of Columbia, Puerto Rico and the U.S. Virgin Islands, to "draft proposals for uniform and model laws on subjects where uniformity is desirable and practicable, and work toward their enactment in legislatures".[4] Uniform acts include the Uniform Probate Code, the Uniform Child Custody Jurisdiction Act, the Uniform Partnership Act, the Uniform Anatomical Gift Act, the Uniform Limited Partnership Act, and the Uniform Interstate Family Support Act.[5] Pending proposals for uniform acts include subjects such as Third Party Access/Visitation of Children and Domestic Partnership/Civil Union.[6] As with the Restatements (discussed *supra* at pp. 9–11), the Conference can only propose laws, and no uniform law is effective until adopted by a state legislature. Since 1892, New York has adopted 54 uniform laws in addition to several articles of the UCC, and most states have adopted even more.[7]

## 2.   THE LEGISLATIVE PROCESS

At the beginning of this introductory section, we devoted substantial attention to the organization and operation of courts in order to provide a basis for a better understanding of the case law the courts produce. In the same way, we now consider legislative institutions and processes to assist in the understanding of legislative law. After reviewing the legislative process we will take up the interpretation of statutes in Part III of this Casebook.

### a.   INTRODUCTION

Of all the professional tasks a lawyer is called on to perform, one of the most frequent is that of interpreting legislation. She may be called on for interpretation, for example, as counsel advising clients of their rights under statutes, or as advocate urging, or defending against, a statutory claim, or as a judge or administrator ruling on the application of legislative language, or as a scholar explaining or appraising its significance. Many of the cases in Part III offer notable examples of judicial inquiry into legislative history in aid of interpretation.[8]

In going through the material that follows, especially as the stages of the federal legislative process are reviewed, it may be helpful to keep in view some general and specific questions. As a general question, a reader

---

**4.**   http://www.nccusl.org.

**5.**   The texts of all acts and drafts can be found at the Uniform Law Commissioner's website hosted by the University of Pennsylvania:   http://www.law.upenn.edu/bll/ulc/ulc_frame.htm.

**6.**   See http://www.nccusl.org.

**7.**   See ibid for a history of enactment by state.

**8.**   Some of the decisions debate the relevance of legislative history in the interpretation of statutes. An understanding of the legislative process should also help you appreciate why this debate is occurring.

might well ask himself at each stage—what does this aspect of the legislature or its procedures disclose about the nature of the legislative institution, about the special advantages and disadvantages of legislative lawmaking and its part in the American legal system? More specifically, and with an eye to the practical use of the process, he should also ask himself the legislative advocate's (lobbyist's) question—what can be done at this stage to speed a bill on its way or obstruct its advance? The effort to answer this last question will surely shed light on the more general question first suggested. Finally, with an eye to interpretive considerations, it is instructive to ask—what does this phase of the process yield in the way of records of legislative deliberations and where are they to be found? What is or should be the weight of these particular records in the search for "legislative intent"?

## b.  STRUCTURE, POWERS, FUNCTIONS OF CONGRESS

The primary function of Congress is to make laws. All the legislative power entrusted by the Constitution to the national government is conferred upon the Congress in Article I, Section 1. In our American scheme, the citizenry looks to Congress for the major declarations and shifts of public policy. The most difficult and substantial problems of society commonly come to this forum for negotiation, compromise and authoritative settlement. The enumeration of Congress's legislative powers in Article I, Section 8 of the Constitution—including familiar powers to tax, borrow, and spend, to regulate commerce, to provide for defense and for the general welfare, etc.—merely sketches the underpinning of the vast power Congress today wields. On this constitutional foundation of granted powers, generously construed by the courts, Congress legislates today for the ongoing needs of a huge government establishment and for substantive concerns as diverse as tariffs, public lands, currency, transportation, highways, aviation, nuclear energy, space exploration, urban renewal, communications, environmental protection, social security, welfare, housing, education, industrial safety, wages and hours, labor-management relations, agriculture, foreign aid, defense, sale of securities, armed services, and so forth. Its responsibilities for public finance, for taxes and other revenue, for borrowing and for appropriations inevitably require it to scrutinize and deal with an enormous range of activities embracing all those just mentioned by way of illustration and others too numerous to itemize. Lawyers, in particular, should be mindful too that Congressional responsibilities include the revision and updating of the substantial body of federal statute law, to say nothing of "back-up" work in dealing with unsatisfactory lawmaking or interpretation by judicial and administrative agencies. Beyond all these aspects of general legislation, there is a continuing and not negligible concern with private legislation in settlement, for example, of individual claims against the government or individual immigration or naturalization cases.

Lawmaking is not the only function of Congress or Congressmen. There is too, for example, the conduct of investigations—commonly in aid of lawmaking and often in pursuit of another major Congressional concern, that of checking on the administration of the laws. The Legislative Reorganization Act of 1946 focused a spotlight on this last concern and called for "continuous oversight" by Congressional committees of the administrative arms of government. Such checking seemed to the sponsors and has seemed to many since to be particularly necessary at a time when the speed and complexity of modern industrial society have required Congress to delegate much power to administrators. "Oversight" permits Congress to appraise administrative performance and to revise the machinery and rules and to provide funds for administrative activity as appropriate.

c.  SOURCE AND DEVELOPMENT OF LEGISLATIVE PROPOSALS

**Charles W. Johnson, "How Our Laws Are Made," H. Doc. 101–139 (2000) (excerpt)**

Sources of ideas for legislation are unlimited and proposed drafts of bills originate in many diverse quarters. Primary among these is the idea and draft conceived by a Member or Delegate. This may emanate from the election campaign during which the Member had promised, if elected, to introduce legislation on a particular subject. The Member may have also become aware after taking office of the need for amendment to or repeal of an existing law or the enactment of a statute in an entirely new field.

In addition, the Member's constituents, either as individuals or through citizen groups may avail themselves of the right to petition and transmit their proposals to the Member. The right to petition is guaranteed by the First Amendment to the Constitution. Many excellent laws have originated in this way, as some organizations, because of their vital concern with various areas of legislation, have considerable knowledge regarding the laws affecting their interests and have the services of legislative draftspersons for this purpose. Similarly, state legislatures may "memorialize" Congress to enact specified federal laws by passing resolutions to be transmitted to the House and Senate as memorials. If favorably impressed by the idea, the Member may introduce the proposal in the form in which it has been submitted or may redraft it. In any event, the Member may consult with the Legislative Counsel of the House or the Senate to frame the ideas in suitable legislative language and form.

In modern times, the "executive communication" has become a prolific source of legislative proposals. The communication is usually in the form of a message or letter from a member of the President's Cabinet, the head of an independent agency, or the President transmitting a draft of a proposed bill to the Speaker of the House of Representatives and the President of the Senate. Despite the structure of separation of powers, Article II, Section 3, of the Constitution imposes an obligation on the President to report to Congress from time to time on the "State of the Union" and to recommend for consideration such measures as the President considers necessary and expedient. Many of these executive communications follow on the President's message to Congress on the state of the Union. The communication is then referred to the standing committee or committees having jurisdiction of the subject matter of the proposal. The chairman or the ranking minority member of the relevant committee usually introduces the bill promptly either in the form in which it was received or with desired changes. This practice is usually followed even when the majority of the House and the President are not of the same political party, although there is no constitutional or statutory requirement that a bill be introduced to effectuate the recommendations. The committee or one of its subcommittees may also decide to examine the communication to determine whether a bill should be introduced. The most important of the regular executive communications is the annual message from the President transmitting the proposed budget to Congress. The President's budget proposal, together with testimony by officials of the various branches of the government before the Appropriations Committees of the House and Senate, is the basis of the several appropriation bills that are drafted by the Committee on Appropriations of the House.

Many of the executive departments and independent agencies employ legislative counsels who are charged with the drafting of bills. These legislative proposals are forwarded to Congress with a request for their enactment.

The drafting of statutes is an art that requires great skill, knowledge, and experience. In some instances, a draft is the result of a study covering a period of a year or more by a commission or committee designated by the President or a member of the cabinet. The Administrative Procedure Act and the Uniform Code of Military Justice are two examples of enactments resulting from such studies. In addition, congressional committees sometimes draft bills after studies and hearings covering periods of a year or more.

## d.   INTRODUCTION AND REFERENCE

Once the drafting of the legislative proposal has been completed and the bill is ready for Congressional consideration, it is necessary to take the appropriate formal steps to lay it before the Congress—i.e., to introduce the bill in one or both chambers. In contrast to the British Parliament where cabinet members may introduce bills, only a Representative can introduce legislation in the House of Representatives, only a Senator in the Senate. Thus the supporters of a proposal must find one or more sponsors in one or both chambers to assume responsibility for the bill and accomplish its introduction.

The choice of a sponsor or sponsors can be important. Sponsorship may represent a burdensome commitment and sponsors not infrequently have a degree of power over the fate of a measure. The sponsor identified with a bill is assumed to have taken a position in its favor (to avoid this, members sometimes insist on adding the phrase "on request" to the notice of their sponsorship) and frequently must defend this position in correspondence, in the Congress and in public discussion and in meeting proposals for amendment. From the proponents' point of view it is vital to know whether a potential sponsor or sponsors is truly in favor of the proposal. Will he take his commitment seriously? Is he strategically placed—say as a member of the Congressional leadership or as chairman of a standing committee (or, at least, as an influential member of it) and as a member of the majority party—so as to make his support most telling? Is he a tenacious and effective fighter if there are storms in the offing, as, for example, New York's Senator Wagner was in sponsoring the National Labor Relations Act and the Social Security Act? Significant Administration bills, which account for much of Congressional time and effort, are commonly introduced by the chairmen of the committees or subcommittees concerned with the subject-matter or, especially if the committee's support is in question, by a leader of the President's party in Congress. Multiple sponsorship of bills is possible in both houses. Whether co-sponsorship is desirable or not in a given case may depend on the circumstances. Dilution of responsibility and prestige must be weighed against a possible broadening of the base of support.

Once the issue of sponsorship has been settled, the sponsor or one of them introduces the legislative proposal. Assume that the proposal is to begin its legislative career in the House. In this case introduction involves nothing more than dropping the proposed bill, with the sponsor's name endorsed upon it, into the hopper at the clerk's desk in the chamber of the House of Representatives. Although there is no opportunity for sponsors to make statements as they introduce legislation in the House, most sponsors will insert an explanatory statement about their bills in the Congressional Record at some time on the day of introduction. In the Senate, the sponsor may make a statement about the bill, if she is present on the floor of the Senate and is recognized. If the bill is ultimately enacted, the statement made about it by the Senate sponsor at the time of Senate introduction, and the explanatory remarks of the House sponsor some time after House introduction, will be components of the bill's legislative history that the courts will weigh in ascertaining legislative intent. Lawyers need to be aware that such materials will generally be found in the Congressional Record.

The first action on our bill after introduction is an important one: the referring of the bill to the appropriate House standing committee for consideration. The committees and their operation will be discussed in some detail in section e, below. For the moment it is enough to point out that bills are normally referred to whichever of the numerous House standing committees has jurisdiction, under House rules, of the bill's subject-matter. See the Table, infra pp. 44–46. A sponsor may request a desired reference. The decision on reference, usually a routine one, is made by the Speaker with the assistance of the Parliamentarian and is recorded in the Congressional Record. From time to time difficult problems of choice arise where bills arguably fall within the jurisdiction of more than one committee. Occasionally, a disputed reference, when the Speaker's ruling is not accepted, has led to a floor fight and a decision by the House itself.

107TH CONGRESS
1ST SESSION

# H. R. 3543

To modify the application of the antitrust laws to authorize collective negotiations among playwrights and producers regarding the development, licensing, and production of plays.

---

## IN THE HOUSE OF REPRESENTATIVES

DECEMBER 19, 2001

Mr. HYDE (for himself and Mr. FRANK) introduced the following bill; which was referred to the Committee on the Judiciary

---

# A BILL

To modify the application of the antitrust laws to authorize collective negotiations among playwrights and producers regarding the development, licensing, and production of plays.

1    *Be it enacted by the Senate and House of Representa-*

2    *tives of the United States of America in Congress assembled,*

3    **SECTION 1. SHORT TITLE.**

4        This Act may be cited as the "Fair Play for Play-

5    wrights Act of 2001".

6    **SEC. 2. MODIFICATION OF APPLICATION OF ANTITRUST**

7                **LAWS.**

8        The antitrust laws shall not apply to—

A House rule calls on the Speaker to refer bills in such a way that, as far as may be, each committee that has jurisdiction over any provision of a bill will have responsibility for considering and reporting on that provision. This may be accomplished by having committees consider legislation concurrently or successively, or by dividing up the bill, or by creating a special ad hoc committee with members drawn from the various standing committees interested in the measure.

In the Senate, the reference process is much the same as in the House, with the decision on reference being made by the presiding officer at the time. Under the Senate rules any controversy as to jurisdiction is to be decided by the presiding officer (subject to an appeal) in favor of that committee which has jurisdiction over the subject matter which predominates in the bill. Upon motion by both the Majority and Minority Leaders or their designees, the bill may be referred to two or more committees jointly or sequentially and may be divided up between the committees.

After introduction and reference, the proposed bill is given a number and sent to the Government Printing Office. The next morning printed copies are available in the Senate and House document rooms. The print of the bill following introduction appears as indicated by the example above. The designation—e.g. H.R.4 (note that H.R. means House of Representatives)—will often be used to refer to the bill thereafter. Had it been a Senate bill the designation would have been the letter "S" followed by the bill number.

As you become accustomed to seeing or reading bills or statutes, you will note that their structure commonly contains such elements as these (items 1, 2, 4, and 8 always being present):

1. *Identifying Designation*—"H.R." or "S." and a number for federal bills, "Chapter" or "Public Law" and a number for federal statutes. State bills have comparable designations.

2. *Title*—This succinctly states the subject or aim of the legislation.

3. *Preamble*—This is found mainly in older legislation. Utilizing one or more "whereas" clauses, a preamble typically has purposes similar to those of the now more widely used Legislative Findings, Purpose or Policy (see below).

4. *Enacting Clause*—This states that the legislature adopts as law what follows.

5. *Short Title*—This gives an easy "handle" or name to the legislation.

6. *Legislative Findings, Purpose or Policy*—This embraces some or all of the following: The reasons or the occasion for the legislation, or the facts found as a basis for it, or arguments for its adoption or constitutionality. Unlike a preamble, it is a part of the Act, since it follows the enacting clause, and, unlike a preamble, it is frequently carried into codifications.

7. *Definitions*—These save repetition and attempt to clarify meaning. Sometimes they are found at the end of a bill or statute.

8. *Purview*—This is the main body of the law containing the administrative, substantive and remedial provisions, etc.

9. *Standard Clauses*—These may comprehend all or some of the following commonly encountered types of clauses:

   a.  Severability Clause–This is a clause that keeps the remaining provisions of the bill or statute in force if any portion of it is judicially declared void or unconstitutional.

   b.  Liberal Interpretation Clause–This is a clause explaining that the bill or statute is to be interpreted according to what the reader believes the author reasonably intended, so as to effectuate the spirit and purpose of the writing.

c.   Saving Clause–This is a clause exempting from coverage something that would otherwise be included. It is generally used in a repealing act to preserve rights and claims that would otherwise be lost.

d.   Repealer Clause—This may be (1) a general repealer repealing in general terms all laws inconsistent with the legislation in question, or (2) a specific schedule explicitly listing laws repealed or (3) both.

e.   Effective Date Clause—This designates the time when the legislation takes effect.

We have spoken only of bills but it is well to note that legislative action by the Congress or its chambers can take other legislative forms. These include joint resolutions, designated as "H.J.Res." or "S.J.Res.," which go through the same legislative process as bills, including signature by the President, and have the same effect, except in the case of joint resolutions proposing constitutional amendments which must be approved by two-thirds of each house and are not signed by the President. There is little, if any, practical difference between bills and those joint resolutions that do not propose constitutional amendments and these forms are sometimes used interchangeably. The bill form tends to be used routinely for general legislation. The Joint Resolution tends to be used for miscellaneous special cases such as authorizing invitations to foreign governments, or extending statutes due to expire.

There are, in addition, concurrent resolutions, designated as "H.Con. Res." or "S.Con.Res.," which are not submitted to the President and so are not equal in status or legal effect to bills or joint resolutions. They are not used for general legislation but normally deal with matters affecting only the Congress and express principles, opinions and purposes of the two Houses. And there are, finally, simple resolutions, designated "H.Res." and "S.Res.," which are promulgated by one House only and deal with concerns of the enacting House such as the establishment of a committee or the expression of the sense of one House on some public or intra-mural issue.

Joint and Concurrent Resolutions, like enacted bills, are printed in the Statutes at Large after adoption; simple Resolutions are not but may be found in the Congressional Record.

e.   THE COMMITTEE STAGE

**Charles W. Johnson, "How Our Laws Are Made," H.Doc. 101–139 (2000) (excerpt):**

Perhaps the most important phase of the legislative process is the action by committees. The committees provide the most intensive consideration to a proposed measure as well as the forum where the public is given their opportunity to be heard. A tremendous volume of work, often overlooked by the public, is done by the Members in this phase. There are, at present, 19 standing committees in the House and

16 in the Senate as well as several select committees. In addition, there are four standing joint committees of the two Houses, that have oversight responsibilities but no legislative jurisdiction. The House may also create select committees or task forces to study specific issues and report on them to the House. A task force may be established formally through a resolution passed by the House or informally through an organization of interested Members and committees by the House leadership.

Each committee's jurisdiction is divided into certain subject matters under the rules of each House and all measures affecting a particular area of the law are referred to the committee with jurisdiction over the particular subject matter. For example, the Committee on the Judiciary in the House has jurisdiction over measures relating to judicial proceedings generally, and 17 other categories, including constitutional amendments, immigration and naturalization, bankruptcy, patents, copyrights, and trademarks. In total, the rules of the House and of the Senate each provide for over 200 different classifications of measures to be referred to committees. Until 1975, the Speaker of the House could refer a bill to only one committee. In modern practice, the Speaker may refer an introduced bill to multiple committees for consideration of those provisions of the bill within the jurisdiction of each committee concerned. The Speaker must designate a primary committee of jurisdiction on bills referred to multiple committees. The Speaker may place time limits on the consideration of bills by all committees, but usually time limits are placed only on additional committees. Additional committees are committees other than the primary committee to which a bill has been referred, either initially on its introduction or sequentially following the report of the primary committee. A time limit would be placed on an additional committee only when the primary committee has reported its version to the House.

Membership on the various committees is divided between the two major political parties. The proportion of the Members of the minority party to the Members of the majority party is determined by the majority party, except that half of the members on the Committee on Standards of Official Conduct are from the majority party and half from the minority party. The respective party caucuses nominate Members of the caucus to be elected to each standing committee at the beginning of each Congress. Membership on a standing committee during the course of a Congress is contingent on continuing membership in the party caucus that nominated the Member for election to the committee. If the Member ceases to be a Member of the party caucus, the Member automatically ceases to be a member of the standing committee.

Members of the House may serve on only two committees and four subcommittees with certain exceptions. However, the rules of the caucus of the majority party in the House provide that a Member may be chairman of only one subcommittee of a committee or select committee with legislative jurisdiction, except for certain committees performing housekeeping functions and joint committees.

A Member usually seeks election to the committee that has jurisdiction over a field in which the Member is most qualified and interested. For example, the Committee on the Judiciary traditionally is composed almost entirely of lawyers. Many Members are nationally recognized experts in the specialty of their particular committee or subcommittee.

Members rank in seniority in accordance with the order of their appointment to the full committee and the ranking majority member with the most continuous service is usually elected chairman. The rules of the House require that committee chairmen be elected from nominations submitted by the majority party caucus at the commencement of each Congress. No Member of the House may serve as chairman of the same standing committee or of the same subcommittee thereof for more than three consecutive Congresses.

The rules of the House prohibit a committee that maintains a subcommittee on oversight from having more than six subcommittees with the exception of the Committee on Appropriations and the Committee on Government Reform.

Each committee is provided with a professional staff to assist it in the innumerable administrative details involved in the consideration of bills and its oversight responsibilities. For standing committees, the professional staff is limited to 30 persons appointed by a vote of the committee. Two-thirds of the committee staff are selected by a majority vote of the majority committee members and one-third of the committee staff are selected by a majority vote of minority committee members. All staff appointments are made without regard to race, creed, sex, or age. The minority staff provisions do not apply to the Committee on Standards of Official Conduct because of its bipartisan nature. The Committee on Appropriations has special authority under the rules of the House for appointment of staff for the minority.

### Standing House Committees, 108th Congress, (2003–2004)

| Committee | Total Members | R | D | Other | No. of Subcom. |
|---|---|---|---|---|---|
| Agriculture | 51 | 27 | 24 | | 5 |
| Appropriations | 65 | 36 | 29 | | 13 |
| Armed Services | 61 | 33 | 28 | | 5 |
| Budget | 43 | 24 | 19 | | 0 |
| Education and the Work-force | 49 | 27 | 22 | | 5 |
| Energy and Commerce | 57 | 31 | 26 | | 6 |
| Financial Services | 70 | 37 | 32 | 1 | 6 |
| Government Reform | 44 | 24 | 19 | 1 | 7 |
| House Administration | 9 | 6 | 3 | | 0 |
| International Relations | 49 | 26 | 23 | | 6 |

| | | | | |
|---|---|---|---|---|
| Judiciary | 37 | 21 | 16 | 5 |
| Resources | 52 | 28 | 24 | 5 |
| Rules | 13 | 9 | 4 | 2 |
| Science | 47 | 25 | 22 | 4 |
| Small Business | 36 | 19 | 17 | 4 |
| Standards of Official Conduct | 10 | 5 | 5 | 0 |
| Transportation and Infrastructure | 75 | 41 | 34 | 6 |
| Veterans' Affairs | 31 | 17 | 14 | 3 |
| Ways and Means | 41 | 24 | 17 | 6 |

Select Committee of the House
Permanent Select Committee on Intelligence
Select Committee on Homeland Security

### Standing Senate Committees, 108th Congress (2003–2004)

| Committee | Total Members | R | D | Other | No. of Subcom. |
|---|---|---|---|---|---|
| Agriculture, Nutrition and Forestry | 21 | 11 | 10 | | 4 |
| Appropriations | 29 | 15 | 14 | | 13 |
| Armed Services | 25 | 13 | 12 | | 6 |
| Banking, Housing, and Urban Affairs | 21 | 11 | 10 | | 5 |
| Budget | 23 | 12 | 11 | | 0 |
| Commerce, Science and Transportation | 23 | 12 | 11 | | 6 |
| Energy and Natural Resources | 23 | 12 | 11 | | 4 |
| Environment and Public Works | 19 | 10 | 9 | | 4 |
| Finance | 21 | 11 | 10 | | 5 |
| Foreign Relations | 19 | 10 | 9 | | 8 |
| Government Affairs | 17 | 9 | 8 | | 3 |
| Health, Education, Labor and Pensions | 21 | 11 | 10 | | 4 |
| Judiciary | 19 | 10 | 9 | | 6 |
| Rules and Administration | 19 | 10 | 9 | | 0 |
| Small Business and Entrepreneurship | 19 | 10 | 9 | | 0 |
| Veterans' Affairs | 15 | 8 | 7 | | 0 |

### Select Committee of Senate
Select Committee on Ethics
Select Committee on Intelligence

Special Committee on Aging
Committee on Indian Affairs
Select Committee on Homeland Security

**Joint Committee**
Joint Economic Committee
Joint Committee on the Library
Joint Committee on Printing
Joint Committee on Taxation

What happens when a bill has been referred to a standing committee? In most cases, the standing committee chairman will refer the bill to a subcommittee for consideration, if the committee has subcommittees, as most do. Also, copies will often be transmitted to the executive departments or agencies with a request for their views. One must remark at this point, on the power of the committee as a whole and the power of the standing committee chair in particular. Only a small percentage of bills referred to committees is reported out. The power it possesses to block or to report legislation, with or without amendment—and we shall later see further reasons why its life and death powers are so great—helps to make the committee a crucial factor in any bill's history.

The Committee chair has other practical powers stemming from his other functions—such as calling and presiding over meetings and hearings, setting the agenda, developing and controlling staff, negotiating for floor consideration, designating the floor manager for the bill and participating in conference proceedings. In her turn, the subcommittee chair will have major power over the fate of the bill and much to say, subject to the power of the full committee and its chairman, over whether the measure is to languish or be pursued with more or less vigor. The subcommittee's decision to table or to endorse or to reshape is often accepted by the full committee and ultimately by the Congress. The Appropriations Committees, for example, regularly endorse the work of their subcommittees. Thus the work of a very few Senators or Representatives and of the chairman may be decisive. The extraordinary fragmentation of Congressional power becomes evident.

Whether the bill is considered by the full committee or a subcommittee, and especially if it is a significant bill and in some degree controversial, the chair or subcommittee chair as the case may be will probably decide to hold public hearings on it; he or she has much discretion as to whether and how such hearings will be conducted. With the staff, who are subject to his or her control, the chair concerned will schedule the hearings, give notice, plan the pattern of witnesses, and issue requests to testify or, perhaps, subpoenas. On the appointed hearing day, an official reporter will be present to record testimony. After introductory statements by committee or subcommittee members, the Senators and Representatives who seek to be heard will receive preference as witnesses; officials of the executive departments or agencies may also then be heard, as well as the representatives of interest groups and other private persons. Prepared statements will often be submitted and witnesses will be questioned. Owing to the multiple burdens of committee work that affect legislators, the hearing may only be sparsely attended by members of the sponsoring committee or subcommittee.

The purposes of hearings may vary widely depending on the measure and the aims of the legislators. If well organized by chairman and staff to that end, they can serve as a valuable means for gathering information and for testing the proposal's impact on segments of the public. In this aspect it is instructive to compare the modest research and data-gathering capability of the courts to the capabilities of Congressional committees, with their staffs, their access to the Congressional Research Service and the Offices of Legislative Counsel, and their access through hearings and otherwise to the expertise of governmental and private sources. But hearings are not always well managed to serve this informational purpose and may be used to serve, instead or in addition, such other purposes as mobilizing public support or opposition, providing publicity for legislators, stalling the legislative progress of a bill, furnishing a "safety valve" for disturbances, and so forth.

After the hearings, the hard work begins on the bill. A transcript of the hearings is made available. With the help of staff, other data, analyses and drafts are assembled. The legislators then meet, with or without preliminary caucusing and with staff personnel and sometimes representatives of governmental departments (and sometimes representatives of private interests) in attendance. They discuss the bill and any amendments and decide whether and on what terms to report it out. If the vote is to table, that will often be the end of a bill unless pressures in the full committee (in the case of a bill first considered by a subcommittee) or in the chamber as a whole can force a different result. If the bill is not tabled, the next step is to "mark up" the bill and it will often receive its definitive shape in the course of compromises and negotiations on this level at the hands of members and staff and drafters. Note must be taken here of the ease with which a proposal can be blocked by a strategically placed minority at this stage—unless the pressures against it can be overcome by intense pressures in its behalf.

When a bill is reported out, with or without amendment, by a subcommittee, it must run the gauntlet of the full committee, which typically has regular meeting days on which subcommittee reports are taken up. Sometimes the subcommittee's work will be accepted; at other times, the whole process of hearings and "marking up" or revision will be repeated in the full committee, which in any event must ultimately vote on its own to table the bill or to report it in some form. Again, there is opportunity for delay and defeat and much may depend on the attitude and practice of the full committee chair toward the proposal. From the standpoint of the lobbyist, of course, the subcommittee and committee phases of action are key points for the application of favorable or adverse pressures and the same is apt to be true at other points of the process where a small number of persons exercise great power over a measure's progress.

Notice at the committee stage that three kinds of documents emerge that may be vital elements in the legislative history of the bill when its meaning is later sought by lawyers, administrators, judges or by the public. The first of these is the hearings, if they are printed and made generally available to the Congress and the public.[9] These may contain important clues to the impact or sense of legislative provisions, especially, for example, when amendments are made in response to points made at the hearings. The second is the different versions of the bill considered by the committee. Changes in language between the bill as referred to the committee and the bill as reported out may shed significant light on the bill's final meaning. The third and perhaps most important document at this stage is the full committee's formal report accompanying the bill when it is transmitted by the committee to the chamber as a whole. This formal report normally discusses the purposes of and reasons for the bill and analyzes its provisions. Committee amendments are indicated and communications from the executive regarding the bill are commonly incorporated in the report. There may be a minority report—i.e., dissenting views—on the same bill. Both the committee report (which will be given a number) and the bill as reported will be printed up and made available promptly after filing. The report has special significance for interpretive purposes, representing, as it does, an expression of views about the bill by the Congressional group charged with detailed knowledge and responsibility. It constitutes a prime source of information about the bill for the members of Congress as well, a source to which they can refer as a basis for their vote. So important is it for this purpose that House and Senate normally require that committee reports be available to the membership for several days before consideration of the measures to which they are addressed.

We have been considering the committee stage in relation to a bill. But if it is to become law, the bill must somehow be laid before the chambers themselves to be voted on and approved by the membership as a whole. In the House, serious risks of delay and obstruction attend the process of getting to the floor but rigid, expeditious procedures speed it to its fate thereafter; on the other hand, in the Senate, getting to the floor is notably less difficult, but serious risks of delay and obstruction arise in connection with floor consideration.

## f. FLOOR ACTION ON THE BILL

### i. *On the House Floor*

Let us look first at the patterns of floor action in the House. Assuming the bill is important and controversial, it will in all probability, as we saw,

---

**9.** A printed version of the hearings may not be available until many months after the hearings have taken place.

be the subject of a special rule from the Rules Committee. Even bills privileged in their own right, such as revenue bills, not infrequently are brought before the House by preference under a special rule from the Rules Committee limiting the terms of debate. The initial step then in the floor proceedings on our bill—unlike privileged bills or bills coming up on the Private or Consent or Discharge Calendar or Suspension of the Rules or as District of Columbia business—will be the Speaker's recognition of a member of the Rules Committee to call up the rule relating to our bill. Special rules of this kind may be debated for an hour but the debate does not normally consume the allotted time and such rules are often adopted without difficulty by voice vote. Following is an example of a typical special rule, of the "open" kind, for a bill on the Union Calendar:

> *Resolved,* That upon the adoption of this resolution it shall be in order to move that the House resolve itself into the Committee of the Whole House on the State of the Union for the consideration of the bill (H.R. ___) to (here insert the purpose of the bill). After general debate, which shall be confined to the bill and shall continue not to exceed two hours, to be equally divided and controlled by the chairman and ranking minority member of the Committee on ___, the bill shall be read for amendment under the five-minute rule. At the conclusion of the consideration of the bill for amendment, the Committee shall rise and report the bill to the House with such amendments as may have been adopted, and the previous question shall be considered as ordered on the bill and amendments thereto to final passage without intervening motion except one motion to recommit.

The text of the resolution is of great importance as it sets the pattern for what follows.

Upon adoption of the special rule the House resolves itself into the Committee of the Whole House on the State of the Union. This step, applicable to most significant pieces of legislation, has a number of consequences. In essence it makes less formal, and speeds, the action of the House. In the Committee of the Whole, the House can operate with a quorum of 100 members (as against 218 for the House itself). Time-consuming yea and nay votes are avoided. For the deliberations of the Committee of the Whole, the Speaker steps down from the chair, appointing another chairman in his place.

As the above special rule indicates, the next step in relation to our bill is general debate. The time the rule allows is equally divided between (a) the bill's floor manager, who is normally the chair of the responsible standing committee or subcommittee, and, (b) his or her principal opponent, who is usually a ranking minority member of the same committee or subcommittee. The floor manager speaks first, followed by his or her opposite number. Both yield time to others for further speeches regarding the bill. Note once again the pervasive role of the standing committee and its leaders in the legislative process.

Following the general debate, the bill is open to amendment, committee amendments having priority. The sponsor of an amendment has five minutes to explain and support his or her amendment; additional time requires unanimous consent. The floor manager has five minutes to respond. If other members want time to discuss an amendment, they offer fictional or pro forma amendments (motions to "strike the last word") as a basis for receiving five minutes of speaking time. Members of the standing committee are also entitled to preference in recognition. Debate on an amendment can continue for some little time under this system and may be closed by unanimous consent or by motion requiring a majority vote. While there are possibilities for delay in House procedure, there is no real opportunity to stop a bill or amendment from being voted on.

Votes on amendments in the Committee of the Whole may be voice votes. If the vote is close or doubtful, a vote by division (proponents and opponents stand in turn to be counted) may be demanded. A roll call vote may be had if the division reveals the lack of a quorum.

The amending stage is crucial in the progress of a bill. The amendments offered may be and often are of such character as to change the bill substantially or weaken it drastically. Their adoption might undermine such support for the bill as already exists. In any case, the skill, dedication and prestige of the floor manager may make the difference between success and failure in warding off crippling revisions. Once again it is appropriate to point to the life and death role of the committee personnel who, having addressed the bill in the committee itself and championed it before the Rules Committee, are now proponents for the bill on the floor. The support or opposition of the bill's standing committee proponents with respect to a particular amendment may influence a member of Congress' vote on the amendment. In theory, doubts should be resolved in favor of the committee that has done the detailed work on the bill. If the committee represents a cross-section of the House, it may have foreseen and met the need to compromise adequately the divergent interests represented in the full House. Weight may attach, too, to the position of the leadership; and in the case of amendments proposed by minority party spokespersons, party loyalty may play a role. Incidentally, one of the most difficult tasks of those managing bills is to see that needed supporters are available on the floor when critical votes are taken.

Note, for purposes of later comparison with the Senate, that amendments put forward in the Committee of the Whole must be germane to the bill and to that portion of the bill they purport to revise. It may be possible to tack a non-germane amendment to a bill when the Rules Committee's special rule waives points of order against the bill or when the amendment concerned has specifically been made in order.

Not only is the bill open to amendment under the procedures we have been discussing, but it is also possible—though rare—to kill the bill in its entirety if a motion to strike the enacting clause is offered and sustained. If this preferential motion—which must be considered at once and allows ten minutes of debate—is upheld in the Committee of the Whole, the Committee rises and reports back to the full House which then has an opportunity to vote on the same question. If the full House sustains the defeat, the bill is killed; if not, the House resolves itself back into Committee of the Whole and resumes debate.

The process of amending the bill in Committee of the Whole, if not limited by the provisions of the special rule, will normally continue until there are no amendments left to consider, but it may be brought to an end by a unanimous consent agreement or by a motion disposed of by majority vote. Here, too, the inexorable march and expedition of House procedures deserve comparison with the Senate.

When the process of reading the bill for amendment has concluded, the Committee of the Whole rises, its action is reported to the House itself, the Speaker resumes the chair, the quorum requirement is once again 218 members, and the House itself takes over consideration at this point. Note again the terms of the special rule, supra, governing the remaining steps, and these steps will generally be quite similar as a practical matter even when a privileged measure—such as an appropriation bill—is being considered without a special rule. Under the rule the "previous question" is deemed ordered, a highly privileged procedure which calls for final vote forthwith on the merits.

The House itself now takes up without debate the amendments, if any, reported by the Committee of the Whole and usually, though not necessarily, votes on them en bloc. Amendments rejected in Committee of the Whole are not reported and, in practice, they are lost and may not be voted on again. Once the amendments approved in Committee of the Whole have been voted on by the House—and the House commonly approves the work of the Committee of the Whole—the question before the House is the adoption of the amended bill itself. After vote on engrossment and third reading of the bill a member of the opposition may make a motion to recommit the bill to the original standing committee with or without instructions. If such a motion without instructions carries, the bill is stopped *pro tem* and goes back to the committee which may however report it back again at some later date for another attempt at passage. If the motion is made and approved with instructions to amend the bill in specified ways—often ways that were defeated in the Committee of the Whole—and to report forthwith, the bill as revised by the standing committee in accordance with the instructions is reported back to the House and put to a vote. When the motion to recommit is defeated, as it normally is, the question before the House becomes the final passage of the bill. The final vote will be a roll-call vote if one fifth of the members so demand.

House floor procedure, taken as a whole, is notable then for the power it gives the majority, the continuing power exercised by the committee, the short shrift (e.g., the 5–minute rule, the "previous question") given to dilatory tactics and to efforts to block a final vote. While the amending process can be used to delay and perhaps destroy, such action is subject to majority approval and is part and parcel of the ongoing Congressional task of reconciling divergent interests as a basis for social action.

### ii.  On the Senate Floor

Compare the operation of the Senate when it takes up a bill on the floor, especially its handling of amendments and the limitation of debate. Commonly a bill will come before the Senate pursuant to a unanimous consent arrangement worked out by the majority leader in consultation with the minority leader and other interested Senators. Failing that, a motion may be made to take up the bill. Such a motion is vulnerable to the filibuster tactic (see below). Pursuant to such a motion, if adopted, or to a unanimous consent agreement, floor consideration of the bill begins—usually with an opening statement by the floor manager who will probably be either the responsible subcommittee chair or, especially on major bills, the chair of the standing committee itself. Members of the committee will most likely be on hand on the floor at this point and the opposition will be led by the appropriate ranking minority committee member. There is no reserved time for general debate as in the House and the amendment of the bill is in order at once. Committee amendments are taken up first, then non-committee amendments. This amendment stage is no less critical, no less dependent on the skill and prestige of the floor managers, than it is in the House. Note, however, that in contrast to the House, where the requirement of germaneness regulates the amending process, in the Senate an amendment to a bill need not be germane to a bill, unless it is a general appropriation bill.

The central characteristic of Senate floor procedure that differentiates it from that of the House and, indeed, from that of most other legislative bodies, is the difficulty of limiting debate. At this time, there are only three ways in which debate may close. First, when all Senators have said all they wish to say on a proposal the debate will come to a halt. Second, there is the possibility of a unanimous consent agreement to limit debate on a particular measure. Even on many relatively controversial bills, the discussion is ended pursuant to such agreements. But such a device is not available to close debate against the wishes of even a single Senator. Absent unanimous consent, or the exhaustion of all desires to speak, the only recourse is the so-called cloture rule.

**Charles W. Johnson, "How Our Laws Are Made," H. Doc. 101–139 (2000) (excerpt):**

> On occasion, Senators opposed to a measure may extend debate by making lengthy speeches or a number of speeches at various stages of consideration intended to prevent or defeat action on the measure. This is the tactic known as "filibustering." Debate, however, may be closed if 16 Senators sign a motion to that effect and the motion is carried by three-fifths of the Senators duly chosen and sworn. Such a motion is voted on one hour after the Senate convenes, following a quorum call on the next day after a day of session has intervened. This procedure is called "invoking cloture." In 1986, the Senate amended its rules to limit "post-cloture" consideration to 30 hours. A Senator may speak for not more than one hour and may yield all or a part of that time to the majority or minority floor managers of the bill under

consideration or to the Majority or Minority leader. The Senate may increase the time for "post-cloture" debate by a vote of three-fifths of the Senators duly chosen and sworn. After the time for debate has expired, the Senate may consider only amendments actually pending before voting on the bill.

There has been much argument over the merits of unlimited debate, or filibustering, and the weak cloture rule. On the one hand, the arguments made have cited the importance of unfettered debate in at least one chamber and have stressed the desirability of assuring that legislation with drastic consequences cannot be adopted by ruthless majorities over the intense opposition of a numerous minority. On the other hand there have been arguments based on the desirability of a majority's being ultimately able to prevail in a democratic society. The upshot of the present rule certainly is, in any case, to allow an intense minority to prevail, to block action, unless an extraordinary majority can be mobilized on the other side. And this state of affairs has pervasive implications for Senate procedure and decision-making. A majority cannot act if a large and determined minority opposes. The filibuster and threat of filibuster—even by individuals—offer a tremendous weapon for extracting concessions and compromises in legislative bargaining, especially in the crowded hours before sessions draw to a close. The difficulty of building winning coalitions is greatly increased. The further dispersion of already dispersed Congressional power should be plain enough to any observer.

The Senate conducts a great deal of business, nonetheless, without encountering the occasional barrier of an actual filibuster. Assuming the bill is a part of such normal business, it will come in due course to a vote. Unlike the House, the Senate does not deliberate in a Committee of the Whole, but it conducts its voting as the House does—by voice, by division and, on the request of one-fifth of a quorum, by roll-call (the yeas and nays). Roll-call votes, due to the chamber's smaller size, are easier and more frequent in the Senate.

When the vote has been taken, any Senator on the prevailing side may move to reconsider it within two days. In order to make the result definite and final, this motion to reconsider is generally made promptly after the final vote and another Senator moves to table the motion while the supporters of the final vote are still on hand. Tabling the motion has the effect of making the final vote conclusive; it usually is approved by voice vote. Once in a while, after a close vote, a change of heart or the arrival of new troops can dramatically upset the result. In the House, as we saw, it is common for the opponents of a bill to move to recommit; the same motion is possible in the Senate, but infrequent. Generally when the motion to reconsider is tabled, the Senate's deliberations—short of conference—on a bill are finished. Such deliberations, it should now be apparent, are far more flexible and leisurely than the House's, more prone to delay and liable as well to serious minority obstruction.

The student of votes in the Congressional Record will note references to "pairs." The practice of pairing is followed in both chambers. Pairing permits absent, or otherwise nonvoting, Senators to record their position. Thus, two absent Senators on opposite sides may "pair" with each other and their positions will be noted but will not be counted in the voting tallies.

*iii.*  *The Congressional Record*

Lawyers investigating the history of bills, and other students of the legislative process will inevitably make extensive use of the Congressional Record, which reports the floor proceedings of Congress and contains other information as well. The Record has been published since 1873. Before that time the proceedings of Congress were published in the Annals of Congress (1789–1824), the Register of Debates (1824–1837) and the Congressional Globe (1833–1873). The modern Record is published daily while Congress is in session. Bound volumes appear later. The bound volumes do not necessarily match the daily edition exactly and, as to both, it must be noted that the Record purports only to be "substantially a verbatim report of proceedings." Unfortunately, the practice of Representatives and Senators in revising or extending their remarks or inserting undelivered speeches has marred the accuracy of the Record as a transcript of what occurred on the floor. A modest step was taken on March 1, 1978 in both House and Senate toward identifying in the Record materials not actually uttered on the floor. Now, in the House section of the Congressional Record, undelivered speeches and other extraneous material are printed in a different type style to distinguish them from speeches actually given on the Floor; in the Senate section, statements or insertions that are not spoken by a Senator from the Floor are preceded by a "bullet." However, because in the Senate, with unanimous consent, remarks are printed as if spoken, the system adopted falls far short of enabling the reader reliably to know how much of what is printed was in fact said in debate. Although only substantially verbatim, the Record is the best source available and lawyers must learn to make effective use of it. It is necessary to remember that the Record fulfills many purposes for the legislator besides that of providing an accurate record for judicial use. A glance at its pages seasoned with articles, occasional speeches, editorials, etc. and at its swollen Appendix will give some idea of the problem. But it does provide a record of some kind of the floor proceedings, the texts of amendments (which may also be available separately and may be crucial for interpretive purposes), and conference reports, and it contains indices invaluable to the researcher such as the Daily Digest, and, in the permanent edition, the History of Bills and Resolutions. In the Congressional Record and in the headings of bills, one peculiarity appears (particularly in the Senate proceedings) which should be mentioned. That is the phenomenon of the "legislative day." Because the Senate is apt to recess, rather than adjourn, from day to day and because recessing overnight does not trigger a new legislative day when the Senate reconvenes in the morning, the Senate may be still operating on a legislative day, begun much earlier, which does not coincide with the calendar day. In the study of the rules this can be important as they may provide for lapses of time in terms of legislative days or calendar days and the difference must be noted.

## g.  INTER–HOUSE COORDINATION

The House and Senate, acting successively or concurrently in accordance with the procedures already described, may adopt identical measures. When they do, there is nothing to prevent or delay presentation of the legislation to the President for his signature. The same is true, even when the chambers pass different versions of a bill, if one chamber is willing, without more, to accept the other's version.

When the differences between the chambers regarding a bill are controversial in character, however, and neither chamber is, or seems, likely to yield its position, special action to compose differences may be needed. Normally a conference will be requested. Conferees or managers from each chamber are appointed by, respectively, the Speaker of the House and the presiding officer of the Senate. At least three conferees—but there may be more—are designated in each chamber. In selecting them, the presiding officer generally follows the recommendations of the appropriate standing committee chair. Each chamber's team of conferees or managers is very likely to include senior members of the standing committee. Such persons as the standing committee chair, the ranking majority and minority members, the appropriate subcommittee chair and the ranking minority subcommittee member will probably be selected. A House rule provides that in appointing conference committee members the Speaker "shall appoint no less than a majority of members who generally supported the House position as determined by the Speaker." Another rule requires the Speaker, to the extent feasible, to name as conferees the authors of the principal amendments to the proposed bill. Both political parties are commonly represented on the committee, with the majority party having the larger representation. Because the Senate and House delegations vote separately on all questions arising in the conference committee and because a majority of each delegation must approve every action, it is not essential that the two delegations be of the same size and they frequently are not. Note here, as elsewhere in the federal legislative process the pervasive influence of the standing committee and its chair.

The designated conferees meet to discuss the bill, typically under great pressure to reach an accommodation and often under great pressure of time. On rare occasions, conference delegations operate under direction from the parent chamber, but generally there are no instructions. The conferees are generally free to negotiate and resolve all matters in dispute between the chambers, although House rules restrict the power of House conferees to agree to non-germane Senate amendments. The conferees may trade off Senate provisions against House provisions and vice versa; they may seek a middle ground between the Senate and House provisions. They may not add new provisions or change provisions already agreed on by both chambers. Nonetheless they have, in practice, substantial leeway to compose differences; moreover it is difficult to enforce strict limitations. Sometimes, one chamber will have amended a bill originating in the other by striking out all that follows the enacting clause and inserting its own provisions. When such an amendment "in the nature of a substitute" comes before the conference, the conferees have the entire subject matter before them and are much more free to make changes, even to draw a new bill. In such cases, the conferees may not include in their report matter not committed to them by either house; but they may include matter which is a germane modification of subjects in disagreement.

The deliberations of a small group with a large measure of power over the shape and fate of a controversial bill are a natural target for pressure from special interests for this or that modification of the bill's provisions. By any yardstick, the conference is crucial for a bill, and any experienced lobbyist cannot fail to be aware of this. Once more there is a major opportunity for blocking action.

As the figures quoted earlier suggest, conference committees are usually able to arrive at some sort of accommodation of Senate–House differences and to agree on provisions to be recommended to the chambers. If the chambers cannot be thus brought to agreement, the bill is lost. Assuming, however, that the conferees do concur in recommendations for adjusting the differences, they incorporate these recommendations in a report which must be signed by a majority of each delegation of the conferees and filed with their respective houses. The dissenting managers have no authority to file statements of minority views. The recommendations are accompanied by a statement on the part of the managers explaining the effect of actions recommended. The conference report containing the recommendations and statement is made available in print separately and in the Congressional Record. As a document representing the late and detailed views of representatives of both chambers it is a very important aid to judicial interpretation of the enacted bill.

The engrossed bill and amendments, together with a copy of the report of the conference committee, are transmitted to the chamber which is to act first on the conference report (normally to the house other than the one requesting the conference). Whichever chamber takes up the conference report, it represents a matter of high privilege. In the House of Representatives, for example, the report and bill do not need help from the Rules Committee to reach the floor quickly.

The chamber first approving the conference report sends the documents to the other house for final action. When both chambers have approved the conference bill it is sent to the enrolling clerk of the chamber in which the bill had its origin. It is then ready for the last stage of its journey to enactment.

## h.  EXECUTIVE ACTION

When the bill has weathered the stages of committee review, of getting to the floor, of floor consideration, of inter-house coordination, it faces at least one more critical test—that of Presidential review. In fact, the

President's concern with an important bill is not something that merely springs into being at the end of the long process just described. When discussing the sources of legislation, we noted the President's major role as an initiator of enactments. Through public statements and personal communications, through Cabinet members, staff aides, administrative agency officials and otherwise, the President maintains active contact with the Congress in regard to bills important to him as they make their way forward from stage to stage of the process. His participation in that process comes to a climax or focus, however, when the moment arrives for exercise of the power to approve or veto conferred on him by the Constitution.

Once the bill is approved in identical form by both House and Senate, it is transmitted to the enrolling clerk of the chamber in which it originated, who undertakes the often complex and difficult task of preparing the so-called enrolled bill, incorporating as accurately as may be all amendments adopted along the way. The enrolled bill is printed and when the proper committee approves the bill as truly enrolled, it is transmitted for signature first to the Speaker of the House, then to the President of the Senate. When both have affixed their signatures to the enrolled bill, it is delivered to the White House and a receipt is secured for it. This delivery is normally regarded as presentation to the President and as triggering the start of the ten day period allowed for Presidential action by the Constitution. Occasionally, in the past, when a President has had to be absent for an extended period—as Wilson was in 1919 and as Franklin D. Roosevelt was some decades later—the step of delivery to the White House has been deferred for a time so as not to trigger the ten day period at an inconvenient moment.

The President has several choices in dealing with a bill presented to him. If he decides to approve the measure, he may do so affirmatively by signing it, or passively, if Congress is still in session at the end of ten days following presentation, by leaving it unsigned. In either case the bill becomes a law. In neither of these cases does the Constitution require any statement by the President. There have, however, been a few special occasions—for example, President Truman's approval of the Hobbs Anti–Racketeering Act of 1946 and the Portal-to-Portal Act of 1947—when the chief executive upon approving a bill has in fact sent a formal message to Congress explaining his approval and discussing the provisions of the legislation concerned. Whether or not there is a formal communication to Congress, the President may in any case issue a more or less detailed public statement on signing the bill. (Part III includes an example of such a statement.)

If the President objects to a bill, the Constitution provides that within ten days after presentation "he shall return it, with his objections to the House in which it shall have originated, who shall enter the objections at large on their Journal and proceed to reconsider it." The veto thus delivered may be overridden by a two-thirds vote of both Senate and House. In that event the bill becomes a law; without such overriding it does not. There is also the possibility of a "pocket veto." This occurs when the

President fails to sign a measure and Congress adjourns before the end of the ten-day period allowed for Presidential action. In this case the bill is lost; Congress has no opportunity to override the veto. When the President vetoes by returning a bill to Congress, there is an obligatory Presidential message that goes with it. Although such a message is not required with a "pocket veto," it has been a Presidential practice to give the press and the public a full statement of reasons for each "pocket veto."

How is the decision made to veto or approve a bill? At the point where an enrolled bill is presented to the President, the Legislative Reference Division of the President's Office of Management and Budget undertakes a searching review process. Copies of the bill are sent to the executive departments and agencies concerned with its provisions and their recommendations are sought within forty-eight hours as to whether the President should veto or approve. While this may sound like a short period for response, it must be remembered that the departments and agencies in question will generally have been active in the legislative process on the bill—e.g., providing expert views and aid to the Congressional committees in hearings and otherwise—and so will commonly be very familiar with the measure. When agency responses are received, the Legislative Reference Division has several days to prepare its own "enrolled bill memorandum" for the chief executive. In that memorandum will be the arguments advanced by the agencies for and against the bill, together with the Division's own analysis and recommendations. In the end the President must weigh all this argumentation in relation to his perception of the national interest, his programs and promises, his obligations, his party position, the counsels of staff and other close advisers, and so forth. Note that the lobbying pressures on the President and his advisers may be as intense at this point as they are at earlier critical points in the legislative process. Note also that the President with his national constituency and his own objectives and resources, brings to the decisional process still another perspective from that applied by the Senators and Representatives who have previously passed on it.

One way or another, the President must decide. Much of the time, the decision is to approve. The number of Presidential vetoes is not in fact very large in comparison to the total number of bills which are presented for signature and become law without exercise of the veto power. But the number of vetoes should not be taken as an index of the veto power's importance. The existence of the veto power and the threat of its possible use extend the President's influence throughout the legislative process. His position must be reckoned with by proponents and opponents at every stage. Here is one more center of power in the panorama of dispersed and divided powers that the Federal legislative processes offer to view. Here is one more opportunity to block action.

If the decision is to approve, and unless the President allows the bill to become law without his signature, there may be more or less elaborate signing ceremonies. Notice of the signing is generally sent by message to the chamber where the bill originated and that chamber informs the other. The action is noted in the Congressional Record.

If the President vetoes a bill, other than by "pocket veto," the bill and his veto message are, as we saw, returned to the chamber of origin. A vetoed bill returned to the Congress in this way is accorded high privilege (there is no need for recourse to the Rules Committee in the House) and will generally be disposed of quickly. Amendments are not in order; in the House, only a limited time is allowed for debate. If there is no real possibility the veto may be overridden, the bill may be tabled or sent back to committee. Otherwise the question is put, "Shall the bill pass, the objections of the President to the contrary notwithstanding?" To override the veto, each chamber must separately vote to do so by a vote of at least two-thirds of those present, a quorum being required to be on hand. A negative vote kills the bill and if it occurs in the first chamber a message is normally sent to the other advising of the decision that the bill is not to pass.

If the President signs the bill or allows it to become law without signature, or if the chambers vote to override a veto, then, as the case may be, the President or the chamber last voting to override will transmit the bill to the General Services Administration for publication. There, a public law number will be given to the bill (the public law number contains the number of the enacting Congress and a number indicating the order in which the bill was adopted as compared with other enactments by the same Congress). The bill is forthwith made available in published form. First, it is made available as a slip law (see *infra*) in unbound pamphlet form printed by offset process from the enrolled bill. Later, this and other new laws will be published in bound volumes of the Statutes at Large, an official authoritative compilation containing the laws of each Congress in the chronological order of their enactment. Later also, the bill will be incorporated in the United States Code, a compilation consolidating and codifying the general and permanent laws of the United States and arranging them by subject-matter under 50 titles. For the lawyer, the Code is a much more readily usable research tool than the chronologically arranged Statutes at Large. Certain titles of the Code have been enacted into positive law in an ongoing codification effort; as to these titles the Code is the official and authoritative source of the statute law. The Statutes at Large and the Revised Statutes (an early compilation of the laws in force as of Dec. 1, 1873) remain the official and authoritative source, however, for laws not included in these titles. These versions of the bill—the slip law, the text in the Statutes at Large, the version in the U.S. Code—are primary sources for lawyers working with legislation. Other materials, such as veto or approval messages, may be of high importance as aids to understanding the bill, now a statute, when it comes before lawyers, courts or administrators for interpretation.

## C.   ADMINISTRATIVE LAW

While case and statutory law will preoccupy almost all of your studies during your first year, administrative law is an important and increasingly pervasive source of law in practice. Administrative agencies run adjudicatory proceedings which, for the parties involved, are essentially indistinguishable from court proceedings. And administrative agencies also promulgate rules, which for all intents and purposes, function as statutes. The following provides an overview of these administrative functions in the U.S. legal system.

## 1.   BACKGROUND AND HISTORY

Ernest Gellhorn and Ronald M. Levin, Administrative Law and Process 1–3, (4th ed. 1997) offer the following observations on the reasons for establishing administrative agencies (instead of relying on the courts and the legislature):

Administrative agencies are usually created to deal with current crises or to redress serious social problems. Throughout the modern era of administrative regulation, which began approximately a century ago, the government's response to a public demand for action has often been to establish a new agency, or to grant new powers to an existing bureaucracy. Near the turn of the century, agencies like the Interstate Commerce Commission and the Federal Trade Commission were created in an attempt to control the anticompetitive conduct of monopolies and powerful corporations.... In the 1960's when the injustices of poverty and racial discrimination became an urgent national concern, the development of programs designed to redress these grievances expanded the scope of government administration. More recently, increased public concern about risks to human health and safety and threats to the natural environment have resulted in new agencies and new regulatory programs.

The primary reason why administrative agencies have so frequently been called upon to deal with such diverse social problems is the great flexibility of the regulatory process. In comparison to courts or legislatures or elected executive officials, administrative agencies have several institutional strengths that equip them to deal with complex problems. Perhaps the most important of these strengths is staffing: an agency is authorized to hire people with whatever mix of talents, skills and experience it needs to get the job done. Moreover, because the agency has responsibility for a limited area of public policy, it can develop the expertise that comes from continued exposure to a problem area....

However, these potential strengths of the administrative process can also be viewed as a threat to other important values. Administrative "flexibility" may simply be a mask for unchecked power, and in our society unrestrained government power has traditionally been viewed with great and justifiable suspicion. Thus, the fundamental policy problem of the administrative process is how to design a system of checks which will minimize the risks of bureaucratic arbitrariness and overreaching, while preserving for the agencies the flexibility they need to act effectively.

For the historical context of the shift in lawmaking from legislatures to administrative agencies, consider the following developments traced in Kenneth C. Davis & Richard J. Pierce, *Administrative Law Treatise* § 1.4 (4th ed. 2002):

> For a broad perspective about the early development of American administrative law, one must seek help from a leading legal and social historian, such as James Willard Hurst. Here are a few excerpts from Hurst's Law and Social Order in the United States 35–41 (1977):

> > One can plot a curve of statute law that begins at a modest and yet substantial level, rises considerably from the 1830's to the 1880's, then shows a marked increase of pitch and takes off into an ascending line, which in the 1970's shows no sign of turning down . . . From the 1880's, but most markedly from the take-off decade of 1905–1915, the regulatory component of statute law became much more prominent and added considerably to the volume of legislation, a shift of emphasis that brought a new type of statute law concerning organized relationships. The focus changed from enabling organized action to injecting more public management or supervision of affairs and providing more sustained, specialized means of defining and enforcing public policy. Symbolic of this turn of affairs were the statutes creating the modern federal and state administrative apparatus; typical was the shift from factory safety laws that simply commanded employers to provide safe work places to law implemented by provision for administrative rule-making and inspection. . . . United States legal history began with distrust of and hence deliberate restriction of executive power and with only rudimentary administrative machinery. . . . Well into the last quarter of the nineteenth century legislative processes—especially in the states—were crude. Legislators worked with little experience and little precedent to guide their jobs; sessions were short; legislators were part-time amateurs at public policy making; only slowly did a standing committee system develop. . . . Our chart will show no great contribution to the body of law from executive offices or administrative agencies until the 1890's. . . . We can plot major executive administrative contributions from the decade 1905–1915, which first saw the grant of substantial rule-making, rule-enforcement, and adjudicative powers to executive offices and independent administrative agencies. . . . Indeed, by the mid-twentieth century the curve for administrative legislation perhaps topped that for statute law: by the 1950's lawyers with business clients and individuals with demands on the increasing service functions of government had to turn more to administrative rule books than to statute books to locate the legal frame of reference for their affairs.

Peter Strauss illustrates this historic change in methods of lawmaking by comparing the Federal Railway Safety Appliances Act of 1893 with the National Traffic and Motor Vehicle Safety Act of 1966. Strauss,

Legislative Theory and the Rule of Law: Some Comments on Rubin, 89 Colum.L.Rev. 427, 428–30 (1989). In both cases Congress responded to the widespread perception that the then-dominant form of transportation was unsafe. Its 1966 response differed significantly from its 1893 response. In the process of enacting the Rail Safety Act, Congress debated and resolved the major policy issues concerning rail safety; it specified detailed safety rules by statute. Seventy years later when Congress passed the Motor Vehicle Safety Act, it debated and resolved none of the major policy issues; rather, Congress instructed an agency to further motor vehicle safety subject only to loosely worded general guidance in the statute delegating power to the agency.

In 1916 Elihu Root in an address as President of the American Bar Association made a statement that could hardly be improved upon with the hindsight of a half century later:

> There is one special field of law development which has manifestly become inevitable. We are entering upon the creation of a body of administrative law quite different in its machinery, its remedies, and its necessary safeguards from the old methods of regulation by specific statutes enforced by the courts.... The necessities of our situation have already led to an extensive employment of that method.... Before these agencies the old doctrine prohibiting the delegation of legislative power has virtually retired from the field and given up the fight. There will be no withdrawal from these experiments. We shall go on; we shall expand them, whether we approve theoretically or not, because such agencies furnish protection to rights and obstacles to wrong doing which under our new social and industrial conditions cannot be practically accomplished by the old and simple procedure of legislatures and courts as in the last generation. 41 A.B.A.R. 355, 368–369 (1916).

In his clarity of perception, Elihu Root may have been a generation or more ahead of other leaders of the bar. At the same time he uttered important words of caution:

> If we are to continue a government of limited powers, these agencies of regulation must themselves be regulated.... The rights of the citizen against them must be made plain. A system of administrative law must be developed, and that with us is still in its infancy, crude and imperfect.

## 2.   ADMINISTRATIVE ADJUDICATION

The courts are our society's traditional instrumentalities for the authoritative disposition of controversies and, at the start of this century, seemed to have a virtual monopoly of the public business of dispute-settlement. But just as legislation has made great inroads into what were once the largely exclusive preserves of the case law, administrative agencies like the National Labor Relations Board and the Federal Trade Commission have come to exercise powers of adjudication in many areas of American social and economic life.

The following are examples of disputes remitted to administrative adjudication. If a person has a disputed claim for federal retirement benefits, he or she does not begin by going to court to sue on it; the claim will be judged and authoritatively determined, at least as a matter of first instance, by an adjudicatory official in the Social Security Administration of the Department of Health and Human Services. A power company that wishes to construct a nuclear reactor applies for the required license not to a court but to the Nuclear Regulatory Commission, which, after proper hearing and deliberation by its atomic safety and licensing board, will grant or deny the application. Administrative agencies entrusted with power to hear and pass upon claims, applications and charges of law violation are found everywhere in the federal governmental structure, sometimes as divisions within cabinet departments, sometimes as independent regulatory establishments. Quantitatively, far more controversies are decided by federal administrative agencies than by all the federal courts.

Administrative adjudication has similarly been a growth industry in the state and local governments. Administrative bodies are empowered to issue or refuse, and to revoke or suspend, the licenses required to engage in a wide variety of professions and businesses. Workers' compensation commissions hear and decide claims arising from industrial accidents, and public utility commissions pass on applications for rate increases submitted by gas, light and water companies. Every municipal government has its administrative complex of local tax boards, licensing officials, zoning appeals boards and the like, all performing in one way or another the essentially judicial function—or quasi-judicial function—of hearing and deciding particular claims, charges and disputes. The decisions reached by federal, state and local administrative agencies are, to one or another extent, subject to judicial review in the (regular) courts, but the scope of this review is usually limited and constitutes not a retrial of the case or claim but an inquiry into whether the administrative adjudicative agency has acted illegally, arbitrarily or without sufficient evidence to support its findings.

For many decades, well into the 1940's, most lawyers looked with distrust and hostility on the proliferation of administrative agencies and the extension of their decision-making powers. The ultimate consensus, it would appear, was that administrative adjudication is inevitable, given the vastly increased range of government's regulatory and public welfare programs, and, being here to stay, should be ordered and regularized. The great step in this direction, insofar as the federal agencies are concerned, was the enactment in 1946 of the Administrative Procedure Act. By this Act, which was passed by the unanimous vote of both houses of Congress, the adjudicative processes of the federal agencies were largely "judicialized," that is, subjected to uniform procedural standards designed to secure fairness in the hearing, determination and review of particular cases. Many states have enacted similar legislation to regularize the processes of administrative adjudication in the state and local governments.

## 3.   RULE PROMULGATION

### a.   FEDERAL ADMINISTRATIVE REGULATIONS

Administrative adjudication is an important element in the contemporary American pattern of controversy-settlement. But administrative agencies do not only apply law in particular cases; they also make law, and the general rules formulated and prescribed by the agencies constitute a major ingredient of American legislation. Approximately ninety federal agencies, some of them established as independent commissions and others as more or less separate branches within cabinet departments, are now involved in the regulation of business and other private activities. Many, perhaps most of the ninety have been entrusted by Acts of Congress with subordinate legislative power, subordinate in the sense that the regulations made and issued by an administrative agency must be within the scope of the authority delegated to the agency by Congress.

Regulations prescribed by a federal agency within the scope of its delegated rule-making power are authoritative norms of the legal order and, assuming the constitutional validity of the underlying federal statute, superior in authoritativeness to state law. Thus a properly issued regulation of the Securities and Exchange Commission, the National Labor Relations Board, or the Food and Drug Administration has legal effect everywhere in the United States, and any conflicting rule on the same subject in a state's case law or statutes, or even in its constitution, must yield to the superior authority of the federal regulation. The rule-making processes of the federal administrative agencies, like their adjudicatory processes, are governed by the Administrative Procedure Act. Acts of Congress require publication of administrative regulations in a daily and official gazette called the Federal Register, and further require that regulations be systematically arranged and codified, by a continuing process, in the Code of Federal Regulations. The rule-making functions of administrative agencies, as well as their adjudicatory and executive (largely enforcement) functions, are examined intensively in law school courses on Administrative Law.

### b.   STATE ADMINISTRATIVE REGULATIONS

State governments have committed many businesses and pursuits to administrative supervision, much of which calls for rule-making by state agencies. The list of regulated activities differs from state to state, reflecting differences in economic conditions and in prevailing political attitudes, but it is everywhere a long list. Regulations are prescribed by state and local agencies and officials on an enormous variety of subjects: agriculture, civil service, fishing, horse racing, water resources and zoning, to mention just a few. State administrative regulations, in their vast aggregate, loom large in the picture of American legislation.

## D.   Comparative Law

## THE U.S. LEGAL TRADITION AMONG THE LEGAL TRADITIONS OF THE WORLD

—Gary F. Bell[1]

Because the United States are a federation, Americans are usually well aware that the law does vary from jurisdiction to jurisdiction. One should note however that all States except Louisiana belong to the common law tradition and therefore their laws are very similar. Even if politically each State is independent and has its own legal system, all States except Louisiana share the same legal tradition and method.

At the international level however, there is much more diversity in legal traditions and methods. Most of the world's national legal systems have been influenced by one of a few legal traditions. In the Western world, there are two main legal traditions—the civil law and the common law. The laws of France and Holland are in some respects different but they both belong to the civil law tradition and share similar assumptions, in the same way California law is in the end not that different from New York law. Mortgage rules may be different in California, New York and England but all have mortgages as opposed to hypothecs as would be the case in France and Holland. And if you want to set up a mortgage you would go to an attorney in both California and New York, and a solicitor in England, but definitely not a notary as you would in France and Holland for a hypothec. Belonging to the same legal tradition means you share the same legal concepts and institutions. And in the case of the common law tradition, you share a common language, English, something the civil law sorely misses since Latin was abandoned as its common language a few centuries ago.

Mainly through colonization, either the civil law or the common law has influenced, at least in part, the laws of almost all countries in the world. Outside of the Western world however, the civil law or the common law often co-exists with other legal traditions, such as the Islamic law tradition, the Jewish law tradition, the Hindu legal tradition, as well as many other legal traditions including many indigenous traditions.[2]

For commerce and trade, most national legal systems rely mainly on either the civil law or the common law. This note will therefore introduce you to the origins and development of the common law and the civil law and to the main distinctions between these two systems, especially in terms of legal methods.

---

**1.**  Thanks to Associate Professor Gary F. Bell of the National University of Singapore for contributing this Note.

**2.**  For a fascinating and detailed description of the different legal traditions read H. Patrick Glenn, Legal Traditions of the World (2000).

## 1.  ORIGINS OF THE TWO LEGAL TRADITIONS AND THEIR DIFFUSION AROUND THE WORLD

### a.  THE COMMON LAW

The common law tradition originated in England. A new legal order was established as early as 1066 by the Norman Conquest, but the common law did not exist in 1066. William the Conqueror did not abolish the local customs and the local courts.[3] Local courts continued to apply local customs. There was no law common to the whole kingdom. The King did however establish some royal courts at Westminster. Their jurisdiction was at first very limited but eventually expanded to the point where the local courts fell into disuse. The decisions of the royal courts became the law common to the whole kingdom, the common law.

The common law has its source in previous court decisions. The main traditional source of the common law is therefore not legislation but cases. This is so true that when the common law evolved into an unfair set of rigid and formal procedural rules the King, rather than legislate to amend the law, created a new court. When a subject thought that a common law decision led to an unfair result he (and at the time usually not she) would petition the King. There were so many petitions that the King created the court of Chancery which could grant a discretionary relief "in equity" to correct the common law. The decisions of this court gave birth to a body of law called equity which is also based on previous judicial decisions.[4] Both law and equity are now part of what is called the common law tradition.

The British Empire brought the common law to all continents. The common law was "received"[5] in many countries but its reception has been most successful in countries where the European settlers became a majority and imposed (usually unfairly through force) their law over indigenous populations. This was the case in Australia, English Canada, New Zealand and the United States (except Louisiana where the civil law was in place before the United States gained jurisdiction). The common law was also imposed on many other colonies but usually with some adaptation to take into account the local law and customs. For example, Singapore and Malaysia which are now independent common law countries still apply Muslim law to the Muslims in family matters. In fact family law or more generally what is referred to as personal laws are often to this day governed by indigenous laws rather than the common law. Nevertheless, still today in Africa and Asia, former British colonies for the most part continue to apply the common law. Today, India is the most populous common law country.

---

**3.** William wanted to be seen as the successor of the previous king and not as a conqueror.

**4.** Today, in almost all common law countries, the same court exercises both the common law and the equity jurisdictions.

**5.** "Reception" refers to the process by which one political entity adopts the law of another.

In some instances, the new colonial power imposed parts of the common law on newly entrusted territories that used to be civil law jurisdictions under the previous colonial masters (e.g. the USA in the Philippines after years of Spanish colonialism, England in South Africa and Quebec after years of Dutch and French settlements). This led to mixed legal systems.

Following the second world war, the economic hegemony of the United States also contributed to the expansion of the common law. International contracts were often drafted in a common law style with the use of common law terms and international arbitrators often applied common law principles.

*A note about the common law in the United States.* Because of the early independence of the United States, the US common law has evolved separately from the common law of England and of other Commonwealth countries. Commonwealth nations became independent only fairly recently, and even long after they were independent, some nations continued to allow appeals to the Judicial Committee of the Privy Council in London (some countries still allow such appeals). This has had a unifying effect on the law of these countries and still today the courts of one country will consider the decisions of the courts of another Commonwealth country as very persuasive. By contrast, only rarely, if ever, does a United States court determining a matter of domestic law invoke a decision of a foreign country's courts. It is therefore even more striking that notwithstanding years of "legal separation" the law of this country still has so much in common with the law of other common law countries.

## b.   THE CIVIL LAW

The origins of the civil law go further back. They can be traced to the Twelve Tables of the Republic of Rome (probably in the fifth century B.C.). In its origins, it is the law of the city of Rome, the law applied to a citizen (in Latin, *civis*) of Rome as opposed to the law applied to a non-citizen.[6] The expression "civil law", in Latin *ius civilis,* literally means the law of the citizens of Rome.

After the fall of the Western Roman Empire (476 A.D.), the so-called barbarians brought their law to Rome, and although Roman law continued to apply to the Romans, the Germanic influence grew quickly and the law became more and more a mixture of Germanic and Roman law. This would later be known as the vulgarized Roman law. This law was different from the classical Roman law. Canon law, the law of the Catholic Church, was the only Western legal system that kept relatively intact many elements of the Roman law. In 529–34, the Eastern Roman Emperor Justinian published the *Corpus Iuris Civilis,* an articulation and reformulation of Roman law

---

**6.**   Those of you familiar with the New Testament will remember that St. Paul, because he was a citizen of Rome, was entitled to be tried according to Roman law (Acts 23, 27). In fact, according to the New Testament, Paul was even entitled to be tried in Rome in front of an imperial court (Acts 25, 11–12).

based on an extensive study of the original documents. The Justinian Code and accompanying compendia remained in force in Byzantium until and even after the fifteenth-century conquest by the Ottoman Turks.

At the end of the eleventh century, the University of Bologna started teaching Roman law, more specifically the *Corpus Iuris Civilis*. This was at first a purely intellectual endeavor since Roman law was no longer the law anywhere in Western Europe. This marked the beginning of what would later be known as the resurgence of Roman law. Soon other Western European universities followed Bologna's lead and after a few centuries and for reasons too complex to be considered here, the Roman law was received almost everywhere in continental Europe. It became the *ius commune* (the "common law") of continental Europe.

The Roman law actually "received" was in fact limited to what we call "private law" (persons, property, torts, contracts etc.). That is why civilian jurists refer to what we call private law simply as "the civil law" (persons, property and obligations).

Although most civil law countries now have a civil code,[7] codification is in fact a fairly recent phenomenon. The first modern code, the French Civil Code dates back only to 1804 and the German Civil Code, to 1896 (in force in 1900).

The French and German Codes are the two main civil law models. Napoleon brought his Code wherever he and his armies traveled. The French model has been influential in Latin countries both in Europe and in America (Central and South America, Louisiana and Quebec). It has also influenced former French, Portuguese, Spanish and Dutch colonies in Africa, the Middle East and Asia, countries as diverse as Indonesia and the Ivory Coast, Vietnam and Peru.

The German model has influenced the Austrian and Swiss codes as well as the law of many Eastern European countries before the Soviet occupation. German Law has also been received in Japan, Korea and Taiwan and to some extent in pre-Maoist China.

## 2.   LEGAL METHODS—A COMPARISON

You must understand that a civil-law legal methods course (if there were such a thing) would be completely different from the course you are now taking. It is important at the beginning of your legal career that you realize that law can take different forms and play different roles in different societies and cultures. What you will be studying is not the law as it necessarily has to be but the law as it is in the United States. Here are a few methodological differences between the civil law and the common law.

*Case law v. "Jurisprudence"*

First and foremost, in common law countries, cases are usually considered to be the primary source of law. Your legal methods class starts with

---

**7.** Scotland—in many respects a civil law jurisdiction—does not have a civil code.

the study of cases. In civil law countries, cases are simply not a source of law—at least not in theory. The reality might well be that legislation has become extremely relevant in common law countries and that cases are becoming more and more relevant in civil law countries, but the attitudes of civilians and common lawyers toward legislation and cases differ greatly.

You will soon get to read a typical French case. When you read the reasons of the court, you will not find a long and detailed exposition of the facts of the case. Instead the court states a few general principles, usually stemming from articles of the civil code or of the law and then concludes "therefore ..." Typically, French cases have one sentence: "whereas article 100 of the civil code states ..., whereas it is a general principle of law that ..., therefore the court decides ...". Even if the civil law had a principle of *stare decisis* (which it does not) it would be hard to apply the decision in one case to other cases with similar facts since the facts of the original case are not stated in full. This is not to say that French jurists do not look at cases, or as they call them collectively, at the *"jurisprudence"*. Quite to the contrary, they very often look at cases, and the civil code is typically published with copious annotations and summaries of court decisions. French jurists however look at jurisprudence not for binding precedents with similar facts but rather for general principles of law and for specific interpretations of particular provisions of law. Typically the case law annotations of the civil code state in one sentence a principle of law rather than a set of facts. Understandably therefore the common law technique of distinguishing cases based on facts is not part of the method taught in French law school.

The practice with regards to cases may vary to a certain extent in civil law countries other than France–for example German cases tend to be longer and give a more detailed account of the facts. It remains however that the cases never have in civil law countries the importance they have in common law countries. The law is perceived as enunciated in codes and statutes and the main function of the jurist is to interpret the codes directly, rather than to distinguish or apply previous cases *in concreto*.

*Legislative interpretation and drafting*

Civil law jurists tend to see the civil code as an all-encompassing document. They will interpret it generously in order to allow it to reach its goal of regulating the whole private law. The code lends itself to this kind of interpretation since its articles are usually drafted in very general and abstract terms.[8] The judges would readily give to the law a teleological interpretation–a purposive interpretation that is not going to be limited to the actual purpose of the legislator in enacting a particular provision, but

**8.** This is especially true of the French model. The German code tends to be a little more detailed. The degree of generality and of abstraction can be stunning. For example, the whole French law of tort (called "delictual obligations") finds its source in this very abstract provision of the French civil code:

Art. 1382 Every act of a person which causes damage to another obliges the person through whose fault the damage occurred to repair it.

which will extend to the purpose of the law and of the code in general in regulating private law. The judges will look at the spirit of the law beyond its letter. As the Swiss Civil Code puts it, in the most radical way:

(1) The Law must be applied in all cases which come within the letter or the spirit of any of its provisions.

(2) Where no provision is applicable, the judge shall decide according to the existing Customary Law and, in default thereof, according to the rule which he would lay down if he had himself to act as legislator.[9]

It is unlikely that the judge will narrowly interpret a provision. Even though in the past there have been some civil law judges who were narrow black letter jurists, it is fair to says that generally the civil law judge will look beyond the letter of the law and will often apply some principles by analogy, even though the letter of the law does not apply. He will however nonetheless be rather reluctant to extend a particular provision of the code in a certain direction unless he or she can be convinced that this does not go against the systematic edifice of the code. The code is perceived as a whole and one must try to foresee in advance the effect of a decision on the whole organization or economy of the code. Therefore, in seminal cases, the court will not decide simply to extend a practice to a new set of facts but will decide whether this matter should be regulated by this part or that part of the code or, to put it differently, whether a particular development is consistent with the very structure of the code. The civil law jurist wants a systematic and consistent approach to the law, but is willing to interpret the code generously to achieve such a systematic and all encompassing approach.

In common law jurisdictions one often has the impression that legislation tends to be considered as an exception to the case law. Of course, in theory, legislation is a higher source of law than cases and courts are bound by what Congress has decided. In fact however, the courts often have a tendency to interpret legislation rather restrictively. We often hear judges say that had the legislator intended to cover a certain situation he could have said so more clearly in the statute. In consequence the legislator tends to enunciate legal rules in very specific terms so as to be "clear". This makes for a legislative style that tends to enunciate a list of possible situations, or facts:

Every person who marks or brands, alters, conceals, disfigures, obliterates, or defaces the mark or brand of any horse, mare, colt, jack, jennet, mule, bull, ox, steer, cow, calf, sheep, goat, hog, shoat or pig belonging to another, with intent thereby to steal the same or to prevent identification thereof by the true owner, shall be guilty of a felony.[10]

Such long lists are almost never heard of in civil law drafting style. Since the judge will not interpret the statute narrowly, there is no need for a

**9.** Swiss Civil Code, art. 1 (1907) (translation).     **10.** Idaho Code § 25–1901

detailed list–a general statement will suffice. It is true that common law also has recourse to the purposive interpretation of statutes,[11] but one should recognize that it does so in a more narrow way than the civil law.

One should not conclude that one drafting style is better than the other. I do not draft a letter to my parents in the same way I draft a letter to my nephew. Different drafting style must be adopted to take into account the interpretative style of the reader. The detailed drafting style of the common law is justified by the way statute, and even contracts, are interpreted by common law judges generally. In the same way the drafting style of the civil law, which sticks to general principles in both statutes and contracts, is also justified by the fact that the judge will interpret the provisions generously. Each drafting style is justified by the legal method of each legal system.

### Other differences

Civil law students will read "la doctrine" more than cases. The "doctrine" is the cumulated writings of law professors on what the law is or should be. In civil law the "doctrine" is highly respected. You have to remember that the University, not the courts, reintroduced the civil law in Continental Europe. It is therefore not surprising that law professors still have an important role in defining the law. Common law professors generally do not enjoy a similar prestige within their own jurisdiction. Here the judges get most of the prestige.

Legal education differs a lot from country to country but it is fair to say that American legal education is very original and in many respects unique. The "case method" or "Socratic method" is peculiar to this country. It must be clear to you by now that the "case" method could not have been devised in a civil law country. One should also note that in those countries (as is the case in England, and in fact everywhere except in the USA and Canada) law is an undergraduate degree. As a result, legal education tends to last longer than the three years typically required in the United States (though generally not as long as the combined seven years of U.S. undergraduate and law school training). The teaching style is magisterial—the professor exposes the law to his or her students, who take notes and do not intervene in class.

### Conclusion

In this era of globalization, one might expect that the differences among legal systems would markedly diminish as the world moves toward greater harmonization and uniformization of law. Though there may be many areas in which uniformity of law may be useful and desirable (trade and commerce for example), in my view, the diversity of legal traditions will and should remain. Moreover, in some respects those differences will become even more apparent. As people travel and migrate around the

---

**11.** See the section below on Acts Interpretation Acts, Part III.C4 ("Statutory Guides to Statutory Interpretation").

world, it is increasingly likely that different traditions will meet and sometimes even clash. Legal traditions are part of a person's identity, maybe not as much as her religious or cultural (including linguistic) traditions, but nonetheless part of that identity. For example, one's Jewishness is in part defined by Jewish law, one's Catholicism, in part by canon law. Recognizing other legal traditions means recognizing an important component of other people's societies. An understanding and appreciation of other legal traditions is likely to be more and more relevant to the practice of law in the future. Learning more about the civil law tradition and other legal traditions is like learning another language: to do it well, you don't just learn the words, you try to appreciate the culture the words import. That in turn, should not only enliven your education but enrich your practical juridical experience as well.

\* Cartoon from PASCAL ÉLIE, HUMOUR: FORMAT LEGAL (1987). Reproduced with the permission of the author and of the publisher (Les Éditions Yvon Blais).

# PART II

# CASE LAW: THE ANALYSIS AND SYNTHESIS OF JUDICIAL DECISIONS

## A. COMMON LAW DECISION-MAKING IN THE PRESENCE OR ABSENCE OF PRECEDENT

### 1. COMMON LAW DECISION-MAKING: SELECTED CONTROVERSIES

#### a. OWNERSHIP OF WRITTEN AND SPOKEN WORDS

## Baker v. Libbie

Supreme Judicial Court of Massachusetts, 1912.
210 Mass. 599, 97 N.E. 109.

Bill in Equity, filed in the Superior Court on February 17, 1911, by the executor of the will of Mary Baker G. Eddy, late of Concord in the State of New Hampshire, against the members of a firm engaged in business in Boston as auctioneers of books and manuscripts, alleging that a number of private unpublished letters written by the plaintiff's testatrix had come into the possession of the defendants in the course of their business, that the defendants had advertised such letters for public sale in their auction rooms in Boston and already had printed and published material and substantial parts of the letters in their sale catalogue, that the catalogue was being distributed by the defendants, and would be further distributed to the persons in attendance at such auction and that portions of the letters also had been published in the newspapers of Boston, New York and other cities of the country; and praying that the defendants might be enjoined and restrained "from further printing, publishing, selling, circulating, or in any manner making public or showing said letters, or any of them, or any copy or copies, extract or extracts therefrom, or any of them, to any person or persons," and "from further circulating or distributing or making public in any manner copies of said catalogue containing extracts from any of said letters."

The case came on to be heard before Richardson, J., who by agreement of the parties reserved and reported it, upon the bill and answer, and all questions of law therein, for determination by this court.

■ RUGG, C.J. The plaintiff as executor of the will of Mary Baker G. Eddy, the founder of "Christian Science" so called, seeks to restrain an auctioneer of manuscripts from publishing for advertising purposes and from selling certain autographed letters of his testatrix. These letters were written in her own hand by Mrs. Eddy, as is said, "during one of the most interesting periods of her career, that is, just after the first publication of her 'Science and Health with Key to the Scriptures,'" in 1875. It is averred in the answer that the letters have no attribute of literature, but are merely friendly letters written to a cousin about domestic and business affairs. Extracts from the letters show that they refer to household matters, to health and to the work she was doing. The questions raised relate to the existence, extent and character of the proprietary right of the writer of private letters upon indifferent subjects not possessing the qualities of literature and to the degree of protection to be given in equity to such rights as are found to exist. These points have never been presented before for decision in this Commonwealth. The nearest approach was in Tomkins v. Halleck, 133 Mass. 32, 43 Am.Rep. 480, where the rights of an author of a dramatic composition put upon the stage but not printed were protected against a rival presentation made possible by human memory (overruling upon this point the earlier case of Keene v. Kimball, 16 Gray, 545, 77 Am.Dec. 426) and Dodge Co. v. Construction Information Co., 183 Mass. 62, 66 N.E. 204, 60 L.R.A. 810, 97 Am.St.Rep. 412, where property rights in valuable commercial information distributed to subscribers in writing, in print, by telegraph or orally, were recognized and protected against use by a rival concern. Neither of these decisions touches at all closely the points involved in the case at bar.

The rights of the authors of letters of a private or business nature have been the subject of judicial determination in courts in England and this country for a period of at least one hundred and seventy years. The first English case was Pope v. Curl, 2 Atk. 341, which was in 1741. It was a suit by Alexander Pope to restrain the publication of letters written by him to Swift and others. In continuing an injunction Lord Chancellor Hardwicke, after remarking that no distinction could be drawn between letters and books or other learned works, said, "Another objection has been made . . . that where a man writes a letter, it is in the nature of a gift to the receiver. But I am of opinion that it is only a special property in the receiver, possibly the property of the paper may belong to him; but this does not give a license to any person whatsoever to publish them to the world, for at most the receiver has only a joint property with the writer. . . . It has been insisted . . . that this is a sort of work which does not come within the meaning of the act of Parliament [as to copyright], because it contains only letters on familiar subjects, and inquiries after the health of friends, and cannot properly be called a learned work. It is certain that no works have done more service to mankind, than those which have appeared in this shape, upon familiar subjects, and which perhaps were never intended to be published; and it is this [that] makes them so valuable."

Thompson v. Stanhope, 2 Ambl. 737 (1774) was a suit by the executors of Lord Chesterfield to restrain the publication of his now famous letters to his son, which the widow of the latter proposed to print and sell. Some of these possessed literary merit of a high order. Lord Chancellor Apsley was "very clear" that an injunction should be granted, upon the authority of the foregoing decision and the somewhat kindred cases of Forrester v. Waller, cited 4 Burr. 2331, and Webb v. Rose, cited 4 Burr. 2330, where notes and conveyancer's draughts were held to be the literary property of the writer or his representatives, and Duke of Queensbury v. Shebbeare, 2 Eden, 329, where the publication of a part of Lord Clarendon's History by a possessor of the manuscript was restrained.

Gee v. Pritchard, 2 Swanst. 402, 426, was decided by Lord Eldon in 1818. Letters apparently without literary or other special interest by the plaintiff to the son of her husband were the subject of the suit, and publication was restrained on the ground of the property right of the writer. In Lytton v. Devey, 54 L.J. (N.S.) Ch. 293, 295, it was said: "The property in the letters remains in the person to whom they are sent. The right to retain them remains in the person to whom the letters are sent; but the sender of the letters has still that kind of interest, if not property, in the letters that he has a right to restrain any use being made of the communication which he has made in the letters so sent by him." See also Prince Albert v. Strange, 2 DeG. & Sm. 652; S.C. 1 MacN. & G. 25, 43. This same principle was followed expressly in the Irish case of Earl of Granard v. Dunkin, 1 Ball & Beatty, 207, and in Labouchere v. Hess, 77 L.T. (N.S.) Ch. 559. There are several dicta to the same effect by great English judges. For example, Lord Campbell said in Boosey v. Jefferys, 6 Exch. 580, at 583, "A court of equity will grant an injunction to prevent the publication of a letter by a correspondent against the will of the writer. That is a recognition of property in the writer, although he has parted with the manuscript; since he wrote to enable his correspondent to know his sentiments, not to give them to the world." Lord Cairns said, respecting correspondence in Hopkinson v. Burghley, L.R. 2 Ch. 447, at 448: "The writer is supposed to intend that the receiver may use it for any lawful purpose, and it has been held that publication is not such a lawful purpose." See also Jefferys v. Boosey, 4 H.L.Cas. 815, 867, 962. The latest English case on the subject recognizes this as the well settled rule. Philip v. Pennell, [1907] 2 Ch. 577. In 1804 the Scottish court on the suit of his children interdicted the publication of manuscript letters of Robert Burns. Cadell & Davies v. Stewart, 1 Bell's Com. 116 n.

The earliest case in this country, Denis v. Leclerc, 1 Martin O.S., La., 297, arose in 1811. A single letter of no literary pretension was there in question and its publication was enjoined, and the writer's property interest in the letter was distinctly upheld.

The question was elaborately discussed by Mr. Justice Story in Folsom v. Marsh, Fed.Cas.No. 4901, 2 Story 100, 110 [D.Mass.1841], who held that "The author of any letter or letters, (and his representatives), whether they are literary compositions, or familiar letters, or letters of business, possess the sole and exclusive copyright therein; and that no persons, neither those to whom they are addressed, nor other persons, have any right or authority, to publish the same upon their own account, or for their own benefit."

In Bartlett v. Crittenden, Fed.Cas.No. 1076, 5 McLean, 32, at 42 [D.Ohio 1849], Mr. Justice McLean said: "Even the publication of private letters by the person to whom they were addressed, may be enjoined. This is done upon the ground that the writer has a right of property in the purpose for which they were written."

In Woolsey v. Judd, 11 How.Prac. 49, 4 Duer, 379 [N.Y.1855], the question was considered exhaustively, and all the earlier cases were reviewed. The conclusion was reached that the writer of even private letters of no literary value has such a proprietary interest as required a court of equity at his instance to prohibit their publication by the receiver.

Grigsby v. Breckinridge, 2 Bush, Ky., 480 [65 Ky. 481 (1867) ], decided that "the recipient of a private letter, sent without any reservation, express or implied, 'held' the general property, qualified only by the incidental right in the author to publish and prevent publication by the recipient, or any other person."

In Barrett v. Fish, 72 Vt. 18, at 20, 47 A. 174, 51 L.R.A. 754, 82 Am.St.Rep. 914 [1899], it was said "that a court of equity will protect the right of property in such [private] letters, by enjoining their unauthorized publication." The same doctrine has been held, either expressly or by way of dictum, in Dock v. Dock, 180 Pa. 14, 22, 36 A. 411, 57 Am.St.Rep. 617 [1897]; Rice v. Williams, 32 F. 437 [E.D.Wisc.1887]; Eyre v. Higbee, 22 How.Pr. 198, 35 Barb. 502 [N.Y.1861]; Palmer v. DeWitt, 47 N.Y. 532, 536, 7 Am.Rep. 480 [1872].

Against these opinions are Wetmore v. Scovell, 3 Edw.Ch. 515 [N.Y. 1842], and Hoyt v. Mackenzie, 3 Barb.Ch. 320, 49 Am.Dec. 178 [N.Y.1848]; decided respectively by Vice–Chancellor McCoun and Chancellor Walworth while sitting alone. They were criticised and overruled in Woolsey v. Judd, 11 How.Prac. 49, 4 Duer, 379, by a court of six judges. There are also certain doubtful dicta by a vice-chancellor in Percival v. Phipps, 2 V. & B. 19, 28 [35 Eng.Rep. 225 (1813) ], which are relied upon as asserting a somewhat similar view. But it is not necessary to discuss them in detail, for this review of cases demonstrates that the weight of decisions by courts of great authority, speaking often through judges of high distinction for learning and ability, supports the conclusion that equity will afford injunctive relief to the author against the publication of his private letters upon commonplace subjects without regard to their literary merit or the popular attention or special curiosity aroused by them.

The same conclusion is reached on principle and apart from authority. It is generally recognized that one has a right to the fruits of his labor. This is equally true, whether the work be muscular or mental or both combined. Property in literary productions, before publication and while they rest in manuscript, is as plain as property in the game of the hunter or in the grain of the husbandman. The labor of composing letters for private and familiar correspondence may be trifling, or it may be severe, but it is nonetheless the result of an expenditure of thought and time. The market value of such an effort may be measured by the opinions of others, but the fact of property is not created thereby. A canvas upon which an obscure or unskilful painter has toiled does not cease to be property merely because by conventional standards it is valueless as a work of art. Few products of the intellect reveal individual characteristics more surely than familiar correspondence, entries in diaries or other unambitious writings. No sound distinction in this regard can be made between that which has literary merit and that which is without it. Such a distinction could not be drawn with any certainty. While extremes might be discovered, compositions near the dividing line would be subject to no fixed criterion at any given moment, and scarcely anything is more fluctuating than the literary taste of the general public. Even those counted as experts in literature differ widely in opinion both in the same and in successive generations as to the relative merits of different authors. The basic principle on which the right of the author is sustained even as to writings confessedly literature is not their literary quality, but the fact that they are the product of labor.

The existence of a right in the author over his letters, even though private and without worth as literature, is established on principle and authority. The right is property in its essential features. It is, therefore, entitled to all the protection which the Constitution and laws give to property.

The extent of this proprietary right, as between the writer and the recipient of letters, requires a closer analysis. It depends upon implications raised by law from the circumstances. This test is a general one, and has been applied to the public delivery of lectures, the presentation of dramas, and other analogous cases. Abernethy v. Hutchinson, 3 L.J.Ch. 209; S.C. 1 Hall & Tw. 28. Tompkins v. Halleck, 133 Mass. 32, 43 Am.Rep. 480. Nicols v. Pitman, 26 Ch.D. 374, 380. The relative rights of the writer and receiver may vary with different conditions. If there be a request for return or if the correspondence is marked in definite terms, as personal or confidential, such special considerations would need to be regarded. The case at bar presents the ordinary example of friendly correspondence between kinswomen upon topics of mutual private interest. Under such circumstances, what does the writer retain and what does he give to the person to whom the letter is sent? The property right of the author has been described as "an incorporeal right to print [and it should be added to prevent the printing of, if he desires] a set of intellectual ideas or modes of thinking, communicated in a set of words and sentences and modes of expression. It is equally detached from the manuscript, or any other physical existence whatsoever." Millar v. Taylor, 4 Burr. 2303, at 2396. It has been called also "the order of words in the * * * composition." Jefferys v. Boosey, 4 H.L.Cas. 815, 867. Holmes v. Hurst, 174 U.S. 82, 86, 19 S.Ct. 606, 43 L.Ed. 904. Kalem Co. v. Harper Bros., 222 U.S. 55, 63, 32 S.Ct. 20, 56 L.Ed. 92, Ann.Cas. 1913A, 1285. The right of the author to publish or suppress publication of his correspondence is absolute in the absence of special considerations, and is independent of any desire or intent at the time of writing. It is an interest in the intangible and impalpable thought and the particular verbal garments in which it has been clothed. Although independent of the manuscript, this right involves a right to copy or secure copies. Otherwise, the author's right of publication might be lost. The author parts with the physical and material elements which are conveyed by and in the envelope. These are given to the receiver. The paper upon which the letter is written belongs to the receiver. Oliver v. Oliver, 11 C.B. (N.S.) 139. Grigsby v. Breckinridge, 2 Bush, Ky., 480, 486, 92 Am.Dec. 509. Pope v. Curl, 2 Atk. 341. Werckmeister v. American Lithographic Co., 142 F. 827, 830. A duty of preservation would impose an unreasonable burden in most instances. It is obvious that no such obligation rests upon the receiver, and he may destroy or keep at pleasure. Commonly there must be inferred a right of reading or showing to a more or less limited circle of friends and relatives. But in other instances the very nature of the correspondence may be such as to set the seal of secrecy upon its contents. See Kenrick v. Danube Collieries & Minerals Co., 39 W.R. 473. Letters of extreme affection and other fiduciary communications may come within this class. There may be also a confidential relation existing between the parties, out of which would arise an implied prohibition against any use of the letters, and a breach of such trust might be restrained in equity. On the other hand, the conventional autograph letters by famous persons signify on their face a license to transfer. Equitable rights may exist in the author against one who by fraud, theft or other illegality obtains possession of letters. The precise inquiry is whether indifferent letters written by one at the time perhaps little known or quite unknown which subsequently acquire value as holographic manuscripts, may be marketed as such. This case does not involve personal feelings or what has been termed the right to privacy. 4 Harvard Law Review, 193. The author has deceased. Moreover, there appears to be nothing about these letters, knowledge of which by strangers would violate even delicate feelings. Although the particular form of the expression of the thought remains the property of the writer, the substance and material on which this thought has been expressed have passed to the recipient of the letter. The paper has received the impression of the pen, and the two in combination have been given away. The thing which has value as an autograph is not the intactable thought, but the material substance upon which a particular human hand has been placed, and has traced the intelligible symbols. Perhaps the autographic value of letters may fluctuate in accordance with their length or the nature of their subject matter. But whatever such value may be, in its essence it does not attach to the intellectual but material part of the letter.

This exact question has never been presented for adjudication, so far as we are aware. There are some expressions in opinions, which dissociated from their connection may be laid hold of to support the plaintiff's contention. See Dock v. Dock, 180 Pa. 14, 22, 36 A. 411, 57 Am.St.Rep. 617; Eyre v. Higbee, 22 How.Pr. 198, 35 Barb. 502; Palin v. Gathercole, 1 Collyer, 565. But on principle it seems to flow from the nature of the right transferred by the author to the receiver and of that retained by the writer in ordinary correspondence, that the extent of the latter's proprietary power is to make or to restrain a publication, but not to prevent a transfer. The rule applicable to the facts of this case, as we conceive it to be, is that in the absence of some special limitation imposed either by the subject matter of the letter or the circumstances under which it is sent, the right in the receiver of an ordinary letter is one of unqualified title in the material on which it is written. He can deal with it as absolute owner subject only to the proprietary right retained by the author for himself and his representatives to the publication or non-publication of idea in its particular verbal expression. In this opinion publication has been used in the sense of making public through printing or multiplication of copies.

The result is that an injunction may issue against publication or multiplication in any way, in whole or in part, for advertising or other purposes, of any of the letters described in the bill, and allowing the plaintiff, if he desires, to make copies thereof within a reasonable time, but going no further.

## Questions

**1.** What new questions does this case present? Why does it matter?

**2.** Why does the court seek support from "authority" before inquiring whether the writer's claims are justified in "principle"?

**3.** What kind of authority does the court invoke? How does the court deal with contrary pronouncements?

**4.** Why do the two prior Massachusetts decisions cited by the court not "touch at all closely the points involved in the case at bar"?

**5.** How does the court identify the respective rights of the letter writer and the recipient? To the extent that the rights overlap, how does the court resolve the conflict?

**6.** Why does the court decline to make literary merit a requirement for protection? What does this tell you about the role of judges?

## Estate of Hemingway v. Random House, Inc.

Court of Appeals of New York, 1968.
23 N.Y.2d 341, 296 N.Y.S.2d 771, 244 N.E.2d 250.

■ Fuld,C.J. On this appeal—involving an action brought by the estate of the late Ernest Hemingway and his widow against the publisher and author of a book, entitled "Papa Hemingway"—we are called upon to decide, primarily, whether conversations of a gifted and highly regarded writer may become the subject of common-law copyright, even though the speaker himself has not reduced his words to writing.

Hemingway died in 1961. During the last 13 years of his life, a close friendship existed between him and A.E. Hotchner, a younger and far less well-known writer. Hotchner, who met Hemingway in the course of writing articles about him became a favored drinking and traveling companion of the famous author, a frequent visitor to his home and the adapter of some of his works for motion pictures and television. During these years, Hemingway's conversation with Hotchner, in which others sometimes took part, was filled with anecdote, reminiscence, literary opinion and revealing comment about actual persons on whom some of Hemingway's fictional characters were based. Hotchner made careful notes of these conversations soon after they occurred, occasionally recording them on a portable tape recorder.

During Hemingway's lifetime, Hotchner wrote and published several articles about his friend in which he quoted some of this talk at length. Hemingway, far from objecting to this practice, approved of it. Indeed, the record reveals that other writers also quoted Hemingway's conversation without any objection from him, even when he was displeased with the articles themselves.

After Hemingway's death, Hotchner wrote "Papa Hemingway," drawing upon his notes and his recollections, and in 1966 it was published by the defendant Random House. Subtitled "a personal memoir", it is a serious and revealing biographical portrait of the world-renowned writer. Woven through the narrative, and giving the book much of its interest and character, are lengthy quotations from Hemingway's talks as noted or remembered by Hotchner. Included also are two chapters on Hemingway's final illness and suicide in which Hotchner writing of his friend with obvious feeling and sympathy, refers to events, and even to medical information, to which he was privy as an intimate of the family. Hemingway's widow, Mary, is mentioned frequently in the book, and is sometimes quoted, but only incidentally.

The complaint, which seeks an injunction and damages, alleges ... that "Papa Hemingway" consists, in the main, of literary matter composed by Hemingway in which he had a common-law copyright ....

The plaintiffs moved for a preliminary injunction. The motion was denied (49 Misc.2d 726, affd. 25 A.D.2d 719), and the book was thereafter published. After its publication, the defendants sought and were granted summary judgment. The Appellate Division unanimously affirmed the resulting orders and granted the plaintiffs leave to appeal to this court.

Turning to the first cause of action, we agree with the disposition made below but on a ground more narrow than that articulated by the court at Special Term. It is the position of the plaintiffs ... that Hemingway was entitled to a common-law copyright on the theory that his directly quoted comment, anecdote and opinion were his "literary creations", his "literary property", and that the defendant Hotchner's note-taking only performed the mechanics of recordation. And, in a somewhat different vein, the plaintiffs argue that "[w]hat for Hemingway was oral one day would be or could become his written manuscript the next day", that his speech, constituting not just a statement of his ideas but the very form in which he conceived and expressed them, was as much the subject of common-law copyright as what he might himself have committed to paper.

Common-law copyright is the term applied to an author's proprietary interest in his literary or artistic creations before they have been made generally available to the public. It enables the author to exercise control over the first publication of his work or to prevent publication entirely—hence, its other name, the "right of first publication". (Chamberlain v. Feldman, 300 N.Y. 135, 139).[1] No cases deal directly with the question

---

**1.** Although common-law copyright in an unpublished work lasts indefinitely, it is extinguished immediately upon publication of the work by the author. He must then rely, for his protection, upon Federal statutory copyright. (See Nimmer, Copyright, § 11, pp. 38, 42 and ch. 4, p. 183 et seq.) Section 2 of the Copyright Act (U.S.Code, tit. 17) expressly preserves common-law rights in *unpub-* *lished* works against any implication that the field is pre-empted by the Federal statute. [While the court's statements with respect to common law copyright in unpublished works were accurate when this opinion was written, the Copyright Act of 1976 made unpublished, as well as published, works of authorship exclusively subject to Federal statutory pro-

whether it extends to conversational speech and we begin, therefore, with a brief review of some relevant concepts in this area of law.

It must be acknowledged—as the defendants point out—that nearly a century ago our court stated that common-law copyright extended to " '[e]very new and innocent product of mental labor which has been *embodied in writing, or some other material form* ' ". (Palmer v. De Witt, 47 N.Y. 532, 537; emphasis supplied.) And, more recently, it has been said that "an author has no property right in his ideas unless * * * given embodiment in a tangible form." (O'Brien v. RKO Radio Pictures, 68 F.Supp. 13, 14.) However, as a *noted scholar* in the field has observed, "the underlying rationale for common law copyright (i.e., the recognition that a property status should attach to the fruits of intellectual labor) is applicable regardless of whether such labor assumes tangible form" (Nimmer, Copyright, § 11.1, p. 40). The principle that it is not the tangible embodiment of the author's work but the creation of the work itself which is protected finds recognition in a number of ways in copyright law.

One example, with some relevance to the problem before us, is the treatment which the law has accorded to personal letters—a kind of half-conversation in written form. Although the paper upon which the letter is written belongs to the recipient, it is the author who has the right to publish them or to prevent their publication. (See Baker v. Libbie, 210 Mass. 599, 605, 606.) In the words of the Massachusetts court in the *Baker* case (210 Mass., at pp. 605–606), the author's right "is an interest in the intangible and impalpable thought and the particular verbal garments in which it has been clothed." Nor has speech itself been entirely without protection against reproduction for publication. The public delivery of an address or a lecture or the performance of a play is not deemed a "publication," and, accordingly, it does not deprive the author of his common-law copyright in its contents. (See Ferris v. Frohman, 223 U.S. 424; King v. Mister Maestro, Inc., 224 F.Supp. 101, 106; Palmer v. De Witt, 47 N.Y. 532, 543, supra; see, also, Nimmer, Copyright, § 53, p. 208.)

Letters, however—like plays and public addresses, written or not—have distinct, identifiable boundaries and they are, in most cases, only occasional products. Whatever difficulties attend the formulation of suitable rules for the enforcement of rights in such works (see, e.g., Note, Personal Letters: In Need of a Law of Their Own, 44 Iowa L.Rev. 705), they are relatively manageable. However, conversational speech, the distinctive behavior of man, is quite another matter, and subjecting any part of it to the restraints of common-law copyright presents unique problems.

One such problem—and it was stressed by the court at Special Term (SCHWEITZER, J.)[2]—is that of avoiding undue restraints on the freedoms

tection. See Act of Oct. 19, 1976, Pub.L. No. 94–553, 90 Stat. 2541.—Ed.].

**2.** Another problem—also remarked by the court—is the difficulty of measuring the relative self-sufficiency of any one party's contributions to a conversation, although it may be, in the case of some kinds of dialogue or interview, that the difficulty would not be greater than in deciding other questions of degree, such as plagiarism. (See, e.g., Nichols v. Universal Pictures Corp., 45 F.2d 119.)

of speech and press and, in particular, on the writers of history and of biographical works of the genre of Boswell's "Life of Johnson". The safeguarding of essential freedoms in this area is, though, not without its complications. The indispensable right of the press to report on what people have *done,* or on what has *happened* to them or on what they have *said in public* (see Time, Inc. v. Hill, 385 U.S. 374; Curtis Pub. Co. v. Butts, 388 U.S. 130; Associated Press v. Walker, 388 U.S. 130) does not necessarily imply an unbounded freedom to publish whatever they may have *said in private conversation,* any more than it implies a freedom to copy and publish what people may have put down in *private writings.*

Copyright, both common-law and statutory, rests on the assumption that there are forms of expression, limited in kind, to be sure, which should not be divulged to the public without the consent of their author. The purpose, far from being restrictive, is to encourage and protect intellectual labor. (See Note, Copyright: Right to Common Law Copyright in Conversation of a Decedent, 67 Col.L.Rev. 366, 367, commenting on the decision denying the plaintiffs before us a preliminary injunction, 49 Misc.2d 726.) The essential thrust of the First Amendment is to prohibit improper restraints on the *voluntary* public expression of ideas; it shields the man who wants to speak or publish when others wish him to be quiet. There is necessarily, and within suitably defined areas, a concomitant freedom *not* to speak publicly, one which serves the same ultimate end as freedom of speech in its affirmative aspect.

The rules of common-law copyright assure this freedom in the case of written material. However, speech is now easily captured by electronic devices and, consequently, we should be wary about excluding all possibility of protecting a speaker's right to decide when his words, uttered in private dialogue, may or may not be published at large. Conceivably, there may be limited and special situations in which an interlocutor brings forth oral statements from another party which both understand to be the unique intellectual product of the principal speaker, a product which would qualify for common-law copyright if such statements were in writing. Concerning such problems, we express no opinion; we do no more than raise the questions, leaving them open for future consideration in cases which may present them more sharply than this one does.

On the appeal before us, the plaintiffs' claim to common-law copyright may be disposed of more simply and on a more narrow ground.

The defendant Hotchner asserts—without contradiction in the papers before us—that Hemingway never suggested to him or to anyone else that he regarded his conversational remarks to be "literary creations" or that he was of a mind to restrict Hotchner's use of the notes and recordings which Hemingway knew him to be accumulating. On the contrary, as we have already observed, it had become a continuing practice, during Hemingway's lifetime, for Hotchner to write articles about Hemingway, consisting largely of quotations from the latter's conversation—and of all of this

Hemingway approved. In these circumstances, authority to publish must be implied, thus negativing the reservation of any common-law copyright.

Assuming, without deciding, that in a proper case a common-law copyright in certain limited kinds of spoken dialogue might be recognized, it would, at the very least, be required that the speaker indicate that he intended to mark off the utterance in question from the ordinary stream of speech, that he meant to adopt it as a unique statement and that he wished to exercise control over its publication. In the conventional common-law copyright situation, this indication is afforded by the creation of the manuscript itself. It would have to be evidenced in some other way if protection were ever to be accorded to some forms of conversational dialogue.

Such an indication is, of course, possible in the case of speech. It might, for example, be found in prefatory words or inferred from the circumstances in which the dialogue takes place.[3] Another way of formulating such a rule might be to say that, although, in the case of most intellectual products, the courts are reluctant to find that an author has "published," so as to lose his common-law copyright (see Nimmer, Copyright, § 58.2, pp. 226–228), in the case of conversational speech,—because of its unique nature—there should be a presumption that the speaker has not reserved any common-law rights unless the contrary strongly appears. However, we need not carry such speculation further in the present case since the requisite conditions are plainly absent here.

For present purposes, it is enough to observe that Hemingway's words and conduct, far from making any such reservation, left no doubt of his willingness to permit Hotchner to draw freely on their conversation in writing about him and to publish such material. . . . It follows, therefore, that the courts below were eminently correct in dismissing the [___] cause of action.

In brief, then, it is our conclusion that, since no triable issues have been raised, the courts below very properly dismissed the complaint.

The orders appealed from should be affirmed, with costs.

■ JUDGES BURKE, SCILEPPI, BERGAN, KEATING, BREITEL and JASEN concur.

Orders affirmed.

## Questions

**1.** What new questions does this case present? Are they any newer than those presented in *Baker v. Libbie?*

---

**3.** This was the situation in Jenkins v. News Syndicate Co. (128 Misc. 284). The plaintiff alleged that she had had a conference with a newspaper editor in which she described in detail the proposed content of some articles she was requested to write. Later, she decided not to write them and the newspaper thereupon published an "interview" with her, precisely quoting much of her conversation with the editor. The court held that she had stated a cause of action for damages on the theory of common-law copyright.

**2.**   What use does the New York Court of Appeals make of *Baker v. Libbie?*

**3.**   Why does the Court of Appeals in *Hemingway* resolve the case on a narrower ground than that invoked by the lower court?

**4.**   What *is* the court's disposition of the case?

b.   THE RIGHT OF PRIVACY

# Roberson v. Rochester Folding Box Co.

Court of Appeals of New York, 1902.
171 N.Y. 538, 64 N.E. 442.

■ PARKER, C.J. The Appellate Division has certified that the following questions of law have arisen in this case, and ought to be reviewed by this court: 1. Does the complaint herein state a cause of action at law against the defendants or either of them? 2. Does the complaint herein state a cause of action in equity against the defendants or either of them? These questions are presented by a demurrer to the complaint, which is put upon the ground that the complaint does not state facts sufficient to constitute a cause of action.

The complaint alleges that the Franklin Mills Co., one of the defendants, was engaged in a general milling business and in the manufacture and sale of flour; that before the commencement of the action, without the knowledge or consent of plaintiff, defendants, knowing that they had no right or authority so to do, had obtained, made, printed, sold and circulated about 25,000 lithographic prints, photographs and likenesses of plaintiff, made in a manner particularly set up in the complaint; that upon the paper upon which the likenesses were printed and above the portrait there were printed, in large, plain letters, the words, "Flour of the Family," and below the portrait in large capital letters, "Franklin Mills Flour," and in the lower right-hand corner in smaller capital letters, "Rochester Folding Box Co., Rochester, N.Y.;" that upon the same sheet were other advertisements of the flour of the Franklin Mills Co.; that those 25,000 likenesses of the plaintiff thus ornamented have been conspicuously posted and displayed in stores, warehouses, saloons and other public places; that they have been recognized by friends of the plaintiff and other people with the result that plaintiff has been greatly humiliated by the scoffs and jeers of persons who have recognized her face and picture on this advertisement and her good name has been attacked, causing her great distress and suffering both in body and mind; that she was made sick and suffered a severe nervous shock, was confined to her bed and compelled to employ a physician, because of these facts; that defendants had continued to print, make, use, sell and circulate the said lithographs, and that by reason of the foregoing facts plaintiff had suffered damages in the sum of $15,000. The complaint prays that defendants be enjoined from making, printing, publishing, circulating or using in any manner any likenesses of plaintiff in any form whatever, for further relief (which it is not necessary to consider here) and for damages.

It will be observed that there is no complaint made that plaintiff was libeled by this publication of her portrait. The likeness is said to be a very good one, and one that her friends and acquaintances were able to recognize; indeed, her grievance is that a good portrait of her, and, therefore, one easily recognized has been used to attract attention toward the paper upon which defendant mill company's advertisements appear. Such publicity, which some find agreeable, is to plaintiff very distasteful, and thus, because of defendants' impertinence in using her picture without her consent for their own business purposes, she has been caused to suffer mental distress where others would have appreciated the compliment to their beauty implied in the selection of the picture for such purposes; but as it is distasteful to her, she seeks the aid of the courts to enjoin a further circulation of the lithographic prints containing her portrait made as alleged in the complaint, and as an incident thereto, to reimburse her for the damages to her feelings, which the complaint fixes at the sum of $15,000.

There is no precedent for such an action to be found in the decisions of this court; indeed the learned judge who wrote the very able and interesting opinion in the Appellate Division said, while upon the threshold of the discussion of the question: "It may be said in the first place that the theory upon which this action is predicated is new, at least in instance if not in principle, and that few precedents can be found to sustain the claim made by the plaintiff, if indeed it can be said that there are any authoritative cases establishing her right to recover in this action." Nevertheless, that court reached the conclusion that plaintiff had a good cause of action against defendants, in that defendants had invaded what is called a "right of privacy"—in other words, the right to be let alone. Mention of such a right is not to be found in Blackstone, Kent or any other of the great commentators upon the law, nor so far as the learning of counsel or the courts in this case have been able to discover, does its existence seem to have been asserted prior to the year 1890, when it was presented with attractiveness and no inconsiderable ability in the Harvard Law Review (Vol. IV., page 193) in an article entitled, "The Right of Privacy."

The so-called right of privacy is, as the phrase suggests, founded upon the claim that a man has the right to pass through this world, if he wills, without having his picture published, his business enterprises discussed, his successful experiments written up for the benefit of others, or his eccentricities commented upon either in handbills, circulars, catalogues, periodicals or newspapers, and, necessarily, that the things which may not be written and published of him must not be spoken of him by his neighbors, whether the comment be favorable or otherwise. While most persons would much prefer to have a good likeness of themselves appear in a responsible periodical or leading newspaper rather than upon an advertising card or sheet, the doctrine which the courts are asked to create for this case would apply as well to the one publication as to the other, for the principle which a court of equity is asked to assert in support of a recovery in this action is that the right of privacy exists and is enforceable in equity, and that the publication of that which purports to be a portrait of another person, even if obtained upon the street by an impertinent individual with a camera, will be restrained in equity on the ground that an individual has the right to prevent his features from becoming known to those outside of his circle of friends and acquaintances.

If such a principle be incorporated into the body of the law through the instrumentality of a court of equity, the attempts to logically apply the principle will necessarily result, not only in a vast amount of litigation, but in litigation bordering upon the absurd, for the right of privacy, once established as a legal doctrine, cannot be confined to the restraint of the publication of a likeness but must necessarily embrace as well the publication of a word-picture, a comment upon one's looks, conduct, domestic relations or habits. And were the right of privacy once legally asserted, it would necessarily be held to include the same things if spoken instead of printed, for one, as well as the other, invades the right to be absolutely let alone. An insult would certainly be in violation of such a right and with many persons would more seriously wound the feelings than would the publication of their picture. And so we might add to the list of things that are spoken and done day by day which seriously offend the sensibilities of good people to which the principle which the plaintiff seeks to have imbedded in the doctrine of the law would seem to apply. I have gone only far enough to barely suggest the vast field of litigation which would necessarily be opened up should this court hold that privacy exists as a legal right enforceable in equity by injunction, and by damages where they seem necessary to give complete relief.

The legislative body could very well interfere and arbitrarily provide that no one should be permitted for his own selfish purpose to use the picture or the name of another for advertising purposes without his consent. In such event, no embarrassment would result to the general body of the law, for the rule would be applicable only to cases provided for by the statute. The courts, however, being without authority to legislate, are required to decide cases upon principle, and so are necessarily embarrassed by precedents created by an extreme, and, therefore, unjustifiable application of an old principle.

The court below properly said that "while it may be true that the fact that no precedent can be found to sustain an action in any given case, is cogent evidence that a principle does not exist upon which the right may be based, it is not the rule that the want of a precedent is a sufficient reason for turning the plaintiff out of court," provided—I think should be added—there can be found a clear and unequivocal principle of the common law which either directly or mediately governs it or which by analogy or parity of reasoning ought to govern it.

The case that seems to have been more relied upon than any other by the learned Appellate Division in reaching the conclusion that the complaint in this case states a cause of action is Schuyler v. Curtis, 147 N.Y. 434, 31 L.R.A. 286, 49 Am.St. 671. In that case certain persons attempted to erect a statue or bust of a woman no longer living, and one of her relatives commenced an action in equity to restrain such erection, alleging that his feelings and the feelings of other relatives of deceased would be injured thereby. At Special Term an injunction was granted on that ground. 19 N.Y.Supp. 264. The General Term affirmed the decision. 64 Hun, 594. This court reversed the judgment, Judge Peckham writing, and so far as the decision is concerned, therefore, it is not authority for the existence of a right of privacy which entitles a party to restrain another from doing an act which, though not actionable at common law, occasions plaintiff mental distress. In the course of the argument, however, expressions were used which it is now claimed indicate that the court recognized the existence of such a right. A sufficient answer to that contention is to be found in the opinion written on the motion for reargument in Colonial City Tr. Co. v. Kingston City R. Co., 154 N.Y. 493, in which it was said: "It was not our intention to decide any case but the one before us.... If, as sometimes happens, broader statements were made by way of argument or otherwise than were essential to the decision of the questions presented, they are the dicta of the writer of the opinion and not the decision of the court. A judicial opinion, like evidence, is only binding so far as it is relevant, and when it wanders from the point at issue it no longer has force as an official utterance." The question up for decision in the Schuyler case was whether the relatives could restrain the threatened action of defendants, and not whether Mrs. Schuyler could have restrained it had she been living. The latter question not being before the court it was not called upon to decide it, and, as we read the opinion, there is no expression in it which indicates an intention either to decide it or to seriously consider it, but rather, it proceeds upon the assumption that if such a right did exist in

Mrs. Schuyler, her relatives did not succeed to it upon her death; all of which will sufficiently appear from the following extracts from the opinion:

"This action is of a nature somewhat unusual and dependent for its support upon the application of certain principles which are themselves not very clearly defined or their boundaries very well recognized or plainly laid down. Briefly described, the action is founded upon the alleged violation of what is termed the right of privacy."

"It is not necessary, however, to the view which we take of this case, to lay down precise and accurate rules which shall apply to all cases touching upon this alleged right."

"For the purposes we have in view, it is unnecessary to wholly deny the existence of the right of privacy to which the plaintiff appeals as the foundation of his cause of action."

"While not assuming to decide what this right of privacy is in all cases, we are quite clear that such a right would not be violated by the proposed action of the defendants."

There are two other cases in this state bearing upon this question: Marks v. Jaffa, 26 N.Y.Supp. 908, decided at Special Term, and Murray v. Gast Lithographic & Engraving Co., 8 Misc.Rep. 36, 28 N.Y.Supp. 271, decided at an Equity Term of the Court of Common Pleas at New York. In the first case the relief prayed for was granted upon the authority of the decision of the General Term in the *Schuyler* case, which was subsequently reversed in this court. In the Murray case, in a well-reasoned opinion by Judge Bischoff, it is held that a parent cannot maintain an action to enjoin an unauthorized publication of the portrait of an infant child, and for damages for injuries to his sensibilities caused by the invasion of his child's privacy, because "the law takes no cognizance of a sentimental injury, independent of a wrong to person or property." In the course of his opinion he quotes from the opinion of Lumpkin, J., in Chapman v. West. U.T. Co., 88 Ga. 763, 30 Am.St. 183, 17 L.R.A. 430, as follows: "The law protects the person and the purse. The person includes the reputation. The body, reputation and property of the citizen are not to be invaded without responsibility in damages to the sufferer. But, outside these protected spheres, the law does not yet attempt to guard the peace of mind, the feelings or the happiness of everyone by giving recovery of damages for mental anguish produced by mere negligence. There is no right, capable of enforcement by process of law, to possess or maintain, without disturbance, any particular condition of feeling. The law leaves feeling to be helped and vindicated by the tremendous force of sympathy. The temperaments of individuals are various and variable, and the imagination exerts a powerful and incalculable influence in injuries of this kind. There are many moral obligations too delicate and subtle to be enforced in the rude way of giving money compensation for their violation. Perhaps the feelings find as full protection as it is possible to give in moral law and a responsive public opinion. The civil law is a practical business system, dealing with what is tangible, and does not undertake to redress psychological injuries."

Outside of this jurisdiction the question seems to have been presented in two other cases in this country: Corliss v. E.W. Walker Co., 57 Fed. 434; 64 Fed. 280, 31 L.R.A. 283, and Atkinson v. Doherty, 121 Mich. 372, 80 Am.St.Rep. 507, 46 L.R.A. 219. The *Corliss* case was an action in equity to restrain the publication of the biography and picture of Mr. Corliss. It was based upon an alleged invasion of the right of privacy. The court denied the injunction as to the publication of the biography but granted it as to the use of certain plates from which the defendant was to make a picture of Mr. Corliss, upon the ground that they had been obtained upon conditions which defendant had not complied with. In the course of the opinion the court said: "Under our laws one can speak and publish what he desires, provided he commit no offense against public morals or private reputation.... There is another objection which meets us at the threshold of this case. The subject-matter of the jurisdiction of a court of equity is civil property, and injury to property, whether actual or prospective is the foundation on which its jurisdiction rests. Re Sawyer, 124 U.S. 200, 210, 31 L.Ed. 402; Kerr, Inj. (2d ed.) p. 1. It follows from this principle that a court of equity has no power to restrain a libelous publication." Both the opinion and the decision necessarily negative the existence of an actionable right of privacy; but subsequently upon a motion to dissolve the injunction, which was granted upon the ground that Mr. Corliss was a public character, and hence the publishers were entitled to use his picture, the learned court expressed the opinion that a private individual has the right to be protected from the publication of his portrait in any form. Now, while this suggestion was obiter, it merits discussion, and an examination of that which it promulgates as doctrine discloses what we deem a fatal objection to the establishment of a rule of privacy. The learned judge says: "I believe the law to be that a private individual has a right to be protected in the representation of his portrait in any form; that this is a property as well as a personal right, and that it belongs to the same class of rights which forbids the reproduction of a private manuscript or painting, or the publication of private letters, or of oral lectures delivered by a teacher to his class, or the revelation of the contents of a merchant's book by a clerk.... But, while the right of a private individual to prohibit the reproduction of his picture or photograph should be recognized and enforced, this right may be surrendered or dedicated to the public by the act of the individual, just the same as a private manuscript, book or painting becomes (when not protected by copyright) public property by the act of publication. The distinction in the case of a picture or photograph lies, it seems to me, between public and private characters. A private individual should be protected against the publication of any portrait of himself, but where an individual becomes a public character the case is different. A statesman, author, artist or inventor, who asks for and desires public recognition, may be said to have surrendered his right to the public." This distinction between public and private characters cannot possibly be drawn. On what principle does an author or artist forfeit his right of privacy and a great orator, a great preacher, or a great advocate retain his? Who can draw a line of demarcation between public characters and private characters, let that line be as wavering and irregular as you please? In the very case then before the judge, what had Mr. Corliss done by which he surrendered his right of privacy? In what respect did he by his inventions "ask for and desire public recognition" any more than a banker or merchant who prosecutes his calling? Or is the right of privacy the possession of mediocrity alone, which a person forfeits by giving rein to his ability, spurs to his industry or grandeur to his character? A lady may pass her life in domestic privacy when, by some act of heroism or self-sacrifice, her name and fame fill the public ear. Is she to forfeit by her good deed the right of privacy she previously possessed? These considerations suggest the answer we would make to the position of the learned judge and at the same time serve to make more clear what we have elsewhere attempted to point out, namely, the absolute impossibility of dealing with this subject save by legislative enactment, by which may be drawn arbitrary distinctions which no court should promulgate as a part of general jurisprudence.

Atkinson v. Doherty was a suit in equity brought by the widow of Colonel John Atkinson, a well-known lawyer in Detroit, to enjoin the defendant, a cigar manufacturer, from using the name and portrait of Colonel Atkinson upon boxes of cigars manufactured by defendant. The suit was dismissed by the Circuit Court, and its decree was unanimously affirmed by the Supreme Court. The case quite closely resembles the *Schuyler* case, which was brought to the attention of that court, and in the course of the opinion the contention that the *Schuyler* case intimated the existence of a right of privacy was met as follows: "We think it should not be considered as containing a dictum even in support of the doctrine contended for." The method adopted by the court in the *Atkinson* case in treating the question was different from that employed by this court in the *Schuyler* case, however, for the opinion proceeds to a review of the authorities upon which the right of privacy is said to rest, reaching the conclusion that all of the authorities which are entitled to respect are based upon property or contract rights, and hence "that Colonel Atkinson would himself be remediless were he alive, and the same is true of his friends who survive." The opinion concludes as follows: "This law of privacy seems to have gained a foothold at one time in the history of our jurisprudence—not by that name, it is true—but in effect. It is evidenced by the old maxim, 'the greater the truth the greater the libel,' and the result has been the emphatic expression of public disapproval, by the emancipation of the press and the establishment of freedom of speech, and the abolition in most of the states of the maxim quoted by constitutional provisions. The limitations upon the exercise of these rights being the law of slander and libel, whereby the publication of an untruth that can be presumed or shown to the satisfaction, not of the plaintiff, but of others (i.e., an impartial jury), to be injurious, not alone to the feelings, but to the reputation, is actionable. Should it be thought that it is a hard rule that is applied in this case, it is only necessary to call attention to the fact that a ready remedy is to be found in legislation. We are not satisfied, however, that the rule is a hard one, and think that the consensus of opinion must be that the complainants contend for a much harder one. The law does not remedy all evils. It cannot, in the nature of things; and deliberation may well be used in considering the propriety of an innovation such as this case suggests. We do not wish to be understood as belittling the complaint. We have no reason to doubt the feeling of annoyance alleged. Indeed, we sympathize with it, and marvel at the impertinence which does not respect it. We can only say that it is one of the ills that under the law cannot be redressed."

An examination of the authorities leads us to the conclusion that the so-called "right of privacy" has not as yet found an abiding place in our jurisprudence, and, as we view it, the doctrine cannot now be incorporated without doing violence to settled principles of law by which the profession and the public have long been guided.

The judgment of the Appellate Division and of the Special Term should be reversed and questions certified answered in the negative, without costs, and with leave to the plaintiff to serve an amended complaint within twenty days, also without costs.

■ GRAY, J., dissenting.

These defendants stand before the court, admitting that they have made, published and circulated, without the knowledge or the authority of the plaintiff, 25,000 lithographic portraits of her, for the purpose of profit and gain to themselves; that these portraits have been conspicuously posted in stores, warehouses and saloons, in the vicinity of the plaintiff's residence and throughout the United States, as advertisements of their goods; that the effect has been to humiliate her and to render her ill and, yet, claiming that she makes out no cause of action. They say that no law on the statute books gives her a right of action and that her right to privacy is not an actionable right, at law or in equity.

Our consideration of the question thus presented has not been foreclosed by the decision in Schuyler v. Curtis, 147 N.Y. 434, 49 Am.St.Rep. 671, 31 L.R.A. 286. In that case, it appeared that the defendants were intending to make, and to exhibit, at the Columbian Exposition of 1893, a statue of Mrs. Schuyler, formerly Miss Mary M. Hamilton and conspicuous in her lifetime for her philanthropic work, to typify "Woman as the Philanthropist" and, as a companion piece, a statute of Miss Susan B. Anthony, to typify the "Representative Reformer." The plaintiff, in behalf of himself, as the nephew of Mrs. Schuyler, and of other immediate relatives, sought by the action to restrain them from carrying out their intentions as to the statue of Mrs. Schuyler; upon the grounds, in substance, that they were proceeding without his consent, (whose relationship was conceded to be such as to warrant such an action, if it were maintainable at all), or that of the other immediate members of the family; that their proceeding was disagreeable to him, because it would have been disagreeable and obnoxious to his aunt, if living, and that it was annoying to have Mrs. Schuyler's memory associated with principles, which Miss Susan B. Anthony typified and of which Mrs. Schuyler did not approve. His right to maintain the action was denied and the denial was expressly placed upon the ground that he, as a relative, did not represent any right of privacy which Mrs. Schuyler possessed in her lifetime and that, whatever her right had been, in that respect, it died with her. The existence of the individual's right to be protected against the invasion of his privacy, if not actually affirmed in the opinion, was, very certainly, far from being denied. "It may be admitted," Judge Peckham observed, when delivering the opinion of the court, "that courts have power, in some cases, to enjoin the doing of an act, where the nature, or character, of the act itself is well calculated to wound the sensibilities of an individual, and where the doing of the act is wholly unjustifiable, and is, in legal contemplation, a wrong, even though the existence of no property, as that term is usually used, is involved in the subject."

That the individual has a right to privacy, which he can enforce and which equity will protect against the invasion of, is a proposition which is not opposed by any decision in this court and which, in my opinion, is within the field of accepted legal principles. It is within the very case supposed by Judge Peckham in Schuyler v. Curtis. In the present case, we may not say that the plaintiff's complaint is fanciful, or that her alleged injury is, purely, a sentimental one. Her objection to the defendants' acts is not one born of caprice; nor is it based upon the defendants' act being merely "distasteful" to her. We are bound to assume, and I find no difficulty in doing so, that the conspicuous display of her likeness, in various public places, has so humiliated her by the notoriety and by the public comments it has provoked, as to cause her distress and suffering, in body and in mind, and to confine her to her bed with illness.

If it were necessary, to be entitled to equitable relief, that the plaintiff's sufferings, by reason of the defendants' acts, should be serious, and appreciable by a pecuniary standard, clearly, we might well say, under the allegations of the complaint, that they were of such degree of gravity. However, I am not of the opinion that the gravity of the injury need be such as to be capable of being estimated by such a standard. If the right of privacy exists and this complaint makes out a case of its substantial violation, I think that the award of equitable relief, by way of an injunction, preventing the continuance of its invasion by the defendants, will not depend upon the complainant's ability to prove substantial pecuniary damages and, if the court finds the defendants' act to be without justification and for selfish gain and purposes, and to be of such a character, as is reasonably calculated to wound the feelings and to subject the plaintiff to the ridicule, or to the contempt of others, that her right to the preventive relief of equity will follow; without considering how far her sufferings may be measurable by a pecuniary standard.

The right of privacy, or the right of the individual to be let alone, is a personal right, which is not without judicial recognition. It is the complement of the right to the immunity of one's person. The individual has always been entitled to be protected in the exclusive use and enjoyment of that which is his own. The common law regarded his person and property as inviolate, and he has the absolute right to be let alone. Cooley, Torts, p. 29. The principle is fundamental and essential in organized society that every one, in exercising a personal right and in the use of his property, shall respect the rights and properties of others. He must so conduct himself, in the enjoyment of the rights and privileges which belong to him as a member of society, as that he shall prejudice no one in the possession and enjoyment of those which are exclusively his. When, as here, there is an alleged invasion of some personal right, or privilege, the absence of exact precedent and the fact that early commentators upon the common law have no discussion upon the subject are of no material importance in awarding equitable relief. That the exercise of the preventive power of a court of equity is demanded in a novel case, is not a fatal objection. Niagara Falls Int. Bridge Co. v. Great Western Ry. Co., 39 Barb. 212; Sherman v. Skuse, 166 N.Y. 352; Hamilton v. Whitridge, 11 Md. 145, 69 Am.Dec. 184. In the social evolution, with the march of the arts and sciences and in the resultant effects upon organized society, it is quite intelligible that new conditions must arise in personal relations, which the rules of the common law, cast in the rigid mould of an earlier social status, were not designed to meet. It would be a reproach to equitable jurisprudence, if equity were powerless to extend the application of the principles of common law, or of natural justice, in remedying a wrong, which, in the progress of civilization, has been made possible as the result of new social, or commercial conditions.

Instantaneous photography is a modern invention and affords the means of securing a portraiture of an individual's face and form, in invitum their owner. While, so far forth as it merely does that, although a species of aggression, I concede it to be an irremediable and irrepressible feature of the social evolution. But, if it is to be permitted that the portraiture may be put to commercial, or other, uses for gain, by the publication of prints therefrom, then an act of invasion of the individual's privacy results, possibly more formidable and more painful in its consequences, than an actual bodily assault might be. Security of person is as necessary as the security of property; and for that complete personal security, which will result in the peaceful and wholesome enjoyment of one's privileges as a member of society, there should be afforded protection, not only against the scandalous portraiture and display of one's features and person, but against the display and use thereof for another's commercial purposes or gain. The proposition is, to me, an inconceivable one that these defendants may, unauthorizedly, use the likeness of this young woman upon their advertisement, as a method of attracting widespread public attention to their wares, and that she must submit to the mortifying notoriety, without right to invoke the exercise of the preventive power of a court of equity.

Such a view, as it seems to me, must have been unduly influenced by a failure to find precedents in analogous cases, or some declaration by the great commentators upon the law of a common-law principle which would, precisely, apply to and govern the action; without taking into consideration that, in the existing state of society, new conditions affecting the relations of persons demand the broader extension of those legal principles, which underlie the immunity of one's person from attack. I think that such a view is unduly restricted, too, by a search for some property, which has been invaded by the defendants' acts. Property is not, necessarily, the thing itself, which is owned; it is the right of the owner in relation to it. The right to be protected in one's possession of a thing, or in one's privileges, belonging to him as an individual, or secured to him as a member of the commonwealth, is property, and as such entitled to the protection of the law. The protective power of equity is not exercised upon the tangible thing, but upon the right to enjoy it; and, so, it is called forth for the protection of the right to that which is one's exclusive possession, as a property right. It seems to me that the principle, which is applicable, is analogous to that upon which courts of equity have interfered to protect the right of privacy, in cases of private writings, or of other unpublished products of the mind. The writer, or the lecturer, has been protected in his right to a literary property in a letter, or a lecture, against its unauthorized publication; because it is property, to which the right of privacy attaches. Woolsey v. Judd, 4 Duer, 399; Gee v. Pritchard, 2 Swanst. 402; Abernathy v. Hutchinson, 3 L.J.Ch. 209; Folsom v. Marsh, 2 Story, 100. I think that this plaintiff has the same property in the right to be protected against the use of her face for defendants' commercial purposes, as she would have, if they were publishing her literary compositions. The right would be conceded, if she had sat for her photograph; but if her face, or her portraiture, has a value, the value is hers exclusively; until the use be granted away to the public. Any other principle of decision, in my opinion, is as repugnant to equity, as it is shocking to reason.

The right to grant the injunction does not depend upon the existence of property, which one has in some contractual form. It depends upon the existence of property in any right which belongs to a person. In Pollard v. Photographic Co., 40 Ch.Div. 345, it was held that the right to grant an injunction against selling copies of plaintiff's photographs did not depend upon the existence of property and that "it is quite clear that independently of any question as to the right at law, the Court of Chancery always had an original and independent jurisdiction to prevent what that court considered and treated as a wrong, whether arising from a violation of an unquestionable right, or from breach of confidence, or contract, as was pointed out by Lord Cottenham in Prince Albert v. Strange, 1 Macn. & G. 25." In Prince Albert v. Strange, Lord Chancellor Cottenham sustained the issuance of an injunction, upon the ground that the right of privacy had been invaded by the publication and sale of etchings, made by Prince Albert and Queen Victoria. Upon the original hearing, Vice–Chancellor Knight–Bruce, in granting the injunction, observed that, "upon the principle of protecting property, it is that the common law, in cases not aided or prejudiced by statute, shelters the privacy and seclusion of thoughts and sentiments committed to writing, and desired by the author to remain not generally known."

It would be, in my opinion, an extraordinary view which, while conceding the right of a person to be protected against the unauthorized circulation of an unpublished lecture, letter, drawing, or other ideal property, yet, would deny the same protection to a person, whose portrait was unauthorizedly obtained, and made use of, for commercial purposes. The injury to the plaintiff is irreparable; because she cannot be wholly compensated in damages for the various consequences entailed by defendants' acts. The only complete relief is an injunction restraining their continuance. Whether, as incidental to that equitable relief, she should be able to recover only nominal damages is not material; for the issuance of the injunction does not, in such a case, depend upon the amount of the damages in dollars and cents.

A careful consideration of the question presented upon this appeal leads me to the conclusion that the judgment appealed from should be affirmed.

■ O'BRIEN, CULLEN and WERNER, JJ., concur with PARKER, CH.J.; BARTLETT and HAIGHT, JJ., concur with GRAY, J.

Judgment reversed, etc.

## Pavesich v. New England Life Insurance Co.

Supreme Court of Georgia, 1905.
122 Ga. 190, 50 S.E. 68.

Paolo Pavesich brought an action against the New England Mutual Life Insurance Company, a non-resident corporation, Thomas B. Lumpkin, its general agent, and J.Q. Adams, a photographer, both residing in the city of Atlanta. The allegations of the petition were, in substance, as follows: In an issue of the Atlanta Constitution, a newspaper published in the city of Atlanta, there appeared a likeness of the plaintiff, which would be easily recognized by his friends and acquaintances, placed by the side of the likeness of an ill-dressed and sickly looking person. Above the likeness of the plaintiff were the words, "Do it now. The man who did." Above the likeness of the other person were the words, "Do it while you can. The man who didn't." Below the two pictures were the words, "These two pictures tell their own story." Under the plaintiff's picture the following appeared: "In my healthy and productive period of life I bought insurance in the New England Mutual Life Insurance Co., of Boston, Mass., and to-day my family is protected and I am drawing an annual dividend on my paid-up policies." Under the other person's picture was a statement to the effect that he had not taken insurance, and now realized his mistake. The statements were signed, "Thomas B. Lumpkin, General Agent." The picture of the plaintiff was taken from a negative obtained by the defendant Lumpkin, or someone by him authorized, from the defendant Adams, which was used with his consent and with knowledge of the purpose for which it was to be used. The picture was made from the negative without the plaintiff's consent, at the instance of the defendant insurance company, through its agent Lumpkin. Plaintiff is an artist by profession, and the publication is peculiarly offensive to him. The statement attributed to plaintiff in the publication is false and malicious. He never made any such statement, and has not and never has had a policy of life-insurance with the defendant company. The publication is malicious and tends to bring plaintiff into ridicule before the world, and especially with his friends and acquaintances who know that he has no policy in the defendant company. The publication is "a trespass upon plaintiff's right of privacy, and was caused by breach of confidence and trust reposed" in the defendant Adams. The prayer was for damages in the sum of $25,000. The petition was demurred to generally [ . . . ]. The court sustained the general demurrer, and the plaintiff excepted.

■ COBB, J. The question to be determined is whether an individual has a right of privacy which he can enforce and which the courts will protect against invasion. It is to be conceded that prior to 1890 every adjudicated case, both in this country and in England, which might be said to have involved a right of privacy, was not based upon the existence of such right, but was founded upon a supposed right of property, or a breach of trust or confidence, or the like; and that therefore a claim to a right of privacy, independent of a property or contractual right or some right of a similar nature, had, up to that time, never been recognized in terms in any decision. The entire absence for a long period of time, even for centuries, of a precedent for an asserted right should have the effect to cause the courts to proceed with caution before recognizing the right, for fear that they may thereby invade the province of the lawmaking power; but such absence, even for all time, is not conclusive of the question as to the existence of the right. The novelty of the complaint is no objection when an injury cognizable by law is shown to have been inflicted on the plaintiff. In such a case "although there be no precedent, the common law will judge according to the law of nature and the public good." Where the case is new in principle, the courts have no authority to give a remedy, no matter how great the grievance; but where the case is only new in instance, and the sole question is upon the application of a recognized principle to a new case, "it will be just as competent to courts of justice to apply the principle to any case that may arise two centuries hence as it was two centuries ago." Broom's Legal Maxims (8th ed.), 193.

The individual surrenders to society many rights and privileges which he would be free to exercise in a state of nature, in exchange for the benefits which he receives as a member of society. But he is not presumed to surrender all those rights, and the public has no more right, without his consent, to invade the domain of those rights which it is necessarily to be presumed he has reserved than he has to violate the valid regulations of the organized government under which he lives. The right of privacy has its foundation in the instincts of nature. It is recognized intuitively, consciousness being the witness that can be called to establish its existence. Any person whose intellect is in a normal condition recognizes at once that as to each individual member of society there are matters private and there are matters public so far as the individual is concerned. Each individual as instinctively resents any encroachment by the public upon his rights which are of a private nature as he does the withdrawal of those of his rights which are of a public nature. A right of privacy in matters purely private is therefore derived from natural law.

It is one of those rights referred to by some law-writers as absolute; "such as would belong to their persons merely in a state of nature, and which every man is entitled to enjoy, whether out of society or in it."

Among the absolute rights referred to by the commentator just cited is the right of personal security and the right of personal liberty. In the first is embraced a person's right to a "legal and uninterrupted enjoyment of his life, his limbs, his body, his health, and his reputation;" and in the second is embraced "the power of locomotion, of changing situation, or moving one's person to whatsoever place one's own inclination may direct, without imprisonment or restraint, unless by due course of law." 1 Bl. 129, 134. While neither Sir William Blackstone nor any of the other writers on the principles of the common law have referred in terms to the right of privacy, the illustrations given by them as to what would be a violation of the absolute rights of individuals are not to be taken as exhaustive, but the language should be allowed to include any instance of a violation of such rights which is clearly within the true meaning and intent of the words used to declare the principle. When the law guarantees to one the right to the enjoyment of his life, it gives to him something more than the mere right to breathe and exist. While of course the most flagrant violation of this right would be deprivation of life, yet life itself may be spared and the enjoyment of life entirely destroyed. An individual has a right to enjoy life in any way that may be most agreeable and pleasant to him, according to his temperament and nature, provided that in such enjoyment he does not invade the rights of his neighbor or violate public law or policy.

All will admit that the individual who desires to live a life of seclusion can not be compelled, against his consent, to exhibit his person in any public place, unless such exhibition is demanded by the law of the land. He may be required to come from his place of seclusion to perform public duties,—to serve as a juror and to testify as a witness, and the like; but when the public duty is once performed, if he exercises his liberty to go again into seclusion, no one can deny him the right. One who desires to live a life of partial seclusion has a right to choose the times, places, and manner in which and at which he will submit himself to the public gaze. Subject to the limitation above referred to, the body of a person can not be put on exhibition at any time or at any place without his consent. The right of one to exhibit himself to the public at all proper times, in all proper places, and in a proper manner is embraced within the right of personal liberty. The right to withdraw from the public gaze at such times as a person may see fit, when his presence in public is not demanded by any rule of law is also embraced within the right of personal liberty. Publicity in one instance and privacy in the other is each guaranteed. If personal liberty embraces the right of publicity, it no less embraces the correlative right of privacy; and this is no new idea in Georgia law. In Wallace v. Railway Company, 94 Ga. 732, it was said: "Liberty of speech and of writing is secured by the constitution, and incident thereto is the correlative liberty of silence, not less important nor less sacred."

Instances might be multiplied where the common law has both tacitly and expressly recognized the right of an individual to repose and privacy. The right of the people to be secure in their persons, houses, papers, and effects against unreasonable searches and seizures, which is so fully protected in the constitutions of the United States and of this State (Civil

Code, §§ 6017, 5713), is not a right created by these instruments, but is an ancient right which, on account of its gross violation at different times, was preserved from such attacks in the future by being made the subject of constitutional provisions.

It may be said that to establish a liberty of privacy would involve in numerous cases the perplexing question to determine where this liberty ended and the rights of others and of the public began. This affords no reason for not recognizing the liberty of privacy and giving to the person aggrieved legal redress against the wrong-doer in a case where it is clearly shown that a legal wrong has been done. It may be that there will arise many cases which lie near the border line which marks the right of privacy on the one hand and the right of another individual or of the public on the other. But this is true in regard to numerous other rights which the law recognizes as resting in the individual. In regard to cases that may arise under the right of privacy, as in cases that arise under other rights where the line of demarkation is to be determined, the safeguard of the individual on the one hand and of the public on the other is the wisdom and integrity of the judiciary. Each person has a liberty of privacy, and every other person h to assess the damage if their finding is in favor of the plaintiff. This burden which rests upon the court in every case of the character referred to is all that will be imposed upon it in actions brought for a violation of the right of privacy. No greater difficulties will be encountered in such cases in determining the existence of the right than often will be encountered in determining the existence of other rights sought to be enforced by action. The courts may proceed in cases involving the violation of a right of privacy as in other cases of a similar nature, and the juries may in the same manner proceed to a determination of those questions which the law requires to be submitted for their consideration. With honest and fearless trial judges to pass in the first instance upon the question of law as to the existence of the right in each case, whose decisions are subject to review by the court of last resort, and with fair and impartial juries to pass upon the questions of fact involved and assess the damages in the event of a recovery, whose verdict is, under our law, in all cases subject to supervision and scrutiny by the trial judge, who may, within the limits of a legal discretion, control their findings, there need be no more fear that the right of privacy will be the occasion of unjustifiable litigation, oppression, or wrong than that the existence of many other rights in the law would bring about such results.

[The Court reviewed prior decisions, concluding with Roberson v. Rochester Folding Box Co.]

We have no fault to find with what is said by the distinguished and learned judge who voiced the views of the majority, as to the existence of decided cases, and agree with him in his analysis of the various cases which he reviews, that the judgment in each was based upon other grounds than the existence of a right of privacy. We also agree with him so far as he asserts that the writers upon the common law and the principles of equity do not in express terms refer to this right. But we are utterly at variance with him in his conclusion that the existence of this right can not be legitimately inferred from what has been said by commentators upon the legal rights of individuals, and from expressions which have fallen from judges in their reasoning in cases where the exercise of the right was not directly involved. So far as the judgment in the case is based upon the argument ab inconvenienti, all that is necessary to be said is that this argument has no place in the case if the right invoked has an existence in the law. But if it were proper to use this argument at all, it could be said with great force that as to certain matters the individual feels and knows that he has a right to exercise the liberty of privacy, and that he has a right to resent any invasion of this liberty; and if the law will not protect him against invasion, the individual will, to protect himself and those to whom he owes protection, use those weapons with which nature has provided him as well as those which the ingenuity of man has placed within his reach. Thus the peace and good order of society would be disturbed by each individual becoming a law unto himself to determine when and under what circumstances he should avenge the outrage which has been perpetrated upon him or a member of his family. The true lawyer, when called to the discharge of judicial functions, has in all times, as a general rule, displayed remarkable conservatism; and wherever it was legally possible to base a judgment upon principles which had been recognized by a long course of judicial decision, this has been done, in preference to applying a principle which might be considered novel. It was for this reason that the numerous cases, both in England and in this country, which really protected the right of privacy were not placed upon the existence of this right, but were allowed to rest upon principles derived from the law of property, trust, and contract. Any candid mind will, however, be compelled to concede that in order to give relief in many of those cases it required a severe strain to bring them within the recognized rules which were sought to be applied. The desire to avoid the novelty of recognizing a principle which had not been theretofore recognized was avoided in such cases by the novelty of straining a well-recognized principle to cover a state of facts to which it had never before been applied. This conservatism of the judiciary has sometimes unconsciously led judges to the conclusion that because the case was novel the right claimed did not exist. With all due respect to Chief Judge Parker and his associates who concurred with him, we think the conclusion reached by them was the result of an unconscious yielding to the feeling of conservatism which naturally arises in the mind of a judge who faces a proposition which is novel. The valuable influence upon society and upon the welfare of the public of the conservatism of the lawyer, whether at the bar or upon the bench, can not be overestimated; but this conservatism should not go to the extent of refusing to recognize a right which the instincts of nature prove to exist, and which nothing in judicial decision, legal history, or writings upon the law can be called to demonstrate its non-existence as a legal right.

We think that what should have been a proper judgment in the *Roberson* case was that contended for by Judge Gray in his dissenting opinion,

[quotations from Judge Gray's opinion omitted]

The effect of the reasoning of the learned judge is to establish conclusively the correctness of the conclusion which we have reached, and we prefer to adopt as our own his reasoning in his own words rather than to paraphrase them into our own. The decision of the Court of Appeals of New York in the *Roberson* case gave rise to numerous articles in the different law magazines of high standing in the country, some by the editors and others by contributors. In some the conclusion of the majority of the court was approved; in others the views of the dissenting judges were commended; and in still others the case and similar cases were referred to as apparently establishing that the claim of the majority was correct, but regret was expressed that the necessity was such that the courts could not recognize the right asserted. An editorial in the American Law Review (vol. 36, p. 636) said: "The decision under review shocks and wounds the ordinary sense of justice of mankind. We have heard it alluded to only in terms of regret."

So thoroughly satisfied are we that the law recognizes within proper limits, as a legal right, the right of privacy, and that the publication of one's picture without his consent by another as an advertisement, for the mere purpose of increasing the profits and gains of the advertiser, is an invasion of this right, that we venture to predict that the day will come when the American bar will marvel that a contrary view was ever entertained by judges of eminence and ability; just as in the present day we stand amazed that Lord Hale, with perfect composure of manner and complete satisfaction of soul, imposed the death penalty for witchcraft upon ignorant and harmless women.

### Notes and Questions

**1.** Articulate the differences in the starting points of the *Roberson* majority's and the *Pavesich* court's analyses.

**2.** How do the two decisions treat prior authority? Whose treatment is more persuasive? Why?

**3.** If, following *Pavesich,* the New York Court of Appeals had to rule on another claim involving the unauthorized publication of personal photographs for purposes of trade, would the New York court adopt the Georgia court's approach? Why or why not?

### c.  THE DUTY OF CARE

## Hynes v. New York Cent. R. Co.

Court of Appeals of New York, 1921.
231 N.Y. 229, 131 N.E. 898.

Appeal from a judgment of the Appellate Division of the Supreme Court in the second judicial department, entered January 12, 1920, affirming a judgment in favor of defendant entered upon a dismissal of the complaint by the court at a Trial Term.

■ Cardozo, J. On July 8, 1916, Harvey Hynes, a lad of sixteen, swam with two companions from the Manhattan to the Bronx side of the Harlem river or United States Ship Canal, a navigable stream. Along the Bronx side of the river was the right of way of the defendant, the New York Central Railroad, which operated its trains at that point by high tension wires, strung on poles and crossarms. Projecting from the defendant's bulkhead above th oard was beyond the line of the defendant's property, and above the public waterway. Its height measured from the stream was three feet at the bulkhead, and five feet at its outermost extremity. For more than five years swimmers had used it as a diving board without protest or obstruction.

On this day Hynes and his companions climbed on top of the bulkhead intending to leap into the water. One of them made the plunge in safety. Hynes followed to the front of the springboard, and stood poised for his dive. At that moment a cross-arm with electric wires fell from the defendant's pole. The wires struck the diver, flung him from the shattered board, and plunged him to his death below. His mother, suing as administratrix, brings this action for her damages. Thus far the courts have held that Hynes at the end of the springboard above the public waters was a trespasser on the defendant's land. They have thought it immaterial that the board itself was a trespass, an encroachment on the public ways. They have thought it of no significance that Hynes would have met the same fate if he had been below the board and not above it. The board, they have said, was annexed to the defendant's bulkhead. By force of such annexation, it was to be reckoned as a fixture, and thus constructively, if not actually, an extension of the land. The defendant was under a duty to use reasonable care that bathers swimming or standing in the water should not be electrocuted by wires falling from its right of way. But to bathers diving from the springboard, there was no duty, we are told, unless the injury was the product of mere willfulness or wantonness, no duty of active vigilance to safeguard the impending structure. Without wrong to them, cross-arms might be left to rot; wires highly charged with electricity might sweep them from their stand, and bury them in the subjacent waters. In climbing on the board, they became trespassers and outlaws. The conclusion is defended with much subtlety of reasoning, with much insistence upon its inevitableness as a merely logical deduction. A majority of the court are unable to accept it as the conclusion of the law.

We assume, without deciding, that the springboard was a fixture, a permanent improvement of the defendant's right of way. Much might be said in favor of another view. We do not press the inquiry, for we are persuaded that the rights of bathers do not depend upon these nice distinctions. Liability would not be doubtful, we are told, had the boy been diving from a pole, if the pole had been vertical. The diver in such a situation would have been separated from the defendant's freehold. Liability, it is said, has been escaped because the pole was horizontal. The plank when projected lengthwise was an extension of the soil. We are to concentrate our gaze on the private ownership of the board. We are to ignore the public ownership of the circumambient spaces of water and of air. Jumping from a boat or a barrel, the boy would have been a bather in the river. Jumping from the end of a springboard, he was no longer, it is said, a bather, but a trespasser on a right of way.

Rights and duties in systems of living law are not built upon such quicksands.

Bathers in the Harlem river on the day of this disaster were in the enjoyment of a public highway, entitled to reasonable protection against destruction by the defendant's wires. They did not cease to be bathers entitled to the same protection while they were diving from encroaching objects or engaging in the sports that are common among swimmers. Such acts were not equivalent to an abandonment of the highway, a departure from its proper uses, a withdrawal from the waters, and an entry upon land. A plane of private right had been interposed between the river and the air, but public ownership was unchanged in the space below it and above. The defendant does not deny that it would have owed a duty to this boy if he had been leaning against the springboard with his feet upon the ground. He is said to have forfeited protection as he put his feet upon the plank. Presumably the same result would follow if the plank had been a few inches above the surface of the water instead of a few feet. Duties are thus supposed to arise and to be extinguished in alternate zones or strata. Two boys walking in the country or swimming in a river stop to rest for a moment along the side of the road or the margin of the stream. One of them throws himself beneath the overhanging branches of a tree. The other perches himself on a bough a foot or so above the ground. Hoffman v. Armstrong, 48 N.Y. 201, 8 Am.Rep. 537. Both are killed by falling wires. The defendant would have us say that there is a remedy for the representatives of one, and none for the representatives of the other. We may be permitted to distrust the logic that leads to such conclusions.

The truth is that every act of Hynes, from his first plunge into the river until the moment of his death, was in the enjoyment of the public waters, and under cover of the protection which his presence in those waters gave him. The use of the springboard was not an abandonment of his rights as bather. It was a mere by-play, an incident, subordinate and ancillary to the execution of his primary purpose, the enjoyment of the highway. The by-play, the incident, was not the cause of the disaster. Hynes would have gone to his death if he had been below the springboard or beside it. Laidlaw v. Sage, 158 N.Y. 73, 97, 52 N.E. 679, 44 L.R.A. 216. The wires were not stayed by the presence of the plank. They followed the boy in his fall, and overwhelmed him in the waters. The defendant assumes that the identification of ownership of a fixture with ownership of land is complete in every incident. But there are important elements of difference. Title to the fixture, unlike title to the land, does not carry with it rights of ownership usque ad coelum. There will hardly be denial that a cause of action would have arisen if the wires had fallen on an aeroplane proceeding above the river, though the location of the impact could be identified as the space above the springboard. The most that the defendant can fairly ask is exemption from liability where the use of the fixture is itself the efficient peril. That would be the situation, for example, if the weight of the boy upon the board had caused it to break and thereby throw him into the river. There is no such causal connection here between his position and his injuries. We think there was no moment when he was beyond the pale of the defendant's duty—the duty of care and vigilance in the storage of destructive forces.

This case is a striking instance of the dangers of "a jurisprudence of conceptions" (Pound, Mechanical Jurisprudence, 8 Columbia Law Review, 605, 608, 610), the extension of a maxim or a definition with relentless disregard of consequences to a "dryly logical extreme." The approximate and relative become the definite and absolute. Landowners are not bound to regulate their conduct in contemplation of the presence of trespassers intruding upon private structures. Landowners are bound to regulate their conduct in contemplation of the presence of travelers upon the adjacent public ways. There are times when there is little trouble in marking off the field of exemption and immunity from that of liability and duty. Here structures and ways are so united and commingled, super-imposed upon each other, that the fields are brought together. In such circumstances, there is little help in pursuing general maxims to ultimate conclusions. They have been framed alio intuitu. They must be reformulated and readapted to meet exceptional conditions. Rules appropriate to spheres which are conceived of as separate and distinct cannot, both, be enforced when the spheres become concentric. There must then be readjustment or collision. In one sense, and that a highly technical and artificial one, the diver at the end of the springboard is an intruder on the adjoining lands. In another sense, and one that realists will accept more readily, he is still on public waters in the exercise of public rights. The law must say whether it will subject him to the rule of the one field or of the other, of this sphere or of that. We think that considerations of analogy, of convenience, of policy, and of justice, exclude him from the field of the defendant's immunity and exemption, and place him in the field of liability and duty. Beck v. Carter, 68 N.Y. 283, 23 Am.Rep. 175; Jewhurst v. City of Syracuse, 108 N.Y. 303, 15 N.E. 409; McCloskey v. Buckley, 223 N.Y. 187, 192, 119 N.E. 395.

The judgment of the Appellate Division and that of the Trial Term should be reversed, and a new trial granted, with costs to abide the event.

■ Hogan, Pound and Crane, JJ., concur; Hiscock, Ch.J., Chase and McLaughlin, JJ., dissent.

### Notes and Questions

**1.** Judge Cardozo in The Growth of the Law 99–103 (1924) thus comments on the above decision:

> We had in my court a year or more ago a case that points my meaning. A boy was bathing in a river. He climbed upon a springboard which projected from a bank. As he stood there, at the end of the board, poised for his dive into the stream, electric wires fell upon him, and swept him to his death below. In the suit for damages that followed, competitive analogies were invoked by counsel for the administratrix

and counsel for the railroad company, the owner of the upland. The administratrix found the analogy that suited her in the position of travelers on a highway. The boy was a bather in navigable waters; his rights were not lessened because his feet were on the board. The owner found the analogy to its liking in the position of a trespasser on land. The springboard, though it projected into the water, was, nonetheless, a fixture, and as a fixture it was constructively a part of the land to which it was annexed. The boy was thus a trespasser upon land in private ownership; the only duty of the owner was to refrain from wanton and malicious injury; if these elements were lacking, the death must go without requital. Now, the truth is that, as a mere bit of dialectics, these analogies would bring a judge to an impasse. No process of merely logical deduction could determine the choice between them. Neither analogy is precise, though each is apposite. There had arisen a new situation which could not force itself without mutilation into any of the existing moulds. When we find a situation of this kind, the choice that will approve itself to this judge or to that, will be determined largely by his conception of the end of the law, the function of legal liability; and this question of ends and functions is a question of philosophy.

In the case that I have instanced, a majority of the court believed that liability should be adjudged. The deductions that might have been made from preestablished definitions were subordinated and adapted to the fundamental principles that determine, or ought to determine, liability for conduct in a system of law wherein liability is adjusted to the ends which law should serve. Hynes v. The New York Central Railroad Co., was decided in May, 1921. Dean Pound's Introduction to the Philosophy of Law had not yet been published. It appeared in 1922. In these lectures, he advances a theory of liability which it may be interesting to compare with the theory of liability reflected in our decision. 'The law,' he says, 'enforces the reasonable expectations arising out of conduct, relations and situations.' I shall leave it to others to say whether the cause of the boy diving from the springboard would be helped or hindered by resort to such a test. This much I cannot doubt. Some theory of liability, some philosophy of the end to be served by tightening or enlarging the circle of rights and remedies, is at the root of any decision in novel situations when analogies are equivocal and precedents are silent. As it stands today, the judge is often left to improvise such a theory, such a philosophy, when confronted overnight by the exigencies of the case before him. Often he fumbles about, feeling in a vague way that some such problem is involved, but missing the universal element which would have quickened his decision with the inspiration of a principle. If he lacks an adequate philosophy, he either goes astray altogether, or at least does not rise above the empiricism that pronounces judgment upon particulars. We must learn that all methods are to be viewed not as idols but as tools. We must test one of them by the others, supplementing and reenforcing where there is weakness, so that what is strong and best in each will be at our service in the hour of need. Thus viewing them we shall often find that they are not antagonists but allies.

What *was* the "theory of liability" of the majority of the Court of Appeals in Hynes?

**2.**   Suppose that, following the Hynes decision, one of Harvey's friends swam across the Harlem River to the Bronx side and clambered up on the New York Central Rail Road's bulkhead. Poised for his dive from the edge of the bulkhead, the young man was struck by yet another falling wire, and was swept to his death. Had he already been in the water, he would have suffered the same fate. How should the court rule on the boy's parents' wrongful death claim against the NYCRR?

**3.**   Suppose that, following the Hynes decision, another of Harvey's friends swam across the Harlem River to the Bronx side, clambered onto the NYCRR's land, and was making his way to the diving board along a path on the NYCRR's land, when yet another wire broke loose, sweeping the boy out past the path and the bulkhead, into the river, where he drowned. Had he already been in the water, he would have suffered the same fate. How should the court rule on the boy's parents' wrongful death claim against the NYCRR?

**4.**   Suppose that, following the Hynes decision, yet another of Harvey's friends swam across the Harlem River to the Bronx side, clambered onto the NYCRR's land, where he decided to have a picnic, before returning to enjoy the waters. As he was spreading out his lunch, still another wire snapped, sweeping the boy, and his lunch, out past the path and the bulkhead, into the river, where he drowned. Had he already been in the water, he would have suffered the same fate. How should the court rule on the boy's parents' wrongful death claim against the NYCRR?

# Judgment of February 13, 1930
**(Jand'heur v. Aux Galeries Belfortaises)**

## France: Court of Cassation (all chambers assembled), 1930

## Cass ch. Réuns., Feb. 13, 1930, D.P. I, 57, concl. Marc'hadour

**THE COURT**:–Having seen article 1384 [of the Civil Code] clause 1 [which states: "One is liable not only for the harm that one causes by one's own fault, but also for that which is caused by the acts of persons for whom one is responsible, or by the things one has under one's care."]

– Whereas the presumption of liability established by this article against the person who has under his care the inanimate thing which has caused harm to another may not be rebutted except by proof of an unforeseeable and unavoidable event ("*cas fortuit*") or of an Act of God ("*force majeure*"), or of a foreign cause not imputable to him; that it does not suffice to prove that such person has committed no wrongful act ("*faute*"), or that the cause of the harmful act remains unknown;

– Whereas, on April 22, 1925, a truck belonging to the *Société Aux Galeries Belfortaises* overturned and wounded the minor child Lise Jand'heur; that the decision appealed from refused to apply the above text on the ground that the accident caused by a moving car, under the impulse and direction of a man, did not constitute, when no proof existed that it was due to an inherent defect in the car, the act of a thing which one has under one's care in the terms of art. 1384 clause 1, and that, as a result, the victim was obliged, in order to recover for her harm, to establish with regard to the driver a wrongful act imputable to him;

– But whereas the law, by application of the presumption which it edicts, does not distinguish according to whether the thing was or was not activated by man's hand; that it is not necessary that there have been an inherent defect in the nature of the thing which was susceptible to cause harm, art. 1384 attaching liability to having the care of the thing, not to the thing itself;

– Therefore it follows that, in ruling as it did, the decision appealed from has reversed the legal text's order of proof and violated the text of the above-referenced law.

– By these reasons, the decision below is broken and the decision is remanded to the Court of Appeals of Dijon.

**Notes and Questions**

(English translation by Jane C. Ginsburg; the translation endeavors to capture the original's stilted style.)

**1.**   This is a decision of France's highest private law court, the Court of Cassation–literally "breaking": when the court reverses the intermediate appellate court's decision, it "breaks" it and remands to another appellate court to apply the law as articulated by the high court.

**2.**   How does the court present the facts and the applicable law? In what order?

**3.**   What can you infer about the state of the law before this case? How does the court address the prior caselaw? Who wrote the decision?

**4.**   *Jand'heur* was in fact a landmark decision, though its presentation typically discloses neither its departures from prior judicial exposition, nor the heated doctrinal debate surrounding the bases of tort liability. France's High Court was at this time expansively reading art. 1384 of the Civil code, beginning a shift in tort law from fault-based liability toward risk allocation based on dominion and control over the harm-causing object. Thus, the court's formulation of the basis for liability under art. 1384 foregoes mention of "fault." Commentators disputed whether liability henceforth would be founded simply on ownership of the harm-causing object, or instead on a legal obligation to maintain and control it. *Compare* L. Josserand, La responsabilité du fait des automobiles devant les chambres réunies de la Cour de cassation, 1930 D.H. Chr. 25, 28 *with* Cass. ch. Réuns., Feb. 13, 1930, D.P. I, 57, note Ripert. Under one interpretation, the court would have adopted a strict liability risk allocation approach, while under the other, fault would in effect have been presumed: if the object caused harm, its owner must have failed to fulfill its legal obligation to "care" for the object. Under neither approach, however, would the victim have had to prove acts by the defendant demonstrating breach of its duty of care.

**5.** How might the French court have decided a case presenting the *Hynes* facts? How might the *Hynes* majority have analyzed *Jand'heur*?

## 2. THE EFFECT OF PRECEDENT ON A SUBSEQUENT CASE

In this and other courses during your first year in law school, you will begin to develop a "feel" for certain of the basic skills and arts of the case lawyer: for example, the distinguishing of cases on their facts, the narrowing of an asserted precedent in terms of its procedural issue, the following of the distinguishable case. But the role of precedents in the common law judicial process cannot be grasped unless you know what a judge or a lawyer means when he speaks of the "holding" or *ratio decidendi* of a case and what he means when he says that a statement in a judicial opinion is "dictum" or "obiter dictum." The distinction between "holding" and "dictum" runs through Anglo–American legal literature and is a recurring theme in case method law classes.

If you have ever heard an oral argument in an appellate court, you undoubtedly have heard counsel for one side or the other quote a statement from some past judicial opinion in support of his legal argument in the case then before the court. And, it is almost equally certain, you have heard some member of the court interrupt the quoting counsel and ask: "Yes, but what were the *facts* of that case?" Why do judges—and law professors, for that matter—insist on asking that question? If the statement being quoted was, in truth, made in the earlier judicial opinion, what difference does it make what the *facts* of that case were? After you have read and thought through the cases and other materials in this Section, you should be able to see that the question, "What were the facts of that [earlier] case?" is, essentially, another way of asking, "Was the statement in the past judicial opinion 'holding' or 'dictum' in that case?"

By then, too, you will have realized that the question is deceptively simple. Central as it is to our system of precedent, the concept of holding and dictum is elusive.

Let us start our analysis by accepting at face value the importance of the distinction. The holding of a case, under our system, must be followed in similar cases, until overruled. Dicta are pronouncements which may be persuasive, but are not binding. You will soon realize that this is a somewhat oversimplified view of case law but let us start there.

How does one tell the difference? The conventional definition is that dictum is any statement in a judicial opinion not necessary to the decision of the case actually before the court. The following is a typical statement of the matter:

> if it [the point of law commented on in the opinion] might have been
> decided either way without affecting any right brought into question,

then, according to the principles of the common law, an opinion on such a question is not a decision. To make it so, there must have been an application of the judicial mind to the precise question necessary to be determined, to fix the rights of the parties, and to decide to whom the property in contestation belongs. And, therefore, this court, and other courts organized under the common law, has never held itself bound by any part of an opinion, in any case, which was not needful to the ascertainment of the right or title in question between the parties.

Curtis, J. in Carroll v. Carroll's Lessee, 57 U.S. (16 How.) 275, 286–287, 14 L.Ed. 936 (1853). A good example of dictum in this sense is the statement in Grand Lodge v. Farnham, 70 Cal. 158, 11 P. 592 (1886): "The rule is otherwise where subscribers agree together to make up a specified sum. * * * In such case, as between the subscribers, there is mutual liability, and the co-subscribers may maintain an action against one who refuses to pay." Since the Farnham case did not involve a suit by co-subscribers, the statement is clearly dictum.

You may well ask why any distinction should be made between holding and dictum. We have designated certain officials judges and made them, subject to legislative overruling, the final law makers in certain spheres. Why should we not give binding effect to all their official pronouncements? Is the following a sufficient answer?

No *dictum* is authority of the highest sort. To give it such weight would be to give judges power to decide in advance a case not before them for adjudication, a merely hypothetical case, and to bind by their opinion the court before which that hypothetical case may eventually become a practical problem. This would be a legislative power, and, still worse, a power exercised in the absence of full argument of the hypothetical case.

Wambaugh, The Study of Cases 19 (2d ed.1894).

The last clause deserves reemphasis. It is a cardinal tenet of the Anglo–American judicial system that the best result will be produced through "the fire of controversy." At least in theory, given adequate legal representation on both sides, the court will have presented to it the best possible arguments for alternative decisions on a disputed point; the defects of either position will be shown up and the best course to pursue be made apparent. The critical word is "disputed" and therein lies the reason for the distinction between holding and dictum: Dicta are pronouncements on points which need not be considered in order to reach a decision and are, therefore, in most cases, pronouncements on points on which the court has not had the benefit of argument.

## Humphrey's Executor v. United States

Supreme Court of the United States, 1935.
295 U.S. 602, 55 S.Ct. 869, 79 L.Ed. 1611.

[Plaintiff brought suit in the Court of Claims to recover a sum of money alleged to be due to the deceased, William E. Humphrey, for salary as a

Federal Trade Commissioner from October 8, 1933, when President Roosevelt undertook to remove him from office, to the time of his death, on February 14, 1934. At the time of the attempted removal, Humphrey had almost five years left to serve of the seven year term to which he had been appointed by President Hoover in 1931. The Court of Claims certified the following two questions to the Supreme Court:

"1.  Do the provisions of Section 1 of the Federal Trade Commission Act, stating that 'any commissioner may be removed by the President for inefficiency, neglect of duty, or malfeasance in office' restrict or limit the power of the President to remove a commissioner except upon one or more of the causes named?

"If the foregoing question is answered in the affirmative, then—

"2.  If the power of the President to remove a commissioner is restricted or limited as shown by the foregoing interrogatory and the answer made thereto, is such a restriction or limitation valid under the Constitution of the United States?"]

■ MR. JUSTICE SUTHERLAND delivered the opinion of the Court.

> \* \* \*

\* \* \* the language of the act, the legislative reports, and the general purposes of the legislation as reflected by the debates, all combine to demonstrate the Congressional intent to create a body of experts who shall gain experience by length of service—a body which shall be independent of executive authority, except in its selection, and free to exercise its judgment without the leave or hindrance of any other official or any department of the government. To the accomplishment of these purposes, it is clear that Congress was of opinion that length and certainty of tenure would vitally contribute. And to hold that, nevertheless, the members of the commission continue in office only at the mere will of the President, might be to thwart, in large measure, the very ends which Congress sought to realize by definitely fixing the term of office.

We conclude that the intent of the act is to limit the executive power of removal to the causes enumerated, the existence of none of which is claimed here; and we pass to the second question.

Second. To support its contention that the removal provision of section 1, as we have just construed it, is an unconstitutional interference with the executive power of the President, the government's chief reliance is Myers v. United States, 272 U.S. 52, 47 S.Ct. 21, 71 L.Ed. 160. That case has been so recently decided, and the prevailing and dissenting opinions so fully review the general subject of the power of executive removal, that further discussion would add little of value to the wealth of material there collected. These opinions examine at length the historical, legislative, and judicial data bearing upon the question, beginning with what is called "the decision of 1789" in the first Congress and coming down almost to the day when the opinions were delivered. They occupy 243 pages of the volume in which they are printed. Nevertheless, the narrow point actually decided was only that the President had power to remove a postmaster of the first class, without the advice and consent of the Senate as required by act of Congress. In the course of the opinion of the court, expressions occur which tend to sustain the government's contention, but these are beyond the point involved and, therefore, do not come within the rule of stare decisis. Insofar as they are out of harmony with the views here set forth, these expressions are disapproved. A like situation was presented in the case of Cohens v. Virginia, 6 Wheat. 264, 399, 5 L.Ed. 257, in respect of certain general expressions in the opinion in Marbury v. Madison, 1 Cranch, 137, 2 L.Ed. 60. Chief Justice Marshall, who delivered the opinion in the Marbury Case, speaking again for the court in the Cohens Case, said: "It is a maxim, not to be disregarded, that general expressions, in every opinion, are to be taken in connection with the case in which those expressions are used. If they go beyond the case, they may be respected, but ought not to control the judgment in a subsequent suit, when the very point is presented for decision. The reason of this maxim is obvious. The question actually before the court is investigated with care, and considered in its full extent. Other principles which may serve to illustrate it, are considered in their relation to the case decided, but their possible bearing on all other cases is seldom completely investigated."

And he added that these general expressions in the case of Marbury v. Madison were to be understood with the limitations put upon them by the opinion in the Cohens Case. See, also, Carroll v. Lessee of Carroll et al., 16 How. 275, 286–287, 14 L.Ed. 936; O'Donoghue v. United States, 289 U.S. 516, 550, 53 S.Ct. 740, 77 L.Ed. 1356.

The office of a postmaster is so essentially unlike the office now involved that the decision in the Myers Case cannot be accepted as controlling our decision here. A postmaster is an executive officer restricted to the performance of executive functions. He is charged with no duty at all related to either the legislative or judicial power. The actual decision in the Myers Case finds support in the theory that such an officer is merely one of the units in the executive department and, hence, inherently subject to the exclusive and illimitable power of removal by the Chief Executive, whose subordinate and aid he is. Putting aside dicta, which may be followed if sufficiently persuasive but which are not controlling, the necessary reach of the decision goes far enough to include all purely executive officers. It goes no farther; much less does it include an officer who occupies no place in the executive department and who exercises no part of the executive power vested by the Constitution in the President.

　　　* * *

The result of what we now have said is this: Whether the power of the President to remove an officer shall prevail over the authority of Congress to condition the power by fixing a definite term and precluding a removal except for cause will depend upon the character of the office; the Myers decision affirming the power of the President alone to make the removal, is confined to purely executive officers; and as to officers of the kind here under consideration, we hold that no removal can be made during the prescribed term for which the officer is appointed, except for one or more of the causes named in the applicable statute.

To the extent, that between the decision in the Myers Case, which sustains the unrestrictable power of the President to remove purely executive officers, and our present decision that such power does not extend to an office such as that here involved, there shall remain a field of doubt, we leave such cases as may fall within it for future consideration and determination as they may arise.

In accordance with the foregoing, the questions submitted are answered:

Question No. 1, Yes.

Question No. 2, Yes.

Mr. Justice McReynolds agrees that both questions should be answered in the affirmative. A separate opinion in Myers v. United States, 272 U.S. 52, at page 178, 47 S.Ct. 21, at page 46, 71 L.Ed. 160, states his views concerning the power of the President to remove appointees.

## Notes and Questions

**1.** The opinion in the *Myers* case occupies about 70 pages of Volume 272 of the United States Reports. To what language in that case does the court in *Humphrey's Executor* point as embodying the "holding"?

Would it have changed the situation if the Court in *Myers* had said, on one of those 70 pages: "We hold that the President may at his discretion, remove from office any person appointed by him or a predecessor."?

The point of these questions is to emphasize that when we speak of the holding of a case we refer not to anything which was *said,* but to what was decided. It is true that we may conclude that a particular formulation of words in a decision is an accurate statement of the holding of the case but, as we shall see, the fact that the court states its "holding" in a particular way does not control in subsequent cases.

**2.** Is the following statement on page 111, supra, holding or dictum? "In so far as they are out of harmony with the views here set forth, these expressions are disapproved."

**3.** Suppose that after the decision in the *Myers* case, but before the *Humphrey's Executor* case, you had been writing a law review article and had stated that in *Myers* the Supreme Court held that Congress may not constitutionally limit the President's power to remove a presidential appointee from office. Would you have been wrong?

Suppose that during that same period you were working in the Justice Department and the President had asked you whether he could fire Humphrey. If you had told him that *Myers* held he could, would you have been wrong?

Suppose, instead, you had been Humphrey's lawyer, and he asked you if he should take another job. If you had said, "Yes, under *Myers* you don't have a claim for your salary," would you have been wrong?

# Morrison v. Olson

Supreme Court of the United States, 1988.
487 U.S. 654, 108 S.Ct. 2597, 101 L.Ed.2d 569.

[The Ethics in Government Act of 1978 allowed the Attorney General to ask a special federal court to appoint an independent counsel to investigate allegations against high level members of the Executive Branch (e.g. an official in the Attorney General's office). Under the statute, only the Attorney General had the power to remove the independent counsel; this power was further limited to discharge on the basis of "good cause, physical disability, mental incapacity, or any other condition that substantially impairs the performance of [her] duties."

In Morrison, appellee Olson, an official of the Attorney General's Office, allegedly gave false testimony during an Environmental Protection Agency investigation. As a result of the Attorney General's request, the special court appointed a special prosecutor, appellant Morrison. A dispute subsequently arose between the Attorney General and the special prosecutor. Olson moved in Federal District Court to declare the independent counsel provision unconstitutional, on the ground that the provision limited the removal power of the Executive Branch. The district court upheld the provision. The Court of Appeals reversed. The Supreme Court reversed the Court of Appeals' disposition.]

Chief Justice Rehnquist delivered the opinion of the Court

* * *

## V

We now turn to consider whether the Act is invalid under the constitutional principle of separation of powers. Two related issues must be addressed: The first is whether the provision of the Act restricting the Attorney General's power to remove the independent counsel to only those instances in which he can show "good cause," taken by itself, impermissibly interferes with the President's exercise of his constitutionally appointed functions . . .

## A

Two Terms ago we had occasion to consider whether it was consistent with the separation of powers for Congress to pass a statute that authorized a Government official who is removable only by Congress to participate in what we found to be "executive powers." Bowsher v. Synar, 478 U.S. 714, 730 (1986). We held in Bowsher that "Congress cannot reserve for itself the power of removal of an officer charged with the execution of the laws except by impeachment." Id., at 726. A primary antecedent for this ruling was our 1926 decision in Myers v. United States, 272 U.S. 52.

Myers had considered the propriety of a federal statute by which certain postmasters of the United States could be removed by the President only "by and with the advice and consent of the Senate." There too, Congress' attempt to involve itself in the removal of an executive official was found to be sufficient grounds to render the statute invalid. As we observed in Bowsher, the essence of the decision in Myers was the judgment that the Constitution prevents Congress from "draw[ing] to itself . . . the power to remove or the right to participate in the exercise of that power. To do this would be to go beyond the words and implications of the [Appointments Clause] and to infringe the constitutional principle of the separation of governmental powers." Myers, supra, at 161.

Unlike both Bowsher and Myers, this case does not involve an attempt by Congress itself to gain a role in the removal of executive officials other than its established powers of impeachment and conviction. The Act instead puts the removal power squarely in the hands of the Executive Branch; an independent counsel may be removed from office, "only by the personal action of the Attorney General, and only for good cause." § 596(a)(1). There is no requirement of congressional approval of the Attorney General's removal decision, though the decision is subject to judicial review. § 596(a)(3). In our view, the removal provisions of the Act make this case more analogous to Humphrey's Executor v. United States, 295 U.S. 602 (1935), than to Myers or Bowsher.

In Humphrey's Executor, the issue was whether a statute restricting the President's power to remove the Commissioners of the Federal Trade Commission (FTC) only for "inefficiency, neglect of duty, or malfeasance in office" was consistent with the Constitution. 295 U.S., at 619. We stated that whether Congress can "condition the [President's power of removal] by fixing a definite term and precluding a removal except for cause, will depend upon the character of the office." Id., at 631. Contrary to the implication of some dicta in Myers, the President's power to remove Government officials simply was not "all-inclusive in respect of civil officers with the exception of the judiciary provided for by the Constitution." 295 U.S., at 629. At least in regard to "quasi-legislative" and "quasi-judicial" agencies such as the FTC, "[t]he authority of Congress, in creating [such] agencies, to require them to act in discharge of their duties independently of executive control . . . includes, as an appropriate incident, power to fix the period during which they shall continue in office, and to forbid their removal except for cause in the meantime." Ibid. In Humphrey's Executor, we found it "plain" that the Constitution did not give the President "illimitable power of removal" over the officers of independent agencies. Ibid. Were the President to have the power to remove FTC Commissioners at will, the "coercive influence" of the removal power would "threate[n] the independence of [the] commission." Id., at 630.

\* \* \*

Appellees contend that Humphrey's Executor [is] distinguishable from this case because they did not involve officials who performed a "core executive function." They argue that our decision in Humphrey's Executor rests on a distinction between "purely executive" officials and officials who exercise "quasi-legislative" and "quasi-judicial" powers. In their view, when a "purely executive" official is involved, the governing precedent is Myers, not Humphrey's Executor. See Humphrey's Executor, supra, at 628. And, under Myers, the President must have absolute discretion to discharge "purely" executive officials at will. See Myers, 272 U.S., at 132–134.

We undoubtedly did rely on the terms "quasi-legislative" and "quasi-judicial" to distinguish the officials involved in Humphrey's Executor from those in Myers, but our present considered view is that the determination of whether the Constitution allows Congress to impose a "good cause"-type restriction on the President's power to remove an official cannot be made to turn on whether or not that official is classified as "purely executive." The analysis contained in our removal cases is designed not to define rigid categories of those officials who may or may not be removed at will by the President, but to ensure that Congress does not interfere with the President's exercise of the "executive power" and his constitutionally appointed duty to "take care that the laws be faithfully executed" under Article II. Myers was undoubtedly correct in its holding, and in its broader suggestion that there are some "purely executive" officials who must be removable by the President at will if he is to be able to accomplish his constitutional role. See 272 U.S., at 132–134. But as the Court noted in Wiener v. United States, 357 U.S. 349 (1958):

> "The assumption was short-lived that the Myers case recognized the President's inherent constitutional power to remove officials no matter what the relation of the executive to the discharge of their duties and no matter what restrictions Congress may have imposed regarding the nature of their tenure." 357 U.S., at 352.

At the other end of the spectrum from Myers, the characterization of the agencies in Humphrey's Executor as "quasi-legislative" or "quasi-judicial" in large part reflected our judgment that it was not essential to the President's proper execution of his Article II powers that these agencies be headed up by individuals who were removable at will. We do not mean to suggest that an analysis of the functions served by the officials at issue is irrelevant. But the real question is whether the removal restrictions are of such a nature that they impede the President's ability to perform his constitutional duty, and the functions of the officials in question must be analyzed in that light.

Considering for the moment the "good cause" removal provision in isolation from the other parts of the Act at issue in this case, we cannot say that the imposition of a "good cause" standard for removal by itself unduly trammels on executive authority. There is no real dispute that the functions performed by the independent counsel are "executive" in the sense that they are law enforcement functions that typically have been undertaken by officials within the Executive Branch. As we noted above, however, the independent counsel is an inferior officer under the Appointments Clause, with limited jurisdiction and tenure and lacking policymaking or significant administrative authority. Although the counsel exercises no small amount of discretion and judgment in deciding how to carry out his or her duties under the Act, we simply do not see how the President's need to control the exercise of that discretion is so central to the functioning of the Executive Branch as to require as a matter of constitutional law that the counsel be terminable at will by the President.

Nor do we think that the "good cause" removal provision at issue here impermissibly burdens the President's power to control or supervise the independent counsel, as an executive official, in the execution of his or her duties under the Act. This is not a case in which the power to remove an executive official has been completely stripped from the President, thus providing no means for the President to ensure the "faithful execution" of the laws. Rather, because the independent counsel may be terminated for "good cause," the Executive, through the Attorney General, retains ample authority to assure that the counsel is competently performing his or her statutory responsibilities in a manner that comports with the provisions of the Act. Although we need not decide in the case exactly what is encompassed within the term "good cause" under the Act, the legislative history of the removal provision also makes clear that the Attorney General may remove an independent counsel for "misconduct." See H.R.Conf.Rep. No. 100–452, p. 37 (1987). Here, as with the provision of the Act conferring the appointment authority of the independent counsel on the special court, the congressional determination to limit the removal power of the Attorney General was essential, in the view of Congress, to establish the necessary independence of the office. We do not think that this limitation as it presently stands sufficiently deprives the President of control over the independent counsel to interfere impermissibly with his constitutional obligation to ensure the faithful execution of the laws.

* * *

### Questions

**1.** In light of the following statement, do the categories of "purely executive," "quasi-legislative," and "quasi-judicial" officials still have relevance?

> We do not mean to suggest that an analysis of the functions served by the officials at issue is irrelevant. But the real question is whether the removal restrictions are of such a nature that they impede the President's ability to perform his ... duty.

487 U.S. at 691. What, in light of *Morrison* did *Humphrey's Executor* hold? What did *Myers* hold?

**2.** Suppose Congress passed a law restricting to good cause the ability of the President to remove the Secretary of State or the Secretary of Defense. Would this be held valid under *Morrison*? Under *Humphrey's Executor*? Under *Myers*?

**3.** After *Morrison*, suppose that Congress imposed a good cause limitation on the removal of a postmaster of the first class (or modern equivalent); would this violate the constitutional principle of separation of powers?

# Cullings v. Goetz

Court of Appeals of New York, 1931.
256 N.Y. 287, 176 N.E. 397.

Action by Joseph Cullings against Edward Goetz and others. From a judgment (231 App.Div. 266, 247 N.Y.S. 109), reversing a judgment of the Trial Term in favor of the plaintiff, and dismissing the complaint, the plaintiff appeals.

■ Cardozo, C.J. Plaintiff brought his automobile to a garage, intending to drive in. There were two sliding doors at the entrance, one open, the other closed. He tried to push the closed one open, but it did not move upon its track. When he shook it with some force, it fell upon his back, causing injuries for which he sues. His action is against Goetz, lessee of the garage, and the Nickleys, the owners, who were also the lessors. The lease was an oral one, and ran from month to month. The trial judge left the question to the jury whether as one of its provisions the owners had agreed to make the necessary repairs. In the event of that agreement and of failure to repair after notice of the need, owners as well as lessee were to be held for any negligence in the unsafe condition of the doors. The jury found a verdict against all the parties sued. On the appeal by the owners, the Appellate Division reversed, and dismissed the complaint upon the ground that the failure of the owners to keep the promise to repair was unavailing to charge them with liability in tort.

The evidence of the supposed promise is at best confused and uncertain, if there be evidence at all. For the purpose of this appeal we assume without deciding that it permits conflicting inferences. We assume also that there was freedom from contributory negligence, though another entrance was available, and there is evidence of notice that the one chosen was out of use. Giving the plaintiff's case the aid of these assumptions, we concur with the Appellate Division in its ruling that liability in tort must be confined to the lessee, whose possession and dominion were exclusive and complete.

The subject has divided juridical opinion. Generally, however, in this country as in England, a covenant to repair does not impose upon the lessor a liability in tort at the suit of the lessee or of others lawfully on the land in the right of the lessee. See, e.g., Tuttle v. Gilbert Mfg. Co., 145 Mass. 169, 13 N.E. 465; Miles v. Janvrin, 196 Mass. 431, 82 N.E. 708, 13 L.R.A. (N.S.) 378, 124 Am.St.Rep. 575; Fiorntino v. Mason, 233 Mass. 451, 454, 124 N.E. 283; Carroll v. Intercolonial Club of Boston, 243 Mass. 380, 383, 137 N.E. 656; Dustin v. Curtis, 74 N.H. 266, 67 A. 220, 11 L.R.A. (N.S.) 504, 13 Ann.Cas. 169; Davis v. Smith, 26 R.I. 129, 58 A. 630, 66 L.R.A. 478, 106 Am.St.Rep. 691, 3 Ann.Cas. 832; Brady v, Klein, 133 Mich. 422, 95 N.W. 557, 62 L.R.A. 909, 103 Am.St.Rep. 455, 2 Ann.Cas. 464; Cavalier v. Pope, [1905] 2 K.B. 757, 762, 764; Cavalier v. Pope, [1906] A.C. 428, 433; Cameron v. Young, [1908] A.C. 176; and see, also, 8 A.L.R. 766, collating the decisions. There are decisions to the contrary (Flood v. Pabst Brewing Co., 158 Wis. 626, 149 N.W. 489, L.R.A. 1916F, 1101; Merchants' Cotton Press & Storage Co. v. Miller, 135 Tenn. 187, 186 S.W. 87, L.R.A.1916F, 1137; Barron v. Liedloff, 95 Minn. 474, 104 N.W. 289), but they speak the voice of a minority. Liability in tort is an incident to occupation or control. American Law Inst., Restatement of the Law of Torts, § 227. By preponderant opinion, occupation and control are not reserved through an agreement that the landlord will repair. Cavalier v. Pope, [1906] A.C. 428, at page 433; Pollock, Torts (13th Ed.) 532; Salmond, Torts (7th Ed.) 477. The tenant and no one else may keep visitors away till the danger is abated, or adapt the warning to the need. The landlord has at most a privilege to enter for the doing of the work, and at times not even that if the occupant protests. "The power of control necessary to raise the duty * * * implies something more than the right or liability to repair the premises. It implies the power and the right to admit people to the premises and to exclude people from them." Cavalier v. Pope, supra. In saying this we assume the possibility of so phrasing and enlarging the rights of the lessor that occupation and control will be shared with the lessee. There are decisions in Massachusetts that draw a distinction between a covenant merely to repair and one to maintain in safe condition with supervision adequate to the end to be archieved. Miles v. Janvrin, supra; Fiorntino v. Mason, supra; Carroll v. Intercolonial Club, supra; see, also, Robinson v. Heil, 128 Md. 645, 98 A. 195; Collison v. Curtner, 141 Ark. 122, 216 S.W. 1059, 8 A.L.R. 760. In the case now at hand, the promise, if there was any, was to act at the request of the lessee. What resulted was not a reservation by an owner of one of the privileges of ownership. It was the assumption of a burden for the benefit of the occupant with consequences the same as if there had been a promise to repair by a plumber or a carpenter. Cf. Zurich General Accident & Liability Ins. Co. v. Watson Elevator Co., 253 N.Y. 404, 409, 171 N.E. 688; Mollino v. Ogden & Clarkson Corporation, 243 N.Y. 450, 154 N.E. 307, 49 A.L.R. 518.

The rule in this state is settled in accord with the prevailing doctrine. Dicta, supposed to be inconsistent, are summoned to the support of a contrary position. They will be considered later on. Whatever their significance, they cannot overcome decisions directly to the point. As often as the question has been squarely up, the answer has been consistent that there is no liability in tort. Some of the decisions rejecting liability are judgments of this court. Kushes v. Ginsberg, 188 N.Y. 630, 81 N.E. 1168, affirming 99 App.Div. 417, 91 N.Y.S. 216; Sterger v. Van Sicklen, 132 N.Y. 499, 30 N.E. 987, 16 L.R.A. 640, 28 Am.St.Rep. 594; cf. Reynolds v. Van Beuren, 155 N.Y. 120, 125, 49 N.E. 763, 42 L.R.A. 129; Wolf v. American Tract Soc., 164 N.Y. 30, 35, 58 N.E. 31, 51 L.R.A. 241; Golob v. Pasinsky, 178 N.Y. 458, 461, 70 N.E. 973. Others, too many to be fully numbered, are in courts of intermediate appeal. Schick v. Fleischhauer, 26 App.Div. 210, 49 N.Y.S. 962; Frank v. Mandel, 76 App.Div. 413, 417, 78 N.Y.S. 855; Stelz v. Van Dusen, 93 App.Div. 358, 87 N.Y.S. 716; Boden v. Scholtz, 101 App.Div. 1, 2, 91 N.Y.S. 437; Pernick v. Central Union Gas Co., 183 App.Div. 543, 170 N.Y.S. 245. The doctrine, wise or unwise in its origin, has worked itself by common acquiescence into the tissues of our law. It is too deeply imbedded to be superseded or ignored. Hardly a day goes by in our great centers of population but it is applied by judges and juries in cases great and small. Countless tenants, suing for personal injuries and proving nothing more than the breach of an agreement, have been dismissed without a remedy in adherence to the authority of Schick v. Fleischhauer and Kushes v. Ginsberg. Countless visitors of tenants and members of a tenant's family have encountered a like fate. If there is no remedy for the tenant, there is none for visitors or relatives present in the tenant's right. Miles v. Janvrin, supra, 196 Mass. at page 440, 82 N.E. 708, 13 L.R.A. (N.S.) 378, 124 Am.St.Rep. 575; Elefante v. Pizitz, 182 App.Div. 819, 821, 169 N.Y.S. 910. Liability has been enlarged by statute where an apartment in an tenement house in a city of the first class is the subject of the lease. Altz v. Leiberson, 233 N.Y. 16, 134 N.E. 703. The duty in such instances is independent of the contract. It is one imposed by law, with liability in tort where the duty is ignored. Here the plaintiff was injured in the use of a garage. His remedy is against the tenant at whose invitation he was there.

We have spoken of dicta that are cited to the contrary. They do not touch the liability of the landlord for conditions within the premises affecting only the lessee or those who enter upon the premises in the right of the lessee. They have to do with nuisances threatening danger to the public beyond the land demised. Cf. Sterger v. Van Sicklen, supra, 132 N.Y. at page 501, 30 N.E. 987, 16 L.R.A. 640, 28 Am.St.Rep. 594; Ahern v. Steele, 115 N.Y. 203, 209, 22 N.E. 193, 5 L.R.A. 449, 12 Am.St.Rep. 778; City of Brooklyn v. Brooklyn City R. Co., 47 N.Y. 475, 483, 7 Am.Rep. 469; Clancy v. Byrne, 56 N.Y. 129, 15 Am.Rep. 391; Jaffe v. Harteau, 56 N.Y. 398, 15 Am.Rep. 438; Brady v. Klein, supra; 18 Halsbury, Laws of England, § 989; 21 Id. §§ 651, 955. Even when thus confined, they are dicta, and nothing more, at least in this state, though reiteration may have given them an authority not otherwise belonging to them. Be that as it may, the fact remains that the decision in every instance exonerated the lessor. One case, it is true, there is (Kilmer v. White, 254 N.Y. 64, 69, 171 N.E. 908), which had to do with conditions within the premises, and not with those outside, but it cites Jaffe v. Harteau, supra, and does not suggest even remotely a purpose to establish a new rule. There is merely a cautious reservation of the doctrine to be applied in situations different from any before us at the time.

\* \* \*

Other grounds of liability suggested in the plaintiff's argument have been considered and are found to be untenable.

We state for greater caution, though the caution should be needless, that nothing said in this opinion has relation to a case where a part only of the building is in the possession of the lessee, and the dangerous condition is in the ways or other parts retained by the lessor. Dollard v. Roberts, 130 N.Y. 269, 29 N.E. 104, 14 L.R.A. 238; Kilmer v. White, supra; American Law Inst., Restatement of the Law of Torts, § 230.

The judgment should be affirmed with costs.

■ POUND, CRANE, LEHMAN, KELLOGG, O'BRIEN, and HUBBS, JJ., concur.

Judgment affirmed.

## Notes and Questions

**1.** One can infer from the opinion of the court in Cullings v. Goetz that counsel for the plaintiff-appellant Cullings had cited past decisions of the Court of Appeals in which the opinions had contained statements generally supporting the plaintiff-appellant's position in the principal case. What is the theory on which Judge Cardozo, in his opinion for the court in the principal case, characterizes these past judicial utterances as dicta?

**2.** Note the care with which Judge Cardozo, in the final paragraph of his opinion, attempts to make it certain that Cullings v. Goetz will not, in its turn, be cited out of context by counsel for the defendant in some future suit against a lessor in part possession of a building.

## Stare Decisis in Operation: The Scope of a Precedent

It should be apparent by now that to ask the question, "What is the holding of a case?" is really to ask, "What fact situations can the rule of law of that case be said to govern?" i.e., "As to what future cases does the decision of the case constitute binding authority?" Since the decision as to whether or not a precedent governs a particular case rests, in the last analysis, with the court deciding the later case, the answer to the question "What is the holding?" is a prediction that as to certain future fact situations the court will consider the decision governing. Whether the prediction is accurate will not be known until the question is finally adjudicated.

Perhaps the best definition of a holding for you as an advocate is that the holding of a case is what you can persuade the court in a later case the court in the first case held. Such a definition is misleading, however, and, especially to the neophyte, is too atomistic to be of much value. It leads to the too quick conclusion that stare decisis is a myth, that judges are not really governed by precedent and that there is no minimum or maximum to what can be called the holding of a case. This is not true. The very fact that judges believe in stare decisis and are trying to make it work gives the doctrine validity and gives us a standard by means of which we can usually predict that as to certain fact situations a decision must be considered a holding and as to others it cannot be so considered.

The principle of stare decisis, simply stated, is that the decision in a case should govern the decision in all like cases—but only in like cases. The best guide in the determination of what are "like cases" is a constant awareness of the underlying assumption of the Anglo–American system of case-by-case progress: that the court in every case will have before it all the facts necessary to a decision and that it will make its decision cognizant of all factors that should be considered. Here we have a standard by which to judge what are "like cases"—they are those whose fact situations present to the court the same factors to be considered in reaching a decision.

There are in any case a number of facts which obviously play no part in the determination, i.e., facts whose absence will not change the factors that the court must consider in reaching its decision. In formulating our

statement of the rule of law established by that case, we can safely exclude these obviously nonsignificant (immaterial) facts from our consideration. So stated, the rule of law derived from that case will cover only fact situations so similar to that case that no court can distinguish it without resorting to painfully obvious sophistry, a course courts are ususaly reluctant to pursue. Here we have the minimum of what can be called the holding.

As we continue to abstract from the facts of our case we eventually reach a level of generalization that clearly includes fact situations materially different from that of the case, i.e., fact situations containing facts that present different considerations for the court to take account of in reaching its decision. When we reach this level of generalization we have gone beyond the maximum of what can be called the holding. An example of such a generalization is that of Baker v. Libbie that all men are entitled to the fruits of their labors.

These limits, however, guide us only in the easy cases. Between these limits lies a large area in which no one can be sure that his statement of the holding is not too general or too specific—that his view of what the material facts were is the right one—until the court has decided his case. This is the area in which most litigated cases fall. The best that can be done in this area is to state a reasonable rule of law abstracted from the precedent case. Your job as a counselor will be to make a reasonable prediction as to the extent to which a precedent will control. Your initial job as an advocate will be to state the holding of the precedent case in sufficiently general terms so that it covers the facts of your case. Your opponent will be stating the holding in much narrower terms—sufficiently narrow so that it does not cover the facts of your case (he will be "distinguishing the case on its facts"). Until the new case is decided, no one can say with certainty that either statement of the holding is right or wrong. Each statement may be eminently reasonable and until the court has been persuaded to adopt one or the other no flat answer can be given to the question of which statement more nearly approximated the holding of the precedent case. It may (or may not) be some consolation that judges often disagree as to what the prior case held. See, for example, Mitchell v. W.T. Grant Co., 416 U.S. 600, 94 S.Ct. 1895, 40 L.Ed.2d 406 (1974) where the majority and minority differed as to whether the Court was overruling an earlier decision.

The job of stating a reasonable rule of law—of predicting the decision of the court on the new facts—is not easy; it is an art rather than a science and as such is primarily a matter of feel—a feel you will develop as you read and use more cases, know your courts better and know better the circumstances out of which the first decision came and the different circumstances, if any, of your own case.

The key to the determination is policy. What was the policy (or policies) underlying the earlier decision? Are there facts in the new case that raise different policy considerations? Of course, if the court believes the policy of the original decision was wrong, it may overrule it or, as we shall see, "confine it to its special facts," but usually one stands a better

chance to win by arguing that the facts are "materially different." How do we know what the policies underlying the first decision were?

An important guide is the language of the court deciding the case; while not absolutely controlling, it often shows you which facts the court thought significant and makes the job of distinguishing a subsequent case much more difficult where that job involves emphasizing facts other than those the court thought significant. It is not, as you will see in the cases on intentional infliction of emotional distress, an insurmountable handicap, but no good lawyer fails to take the language of the court into account.

But useful as the language may be, the most important element of any case is its facts; the first job you must do is to compare the facts of your case with the facts of those cases upon which you intend to rely as precedent; you must be prepared to reconcile factual differences if any exist.

### Problem Case

The following is the opinion of the court in the recent case of Radin v. Ellis, decided by the Supreme Court of the [hypothetical] State of New Hazard in January, 2003.

WANG, J. The facts in this case can be simply stated. Early in 2000, the defendant Olivia Ellis purchased a new Ford automobile for the use of herself and the members of her immediate family. On March 6, 2000, the defendant Ellis gave her 16–year–old daughter, Catherine, permission to drive the Ford to the lab where she works after school. As is well known, the law of this State forbids the issuance of a driver's license to any person under 18 years of age. While Catherine was driving through the streets of Taylorville on the way to the lab, she lost control of the car, which ran up on the curb and seriously injured the plaintiff Radin.

The facts stated in the foregoing paragraph are alleged in the plaintiff Radin's complaint in this action. The jury brought in a verdict for $150,000 damages in plaintiff Radin's favor, and the defendant Ellis moved for a new trial. The motion for a new trial was denied by the trial court, and the defendant appeals to this Court.

The development of the law on this subject has been attended by a slow process of clarification. When the automobile was new and regarded as no more dangerous than the horse and buggy, courts were disposed to hold that no strict liability attached to a registered car owner. Today, mounting traffic accident statistics have brought home to us that the modern, 100–mile–an–hour automobile is, indeed, fraught with such possibility for harm that the owner must bear strict responsibility for its use. When a person purchases a high-powered automobile and allows her spouse or child to use it, she is responsible for all injuries to pedestrians which may result from the spouse's or child's negligence in the operation of the automobile. The question of

law is, remarkably, one of first impression in this jurisdiction, but we have no doubt at all about it.

Because, as stated in Judge Wang's opinion, the decision in Radin v. Ellis is the first decision in New Hazard on the subject of the liability of a car owner for injuries resulting from another's operation of the car, it is important to determine the scope of the principle of law for which Radin v. Ellis can be taken as authority. What *is* the holding of Radin v. Ellis?

## The Uses of Dictum

Should a competent advocate cite dicta supporting his position, particularly when there is no past case squarely in point? As you read these cases, is a dictum merely to be discounted—or to be disregarded altogether? Note Justice Sutherland's reference, (Humphrey's Executor, supra) to " * * * dicta, which may be followed if sufficiently persuasive, but which are not controlling." And compare Chief Justice Marshall's statement in Cohens v. Virginia, 19 U.S. 264, 399, 5 L.Ed. 257 (1821) that "they [i.e., dicta] may be respected, but ought not to control the judgment in a subsequent suit when the very point is presented for decision." Another formulation often seen is the following:

> Nevertheless some weight is very properly given to a dictum, a weight similar to that assigned to the sayings of learned text-writers; and in this sense a dictum is authority, its weight varying with the learning of the court and with the amount of thought bestowed by the court upon the point covered by the dictum.

Wambaugh, The Study of Cases 19 (2d Ed.1894).

But these formulations tend to stress the mechanistic aspects. While Courts are not required to follow dictum, if one is looking for guidance as to what courts will do, a well-considered recent dictum may be a better guide than an old holding. Consider in this respect the decision of the United States Supreme Court in Banco Nacional de Cuba v. Sabbatino, 376 U.S. 398, 84 S.Ct. 923, 11 L.Ed.2d 804 (1964). One of the unsettled questions involved in the controversy was whether state or federal law controlled. In Sabbatino it did not matter since New York law (which would have been applicable if state law controlled) and federal law were the same. Nevertheless the Court said:

> We could perhaps in this diversity action avoid the question whether federal or state law is applicable. . . . However, we are constrained to make it clear that an issue concerned with a basic choice regarding the competence and function of the Judiciary . . . must be treated exclusively as an aspect of federal law.

376 U.S. at 424–5. Who in a subsequent case would be brave enough to tell the Court that its statement should be ignored as mere dictum—or so foolish as to advise a client that the dictum did not represent "the law"?

## The Positive Aspects of the Doctrine

Do you agree with the following statement of Judge Jerome Frank?

> Stare decisis has no bite when it means merely that a court adheres to a precedent it considers correct. It is significant only when a court feels constrained to stick to a former ruling although the Court has come to regard it as unwise or unjust.

United States v. Shaughnessy, 234 F.2d 715, 719 (2d Cir.1955).

Most discussions of holding and dictum focus exclusively on the negative aspects of the concept: the extent to which the holding of a case is "binding" on subsequent cases. But the concept has another, very important aspect. As noted above, it is possible to phrase the holding of a case at many levels of generality. By restricting the prior "holding" to its narrowest formulation, judges can avoid the binding effect; but they also can, by using the broadest formulation, move the law significantly without seeming to do violence to the doctrine of precedent. When you study the cases on intentional infliction of emotional distress, observe how much flexibility there is in the system and how much courts move the law while they purport to be following binding precedent.

## Malone v. Fons

Court of Appeals of Wisconsin, 1998
217 Wis.2d 746, 580 N.W.2d 697, *rev. denied*, 219 Wis.2d 922, 584 N.W.2d 123 (1998)

■ CURLEY, J. Sarah Malone, by her guardian ad litem, and her parents, Laurie and Todd Malone (collectively, "the Malones"), appeal from summary judgment entered in favor of the respondents which dismissed all their causes of action against Joseph Fons and his insurance company. The causes of action were brought against Fons because a dog owned by his tenant bit Sarah Malone. The Malones contend the trial court erred because: Fons's conduct fell within the parameters of a claim for common law negligence; Fons was a "harborer" of his tenant's dog, as that term is defined in § 174.001, Stats., and was subject to the double damages provision found in § 174.02(1)(b) because Fons had notice that the dog previously injured a person; and Sarah Malone, the dog-bite victim, was a third-party beneficiary of either Fons's contract, requiring him to provide liability insurance to his tenant, or of his misrepresentation to the tenant that her rent payment included a sum for liability insurance for her. Because we conclude that the holding enunciated in *Gonzales v. Wilkinson*, 68 Wis. 2d 154, 227 N.W.2d 907 (1975), which held that a landlord is not an insurer for the acts of his tenant's dog in a common law negligence claim, controls ... we affirm.

### I.  Background.

Sarah Malone was eight years old on March 22, 1994, when she was bitten by a Rottweiler belonging to Barbara Garner. As a result of the bite, she sustained serious injury. Garner rented her single family home from Fons; however, Sarah was not bitten on this property. She was in a driveway adjacent to the Garner residence when the dog broke free of the leash being held by one of Barbara Garner's children, mauling Sarah. Although disputed by Fons, but considered true by the trial court for summary judgment purposes, the Malones also claimed that the dog had previously broken free of his leash, run across the street and placed his jaws around the arm of another young child. Further, the Malones claimed, again disputed by Fons, but accepted as true by the trial court, that the father of the child involved in this first incident related the occurrence to Fons and complained about the dog. As further proof of Fons's negligence, the Malones submitted a rental agreement between Fons and Garner which prohibited pets, which Fons failed to enforce. With respect to their third-party beneficiary claim, the Malones assert that Fons either contracted with Garner to provide her with liability insurance, or, in the alternative, that Fons misrepresented to her that he would be providing this type of insurance when originally renting her the property.

The Malones's original complaint named only Garner, the owner of the dog, as a defendant. Later, the complaint was amended twice to include Fons, and his insurer, as defendants. The second amended complaint alleged claims of common law negligence ... against both Garner and Fons.... Fons brought a summary judgment motion which the trial court granted, finding that Fons owed no duty to Sarah Malone as a matter of law and dismissing all of the Malones's claims against Fons and his insurer.

II.   Analysis.

\* \* \*

### A.   *Common law negligence claim.*

The Malones contend that Fons, as the landlord of the dog's owner, was liable under common law negligence for injuries sustained from the dog bite because he had a "no pets" rule which he failed to enforce, he knew of the dog's existence, and he had been notified of an earlier incident where the dog exhibited mischievous behavior. The trial court ruled that *Gonzales v. Wilkinson*, 68 Wis. 2d 154, 227 N.W.2d 907 (1975), prevents the Malones from recovering from Fons on their common law negligence theory. In *Gonzales*, a young child wandered onto a neighboring tenant's property and was attacked and bitten in the head by the tenant's basset hound. The plaintiffs sought to impose liability on both the tenant and the landlord under a claim of maintaining an attractive nuisance. *Id.* at 155, 227 N.W.2d at 909. The supreme court, reviewing only the claim against the landlord, held that the attractive nuisance doctrine was unavailable to the plaintiffs. *Id.* at 157, 227 N.W.2d at 909. The dissenting minority, however, stated that it would not reverse because the complaint, liberally construed, alleged a common law negligence claim against the landlord. In response, the *Gonzales* majority stated:

> Although not argued by the parties, a minority of the court would hold the complaint sufficient to state a cause of action against the landowner Wilkinson upon the basis of common-law negligence. The majority does not agree.

> In examining the complaint we find no allegation that James Wilkinson was either the owner or the keeper of the dog, nor is it

alleged that he in any way had any dominion over the dog. There is an allegation that he knew his tenant, Ray Prueher, maintained a vicious dog on the premises but the law does not require him, as the owner of the building, to be an insurer for the acts of his tenant. Under the allegations of this complaint, we hold that the ownership and control of the premises created no duty on the part of the owner of the premises to the plaintiffs.

*Id.* at 158, 227 N.W.2d at 910.

The Malones argue that the trial court erred in finding this statement dispositive of the case because, in their view, the language in *Gonzales* addressing the common law negligence claim was purely dicta as it was unnecessary to the issue presented in the case. Further, if this court concludes the language from *Gonzales* is a holding, rather than dicta, the Malones argue that more recent cases appear to blur the efficacy of the *Gonzales* ruling. They cite *Pagelsdorf v. Safeco Ins. Co. of America*, 91 Wis. 2d 734, 284 N.W.2d 55 (1979), and *Pattermann v. Pattermann*, 173 Wis. 2d 143, 496 N.W.2d 613 (Ct.App.1992), in support of this argument.

We conclude that: (1) the relevant statements in *Gonzales* were not a dicta, but rather, expressed the court's holding; (2) according to the plain language of *Gonzales*, Fons is not liable, on common law negligence grounds, for the bite which Sarah received from Fons's tenant's dog; and (3) neither *Pagelsdorf* nor *Pattermann* have modified *Gonzales*'s holding as it relates to the facts of this particular case.

1.  *Gonzales*-dicta or holding?

As the Malones point out, the complaint in the *Gonzales* case concerned an attractive nuisance claim, not a common law negligence claim. See *Gonzales*, 68 Wis. 2d at 155–57, 227 N.W.2d at 909. The supreme court, however, in response to the dissent, went on to discuss, *sua sponte*, whether the facts set forth a cause of action in common law negligence. See id. at 158, 227 N.W.2d at 910. They determined that they did not. See id. The Malones claim that this determination is dicta. We disagree.

"Dicta" is language which is broader than necessary to determine an issue. *See State ex rel. Schultz v. Bruendl*, 168 Wis. 2d 101, 112, 483 N.W.2d 238, 241 (Ct.App.1992). However, "when an appellate court intentionally takes up, discusses and decides a question germane to a controversy, such a decision is not a *dictum* but is a judicial act of the court which it will thereafter recognize as a binding decision." *State v. Taylor*, 205 Wis. 2d 664, 670, 556 N.W.2d 779, 782 (Ct.App.1996). Applying that test, we determine that the language in *Gonzales* pertaining to its ruling on the common-law negligence is not dicta, but rather, a holding. We base this on our reading of *Gonzales* where, we note, the majority intentionally took up, discussed and decided the question of whether the defendant-landlord could be liable on a common-law negligence theory. That question was germane to the controversy because, had the majority adopted the minority position, reversal would not have been necessary. Thus, the *Gonzales* ruling on common law negligence is not dicta.

2.   Fons is not liable for common-law negligence under *Gonzales*.

We note that the facts of *Gonzales* are strikingly similar to the facts in the instant case. As in this case, the landlord in *Gonzales* was sued after a tenant's dog bit a child who lived nearby. Here, as in *Gonzales*, the landlord was neither the owner nor the keeper of the dog, which belonged to the tenant. In *Gonzales* the supreme court held that the landlord could not be held liable on a common-law negligence theory for the acts of his tenant's dog, stating:

> In examining the complaint we find no allegation that James Wilkinson was either the owner or the keeper of the dog, nor is it alleged that he in any way had any dominion over the dog. There is an allegation that he knew his tenant, Ray Prueher, maintained a vicious dog on the premises but the law does not require him, as the owner of the building, to be an insurer for the acts of his tenant. Under the allegations of this complaint, we hold that the ownership and control of the premises created no duty on the part of the owner of the premises to the plaintiffs.

*Gonzales*, 68 Wis. 2d at 158, 227 N.W.2d at 910. Aside from their contention that this language is dicta, the Malones do not seriously dispute that this language, standing alone and apart from other cases, when applied to the very similar facts in the instant case, absolves Fons of liability for common-law negligence. Clearly, Gonzales holds that a landlord, who is not an owner or keeper of a tenant's dog, and who does not exercise dominion and control over the dog, is not liable on common-law negligence grounds for the acts of his tenant's dog.

The rule promulgated in *Gonzales* is also consistent with cases concerning non-landlord-related common-law negligence dog-bite claims, . . . [that] hold that only an owner or a keeper of an animal can be held liable for common-law negligence.

. . .

Thus, it would appear that *Gonzales* simply extends the common law rule to a landlord-tenant situation. A landlord is normally neither an owner nor a keeper of his or her tenants' dogs, nor does a landlord usually exercise any control over those dogs. Hence, a landlord is not liable under the common law for any injuries caused by a tenant's dog. Therefore, we conclude that, according to the plain language of Gonzales, Fons is not liable on common-law negligence grounds for the dog bite inflicted upon Sarah by his tenant's dog.

3.   Has *Gonzales* been modified or overruled by later cases?

The Malones also claim that even if the language of *Gonzales* is not dicta, and would absolve Fons of liability for common-law negligence, subsequent Wisconsin cases have modified *Gonzales*'s effect. The Malones do not claim that *Gonzales* has been expressly overruled or modified; rather, they assert that, since *Gonzales*, the law of negligence has "evolved" to "create [a] common law duty on the part of a landlord for a vicious dog kept by his tenants." We disagree.

The Malones bolster their argument with two cases. The first is the *Pattermann* case. In *Pattermann*, the Pattermann family gathered at Sallie Pattermann's home in preparation for a family reunion. Scott Pattermann and his family arrived from Florida with their dog, Mandy, a chow chow. Sallie allowed the dog to be placed in a hallway, and shortly thereafter, Erin Pattermann, another guest, arrived. When she bent down to pet the dog, the dog jumped up and bit her in the face. See *Pattermann*, 173 Wis. 2d at 148, 496 N.W.2d at 615. The plaintiff's complaint alleged both a common-law negligence claim and a strict liability claim under § 174.02, Stats., against Sallie. See id. The trial court directed a verdict in Sallie's favor. Id. at 148–49, 496 N.W.2d at 615. Although the appellate court affirmed the trial court's grant of a directed verdict with respect to both claims, the appellate court stated, with regard to the common-law negligence claim: "Even if Sallie were not the owner or keeper of the animal, as the landowner she may be liable for negligence associated with a known dangerous dog allowed on her premises." Id. at 151, 496 N.W.2d at 616 (citing Klimek v. Drzewiecki, 135 Mich. App. 115, 352 N.W.2d 361 (1984)). The Malones seize upon this statement and argue that *Pattermann* "makes clear that a dog may be considered a dangerous condition of the premises and a landowner may be held liable if he knows the dog had previously bitten someone even though he is not the owner or keeper of the dog." The Malones also argue that "landowner," as the term was used in *Pattermann*, applies to landlords as well as other landowners, and, as a consequence, Fons may be liable for common-law negligence in the instant case. We disagree.

First, in contrast to *Gonzales*, *Pattermann*'s facts are markedly different from the facts in this case. Although *Pattermann* involved a dog-bite and a landowner, nowhere in the case is there a discussion about the duties of a landlord. Therefore, we find the suggestion that the *Pattermann* court intended its holding to apply to landlords speculative at best. Second, we note that the court in *Pattermann* merely assumed, without deciding, that the plaintiff had correctly cited the law. Finally, the court of appeals's statements in *Pattermann* cannot be read to allow common-law negligence claims against landlords for injuries caused by dangerous dogs on their premises because such a holding would expressly conflict with the supreme court's prior holding in *Gonzales*. The court of appeals has no authority to overrule, modify or withdraw language from even its own decisions, see Cook v. Cook, 208 Wis. 2d 166, 185–90, 560 N.W.2d 246, 254–56 (1997), and obviously has no authority to overrule or modify decisions of the supreme court. See id. at 189, 560 N.W.2d at 256. Therefore, we conclude that *Pattermann* is factually distinguishable from the instant case and that *Pattermann* did not overrule or modify Gonzales. Thus, we conclude that Gonzales's holding is unaffected by *Pattermann*.

The Malones also cite *Pagelsdorf* to support their theory. In *Pagelsdorf*, the plaintiff, a neighbor, was injured when a rotted railing collapsed due to the landlord's failure to maintain the premises. *Pagelsdorf,* 91 Wis. 2d at 735–37, 284 N.W.2d at 56–57. Although not a dog-bite case, *Pagelsdorf* broke new ground and set a new standard for landlords in the maintenance of their rental property. Prior to *Pagelsdorf,* a landlord, with certain exceptions, enjoyed a general rule of nonliability for injuries to his tenants and their visitors resulting from defects in the premises. See id. at 740, 284 N.W.2d at 58 (citing Skrzypezak v. Konieczka, 224 Wis. 455, 272 N.W. 659 (1937)); *Pagelsdorf,* however, abrogated that general rule, stating:

> We believe, however, that the better public policy lies in the abandonment of the general rule of nonliability and the adoption of a rule that a landlord is under a *duty to exercise ordinary care in the maintenance of the premises.*

Id. at 741, 284 N.W.2d at 59 (emphasis added). The Malones essentially argue that, by abandoning the general rule of nonliability for landlords, *Pagelsdorf* overruled *Gonzales*'s holding that a landlord may not be liable, on common-law negligence grounds, for injuries caused by his tenants' dogs. *Pagelsdorf* does contain two sweeping sentences which, if read out of context, would seem to support the Malones's position. In the beginning of the opinion, the court stated: "Abrogating the landlord's general cloak of immunity at common law, we hold that a landlord must exercise ordinary care toward his tenant and others on the premises with permission." Id. at 735, 284 N.W.2d at 56. Similarly, near the end of the opinion, the court stated: "In conclusion, a landlord owes his tenant or anyone on the premises with the tenant's consent a duty to exercise ordinary care." Id. at 745, 284 N.W.2d at 61. After examining the facts of the case and the context of those statements, however, we conclude that *Pagelsdorf*'s rule is limited to situations dealing with property maintenance issues and defects in the premises, and thus, that *Pagelsdorf* did not overrule *Gonzales*'s rule regarding dog bites.

*Pagelsdorf* involved a defective wooden porch railing, not a dog bite. Throughout the opinion, the *Pagelsdorf* court repeatedly refers to "defects" and "defective premises," and to the landlord's duty to "maintain" the premises. For instance, in the first sentence of the opinion, the court states, "We dispose of this appeal by addressing the single issue of the scope of a landlord's duty toward his tenant's invitee who is injured *as a result of defective premises.*" Id. at 735, 284 N.W.2d at 56 (emphasis added). Also, the court states: "The question on which the appeal turns is whether the trial court erred in failing to instruct the jury that Mahnke [the landlord] owed *Pagelsdorf* a duty to exercise ordinary care *in maintaining the premises.*" Id. at 738, 284 N.W.2d at 58 (emphasis added). Later, the court states: "We conclude that there is no remaining justification for the landlord's general cloak of common law immunity and hereby abolish the general common law principle of nonliability of landlords toward persons injured *as a result of their defective premises.*" Id.at 744, 284 N.W.2d at 60 (emphasis added). Finally, the court concludes by stating:

In conclusion, a landlord owes his tenant or anyone on the premises with the tenant's consent a duty to exercise ordinary care. If a person lawfully on the premises is injured as a result of the landlord's negligence *in maintaining the premises*, he is entitled to recover from the landlord under general negligence principles. Issues of notice of *the defect*, its obviousness, control of the premises, and so forth are all relevant only insofar as they bear on the ultimate question: Did the landlord exercise ordinary care *in the maintenance of the premises under all the circumstances*?

Id. at 745, 284 N.W.2d at 61. The Malones have cited no persuasive authority for the proposition that a tenant's dog should be considered a "defect" of the premises, or that a landlord's act of permitting a tenant to own a dog should be equated with a landlord's failure to repair a defect, or to properly "maintain the premises." Although the Malones cite *Pattermann* as support for their claim that a dog can be considered a dangerous condition, that case did not involve a landlord, and, contrary to the Malones's assertions, did not in any way hold that a tenant's dog is a "defect" in the premises similar to a rotted wooden railing. Therefore, we conclude that Pagelsdorf has not affected the validity of the rule of law enunciated in *Gonzales*, and that the trial court correctly granted summary judgment with respect to the Malones's common-law negligence claim against Fons.

* * *

■ FINE, J. (dissenting). The majority holds that when a landlord is on notice that his or her tenant is keeping a dangerous dog on the rented premises in violation of the lease, the landlord is not responsible if that dog attacks and injures someone within the foreseeable zone of danger even though the parents of an earlier victim had warned the landlord before the latest attack that the dog was dangerous and asked the landlord to make his tenants get rid of the dog. I respectfully dissent.

Under the facts as alleged in this case, I believe that Joseph Fons, the landlord here, had a duty to enforce the "no pets" clause in the lease after he learned that his tenants were harboring a dangerous dog. "A defendant's duty is established when it can be said that it was foreseeable that his act or omission to act may cause harm to someone." A.E. Investment Corp. v. Link Builders, Inc., 62 Wis. 2d 479, 484, 214 N.W.2d 764, 766 (1974). This is true "even though the nature of that harm and the identity of the harmed person or harmed interest is unknown at the time of the act." Id., 62 Wis. 2d at 483, 214 N.W.2d at 766. Here, although the ultimate victim was unknown, the nature of the harm was patent.

Under Wisconsin law, a tortfeasor is liable to an injured plaintiff "if there is an unbroken chain of causation from the negligent act to the injury sustained and if the negligence is a substantial factor," unless public-policy considerations intervene. Howard v. Mt. Sinai Hospital, Inc., 63 Wis. 2d 515, 217 N.W.2d 383, on rehearing, 63 Wis. 2d 515, 523, 219 N.W.2d 576, 577 (1974) (per curiam, on reconsideration). There was such an unbroken chain here. The crux of the public-policy analysis is whether the imposition of liability would "shock the conscience of society." Rolph v. EBI Companies, 159 Wis. 2d 518, 534, 464 N.W.2d 667, 672–673 (1991). Imposition of liability here is well within the ambit of the doctrine announced by A.E. Investment Corp., and, in my view, is not barred by public-policy considerations.

The majority, as did the trial court, reads Gonzales v. Wilkinson, 68 Wis. 2d 154, 227 N.W.2d 907 (1975), as barring the plaintiffs' action. Accepting for the sake of this discussion the majority's conclusion that the portion of *Gonzales* upon which it relies is a "holding" and not dictum, I do not agree that *Gonzales* is dispositive under the facts of this case that we must accept as true.

As the majority recognizes, *Gonzales* was an attractive-nuisance case. Id., 68 Wis. 2d at 155–156, 227 N.W.2d at 909. In *Gonzales*'s passing reference to the landlord's common-law negligence, it noted, without even discussing the broad principle it had so recently set out in *A.E. Investment*, that the landlord had no "dominion over the dog," and that any liability under a common-law negligence theory rested merely on "the ownership and control of the premises," which, by themselves, did not create a duty to the plaintiffs. Id., 68 Wis. 2d at 158, 227 N.W.2d at 910. Here, in contrast, the dog should not have been on the premises. The dog would not have been on the premises if Fons had enforced the lease and heeded the warning given to him by the parents of the earlier victim. Unlike the situation in *Gonzales*, the plaintiffs here are not seeking to hold Fons liable as "an insurer for the acts of his tenant," ibid., but, rather, for refusing to enforce the lease provision under circumstances when it was "foreseeable" that his refusal "may cause harm to someone," *A.E. Investment*, 62 Wis. 2d at 484, 214 N.W.2d at 766 ("A defendant's duty is established when it can be said that it was foreseeable that his act or omission to act may cause harm to someone.").

. . .

## Questions

**1.** Do you agree that the *Gonzales* excerpts quoted above represent the court's "holding"? Is it significant that the issue in *Gonzales*—the issue argued by the parties—was the attractive nuisance doctrine, which was not at issue in *Malone*?

**2.** Notice that the *Malone* court "holds" what the holding of *Gonzales* is, and then applies that holding to the case at hand. What does this type of analysis say about the doctrine of *stare decisis*?

**3.** What policies support the majority's apparent view that changes in the law must occur expressly, rather through a more general "evolution?"

## 3.   DEFINING THE MEANING OF PRECEDENT

# Anastasoff v. United States

United States Court of Appeals for the Eighth Circuit, 2000.
223 F.3d 898.

■ RICHARD S. ARNOLD, CIRCUIT JUDGE.

Faye Anastasoff seeks a refund of overpaid federal income tax. On April 13, 1996, Ms. Anastasoff mailed her refund claim to the Internal Revenue Service for taxes paid on April 15, 1993. The Service denied her claim under 26 U.S.C. § 6511(b), which limits refunds to taxes paid in the three years prior to the filing of a claim. Although her claim was mailed within this period, it was received and filed on April 16, 1996, three years and one day after she overpaid her taxes, one day late. In many cases, "the Mailbox Rule," 26 U.S.C. § 7502, saves claims like Ms. Anastasoff's that would have been timely if received when mailed; they are deemed received when postmarked. But § 7502 applies only to claims that are untimely, and the parties agree that under 26 U.S.C. § 6511(a), which measures the timeliness of the refund claim itself, her claim was received on time. The issue then is whether § 7502 can be applied, for the purposes of § 6511(b)'s three-year refund limitation, to a claim that was timely under § 6511(a). The District Court held that § 7502 could not apply to any part of a timely claim, and granted judgment for the Service. On appeal, Ms. Anastasoff argues that § 7502 should apply whenever necessary to fulfill its remedial purpose, i.e., to save taxpayers from the vagaries of the postal system, even when only part of the claim is untimely. We affirm the judgment of the District Court.

I.

We rejected precisely the same legal argument in Christie v. United States, No. 91–2375MN (8th Cir. Mar. 20, 1992) (per curiam) (unpublished). In *Christie,* as here, we considered a refund claim mailed just prior to § 6511(b)'s three-year bar and received just after. Like Ms. Anastasoff, the *Christie* taxpayers argued that § 7502 should operate regardless of the claim's timeliness under § 6511(a) to save their claim under § 6511(b). We held that even if § 7502 could apply to a timely claim, it would not help in this situation: If § 7502 were applied to the claim, it would be deemed received before the return. But § 6511(a) provides that a claim must be submitted within two years of overpayment if no return has yet been filed—not three years. In other words, to save the claim under § 6511(b) only makes it untimely under § 6511(a). Ms. Anastasoff does not attempt to distinguish *Christie.* She does argue that a relevant regulation was not cited in *Christie,* but the reasoning of the *Christie* opinion is squarely inconsistent with the effect taxpayer desires to attribute to the regulation.

Although it is our only case directly in point, Ms. Anastasoff contends that we are not bound by *Christie* because it is an unpublished decision and thus not a precedent under 8th Circuit Rule 28A(i). We disagree. We hold that the portion of Rule 28A(i) that declares that unpublished opinions are not precedent is unconstitutional under Article III, because it purports to confer on the federal courts a power that goes beyond the "judicial."

The Rule provides:

> Unpublished opinions are not precedent and parties generally should not cite them. When relevant to establishing the doctrines of res judicata, collateral estoppel, or the law of the case, however, the parties may cite any unpublished opinion. Parties may also cite an unpublished opinion of this court if the opinion has persuasive value on a material issue and no published opinion of this or another court would serve as well. . . .

Inherent in every judicial decision is a declaration and interpretation of a general principle or rule of law. Marbury v. Madison, 5 U.S. 137, 1 Cranch 137, 177–78, 2 L.Ed. 60 (1803). This declaration of law is authoritative to the extent necessary for the decision, and must be applied in subsequent cases to similarly situated parties. James B. Beam Distilling Co. v. Georgia, 501 U.S. 529, 544, 111 S.Ct. 2439, 115 L.Ed.2d 481 (1991); Cohens v. Virginia, 6 Wheat. 264, 399, 5 L.Ed. 257 (1821). These principles, which form the doctrine of precedent, were well established and well regarded at the time this nation was founded. The Framers of the Constitution considered these principles to derive from the nature of judicial power, and intended that they would limit the judicial power delegated to the courts by Article III of the Constitution. Accordingly, we conclude that 8th Circuit Rule 28A(i), insofar as it would allow us to avoid the precedential effect of our prior decisions, purports to expand the judicial power beyond the bounds of Article III, and is therefore unconstitutional. That rule does not, therefore, free us from our duty to follow this Court's decision in *Christie*.

## II.

The doctrine of precedent was well-established by the time the Framers gathered in Philadelphia. Morton J. Horwitz, *The Transformation of American Law: 1780–1860* 8–9 (1977); J.H. Baker, *An Introduction to English Legal History* 227 (1990); Sir William Holdsworth, *Case Law*, 50 L.Q.R. 180 (1934). See, *e.g.*, 1 Sir William W. Blackstone, *Commentaries on the Laws of England* * 69 (1765) ("it is an established rule to abide by former precedents"). To the jurists of the late eighteenth century (and thus by and large to the Framers),[4] the doctrine seemed not just well established but an immemorial custom, the way judging had always been carried out, part of the course of the law.[5] In addition, the Framers had inherited a very

**4.** Lawyers made up majorities of the Continental Congress, the signers of the Declaration of Independence, and the Framers of the Constitution. Perry Miller, *The Legal Mind in America* 16 (1962).

**5.** James Wilson suggested that the doctrine of precedent was brought to England by the Romans. 1 *The Works of James Wilson*

343 (1967). Chancellor Kent traced it "from the earliest periods of English history." James Kent, *Commentaries on American Law* 473–78 (12th ed. 1873). Blackstone found it "even so early as the conquest." 1 William Blackstone, *Commentaries* *69. Before them, in Slade v. Morley, Sir Edward Coke suggested simply that "precedents have always been

favorable view of precedent from the seventeenth century, especially through the writings and reports of Sir Edward Coke; the assertion of the authority of precedent had been effective in past struggles of the English people against royal usurpations, and for the rule of law against the arbitrary power of government.[6] In sum, the doctrine of precedent was not merely well established; it was the historic method of judicial decision-making, and well regarded as a bulwark of judicial independence in past struggles for liberty.

Modern legal scholars tend to justify the authority of precedents on equitable or prudential grounds.[7] By contrast, on the eighteenth-century view (most influentially expounded by Blackstone), the judge's duty to follow precedent derives from the nature of the judicial power itself.[8] As Blackstone defined it, each exercise of the "judicial power" requires judges "to determine the law" arising upon the facts of the case. 3 Blackstone, *Commentaries* *25. "To determine the law" meant not only choosing the appropriate legal principle but also expounding and interpreting it, so that "the law in that case, being solemnly declared and determined, what before was uncertain, and perhaps indifferent, is now become a permanent rule...." 1 *Commentaries* *69.[9] In determining the law in one case, judges bind those in subsequent cases because, although the judicial power requires judges "to determine law" in each case, a judge is "sworn to determine, not according to his own judgements, but according to the known laws. [Judges are] not delegated to pronounce a new law, but to

respected...." 4 Co.Rep. 91, 76 Eng.Rep. 1074 (K.B.1602), reprinted in *Sources of English Legal History: Private Law to 1750* 428 (1986).

**6.** Coke's struggle against the tyranny of the Stuarts, which the Framers identified with their own against King George, made him the legal authority most admired and most often cited by American patriots. Bernard Bailyn, *The Ideological Origins of the American Revolution* 30 (1967). Coke used precedent, and emphasized it to a greater degree than his predecessors, because it was his main weapon in the fight for the independence of the judiciary and limits on the king's prerogative rights. See Harold J. Berman and Charles J. Reid, Jr., *The Transformation of English Legal Science: From Hale to Blackstone,* 45 Emory L.J. 437, 450 (1996); J.G.A. Pocock, *The Ancient Constitution and the Feudal Law* 46 (1987). By contrast, the only criticism of the doctrine of precedent was associated with Thomas Hobbes, who regarded the authority of precedent as an affront to the absolute power of the Sovereign. See Thomas Hobbes, *Leviathan* 323–26 (Penguin ed.1985).

**7.** See, *e.g.,* Frederick Schauer, *Precedent,* 39 Stan.L.Rev. 571, 595–602 (1987)

(noting that the authority of precedent is commonly supported by arguments: (1) from fundamental fairness, i.e., that like cases should be treated alike; (2) from the need for predictability; and (3) as an aid to judicial decision-making, to prevent unnecessary reconsideration of established matters).

**8.** Blackstone's great influence on the Framers' understanding of law is a familiar fact. See Schick v. United States, 195 U.S. 65, 69, 24 S.Ct. 826, 49 L.Ed. 99 (1904) ("At the time of the adoption of the Federal Constitution, it [Blackstone's work] had been published about twenty years, and it has been said that more copies of the work had been sold in this country than in England; so that undoubtedly, the framers of the Constitution were familiar with it."); Daniel Boorstin, *The Mysterious Science of Law* 265 (1941).

**9.** This need not be done by way of a reported opinion. The record of the judicial proceedings and decision alone is sufficient evidence of the legal principles necessary to support the decision to provide "light or assistance" when "any critical question arises." 1 Blackstone, *Commentaries* *69.

maintain and expound the old." *Id.* The judicial power to determine law is a power only to determine what the law is, not to invent it. Because precedents are the "best and most authoritative" guide of what the law is, the judicial power is limited by them. *Id.* The derivation of precedential authority from the law-declaring nature of the judicial power was also familiar to the Framers through the works of Sir Edward Coke and Sir Matthew Hale. See 4 E. Coke, *Institutes of the Laws of England* 138 (1642) (a prior judicial decision on point is sufficient authority on a question of law because "a judicial decision is to the same extent a declaration of the law."); 1 Coke, *Institutes* 51 (1642) ("[i]t is the function of a judge not to make, but to declare the law, according to the golden mete-wand of the law and not by the crooked cord of discretion."); Sir Matthew Hale, *The History of The Common Law of England* 44–45 (Univ. of Chicago ed., 1971) ("Judicial Decisions [have their] Authority in Expounding, Declaring, and Publishing what the Law of this Kingdom is....").

In addition to keeping the law stable, this doctrine is also essential, according to Blackstone, for the separation of legislative and judicial power. In his discussion of the separation of governmental powers, Blackstone identifies this limit on the "judicial power," i.e., that judges must observe established laws, as that which separates it from the "legislative" power and in which "consists one main preservative of public liberty." 1 Blackstone, *Commentaries* *258–59. If judges had the legislative power to "depart from" established legal principles, "the subject would be in the hands of arbitrary judges, whose decisions would be then regulated only by their own opinions...." *Id.* at *259.

The Framers accepted this understanding of judicial power (sometimes referred to as the declaratory theory of adjudication) and the doctrine of precedent implicit in it.[10] Hamilton, like Blackstone, recognized that a court "pronounces the law" arising upon the facts of each case.[11] *The Federalist No. 81,* at 531 (Alexander Hamilton) (Modern Library ed., 1938). He explained the law-declaring concept of judicial power in the term, "jurisdiction": "This word is composed of JUS and DICTIO, *juris dictio,* or a speaking and pronouncing of the law," *id.,* and concluded that the jurisdiction of appellate courts, as a law-declaring power, is not antagonistic to the fact-finding role of juries. *Id.* Like Blackstone, he thought that "[t]he courts must declare the sense of the law," and that this fact means courts

---

**10.** See Letter from James Madison to Charles Jared Ingersoll (June 25, 1831), reprinted in *The Mind of the Founder: Sources of the Political Thought of James Madison* 390, 390–93 (Marvin Meyers ed., rev. ed.1981) (describing the "authoritative force" of "judicial precedents" as stemming from the "obligations arising from judicial expositions of the law on succeeding judges...."); James Wilson, II *The Works of James Wilson* 502 (1967) ("Judicial decisions are the principal and most authentic" proof of what the law is and ... "every prudent and cautious

judge will appreciate them [because] ... his duty and his business is not to make the law, but to interpret and apply it.") *Id.* See also Christopher Wolfe, *The Rise of Modern Judicial Review: From Constitutional Interpretation to Judge–Made Law* 74 (1986); David M. O'Brien, *Constitutional Law and Politics* 73 (1995).

**11.** James Wilson agreed: "judicium is quasi juris dictum ... a judgment is a declaration of the law." II *The Works of James Wilson* 524 (1967).

must exercise "judgment" about what the law is rather than "will" about what it should be. *The Federalist No. 78*, at 507–08. Like Blackstone, he recognized that this limit on judicial decision-making is a crucial sign of the separation of the legislative and judicial power. *Id.* at 508. Hamilton concludes that "[t]o avoid an arbitrary discretion in the courts, it is indispensable that they should be bound down by strict rules and precedents, which serve to define and point out their duty in every particular case that comes before them...." *Id.* at 510.[12]

The Framers thought that, under the Constitution, judicial decisions would become binding precedents in subsequent cases. Hamilton anticipated that the record of federal precedents "must unavoidably swell to a very considerable bulk...." *Id.* But precedents were not to be recorded for their own sake. He expected judges to give them "long and laborious study" and to have a "competent knowledge of them." *Id.* Likewise, Madison recognized "the obligation arising from judicial expositions of the law on succeeding judges." Letter from James Madison to Charles Jared Ingersoll (June 25, 1831), reprinted in *The Mind of the Founder: Sources of the Political Thought of James Madison* 390, 390–93 (Marvin Meyers ed., rev. ed.1981). Madison expected that the accumulation of precedents would be beneficial: "[a]mong other difficulties, the exposition of the Constitution is frequently a copious source, and must continue so until its meaning on all great points shall have been settled by precedents." Letter from James Madison to Samuel Johnson (June 21, 1789), in *12 Papers of James Madison* 250 (Robert A. Rutland et al. eds., 1977). Although they drew different conclusions from the fact, the Anti–Federalists also assumed that federal judicial decisions would become authorities in subsequent cases.[13] Finally, early Americans demonstrated the authority which they assigned to judicial decisions by rapidly establishing a reliable system of American reporters in the years following the ratification of the Constitution. Grant

---

**12.**  Other early authorities confirm the connection between the doctrine of precedent and the separation of powers. See 1 *Kent's Commentaries,* Lect. XXI at 479: "Those nations, which have adopted the civil law as the main foundation of their own [recognize precedent to a far less degree than our own].... With them the necessity of judiciary independence upon the executive, is not so clearly acknowledged.... It has been shown already that this independence requires, in a considerable degree, the acknowledgment of precedential authority."; William Cranch, Preface, 1 Cranch iii (1804): "In a government which is emphatically styled a government of laws, the least possible range ought to be left for the discretion of the judge ... perhaps nothing conduces more to that object than the publication of reports. Every case decided is a check upon the judge. He can not decide a similar case differently, without strong rea-

sons, which, for his own justification, he will wish to make public."

**13.**  See, *e.g.,* Essays of Brutus, XV (Mar. 20, 1788) in 2 *The Complete Anti–Federalist,* 441 (Herbert J. Storing ed., 1981): "one adjudication will form a precedent to the next, and this to a following one. These cases will immediately affect individuals only; so that a series of determinations will probably take place before even the people will be informed of them." By contrast, the danger in the Federal Farmer's view was that the federal courts had "no precedents in this country, as yet, to regulate the divisions in equity as in Great Britain; equity, therefore, in the supreme court for many years will be mere discretion." Letters from The Federal Farmer No. 3 (Oct. 10, 1787), in 2 *The Complete Anti–Federalist* at 244.

Gilmore, *The Ages of American Law* 23 (1977); Peter Karsten, *Heart Versus Head: Judge–Made Law in Nineteenth–Century America* 28–32 (1997).

We do not mean to suggest that the Framers expected or intended the publication (in the sense of being printed in a book) of all opinions. For the Framers, limited publication of judicial decisions was the rule, and they never drew that practice into question. Before the ratification of the Constitution, there was almost no private reporting and no official reporting at all in the American states. Frederick G. Kempin, Jr., *Precedent and Stare Decisis: The Critical Years, 1800–1850,* 3 Am.J.Leg.Hist. 28, 34 (1959) (reviewing the history of American reports). As we have seen, however, the Framers did not regard this absence of a reporting system as an impediment to the precedential authority of a judicial decision. Although they lamented the problems associated with the lack of a reporting system and worked to assure more systematic reporting, judges and lawyers of the day recognized the authority of unpublished decisions even when they were established only by memory or by a lawyer's unpublished memorandum. Karsten, *Heart Versus Head* 30; Jesse Root, *The Origin of Government and Laws in Connecticut* (1798), reprinted in *The Legal Mind in America* 38–39 (Perry Miller ed., 1962).[14]

To summarize, in the late eighteenth century, the doctrine of precedent was well-established in legal practice (despite the absence of a reporting system), regarded as an immemorial custom, and valued for its role in past struggles for liberty. The duty of courts to follow their prior decisions was understood to derive from the nature of the judicial power itself and to separate it from a dangerous union with the legislative power. The statements of the Framers indicate an understanding and acceptance of these principles. We conclude therefore that, as the Framers intended, the doctrine of precedent limits the "judicial power" delegated to the courts in Article III. No less an authority than Justice (Professor) Joseph Story is in accord. See his *Commentaries on the Constitution of the United States* §§ 377–78 (1833):

> The case is not alone considered as decided and settled; but the principles of the decision are held, as precedents and authority, to bind future cases of the same nature. This is the constant practice under our whole system of jurisprudence. Our ancestors brought it with them, when they first emigrated to this country; and it is, and always has been considered, as the great security of our rights, our liberties,

---

**14.** In this, they were following the common-law view, which considered entry on the official court record sufficient to give a decision precedential authority whether or not the decision was subsequently reported. See, *e.g.,* Coke, 2 *Institutes,* Proeme, last paragraph (stating that judicial decisions are reliable authority whether they are published, i.e., "related and reported in our Bookes," or only "extant in judicial Records....."). This remained true even after reporting be-

came more systematic. See James Ram, *Science of Legal Judgement* (1834) ("A manuscript note of a case is authority. It may be more full, or accurate, than a printed report of the same case. The existence of such manuscript may be little known. When cited by a party in a cause ... it may be 'an authority precisely applicable' (18 Ves. 347); but the opposite party, or the Court, may never have heard of it before; it may then come as a great surprise upon both.").

and our property. It is on this account, that our law is justly deemed certain, and founded in permanent principles, and not dependent upon the caprice or will of judges. A more alarming doctrine could not be promulgated by any American court, than that it was at liberty to disregard all former rules and decisions, and to decide for itself, without reference to the settled course of antecedent principles.

This known course of proceeding, this settled habit of thinking, this conclusive effect of judicial adjudications, was in the full view of the framers of the constitution. It was required, and enforced in every state in the Union; and a departure from it would have been justly deemed an approach to tyranny and arbitrary power, to the exercise of mere discretion, and to the abandonment of all the just checks upon judicial authority.

III.

Before concluding, we wish to indicate what this case is not about. It is not about whether opinions should be published, whether that means printed in a book or available in some other accessible form to the public in general. Courts may decide, for one reason or another, that some of their cases are not important enough to take up pages in a printed report. Such decisions may be eminently practical and defensible, but in our view they have nothing to do with the authoritative effect of any court decision. The question presented here is not whether opinions ought to be published, but whether they ought to have precedential effect, whether published or not. We point out, in addition, that "unpublished" in this context has never meant "secret." So far as we are aware, every opinion and every order of any court in this country, at least of any appellate court, is available to the public. You may have to walk into a clerk's office and pay a per-page fee, but you can get the opinion if you want it. Indeed, most appellate courts now make their opinions, whether labeled "published" or not, available to anyone on line. This is true of our Court.

Another point about the practicalities of the matter needs to be made. It is often said among judges that the volume of appeals is so high that it is simply unrealistic to ascribe precedential value to every decision. We do not have time to do a decent enough job, the argument runs, when put in plain language, to justify treating every opinion as a precedent. If this is true, the judicial system is indeed in serious trouble, but the remedy is not to create an underground body of law good for one place and time only. The remedy, instead, is to create enough judgeships to handle the volume, or, if that is not practical, for each judge to take enough time to do a competent job with each case. If this means that backlogs will grow, the price must still be paid. At bottom, rules like our Rule 28A(i) assert that courts have the following power: to choose for themselves, from among all the cases they decide, those that they will follow in the future, and those that they need not. Indeed, some forms of the non-publication rule even forbid citation. Those courts are saying to the bar: "We may have decided this question the opposite way yesterday, but this does not bind us today, and, what's more, you cannot even tell us what we did yesterday." As we have tried to explain in this opinion, such a statement exceeds the judicial power, which is based on reason, not *fiat*.

Finally, lest we be misunderstood, we stress that we are not here creating some rigid doctrine of eternal adherence to precedents. Cases can be overruled. Sometimes they should be. On our Court, this function can be performed by the en banc Court, but not by a single panel. If the reasoning of a case is exposed as faulty, or if other exigent circumstances justify it, precedents can be changed. When this occurs, however, there is a burden of justification. The precedent from which we are departing should be stated, and our reasons for rejecting it should be made convincingly clear. In this way, the law grows and changes, but it does so incrementally, in response to the dictates of reason, and not because judges have simply changed their minds.

### IV.

For these reasons, we must reject Ms. Anastasoff's argument that, under 8th Cir.R. 28A(i), we may ignore our prior decision in *Christie*. Federal courts, in adopting rules, are not free to extend the judicial power of the United States described in Article III of the Constitution. Willy v. Coastal Corp., 503 U.S. 131, 135, 112 S.Ct. 1076, 117 L.Ed.2d 280 (1992). The judicial power of the United States is limited by the doctrine of precedent. Rule 28A(i) allows courts to ignore this limit. If we mark an opinion as unpublished, Rule 28A(i) provides that is not precedent. Though prior decisions may be well-considered and directly on point, Rule 28A(i) allows us to depart from the law set out in such prior decisions without any reason to differentiate the cases. This discretion is completely inconsistent with the doctrine of precedent; even in constitutional cases, courts "have always required a departure from precedent to be supported by some 'special justification.' " United States v. International Business Machines Corp., 517 U.S. 843, 856, 116 S.Ct. 1793, 135 L.Ed.2d 124 (1996), quoting Payne v. Tennessee, 501 U.S. 808, 842, 111 S.Ct. 2597, 115 L.Ed.2d 720 (1991) (Souter, J., concurring). Rule 28A(i) expands the judicial power beyond the limits set by Article III by allowing us complete discretion to determine which judicial decisions will bind us and which will not. Insofar as it limits the precedential effect of our prior decisions, the Rule is therefore unconstitutional.

Ms. Anastasoff's interpretation of § 7502 was directly addressed and rejected in *Christie*. Eighth Cir.R. 28A(i) does not free us from our obligation to follow that decision. Accordingly, we affirm the judgment of the District Court.

### Note—Subsequent History

Ms. Anastasoff successfully petitioned the court for a rehearing en banc. In response to the petition, the government agreed to pay her the refund she sought, and also declared that it would follow the rule in Weisbart v. United States, 222 F.3d 93 (2d Cir.2000), in which the Second

Circuit had reached a result contrary to the Eight Circuit's unpublished *Christie* decision discussed in the *Anastasoff* opinion.

The en banc Court of Appeal held that Ms Anastasoff's case was moot, as she had received her refund, and the government had changed its policy. "The controversy over the status of unpublished opinions, is to be sure, of great interest and importance, but this sort of factor will not save a case from becoming moot. We sit to decide cases, not issues, and whether unpublished opinions have precedential effect no longer has any relevance for the decision of this tax-refund case." 235 F.3d 1054 (8th Cir.2000). Following customary practice, the Court vacated its previous opinion and judgment. "The constitutionality of that portion of Rule 28A(i) which says that unpublished opinions have no precedential effect remains an open question in this Circuit." Id. at *5.

## Questions

**1.** Suppose, following the resolution in *Anastasoff*, another case raises the issue of the precedential effect of an unpublished opinion in the 8th Circuit. The unpublished opinion is dispositive of the issue in the later case. What effect should the judge in that Circuit now give the unpublished opinion?

**2.** Does Judge Arnold understate the relationship between publication and precedent? How can a prior decision be binding if the parties do not know what the court previously decided? Or if the court itself does not know what it previously decided?

**3.** *Anastasoff* sparked considerable scholarly and practitioner commentary. See, e.g., volume 1 of the Journal of Appellate Practice & Process (1999), a special issue devoted to *Anastasoff* and its implications. Among the strongest critics of Judge Arnold's opinion is Judge Alex Kozinski of the 9th Circuit, whose rebuttal follows.

## Hart v. Massanari

United States Court of Appeals for the Ninth Circuit, 2001.
266 F.3d 1155.

■ KOZINSKI, CIRCUIT JUDGE.

Appellant's opening brief cites Rice v. Chater, No. 95–35604, 1996 WL 583605 (9th Cir. Oct.9, 1996). *Rice* is an unpublished disposition, not reported in the Federal Reporter except as a one-line entry in a long table of cases. *See* Decisions Without Published Opinions, 98 F.3d 1345, 1346 tbl. (9th Cir.1996). The full text of the disposition can be obtained from our clerk's office, and is available on Westlaw® and LEXIS®. However, it is marked with the following notice: "This disposition is not appropriate for publication and may not be cited to or by the courts of this circuit except as provided by 9th Cir.R. 36–3." Our local rules are to the same effect: "Unpublished dispositions and orders of this Court are not binding precedent ... [and generally] may not be cited to or by the courts of this circuit...." 9th Cir. R. 36–3.

We ordered counsel to show cause as to why he should not be disciplined for violating Ninth Circuit Rule 36–3. Counsel responds by arguing that Rule 36–3 may be unconstitutional. He relies on the Eighth Circuit's opinion in Anastasoff v. United States, 223 F.3d 898, *vacated as moot on reh'g en banc*, 235 F.3d 1054 (8th Cir.2000). *Anastasoff,* while vacated, continues to have persuasive force. *See, e.g.*, Williams v. Dallas Area Rapid Transit, 256 F.3d 260 (5th Cir.2001) (Smith, J., dissenting from denial of reh'g en banc). It may seduce members of our bar into violating our Rule 36–3 under the mistaken impression that it is unconstitutional. We write to lay these speculations to rest.

## I

**A.** *Anastasoff* held that Eighth Circuit Rule 28A(i), which provides that unpublished dispositions are not precedential—and hence not binding on future panels of that court—violates Article III of the Constitution. *See* 223 F.3d at 899. According to *Anastasoff,* exercise of the "judicial Power" precludes federal courts from making rulings that are not binding in future cases. Or, to put it differently, federal judges are not merely required to follow the law, they are also required to *make* law in every case. To do otherwise, *Anastasoff* argues, would invite judicial tyranny by freeing courts from the doctrine of precedent: " 'A more alarming doctrine could not be promulgated by any American court, than that it was at liberty to disregard all former rules and decisions, and to decide for itself, without reference to the settled course of antecedent principles.' " *Id.* at 904 (quoting Joseph Story, *Commentaries on the Constitution of the United States* § 377 (1833)).[3]

We believe that *Anastasoff* overstates the case. Rules that empower courts of appeals to issue nonprecedential decisions do not cut those courts free from all legal rules and precedents; if they did, we might find cause for alarm. But such rules have a much more limited effect: They allow panels of the courts of appeals to determine whether future panels, as well as judges of the inferior courts of the circuit, will be bound by particular rulings. This is hardly the same as turning our back on all precedents, or on the concept of precedent altogether. Rather, it is an effort to deal with precedent in the context of a modern legal system, which has evolved considerably since the early days of common law, and even since the time the Constitution was adopted.

The only constitutional provision on which *Anastasoff* relies is that portion of Article III that vests the "judicial Power" of the United States in the federal courts. U.S. Const. art. III, § 1, cl. 1. *Anastasoff* may be the first case in the history of the Republic to hold that the phrase "judicial Power"

---

**3.** In the passage cited by *Anastasoff,* Justice Story argued only that the judicial decisions of the Supreme Court were "conclusive and binding," and that inferior courts were not free to disregard the "decisions of the highest tribunal." He said nothing to suggest that the principle of binding authori-ty constrained the "judicial Power," as *Anastasoff* does; rather, he recognized that the decisions of the Supreme Court were binding upon the states because they were the "supreme law of the land." Story, *supra,* §§ 376–78.

encompasses a specific command that limits the power of the federal courts. There are, of course, other provisions of Article III that have received judicial enforcement, such as the requirement that the courts rule only in "Cases" or "Controversies," *see, e.g.*, Lujan v. Defenders of Wildlife, 504 U.S. 555, 559, 112 S.Ct. 2130, 119 L.Ed.2d 351 (1992), and that the pay of federal judges not be diminished during their good behavior. *See, e.g.*, United States v. Hatter, 532 U.S. 557, 532–557, 121 S.Ct. 1782, 1790–91, 149 L.Ed.2d 820 (2001). The judicial power clause, by contrast, has never before been thought to encompass a constitutional limitation on how courts conduct their business.

* * *

*Anastasoff* focused on one aspect of the way federal courts do business—the way they issue opinions—and held that they are subject to a constitutional limitation derived from the Framers' conception of what it means to exercise the judicial power. Given that no other aspect of the way courts exercise their power has ever been held subject to this limitation, we question whether the "judicial Power" clause contains any limitation at all, separate from the specific limitations of Article III and other parts of the Constitution. The more plausible view is that when the federal courts rule on cases or controversies assigned to them by Congress, comply with due process, accord trial by jury where commanded by the Seventh Amendment and generally comply with the specific constitutional commands applicable to judicial proceedings, they have ipso facto exercised the judicial power of the United States. In other words, the term "judicial Power" in Article III is more likely descriptive than prescriptive.

If we nevertheless were to accept *Anastasoff* 's premise that the phrase "judicial Power" contains limitations separate from those contained elsewhere in the Constitution, we should exercise considerable caution in recognizing those limitations, lest we freeze the law into the mold cast in the eighteenth century. The law has changed in many respects since the time of the Framing, some superficial, others quite fundamental. For example, as Professor William Nelson has convincingly demonstrated, colonial juries "usually possessed the power to find both law and fact in the cases in which they sat," and were not bound to follow the instructions given to them by judges. *See* William E. Nelson, *Marbury v. Madison: The Origins and Legacy of Judicial Review* 16–17 (2000). Today, of course, we would consider it unfair—probably unconstitutional—to allow juries to make up the law as they go along.

Another example: At the time of the Framing, and for some time thereafter, the practice that prevailed both in the United States and England was for judges of appellate courts to express separate opinions, rather than speak with a single (or at least majority) voice. The practice changed around the turn of the nineteenth century, under the leadership of Chief Justice Marshall. *See* George L. Haskins & Herbert A. Johnson, *Foundations of Power: John Marshall, 1801–15, in* 2 The Oliver Wendell Holmes Devise: History of the Supreme Court of the United States 382–89 (Paul A. Freund ed., 1981).

And yet another example: At the time of the Framing, and for some time thereafter, it was considered entirely appropriate for a judge to participate in the appeal of his own decision; indeed, before the creation of the Circuit Courts of Appeals, appeals from district court decisions were often taken to a panel consisting of a Supreme Court Justice riding circuit, and the district judge from whom the decision was taken. Act of March 2, 1793, ch. 22, § 1, 1 Stat. 333; *see also* Charles Alan Wright, Arthur R. Miller & Edward H. Cooper, *Federal Practice and Procedure* § 3504 (2d ed.1984). Today, of course, it is widely recognized that a judge may not hear the appeal from his own decision. There are doubtless many more such examples.[6]

One danger of giving constitutional status to practices that existed at common law, but have changed over time, is that it tends to freeze certain aspects of the law into place, even as other aspects change significantly. *See* note 6 *supra*. This is a particularly dangerous practice when the constitutional rule in question is not explicitly written into the Constitution, but rather is discovered for the first time in a vague, two-centuries-old provision. The risk that this will allow judges to pick and choose those ancient practices they find salutary as a matter of policy, and give them constitutional status, is manifest. *Compare* Richard S. Arnold, *Unpublished Opinions: A Comment,* 1 J.App. Prac. & Process 219 (1999) (suggesting that all opinions be published and given precedential value), *with Anastasoff,* 223 F.3d 898 (holding that the Eighth Circuit's rule barring citation to unpublished opinions violates Article III). Thus, in order to follow the path forged by *Anastasoff,* we would have to be convinced that the practice in question was one the Framers considered so integral and well-understood that they did not have to bother stating it, even though they spelled out many other limitations in considerable detail. Specifically, to adopt *Anastasoff* 's position, we would have to be satisfied that the Framers had a very rigid

---

**6.** The three examples we have given, though apparently disparate, actually bear on the question of what weight was given to precedent at the time of the Framing. In a regime where juries have power to decide the law, the concept of "binding" precedent has a very different, and much more diluted, meaning than in the current regime where jury verdicts are routinely reversed if they are not supported by the evidence in light of the applicable law. Similarly, binding precedent means something different altogether when a court speaks with seven or nine voices than with a single voice. Nine judges speaking separately may well agree on the outcome of a case, but they cannot give the kind of specific guidance as to the conduct of future cases that can be found in a single opinion speaking for the court. Finally, during the time when appeals were conducted by two-judge panels consisting of the circuit justice flanked by the district judge whose ruling was being appealed produced remarkably few—if any—written rulings. The precedential value of rulings from such panels was, for obvious reasons, not particularly valuable guidance in future cases. *Anastasoff* 's view that the judicial process underwent such fundamental changes, yet the process of producing precedential opinions remained essentially unchanged, strikes us as inherently doubtful. *Anastasoff* 's historical analysis has been called into question even by academics who generally agree with the result. *See, e.g.,* Polly J. Price, *Precedent and Judicial Power After the Founding,* 42 B.C. L.Rev. 81, 84, 90–93 (2000); Salem M. Katsh & Alex V. Chachkes, *Constitutionality of "No-Citation" Rules,* 3 J.App. Prac. & Process 287, 288 & n. 5 (2001).

conception of precedent, namely that all judicial decisions necessarily served as binding authority on later courts.

This is, in fact, a much more rigid view of precedent than we hold today. As we explain below, most decisions of the federal courts are not viewed as binding precedent. No trial court decisions are; almost four-fifths of the merits decisions of courts of appeals are not. *See* p. 1177 *infra*.[7] To be sure, *Anastasoff* challenges the latter practice. We find it significant, however, that the practice has been in place for a long time, yet no case prior to *Anastasoff* has challenged its constitutional legitimacy. The overwhelming consensus in the legal community has been that having appellate courts issue nonprecedential decisions is not inconsistent with the exercise of the judicial power.

To accept *Anastasoff* 's argument, we would have to conclude that the generation of the Framers had a much stronger view of precedent than we do. In fact, as we explain below, our concept of precedent today is far stricter than that which prevailed at the time of the Framing. The Constitution does not contain an express prohibition against issuing nonprecedential opinions because the Framers would have seen nothing wrong with the practice.

**B.**   Modern federal courts are the successors of the English courts that developed the common law, but they are in many ways quite different, including how they understand the concept of precedent. Common law judges did not make law as we understand that concept; rather, they "found" the law with the help of earlier cases that had considered similar matters. An opinion was evidence of what the law is, but it was not an independent source of law. *See* Theodore F.T. Plucknett, *A Concise History of the Common Law* 343–44 (5th ed.1956). The law was seen as something that had an existence independent of what judges said: "a miraculous something made by nobody . . . and merely declared from time to time by the judges." 2 John Austin, *Lectures on Jurisprudence or The Philosophy of Positive Law* 655 (4th ed. 1873) (emphasis omitted). Opinions were merely judges' efforts to ascertain the law, much like scientific experiments were efforts to ascertain natural laws. If an eighteenth-century judge believed that a prior case was wrongly decided, he could say that the prior judge had erred in his attempt to discern the law. *See* Bole v. Horton, 124 Eng. Rep. 1113, 1124 (C.P.1673). Neither judges nor lawyers understood precedent to be binding in *Anastasoff*'s strict sense.[9]

**7.**   Rules limiting the precedential effect of unpublished decisions exist in every federal circuit and all but four states (Connecticut, Delaware, New York and North Dakota). [citation omitted.] *But see* Eaton v. Chahal, 146 Misc.2d 977, 553 N.Y.S.2d 642, 646 (N.Y.Sup. Ct.1990) ("[U]nreported decisions issued by judges of coordinate jurisdiction . . . are not binding precedent upon this court. . . .") The near-universal adoption of the practice illustrates not only that the practice is consistent with the prevailing conception of the judicial power, but also that it reflects sound judicial policy.

**9.**   As Holdsworth put it:

The general rule is clear. Decided cases which lay down a rule of law are authoritative and must be followed. But in very many of the statements of this general rule there are reservations of different kinds. . . . The fundamental principle,

One impediment to establishing a system of strict binding precedent was the absence at common law of a distinct hierarchy of courts. *See* Plucknett, *supra,* at 350.[10] Only towards the end of the nineteenth century, after England had reorganized its courts, was the position of the House of Lords at the head of its judicial hierarchy confirmed. Before that, there was no single high court that could definitively say what the law was. Thus, as late as the middle of the nineteenth century, an English judge might ignore decisions of the House of Lords, and the Exchequer and Queen's Bench held different views on the same point as late as 1842.[12] *See id.* at 350. Common law judges looked to earlier cases only as examples of policy or practice, and a single case was generally not binding authority. Eighteenth-century judges did not feel bound to follow most decisions that might lead to inconvenient results, and judges would even blame reporters for cases they disliked. *See* Plucknett, *supra,* at 349.

The idea that judges declared rather than made the law remained firmly entrenched in English jurisprudence until the early nineteenth century. David M. Walker, *The Oxford Companion to Law* 977 (1980). Blackstone, who wrote his Commentaries only two decades before the Constitutional Convention and was greatly respected and followed by the generation of the Framers, noted that "the 'law,' and the 'opinion of the

upon which all these reservations ultimately rest, is the principle stated by Coke, Hale and Blackstone, that these cases do not make law, but are only the best evidence of what the law is. They are not, as Hale said, "law properly so called," but only very strong evidence of the law. They are evidence, as Coke said, of the existence of those usages which go to make up the common law; and, conversely, the fact that no case can be produced to prove the existence of an alleged usage is evidence that there is no such usage. This principle is the natural, though undesigned, result of the unofficial character of the reports; and it is clear that its adoption gives the courts power to mould as they please the conditions in which they will accept a decided case or a series of decided cases as authoritative. If the cases are only evidence of what the law is the courts must decide what weight is to be attached to this evidence in different sets of circumstances. *The manner in which they have decided this question has left them many means of escape from the necessity of literal obedience to the general rule that decided cases must always be followed.* They have allowed many exceptions to, and modifications of, this rule if, in their opinion, a literal obedience to it would produce either technical departures from established principles, or substantial inconveniences which would be contrary to public policy.

Sir William Holdsworth, 12 *A History of English Law* 150–51 (1938) (footnotes omitted) (emphasis added).

**10.**  As one commentator has noted:

[T]wo conditions had to be satisfied before the doctrine of *stare decisis* could be established. (1) There had to exist reliable reports of cases. It is obvious that if cases are to be binding, there should be precise records of what they lay down. (2) There had also to be a settled judicial hierarchy. Equally obvious is it that until this was settled it could not be known which decisions were binding. Not until roughly the middle of the last century were these conditions fulfilled, and it is from about then that the modern doctrine [of stare decisis] emerges.

R.W.M. Dias, *Jurisprudence* 30–31 (2d ed.1964).

**12.**  The three common law courts of first instance—the King's (or Queen's) Bench, Common Pleas and Exchequer—had overlapping jurisdiction in many common classes of cases. *See* Plucknett, *supra,* at 210.

judge' are not ... one and the same thing; since it sometimes may happen that the judge may mistake the law"; in such cases, the precedent simply "was not law." 1 William Blackstone, *Commentaries* *70–71 (1765).

For centuries, the most important sources of law were not judicial opinions themselves, but treatises that restated the law, such as the commentaries of Coke and Blackstone. Because published opinions were relatively few, lawyers and judges relied on commentators' synthesis of decisions rather than the verbatim text of opinions.

Case reporters were entrepreneurs who scribbled down jury charges as they were delivered by judges, then printed and sold them. Or, reporters might cobble together case reports from secondhand sources and notes found in estates, sometimes years after the cases were decided.... Not surprisingly, case reports often contradicted each other in describing the reasoning, and even the names, of particular cases....

　　　* * *

A survey of the legal landscape as it might have been viewed by the generation of the Framers casts serious doubt on the proposition—so readily accepted by *Anastasoff*—that the Framers viewed precedent in the rigid form that we view it today. Indeed, it is unclear that the Framers would have considered our view of precedent desirable.[19] The common law, at its core, was a reflection of custom, and custom had a built-in flexibility that allowed it to change with circumstance. Thus, "when Lord Mansfield incorporated the custom of merchants into the common law, it was a living flexible custom, responding to the growth and change of mercantile habits." Plucknett, *supra,* at 350. Embodying that custom into a binding decision raised the danger of ossifying the custom: "[I]f perchance a court has given a decision on a point of that custom, it loses for ever its flexibility and is fixed by the rule of precedent at the point where the court touched it." *Id.* It is entirely possible that lawyers of the eighteenth century, had they been confronted with the regime of rigid precedent that is in common use today, would have reacted with alarm.

The modern concept of binding precedent—where a single opinion sets the course on a particular point of law and must be followed by courts at the same level and lower within a pyramidal judicial hierarchy—came about only gradually over the nineteenth and early twentieth centuries. Lawyers began to believe that judges made, not found, the law. This coincided with monumental improvements in the collection and reporting of case authorities. As the concept of law changed and a more comprehen-

---

**19.** As another commentator has noted:

The Framers were familiar with the idea of precedent. But ... [t]he whole idea of just what precedent entailed was unclear. The relative uncertainty over precedent in 1789 also reflects the fact that "many state courts were manned by laymen, and state law and procedure were frequently in unsettled condition. The colonial and state courts did not enjoy high prestige, and their opinions were not even deemed worthy of publication."

Henry Paul Monaghan, *Stare Decisis and Constitutional Adjudication,* 88 Colum. L.Rev. 723, 770 n. 267 (1988) (citations omitted)....

sive reporting system began to take hold, it became possible for judicial decisions to serve as binding authority.

Early American reporters resembled their English ancestors—disorganized and meager—but the character of the reporting process began to change, after the Constitution was adopted, with the emergence of official reporters in the late eighteenth century and the early nineteenth century. And, later in the nineteenth century, the West Company began to publish standardized case reporters, which were both accurate and comprehensive, making "it possible to publish in written form all of the decisions of courts." [Citation omitted.] Case reports grew thicker, and the weight of precedent began to increase—weight, that is, in terms of volume.

* * *

# II

Federal courts today do follow some common law traditions. When ruling on a novel issue of law, they will generally consider how other courts have ruled on the same issue. This consideration will not be limited to courts at the same or higher level, or even to courts within the same system of sovereignty. Federal courts of appeals will cite decisions of district courts, even those in other circuits; the Supreme Court may cite the decisions of the inferior courts, *see, e.g.*, City of Richmond v. J.A. Croson Co., 488 U.S. 469, 491, 109 S.Ct. 706, 102 L.Ed.2d 854 (1989) (citing Associated Gen. Contractors of Cal. v. City & County of San Francisco, 813 F.2d 922, 929 (9th Cir.1987)), or those of the state courts, *see, e.g.*, Lujan v. G & G Fire Sprinklers, Inc., 532 U.S. 189, 121 S.Ct. 1446, 1452, 149 L.Ed.2d 391 (2001)(citing J & K Painting Co. v. Bradshaw, 45 Cal.App.4th 1394, 1402, 53 Cal.Rptr.2d 496 (Cal.Ct.App.1996)). It is not unusual to cite the decision of courts in foreign jurisdictions, so long as they speak to a matter relevant to the issue before us. *See, e.g.*, Mozes v. Mozes, 239 F.3d 1067, 1071 (9th Cir.2001). The process even extends to non-case authorities, such as treatises and law review articles. *See id.* at 1071 & n. 7.

Citing a precedent is, of course, not the same as following it; "respectfully disagree" within five words of "learned colleagues" is almost a cliche. After carefully considering and digesting the views of other courts and commentators—often giving conflicting guidance on a novel legal issue—courts will then proceed to follow one line of authority or another, or sometimes strike out in a completely different direction. While we would consider it bad form to ignore contrary authority by failing even to acknowledge its existence, it is well understood that—in the absence of binding precedent—courts may forge a different path than suggested by prior authorities that have considered the issue. So long as the earlier authority is acknowledged and considered, courts are deemed to have complied with their common law responsibilities.

But precedent also serves a very different function in the federal courts today, one related to the horizontal and vertical organization of those courts. *See* John Harrison, *The Power of Congress Over The Rules of Precedent*, 50 Duke L.J. 503 (2000). A district judge may not respectfully (or disrespectfully) disagree with his learned colleagues on his own court of appeals who have ruled on a controlling legal issue, or with Supreme Court Justices writing for a majority of the Court. Binding authority within this regime cannot be considered and cast aside; it is not merely evidence of what the law is. Rather, caselaw on point *is* the law. If a court must decide an issue governed by a prior opinion that constitutes binding authority, the later court is bound to reach the same result, even if it considers the rule unwise or incorrect. Binding authority must be followed unless and until overruled by a body competent to do so.

In determining whether it is bound by an earlier decision, a court considers not merely the "reason and spirit of cases" but also "the letter of particular precedents." *Fisher v. Prince,* 97 Eng. Rep. 876, 876 (K.B.1762). This includes not only the rule announced, but also the facts giving rise to the dispute, other rules considered and rejected and the views expressed in response to any dissent or concurrence. Thus, when crafting binding authority, the precise language employed is often crucial to the contours and scope of the rule announced.[26]

Obviously, binding authority is very powerful medicine. A decision of the Supreme Court will control that corner of the law unless and until the Supreme Court itself overrules or modifies it. Judges of the inferior courts may voice their criticisms, but follow it they must. *See, e.g.,* Ortega v. United States, 861 F.2d 600, 603 & n. 4 (9th Cir.1988) ("This case is squarely controlled by the Supreme Court's recent decision.... [We] agree[ ] with the dissent that [appellant] deserves better treatment from our Government. Unfortunately, legal precedent deprives us of discretion to do equity."). The same is true as to circuit authority, although it usually covers a much smaller geographic area. Circuit law, a concept wholly unknown at the time of the Framing, *see* Danny J. Boggs & Brian P. Brooks, *Unpublished Opinions & the Nature of Precedent,* 4 Green Bag 2d 17, 22 (2000), binds all courts within a particular circuit, including the court of appeals itself. Thus, the first panel to consider an issue sets the law not only for all the inferior courts in the circuit, but also future panels of the court of appeals.

Once a panel resolves an issue in a precedential opinion, the matter is deemed resolved, unless overruled by the court itself sitting en banc, or by the Supreme Court.[28] As *Anastasoff* itself states, a later three-judge panel considering a case that is controlled by the rule announced in an earlier panel's opinion has no choice but to apply the earlier-adopted rule; it may not any more disregard the earlier panel's opinion than it may disregard a ruling of the Supreme Court. *Anastasoff,* 223 F.3d at 904; *see also* Santamaria v. Horsley, 110 F.3d 1352, 1355 (9th Cir.1997) ("It is settled law that one three-judge panel of this court cannot ordinarily reconsider or overrule

**26.** This is consistent with the practice in our court—and all other collegial courts of which we are aware—in which the judges who join an opinion authored by another judge make substantive suggestions, often conditioning their votes on reaching agreement on mutually acceptable language.

**28.** Or, unless Congress changes the law....

the decision of a prior panel."), *rev'd,* 133 F.3d 1242 (9th Cir.) (en banc), *amended by* 138 F.3d 1280 (9th Cir.), *cert. denied,* 525 U.S. 823–24, 119 S.Ct. 68, 142 L.Ed.2d 53 (1998); Montesano v. Seafirst Commercial Corp., 818 F.2d 423, 425–26 (5th Cir.1987) (A "purpose of institutional orderliness [is served] by our insistence that, in the absence of intervening Supreme Court precedent, one panel cannot overturn another panel, regardless of how wrong the earlier panel decision may seem to be."). Designating an opinion as binding circuit authority is a weighty decision that cannot be taken lightly, because its effects are not easily reversed. Whether done by the Supreme Court or the court of appeals through its "unwieldy" and time-consuming en banc procedures, Richard A. Posner, *The Federal Courts: Crisis and Reform* 101 (1985), overruling such authority requires a substantial amount of courts' time and attention—two commodities already in very short supply.

    \* \* \*

## III

While we agree with *Anastasoff* that the principle of precedent was well established in the common law courts by the time Article III of the Constitution was written, we do not agree that it was known and applied in the strict sense in which we apply binding authority today. It may be true, as *Anastasoff* notes, that "judges and lawyers of the day recognized the authority of unpublished decisions even when they were established only by memory or by a lawyer's unpublished memorandum," 223 F.3d at 903, but precedents brought to the attention of the court in that fashion obviously could not serve as the kind of rigid constraint that binding authority provides today. Unlike our practice today, a single case was not sufficient to establish a particular rule of law, and case reporters often filtered out cases that they considered wrong, or inconsistent with their view of how the law *should* develop. The concept of binding case precedent, though it was known at common law, was used exceedingly sparingly. For the most part, common law courts felt free to depart from precedent where they considered the earlier-adopted rule to be no longer workable or appropriate.

Case precedent at common law thus resembled much more what we call persuasive authority than the binding authority which is the backbone of much of the federal judicial system today. The concept of binding precedent could only develop once two conditions were met: The development of a hierarchical system of appellate courts with clear lines of authority, and a case reporting system that enabled later courts to know precisely what was said in earlier opinions. As we have seen, these developments did not come about—either here or in England—until the nineteenth century, long after Article III of the Constitution was written....

A system of strict binding precedent also suffers from the defect that it gives undue weight to the first case to raise a particular issue. This is especially true in the circuit courts, where the first panel to consider an issue and publish a precedential opinion occupies the field, whether or not the lawyers have done an adequate job of developing and arguing the issue.

The question raised by *Anastasoff* is whether one particular aspect of the binding authority principle—the decision of which rulings of an appellate court are binding—is a matter of judicial policy or constitutional imperative. We believe *Anastasoff* erred in holding that, as a constitutional matter, courts of appeals may not decide which of their opinions will be deemed binding on themselves and the courts below them. For the reasons explained, the principle of strict binding authority is itself not constitutional, but rather a matter of judicial policy. Were it otherwise, it would cast doubt on the federal court practice of limiting the binding effect of appellate decisions to the courts of a particular circuit. Circuit boundaries—and the very system of circuit courts—are a matter of judicial administration, not constitutional law. If, as *Anastasoff* suggests, the Constitution dictates that every "declaration of law ... must be applied in subsequent cases to similarly situated parties," 223 F.3d at 900, then the Second Circuit would have no authority to disagree with a ruling of the Eighth Circuit that is directly on point, and the first circuit to rule on a legal issue would then bind not only itself and the courts within its own circuit, but all inferior federal courts.

* * *

Nor is it clear, under the reasoning of *Anastasoff,* how courts could limit the binding effect of their rulings to appellate decisions. Under *Anastasoff* 's reasoning, district court opinions should bind district courts, at least in the same district, or even nationwide. After all, the Constitution vests the same "judicial Power" in all federal courts, so *Anastasoff* 's conclusion that judicial decisions must have precedential effect would apply equally to the thousands of unpublished decisions of the district courts.

No doubt the most serious implication of *Anastasoff* 's constitutional rule is that it would preclude appellate courts from developing a coherent and internally consistent body of caselaw to serve as binding authority for themselves and the courts below them. Writing an opinion is not simply a matter of laying out the facts and announcing a rule of decision. Precedential opinions are meant to govern not merely the cases for which they are written, but future cases as well.

In writing an opinion, the court must be careful to recite all facts that are relevant to its ruling, while omitting facts that it considers irrelevant. Omitting relevant facts will make the ruling unintelligible to those not already familiar with the case; including inconsequential facts can provide a spurious basis for distinguishing the case in the future. The rule of decision cannot simply be announced, it must be selected after due consideration of the relevant legal and policy considerations. Where more than one rule could be followed—which is often the case—the court must explain why it is selecting one and rejecting the others. Moreover, the rule must be phrased with precision and with due regard to how it will be applied in future cases. A judge drafting a precedential opinion must not only consider the facts of the immediate case, but must also envision the countless permutations of facts that might arise in the universe of future cases. Modern opinions generally call for the most precise drafting and re-drafting to ensure that the rule announced sweeps neither too broadly nor too narrowly, and that it does not collide with other binding precedent that bears on the issue. *See* Fred A. Bernstein, *How to Write it Right,* Cal. Lawyer, at 42 (June 2000). Writing a precedential opinion, thus, involves much more than deciding who wins and who loses in a particular case. It is a solemn judicial act that sets the course of the law for hundreds or thousands of litigants and potential litigants. When properly done, it is an exacting and extremely time-consuming task.

It goes without saying that few, if any, appellate courts have the resources to write precedential opinions in every case that comes before them.[33] The Supreme Court certainly does not. Rather, it uses its discretionary review authority to limit its merits docket to a handful of opinions per justice, from the approximately 9000 cases that seek review every Term.[34] While federal courts of appeals generally lack discretionary review authority, they use their authority to decide cases by unpublished—and nonprecedential—dispositions to achieve the same end: They select a manageable number of cases in which to publish precedential opinions, and leave the rest to be decided by unpublished dispositions or judgment orders. In our circuit, published dispositions make up approximately 16 percent of decided cases; in other circuits, the percentage ranges from 10 to 44, the national average being 20 percent. Administrative Office of the United States Courts, *Judicial Business of the United States Courts* 44 tbl. S–3 (2000).

That a case is decided without a precedential opinion does not mean it is not fully considered, or that the disposition does not reflect a reasoned analysis of the issues presented. What it does mean is that the disposition is not written in a way that will be fully intelligible to those unfamiliar with the case, and the rule of law is not announced in a way that makes it suitable for governing future cases. As the Federal Judicial Center recognized, "the judicial time and effort essential for the development of an opinion to be published for posterity and widely distributed is necessarily greater than that sufficient to enable the judge to provide a statement so that the parties can understand the reasons for the decision." Federal Judicial Center, *Standards for Publication of Judicial Opinions* 3 (1973). An unpublished disposition is, more or less, a letter from the court to

---

**33.** As Judge Posner has noted:

Given the workload of the federal courts of appeals today, the realistic choice is not between limited publication, on the one hand, and, on the other, improving and then publishing all the opinions that are not published today; it is between preparing but not publishing opinions in many cases and preparing no opinions in those cases. It is a choice, in other words, between giving the parties reasons for the decision of their appeal and not giving them reasons even though the appeal is not frivolous.

Richard A. Posner, *The Federal Courts: Challenge and Reform* 168–69 (1996).

**34.** The United States Supreme Court decided seventy-seven cases in October Term 1999, which represents less than nine opinions per justice. *Statistics for the Supreme Court's October Term 1999,* 69 U.S.L.W. 3076 (BNA 2000). By comparison, in 1999, each active judge in our court heard an average of 450 cases and had writing responsibility for an average of twenty opinions and 130 unpublished dispositions. . . .

parties familiar with the facts, announcing the result and the essential rationale of the court's decision. Deciding a large portion of our cases in this fashion frees us to spend the requisite time drafting precedential opinions in the remaining cases.

Should courts allow parties to cite to these dispositions, however, much of the time gained would likely vanish. Without comprehensive factual accounts and precisely crafted holdings to guide them, zealous counsel would be tempted to seize upon superficial similarities between their clients' cases and unpublished dispositions. Faced with the prospect of parties citing these dispositions as precedent, conscientious judges would have to pay much closer attention to the way they word their unpublished rulings. Language adequate to inform the parties how their case has been decided might well be inadequate if applied to future cases arising from different facts. And, although three judges might agree on the outcome of the case before them, they might not agree on the precise reasoning or the rule to be applied to future cases. Unpublished concurrences and dissents would become much more common, as individual judges would feel obligated to clarify their differences with the majority, even when those differences had no bearing on the case before them. In short, judges would have to start treating unpublished dispositions—those they write, those written by other judges on their panels, and those written by judges on other panels—as mini-opinions. This new responsibility would cut severely into the time judges need to fulfill their paramount duties: producing well-reasoned published opinions and keeping the law of the circuit consistent through the en banc process. The quality of published opinions would sink as judges were forced to devote less and less time to each opinion.

Increasing the number of opinions by a factor of five, as *Anastasoff* suggests, doesn't seem to us a sensible idea, even if we had the resources to do so. Adding endlessly to the body of precedent—especially binding precedent—can lead to confusion and unnecessary conflict. Judges have a responsibility to keep the body of law "cohesive and understandable, and not muddy[ ] the water with a needless torrent of published opinions." [Citation omitted.] Cases decided by nonprecedential disposition generally involve facts that are materially indistinguishable from those of prior published opinions. Writing a second, third or tenth opinion in the same area of the law, based on materially indistinguishable facts will, at best, clutter up the law books and databases with redundant and thus unhelpful authority. Yet once they are designated as precedent, they will have to be read and analyzed by lawyers researching the issue, materially increasing the costs to the client for absolutely no legitimate reason. Worse still, publishing redundant opinions will multiply significantly the number of inadvertent and unnecessary conflicts, because different opinion writers may use slightly different language to express the same idea. As lawyers well know, even small differences in language can have significantly different implications when read in light of future fact patterns, so differences in phrasing that seem trivial when written can later take on a substantive significance.

The risk that this may happen vastly increases if judges are required to write many more precedential opinions than they do now, leaving much less time to devote to each. Because conflicts—even inadvertent ones—can only be resolved by the exceedingly time-consuming and inefficient process of en banc review, *see* Atonio v. Wards Cove Packing Co., 810 F.2d 1477, 1478–79 (9th Cir.1987) (en banc) (conflict in panel opinions must be resolved by en banc court), *cert. denied*, 485 U.S. 989, 108 S.Ct. 1293, 99 L.Ed.2d 503 (1988), an increase in intracircuit conflicts would leave much less time for us to devote to normal panel opinions. Maintaining a coherent, consistent and intelligible body of caselaw is not served by writing more opinions; it is served by taking the time to make the precedential opinions we do write as lucid and consistent as humanly possible.[39]

## IV

Unlike the *Anastasoff* court, we are unable to find within Article III of the Constitution a requirement that all case dispositions and orders issued by appellate courts be binding authority. On the contrary, we believe that an inherent aspect of our function as Article III judges is managing precedent to develop a coherent body of circuit law to govern litigation in our court and the other courts of this circuit. We agree with *Anastasoff* that we—and all courts—must follow the law. But we do not think that this means we must also make binding law every time we issue a merits decision. The common law has long recognized that certain types of cases do not deserve to be authorities, and that one important aspect of the judicial function is separating the cases that should be precedent from those that should not. Without clearer guidance than that offered in *Anastasoff,* we see no constitutional basis for abdicating this important aspect of our judicial responsibility.

Contrary to counsel's contention, then, we conclude that Rule 36–3 is constitutional. We also find that counsel violated the rule. Nevertheless, we are aware that *Anastasoff* may have cast doubt on our rule's constitutional validity. Our rules are obviously not meant to punish attorneys who, in good faith, seek to test a rule's constitutionality. We therefore conclude that the violation was not willful and exercise our discretion not to impose sanctions.

The order to show cause is DISCHARGED.

---

**39.** *Anastasoff* suggests that the appointment of more judges would enable courts to write binding opinions in every case. *See* 223 F.3d at 904. We take no position as to whether there should be more federal judges, that being a policy question for Congress to decide. We note, however, that Congress would have to increase the number of judges by something like a factor of five to allocate to each judge a manageable number of opinions each year. But adding more judges, and more binding precedents, creates its own set of problems by significant-ly increasing the possibility of conflict within the same circuit as each judge will have an increased body of binding caselaw to consider and reconcile.

That problem, in turn, could be ameliorated by increasing the number of circuits, but that would increase the number of inter-circuit conflicts, moving the problem up the chain of command to the Supreme Court, which likewise does not have the capacity to significantly increase the number of opinions it issues each year. . . .

## Questions

**1.** Is the primary reason to reject *Anastasoff*'s understanding of the "Judicial Power" historical or practical?

**2.** How effectively do the examples Judge Kozinski adduces at note 6 undercut Judge Arnold's contentions regarding the force of precedent?

**3.** Do not Circuit rules like the ones at issue in *Anastasoff* and *Hart v. Massanari* allow courts to adjudicate the rights and obligations of the parties before them in a particular case, without binding the courts to apply the same rule to future parties in like cases? Does Judge Kozinski address this concern?

**4.** Should there be any limits on an appellate court's freedom to decide which of its decisions should "count"? If so, what should they be, and why? See, e.g., Polly J. Price, *Precedent and Judicial Power After the Founding*, 42 B.C.L. Rev. 81 (2000).

## Note—The Debate Over Precedent

Judge Arnold's decision in Anastasoff has sparked controversy among judges, commentators and practicing lawyers. As you have seen, Judge Kozinski adopted an opposing view regarding the constitutional meaning of the "Judicial Power" and whether it contains an implied limitation on the judiciary's classification of unpublished opinions as non-citable. This circuit split is the kind of issue that may necessitate resolution by the Supreme Court or even intervention by Congress.[1]

The responses to non-publication of opinions have ranged. At one end of the spectrum, groups like The Committee for the Rule of Law[2] propound an uncompromising adherence to precedent that they perceive to be founded in the Constitution. They contend that, once decided, cases should be binding. At the other end of the spectrum, some respond that whatever history has to say, it is simply impracticable to write all decisions in a way

**1.** Indeed, the House has held hearings on the subject. See Oversight Hearing on Unpublished Judicial Opinions, Committee on the Judiciary, Subcommittee on Courts, the Internet, and Intellectual Property, June 27, 2002 at http://www.house.gov/judiciary/courts.htm. Representative Coble, the Chair of the Subcommittee, explained:

"no branch of the government, including the third branch, is immune from evaluation.... [W]e are assembled here today, to determine if there is in fact a problem with regard to the administration of justice in our country and, if so, to explore how we should fix or repair the problem.... [W]e are trying to determine if the administrative practices of limited publication and noncitation of opinions among the circuits are fair, both to litigants who want to know what a court was thinking when it rendered a decision, as well as to attorneys attempting to scour the law for precedential authority when advising their clients." Hearing Transcript at http://commdocs.house.gov/committees/judiciary/hju80454.000/hju80454_0f.htm;

The subcommittee heard testimony from Judge Kozinski; Kenneth Schmier, Chairman, Committee for the Rule of Law; Law Professor Arthur Hellman, and Judge Alito of the Third Circuit.

**2.** See www.nonpublication.com.

that makes them worthy of citation. Thus, the argument goes, courts should be able to designate those opinions on which they have expended the necessary time and effort as citable, and conversely, the other opinions as non-citable.

Adopting an intermediate view, Prof. Polly Price proposes that while originalist arguments based on historical sources are rarely determinative, the preponderance of the evidence shows that the Framers believed, and therefore intended the term "Judicial Power" to convey, that judges should "at least begin their reasoning process with prior decided cases."[3] This analysis thus distinguishes between precedent, using caselaw as a starting point, and stare decisis, the degree to which such caselaw is binding.

Prof. Price argues that conflating these two ideas confuses the argument about the meaning of the "Judicial Power" and that those who criticize the Arnold position for its broad-sweeping nature have often fallen into this trap. On the other hand, Prof. Thomas Healy adopts the opposite view and, also arguing from history, writes: "the history of precedent in the common law...demonstrates that stare decisis was not an established doctrine by 1789, nor was it viewed as necessary to check the potential abuse of judicial power."[4]

Prof. Price also contends that critiques of the novelty of Judge Arnold's argument are a red herring. The requirement of precedent is not new; she claims; instead, non-citation rules are a radical development which run against constitutional ideas present since the Founding. She writes: "Most of the rules have come into being in the last several decades in response to dramatically rising caseloads.... [T]he new non-citation rules that consider some judicial decisions not to be precedent are an aberration in our historical practice."[5]

Leaving history aside, much of the debate about Judge Arnold's position has focused on the pragmatic implications of such a rule or constitutional provisions other than the Judicial Power of Art. III. "[T]he commentary unleashed on the heels of the *Anastasoff* opinion has largely ignored Judge Arnold's historical premises, focusing instead on questions of pragmatics, or even constitutional implications under provisions outside of Article III."[6] As one author argues: "The [no-citation] rules violate the First Amendment's guarantees of freedom of speech and of the right to petition for redress of grievances. They also diminish confidence in adjudication, eliminate checks on judicial power, and result in government waste because there is no persuasive reason why taxpayers should pay for the production of opinions they cannot use as precedents."[7]

**3.** Polly J. Price, *Precedent and Judicial Power after the Founding*, 42 B.C. L. Rev. 81, 93 (2000).

**4.** Thomas Healy, *Stare Decisis as a Constitutional Requirement*, 104 W. Va. L. Rev. 43, 43 (2001).

**5.** Price, supra note 3, at 107–08.

**6.** Thomas R. Lee & Lance S. Lehnhof, *The Anastasoff Case and the Judicial Power to "Unpublish" Opinions*, 77 Notre Dame L. Rev. 135, 138–39 (2001).

**7.** David Greenwald & Frederick A. O. Schwartz, *The Censorial Judiciary*, 35 U.C. Davis L. Rev. 1133, 1133–34 (2002).

Indeed, a persuasive criticism of Judge Kozinski's position in *Massanari* is based not on history but on the separation of powers decreed by the Constitution. The governmental structure contemplated by the Framers mandates that the judicial power differ from the legislative power. The judicial power is case specific and applied mostly to past conduct,[8] while the legislative power is general and applied mostly prospectively.

To the extent judges can pick which cases should be binding or even citable, the line between legislative and judicial decision-making blurs. The power to select which decisions will have precedential force undermines the grounding of the judicial function in the application of case law and interpretation of statutes. Such judicial selectivity more closely resembles the discretionary nature and policy focus of the legislative function. We have some comfort that the legislature, as a representative body, will attempt to express the will of the electorate. In the case of appointed judges, however, the same checks and balances are not in place. Thus the separation of powers doctrine contemplates that the judiciary will be constrained by precedent while the legislature will be constrained by the electorate.

The *Anastasoff* debate has also led to the formation of a grass roots organization against nonpublication, as evidenced by the website www.nonpublication.com. The site provides links to over 40 law review articles on the debate as well as cases, court transcripts, press clippings, and a mission statement ("common sense and our sacred constitutions require that the unfettered discipline of stare decisis be restored to the judicial system").[9]

How or whether the issue will be resolved remains to be seen. The *Anastasoff* controversy reflects the pressures of burgeoning judicial caseloads, a problem that is not going to go away anytime soon. The debate also highlights the indeterminacy of resolving constitutional controversies through originalist arguments: each side has relied on a historical account of the founding to support its position. Most important for present purposes, however, the *Anastasoff* debate demonstrates some of the subtleties regarding the distinction between precedent and *stare decisis*, concepts that are often conflated even in the academic literature.

## Questions

**1.** On whose "intent" should we rely if we believe that originalism is dispositive? How do you discern the intent of a legislature or Constitutional convention, especially one that took place over two centuries ago?

**2.** From the point of view of separation of powers, is there a difference between a court's choosing among decided cases which ones will "count" for citation, and choosing whether to hear the case at all? Recall that the U.S. Supreme Court grants only a small fraction of the petitions for certiorari; is this practice problematic?

---

**8.** Equitable remedies such as injunctions could be conceived as applying prospectively.

**9.** Mission Statement at http://www.nonpublication.com (last visited Nov. 5, 2002).

**3.** Do you agree with Prof. Price that opinions should be a starting point for judicial decision-making or should there be a stronger requirement of deference to prior opinions?

**4.** Is it true that taxpayers pay judges to write precedential opinons? What is the link between taxes and the publication of judicial opinions? If a court decides a case on a ground narrower than that advanced by the parties (see, e,g, *Estate of Hemingway v. Random House, supra*), has the court cheated the taxpayers who litigated the claim? The more general set of taxpayers who hoped for the resolution of the broader question? Who *should* be resolving the broader issues that a litigation may implicate?

## B. HOW PRECEDENT WORKS OVER TIME

### 1. EXAMPLE OF A CLAIM'S EVOLUTION: INTENTIONAL INFLICTION OF EMOTIONAL DISTRESS

It should be clear by now that one case standing by itself does not tell us much about the law in a particular field.[1] To know "what the law is" we need to put together all the related cases—to "synthesize" them. The process of synthesis is the most important element in working with case law; one synthesizes decisions for a number of purposes: to write scholarly articles, to write opinion letters, to write briefs—indeed, just about every time one makes a statement about what the law is. In real life, before you synthesize you will need to find the cases; here, this section of the casebook gives you a ready-made, albeit not complete, group of cases for you to synthesize.

The primary objective of this section is to show you how over one hundred years the law relating to liability for intentional infliction of emotional distress has changed as new fact situations have been presented for decision or, more fundamentally, as the social, political and economic environment has evolved and how this change has taken place within our doctrine of precedent, largely without benefit of statute. Your emphasis should be on learning *how* the law has changed, although you should gather as much as time permits as to *why*.

In order to get the most out of this exercise, you should put yourself in the position of the lawyers who had to deal with the law during its development. It is easy to find others' descriptions of what happened, and

---

**1.** For the truth of the matter is a truth so obvious and trite that it is somewhat regularly overlooked by students. *That no case can have a meaning by itself!* Standing alone it gives you no guidance. It can give you no guidance as to how far it carries, as to how much of its language will hold water later. What counts, what gives you leads, what gives you sureness, *that is the background of the other cases* in relation to which you must read the one. They color the language, the technical terms, used in the opinion. But above all they give you the wherewithal to find which of the facts are significant, and in what aspect they are significant, and how far the rules laid down are to be trusted.

Karl Llewellyn, The Bramble Bush 48–9.

why, but resort to such sources will be self-defeating. When you are faced with the task of making your own predictions, it will not be possible to peek ahead; all you will have to go on are the cases decided to date and your own understanding of the process by which law is made and unmade in our system. After each case, then, you should try to synthesize that case and the earlier cases as though they were all the information that was available, and to formulate a "rule of law" that will accommodate these cases.[2] Professor Llewellyn described this process in the context of the required simultaneous existence of "offer" and "acceptance" in the law of contracts by Professor Llewellyn, (The Bramble Bush 49–50):

> The first case involves a man who makes an offer and gets in his revocation before his offer is accepted. The court decides that he cannot be sued upon his promise, and says that no contract can be made unless the minds of both parties are at one at once. The second case involves a man who has made a similar offer and has mailed a revocation, but to whom a letter of acceptance has been sent before his revocation was received. The court holds that he can be sued upon his promise, and says that his offer was being repeated every moment from the time that it arrived until the letter of acceptance was duly mailed. Here are two rules which are a little difficult to put together, and to square with sense, and which are, too, a little hard to square with the two holdings in the cases. We set to work to seek a way out which will do justice to the holdings. We arrive perhaps at this, that it is not necessary for the two minds to be at one at once, if the person who has received an offer thinks, and thinks reasonably, as he takes the last step of acceptance, that the offeror is standing by the offer.

a.   CLAIM REJECTED

# Terwilliger v. Wands

Court of Appeals of New York, 1858.
17 N.Y. 54.

ACTION for slander. The plaintiff proved by La Fayette Wands that the defendant asked him, Wands, what the plaintiff was running to Mrs. Fuller's so much for he knew he went there for no good purpose. Mrs. Fuller was a bad woman, and plaintiff had a regular beaten path across his land to Fuller's; defendant said plaintiff went there to have intercourse with Mrs. Fuller, and that plaintiff would do all he could to keep Mrs. Fuller's husband in the penitentiary so that he could have free access there.

---

**2.**  Moreover, you should do it *before* you discuss the cases in class. In the words of Professor Llewellyn (The Bramble Bush 53):

> it is vital, it is the very basic element of case law study, for you to have done your matching of the cases before you meet with his [the instructor's]. For it is not by watching him juggle the balls that you will learn. It is by matching his results against your own, by criticizing the process you have gone through in the light of the process he is going through. Indeed if you have not tried the game yourself, *you will not follow him.*

The plaintiff proved by Neiper that the defendant said about the same words to that witness, and that he, being an intimate friend of the plaintiff's and a brother-in-law of Mrs. Fuller, communicated to the plaintiff what the defendant had told him, and that the story was all over the country. Other witnesses testified to similar imputations by the defendant, but there was no proof that what the defendant said to them was communicated to the plaintiff.

The only damages proved were that the plaintiff was prostrated in health and unable to attend to business after hearing of the reports circulated by the defendant. A motion for a nonsuit was sustained upon the grounds that the damage, if any, was occasioned by the speaking of the words by the defendant. The judgment was affirmed by the General Term. The plaintiff appealed.

■ STRONG, J. The words spoken by the defendant not being actionable of themselves, it was necessary, in order to maintain the action, to prove that they occasioned special damages to the plaintiff. The special damages must have been the natural, immediate and legal consequence of the words. (*Stark. on Sland. by Wend., 2nd ed.,* 203; 2 *id.* 62, 64; Beach v. Ranney, 2 Hill, 309; Crain v. Petrie, 6 *id.* 522; Kendall v. Stone, 5 *N.Y.* 14.)

The special damages relied upon are not of such a nature as will support the action. The action for slander is given by the law as a remedy for "injuries affecting a man's reputation or good name by malicious, scandalous and slanderous words, tending to his damage and derogation." (3 *Bl.Com.* 123; *Stark, on Sland., Prelim. Obs.* 22–29; 1 *id.* 17, 18.) It is injuries affecting the reputation only which are the subject to the action. In the case of slanderous words actionable *per se,* the law, from their natural and immediate tendency to produce injury, adjudges them to be injurious, though no special loss or damage can be proved. "But with regard to words that do not apparently and upon the face of them import such defamation as will of course be injurious, it is necessary that the plaintiff should aver some particular damage to have happened." (3 *Bl.Com.* 124.) As to what constitutes special damages, Starkie mentions the loss of a marriage, loss of hospitable gratuitous entertainment, preventing a servant or bailiff from getting a place, the loss of customers by a tradesman; and says that in general whenever a person is prevented by the slander from receiving that which would otherwise be conferred upon him, though gratuitously, it is sufficient. (1 *Stark. on Sland.* 195, 202; *Cook's Law of Def.* 22–24.) In Olmsted v. Miller (1 Wend. 506), it was held that the refusal of civil entertainment at a public house was sufficient special damage. So in *Williams v. Hill* (19 Wend. 305), was the fact that the plaintiff was turned away from the house of her uncle and charged not to return until she had cleared up her character. So in Beach v. Ranney, was the circumstance that persons, who had been in the habit of doing so, refused longer to provide fuel, clothing, etc. (2 *Stark, on Ev.* 872, 873.) These instances are sufficient to illustrate the kind of special damage that must result from defamatory words not otherwise actionable to make them so; they are damages produced by, or through, impairing the reputation.

It would be highly impolitic to hold all language, wounding the feelings and affecting unfavorably the health and ability to labor, of another, a ground of action; for that would be to make the right of action depend often upon whether the sensibilities of a person spoken of are easily excited or otherwise; his strength of mind to disregard abusive, insulting remarks concerning him; and his physical strength and ability to bear them. Words which would make hardly an impression on most persons, and would be thought by them, and should be by all, undeserving of notice, might be exceedingly painful to some, occasioning sickness and an interruption of ability to attend to their ordinary avocations. There must be some limit to liability for words not actionable *per se*, both as to the words and the kind of damages; and a clear and wise one has been fixed by the law. The words must be defamatory in their nature; and must in fact disparage the character; and this disparagement must be evidenced by some positive loss arising therefrom directly and legitimately as a fair and natural result. In this view of the law words which do not degrade the character do not injure it, and cannot occasion loss. In *Cook's Law of Def.* (p. 24), it is said: "In order to render the consequence of words spoken special damage, the words must be in themselves disparaging; for if they be innocent the consequence does not follow naturally from the cause." In Kelly v. Partington (5 Barn. & Adol. 645), which was an action for slander, the words in the declaration were "she secreted 1*s.* 6*d.* under the till, stating these are not times to be robbed." It was alleged as special damage that by reason of the speaking of the words a third person refused to take the plaintiff into service. The plaintiff recovered one shilling damages, and the defendant obtained a rule *nisi* for arresting the judgment on the ground that the words, taken in their grammatical sense, were not disparaging to the plaintiff and, therefore, that no special damage could result from them. Denman, Ch. J., said: "The words do not of necessity import, any thing injurious to the plaintiff's character, and we think the judgment must be arrested unless there be something on the face of the declaration from which the court can clearly see that the slanderous matter alleged is injurious to the plaintiff. Where the words are ambiguous, the meaning can be supplied by *innuendo;* but that is not the case here. The rule for arresting the judgment must, therefore be made absolute." Littledale, J., said: "I cannot agree that words laudatory of a party's conduct would be the subject of an action if they were followed by special damage. They must be defamatory or injurious in their nature. *In Comyn's Digest, title 'Action on the case for Defamation'* (D., 730), it is said generally that any words are actionable by which the party has a special damage, but all the examples given in illustration of the rule are of words defamatory in themselves, but not actionable, because they do not subject the party to a temporal punishment. In all the instances put the words are injurious to the reputation of the person of whom they were spoken."

It is true that this element of the action for slander in the case of words not actionable of themselves—that the special damages must flow from impaired reputation—has been overlooked in several modern cases, and loss of health and consequent incapacity to attend to business held sufficient special damage (Bradt v. Towsley, 13 Wend. 253; Fuller v. Fenner, 16 Barb. 333); but these cases are a departure from principle and should not be followed.

Where there is no proof that the character has suffered from the words, if sickness results it must be attributed to apprehension of loss of character, and such fear of harm to character, with resulting sickness and bodily prostration, cannot be such special damage as the law requires for the action. The loss of character must be a substantive loss, one which has actually taken place.

■ ROOSEVELT, J., dissented.

## Murray v. Gast Lithographic & Engraving Co.

Common Pleas of New York, 1894.
8 Misc. 36, 28 N.Y.S. 271.

[Re-read the excerpt from this decision included in the majority opinion in *Roberson v. Rochester Folding Box, supra* at pp. 85, 89]

### Questions

**1.**  What is the difference between "special damage" and the harm the *Terwilliger* plaintiff claimed to suffer?

**2.**  Why do the *Terwilliger* and *Murray v. Gast* courts reject the plaintiffs' claims? Does their reasoning foreclose all claims for intentional infliction of emotional distress?

b.   CLAIM SUSTAINED IF DEFENDANT OWED A SPECIAL DUTY TO PLAINTIFF

## Gillespie v. Brooklyn Heights R. Co.

Court of Appeals of New York, 1904.
178 N.Y. 347, 70 N.E. 857.

APPEAL from a judgment of the Appellate Division of the Supreme Court in the second judicial department, entered March 20, 1903, affirming a judgment in favor of defendant entered upon a verdict directed by the court in favor of plaintiff for nominal damages.

On the twenty-sixth of December, 1900, the plaintiff, who was a practicing physician, boarded one of the defendant's cars at the corner of Nostrand avenue and Fulton street at about 10:20 in the morning. As to what thereafter occurred, the plaintiff testified: "I know who the conductor was on that car, Conductor Wright. He came to collect my fare just a few minutes after I got on the car. I gave him a twenty-five cent piece and said to him, 'A transfer, please, to Reid Avenue.' Just at that moment a lady on the opposite side called to him. He crossed and he went to punch a transfer and I thought it was mine, and I said to him, 'Please don't do that until I speak with you.' He paid no attention. After he gave the lady her transfer I said to him, 'Won't you please come here? I wish to speak to you about the transfer?' So he came across very growly and roughly, and wanted to know, 'What is the matter with yez?' I said, 'Won't you please tell me—I don't know much about those streets away up here—which would be the nearest, Reid Avenue or Sumner Avenue, to Stuyvesant Avenue.' He said, 'We don't have any Reid Avenue transfers; we transfer at Sumner Avenue.' 'Well,' I said then, 'I thank you; please give me a transfer for Sumner Avenue and my change,' and he actually hollered at me, 'What change?' I said, 'The money I gave you, twenty-five cents, and I want my change,' and he put his hands in his pocket and he pulled out a whole handful of pennies or nickels; he said, 'do you see any twenty-five cents there?' He said, 'It is the likes of ye—you are a dead beat; you are a swindler. I know the likes of ye;' he said, 'You didn't give me twenty-five cents.' The lady that sat next to me set the conductor right. She said to him, 'I am sure, sir, she gave you a quarter of a dollar; I saw her give it to you,' and he turned—'Well, perhaps you are a friend of hers.' Then he said that dead beats like me, he knew that every day they were traveling on the cars; he knew the swindlers and the dead beats—'But you can't dead beat me. I know you; you belong to them,' and he said then, 'Why, only here the other day, I had just such a woman as you trying to dead beat me out of money,' and I said, 'I want my change and I don't want such insolence.' Then he walked back and two gentlemen got on the car, and he called the attention of those two gentlemen to me and said, pointing to me—I went to the door, and he was telling them how I was trying to swindle him, 'But,' he said, 'I know them; they are all dead beats; she can't beat me.' I said to him, 'Look here, sir, I know President Rossiter, and I shall make a complaint of you,' and he came over close to me—he said, 'Ah, the likes of you,' he said. 'You couldn't make a complaint to President Rossiter,' he said: 'I have been on this road too long for you to have any authority with him—no, no.' 'Well,' I said, 'I shall tell him,' and I went back and sat down.''

The plaintiff further and in substance testified that she noticed that there was a smell of whisky in the conductor's breath; that he did not give her her change at all; that he gave her no transfer; that he said nothing except merely that he had nothing to do with her, and that ''I was a dead beat and a swindler.'' She then testified as to her efforts to see President Rossiter; that when she reached his office she was about four miles from home; that she walked that distance because she had no money with which to pay her fare; that she became sick, was confined to the bed for two days, and as to its effect upon her business. All this evidence was undisputed.

At the close of the plaintiff's case the defendant made a motion for a dismissal of the complaint, and the court said: ''The allegation of the complaint is that it was done maliciously by the servant of the corporation, so that takes it out of the action against the corporation anyway, so far as the slander part of it is concerned. The only question now is whether she is entitled to recover the amount that she paid for the fare.'' The plaintiff claimed she was entitled to recover more. The court thereupon said: ''On the testimony as it stands they (the company) did receive it; it is uncontradicted now that they did receive it. I think I will direct a verdict for the twenty cents if you (referring to the defendant's counsel) want to.''

The plaintiff excepted to the direction of a verdict and asked to go to the jury "upon the facts in the case, upon the wrong and the wrongful detention of this woman's money, and the suffering occasioned by it," and the court directed a verdict for the plaintiff for twenty cents, and held that that was the extent to which the railroad company was liable and that "the other damages, if any have grown out of it, are not the proximate result of the act of the conductor." The verdict was directed with the consent of the defendant's counsel.

■ MARTIN, J. The principal and practically the only question involved upon this appeal is whether the plaintiff was entitled to recover for the tort or breach of contract proved, an amount in excess of the sum she actually overpaid the defendant's conductor. Confessedly the plaintiff was a passenger on the defendant's car and entitled to be carried over its road. That at the time of this occurrence the relation of carrier and passenger existed between the defendant and the plaintiff is not denied. The latter gave the conductor a quarter of a dollar from which to take her fare, he received it, but did not return her the twenty cents change to which she was entitled. She subsequently asked him for it, when he, in an abusive and impudent manner, not only refused to pay it, but also grossly insulted her by calling her a dead beat and a swindler, and by the use of other insulting and improper language, even after a fellow-passenger had informed him that she had given him the amount she claimed.

In this case there was obviously a breach of the defendant's contract and of its duty to its passenger. It was its duty to receive any coin or bill not in excess of the amount permitted to be tendered for fare on its car under its rules and regulations, and to make the change and return it to the plaintiff or person tendering the money for the fare. That certainly must have been a part of the contract entered into by the defendant, and the refusal of the conductor to return her change was a tortious act upon his part, performed by him while acting in the line of his duty as the defendant's servant. To that extent, at least, the contract between the parties was broken, and as an incident to and accompanying that breach, the language and tortious acts complained of were employed and performed by the defendant's conductor.

This brings us to the precise question whether, in an action to recover damages for the breach of that contract and for the tortious acts of the conductor in relation thereto, the conduct of such employee and his treatment of the plaintiff at the time may be considered upon the question of damages and in aggravation thereof. That the plaintiff suffered insult and indignity at the hands of the conductor, and was treated disrespectfully and undecorously by him under such circumstances as to occasion mental suffering, humiliation, wounded pride and disgrace, there can be little doubt. At least the jury might have so found upon the evidence before them.

This question was treated on the argument as a novel one, and as requiring the establishment of a new principle of law to enable the plaintiff to recover damages in excess of the amount retained by the defendant's conductor which rightfully belonged to her. In that, we think counsel were at fault, and that the right to such a recovery is established beyond question, as will be seen by the authorities which we shall presently consider. The consideration of this general question involves two propositions: The first relates to the duties of carriers to their passengers; and the second to the rule of damages when there has been a breach of such duty.

The relation between a carrier and its passenger is more than a mere contract relation, as it may exist in the absence of any contract whatsoever. Any person rightfully on the cars of a railroad company is entitled to protection by the carrier, and any breach of its duty in that respect is in the nature of a tort and recovery may be had in an action of tort as well as for a breach of the contract. (2 Sedgwick on Damages, 637.) In considering the duties of carriers to their passengers, we find that the elementary writers have often discussed this question, and that it has frequently been the subject of judicial consideration. Thus in Booth on Street Railways (§ 372) it is said: "The contract on the part of the company is to safely carry its passengers and to compensate them for all unlawful and tortious injuries inflicted by its servants. It calls for safe carriage, for safe and respectful treatment from the carrier's servants, and for immunity from assaults by them, or by other persons if it can be prevented by them. No matter what the motive is which incites the servant of the carrier to commit an improper act towards the passenger during the existence of the relation, the master is liable for the act and its natural and legitimate consequences. Hence, it is responsible for the insulting conduct of its servants, which stops short of actual violence." * * *

Having thus considered a portion of the elementary authorities relating to this question, we will now consider a few of the many decided cases relating to the same subject. In Chamberlain v. Chandler (3 Mason, 242, 245), Judge STORY, who delivered the opinion of the court, in discussing the duties, relations and responsibilities which arise between the carrier and passenger, said: "In respect to passengers, the case of the master is one of peculiar responsibility and delicacy. Their contract with him is not for mere ship room, and personal existence, on board, but for reasonable food, comforts, necessaries and kindness. It is a stipulation, not for toleration merely, but for respectful treatment, for that decency of demeanor, which constitutes the charm of social life, for that attention, which mitigates evils without reluctance, and that promptitude, which administers aid to distress. In respect to females, it proceeds yet farther, it includes an implied stipulation against general obscenity, that immodesty of approach which borders on lasciviousness, and against that wanton disregard of the feelings, which aggravates every evil, and endeavors by the excitement of terror, and cool malignancy of conduct, to inflict torture upon susceptible minds. * * * It is intimated that all these acts, though wrong in morals, are yet acts which the law does not punish; that if the person is untouched, if the acts do not amount to an assault and battery, they are not to be redressed. The law looks on them as unworthy of its cognizance. The master is at liberty to inflict the most severe mental sufferings, in the most tyrannical manner, and yet if he withholds a blow, the victim may be crushed by his unkindness. He commits nothing within the reach of civil jurisprudence. My opinion is, that the law involves no such absurdity. It is rational and just. It gives compensation for mental sufferings occasioned by acts of wanton injustice, equally whether they operate by way of direct, or of consequential, injuries. In each case the contract of the passengers for the voyage is in substance violated; and the wrong is to be redressed as a cause of damage."

In Cole v. Atlanta and West Point R.R. Co. (102 Ga. 474, 477) it was held that it was the unquestionable duty of a railroad company to protect a passenger against insult or injury from its conductor, and that the unprovoked use by a conductor to a passenger of opprobrious words and abusive language tending to humiliate the passenger or subject him to mortification, gives to the latter a right of action against the company. In that case it was said: "The carrier's liability is not confined to assaults committed by its servants, but it extends also to insults, threats, and other disrespectful conduct." In Goddard v. Grand Trunk R. Co. (57 Maine, 202, 213) it was held that a common carrier of passengers is responsible for the misconduct of his servant towards a passenger. In that case, WALTON, J., delivering the opinion of the court, said: "The carrier's obligation is to carry his passenger safely and properly, and to treat him respectfully, and if he intrusts the performance of this duty to his servants, the law holds him responsible for the manner in which they execute the trust. The law seems to be now well settled that the carrier is obliged to protect his passenger from violence and insult, from whatever source arising. * * * He must not only protect his passenger against the violence and insults of strangers and co-passengers, but *a fortiori*, against the violence and insults of his own servants. If this duty to the passenger is not performed, if this protection is not furnished, but, on the contrary, the passenger is assaulted and insulted, through the negligence or the willful misconduct of the carrier's servant, the carrier is necessarily responsible," citing Howe v. Newmarch (12 Allen, 55); Moore v. Fitchburg R.R. Co. (4 Gray, 465); Seymour v. Greenwood (7 Hurl. & Nor. 355); M. & M.R.R. Co. v. Finney (10 Wis. 388); Penn. R.R. Co. v. Vandiver (42 Penn.St. 365); P. & R.R.R. Co. v. Derby (14 How. [U.S.] 468); P., F.W. & C. Ry. Co. v. Hinds (53 Penn.St. 512); Flint v. N. & N.Y. Transportation Co. (34 Conn. 554); Landreaux v. Bel. (5 La. [O.S.] 434); B. & O. R.R. Co. v. Blocher (27 Md. 277).

The duties arising between a carrier and passenger have been several times discussed in this state, as in Stewart v. Brooklyn and Crosstown R.R. Co. (90 N.Y. 588, 590), where it was said: "By the defendant's contract with the plaintiff, it had undertaken to carry him safely and to treat him respectfully; and while a common carrier does not undertake to insure against injury from every possible danger, he does undertake to protect the passenger against any injury arising from the negligence or willful misconduct of its servants while engaged in performing a duty which the carrier owes to the passenger. * * * 'The carrier's obligation is to carry his passenger safely, and properly, and to treat him respectfully, and if he intrusts this duty to his servants, the law holds him responsible for the manner in which they execute the trust.' " The court then quoted with approval the decision in Nieto v. Clark (1 Cliff. 145, 149) where it was said: "In respect to female passengers, the contract proceeds yet further, and includes an implied stipulation that they shall be protected against obscene conduct, lascivious behavior, and every immodest and libidinous approach. * * * A common carrier undertakes absolutely to protect his passengers against the misconduct of their own servants engaged in executing the contract." Subsequently in Dwinelle v. N.Y.C. & H.R. R.R. Co. (120 N.Y. 117, 125) the same doctrine was held and the foregoing portion of the opinion in the *Stewart* case was quoted and reaffirmed by this court. It was then added: "These and numerous other cases hold that no matter what the motive is which incites the servant of the carrier to commit an unlawful or improper act toward the passenger during the existence of the relation of carrier and passenger, the carrier is liable for the act and its natural and legitimate consequences." Again, in Palmeri v. Manhattan R. Co. (133 N.Y. 261, 266) it was held that the corporation is liable for the acts of injury and insult by an employee, although in departure from the authority conferred or implied, if they occur in the course of the employment. In that case the employee alleged that the plaintiff was a counterfeiter and a common prostitute, placed his hand upon her and detained her for a while, but let her go without having her arrested. The action was to recover damages for unlawful imprisonment accompanied by the words alleged to have been spoken. This court held she was entitled to recover. The judge then said: "Though injury and insult are acts in departure from the authority conferred, or implied, nevertheless, as they occur in the course of the employment, the master becomes responsible for the wrong committed." The foregoing authorities render it manifest that the defendant was not only liable to the plaintiff for the money wrongfully retained by its conductor, but also for any injury she suffered from the insulting and abusive language and treatment received at his hands.

This brings us to the consideration of the elements of damages in such a case, and what may be considered in determining their amount. Among the elements of compensatory damages for such an injury are the humiliation and injury to her feelings which the plaintiff suffered by reason of the insulting and abusive language and treatment she received, not, however, including any injury to her character resulting therefrom.

In Shepard v. Chicago, R.I. & P.R. Co. (77 Iowa, 54) the court charged the jury, "When a passenger is wrongfully compelled to leave a train, and suffer insult and abuse, the law does not exactly measure his damages, but it authorizes the jury to consider the injured feelings of the party, the indignity endured, the humiliation, wounded pride, mental suffering, and the like, and to allow such sum as the jury may say is right," and it was held that his instruction was not subject to the objection that it authorized an allowance of exemplary damages, because damages may properly be allowed for mental suffering caused by indignity and outrage, and such damages are compensatory and not exemplary.

After this somewhat extended review of the authorities bearing upon the subject, we are led irresistibly to the conclusion that the defendant is liable for the insulting and abusive treatment the plaintiff received at the hands of its servant; that she is entitled to recover compensatory damages for the humiliation and injury to her feelings occasioned thereby, and that the trial court erred in directing a verdict for the plaintiff for twenty cents only and in refusing to submit the case to the jury.

The judgments of the Appellate Division and trial court should be reversed and a new trial granted, with costs to abide the event.

■ Gray, J. (dissenting.) I dissent; because I think it is extending unduly the doctrine of a common carrier's liability in making it answerable in damages for the slanderous words spoken by one of its agents.

■ Bartlett, Haight and Cullen, JJ., concur with Martin, J.; Parker, Ch. J., and O'Brien, J., concur with Gray, J.

Judgments reversed, etc.

## De Wolf v. Ford

Court of Appeals of New York, 1908.
193 N.Y. 397, 86 N.E. 527.

■ Werner, J. As no evidence was taken at the trial, the dismissal of the complaint compels us to assume the truth of all the allegations of fact contained in that pleading. Sheridan v. Jackson, 72 N.Y. 170; Baylies Trial Pr. (2d ed.) 247. The facts which must, therefore, be regarded as established for the purposes of this review are that the relation of innkeeper and guest existed between the defendants and the plaintiff at the time when the servant of the former forced his way into the room of the latter; that this forcible entry was made without invitation from the guest and against her protest; that she was there subjected to the mortification of exposing her person in scant attire, and to the ignominy of being accused of immoral conduct; that she and her visitor were ordered to depart from the hotel, and that all this was done by the defendants' servant without justification and in the course of his regular employment. If the defendants, in these circumstances, are not to be held responsible, it must be upon the theory that they owed no duty to the plaintiff in respect of her convenience, privacy, safety and comfort while she was their guest, and that an innkeeper is immune from liability for any maltreatment which he or his servants may inflict upon a guest be it ever so wilful or flagrant. We think it may safely be asserted that this has never been the law, and that no principle so repugnant to common decency and justice can ever find lodgment in any enlightened system of jurisprudence.

The innkeeper holds himself out as able and willing to entertain guests for hire, and, in the absence of a specific contract, the law implies that he will furnish such entertainment as the character of his inn and reasonable attention to the convenience and comfort of his guests will afford. If the guest is assigned to a room upon the express or implied understanding that he is to be the sole occupant thereof during the time that it is set apart for his use, the innkeeper retains a right of access thereto only at such proper times and for such reasonable purposes as may be necessary in the general conduct of the inn or in attending to the needs of the particular guest. When a guest is assigned to a room for his exclusive use, it is his for all proper purposes and at all times until he gives it up. This exclusive right of use and possession is subject to such emergent and occasional entries as the innkeeper and his servants may find it necessary to make in the reasonable discharge of their duties; but these entries must be made with due regard to the occasion and at such times and in such manner as are consistent with the rights of the guest. One of the things which a guest for hire at a public inn has the right to insist upon is respectful and decent treatment at the hands of the innkeeper and his servants. That is an essential part of the contract whether it is express or implied. This right of the guest necessarily implies an obligation on the part of the innkeeper that neither he nor his servants will abuse or insult the guest, or indulge in any conduct or speech that may unnecessarily bring upon him physical discomfort or distress of mind.

Upon the facts of record, considered in the light of this very general statement of the rules which govern the relation of innkeeper and guest, it is clear that the defendants were guilty of a most flagrant breach of duty towards the plaintiff. As a guest for hire in the inn of the defendants the plaintiff was entitled to the exclusive and peaceable possession of the room assigned to her, subject only to such proper intrusions by the defendants and their servants as may have been necessary in the regular and orderly conduct of the inn, or under some commanding emergency. Had such an emergency arisen, calling for immediate and unpremeditated action on the part of the defendants or their servants, in conserving the safety or protection of the plaintiff or of other guests, or of the building in which they were housed, the usual rules of decency, propriety, convenience or comfort might have been disregarded without subjecting the defendants to liability for mistake of judgment or delinquency in conduct; but for all other purposes their occasional or regular entries into the plaintiff's room were subject to the fundamental consideration that it was for the time being her room, and that she was entitled to respectful and considerate treatment at their hands. Such treatment necessarily implied an observance by the defendants of the properties as to the time and manner of entering the plaintiff's room, and of civil deportments towards her when such an entry was either necessary or proper. Instead of acting according to these simple rules the servant of the defendants forced his way into the plaintiff's room, under conditions which would have caused any woman, except the most shameless harlot, a degree of humiliation and suffering that only a pure and modest woman can properly describe. Not content with that, the servant castigated the plaintiff with opprobrious and offensive epithets, imputing to her immorality and unchastity, and, as a fitting climax to such an episode, ordered the plaintiff to leave the inn.

The majority opinion handed down by the Appellate Division, in which the dismissal of the complaint was sustained, seems to be based upon the theory that under the common law the innkeeper is not responsible for the safety of his guest for hire, and as authority for that view it cites Calye's Case, 8 Coke's Rep. 63. All that appears to have been decided in that case is that the innkeeper is under an absolute duty to safely keep the chattels brought to the inn and intrusted to him by his guest. There is a dictum in the opinion to the effect that if the guest be beaten in the inn, the innkeeper shall not answer for it; but under no reasonable construction could that language be held to mean that an innkeeper and his servants might assault a guest and yet not be liable. There may doubtless be many conditions under which a guest at an inn may be assaulted or insulted by another guest or by an outsider without subjecting the innkeeper to liability, but if it ever was thought to be the law that an innkeeper and his servants have the right to wilfully assault, abuse or maltreat a guest, we think the time has arrived when it may very properly and safely be changed to accord with a more modern conception of the relation of innkeeper and guest. We think it would be startling, to say the least, to announce it as the law of this state that an innkeeper and his male servants may invade the room of a female guest at any hour of the day or night without her consent, in utter disregard of every law of decency and modesty, and that the necessity for such an extraordinary right lies in the rule that an innkeeper must be permitted to control every part of his inn for the protection of all his guests. Such a doctrine, so far from holding an innkeeper to a reasonable responsibility in the quasi public business which he is permitted to carry on, would clothe him with dangerous prerogatives permitted to no other class of men.

We conclude, therefore, that the invasion of the plaintiff's room in the defendants' inn and the treatment to which she was there subjected under the circumstances described in the complaint constituted a violation of the duty which the defendants owed to the plaintiff and for which they may be held liable if the facts alleged are established by proof. The complaint, although somewhat in artificial in form, sets forth all the facts necessary to such a cause of action. The measure of liability, if any, will be purely compensatory and not punitive, the plaintiff's right to recover being confined to such injury to her feelings and such personal humiliation as she may have suffered. Gillespie v. Brooklyn Heights R. Co., 178 N.Y. 347, 102 Am.St.Rep. 503, 66 L.R.A. 618. That is the extent to which the defendants' liability may fairly be said to spring from their breach of duty. Any remedy beyond that which the plaintiff may seek to assert must be invoked in a different form of action. The gravamen of the action at bar is not the alleged slanderous defamation of the plaintiff, but the defendants' breach of the duty which it owed to the plaintiff and the injury which was directly caused thereby.

## Questions

**1.**  Is the harm caused by the insulting behavior of a railroad employee any less abstract and ill-defined than the harm caused by the insulting behavior of a neighbor?

**2.**  Why does it make a difference if the person causing the emotional harm is in a special relationship, such as that of a common carrier or an inn-keeper, with the plaintiff?

**3.**  In *Gillespie,* the majority cited Palmeri v. Manhattan R. Co. in support of the liability of the railroad for "acts of injury and insult" committed by its employee in the course of his employment. Judge Gray was the author of the *Palmeri* decision. Yet he dissented in *Gillespie.* Why, do you suppose?

**4.**  In *Gillespie,* the New York Court of Appeals divided 4–3. A mere four years later, in De Wolf v. Ford, the court was unanimous. Why?

c.  CLAIM SUSTAINED IF THE WILLFUL CONDUCT CAUSING THE EMOTIONAL DISTRESS WAS INDEPENDENTLY WRONGFUL

# Garrison v. Sun Printing & Publishing Ass'n

Court of Appeals of New York, 1912.
207 N.Y. 1, 100 N.E. 430.

■ HISCOCK, J. By demurrer to one of the purported causes of action set forth in the complaint, the question is presented whether a husband may recover for loss of services of his wife caused by her sickness resulting from mental distress, which in turn was caused by the defendant's willful and malicious publication concerning her of defamatory words actionable per se. There is no question but that the published words are libelous per se, and, whatever facts may be established on a trial, we must assume for the purposes of this appeal, in accordance with defendant's admissions, concededly to be implied from its demurrer, that the defendant not only published them of and concerning plaintiff's wife, but that it did so "wickedly and maliciously and intentionally and willfully," for thus it is alleged in the complaint.

Inasmuch as plaintiff's right to recover, if at all under the circumstances, must in effect be derived through his wife, it will be important in the first place to inquire whether the wife herself might recover for mental distress and physical sufferings resulting from the willful and malicious publication of such libelous words.

It was early established in this state, by decisions which do not appear to have been overruled or limited, that an action to recover for the utterance of defamatory words, not actionable in themselves, could not be sustained by proof of mental distress and physical pain suffered by the complainant as a result thereof. Terwilliger v. Wands, 17 N.Y. 54, 72 Am.Dec. 420; Wilson v. Goit, 17 N.Y. 442. And the same doctrine seems to have prevailed in England. Alsop v. Alsop, 5 H. & N. 534, 539; Lynch v. Knight, 9 H. of L. Cases, 577, 592.

On a superficial examination of the opinion in Terwilliger v. Wands, and on which rested the decision in Wilson v. Goit, it would seem to be founded on reasons which would be as applicable to a case of defamatory words actionable in themselves as to one where the words were not thus in themselves actionable and required proof of special damages. It was held that special damages of the kind stated and of which recovery was there being sought were not such natural, immediate, and legal consequences of the words spoken as to sustain the action. A more careful examination, however, discloses that the real and full theory on which a recovery was refused was that an action for slander or libel is brought to recover fundamentally for injury to character, and that the special damages necessary to sustain such an action must flow from disparaging and injuring it; that illness "was not, in a legal view, a natural, ordinary one (consequence), as it does not prove that the plaintiff's character was injured. The slander may not have been credited by or had the slightest influence upon any one unfavorable to the plaintiff." It was further remarked that "this element of an action for slander in a case of words not actionable of themselves"—that the special damages must flow from impaired reputation—had been overlooked in several cases, but that, nevertheless, "where there is *no proof that the character has suffered* from the words, if sickness results it must be attributed to apprehension of loss of character, and such fear of harm to character, with resulting sickness and bodily prostration, cannot be such special damage as the law requires for the action. The loss of character must be a substantive loss, one which has actually taken place." 17 N.Y. 62, 63, 72 Am.Dec. 420.

Both the Terwilliger and the Wilson Cases took pains to limit their effect to cases of defamatory words not actionable in themselves. Their plain intent was to declare that an action of libel or slander involves as its very foundation an injury to character; that where the language complained of is not of such a character that the law presumes an injury, but requires proof of special damages, this requirement cannot be satisfied by simply proving that the plaintiff had been made sick, there being no proof whatever of injury to the character, which involves the effect of the defamatory words on third persons rather than on the complainant himself. Hamilton v. Eno, 16 Hun. 599, 601. It will be seen that this reasoning does not apply to a case where the words are actionable in themselves because there the law presumes an injury to character which of itself will sustain an action, and proof of mental or physical suffering is presented as an element of additional or special damages accompanying or resulting from the injury to character thus presumed.

While the further proposition does not appear to have been specifically decided in this state, I have no doubt that a plaintiff, being entitled to recover compensatory damages for mental distress resulting from the publication of defamatory words actionable in themselves, may likewise recover for physical sufferings brought about by or attending such mental distress. It is true that the physical sufferings as in this case may be removed one step further from the wrong than the mental disturbance which gives rise to it; but this fact of itself does not prevent a recovery provided these damages otherwise come within the rules applicable to such a subject.

I think the rule must be regarded as well recognized that in an action brought for the redress of a wrong intentionally, willfully, and maliciously committed, the wrongdoer will be held responsible for the injuries which he has directly caused, even though they lie beyond the limit of natural and apprehended results as established in cases where the injury was unintentional. Eten v. Luyster, 60 N.Y. 252, 260; Williams v. Underhill, 63

App.Div. 223, 226, 71 N.Y.Supp. 291; Putnam v. Broadway & Seventh Ave. R.R. Co., 55 N.Y. 108, 119, 14 Am.Rep. 190; Milwaukee & St. P. Ry. Co. v. Kellogg, 94 U.S. 469, 475, 24 L.Ed. 256; Spade v. Lynn, etc., R.R. Co., 168 Mass. 285, 295, 47 N.E. 88, 38 L.R.A. 512, 60 Am.St.Rep. 393; Lehrer v. Elmore, 100 Ky. 56, 60, 37 S.W. 292; Meagher v. Driscoll, 99 Mass. 281, 96 Am.Dec. 759; Swift v. Dickinson, 31 Conn. 285.

In Spade v. Lynn, etc., R.R. Co., supra, the court, after affirming the rule that in an action for negligence there could be no recovery for physical sufferings resulting from mere fright and mental disturbance, said: "It is hardly necessary to add that this decision does not reach those classes of action where an intention to cause mental distress or to hurt the feelings is shown or is reasonably to be inferred, as for example in cases of * * * slander."

In Burt v. McBain, supra, which was an action to recover damages for the utterance of words similar to those alleged in this case and like the latter made actionable per se by statute, it was held that injury in mind and health were such natural results of such an utterance that they might be shown as an element of damages without even a special declaration thereof.

In Swift v. Dickinson, supra, it was held that a plaintiff might recover damages for physical sufferings caused by the utterance of words actionable per se.

In the *Terwilliger* and *Wilson* cases, already quoted from, it is fairly to be inferred from the pains with which those decisions were limited to cases of words not actionable per se that a different rule would apply and a recovery be allowed for physical sufferings and mental distress resulting from the defamatory utterance of words actionable in themselves.

Reaching the conclusion, as I therefore do, that the wife might have recovered damages for the mental distress and physical sufferings caused by the publication of defendant's libel, it follows that plaintiff as her husband may maintain this action for loss of society and services. He had a right to these. The services were presumably of pecuniary value to him, and any wrong by which he was deprived thereof was a wrong done to his rights and interests for which he may recover damages. Cregin v. Brooklyn Crosstown R.R. Co., 75 N.Y. 192, 31 Am.Rep. 459; Reynolds v. Robinson, 64 N.Y. 589; Wilson v. Goit, cited *supra*; Olmsted v. Brown, 12 Barb. 657.

### Questions

1.  Has *Garrison* followed *Terwilliger,* or quietly overruled it?

2.  What is the basis of the husband's claim?

## Beck v. Libraro

Supreme Court, Appellate Division, Second Department, 1927.
220 App.Div. 547, 221 N.Y.S. 737.

■ KAPPER, J. The action is for damages for alleged personal injuries attributable to the defendant's act in discharging a loaded gun from the window of his home into and through a window of plaintiff's apartment while she was at home. The defendant was successful in his motion, made under rule 106 of the Rules of Civil Practice, to dismiss the complaint for failure to state a cause of action.

The complaint charges that the defendant "assaulted" plaintiff. This conclusion of fact is followed by allegations showing that the defendant fired this gun into the plaintiff's apartment several times, in doing which the windows were broken; the bullets struck various parts of a room in which the plaintiff was, and broke household articles therein. Plaintiff also alleged that, while the defendant did this shooting, she was lying in bed, having but a few moments before given birth to a child. The plaintiff was not shot, but alleged that defendant's act or acts caused her extreme fright, nervous shock, and hysteria, and resulted in serious illness to her. The complaint also sets forth the conclusion that the defendant's conduct was wanton, reckless, unlawful, and mischievous, and was committed without regard for plaintiff's safety, when the defendant knew, from the lighted apartment in which plaintiff was, that she was therein at the time, or that he should have known that an occupant was therein.

\* \* \*

Ignoring the allegation of assault, the other acts charged in the complaint are sufficient to constitute a cause of action, in my opinion. The defendant relies on the well-known case of Mitchell v. Rochester Railway Co., 151 N.Y. 107, 45 N.E. 354, 34 L.R.A. 781, 56 Am.St.Rep. 604, where it was held that a recovery of damages may not be had for injuries sustained by fright occasioned by the negligence of another, where there is no immediate personal injury. In that case, while the plaintiff was standing upon a street crosswalk, awaiting an opportunity to board an approaching street car drawn by horses, the approaching horses turned to the right and so close to the plaintiff as to result in her finding herself standing between the horses' heads when they were stopped, and her testimony was that, from the fright and excitement caused by the approach and proximity of the team, she became unconscious and ill, and that a miscarriage followed.

That case obviously was one of negligence in the want of ordinary prudence, as ordinarily understood and accepted in law, and involved no element of wantonness or willfulness. Here, however, there is a great deal more. The defendant's act of shooting this gun through the lighted windows of plaintiff's apartment was so wanton, reckless, and mischievous as to constitute an apparent disregard of human safety. This is shown by a mere recital of the facts set forth in the complaint, even without the conclusion alleged that such was the character of the defendant's wrongdoing. We have held (Preiser v. Wielandt, 48 App.Div. 569, 570, 62 N.Y.S. 890) that the doctrine of the Mitchell Case, supra, applies only to actions based on negligence, and not to cases of willful tort, and that, where the defendant's act was in and of itself wrongful, the fact that the injury started in fright is not a ground for denying a recovery of damages. Our decision in the case cited was followed by the First Department in Williams

v. Underhill, 63 App.Div. 223, 226, 71 N.Y.S. 291. In this view, I think the complaint states a cause of action, and that its dismissal was error.

### Question

Why should it make a difference that the wrongful conduct underpinning the claim for emotional distress was intentional rather than negligent? We will return to this issue when we consider Battalla v. State, the decision which overruled the *Mitchell* case, infra, part II.B.2

### d.   CLAIM SUSTAINED EVEN IF THE WILLFUL CONDUCT CAUSING THE EMOTIONAL DISTRESS WAS NOT OTHERWISE WRONGFUL

## Flamm v. Van Nierop

Supreme Court, Westchester County, 1968.
56 Misc.2d 1059, 291 N.Y.S.2d 189.

■ DILLON, J.

The defendant moves to dismiss the first two causes of action alleged in the complaint for insufficiency in law. It is alleged in the first cause of action that on numerous occasions since October, 1966, the defendant has done the following: Dashed at the plaintiff in a threatening manner in various public places, with "threatening gestures, grimaces, leers, distorted faces and malign looks," accompanied by "ridiculous utterances and laughs"; driven his automobile behind that of the plaintiff at a dangerously close distance; walked closely behind, or beside, or in front of the plaintiff on the public streets; and constantly telephoned the plaintiff at his home and place of business and either hung up or remained on the line in silence. It is alleged further that all of this has been done maliciously and for the purpose of causing physical and mental damage, and that the plaintiff has suffered severe mental and emotional distress, sleeplessness and physical debilitation.

It seems probable that the complaint states a cause of action for assault (Brown v. Yaspan, 256 App.Div. 991, 10 N.Y.S.2d 502), but the plaintiff does not urge the point. He claims to have stated a cause of action for the intentional infliction of emotional and physical harm. This is a relatively new and unfamiliar cause of action, which requires some discussion.

The law cannot be expected to provide a civil remedy for every personal conflict in this crowded world. Physical injuries to the person, inflicted either intentionally or through negligence, are actionable under familiar principles. Acts causing mental distress are in a different category. Oral or written statements which are false and defamatory, and which upon publication tend to deprive the victim of his good name, may be remedied in actions for libel and slander.

On the other hand, offenses of a minor nature, such as name-calling or angry looks, are not actionable though they may wound the feelings of the victim and cause some degree of emotional upset. This is because the law has no cure for trifles.

But when the actor's conduct is extraordinarily vindictive, it may be regarded as so extreme and so outrageous as to give rise to a cause of action for emotional distress. This is the test laid down in the Restatement 2d, Torts, § 46 (1966). An example of extreme and outrageous conduct may be found in Halio v. Lurie, 15 A.D.2d 62, 222 N.Y.S.2d 759, where the defendant, having jilted his fiancee and married another, addressed a taunting and insulting letter to the forsaken female. The complaint in that case was held to state a cause of action for the intentional infliction of serious mental distress.

In the court's opinion the complaint in this case states a similar cause of action. If a man finds himself perpetually haunted by an enemy; if he is greeted at every turn by baleful looks, sudden sorties which fall short of physical contact, and derisive laughter; if he cannot drive his car without the imminent threat of a collision from the rear; and if he is troubled at all hours by telephone calls followed only by silence, then it can hardly be doubted that he is being subjected to the extreme and outrageous conduct which gives rise to a cause of action in tort. An analogy may be found in the concept of cruelty in a matrimonial action. In holding that such cruelty is not limited to physical injury, the Court of Appeals has said that "if it were, a husband might constantly and without cause publicly call his wife a vile and shameless bawd so long as he did not strike her or threaten to strike her, and might thus intentionally break down her health and destroy her reason without giving her a claim on him for separate maintenance" (Pearson v. Pearson, 230 N.Y. 141, 146, 129 N.E. 349, 350). Conceivably a similar result might follow if the plaintiff can prove what is alleged in this complaint.

Of course, whether the proof can be furnished at the trial is another question. It would seem that evidence connecting the defendant with the speechless telephone calls will be difficult to produce; and whether the plaintiff can prove the remaining allegations to a sufficient degree to establish the cause of action is a question to be determined by the trier of the facts. Upon this motion the court must assume the truth of what is stated in the complaint, and upon that assumption this complaint states a cause of action.

The second cause of action is a repetition of the first, with the additional allegation that the defendant's conduct still continues and will continue in the future, resulting in irreparable injury to the plaintiff. Under that cause of action the plaintiff demands injunctive relief, in addition to the money damages demanded in the first cause of action. The court is of the opinion that both forms of relief are available upon proper proof. The motion is therefore denied as to both causes of action.

## Howell v. New York Post Co.

Court of Appeals of New York, 1993.
81 N.Y.2d 115, 612 N.E.2d 699.

■ CHIEF JUDGE KAYE.

This appeal, involving a newspaper's publication of plaintiff's photograph without her consent, calls upon us to consider the relationship

between two separate but potentially overlapping torts: intentional infliction of emotional distress, and invasion of the right to privacy.

In early September 1988, plaintiff Pamela J. Howell was a patient at
Four Winds Hospital, a private psychiatric facility in Westchester County.
Her complaint and affidavit (accepted as true on this appeal) allege that it
was imperative to her recovery that the hospitalization remain a secret
from all but her immediate family.

Hedda Nussbaum was also at that time a patient at Four Winds.
Nussbaum was the "adoptive" mother of six-year-old Lisa Steinberg, whose
November 1987 death from child abuse generated intense public interest.

On September 1, 1988, a New York Post photographer trespassed onto
Four Winds' secluded grounds and, with a telephoto lens, took outdoor
pictures of a group that included Nussbaum and plaintiff. That night, the
hospital's medical director telephoned a Post editor requesting that the
paper not publish any patient photographs. Nevertheless, on the front page
of next days' edition two photographs appeared—one of Nussbaum taken in
November 1987, shortly after her arrest in connection with Lisa's death,
and another of Nussbaum walking with plaintiff, taken the previous day at
Four Winds.

In the earlier photograph, Nussbaum's face is bruised and disfigured,
her lips split and swollen, and her matted hair is covered with a scarf. By
contrast, in the photograph taken at Four Winds, Nussbaum's facial
wounds have visibly healed, her hair is coiffed, and she is neatly dressed in
jeans, a sweater and earrings. Plaintiff, walking alongside her, smiling, is in
tennis attire and sneakers. The caption reads: "The battered face above
belongs to the Hedda Nussbaum people remember—the former live-in lover
of accused child-killer, Joel Steinberg. The serene woman in jeans at left is
the same Hedda, strolling with a companion in the grounds of the upstate
psychiatric center where her face and mind are healing from the terrible
wounds Steinberg inflicted."

The accompanying article centers on Nussbaum's physical and mental
rehabilitation and quotes her as saying: "I feel good. I'm healthy ...
They're good to me here. The People are nice and I do my photography."
The article concludes by noting that several issues still haunt Nussbaum,
including whether she should cooperate with the prosecution and testify
against Steinberg.

Although plaintiff's name was not mentioned in the caption or article,
her face is readily discernible. Alleging she experienced emotional distress
and humiliation, plaintiff commenced an action against the Post, the
photographer and two writers, seeking multimillion dollar damages for
alleged violations of Civil Rights Law § 50 and 51, intentional and negligent infliction of emotional distress, trespass, harassment and prima facie
tort. Plaintiff's husband, by the same complaint, brought a derivative claim
for loss of consortium.

Supreme Court granted in part defendants' CPLR 3211 (a) (7) motion by dismissing all causes of action except for intentional infliction of emotional distress and the derivative claim, and denied plaintiff's motion for summary judgment. On the parties' cross appeals, the Appellate Division modified by dismissing the entire complaint. This Court granted plaintiff's motion for leave to appeal to consider the dismissal of her claims for violation of the right to privacy and intentional infliction of emotional distress. We now affirm.

### The Legal Backdrop

This appeal brings together two separate bodies of tort law, each with a long history that is relevant to resolution of the issues before us.

### Intentional Infliction of Emotional Distress

Historically, the common law of this State did not recognize emotional injury—even with physical manifestations—as an independent basis for recovery. In Mitchell v. Rochester Ry. Co. (151 NY 107 [1896]), for example, a pregnant woman nearly hit by defendant's horses suffered a miscarriage. The Court noted that since there was no cause of action for fright, "it is obvious that no recovery can be had for injuries resulting therefrom. That the result may be nervous disease, blindness, insanity, or even a miscarriage, in no way changes the principle." (151 NY, at 109–110.) The Court expressed two concerns, present even today, with permitting emotional distress damages: (i) the potential "flood of litigation," and (ii) the ease with which emotional injury "may be . . . feigned without detection" ( id., at 110).

Nevertheless, emotional distress damages as an adjunct, or "parasitic," to recognized torts were allowed (see, e.g., Garrison v. Sun Print. & Publ. Assn., 207 NY 1, 8 [1912] [defamation]). Indeed, courts often struggled to find an established cause of action upon which to base an award of emotional distress damages to a deserving plaintiff. This is exemplified by a line of cases allowing victims of unacceptable behavior to recover under a breach of contract theory (see, e.g., Boyce v. Greeley Sq. Hotel Co., 228 NY 106; Aaron v. Ward, 203 NY 351; de Wolf v. Ford, 193 NY 397).

The Restatement of Torts, first adopted in 1934, generally insulated an actor from liability for causing solely emotional distress: "conduct which is intended or which though not so intended is likely to cause only a mental or emotional disturbance to another does not subject the actor to liability . . . for emotional distress resulting therefrom" (Restatement of Torts § 46 [a]). Shortly thereafter, in an influential article surveying the field—including the New York cases—Calvert Magruder concluded that courts were already giving extensive protection to feelings and emotions, showing an "adaptability of technique" in redressing the more serious invasions (Magruder, *Mental and Emotional Disturbance in the Law of Torts*, 49 Harv L Rev 1033, 1067 [1936]).

Building on the Magruder article, Professor Prosser argued that, without expressly saying so, courts had actually created a new tort consisting of the intentional, outrageous infliction of mental suffering in an extreme form (Prosser, *Intentional Infliction of Mental Suffering: A New Tort*, 37 Mich L Rev 874, 874 [1939]). "Out of the array of technical assaults, batteries, imprisonments, trespasses, 'implied contracts,' invasions of 'privacy' or of doubtful 'property rights,' the real interest which is being protected stands forth very clearly." (Id., at 886–887.) Prosser suggested that there was no longer a reason or necessity for resorting to such "subterfuges," and that it was "high time to abandon them, and to rest the action upon its real ground." (Id., at 881.)

Responding to these and similar importunings, the Restatement in 1948 abandoned its earlier position and declared that "[o]ne who, without a privilege to do so, intentionally causes severe emotional distress to another is liable ... for such emotional distress" (Restatement of Torts § 46 [a] [1948 Supp]).

While working on the Second Restatement of Torts, its Reporter, Dean Prosser, noted that the 1948 version was so broad as to suggest the need for further limitation (Prosser, Insult and Outrage, 44 Cal L Rev 40, 41 [1956]). The requirement of "extreme and outrageous conduct" was the apparent solution. As the Second Restatement reads: "One who by extreme and outrageous conduct intentionally or recklessly causes severe emotional distress to another is subject to liability for such emotional distress" (Restatement [Second] of Torts § 46 [1] [1965]). This Court subsequently adopted the Restatement formulation (see, Fischer v. Maloney, 43 NY2d 553, 557; Murphy v. American Home Prods. Corp., 58 NY2d 293, 303; Freihofer v. Hearst Corp., 65 NY2d 135, 143).

The tort has four elements: (i) extreme and outrageous conduct; (ii) intent to cause, or disregard of a substantial probability of causing, severe emotional distress; (iii) a causal connection between the conduct and injury; and (iv) severe emotional distress. The first element—outrageous conduct—serves the dual function of filtering out petty and trivial complaints that do not belong in court, and assuring that plaintiff's claim of severe emotional distress is genuine (see, Prosser, Insult and Outrage, 44 Cal L Rev, at 44–45; compare, Mitchell v Rochester Ry Co., 151 NY, at 110). In practice, courts have tended to focus on the outrageousness element, the one most susceptible to determination as a matter of law (see, Restatement [Second] of Torts § 46, comment h; Givelber, *The Right to Minimum Social Decency and the Limits of Evenhandedness: Intentional Infliction of Emotional Distress by Outrageous Conduct* ["Social Decency"], 82 Colum L Rev 42, 42–43 [1982]).

Unlike other intentional torts, intentional infliction of emotional distress does not proscribe specific conduct (compare, e.g., Restatement [Second] of Torts § 18 [battery]; id., § 35 [false imprisonment]), but imposes liability based on after-the-fact judgments about the actor's behavior. Accordingly, the broadly defined standard of liability is both a virtue and a vice. The tort is as limitless as the human capacity for cruelty. The price for this flexibility in redressing utterly reprehensible behavior, however, is a tort that, by its terms, may overlap other areas of the law, with potential liability for conduct that is otherwise lawful. Moreover, unlike other torts, the actor may not have notice of the precise conduct proscribed (see, Givelber, Social Decency, 82 Colum L Rev, at 51–52).

Consequently, the "requirements of the rule are rigorous, and difficult to satisfy" (Prosser and Keeton, Torts § 12, at 60–61 [5th ed]; see also, Murphy, 58 NY2d, at 303 [describing the standard as "strict"]). Indeed, of the intentional infliction of emotional distress claims considered by this Court, every one has failed because the alleged conduct was not sufficiently outrageous (see, Freihofer v Hearst Corp., 65 NY2d, at 143–144; Burlew v. American Mut. Ins. Co., 63 NY2d 412, 417–418; Murphy, 58 NY2d, at 303; Fischer v Maloney, 43 NY2d, at 557). " 'Liability has been found only where the conduct has been so outrageous in character, and so extreme in degree, as to go beyond all possible bounds of decency, and to be regarded as atrocious, and utterly intolerable in a civilized community' " (*Murphy*, 58 NY2d, at 303, *quoting* Restatement [Second] of Torts § 46, comment d).

The Right to Privacy

While legal scholarship has been influential in the development of a tort for intentional infliction of emotional distress, it has had less success in the development of a right to privacy in this State. In a famous law review article written more than a century ago, Samuel Warren and Louis Brandeis advocated a tort for invasion of the right to privacy (Warren and Brandeis, *The Right to Privacy*, 4 Harv L Rev 193 [1890]). Relying in part on this article, Abigail Marie Roberson sued a flour company for using her picture, without consent, in the advertisement of its product (Roberson v. Rochester Folding Box Co., 171 NY 538). Finding a lack of support for the thesis of the Warren–Brandeis study, this Court, in a four to three decision, rejected plaintiff's claim.

The *Roberson* decision was roundly criticized. The Legislature responded by enacting the Nation's first statutory right to privacy (L 1903, Ch 132), now codified as sections 50 and 51 of the Civil Rights Law. Section 50 prohibits the use of a living person's name, portrait or picture for "advertising" or "trade" purposes without prior written consent (Civil Rights Law § 50). Section 50 provides criminal penalties and section 51 a private right of action for damages and injunctive relief.

Although the statute itself does not define the terms "advertising" or "trade" purposes, courts have consistently held that the statute should not be construed to apply to publications concerning newsworthy events or matters of public interest (Finger v. Omni Publs. Intl., 77 NY2d 138, 141–142; Stephano v. News Group Publs., 64 NY2d 174, 184). This is both a matter of legislative intent and a reflection of constitutional values in the area of free speech and free press (*Stephano*, 64 NY2d, at 184; Arrington v. New York Times Co., 55 NY2d 433, 440). Thus, a " 'picture illustrating an article on a matter of public interest is not considered used for the purpose of trade or advertising within the prohibition of the statute ... unless it has no real relationship to the article ... or unless the article is an advertisement in disguise' " (Murray v. New York Mag. Co., 27 NY2d 406,

409, *quoting* Dallesandro v. Holt & Co., 4 AD2d 470, 471, *appeal dismissed* 7 NY2d 735; see also, *Finger*, 77 NY2d, at 142; *Stephano*, 64 NY2d, at 185; *Arrington*, 55 NY2d, at 440).

At least three other "privacy" torts have been recognized elsewhere (see, Prosser, Privacy, 48 Cal L Rev 383; Restatement [Second] of Torts § 652A–652E): unreasonable publicity given to another's private life (Restatement [Second] of Torts § 652D); unreasonable intrusion upon seclusion (id., § 652B); and publicity that unreasonably places another in a false light (id., § 652E). While the courts of other jurisdictions have adopted some or all of these torts, in this State the right to privacy is governed exclusively by sections 50 and 51 of the Civil Rights Law; we have no common law of privacy (*Stephano*, 64 NY2d, at 182; *Arrington*, 55 NY2d, at 439–440; Cohen v. Hallmark Cards, 45 NY2d 493, 497, n. 2; Flores v. Mosler Safe Co., 7 NY2d 276, 280). Balancing the competing policy concerns underlying tort recovery for invasion of privacy is best left to the Legislature, which in fact has rejected proposed bills to expand New York law to cover all four categories of privacy protection (see, *Arrington*, 55 NY2d, at 440; Savell, *Right of Privacy–Appropriation*, 48 Alb L Rev, at 3, n 4).

### Application of the Law to the Present Appeal

The core of plaintiff's grievance is that, by publishing her photograph, defendants revealed to her friends, family and business associates that she was undergoing psychiatric treatment—a personal fact she took pains to keep confidential. There is, of course, no cause of action in this State for publication of truthful but embarrassing facts. Thus, a claim grounded in the right to privacy must fall within Civil Rights Law § 50 and 51.

The statutory right to privacy is not transgressed unless defendants used plaintiff's photograph in connection with trade or advertising. Accordingly, if plaintiff's picture accompanied a newspaper article on a matter of public interest, to succeed she must demonstrate that the picture bore no real relationship to the article, or that the article was an advertisement in disguise (see, *Stephano*, 64 NY2d, at 185; *Arrington*, 55 NY2d, at 440; Murray v New York Mag. Co., 27 NY2d, at 409). Plaintiff concedes that, in the aftermath of Lisa Steinberg's death, articles about Hedda Nussbaum were a matter of public interest. Additionally, the Post article plainly was not a veiled advertisement. Thus, analysis of the civil rights claim centers on the "no real relationship" requirement.

We have been reluctant to intrude upon reasonable editorial judgments in determining whether there is a real relationship between an article and photograph (*Finger*, 77 NY2d, at 143; see also, Gaeta v. New York News, 62 NY2d 340, 349). In *Finger*, for example, a magazine without consent used a photograph of plaintiffs and their six children to illustrate a segment about caffeine-enhanced fertility. Although none of the children had been conceived in the manner suggested by the article, we concluded that the requisite nexus between the article and photograph was established because the article's theme—having a large family—was fairly reflected in the picture (see, *Finger,* 77 NY2d, at 142–143).

In the present case, similarly, plaintiff has failed to meet her burden. The subject of the article was Hedda Nussbaum's physical and emotional recovery from the beatings allegedly inflicted by Joel Steinberg. The photograph of a visibly healed Nussbaum, interacting with her smiling, fashionably clad "companion" offers a stark contrast to the adjacent photograph of Nussbaum's disfigured face. The visual impact would not have been the same had the Post cropped plaintiff out of the photograph, as she suggests was required. Thus, there is a real relationship between the article and the photograph of plaintiff, and the civil rights cause of action was properly dismissed.

Defendants would have our analysis end here—without considering whether plaintiff has stated a cause of action for intentional infliction of emotional distress—arguing that the tort may not be used as an end run around a failed right to privacy claim. Insofar as plaintiff's claim is based on the publication of her photograph, we agree, for the publication was qualifiedly privileged—meaning that defendants acted within their legal right—and no circumstances are present that would defeat the privilege.

The distinction between privileged and nonprivileged conduct as it relates to infliction of emotional distress is implicit in our cases and explicit in the Restatement. In Murphy v American Home Prods. Corp. (58 NY2d, at 303), an employment case, we held that plaintiff could not "subvert the traditional at-will contract rule by casting his cause of action in terms of a tort of intentional infliction of emotional distress." If an employer has the right to discharge an employee, the exercise of that right cannot lead to a claim for infliction of emotional distress, however distressing the discharge may be to the employee. In the course of discharging the employee, however, an employer's deliberate reprehensible conduct intentionally or recklessly causing severe emotional distress is not within the employer's right, and may support a claim for intentional infliction of emotional distress.

The 1948 Restatement expressly provided that privileged conduct could not be the basis for liability (Restatement of Torts § 46 [1948 Supp]), and the comments to the current version signify an intent to continue the privileged-conduct exception: "The conduct, although it would otherwise be extreme and outrageous, may be privileged under the circumstances. The actor is never liable, for example, where [the actor] has done no more than to insist upon his [or her] legal rights in a permissible way, even though he [or she] is well aware that such insistence is certain to cause emotional distress." (Restatement [Second] of Torts § 46, comment g.)

A newspaper's publication of a newsworthy photograph is an act within the contemplation of the "privileged-conduct" exception (compare, Hustler Mag. v. Falwell, 485 US 46, 56). Thus, even if defendants were aware that publication would cause plaintiff emotional distress (see, Restatement [Second] of Torts § 46, comment f), publication—without more—could not ordinarily lead to liability for intentional infliction of emotional distress.

We do not mean to suggest, however, that a plaintiff could never defeat the privilege and state a claim for intentional infliction of emotional distress. But because plaintiff's allegations offer no basis for concluding that the privilege has been abused, we need not explore today what circumstances might overcome the privilege.

That does not conclude our analysis, for plaintiff additionally complains that the manner in which her photograph was obtained constituted extreme and outrageous conduct contemplated by the tort of intentional infliction of emotional distress.

Courts have recognized that newsgathering methods may be tortious (see, e.g., Galella v. Onassis, 487 F2d 986, 995 [2d Cir]) and, to the extent that a journalist engages in such atrocious, indecent and utterly despicable conduct as to meet the rigorous requirements of an intentional infliction of emotional distress claim, recovery may be available. The conduct alleged here, however—a trespass onto Four Winds' grounds—does not remotely approach the required standard. That plaintiff was photographed outdoors and from a distance diminishes her claim even further.

Accordingly, the order of the Appellate Division, insofar as it pertains to the individual defendants, should be affirmed, with costs.

## Notes and Questions

**1.** In light of the Court of Appeals' decision in *Howell*, what acts, do you suppose, would satisfy the standard? Have the New York courts ended up recognizing a claim for intentional infliction of emotional distress in principle, but not in fact? Does it make sense for courts to have adopted a theory of liability, if in practice no facts have fulfilled the elements of the claim? On the other hand, does it make sense to allow a claim for intentional infliction of emotional distress if the conduct is otherwise lawful or even privileged?

**2.** Other common law jurisdictions have proved less reluctant to redress a claim for intentional infliction of emotional distress. Consider the following analysis of the Massachusetts Supreme Judicial Court:

> The defendants argue that "there is no authority under existing Massachusetts law for the proposition that the intentional infliction of mental or emotional distress provides a separate and distinct basis of tort liability." That is true only because the precise question has never been presented to this court for decision. That argument is therefore no more valid than would be an argument by the plaintiff that there is no record of any Massachusetts law denying recovery on such facts. No litigant is automatically denied relief solely because he presents a question on which there is no Massachusetts judicial precedent. It would indeed be unfortunate, and perhaps disastrous, if we were required to conclude that at some unknown point in the dim and distant past the law solidified in a manner and to an extent which makes it impossible now to answer a question which had not arisen and been answered prior to that point. The courts must, and do, have

the continuing power and competence to answer novel questions of law arising under ever changing conditions of the society which the law is intended to serve.

The defendants also argue that "this Court has heretofore allowed recovery for these items of damages [mental or emotional distress] only in the cases where the defendant has committed an independent and separate tort recognized at common law." This, if true, is basically the same argument, or a subsidiary of the same argument, discussed and disposed of in the preceding paragraph. The right to recover for these items of damages should not be denied just because they do not fit in any of the existing niches in the ancient walls surrounding the law of torts. If the current needs of society require and justify so doing, the walls may be extended and additional niches built to accomplish justice.

George v. Jordan Marsh Co., 268 N.E.2d 915 (Mass.1971).

In Yeager v. Local Union 20, 453 N.E.2d 666, 670 (Ohio 1983) the Ohio Supreme Court, overruling prior caselaw, became the last jurisdiction to recognize an independent tort of intentional infliction of emotional distress:

[We] discard[] the requirement that intentionally inflicted emotional distress be "parasitic" to an already recognized tort cause of action as in [our prior decision]. [We] also reject[] any requirement that the emotional distress manifest itself in the form of some physical injury. This approach is in accord with the well-reasoned analysis of a substantial number of jurisdictions throughout the nation.

The court remanded for a determination whether the conduct at issue—threats allegedly made by union organizers against a company officer and his family–met the Restatement standard of outrageousness. One of the justices nonetheless offered his view of the quality of defendants' conduct:

Here, the record shows that there was evidence that the defendants did intentionally and maliciously express certain threats which put the plaintiff in fear and terror. There was evidence not only to the effect that the defendants had threatened the plaintiff with injury, but also that the safety of the plaintiff's family had been maliciously threatened by these defendants. All of such evidence would present a cause of action against these defendants and, if proven, would be the basis for a recovery for serious emotional distress.

**3.** The tort claim of intentional infliction of emotional distress has prospered in the area of employment law, particularly in the context of sexual or racial harassment in the workplace. We will encounter that incarnation of the claim in Part III.E.2 of this casebook, in the context of an anti discrimination suit under Title VII of the 1964 Civil Rights Act. See Landgraf v. USI Film Products, 511 U.S. 244 (1994).

## 2. OVERRULING

> It is a maxim among these lawyers, that whatever hath been done before may legally be done again: and therefore they take special care to record all the decisions formerly made against common justice and the general reason of mankind. These, under the name of precedents, they produce as authorities, to justify the most iniquitous opinions; and the judges never fail of directing accordingly.

J. Swift, *Gulliver's Travels* 275 (1726) (The Novel Library 1947), *quoted in* James C. Rehnquist, Note: *The Power That Shall Be Vested in a Precedent: Stare Decisis, the Constitution, and the Supreme Court*, 66 B.U.L.Rev. 345 (1986).

In England, before 1966, the House of Lords (in its judicial capacity) took the position that it could not overrule prior decisions. Whether this position was as rigid as it purported to be is a matter for some argument. However, it is true that the doctrine of *stare decisis* was more strictly applied in England than in the United States, where it has always been accepted that a court could overrule its prior decisions.[1]

A court's option, in the last analysis, to overrule a prior decision makes the concept of "holding" even more elusive than it might otherwise be. What, you may ask, is all of the fuss about "binding decisions" if they aren't really binding (even when they are citable)? Consider the rationale behind adherence to precedent. It has often been argued that *stare decisis* promotes certainty, impartiality, efficiency and the appearance of justice in the legal system. Nonetheless, there are legitimate reasons to overrule precedent. In addition to asking *why* a decision has been overruled, you might also ask yourself *how* the decision was overruled. Did the court explicitly overrule precedent? How much of the "old rule" survives? How much of a difference is there between an outright overruling and a progressive distinction of contrary precedent?

---

**1.** Before judgments were given in the House of Lords on July 26, 1966, Lord Gardiner, L.C., made the following statement on behalf of himself and the Lords of Appeal in Ordinary:

> Their lordships regard the use of precedent as an indispensable foundation upon which to decide what is the law and its application to individual cases. It provides at least some degree of certainty upon which individuals can rely in the conduct of their affairs, as well as a basis for orderly development of legal rules.
>
> Their lordships nevertheless recognise that too rigid adherence to precedent may lead to injustice in a particular case and also unduly restrict the proper devel-

opment of the law. They propose therefore to modify their present practice and, while treating former decisions of this House as normally binding, to depart from a previous decision when it appears right to do so.

In this connexion they will bear in mind the danger of disturbing retrospectively the basis on which contracts, settlements of property and fiscal arrangements have been entered into and also the especial need for certainty as to the criminal law.

This announcement is not intended to affect the use of precedent elsewhere than in this House.

3 All E.R. Ch. D. 77.

# Battalla v. State

Court of Appeals of New York, 1961.
10 N.Y.2d 237, 219 N.Y.S.2d 34, 176 N.E.2d 729.

■ BURKE, JUDGE.

The question presented is whether the claim states a cause of action when it alleges that claimant was negligently caused to suffer "severe emotional and neurological disturbances with residual physical manifestations".

The appellant avers that in September of 1956, at Bellayre Mountain Ski Center, the infant plaintiff was placed in a chair lift by an employee of the State who failed to secure and properly lock the belt intended to protect the occupant. As a result of this alleged negligent act, the infant plaintiff became frightened and hysterical upon the descent, with consequential injuries.

The Court of Claims, on a motion to dismiss the complaint, held that a cause of action does lie. The Appellate Division found itself constrained to follow Mitchell v. Rochester Ry. Co., 151 N.Y. 107, 45 N.E. 354, 34 L.R.A. 781 [1896] and, therefore, reversed and dismissed the claim. The Mitchell case decided that there could be no recovery for injuries, physical or mental, incurred by fright negligently induced.

It is our opinion that Mitchell should be overruled. It is undisputed that a rigorous application of its rule would be unjust, as well as opposed to experience and logic. On the other hand, resort to the somewhat inconsistent exceptions would merely add further confusion to a legal situation which presently lacks that coherence which precedent should possess. "We act in the finest common-law tradition when we adapt and alter decisional law to produce common-sense justice. * * * Legislative action there could, of course, be, but we abdicate our own function, in a field peculiarly nonstatutory, when we refuse to reconsider an old and unsatisfactory court-made rule." Woods v. Lancet, 303 N.Y. 349, 355, 102 N.E.2d 691, 694, 27 A.L.R.2d 1250.

Before passing to a résumé of the evolution of the doctrine in this State, it is well to note that it has been thoroughly repudiated by the English courts which initiated it, rejected by a majority of American jurisdictions, abandoned by many which originally adopted it, and diluted, through numerous exceptions, in the minority which retained it. Moreover, it is the opinion of scholars that *the right* to bring an action should be enforced.[1]

---

**1.** For excellent studies see 1936 Report of N.Y.Law Rev.Comm., pp. 379–450; McNiece, *Psychic Injury and Tort Liability in New York*, 24 St. John's L.Rev. 1; see also, Smith, *Relation of Emotions to Injury and Disease; Legal Liability for Psychic Stimuli*, 30 Va.L.Rev. 193 (1944); Magruder, *Mental and Emotional Disturbance in the Law of* *Torts*, 49 Harv.L.Rev. 1033 (1936); Throckmorton, *Damages for Fright*, 34 Harv.L.Rev. 260 (1921); Wilson, *The New York Rule as to Nervous Shock*, 11 Cornell L.Q. 512 (1926); Edgar, *Foreseeability and Recovery in Tort*, 9 St. John's L.Rev. 84 (1934); Prosser, *Torts* (2d ed.), pp. 38–47, 178, 192; for others, see 1936 Report of N.Y.Law Rev.Comm., p. 448;

It is fundamental to our common-law system that one may seek redress for every substantial wrong. "The best statement of the rule is that a wrong-doer is responsible for the natural and proximate consequences of his misconduct; and what are such consequences must generally be left for the determination of the jury." Ehrgott v. Mayor of City of New York, 96 N.Y. 264, 281. A departure from this axiom was introduced by Mitchell (supra), wherein recovery was denied to plaintiff, a pregnant woman, who, although not physically touched, was negligently caused to abort her child. Defendant's horses were driven in such a reckless manner that, when finally restrained, plaintiff was trapped between their heads. The court indicated essentially three reasons for dismissing the complaint. It stated first that, since plaintiff could not recover for mere fright, there could be no recovery for injuries resulting therefrom. It was assumed, in addition, that the miscarriage was not the proximate result of defendant's negligence, but rather was due to an accidental or unusual combination of circumstances. Finally, the court reasoned that a recovery would be contrary to public policy because that type of injury could be feigned without detection and it would result in a flood of litigation where damages must rest on speculation.

With the possible exception of the last, it seems "[a]ll these objections have been demolished many times, and it is threshing old straw to deal with them." (Prosser, Torts [2d ed.], § 37, pp. 176–177.) Moreover, we have stated that the conclusions of the *Mitchell* case (supra) "cannot be tested by pure logic". Comstock v. Wilson, 1931, 257 N.Y. 231, 234, 177 N.E. 431, 432, 76 A.L.R. 676. Although finding impact and granting recovery, the unanimous court in *Comstock* rejected all but the public policy arguments of the *Mitchell* decision.

We presently feel that even the public policy argument is subject to challenge. Although fraud, extra litigation and a measure of speculation are, of course, possibilities, it is no reason for a court to eschew a measure of its jurisdiction. "The argument from mere expediency cannot commend itself to a Court of justice, resulting in the denial of a logical legal right and remedy in *all* cases because in *some* a fictitious injury may be urged as a real one." Green v. T.A. Shoemaker & Co., 111 Md. 69, 81, 73 A. 688, 692, 23 L.R.A., N.S., 667.

In any event, it seems that fraudulent accidents and injuries are just as easily feigned in the slight-impact cases[2] and other exceptions[3] wherein

---

see, also, 15 Am.Jur., Damages, § 188; 25 C.J.S. Damages § 70; Restatement, Torts, § 436, subds. (1), (2).

**2.** For example, Jones v. Brooklyn Heights R.R. Co., 23 App.Div. 141, 48 N.Y.S. 914, wherein plaintiff was hit on the head by a small incandescent light bulb which fell from a lamp attached to the roof of defendant's car in which plaintiff was a passenger. Plaintiff was allowed to recover for a miscarriage brought on *by the shock* stimulated by

the injury. See, also, Buckbee v. Third Ave. R.R. Co., 64 App.Div. 360, 72 N.Y.S. 217 (slight electric shock); Powell v. Hudson Valley Ry. Co., 88 App.Div. 133, 84 N.Y.S. 237 (slight burn); Comstock v. Wilson, 257 N.Y. 231, 177 N.E. 431, supra (fright induced by prior collision caused passenger to faint and fracture skull); Sawyer v. Dougherty, 286 App.Div. 1061, 144 N.Y.S.2d 746 (blast of air filled with glass).

New York permits a recovery, as in the no-impact cases which it has heretofore shunned.[4] As noted by the Law Revision Commission: "The exceptions to the rule cannot be said to insure recovery to any substantial number of meritorious claimants and there is good ground for believing that they breed dishonest attempts to mold the facts so as to fit them within the grooves leading to recovery." (1936 Report of N.Y.Law Rev. Comm., p. 450.) The ultimate result is that the honest claimant is penalized for his reluctance to fashion the facts within the framework of the exceptions.

Not only, therefore, are claimants in this situation encouraged by the Mitchell disqualification to perjure themselves, but the constant attempts to either come within an old exception, or establish a new one, lead to excess appellate litigation (see Gulf, C. & S.F. Ry. Co. v. Hayter, 93 Tex. 239, 54 S.W. 944, 47 L.R.A. 325). In any event, even if a flood of litigation were realized by abolition of the exception, it is the duty of the courts to willingly accept the opportunity to settle these disputes.

The only substantial policy argument of Mitchell is that the damages or injuries are somewhat speculative and difficult to prove. However, the question of proof in individual situations should not be the arbitrary basis upon which to bar all actions, and "it is beside the point * * * in determining sufficiency of a pleading". Woods v. Lancet, 303 N.Y. 349, 356, 102 N.E.2d 691, 695, supra. In many instances, just as in impact cases, there will be no doubt as to the presence and extent of the damage and the fact that it was proximately caused by defendant's negligence. In the difficult cases, we must look to the quality and genuineness of proof, and rely to an extent on the contemporary sophistication of the medical profession and the ability of the court and jury to weed out the dishonest claims. Claimant should, therefore, be given an opportunity to prove that her injuries were proximately caused by defendant's negligence.

Accordingly, the judgment should be reversed and the claim reinstated, with costs.

■ VAN VOORHIS, JUDGE (dissenting).

In following the Massachusetts rule, which corresponded to that enunciated in this State by Mitchell v. Rochester Ry. Co., 151 N.Y. 107, 45 N.E. 354, Mr. Justice Holmes described it as "an arbitrary exception, based upon a notion of what is practicable, that prevents a recovery for visible illness resulting from nervous shock alone. Spade v. Lynn & Boston Railroad, 168

---

**3.** Injuries from fright are also recoverable generally in: "the burial right cases, the contract relationship cases [innkeeper and common carrier cases], the immediate physical injury cases * * *, the Workmen's Compensation cases, the food cases, the wilful or wanton injury cases, and the right of privacy cases" (brackets mine; McNiece, 24 St. John's L.Rev., pp. 33–65).

**4.** No recovery: Newton v. New York, N.H. & H.R.R. Co., 106 App.Div. 415, 94 N.Y.S. 825 (plaintiff passenger in train collision); Hutchinson v. Stern, 115 App.Div. 791, 101 N.Y.S. 145 (plaintiff could not recover for loss of wife's services when she gave birth to a stillborn child while witnessing an attack on plaintiff); O'Brien v. Moss, 220 App.Div. 464, 221 N.Y.S. 621 (passenger in car collision).

Mass. 285, 288, 47 N.E. 88, 38 L.R.A. 512, 60 Am.St.Rep. 393; Smith v. Postal Telegraph Cable Co., 174 Mass. 576, 55 N.E. 380, 47 L.R.A. 323, 75 Am.St.Rep. 374." Homans v. Boston El. Ry. Co., 180 Mass. 456, 457–458, 62 N.E. 737, 57 L.R.A. 291. Illogical as the legal theoreticians acknowledge this rule to be, it was Justice Holmes who said that the life of the law has not been logic but experience. Experience has produced this rule to prevent the ingenuity of special pleaders and paid expert witnesses from getting recoveries in negligence for nervous shock without physical injury, which was stated as well as possible in Mitchell v. Rochester Ry. Co., supra, 151 N.Y. at page 110, 45 N.E. at page 354 as follows: "If the right of recovery in this class of cases should be once established, it would naturally result in a flood of litigation in cases where the injury easily feigned without detection, and where the damages must rest upon mere conjecture or speculation. The difficulty which often exists in cases of alleged physical injury, in determining whether they exist, and if so, whether they were caused by the negligent act of the defendant, would not only be greatly increased, but a wide field would be opened for fictitious or speculative claims. To establish such a doctrine would be contrary to principles of public policy."

The opinion likewise points out (151 N.Y. at page 109, 45 N.E. at page 354) the speculative nature of the usual evidence of causation where it is contended that mere fright has resulted in "nervous disease, blindness, insanity, or even a miscarriage".

These statements in the Mitchell opinion are not archaic or antiquated, but are even more pertinent today than when they were first stated. At a time like the present, with constantly enlarging recoveries both in scope and amount in all fields of negligence law, and when an influential portion of the Bar is organized as never before to promote ever-increasing recoveries for the most intangible and elusive injuries, little imagination is required to envision mental illness and psychosomatic medicine as encompassed by the enlargement of the coverage of negligence claims to include this fertile field. In Comstock v. Wilson, 257 N.Y. 231, 177 N.E. 431, Mitchell v. Rochester Ry. Co. (supra) is not overruled, but the opinion by Judge Lehman (257 N.Y. at page 238, 177 N.E. at page 433) cites it as well as the Massachusetts rule of Spade v. Lynn & Boston R.R. Co., 168 Mass. 285, 47 N.E. 88, as holding that "for practical reasons there is ordinarily no duty to exercise care to avert causing mental disturbance, and no legal right to mental security." Judge Lehman's opinion continues: "Serious consequences from mere mental disturbance unaccompanied by physical shock cannot be anticipated, and no person is bound to be alert to avert a danger that foresight does not disclose. The conclusion is fortified by the practical consideration that where there has been no physical contact there is danger that fictitious claims may be fabricated. Therefore, where no wrong was claimed other than a mental disturbance, the courts refuse to sanction a recovery for the consequence of that disturbance" (257 N.Y. at pages 238–239, 177 N.E. at page 433).

The problem involved in enlarging the scope of recovery in negligence, even in instances where, as here, an enlargement might be justified on purely theoretical grounds, is that, when once the door has been opened, the new and broader rule is in practice pressed to its extreme conclusion. Courts and juries become prone to accept as established fact that fright has been the cause of mental or physical consequences which informed medical men of balanced judgment find too complicated to trace. Once a medical expert has been found who, for a consideration, expresses an opinion that the relationship of cause and effect exists, courts and juries tend to lay aside critical judgment and accept the fact as stated.

This is the practical reason mentioned by Judges Holmes and Lehman. The Pennsylvania Supreme Court has recently decided that to hold otherwise "would open a Pandora's box." Bosley v. Andrews, 393 Pa. 161, 168, 142 A.2d 263, 266.

In my view the judgment dismissing the claim should be affirmed.

■ FULD, FROESSEL and FOSTER, JJ., concur with BURKE, J.

■ VAN VOORHIS, J., dissents in an opinion in which DESMOND, C.J., and DYE, J., concur.

Judgment reversed and order of the Court of Claims reinstated, with costs in this court and in the Appellate Division.

## Notes and Questions

**1.** What reasons does the court give for overruling precedent? Are these more important than the doctrine of *stare decisis*?

**2.** When and how does a court decide that a rule has become "unjust" and "opposed to experience and logic," as argued in *Battalla?*

**3.** Consider Justice Brandeis' dissent in Burnet v. Coronado Oil & Gas, 285 U.S. 393, 406 (1932):

> Stare decisis is usually the wise policy, because in most matters it is more important that the applicable rule of law be settled than that it be settled right.

## Planned Parenthood v. Casey

Supreme Court of the United States, 1992.
505 U.S. 833, 112 S.Ct. 2791, 120 L.Ed.2d 674.

[Editor's note: In this case, as in several before it, the Supreme Court was asked to overrule Roe v. Wade, 410 U.S. 113 (1973), in which a 7–member majority of the Court held constitutionally invalid a flat ban on all abortions other than those necessary to save the life of the mother. The Court held that restrictions on abortion would be subject to strict scrutiny and must be related to the trimester of pregnancy. The court summarized its holdings as follows:

"1. A state criminal abortion statute of the current Texas type, that excepts from criminality only a *life-saving* procedure on behalf of the mother, without regard to pregnancy stage and without recognition of the other interests involved, is violative of the Due Process Clause of the Fourteenth Amendment.

"(a) For the stage prior to approximately the end of the first trimester, the abortion decision and its effectuation must be left to the medical judgment of the pregnant woman's attending physician.

"(b) For the stage subsequent to approximately the end of the first trimester, the State, in promoting its interest in the health of the mother, may, if it chooses, regulate the abortion procedure in ways that are reasonably related to maternal health.

"(c) For the stage subsequent to viability, the State in promoting its interest in the potentiality of human life may, if it chooses, regulate, and even proscribe, abortion except where it is necessary for the preservation of the life or health of the mother.

"2.   The State may define the term 'physician,' as it has been employed in the preceding paragraphs of this part of the opinion, to mean only a physician currently licensed by the State, and may proscribe any abortion by a person who is not a physician as so defined."

410 U.S. at 164–65.

In *Planned Parenthood v. Casey,* plaintiffs challenged Pennsylvania statutes that imposed a variety of restrictions on the exercise of a woman's right to an abortion. The restrictions applied during the first as well as subsequent trimesters. A plurality of the Court declined to overrule *Roe,* but upheld the following provisions:

1.   Informed consent. The statute requires that at least 24 hours before performing an abortion a physician must inform the woman of the nature and risks of the procedure and inform the woman of the availability of information about the availability of medical assistance with child birth, child support, adoption and other alternatives to adoption. Any woman electing an abortion must certify that the availability of such information was made known to her. The informed consent requirement operates as a forced 24 hour waiting period before an abortion may be performed.

2.   Parental consent. The statute requires any woman under the age of eighteen to obtain the consent of one of her parents or guardians. The consent must be "informed," meaning that the parent or guardian must receive the information described above. If neither parent or guardian give consent, a "judicial bypass" alternative permits the consent required to be given by a court.

3.   Medical emergency definition. The informed and parental consent requirements are subject to a medical emergency exception. The exception waives compliance with these restrictions if an immediate abortion is necessary to "avert ... death or ... [prevent] serious risk of substantial and irreversible impairment of a major bodily function."

4. Record keeping. The statute requires the facility performing the abortion to file a report including such information as the woman's age, number of prior abortions and pregnancies, etc. The woman's name is not required to be reported.

The plurality overturned the following provision of the Pennsylvania statute:

1. Spousal notification. This provision would have required any married woman seeking an abortion to sign a statement that she had notified her spouse of her decision to undergo the procedure. The court also overturned that portion of the record keeping requirement calling for the reporting of a married woman's reason for failing to inform her spouse of her decision to have an abortion.]

O'Connor, Kennedy, and Souter, JJ., announced the judgment of the Court and delivered the opinion of the Court with respect to Parts I, II, III, V–A, V–C, and VI, in which Blackmun and Stevens, JJ., joined, an opinion with respect to Part V–E, in which Stevens, J., joined, and an opinion with respect to Parts IV, V–B, and V–D. Stevens, J., filed an opinion concurring in part and dissenting in part. Blackmun, J., filed an opinion concurring in part, concurring in the judgment in part, and dissenting in part. Rehnquist, C.J., filed an opinion concurring in the judgment in part and dissenting in part, in which White, Scalia, and Thomas, JJ., joined. Scalia, J., filed an opinion concurring in the judgment in part and dissenting in part, in which Rehnquist, C.J., and White and Thomas, JJ., joined.

■ Justice O'Connor, Justice Kennedy, and Justice Souter announced the judgment of the Court and delivered the opinion of the Court with respect to Parts I, II, III, V–A, V–C, and VI, an opinion with respect to Part V–E, in which Justice Stevens joins, and an opinion with respect to Parts IV, V–B, and V–D.

### I*

Liberty finds no refuge in a jurisprudence of doubt. Yet 19 years after our holding that the Constitution protects a woman's right to terminate her pregnancy in its early stages, Roe v. Wade, 410 U.S. 113 (1973), that definition of liberty is still questioned. Joining the respondents as amicus curiae, the United States, as it has done in five other cases in the last decade, again asks us to overrule Roe. See Brief for Respondents 104–117; Brief for United States as Amicus Curiae 8.

At issue in these cases are five provisions of the Pennsylvania abortion Control Act of 1982 as amended in 1988 and 1989. 18 Pa.Cons.Stat. §§ 3203–3220 (1990).... Before any of these provisions took effect, the petitioners, who are five abortion clinics and one physician representing himself as well as a class of physicians who provide abortion services, brought this suit seeking declaratory and injunctive relief. Each provision

---

* [Most of the text of this decision was edited by Professor Peter Strauss for the Columbia Law School first-year Legal Meth- ods course. Many citations have been omitted without indication, for ease of reading. Ellipses (...) mark only the deletion of text.—Ed.]

was challenged as unconstitutional on its face. The District Court entered a preliminary injunction against the enforcement of the regulations, and, after a 3–day bench trial, held all the provisions at issue here unconstitutional, entering a permanent injunction against Pennsylvania's enforcement of them. 744 F.Supp. 1323 (E.D.Pa.1990). The Court of Appeals for the Third Circuit affirmed in part and reversed in part, upholding all of the regulations except for the husband notification requirement. 947 F.2d 682 (1991). We granted certiorari. 502 U.S. (1992).

The Court of Appeals found it necessary to follow an elaborate course of reasoning even to identify the first premise to use to determine whether the statute enacted by Pennsylvania meets constitutional standards. See 947 F.2d, at 687–698. And at oral argument in this Court, the attorney for the parties challenging the statute took the position that none of the enactments can be upheld without overruling Roe v. Wade. Tr. of Oral Arg. 5–6. We disagree with that analysis; but we acknowledge that our decisions after Roe cast doubt upon the meaning and reach of its holding. Further, the CHIEF JUSTICE admits that he would overrule the central holding of Roe and adopt the rational relationship test as the sole criterion of constitutionality. State and federal courts as well as legislatures throughout the Union must have guidance as they seek to address this subject in conformance with the Constitution. Given these premises, we find it imperative to review once more the principles that define the rights of the woman and the legitimate authority of the State respecting the termination of pregnancies by abortion procedures. After considering the fundamental constitutional questions resolved by Roe, principles of institutional integrity, and the rule of stare decisis, we are led to conclude this: the essential holding of Roe v. Wade should be retained and once again reaffirmed.

It must be stated at the outset and with clarity that Roe's essential holding, the holding we reaffirm, has three parts. First is a recognition of the right of the woman to choose to have an abortion before viability and to obtain it without undue interference from the State. Before viability, the State's interests are not strong enough to support a prohibition of abortion or the imposition of a substantial obstacle to the woman's effective right to elect the procedure. Second is a confirmation of the State's power to restrict abortions after fetal viability, if the law contains exceptions for pregnancies which endanger a woman's life or health. And third is the principle that the State has legitimate interests from the outset of the pregnancy in protecting the health of the woman and the life of the fetus that may become a child. These principles do not contradict one another, and we adhere to each. . . .

## II

[The Court expounded at length on the protection afforded substantive liberties by the Due Process Clause of the Fourteenth Amendment, which declares that no State shall "deprive any person of life, liberty, or property, without due process of law." Critical examination of the discussion is best left to the course in Constitutional Law; here it is enough to say that the majority found it "settled" that the clause does protect substantive liberties—not simply procedures, and not only those rights that happen to be enumerated in Amendments 1—8, part of the Bill of Rights. Citing such aspects of liberty as marriage and child-rearing, it concluded:]

It was this dimension of personal liberty that Roe sought to protect, and its holding invoked the reasoning and the tradition of the precedents we have discussed, granting protection to substantive liberties of the person. Roe was, of course, an extension of those cases and, as the decision itself indicated, the separate States could act in some degree to further their own legitimate interests in protecting pre-natal life. The extent to which the legislatures of the States might act to outweigh the interests of the woman in choosing to terminate her pregnancy was a subject of debate both in Roe itself and in decisions following it.

While we appreciate the weight of the arguments ... that Roe should be overruled, the reservations any of us may have in reaffirming the central holding of Roe are outweighed by the explication of individual liberty we have given combined with the force of stare decisis. We turn now to that doctrine.

## III

### A

The obligation to follow precedent begins with necessity, and a contrary necessity marks its outer limit. With Cardozo, we recognize that no judicial system could do society's work if it eyed each issue afresh in every case that raised it. See B. Cardozo, The Nature of the Judicial Process 149 (1921). Indeed, the very concept of the rule of law underlying our own Constitution requires such continuity over time that a respect for precedent is, by definition, indispensable. See Powell, Stare Decisis and Judicial Restraint, 1991 Journal of Supreme Court History 13, 16. At the other extreme, a different necessity would make itself felt if a prior judicial ruling should come to be seen so clearly as error that its enforcement was for that very reason doomed.

Even when the decision to overrule a prior case is not, as in the rare, latter instance, virtually foreordained, it is common wisdom that the rule of stare decisis is not an "inexorable command," and certainly it is not such in every constitutional case, see Burnet v. Coronado Oil Gas Co., 285 U.S. 393, 405–411 (1932) (Brandeis, J., dissenting). See also Payne v. Tennessee, 501 U.S. ___, (1991) (Souter, J., joined by Kennedy, J., concurring); Arizona v. Rumsey, 467 U.S. 203, 212 (1984). Rather, when this Court reexamines a prior holding, its judgment is customarily informed by a series of prudential and pragmatic considerations designed to test the consistency of overruling a prior decision with the ideal of the rule of law, and to gauge the respective costs of reaffirming and overruling a prior case. Thus, for example, we may ask whether the rule has proved to be intolerable simply in defying practical workability, Swift & Co. v. Wickham, 382 U.S. 111, 116 (1965); whether the rule is subject to a kind of reliance that would lend a special hardship to the consequences of overruling and add inequity to the cost of repudiation, e.g., United States v. Title Ins. & Trust Co., 265 U.S. 472, 486 (1924); whether related principles of law have so far developed as to have left the old rule no more than a remnant of abandoned doctrine, see Patterson v. McLean Credit Union, 491 U.S. 164, 173–174 (1989); or whether facts have so changed or come to be seen so differently, as to have robbed the old rule of significant application or justification, e.g., Burnet, supra, at 412 (Brandeis, J., dissenting).

So in this case we may inquire whether Roe's central rule has been found unworkable; whether the rule's limitation on state power could be removed without serious inequity to those who have relied upon it or significant damage to the stability of the society governed by the rule in question; whether the law's growth in the intervening years has left Roe's central rule a doctrinal anachronism discounted by society; and whether Roe's premises of fact have so far changed in the ensuing two decades as to render its central holding somehow irrelevant or unjustifiable in dealing with the issue it addressed.

### 1

Although Roe has engendered opposition, it has in no sense proven "unworkable," see Garcia v. San Antonio Metropolitan Transit Authority, 469 U.S. 528, 546 (1985), representing as it does a simple limitation beyond which a state law is unenforceable. While Roe has, of course, required judicial assessment of state laws affecting the exercise of the choice guaranteed against government infringement, and although the need for such review will remain as a consequence of today's decision, the required determinations fall within judicial competence.

### 2

The inquiry into reliance counts the cost of a rule's repudiation as it would fall on those who have relied reasonably on the rule's continued application. . . . [F]or two decades of economic and social developments, people have organized intimate relationships and made choices that define their views of themselves and their places in society, in reliance on the availability of abortion in the event that contraception should fail. The ability of women to participate equally in the economic and social life of the Nation has been facilitated by their ability to control their reproductive lives. See, e.g., R. Petchesky, Abortion and Woman's Choice 109, 133, n. 7 (rev. ed. 1990). The Constitution serves human values, and while the effect of reliance on Roe cannot be exactly measured, neither can the certain cost of overruling Roe for people who have ordered their thinking and living around that case be dismissed.

### 3

No evolution of legal principle has left Roe's doctrinal footings weaker than they were in 1973. No development of constitutional law since the case was decided has implicitly or explicitly left Roe behind as a mere survivor of obsolete constitutional thinking.

It will be recognized, of course, that Roe stands at an intersection of two lines of decisions ... The Roe Court itself placed its holding in the succession of cases ... [recognizing constitutionally protected rights of privacy in intimate relationships. S]ubsequent constitutional developments have neither disturbed, nor do they threaten to diminish, the scope of recognized protection accorded to the liberty relating to intimate relationships, the family, and decisions about whether or not to beget or bear a child. See, e.g., Carey v. Population Services International, 431 U.S. 678 (1977); Moore v. East Cleveland, 431 U.S. 678 (1977).

Roe, however, [may also be seen as] ... a rule (whether or not mistaken) of personal autonomy and bodily integrity, with doctrinal affinity to cases recognizing limits on governmental power to mandate medical treatment or to bar its rejection. If so, our cases since Roe accord with Roe's view that a State's interest in the protection of life falls short of justifying any plenary override of individual liberty claims. Cruzan v. Director, Missouri Dept. of Health, 497 U.S. 261, 278 (1990)....

Finally, one could classify Roe as sui generis. If the case is so viewed, then there clearly has been no erosion of its central determination. The original holding resting on the concurrence of seven Members of the Court in 1973 was expressly affirmed by a majority of six in 1983, see Akron v. Akron Center for Reproductive Health, Inc., 462 U.S. 416 (1983) (Akron I), and by a majority of five in 1986, see Thornburgh v. American College of Obstetricians and Gynecologists, 476 U.S. 747 (1986).... More recently, in Webster v. Reproductive Health Services, 492 U.S. 490 (1989), although two of the present authors questioned the trimester framework in a way consistent with our judgment today, a majority of the Court either decided to reaffirm or declined to address the constitutional validity of the central holding of Roe.

Nor will courts building upon Roe be likely to hand down erroneous decisions as a consequence. Even on the assumption that the central holding of Roe was in error, that error would go only to the strength of the state interest in fetal protection, not to the recognition afforded by the Constitution to the woman's liberty.... The soundness of this prong of the Roe analysis is apparent from a consideration of the alternative. If indeed the woman's interest in deciding whether to bear and beget a child had not been recognized as in Roe, the State might as readily restrict a woman's right to choose to carry a pregnancy to term as to terminate it, to further asserted state interests in population control, or eugenics, for example.... In any event, because Roe's scope is confined by the fact of its concern with postconception potential life, a concern otherwise likely to be implicated only by some forms of contraception protected independently under Griswold and later cases, any error in Roe is unlikely to have serious ramifications in future cases.

## 4

We have seen how time has overtaken some of Roe's factual assumptions: advances in maternal health care allow for abortions safe to the mother later in pregnancy than was true in 1973, see Akron I, supra, at 429, n. 11, and advances in neonatal care have advanced viability to a point somewhat earlier. But these facts go only to the scheme of time limits on the realization of competing interests, and the divergences from the factual premises of 1973 have no bearing on the validity of Roe's central holding, that viability marks the earliest point at which the State's interest in fetal life is constitutionally adequate to justify a legislative ban on nontherapeutic abortions. . . .

### 5

The sum of the precedential inquiry to this point shows Roe's underpinnings unweakened in any way affecting its central holding. While it has engendered disapproval, it has not been unworkable. An entire generation has come of age free to assume Roe's concept of liberty in defining the capacity of women to act in society, and to make reproductive decisions; no erosion of principle going to liberty or personal autonomy has left Roe's central holding a doctrinal remnant; Roe portends no developments at odds with other precedent for the analysis of personal liberty; and no changes of fact have rendered viability more or less appropriate as the point at which the balance of interests tips. Within the bounds of normal stare decisis analysis, then, and subject to the considerations on which it customarily turns, the stronger argument is for affirming Roe's central holding, with whatever degree of personal reluctance any of us may have, not for overruling it.

### B

In a less significant case, stare decisis analysis could, and would, stop at the point we have reached. But the sustained and widespread debate Roe has provoked calls for some comparison between that case and others of comparable dimension that have responded to national controversies and taken on the impress of the controversies addressed. Only two such decisional lines from the past century present themselves for examination, and in each instance the result reached by the Court accorded with the principles we apply today.

The first example is that line of cases identified with Lochner v. New York, 198 U.S. 45 (1905), which imposed substantive limitations on legislation limiting economic autonomy in favor of health and welfare regulation, adopting, in Justice Holmes' view, the theory of laissez-faire. Id., at 75 (Holmes, J., dissenting). The *Lochner* decisions were exemplified by Adkins v. Children's Hospital of D.C., 261 U.S. 525 (1923), in which this Court held it to be an infringement of constitutionally protected liberty of contract to require the employers of adult women to satisfy minimum wage standards. Fourteen years later, West Coast Hotel Co. v. Parrish, 300 U.S. 379 (1937), signalled the demise of *Lochner* by overruling *Adkins*. In the meantime, the Depression had come and, with it, the lesson that seemed unmistakable to most people by 1937, that the interpretation of contractual freedom protected in *Adkins* rested on fundamentally false factual assumptions about the capacity of a relatively unregulated market to satisfy minimal levels of human welfare.... [T]he clear demonstration that the facts of economic life were different from those previously assumed warranted the repudiation of the old law.

The second comparison that 20th century history invites is with the cases employing the separate-but-equal rule for applying the Fourteenth Amendment's equal protection guarantee. They began with Plessy v. Ferguson, 163 U.S. 537 (1896), ... rejecting the argument that racial separation enforced by the legal machinery of American society treats the black race as inferior.... [T]his understanding of the facts and the rule it was stated to justify were repudiated in Brown v. Board of Education, 347 U.S. 483 (1954) ... [which observed] that whatever may have been the understanding in *Plessy's* time of the power of segregation to stigmatize those who were segregated with a "badge of inferiority," it was clear by 1954 that legally sanctioned segregation had just such an effect.... While we think *Plessy* was wrong the day it was decided, we must also recognize that the *Plessy* Court's explanation for its decision was so clearly at odds with the facts apparent to the Court in 1954 that the decision to reexamine *Plessy* was on this ground alone not only justified but required. *West Coast Hotel* and *Brown* each rested on facts, or an understanding of facts, changed from those which furnished the claimed justifications for the earlier constitutional resolutions.... In constitutional adjudication as elsewhere in life, changed circumstances may impose new obligations, and the thoughtful part of the Nation could accept each decision to overrule a prior case as a response to the Court's constitutional duty.

Because the case before us presents no such occasion ... the Court could not pretend to be reexamining the prior law with any justification beyond a present doctrinal disposition to come out differently from the Court of 1973. To overrule prior law for no other reason than that would run counter to the view repeated in our cases, that a decision to overrule should rest on some special reason over and above the belief that a prior case was wrongly decided. [Citing only two dissents by recent conservative Justices, Mitchell v. W.T. Grant, 416 U.S. 600, 636 (1974) (Stewart, J., dissenting) ("A basic change in the law upon a ground no firmer than a change in our membership invites the popular misconception that this institution is little different from the two political branches of the Government. No misconception could do more lasting injury to this Court and to the system of law which it is our abiding mission to serve") and Mapp v. Ohio, 367 U.S. 643, 677 (1961) (Harlan, J., dissenting).]

## C

... Our analysis would not be complete ... without explaining why overruling Roe's central holding would ... seriously weaken the Court's capacity to exercise the judicial power and to function as the Supreme Court of a Nation dedicated to the rule of law....

The root of American governmental power is revealed most clearly in the instance of the power conferred by the Constitution upon the Judiciary of the United States and specifically upon this Court. As Americans of each succeeding generation are rightly told, the Court cannot buy support for its decisions by spending money and, except to a minor degree, it cannot independently coerce obedience to its decrees. The Court's power lies, rather, in its legitimacy, a product of substance and perception that shows itself in the people's acceptance of the Judiciary as fit to determine what the Nation's law means and to declare what it demands.

The underlying substance of this legitimacy [lies] . . . in the Constitution and the lesser sources of legal principle on which the Court draws. . . . [A] decision without principled justification would be no judicial act at all. But even when justification is furnished by apposite legal principle, something more is required. Because not every conscientious claim of principled justification will be accepted as such, the justification claimed must be beyond dispute. The Court must take care to speak and act in ways that allow people to accept its decisions on the terms the Court claims for them, as grounded truly in principle, not as compromises with social and political pressures having, as such, no bearing on the principled choices that the Court is obliged to make. . . .

The need for principled action to be perceived as such is implicated to some degree whenever this, or any other appellate court, overrules a prior case. . . . [To be sure,] the country can accept some correction of error without necessarily questioning the legitimacy of the Court. . . . [H]owever, the Court would almost certainly fail to receive the benefit of the doubt in overruling prior cases [in two circumstances]. There is, first, a point beyond which frequent overruling would overtax the country's belief in the Court's good faith. . . . If that limit should be exceeded, disturbance of prior rulings would be taken as evidence that justifiable reexamination of principle had given way to drives for particular results in the short term. The legitimacy of the Court would fade with the frequency of its vacillation.

[Second, w]here, in the performance of its judicial duties, the Court decides a case in such a way as to resolve the sort of intensely divisive controversy reflected in Roe . . . its decision has a dimension that the resolution of the normal case does not carry. It is the dimension present whenever the Court's interpretation of the Constitution calls the contending sides of a national controversy to end their national division by accepting a common mandate rooted in the Constitution.

The Court is not asked to do this very often, having thus addressed the Nation only twice in our lifetime, in the decisions of Brown and Roe. But when the Court does act in this way, its decision requires an equally rare precedential force to counter the inevitable efforts to overturn it and to thwart its implementation. Some of those efforts may be mere unprincipled emotional reactions; others may proceed from principles worthy of profound respect. But whatever the premises of opposition may be, only the most convincing justification under accepted standards of precedent could suffice to demonstrate that a later decision overruling the first was anything but a surrender to political pressure, and an unjustified repudiation of the principle on which the Court staked its authority in the first instance. So to overrule under fire in the absence of the most compelling reason to reexamine a watershed decision would subvert the Court's legitimacy beyond any serious question. Cf. Brown v. Board of Education, 349 U.S. 294, 300 (1955) (Brown II)

The country's loss of confidence in the judiciary would be underscored by an equally certain and equally reasonable condemnation for another failing in overruling unnecessarily and under pressure. Some cost will be paid by anyone who approves or implements a constitutional decision where it is unpopular, or who refuses to work to undermine the decision or to force its reversal. The price may be criticism or ostracism, or it may be violence. An extra price will be paid by those who themselves disapprove of the decision's results when viewed outside of constitutional terms, but who nevertheless struggle to accept it, because they respect the rule of law. To all those who will be so tested by following, the Court implicitly undertakes to remain steadfast, lest in the end a price be paid for nothing. The promise of constancy, once given, binds its maker for as long as the power to stand by the decision survives and the understanding of the issue has not changed so fundamentally as to render the commitment obsolete. From the obligation of this promise this Court cannot and should not assume any exemption when duty requires it to decide a case in conformance with the Constitution. A willing breach of it would be nothing less than a breach of faith, and no Court that broke its faith with the people could sensibly expect credit for principle in the decision by which it did that.

It is true that diminished legitimacy may be restored, but only slowly. Unlike the political branches, a Court thus weakened could not seek to regain its position with a new mandate from the voters, and even if the Court could somehow go to the polls, the loss of its principled character could not be retrieved by the casting of so many votes. Like the character of an individual, the legitimacy of the Court must be earned over time. So, indeed, must be the character of a Nation of people who aspire to live according to the rule of law. Their belief in themselves as such a people is not readily separable from their understanding of the Court invested with the authority to decide their constitutional cases and speak before all others for their constitutional ideals. If the Court's legitimacy should be undermined, then, so would the country be in its very ability to see itself through its constitutional ideals. The Court's concern with legitimacy is not for the sake of the Court but for the sake of the Nation to which it is responsible.

The Court's duty in the present case is clear. In 1973, it confronted the already-divisive issue of governmental power to limit personal choice to undergo abortion, for which it provided a new resolution based on the due process guaranteed by the Fourteenth Amendment. Whether or not a new social consensus is developing on that issue, its divisiveness is no less today than in 1973, and pressure to overrule the decision, like pressure to retain it, has grown only more intense. A decision to overrule Roe's essential holding under the existing circumstances would address error, if error there was, at the cost of both profound and unnecessary damage to the Court's legitimacy, and to the Nation's commitment to the rule of law. It is therefore imperative to adhere to the essence of Roe's original decision, and we do so today.

... [The ensuing very lengthy, and somewhat fractured, discussion of the merits of the several challenges to the Pennsylvania statutes is omitted.]

[The separate opinions of Justice Blackmun and Justice Stevens, the strongest proponents of *Roe,* had little to say on the subject of stare decisis, and are omitted, save for this footnote from Justice Stevens' opinion.**]

■ CHIEF JUSTICE REHNQUIST, with whom JUSTICE WHITE, JUSTICE SCALIA, and JUSTICE THOMAS join, concurring in the judgment in part and dissenting in part.

The joint opinion, following its newly-minted variation on stare decisis, retains the outer shell of Roe v. Wade, 410 U.S. 113 (1973), but beats a wholesale retreat from the substance of that case. We believe that Roe was wrongly decided, and that it can and should be overruled consistently with our traditional approach to stare decisis in constitutional cases. We would adopt the approach of the plurality in Webster v. Reproductive Health Services, 492 U.S. 490 (1989), and uphold the challenged provisions of the Pennsylvania statute in their entirety.

## I

[The Chief Justice explained at length his conclusion that *Roe* should be overruled: The opinion was ill-founded in reason, subsequent decisions had tended to extend its reach, and the plurality's "undue burden" test was both unfounded in the Constitution and unworkable. His opinion acknowledged that "a liberty interest protected under the Due Process Clause of the Fourteenth Amendment will be deemed fundamental if it is 'implicit in the concept of ordered liberty,' ... 'so rooted in the traditions and conscience of our people as to be ranked as fundamental,'" and that the meaning of the Due Process Clause extends beyond freedom from physical restraint. In Pierce v. Society of Sisters, 268 U.S. 510 (1925), we held that it included a parent's right to send a child to private school; in Meyer v. Nebraska, 262 U.S. 390 (1923), we held that it included a right to teach a foreign language in a parochial school. Building on these cases, we have held that that the term "liberty" includes a right to marry, Loving v. Virginia, 388 U.S. 1 (196–7); a right to procreate, Skinner v. Oklahoma ex rel. Williamson, 316 U.S. 535 (1942); and a right to use contraceptives. Griswold v. Connecticut, 381 U.S. 479 (1965); Eisenstadt v. Baird, 405 U.S. 438 (1972). "But ... in terming [the right to abortion] fundamental, the Court in Roe read the earlier opinions upon which it based its decision much too broadly. Unlike marriage, procreation and contraception, abor-

---

** It is sometimes useful to view the issue of stare decisis from a historical perspective. In the last nineteen years, fifteen Justices have confronted the basic issue presented in Roe. Of those, eleven have voted as the majority does today: Chief Justice Burg- er, Justices Douglas, Brennan, Stewart, Marshall, and Powell, and Justices Blackmun, O'Connor, Kennedy, Souter, and myself. Only four—all of whom happen to be on the Court today—have reached the opposite conclusion.

tion 'involves the purposeful termination of potential life.' ... Nor do the historical traditions of the American people support the view that the right to terminate one's pregnancy is 'fundamental.' ... 'The Court is most vulnerable and comes nearest to illegitimacy when it deals with judge-made constitutional law having little or no cognizable roots in the language or design of the Constitution.' ''']***

## II

The joint opinion of Justices O'Connor, Kennedy, and Souter cannot bring itself to say that Roe was correct as an original matter, but the authors are of the view that "the immediate question is not the soundness of Roe's resolution of the issue, but the precedential force that must be accorded to its holding." Instead of claiming that Roe was correct as a matter of original constitutional interpretation, the opinion therefore contains an elaborate discussion of stare decisis. This discussion of the principle of stare decisis appears to be almost entirely dicta, because the joint opinion does not apply that principle in dealing with Roe. Roe decided that a woman had a fundamental right to an abortion. The joint opinion rejects that view. Roe decided that abortion regulations were to be subjected to "strict scrutiny" and could be justified only in the light of "compelling state interests." The joint opinion rejects that view. Roe analyzed abortion regulation under a rigid trimester framework, a framework which has guided this Court's decisionmaking for 19 years. The joint opinion rejects that framework.

Stare decisis is defined in Black's Law Dictionary as meaning "to abide by, or adhere to, decided cases." Black's Law Dictionary 1406 (6th ed. 1990). Whatever the "central holding" of Roe that is left after the joint opinion finishes dissecting it is surely not the result of that principle. While purporting to adhere to precedent, the joint opinion instead revises it. *Roe* continues to exist, but only in the way a storefront on a western movie set exists: a mere facade to give the illusion of reality. Decisions following *Roe*, such as Akron v. Akron Center for Reproductive Health, Inc., 462 U.S. 416 (1983), and Thornburgh v. American College of Obstetricians and Gynecologists, 476 U.S. 747 (1986), are frankly overruled in part under the "undue burden" standard expounded in the joint opinion.

In our view, authentic principles of stare decisis do not require that any portion of the reasoning in Roe be kept intact. "Stare decisis is not ... a universal, inexorable command," especially in cases involving the interpretation of the Federal Constitution. Erroneous decisions in such constitutional cases are uniquely durable, because correction through legislative action, save for constitutional amendment, is impossible. It is therefore our duty to reconsider constitutional interpretations that "depart from a proper understanding" of the Constitution. Our constitutional watch does not cease merely because we have spoken before on an issue; when it becomes

*** [This last passage quotes an epigram of Justice White's opinion for the Court in Bowers v. Hardwick, 478 U.S. 186, 194 (1986), holding that the Constitution does not forbid state criminalization of consensual sodomy between homosexuals—Ed.]

clear that a prior constitutional interpretation is unsound we are obliged to reexamine the question.

The joint opinion discusses several stare decisis factors which, it asserts, point toward retaining a portion of *Roe*. Two of these factors are that the main "factual underpinning" of *Roe* has remained the same, and that its doctrinal foundation is no weaker now than it was in 1973. Of course, what might be called the basic facts which gave rise to *Roe* have remained the same—women become pregnant, there is a point somewhere, depending on medical technology, where a fetus becomes viable, and women give birth to children. But this is only to say that the same facts which gave rise to *Roe* will continue to give rise to similar cases. . . . And surely there is no requirement, in considering whether to depart from stare decisis in a constitutional case, that a decision be more wrong now than it was at the time it was rendered. . . .

The joint opinion also points to the reliance interests involved in this context in its effort to explain why precedent must be followed for precedent's sake. . . . But . . . [no] traditional notion of reliance is . . . applicable here. The Court today cuts back on the protection afforded by *Roe*, and no one claims that this action defeats any reliance interest in the disavowed trimester framework. . . .

The joint opinion thus turns to what can only be described as an unconventional—and unconvincing—notion of reliance, a view based on the surmise that the availability of abortion since *Roe* has led to "two decades of economic and social developments" that would be undercut if the error of *Roe* were recognized. Ibid. . . . Surely it is dubious to suggest that women have reached their "places in society" in reliance upon *Roe*, rather than as a result of their determination to obtain higher education and compete with men in the job market, and of society's increasing recognition of their ability to fill positions that were previously thought to be reserved only for men. . . .

Apparently realizing that conventional stare decisis principles do not support its position, the joint opinion advances a belief that retaining a portion of *Roe* is necessary to protect the "legitimacy" of this Court. Because the Court must take care to render decisions "grounded truly in principle," and not simply as political and social compromises, the joint opinion properly declares it to be this Court's duty to ignore the public criticism and protest that may arise as a result of a decision. . . . But the joint opinion goes on to state that when the Court "resolves the sort of intensely divisive controversy reflected in *Roe* and those rare, comparable cases," its decision is exempt from reconsideration under established principles of stare decisis in constitutional cases. . . . This is a truly novel principle, one which is contrary to both the Court's historical practice and to the Court's traditional willingness to tolerate criticism of its opinions. Under this principle, when the Court has ruled on a divisive issue, it is apparently prevented from overruling that decision for the sole reason that it was incorrect, unless opposition to the original decision has died away.

The first difficulty with this principle lies in its assumption that cases which are "intensely divisive" can be readily distinguished from those that are not.... Although many of the Court's decisions divide the populace to a large degree, we have not previously on that account shied away from applying normal rules of stare decisis when urged to reconsider earlier decisions. Over the past 21 years, for example, the Court has overruled in whole or in part 34 of its previous constitutional decisions.

... It appears to us very odd indeed that the joint opinion chooses as benchmarks two cases in which the Court chose not to adhere to erroneous constitutional precedent, but instead enhanced its stature by acknowledging and correcting its error, apparently in violation of the joint opinion's "legitimacy" principle. See *West Coast Hotel Co. v. Parrish, supra; Brown v. Board of Education, supra.* One might also wonder how it is that the joint opinion puts these, and not others, in the "intensely divisive" category, and how it assumes that these are the only two lines of cases of comparable dimension to *Roe.* There is no reason to think that either *Plessy* or *Lochner* produced the sort of public protest when they were decided that *Roe* did.... [O]ur decision in *West Coast Hotel,* which overruled *Adkins v. Children's Hospital, supra,* and *Lochner,* was rendered at a time when Congress was considering President Franklin Roosevelt's proposal to "reorganize" this Court and enable him to name six additional Justices in the event that any member of the Court over the age of 70 did not elect to retire. It is difficult to imagine a situation in which the Court would face more intense opposition to a prior ruling than it did at that time, and, under the general principle proclaimed in the joint opinion, the Court seemingly should have responded to this opposition by stubbornly refusing to reexamine the *Lochner* rationale, lest it lose legitimacy by appearing to "overrule under fire." ... [T]he opinion contends that the Court was entitled to overrule *Plessy* and *Lochner* in those cases, despite the existence of opposition to the original decisions, only because both the Nation and the Court had learned new lessons in the interim. This is at best a feebly supported, post hoc rationalization for those decisions.... Although the Court [in *West Coast Hotel*] did acknowledge in the last paragraph of its opinion the state of affairs during the then-current Depression, the theme of the opinion is that the Court had been mistaken as a matter of constitutional law when it embraced "freedom of contract" 32 years previously.... The Court in *Brown* simply recognized, as Justice Harlan had recognized beforehand, that the Fourteenth Amendment does not permit racial segregation. The rule of *Brown* is not tied to popular opinion about the evils of segregation; it is a judgment that the Equal Protection Clause does not permit racial segregation, no matter whether the public might come to believe that it is beneficial. On that ground it stands, and on that ground alone the Court was justified in properly concluding that the *Plessy* Court had erred.

There are other reasons why the joint opinion's discussion of legitimacy is unconvincing as well. In assuming that the Court is perceived as "surrendering to political pressure" when it overrules a controversial decision, the joint opinion forgets that there are two sides to any controversy.... If one assumes instead, as the Court surely did in both *Brown* and *West Coast Hotel*, that the Court's legitimacy is enhanced by faithful interpretation of the Constitution irrespective of public opposition, such self-engendered difficulties may be put to one side.

Roe is not this Court's only decision to generate conflict. Our decisions in some recent capital cases, and in Bowers v. Hardwick, 478 U.S. 186 (1986), have also engendered demonstrations in opposition. The joint opinion's message to such protesters appears to be that they must cease their activities in order to serve their cause, because their protests will only cement in place a decision which by normal standards of stare decisis should be reconsidered. Nearly a century ago, Justice David J. Brewer of this Court, in an article discussing criticism of its decisions, observed that "many criticisms may be, like their authors, devoid of good taste, but better all sorts of criticism than no criticism at all." Justice Brewer on "The Nation's Anchor," 57 Albany L.J. 166, 169 (1898). This was good advice to the Court then, as it is today. Strong and often misguided criticism of a decision should not render the decision immune from reconsideration, lest a fetish for legitimacy penalize freedom of expression.

The end result of the joint opinion's paeans of praise for legitimacy is the enunciation of a brand new standard for evaluating state regulation of a woman's right to abortion—the "undue burden" standard. As indicated above, *Roe v. Wade* adopted a "fundamental right" standard under which state regulations could survive only if they met the requirement of "strict scrutiny." While we disagree with that standard, it at least had a recognized basis in constitutional law at the time Roe was decided. The same cannot be said for the "undue burden" standard, which is created largely out of whole cloth by the authors of the joint opinion. It is a standard which even today does not command the support of a majority of this Court.... Despite the efforts of the joint opinion, the undue burden standard presents nothing more workable than the trimester framework which it discards today. Under the guise of the Constitution, this Court will still impart its own preferences on the States in the form of a complex abortion code. The sum of the joint opinion's labors in the name of stare decisis and "legitimacy" is this: *Roe v. Wade* stands as a sort of judicial Potemkin Village, which may be pointed out to passers by as a monument to the importance of adhering to precedent. But behind the facade, an entirely new method of analysis, without any roots in constitutional law, is imported to decide the constitutionality of state laws regulating abortion. Neither stare decisis nor "legitimacy" are truly served by such an effort.

. . .

■ JUSTICE SCALIA, with whom the CHIEF JUSTICE, JUSTICE WHITE, and JUSTICE THOMAS join, concurring in the judgment in part and dissenting in part.

... [T]he issue in this case [is] not whether the power of a woman to abort her unborn child is a "liberty" in the absolute sense; or even whether it is a liberty of great importance to many women. Of course it is both. The issue is whether it is a liberty protected by the Constitution of the United

States. I am sure it is not. I reach that conclusion not because of anything so exalted as my views concerning the "concept of existence, of meaning, of the universe, and of the mystery of human life." Ibid. Rather, I reach it for the same reason I reach the conclusion that bigamy is not constitutionally protected—because of two simple facts: (1) the Constitution says absolutely nothing about it, and (2) the longstanding traditions of American society have permitted it to be legally proscribed....

Beyond that brief summary of the essence of my position, ... I must ... respond to a few of the more outrageous arguments in today's opinion, which it is beyond human nature to leave unanswered. I shall discuss each of them under a quotation from the Court's opinion to which they pertain....

*"Liberty finds no refuge in a jurisprudence of doubt."*

\* \* \*

One might have feared to encounter this august and sonorous phrase in an opinion defending the real *Roe v. Wade,* rather than the revised version fabricated today by the authors of the joint opinion. The shortcomings of *Roe* did not include lack of clarity: Virtually all regulation of abortion before the third trimester was invalid. But to come across this phrase in the joint opinion—which calls upon federal district judges to apply an "undue burden" standard as doubtful in application as it is unprincipled in origin—is really more than one should have to bear....

> *"While we appreciate the weight of the arguments ... that Roe should be overruled, the reservations any of us may have in reaffirming the central holding of Roe are outweighed by the explication of individual liberty we have given combined with the force of stare decisis."*

The Court's reliance upon stare decisis can best be described as contrived. It insists upon the necessity of adhering not to all of *Roe,* but only to what it calls the "central holding." It seems to me that stare decisis ought to be applied even to the doctrine of stare decisis, and I confess never to have heard of this new, keep-what-you-want-and-throw-away-the-rest version....

I am certainly not in a good position to dispute that the Court has saved the "central holding" of *Roe,* since to do that effectively I would have to know what the Court has saved, which in turn would require me to understand (as I do not) what the "undue burden" test means. I must confess, however, that I have always thought, and I think a lot of other people have always thought, that the arbitrary trimester framework, which the Court today discards, was quite as central to *Roe* as the arbitrary viability test, which the Court today retains. It seems particularly ungrateful to carve the trimester framework out of the core of *Roe,* since its very rigidity (in sharp contrast to the utter indeterminability of the "undue burden" test) is probably the only reason the Court is able to say, in urging stare decisis, that *Roe* "has in no sense proven 'unworkable,' " I suppose the Court is entitled to call a "central holding" whatever it wants to call a "central holding"—which is, come to think of it, perhaps one of the difficulties with this modified version of stare decisis. I thought I might note, however, that the following portions of *Roe* have not been saved:

\* Under *Roe*, requiring that a woman seeking an abortion be provided truthful information about abortion before giving informed written consent is unconstitutional, if the information is designed to influence her choice, *Thornburgh*, 476 U.S., at 759–765; *Akron I*, 462 U.S., at 442–445. Under the joint opinion's "undue burden" regime (as applied today, at least) such a requirement is constitutional.

\* Under *Roe*, requiring that information be provided by a doctor, rather than by nonphysician counselors, is unconstitutional, *Akron I, supra*, at 446–449. Under the "undue burden" regime (as applied today, at least) it is not.

\* Under *Roe*, requiring a 24–hour waiting period between the time the woman gives her informed consent and the time of the abortion is unconstitutional, *Akron I, supra*, at 449–451. Under the "undue burden" regime (as applied today, at least) it is not.

\* Under *Roe*, requiring detailed reports that include demographic data about each woman who seeks an abortion and various information about each abortion is unconstitutional, *Thornburgh, supra*, at 765–768. Under the "undue burden" regime (as applied today, at least) it generally is not.

> *"Where, in the performance of its judicial duties, the Court decides a case in such a way as to resolve the sort of intensely divisive controversy reflected in Roe ..., its decision has a dimension that the resolution of the normal case does not carry. It is the dimension present whenever the Court's interpretation of the Constitution calls the contending sides of a national controversy to end their national division by accepting a common mandate rooted in the Constitution."*

The Court's description of the place of *Roe* in the social history of the United States is unrecognizable. Not only did *Roe* not, as the Court suggests, resolve the deeply divisive issue of abortion; it did more than anything else to nourish it, by elevating it to the national level where it is infinitely more difficult to resolve. National politics were not plagued by abortion protests, national abortion lobbying, or abortion marches on Congress, before *Roe v. Wade* was decided. Profound disagreement existed among our citizens over the issue—as it does over other issues, such as the death penalty—but that disagreement was being worked out at the state level. As with many other issues, the division of sentiment within each State was not as closely balanced as it was among the population of the Nation as a whole, meaning not only that more people would be satisfied with the results of state-by-state resolution, but also that those results would be more stable. Pre–*Roe*, moreover, political compromise was possible.... *Roe* fanned into life an issue that has inflamed our national politics in general, and has obscured with its smoke the selection of Justices to this Court in particular, ever since. And by keeping us in the abortion-umpiring business, it is the perpetuation of that disruption, rather than of any *pax Roeana,* that the Court's new majority decrees.

*"To overrule under fire . . . would subvert the Court's legitimacy. . . .*

*"To all those who will be . . . tested by following, the Court implicitly undertakes to remain steadfast. . . . The promise of constancy, once given, binds its maker for as long as the power to stand by the decision survives and . . . the commitment [is not] obsolete. . . .*

*"[The American people's] belief in themselves as . . . a people [who aspire to live according to the rule of law] is not readily separable from their understanding of the Court invested with the authority to decide their constitutional cases and speak before all others for their constitutional ideals. If the Court's legitimacy should be undermined, then, so would the country be in its very ability to see itself through its constitutional ideals."*

The Imperial Judiciary lives. It is instructive to compare this Nietzschean vision of us unelected, life-tenured judges—leading a *Volk* who will be "tested by following," and whose very "belief in themselves" is mystically bound up in their "understanding" of a Court that "speaks before all others for their constitutional ideals"—with the somewhat more modest role envisioned for these lawyers by the Founders. "The judiciary . . . has . . . no direction either of the strength or of the wealth of the society, and can take no active resolution whatever. It may truly be said to have neither FORCE nor WILL but merely judgment. . . ." The Federalist No. 78, 393–394 (G. Wills ed. 1982). Or, again, to compare this ecstasy of a Supreme Court in which there is, especially on controversial matters, no shadow of change or hint of alteration ("There is a limit to the amount of error that can plausibly be imputed to prior courts") with the more democratic views of a more humble man: "The candid citizen must confess that if the policy of the Government upon vital questions affecting the whole people is to be irrevocably fixed by decisions of the Supreme Court, . . . the people will have ceased to be their own rulers, having to that extent practically resigned their Government into the hands of that eminent tribunal." A. Lincoln, First Inaugural Address (Mar. 4, 1861). It is particularly difficult, in the circumstances of the present decision, to sit still for the Court's lengthy lecture upon the virtues of "constancy," of "remaining steadfast," of adhering to "principle." Among the five Justices who purportedly adhere to *Roe*, at most three agree upon the principle that constitutes adherence (the joint opinion's "undue burden" standard)—and that principle is inconsistent with *Roe*. To make matters worse, two of the three, in order thus to remain steadfast, had to abandon previously stated positions. It is beyond me how the Court expects these accommodations to be accepted "as grounded truly in principle, not as compromises with social and political pressures having, as such, no bearing on the principled choices that the Court is obliged to make." The only principle the Court "adheres" to, it seems to me, is the principle that the Court must be seen as standing by *Roe*. That is not a principle of law (which is what I thought the Court was talking about), but a principle of Realpolitik—and a wrong one at that.

I cannot agree with, indeed I am appalled by, the Court's suggestion that the decision whether to stand by an erroneous constitutional decision must be strongly influenced—against overruling, no less—by the substantial and continuing public opposition the decision has generated. The Court's judgment that any other course would "subvert the Court's legitimacy" must be another consequence of reading the error-filled history book that described the deeply divided country brought together by Roe. In my history-book, the Court was covered with dishonor and deprived of legitimacy by Dred Scott v. Sandford, 19 How. 393 (1857), an erroneous (and widely opposed) opinion that it did not abandon, rather than by West Coast Hotel Co. v. Parrish, 300 U.S. 379 (1937), which produced the famous "switch in time" from the Court's erroneous (and widely opposed) constitutional opposition to the social measures of the New Deal. . . .

But whether it would "subvert the Court's legitimacy" or not, the notion that we would decide a case differently from the way we otherwise would have in order to show that we can stand firm against public disapproval is frightening. It is a bad enough idea, even in the head of someone like me, who believes that the text of the Constitution, and our traditions, say what they say and there is no fiddling with them. But when it is in the mind of a Court that believes the Constitution has an evolving meaning, see that the Ninth Amendment's reference to "other" rights is not a disclaimer, but a charter for action, and that the function of this Court is to "speak before all others for [the people's] constitutional ideals" unrestrained by meaningful text or tradition—then the notion that the Court must adhere to a decision for as long as the decision faces "great opposition" and the Court is "under fire" acquires a character of almost czarist arrogance. . . .

In truth, I am as distressed as the Court is—and expressed my distress several years ago, see *Webster*, 492 U.S., at 535—about the "political pressure" directed to the Court: the marches, the mail, the protests aimed at inducing us to change our opinions. How upsetting it is, that so many of our citizens (good people, not lawless ones, on both sides of this abortion issue, and on various sides of other issues as well) think that we Justices should properly take into account their views, as though we were engaged not in ascertaining an objective law but in determining some kind of social consensus. . . . [But] the American people love democracy and the American people are not fools. As long as this Court thought (and the people thought) that we Justices were doing essentially lawyers' work up here—reading text and discerning our society's traditional understanding of that text—the public pretty much left us alone. Texts and traditions are facts to study, not convictions to demonstrate about. But if in reality our process of constitutional adjudication consists primarily of making value judgments; if we can ignore a long and clear tradition clarifying an ambiguous text . . . then a free and intelligent people's attitude towards us can be expected to be (ought to be) quite different. The people know that their value judgments are quite as good as those taught in any law school—maybe better. If, indeed, the "liberties" protected by the Constitution are, as the Court says, undefined and unbounded, then the people should demonstrate, to protest that we do not implement their values instead of ours. Not only that, but confirmation hearings for new Justices should deteriorate into question-

and-answer sessions in which Senators go through a list of their constituents' most favored and most disfavored alleged constitutional rights, and seek the nominee's commitment to support or oppose them. Value judgments, after all, should be voted on, not dictated; and if our Constitution has somehow accidently committed them to the Supreme Court, at least we can have a sort of plebiscite each time a new nominee to that body is put forward.

* * *

## Questions

**1.**  Do you agree with Justice Scalia's description of the plurality's approach to *stare decisis* as "take-what-you-want-and-throw-away-the-rest"?

**2.**  Even assuming that Justice Scalia's characterization, however unkind, is also accurate, what is the difference between that approach to *stare decisis* and distinguishing an inconvenient precedent? What is the difference between that and (re)characterizing a "holding" as "dictum"?

**3.**  Do you think that *stare decisis* acts as an effective check on the personal opinions of the Justices?

## 3.  RETROACTIVITY

When a judicial decision announces a new rule of law, or overrules an old one, to what events does it apply? In addition to determining the rights and/or responsibilities of the parties to the case decided, does the ruling apply forward and/or backward in time as well? Consider the following possibilities:

The Court announces a new rule in response to a new question, e.g. the Georgia Supreme Court recognizes the right of privacy, and holds that the unauthorized publication of a person's photograph for commercial purposes violates that right.

Possibility #1. All unauthorized publications occurring in Georgia from the date of decision (1905) forward are subject to the rule.

Possibility #2. In addition, all unauthorized publications occurring in Georgia before 1905 are also covered (assuming the statute of limitations has not run).

The Court announces a new rule that overrules a prior rule, e.g., the New York Court of Appeals overturns its precedent that barred a claim for negligent infliction of emotional distress.

Possibility #1. All claims alleging emotional distress resulting from negligent conduct occurring as of the decision (1961) are actionable, but the new rule does not apply to the parties in the overruling case.

Possibility #2. All claims alleging emotional distress resulting from negligent conduct occurring as of the decision are actionable, and the new rule applies to the parties in the overruling case.

Possibility #3. In addition, all claims alleging emotional distress resulting from negligent conduct occurring before the decision are also covered (assuming the statute of limitations has not run), so long as such a claim had not already been brought and finally adjudicated under the old rule.

Possibility #4. In addition, old claims may be reopened and readjudicated under the new rule.

As a general matter, judicial decisions in fact do apply to events that occurred before the new or changed rule was declared. However, where prior decisions have been overruled, the parties to those cases are not free to reopen the case, if it has already been the object of a final judgment.

Why do judicial decisions operate in this retroactive way? Should they? Could it, or should it, be otherwise? The materials in this section are intended to introduce some of the considerations involved in these and related questions.

The problem of retroactivity, along with *stare decisis* and *res judicata,* is one of the forces promoting stability and predictability in the judicial process. People act—or are thought to act—in reliance on existing rules, including judge-made rules. Where there was no pre-existing rule, as in the first example above, retroactive application of judicial response to a "new question" unsettles no expectations. But when a court has overruled its precedent, retroactive application of its decision can undermine the expectations of those who acted in accordance with the prior rule, particularly if in cases preceding the overruling the court has not signalled a disposition to change the law. This concern may present a substantial argument for continued adherence to precedent. *See, e.g.,* Cullings v. Goetz, supra, p. 117.

As a result, courts may seek to limit the retroactive impact of a changed rule, so that prior actors not parties to the case are not prejudiced by the change. However, this technique too, encounters criticism. With retroactivity as the base-line rule, courts will hesitate to make abrupt changes in the law. Without the constraint of retroactivity, judges might be inclined to rule on more than the parties' dispute requires. Thus, were courts free to limit their decisions' retroactive effect, some critics fear courts might be tempted to usurp the legislature's functions. Recall that even in a common law system, courts, unlike legislatures, are not constituted as "lawmakers." Rather, judge-made law is the product of the dispute-settling process. Judges, at least in theory, assess and adjust the law in the limited context of the parties and controversy before them; they do not announce sweeping rules of general and abstract application. (Consider the accuracy of that proposition in light of the materials you have studied up till now.)

The following two decisions, one from England's House of Lords, the other from the Supreme Court of Wisconsin, illustrate several approaches to the impact of an overruling on controversies arising before the jurisdiction's highest court changed the common law rule. The note immediately below should assist your reading of the House of Lords' decision.

### The English Court Structure[1]

The English court system can be analyzed with the same conceptual framework used for the US court systems.[2] There are courts of first instance, an intermediate appellate court and a court of last resort. The pre-eminent first instance court is the High Court, which has original jurisdiction to hear all civil claims. It sits in three divisions: Queens Bench, Family and Chancery. Below the High Court is the senior first instance criminal court, called the Crown Court. Criminal trials are not held in the High Court, so in this respect the Crown Court is High Court's equal. However, the Crown Court is ranked below the High Court because in certain circumstances a defendant may appeal from the Crown to the High Court. There are also first instance courts of limited jurisdiction; namely Magistrates Courts for summary criminal offences (misdemeanors), and the County Courts for civil litigation.

The intermediate appellate court is called the Court of Appeal and sits in two divisions: Civil and Criminal.

The court of last resort is known as the judicial branch of the House of Lords, which hears appeals from the Court of Appeal in both civil and criminal matters (and from the High Court in rare cases), and from Scotland and Northern Ireland in civil matters.[3] This court has twelve members (called Lords of Appeal in Ordinary, or "Law Lords"), plus the Lord Chancellor, who usually hear appeals in five-person Appellate Committees. The House of Lords has an interesting dual function—it is also the

---

**1.** Thanks to Daniel Kalderimis, Associate-in-Law, Columbia University, LLB (Hons) Victoria University of Wellington, N.Z.

**2.** Indeed the English court system, which includes Wales, is perhaps easier to understand because the U.K. is a unitary, and not a federal system. Note that Scotland and Northern Ireland, though part of the United Kingdom, have their own legal sys-

tem, which intersects with, but is distinct from, the English system.

**3.** Note that by virtue of the United Kingdom's membership of the European Union, some matters may be referred by the House of Lords to the Court of Justice of the European Communities.

upper house of the English parliament and the Law Lords are also members of this legislative body. In this latter capacity the Law Lords can and do participate in considering legislation. In particular, the Law Lords are recognized as having valuable legal expertise which is especially relevant to technical law reform and consolidation Bills.[4] In this respect, the United Kingdom does not enforce the strict separation of powers enshrined in the US Constitution. On the other hand, the Law Lords are aware of the constitutional delicacy of their dual roles and by convention avoid political controversy, sitting on the crossbenches of the House. It is rare, but not unheard of, for serving Law Lords to take an active part in legislative debate.[5]

For completeness, you should note that there is one additional court, called the Judicial Committee of the Privy Council, which is not part of the English hierarchy, but functions as a court of last resort for certain Commonwealth countries. Its jurisdiction is steadily shrinking, having lost Canada and Australia, but currently includes New Zealand, Jamaica and some Pacific islands. The membership of the Privy Council includes the Law Lords, as well as select Privy Counsellors appointed from Commonwealth countries. As with the House of Lords, the Privy Council usually sits in groups of five.

4. Gavin Drewry and Sir Louis Blom–Cooper, *The Appellate Function, in THE HOUSE OF LORDS : ITS PARLIAMENTA-* *RY AND JUDICIAL ROLES* 123–124 (Paul Carmichael & Brice Dickson eds., 1999).

5. *Ibid*, 124.

The diagram below sets out a simplified version of the English system.[6]

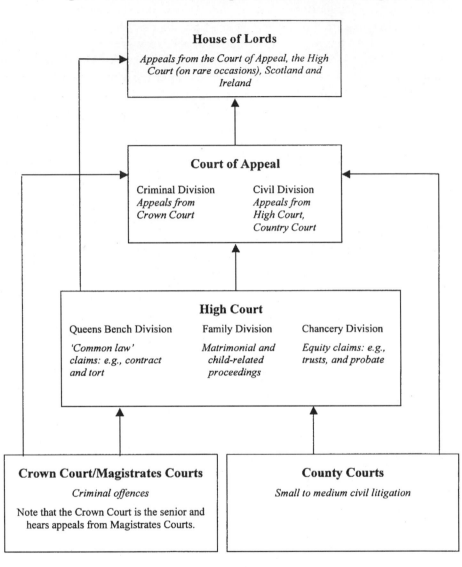

# Kleinwort Benson Ltd v. Lincoln City Council

House of Lords, 1998.
[1998] UKHL 38, [1999] 2 AC 349, [1998] 4 All ER 513, [1998] 3 WLR 1095.

Lord Browne-Wilkinson, Lord Goff of Chieveley, Lord Lloyd of Berwick, Lord Hoffmann, Lord Hope of Craighead

## OPINIONS OF THE LORDS OF APPEAL FOR JUDGMENT IN THE CAUSE

[Editor's Note: In Hazell v. London Borough of Hammersmith and Fulham [1992] 2 A.C. 1, the House of Lords ruled that interest rate swap agreements were void, when entered into by municipal authorities (as such a body is not empowered to engage in financial speculation). In a swap transaction, one party, the "fixed rate payer," agrees to pay to the other party over a certain period interest at a fixed rate on a stated capital sum; and the other party, the "floating rate payer," agrees to pay over the same period to the fixed rate payer interest on the same sum at a market rate determined in accordance with a certain formula. In practice, a balance is struck at each relevant date and the party who then owes the greater sum will pay the difference to the other party.

The Kleinwort Benson bank entered into interest rate swap transactions with four municipal authorities. Following the decision in Hazell, the bank commenced proceedings against each of the authorities claiming restitution of the sums it had paid to them under these transactions. The bank contended that its money should be returned because the bank was operating under a "mistake of law" as to the transactions' validity. Departing from prior decisions that had held contracts voidable for mistakes of fact, but not for mistakes of law, the House of Lords determined that "mistake of law" was indeed a ground for contract avoidance. At the times the swap agreements were entered into, and the payments were made, however, the transactions were generally believed to be lawful.

There could be no "mistake of law" unless the House of Lords' subsequent invalidation of swap transactions were deemed to apply to transactions occurring before the date of the decision. A majority of the Law Lords in Kleinwort Benson ruled that the Hazell decision had the effect of altering the legal rule not only for the future, but also for previously concluded transactions. As a result, the bank was retroactively mistaken about the legal validity of its agreements.

A word about the presentation of the decision: Unlike the practice followed in the U.S. Supreme Court and lower appellate courts, each Law Lord in this case separately presents his own statement of the facts and the legal analysis. There is no majority opinion (or dissenting opinion) synthesizing the reasoning of the several judges who agree on an outcome and its justification. Consider what the practice of separate statements implies for discerning the terms and scope of the "holding" of the decision.]

## LORD BROWNE–WILKINSON

My Lords,

I have had the advantage of reading in draft the speech of my noble and learned friend, Lord Goff of Chieveley which contains yet another major contribution to the law of restitution.

Were it not for one matter, I would be in full agreement with his views. But unfortunately he and the majority of your Lordships take the view that when established law is changed by a subsequent decision of the Courts, money rightly paid in accordance with the old established law is recoverable as having been paid under a mistake of law. I take the view that the monies are not recoverable since, at the time of payment, the payer was not labouring under any mistake.

The majority view is that the decision in Hazell v. London Borough of Hammersmith and Fulham [1992] 2 A.C. 1 established that the swaps agreements were void; that although the decision in Hazell post-dated the last of the payments made by Kleinworts to the local authorities the decision operated retrospectively so that under the law as eventually established Kleinworts were labouring under a mistake at the time they made each payment in thinking that they were liable to make such payment. Therefore, in their view, Kleinworts can recover payments made under a mistake of law. My view, on the other hand, is that although the decision in Hazell is retrospective in its effect, retrospection cannot falsify history: if at the date of each payment it was settled law that local authorities had capacity to enter into swap contracts, Kleinworts were not labouring under any mistake of law at that date. The subsequent decision in Hazell could not create a mistake where no mistake existed at the time.

. . . [W]hen the common law is changed by later judicial decision, have all payments made on the basis of the previous law been made under a mistake of law? . . .

*Where the law is established by judicial decision subsequently overruled*

I will take the case where the law has been established by a single decision of the Court of Appeal made in 1930. In 1990 the payer makes a payment which would only have been due to the payee if the Court of Appeal decision was good law. The payer was advised that the Court of Appeal decision was good law. In 1997 this House overruled the Court of Appeal decision. Is the plaintiff entitled to recover the payment made in 1990 on the ground of mistake of law?

There is, as I understand it, no dispute that in order to recover the plaintiff has to have been labouring under the mistake at the date of payment and to have made the payment because of that mistake. Certainly that position has been accepted by Kleinworts in their written reply and by my noble and learned friend, Lord Goff. The question is whether the subsequent overruling of the 1930 Court of Appeal decision requires the court to hold that at the date of payment (1990) the law (contrary to what the plaintiff had been advised) was not the law established by the Court of Appeal decision of 1930.

The theoretical position has been that judges do not make or change law: they discover and declare the law which is throughout the same.

According to this theory, when an earlier decision is overruled the law is not changed: its true nature is disclosed, having existed in that form all along. This theoretical position is, as Lord Reid said, a fairy tale in which no-one any longer believes. In truth, judges make and change the law. The whole of the common law is judge-made and only by judicial change in the law is the common law kept relevant in a changing world. But whilst the underlying myth has been rejected, its progeny—the retrospective effect of a change made by judicial decision—remains. As Lord Goff in his speech demonstrates, in the absence of some form of prospective overruling, a judgment overruling an earlier decision is bound to operate to some extent retrospectively: once the higher court in the particular case has stated the changed law, the law as so stated applies not only to that case but also to all cases subsequently coming before the courts for decision, even though the events in question in such cases occurred before the Court of Appeal decision was overruled.

Therefore the precise question is whether the fact that the later overruling decision operates retrospectively so far as the substantive law is concerned also requires it to be assumed (contrary to the facts) that at the date of each payment the plaintiff made a mistake as to what the law then was. In my judgment it does not. The main effect of your Lordships' decision in the present case is to abolish the rule that money paid under a mistake of law cannot be recovered, which rule was based on the artificial assumption that a man is presumed to know the law. It would be unfortunate to introduce into the amended law a new artificiality, viz., that a man is making a mistake at the date of payment when he acts on the basis of the law as it is then established. He was not mistaken at the date of payment. He paid on the basis that the then binding Court of Appeal decision stated the law, which it did: the fact that the law was later retrospectively changed cannot alter retrospectively the state of the payer's mind at the time of payment. As Deane J. said in the High Court of Australia in University of Wollongong v. Metwally 158 C.L.R. 447 at p. 478:

> "A parliament may legislate that, for the purposes of the law which it controls, past facts or past laws are to be deemed and treated as having been different to what they were. It cannot however objectively expunge the past or alter the facts of history."

If that be true of statutory legislation, the same must a fortiori be true of judicial decision. In my judgment, therefore, if a man has made a payment on an understanding of the law which was correct as the law stood at the date of such payment he has not made that payment under a mistake of law if the law is subsequently changed.

I am fortified in that view by considering what will be the effect of your Lordships' decision. A payment which was initially irrecoverable will subsequently become recoverable. Consider the hypothetical case I have put. A payment was made in 1990 when the Court of Appeal decision was still valid. Under the existing law, the claim in restitution should apparently have arisen at the date of such payment: see Baker v. Courage & Co. [1910] 1 K.B. 56. Yet at that date there could be no question of any mistake. It would not have been possible to issue a writ claiming restitution on the grounds of mistake of law until the 1997 decision had overruled the 1930 Court of Appeal decision. Therefore a payment which, when made, and for several years thereafter, was entirely valid and irrecoverable would subsequently become recoverable. This result would be subversive of the great public interest in the security of receipts and the closure of transactions. The position is even worse because all your Lordships consider that the claims to recover money paid under a mistake of law are subject to section 32(1)(c) of the Limitation Act 1980, i.e. that in such a case time will not begin to run until the "mistake" is discovered. A subsequent overruling of a Court of Appeal decision by the House of Lords could occur many decades after payments have been made on the faith of the Court of Appeal decision: in such a case "the mistake" would not be discovered until the later overruling. All payments made pursuant to the Court of Appeal ruling would be recoverable subject only to the possible defence of change of position.

. . .

My Lords, in these circumstances I find myself in a quandary. I am convinced that the law should be changed so as to permit monies paid under a mistake of law to be recovered. I also accept, for the reasons given by my noble and learned friend Lord Goff, that the relevant limitation period applicable to such a claim would be that laid down by section 32(1)(c) of the Limitation Act 1980, i.e. six years from the date on which the mistake was, or could with reasonable diligence have been, discovered. The majority of your Lordships consider that such claim will arise when the law (whether settled by existing authority or by common consensus) is changed by a later decision of the courts. The consequence of this House in its judicial capacity introducing such a fundamental change would be as follows. On every occasion in which a higher court changed the law by judicial decision, all those who had made payments on the basis that the old law was correct (however long ago such payments were made) would have six years in which to bring a claim to recover money paid under a mistake of law. All your Lordships accept that this position cannot be cured save by primary legislation altering the relevant limitation period. In the circumstances, I believe that it would be quite wrong for your Lordships to change the law so as to make money paid under a mistake of law recoverable since to do so would leave this gaping omission in the law. In my judgment the correct course would be for the House to indicate that an alteration in the law is desirable but leave it to the Law Commission and Parliament to produce a satisfactory statutory change in the law which, at one and the same time, both introduces the new cause of action and also properly regulates the limitation period applicable to it.

I would dismiss these appeals.

## LORD GOFF OF CHIEVELEY

My Lords,

... the mistake relied upon [by Kleinwort] is a mistake of law; and under the law as it stands at present restitution will in general not be granted in respect of money paid under a mistake of that kind. It follows that, in the present proceedings, Kleinwort Benson is seeking a decision that that long-established rule [the "mistake of law rule" (ed)] should no longer form part of the English law of restitution-a decision which, as all parties to the present litigation recognise, can only be made by your Lordships' House.

. . .

For all these reasons .... I would therefore conclude ... that the mistake of law rule should no longer be maintained as part of English law, and that English law should now recognise that there is a general right to recover money paid under a mistake, whether of fact or law, subject to the defences available in the law of restitution.

. . .

*Issue IA: Payments made under a settled understanding of the law.*

I turn now to a central question in these appeals. This relates to the fact that the payments of which recovery is sought in these cases were made under contracts which at the time were understood by all concerned to be valid and binding, so that the payments themselves were believed to be lawfully due under those contracts. This misunderstanding was, of course, removed by the decision of this House in *Hazell* [1992] 2 A.C. 1 that the contracts were beyond the powers of the local authorities involved and so void. The argument now advanced by the local authorities is that payments so made on the basis of a settled understanding of the law which is later changed by a judicial decision should not be recoverable on the ground of mistake of law.

. . .

*The declaratory theory of judicial decisions.* Historically speaking, the declaratory theory of judicial decisions is to be found in a statement by Sir Matthew Hale over 300 years ago, viz. that the decisions of the courts do not constitute the law properly so called, but are evidence of the law and as such "have a great weight and authority in expounding, declaring and publishing what the law of this Kingdom is": see *Hale's History of the Common Law* (6th ed.) p. 90. To the like effect, *Blackstone (Commentaries,* 6th ed., i, pp. 88–9) stated that "the decisions of courts are the evidence of what is the common law". In recent times, however, a more realistic approach has been adopted, as in Sir George Jessel's celebrated statement that rules of equity, unlike rules of the common law, are not supposed to have been established since time immemorial, but have been invented, altered, improved and refined from time to time: see *In re Hallett's Estate* (1880) 13 Ch. D. 696, 710. There can be no doubt of the truth of this statement; and we all know that in reality, in the common law as in equity, the law is the subject of development by the judges—normally, of course, by appellate judges. We describe as leading cases the decisions which mark the principal stages in this development, and we have no difficulty in identifying the judges who are primarily responsible. It is universally recognised that judicial development of the common law is inevitable. If it had never taken place, the common law would be the same now as it was in the reign of King Henry II; it is because of it that the common law is a living system of law, reacting to new events and new ideas, and so capable of providing the citizens of this country with a system of practical justice relevant to the times in which they live. The recognition that this is what actually happens requires, however, that we should look at the declaratory theory of judicial decision with open eyes and reinterpret it in the light of the way in which all judges, common law and equity, actually decide cases today.

When a judge decides a case which comes before him, he does so on the basis of what he understands the law to be. This he discovers from the applicable statutes, if any, and from precedents drawn from reports of previous judicial decisions. Nowadays, he derives much assistance from academic writings in interpreting statutes and, more especially, the effect of reported cases; and he has regard, where appropriate, to decisions of judges in other jurisdictions. In the course of deciding the case before him he may, on occasion, develop the common law in the perceived interests of justice, though as a general rule he does this "only interstitially", to use the expression of O.W. Holmes J. in *South Pacific Co. v. Jensen* (1917) 244 U.S. 2095, 221. This means not only that he must act within the confines of the doctrine of precedent, but that the change so made must be seen as a development, usually a very modest development, of existing principle and so can take its place as a congruent part of the common law as a whole. In this process, what Maitland has called the "seamless web", and I myself (*The Search for Principle*, Proc. Brit. Acad. vol. LXIX (1983) 170, 186) have called the "mosaic", of the common law, is kept in a constant state of adaptation and repair, the doctrine of precedent, the "cement of legal principle", providing the necessary stability. A similar process must take place in codified systems as in the common law, where a greater stability is provided by the code itself; though as the years pass by, and decided cases assume a greater importance, codified systems tend to become more like common law systems.

Occasionally, a judicial development of the law will be of a more radical nature, constituting a departure, even a major departure, from what has previously been considered to be established principle, and leading to a realignment of subsidiary principles within that branch of the law. Perhaps the most remarkable example of such a development is to be found in the decisions of this House in the middle of this century which led to the creation of our modern system of administrative law. It is into this category that the present case falls; but it must nevertheless be seen as a development of the law, and treated as such.

Bearing these matters in mind, the law which the judge then states to be applicable to the case before him is the law which, as so developed, is perceived by him as applying not only to the case before him, but to all other comparable cases, as a congruent part of the body of the law.

Moreover when he states the applicable principles of law, the judge is declaring these as constituting the law relevant to his decision. Subject to consideration by appellate tribunals, and (within limits) by judges of equal jurisdiction, what he states to be the law will, generally speaking, be applicable not only to the case before him but, as part of the common law, to other comparable cases which come before the courts, whenever the events which are the subject of those cases in fact occurred.

It is in this context that we have to reinterpret the declaratory theory of judicial decision. We can see that, in fact, it does not presume the existence of an ideal system of the common law, which the judges from time to time reveal in their decisions. The historical theory of judicial decision, though it may in the past have served its purpose, was indeed a fiction. But it does mean that, when the judges state what the law is, their decisions do, in the sense I have described, have a retrospective effect. That is, I believe, inevitable. It is inevitable in relation to the particular case before the court, in which the events must have occurred some time, perhaps some years, before the judge's decision is made. But it is also inevitable in relation to other cases in which the law as so stated will in future fall to be applied. I must confess that I cannot imagine how a common law system, or indeed any legal system, can operate otherwise if the law is be applied equally to all and yet be capable of organic change. This I understand to be the conclusion reached in *Cross and Harris on Precedent in English Law*, 4th ed., from which I have derived much assistance, when at p. 33 they ask the question: "what can our judges do but make new law and how can they prevent it from having retrospective effect?" This is also the underlying theme of Lord Coulsfield's evidence to the Scottish Law Commission quoted in para. 3.14 of their Discussion Paper No. 99, Judicial Abolition of the Error of Law Rule and its Aftermath (1996) (which I have read with interest and respect) in which, in the light of the decision of the Inner House in *Morgan Guaranty Trust Co. of New York v. Lothian Regional Council* 1995 S.C. 151, and especially the notable judgment of my noble and learned friend Lord Hope of Craighead in that case, they reconsider and resile from their previous proposal that Scots law should adopt a "settled understanding of the law" provision along the lines proposed by our own Law Commission. The only alternative, as I see it, is to adopt a system of prospective overruling. But such a system, although it has occasionally been adopted elsewhere with, I understand, somewhat controversial results, has no place in our legal system. I wish to add that I do not regard the declaratory theory of judicial decision, as I have described it, as an aberration of the common law. Since I regard it as an inevitable attribute of judicial decision-making, some such theory must, I imagine, be applied in civil law countries, as in common law countries; indeed I understand that a declaratory theory of judicial decision applies in Germany, though I do not know its precise form.

It is in the light of the foregoing that I have to ask myself whether the Law Commission's "settled understanding of the law" proposal forms part of the common law. This, as I understand the position, requires that I should consider whether parties in the position of Kleinwort Benson were mistaken when they paid money to local authorities under interest swap agreements which they, like others, understood to be valid but have later been held to be void. To me, it is plain that the money was indeed paid over under a mistake, the mistake being a mistake of law. The payer believed, when he paid the money, that he was bound in law to pay it. He is now told that, on the law as held to be applicable at the date of the payment, he was not bound to pay it. Plainly, therefore, he paid the money under a mistake of law, and accordingly, subject to any applicable defences, he is entitled to recover it. It comes as no surprise to me that, in the swaps litigation, it appears to have been assumed that money paid pursuant to interest rate swap agreements was paid under a mistake which, in *Westdeutsche Landesbank Girozentrale v. Islington London Borough Council* [1994] 4 All E.R. 890, 931E, was inevitably held by Hobhouse J. to have been a mistake of law and so, on the law as it then stood, irrecoverable on that basis. Not surprisingly, there is very little previous authority on the question whether in such circumstances the money has been paid under a mistake of law; but such authority as there is supports this view. . . .

    .  .  .

The question then arises whether, having regard to the fact that the right to recover money paid under a mistake of law is only now being recognised for the first time, it would be appropriate for your Lordships' House so to develop the law on the lines of the Law Commission's proposed reform as a corollary to the newly developed right of recovery. I can see no good reason why your Lordships' House should take a step which, as I see it, is inconsistent with the declaratory theory of judicial decision as applied in our legal system, under which the law as declared by the judge is the law applicable not only at the date of the decision but at the date of the events which are the subject of the case before him, and of the events of other cases in pari materia which may thereafter come before the courts. I recognise, of course, that the situation may be different where the law is subject to legislative change. That is because legislation takes effect from the moment when it becomes law, and is only retrospective in its effect to the extent that this is provided for in the legislative instrument. Moreover even where it is retrospective, it has the effect that as from the date of the legislation a new legal provision will apply retrospectively in place of that previously applicable. It follows that retrospective legislative change in the law does not necessarily have the effect that a previous payment was, as a result of the change in the law, made under a mistake of law at the time of payment. . . . As I have already pointed out, this is not the position in the case of a judicial development of the law. But, for my part, I cannot see why judicial development of the law should, in this respect, be placed on the same footing as legislative change. In this connection, it should not be forgotten that legislation which has an impact on previous transactions can be so drafted as to prevent unjust consequences flowing from it. That option is not, of course, open in the case of judicial decisions.

    .  .  .

Of course, I recognise that the law of restitution must embody specific defences which are concerned to protect the stability of closed transactions. The defence of change of position is one such defence; the defences of compromise, and settlement of an honest claim (the scope of which is a matter of debate), are others. It is possible that others may be developed from judicial decisions in the future. But the proposed "settled understanding of the law" defence is not, overtly, such a defence. It is based on the theory that a payment made on that basis is not made under a mistake at all. Once that reasoning is seen not to be correct, the basis for the proposed defence is, at least in cases such as the present, undermined.

. . .

*Conclusion*: In the result, I would answer the questions posed for your Lordships under the various Issues as follows:

. . .

*Issue 1A*: There is no principle of English law that payments made under a settled understanding of the law which is subsequently departed from by judicial decision shall not be recoverable in restitution on the ground of mistake of law.

. . .

## LORD LLOYD OF BERWICK

My Lords,

. . .

This brings us to the central question. Nobody now suggests that the common law is static. It is capable of adapting itself to new circumstances. Is it then capable of being changed? or is it only capable of being developed? The common sense answer is that the common law is capable of being changed, not only by legislation, but also by judicial decision. This is nowhere clearer than when a long-standing decision of the Court of Appeal is overruled. Indeed in a system such as ours, where the Court of Appeal is bound by its own previous decisions, the main justification for the existence of a second tier appeal is that it enables the House to re-direct the law when it has taken a wrong turning. . . .

What then is the House doing when it overrules a line of Court of Appeal authority? First and foremost it is determining what the law is in relation to the case which it is deciding. It will then apply that law to the facts of the particular case. Since the transaction giving rise to the case will have occurred in the past, it can be said that to that very limited extent (and the same is true of every decision of every court) it is applying the law retrospectively.

An inevitable consequence of determining the law in relation to a particular case is that the same law will apply to other cases as yet undecided, in which the same point arises. This is so whether the transaction in question lies in the past or the future. So again, to that limited extent, it can be said that the decision operates retrospectively. But that, as it seems to me, is the full extent of any retrospective effect. There is no way in which the decision can be applied retrospectively to cases which have already been decided. Nor is there any logical reason why there should be. It is the function of the court to decide what the law is, not what it was. So when the House of Lords overrules a line of Court of Appeal decisions it does not, and cannot, decide those cases again. The law as applied to those cases was the law as decided at the time by the Court of Appeal. The House of Lords can say that the Court of Appeal took a wrong turning. It can say what the law should have been. But it cannot say that the law actually applied by the Court of Appeal was other than what it was. It cannot, in my learned and noble friend Lord Browne–Wilkinson's vivid expression, falsify history.

It follows that in such a case the House of Lords is doing more than develop the law. It is changing the law, as common sense suggests.... If this view of what happens is inconsistent with the declaratory theory of the Court's function, then it is time we said so. It always was a fairy tale.

If it is right that the House of Lords can change the law by overruling a previous decision of the Court of Appeal, it must follow that a person relying on the old law was under no mistake at the time, and cannot claim to have been under a mistake ex post facto because the law is subsequently changed. This is obviously true where the law is changed by legislation. In my opinion it is equally true when the law is changed by judicial decision. The point is put clearly by the Scottish Law Commission in Discussion Paper No. 99, Judicial Abolition of the Error of Law Rule and its Aftermath (1996) paragraph 3.33 when summarising the views of the Court of Session judges:

> "The Court of Session judges pointed to the oddity of providing that a payment is not to be recoverable by reason of a 'change' in the law. If it is indeed a change, the payment would ex hypothesi not be recoverable. We agree that any provision introducing the bar should not refer to a change in the law. If the courts do change the law, the reference is unnecessary; if they do not (because of the declaratory theory) it would be inappropriate for statute to state that they do."

The next question is whether the same reasoning applies where there is no previous decision of the Court of Appeal directly in point. Can the House of Lords "change" the law in those circumstances, or can it only develop the law? I can see no difference in principle. The English common law is not confined to decided cases. In the field of commercial law, for example, the custom of merchants has always been a fruitful source of law. It is true that a custom can be challenged in a court of law. But it does not need a court of law to establish a custom. Custom is binding on the parties irrespective of any judicial decision. Where therefore a long established custom is rejected by a court of law on the ground that it is inconsistent with statute, the law is "changed" just as much as when a decision of the Court of Appeal is overruled by the House of Lords. I repeat some sentences from the Law Commission Report No. 227 which I have already quoted:

"It is not realistic to restrict 'settled law' to propositions which arise only from statute or from judicial decisions . . . Courts will be free . . . to recognise a proposition as settled irrespective of the source from which it is derived."

I agree with these observations. There may of course be cases where there is a dispute whether the law was settled at the time of the transaction. But as the Law Commission again point out, this is just the sort of common sense question which the courts are particularly well qualified to answer.

There are two policy reasons which support the [local authorities'] view point. The prospect of transactions being reopened many years after the event by a subsequent decision of the Court of Appeal or House of Lords is not one which the law should favour, especially in the field of commerce. It is true that in many cases the defendant would be able to rely on change of position as a defence. But this would not necessarily be so in every case. Certainty and finality, as has been said so often, are twin policy objectives of the highest importance in formulating legal principles.

. . .

Appellate courts ought to be encouraged to change the law in those rare cases where change is needed. They should not be inhibited by the fear of reopening past transactions.

. . .

For the above reasons, I would answer the questions formulated by Lord Goff as follows:

. . .

*Issue 1A:* Monies paid on the basis of a settled view of the law which has been subsequently overturned by judicial decision are not recoverable;

. . .

But a majority of your Lordships are of a different view. What are the consequences? One consequence is that in all those cases where the House of Lords has overruled a previous decision of the Court of Appeal it would be open to those who have entered into transactions in reliance on the previous decision to seek to re-open their transactions. This is a consequence which, in the commercial field at any rate, I view with alarm. My noble and learned friend Lord Hoffmann accepts that there is a problem, but considers that the solution can be left to Parliament. It is reasonable to assume that Parliament would start with the Law Commission's proposals, which, as I have said, successive governments of both main parties have accepted. But in the meantime there will be an inevitable period of intense uncertainty. If your Lordships are not willing to adopt the Law Commission's solution as it stands, it is surely better to let Parliament adopt that solution, or some other solution, *before* our decision rather than after.

. . .

## LORD HOFFMANN

. . .

The problem [as to whether a "mistake" may be said to have occurred] arises because (1) the law requires that a mistake should have been as to some *existing* fact or (on the view which your Lordships now take) the then *existing* state of the law but (2) a judicial statement of the law operates retrospectively. So the question is whether the retrospectivity of the law-making process enables one to say that holding a contrary view of the law at an earlier stage was a mistake. This question cannot be answered simply by taking a robust, common sense definition of a mistake at the time of payment, and saying that one does not believe in fairy stories. It is easy to understand the expostulation of Lord Coleridge C.J. in *Henderson v. Folkestone Waterworks Co.* (1885) 1 T.L.R. 329 at the suggestion that, because his judgment had been reversed by the House of Lords, he had been "ignorant of the law." The common sense notion of a mistake as to an existing state of affairs is that one has got it wrong when, if one had been better informed, one could have got it right. But common sense does not easily accommodate the concept of retrospectivity. This is a legal notion. If the ordinary man was asked whether Lord Coleridge had made a mistake, he would no doubt have said that in the ordinary sense, which might carry some reflection on his competence as a judge, he had not. But if he was asked whether he should be treated for the purposes of some legal rule as having made a mistake, he might say "I don't know. You tell me that the later decision operated retrospectively, which means that at least for some purposes, it must be assumed to have been the law at the time. Therefore it may be that for some purposes a person who held the contrary view should be treated as having made a mistake. It all depends upon the context. You had better ask a lawyer."

The lawyer would, I think, start by considering why, in principle, a person who had paid because he held some mistaken belief should be entitled to recover. The answer is that it is prima facie unjust for the recipient to retain the money when, if the payer had known the true state of affairs, he would not have paid.

. . .

The distinction therefore does not turn upon the fact that the person making the payment could not have discovered the true state of affairs about the law any more than about the facts. It turns upon the purely abstract proposition that in principle ... the truth or falsity of any proposition of existing fact could have been ascertained at the time, whereas the law, as it was subsequently be declared to have been, could not.

One must therefore ask why, in the context of unjust enrichment, this should make a difference. In both cases it has turned out that the state of affairs at the time was not (or was deemed not to have been) what the payer thought. In the case of a mistake of fact, it is because things were actually not what he believed them to be. In the case of a mistake of law, it is by virtue of the retrospectivity of the decision. Does the principle of unjust enrichment require that this retrospectivity should be carried through into the question of whether the payer made a mistake?

In my view, it would be very anomalous if it did not . . .

An analogy was drawn in argument between a retrospective decision of a court and a retrospective Act of Parliament. A failure to predict the latter, it was said, could not possibly be a mistake and therefore why should the former. I do not myself see why, in principle, if an Act of Parliament requires that the law be deemed to have been different on an earlier date, it should not follow that a person who acted in accordance with the law as it then was should be deemed to have made a mistake.

I therefore do not think that there are any reasons of principle for distinguishing cases in which a subsequent decision changes a settled view of the law, or, for that matter, settles what was previously an unsettled view of the law. The enrichment of the recipient is in each case unjust because he has received money which he would not have received if the payer had known the law to be what it has since been declared to have been.

. . .

## LORD HOPE OF CRAIGHEAD

My Lords,

. . .

### Was There a Mistake?

Subject to any defences that may arise from the circumstances, a claim for restitution of money paid under a mistake raises three questions: (1) was there a mistake? (2) did the mistake cause the payment? and (3) did the payee have a right to receive the sum which was paid to him?

The first question arises because the mistake provides the cause of action for recovery of the money had and received by the payee. Unless the payer can prove that he acted under a mistake, he cannot maintain an action for money had and received on this ground. . . .

In the present case the second and third questions do not appear to present any difficulty. But the first question raises an issue of very real importance. The answer which is given to it will have significant implications for the future development of the law of restitution on the ground of unjust enrichment.

In my opinion the proper starting point for an examination of this issue is the principle on which the claim for restitution of these payments is founded, which is that of unjust enrichment. The essence of this principle is that it is unjust for a person to retain a benefit which he has received at the expense of another, without any legal ground to justify its retention, which that other person did not intend him to receive. . . .

. . .

What then is the position where the fact that the payment was not legally due at the time when it was made was only revealed later by subsequent case law? In posing this question I am not dealing with the situation where a judgment of the court that a sum is due has become final and been acted upon, but is afterwards overruled by a higher court in a different case. The law of unjust enrichment does not disturb transactions of that kind. Where the payment is made because the court has held that the sum is due to be paid to the payee, the obligation to pay is to be found in the order which has been made by the court. I am dealing with the case where the payment was made on the understanding that the law on the point was settled and that understanding was shown by subsequent case law to have been wrong.

. . .

The answer to this question may be said to depend upon whether the decision in question has changed the law or has merely declared what the law always was. We were reminded of Lord Reid's observation that to say that the judges never change the law is a fairy tale: (1972–73) J.S.P.T.L. 22. Experience has shown that the judges do from time to time change the law, in order to adapt it to changed social conditions or in response to other factors which show that the law has become out of date. But it would be equally wrong to say that the judges never declare the law. It may simply be that there was a gap which needed to be filled, or that there was a defect in thinking which needed to be revealed so that a point could be clarified. And to overturn an established line of authority is one thing. It is quite another where there was no previous decision on a point which no-one had sought to bring before the court previously. It may be said that a view of the law can be regarded as settled even where there is no case law at all on the subject, because all those interested in it have acted on a common understanding of what the law requires. But I would find it difficult to accept that a judge who said that that common understanding was wrong, and that the law was different from what everyone previously had thought it was, had changed the law. It would seem to be more accurate to say that, as it was for the judge to say what the law was, he was merely declaring what the law was and that he was not changing it.

. . .

On the whole it seems to me to be preferable to avoid being drawn into a discussion as to whether a particular decision changed the law or whether it was merely declaratory. It would not be possible to lay down any hard and fast rules on this point. Each case would have to be decided on what may in the end be a matter of opinion, about which there may be room for a good deal of dispute. It is better to face up to the fact that every decision as to the law by a judge operates retrospectively, and to concentrate instead on the question—which I would regard as the critical question—whether the payer would have made the payment if he had known what he is now being told was the law. It is the state of the law at the time of the payment which will determine whether or not the payment was or was not legally due to be paid, and it is the state of mind of the payer at the time of payment, which will determine whether he paid under a mistake. But there seems to me to be no reason in principle why the law of unjust enrichment should insist that that mistake must be capable of being demonstrated at the same time as the time when the payment was made. A mistake of fact may take some time to discover. If there is a dispute about this, the question whether there was a mistake may remain in doubt until the issue has been resolved by a judge. Why should this not be so where the mistake is one of law?

. . .

If it were necessary to decide this point, I do not think that it would be right to say that the decision in the *Hazell* case "changed" the law. What it did was to clarify a point which had been overlooked and was in need of determination by the court. But the situation seems to me to be no different in principle from one where the facts are shown, as a result of inquiries which at the time of the payment were overlooked or not thought to be necessary, to have been different from what they had been thought to be at the time of the payment by the payer. Prima facie the Bank is entitled to restitution on the ground of mistake.

. . .

## Note

Note the format of the *Kleinwort* decision: each of the five Law Lords delivers a separate opinion. House of Lords opinions are not always as fulsome as those in *Kleinwort*, and often consist only of a short sentence adopting the reasoning expressed in a different opinion. Nevertheless, the convention that each Law Lord separately express his or her view differs from the US Supreme Court practice of concurring and dissenting opinions which accommodate the views of several Justices. A good contrast is *Babbitt v. Sweet Home Chapter of Communities for A Great Oregon*, 515 U.S. 687, 115 S.Ct. 2407, 132 L.Ed.2d 597 (1995) on page 429 of this casebook.

You have probably noticed that you needed to read each opinion in *Kleinwort* carefully to work out the 3–2 result! This is a common complaint. Moreover, the practice of separate opinions which concur as to result but not as to reasoning can create difficulties in determining the "true" holding. On the other hand, the English approach requires that each judge independently consider and articulate his or her own view. You might consider the advantages and disadvantages of the different judicial styles.

## Fitzgerald v. Meissner & Hicks, Inc.

Supreme Court of Wisconsin, 1968.
38 Wis.2d 571, 157 N.W.2d 595.

This appeal involves application of this court's decision in Moran v. Quality Aluminum Casting Co. (1967), 34 Wis.2d 542, 150 N.W.2d 137, which held a wife could bring an action for loss of consortium.

The plaintiff-appellant, Marie E. Fitzgerald, commenced this action on September 18, 1966, to recover for loss of consortium of her husband, Richard T. Fitzgerald. The complaint alleged that on August 7, 1964, Fitzgerald had been seriously injured when he fell from a scaffolding while engaged in his employment at a construction site in the city of Milwaukee. Each of the defendants were owners of the site at the time of the accident.

The defendants demurred to the complaint contending it did not state facts sufficient to constitute a cause of action. The trial court sustained the demurrers. The trial court's reasoning does not appear of record but the parties agree the decision was based upon a prior rule that a wife could not maintain an action for loss of consortium. The demurrers were argued on February 6, 1967. The trial court sustained the demurrers and granted judgment dismissing the complaint on February 15, 1967.

On February 22, 1967, the plaintiff filed a notice of appeal. Five days later the Moran case was argued before this court and on April 28, 1967, the court overturned its previous decision in Nickel v. Hardware Mut. Casualty Co. (1955), 269 Wis. 647, 70 N.W.2d 205, and held that a wife could maintain an action for loss of consortium of her husband who has been injured by the negligent acts of a third person.

■ BEILFUSS, JUSTICE.

The [issue] presented on this appeal [is]:

1.   Does the rule of law recognizing a wife's right to maintain a cause of action for loss of consortium as set forth in Moran v. Quality Aluminum Casting Co., supra, have prospective or retrospective application?

\* \* \*

The general rule adhered to by this court is the "Blackstonian Doctrine." This doctrine provides that a decision which overrules or repudiates an earlier decision is retrospective in operation.\*

There are, however, exceptions to this rule which have long been recognized by this court:

> "While there would seem to be no middle ground in logic, between a complete adherence to or a complete repudiation of the Blackstonian doctrine, the courts nevertheless have established certain exceptions to

---

\* [The doctrine is founded on the idea that judges discover rather than make law. According to Blackstone, a court overruling a prior decision does not announce a new law, but "vindicate[s] the old one from misrepresentation.... [I]t is declared, not that such a sentence was bad law, but that it was not law." Blackstone's Commentaries on the Laws of England—Ed.]

it for the purpose of mitigating hardships created by its literal application. Without attempting to deal exhaustively with the subject, it may be said that, generally speaking, courts adhering to the rule that a later decision operates retrospectively, have created the following exceptions: (1) Where contracts have been entered into in reliance upon a legislative enactment as construed by the earlier decisions. (2) Where a legislative enactment has been declared valid by earlier decisions. and contracts have been entered into in reliance upon the statute and decisions. [Cases cited.] (3) Where a criminal statute, which has received a limited construction by earlier decisions, has been so expanded in meaning by the later overruling decision as to make acts criminal which were not such under the earlier decisions, and the later decision is sought to be applied to one whose acts were committed before the statute was given the enlarged construction." [citations omitted].

Generally, throughout the various American jurisdictions, other exceptions to the Blackstonian doctrine have been utilized. Retroactive operation has been sometimes denied where there has been great reliance on an overruled decision by a substantial number of persons and considerable harm or detriment could result to them. It has also been denied where the purpose of the new ruling cannot be served by retroactivity, and where retroactivity would tend to thrust an excessive burden on the administration of justice. 10 A.L.R.3d 1384.

In this jurisdiction the "reliance" and "administration of justice" considerations have been recognized. In relatively recent years the court has applied exceptions to the Blackstonian doctrine in the tort area of the law where it has determined a compelling judicial reason exists. The reliance factor has been a most prominent consideration in the prospective only abrogation of the various tort immunities.[3] [citations omitted].

Recently in Dupuis v. General Casualty Co. (1967), 36 Wis.2d 42, 45, 152 N.W.2d 884, 885, the court emphasized the importance of the reliance factor in its decisions to limit application of the foregoing list of cases:

"Inherent in a court declaring that a decision should apply prospectively only is a determination that a compelling judicial reason exists for doing so. In many of the cases previously decided which apply this principle, one of the important compelling judicial reasons which has been considered is what has been referred to as the reliance factor, i.e., that the parties involved had relied upon the immunity doctrine and that to make a decision effective retroactively would manifestly adversely affect great numbers of individuals and institutions that had correctly relied upon their expressed immunity in the conduct of their affairs."

Obviously the court was not suggesting a great number of individuals and institutions had committed torts relying upon the immunity. The reason for the prospective application of these decisions, as mentioned in

**3.** The decisions cited were limited to prospective application with the exception that it was determined they would apply to the parties involved in the actual case.

Kojis, was because the court was concerned about the failure of those affected to purchase insurance coverage in reliance upon the immunity.

The possibility of imposing an excessive burden on the administration of justice was a compelling judicial reason for the limitation placed on the retrospective application of this court's decision in Bielski v. Schulze (1962), 16 Wis.2d 1, 114 N.W.2d 105, which changed our contribution rule and discarded the concept of gross negligence. This is best described by former Mr. Justice THOMAS E. FAIRCHILD in his article in 46 Marquette L.Rev. 1, 15:

"In Bielski the court limited the retrospective application of the change in law with respect to contribution and gross negligence. Here again were elements of law which are ordinarily not relied upon by people who are about to engage in tortious conduct. Yet the court was mindful of the fact that if full retrospective application were given, burdens of further litigation would probably be imposed on litigants and the public in cases where claims had been substantially disposed of by litigation or settlement. Such burdens would seem to be wasteful."

The compelling judicial reason for the prospective limitation placed on this court's decision abrogating the doctrine of parental immunity, Goller v. White (1963), 20 Wis.2d 402, 122 N.W.2d 193, contained consideration both for the reliance placed on the doctrine and for the effect retroactive operation would have on the administration of justice. Our statute controlling limitations of actions of minors (sec. 893.33) provides that a child has until one year after he attains majority to bring suit for injuries sustained during his minority. Conceivably, retroactive application of Goller could have resulted in suits for injuries sustained by minors for a period of more than 20 years previous to that decision. There was not only concern over the possibility of overburdening the courts with litigation, but also concern for those who in reliance on the immunity doctrine failed to preserve essential evidence. Dupuis v. General Casualty Co., supra.

In the case at bar none of the considerations presented by the foregoing are present to any significant degree. Obviously the contract and criminal considerations are not present. The degree of reliance a tortfeasor might have placed on a wife's inability to recover consortium damages would be insignificant if existent. Certainly the tort was not committed with this in mind and the degree to which it may have influenced the decision whether or not to purchase liability insurance would be less than minimal. Nor will it affect the monetary limits of liability of the insurance carrier.

The respondents vigorously contend the reliance factor is present because insurance companies have relied on this court's position prior to *Moran* in the calculation of their insurance rates. The degree to which the premiums charged by insurance companies would have differed had a wife always been accorded the right to recover consortium damages is speculative and probably relatively insignificant. In any event, it is not of such proportion to be recognized as a compelling judicial reason.

Mr. Justice Fairchild's statement setting forth the reasons for this court's retroactive application of its decisions abolishing the defense of assumption of risk is apropos:

"In *McConville* and *Colson,* abrogating the defense of assumption of risk, the court did not limit the application of the change in law. The existence of the defense becomes important to most people only in retrospect. A prospective host probably does not consciously rely upon it, either in offering an automobile ride to his guest or deciding whether or not to carry liability insurance. The degree to which the existence of the defense might affect the premiums charged by insurance companies is not clear. Nor is it clear that a farmer would rely on the doctrine in deciding against insurance. In any event, the concurring opinions in Baird v. Cornelius, ((1961), 12 Wis.2d 284, 107 N.W.2d 278), decided one year before *McConville,* had very clearly signalled the probability that the defense was likely to be abrogated." 46 Marquette L.Rev. 1, 15.

The retroactive operation of *Moran* will not unduly burden the administration of justice. With our three-year statute of limitation on such actions (sec. 893.205), retroactive application, considered at this point in time, will only affect those actions arising a little more than two years prior to *Moran.*

Finally, in consideration of the issue it should be noted that the actual monetary amount involved will probably not be substantial. The largest item in loss of consortium damages, no doubt, is the support item. The inability to maintain a wife's support has always been an item for which the husband has been allowed to recover. Consequently, the only items Moran makes recoverable that were not recoverable before are loss of society, affection, and sexual companionship.

Although several of the cases referred to above provide for prospective application for the reasons stated therein, we adhere to the concept that a decision that overrules or changes a rule of law is to be applied retrospectively unless it is established there are compelling judicial reasons for not doing so. No sufficient compelling judicial reasons are apparent nor established to warrant an exception to the rule of retrospective application of the *Moran* decision, which recognizes the right of a wife to assert a claim for loss of consortium. *Moran* is, therefore, to be applied retrospectively.

\* \* \*

Judgment reversed, and remanded for further proceedings.

### Notes and Questions

**1.** As the *Fitzgerald* opinion notes, courts depart from the traditional Blackstonian doctrine in certain situations. For instance, when parties such as charitable, governmental, and religious entities relied on accepted doctrines granting them immunity, they did not purchase liability insurance. Some believe that to impose liability retrospectively on such parties would be unfair. Therefore, in such limited cases, the general rule is to apply the changed law prospectively only, although there is not uniform agreement on this point.

Molitor v. Kaneland Comm. Unit Dist. No. 302, 18 Ill.2d 11, 163 N.E.2d 89 (1959), for example, abolished the rule that a school district is immune from tort liability. (The plaintiff sued the district after he was injured in a school bus accident.) The majority made the new rule prospective but applied it to the parties in the case; otherwise, the court reasoned, plaintiffs would have no incentive to appeal the upholding of an "unjust" precedent since they would not benefit from a reversal. The majority did not decide whether the new rule would apply to other children injured in the same accident. Compare Holytz v. City of Milwaukee, 17 Wis.2d 26, 115 N.W.2d 618 (1962) (making the new rule effective 40 days after the date of the decision); Jones v. State Highway Comm., 557 S.W.2d 225 (Mo. banc 1977) (making the new rule effective almost a year later than the decision); Spanel v. Mounds View School Dist. No. 621, 264 Minn. 279, 118 N.W.2d 795 (1962) (making the new rule apply only to torts committed after the adjournment of the next session of the state legislature).

Does the practice of choosing an effective date other than the date of decision seem more "legislative"? Does that trouble you?

**2.**  What, in your view, are the relative merits and demerits of (a) making the overruling wholly prospective as in *Spanel;* making the overruling prospective except as to the plaintiff in the immediate case, as in *Molitor;* or (c) making the overruling prospective except as to those involved in the same accident, as was advocated by the dissent in *Molitor?*

———

At this point in the course, you may find particular resonance in the following observations of Justice Cardozo

Our survey of judicial methods teaches us, I think, the lesson that the whole subject matter of jurisprudence is more plastic, more malleable, the molds less definitively cast, the bounds of right and wrong less preordained and constant, than most of us, without the aid of some such analysis, have been accustomed to believe. We like to picture ourselves the field of the law as accurately mapped and plotted. We draw our little lines, and they are hardly down before we blur them. As in time and space, so here. Divisions are working hypotheses, adopted for our convenience. We are tending more and more toward an appreciation of the truth that, after all, there are few rules; there are chiefly standards and degrees. It is a question of degree whether I have been negligent. It is a question of degree whether in the use of my own land, I have created a nuisance which may be abated by my neighbor. It is a question of degree whether the law which takes my property and limits my conduct impairs my liberty unduly. So also the duty of a judge becomes a question of degree, and he is a useful judge or a poor one as he estimates the measure accurately or loosely. He must balance all his ingredients, his philosophy, his logic, his analogies, his history, his customs, his sense of right, and all the rest, and adding a little here and taking out a little there, must determine, as wisely as he can, which weight shall tip the scales.

Benjamin Nathan Cardozo, The Nature of the Judicial Process 161–62 (Yale Univ. Press. 1921)

## C.   REVIEW PROBLEMS

### Problem 1

Harris Enterprises is a real estate company that owns several office buildings in Ryanville. Harris rents office space to commercial tenants. On June 1, 1987, at the height of the real estate market, Harris granted the law firm of Bell & Young a ten-year lease on twelve floors in its most prestigious building, Pegasus Place, at $100,000 per month.

In September 1992, in the depths of the real estate market, Bell & Young obtained more favorable rental terms in an office building in the nearby city of Saperstown. Bell & Young therefore vacated Pegasus Place, and stopped paying rent to Harris Ents. Harris Ents. nonetheless continued to send monthly invoices. By the time Bell & Young left Pegasus Place, comparable office space in Ryanville was being leased at $50,000 per month. Bell & Young's departure dismayed Harris not only because of the loss of rental income, but because of the security problems posed by the vacant space. A recent article in the Ryanville Record described several incidents in which visitors and tenants of office buildings similar to Pegasus Place had been accosted, forced into the vacant space, and then robbed. In response to this danger, in December Harris changed the locks to all the doors of the offices it had leased to Bell & Young.

Harris found a new tenant for the Bell & Young space beginning March 1, 1993, and continuing through the end of Bell & Young's lease term (May 31, 1997), at $50,000 per month. Taking into account the six months during which the office space remained vacant, the difference between the rent Harris is now receiving and the rent Harris would have received had Bell & Young remained is $3,650,00. Can Harris recover this sum from Bell & Young? Your research has revealed the following two decisions from the Supreme Court of New Hazard (the State in which Ryanville and Saperstown are located).

### METRO–TV v. DAYAL REALTY CO.

Supreme Court of New Hazard, 1990

■ ZLOTCHEW, CHIEF JUSTICE,

Appellee Dayal Realty brought this action against appellant Metro–TV, an electronics retailer, for outstanding rent on a five-year commercial lease entered into on July 1, 1984. The trial and appellate courts held Metro liable for the 37 months of unpaid rent, from June 1, 1986 through June 30, 1989. We reverse.

The undisputed facts are as follows. On June 1, 1986, Metro failed to make its monthly rent payment, and has made no rent payments since. Over the Fourth of July weekend, while Metro's store was closed for the holiday, Ashima Dayal, President of Dayal Realty, changed the locks on the store, and sent a registered letter to Metro's president, stating "You are still obligated to pay me under our lease agreement, and until you make back payments I will not give you a key to the new lock." Metro did not pay, and the store remained unoccupied through June 30, 1989.

Metro claims that Dayal's changing the locks released Metro from its obligation to pay rent. We agree, holding that when Dayal Realty changed the locks, that act constituted an eviction. An eviction terminates a tenant's duty to pay rent for the remainder of the lease term. Thus, we find Metro liable for only the one month's rent corresponding to the period after which Metro had stopped paying but during which it was still occupying the store.

## UNIVERSITY OF NEW HAZARD v. GIANNOU

### Supreme Court of New Hazard, 1992

■ Kim, Justice

Appellant, the University of New Hazard, brought this action against appellee, a residential tenant, for one years' outstanding rent on a three-year lease. The trial and appellate courts held that appellant's changing of the lock on appellee's apartment discharged his duty to pay rent. We reverse.

The University owns several residential apartment buildings near its main campus in Ryanville. It rents these apartments to students and staff members. In this case, the University granted a three-year lease to appellee, Nicholas Giannou, then-Chairman of the Department of Greek and Classical Philosophy. After two years, Giannou went out of state on sabbatical leave to the Agora Academy. He left his university apartment empty, and left his key in the lock.

Following complaints from neighbors that squatters were living in Giannou's apartment, the university changed the locks, and sent Giannou a letter informing him of the lock change, and instructing him to contact the University real estate office to obtain a new key.

Giannou did not request a new key. Instead, at the conclusion of his sabbatical year, he resigned from the University of New Hazard, in order to remain at Agora Academy. He has refused to respond to the University's demands for back rent.

We hold that, under these circumstances, the landlord's changing of the lock did not constitute an eviction. The University is entitled to one year's back rent.

## Problem 2[1]

Fourteen-year-old Andrew Quale was struck by a truck while riding his bicycle. Although his injuries seemed slight, his mother, Mary Quale, took him to the hospital. His sole complaint was a headache. After Mary described the accident, Dr. Richard Farmer ordered X-rays. The X-rays did not indicate a skull fracture. Farmer did not examine the back of the boy's head, where there was a red mark, nor did he use the other diagnostic procedures that are standard in such cases. Farmer sent the boy home and asked his mother to observe him. Andrew died early the next morning. The coroner concluded from an autopsy that the boy died from hemorrhaging due to a basal skull fracture.

Mary Quale has asked you to sue Farmer for malpractice. You contacted another doctor as a possible expert witness. She told you that there is no doubt the doctor was negligent. In answer to your question about the likelihood of the boy's survival if there had been proper treatment, she said that the mortality rate for such injuries was about 100% without surgery. Then she added, "There certainly is a chance and I can't say exactly what—maybe some place around 50%—that Andrew would have survived with surgery. She cannot give you a more definite answer."

Assume that Farmer was negligent. Did Farmer's negligence proximately cause the boy's death? There are two relevant cases in your state:

### *Moulton v. Ginocchio* (1966)

Craig Moulton, who is the administrator of the decedent's estate, brought this action against Samuel Ginocchio, a physician, for negligence in treating the decedent's illness. The trial court dismissed the complaint on the ground that the doctor's negligence did not proximately cause her death. We disagree and reverse. The decedent, a diabetic, went to Ginocchio's hospital with intense abdominal pain, which Ginocchio diagnosed as a stomach "bug." He gave her pain medication and released her. She died several hours later from massive hemorrhaging caused by an intestinal obstruction. Ginocchio claims that there is no basis for concluding with certainty that his negligent diagnosis and treatment caused her death. The law does not require certainty, however; a physician is answerable if he prevents a substantial possibility of survival. Moulton's experts testified categorically and without contradiction that the decedent would have survived had she undergone prompt surgery. Moulton, therefore, satisfied the "substantial possibility" requirement.

### *Mallard v. Harkin* (1969)

Eleanor Mallard brought suit against Joseph Harkin, a physician, for Harkin's allegedly negligent failure to immediately diagnose and per-

**1.** Reproduced with permission from John C. Dernbach and Richard V. Singleton II, A Practical Guide to Legal Writing and Legal Method (1981) and from John C. Dernbach, Richard V. Singleton II, Cathleen S. Wharton & John Ruhtenberg, A Practical Guide to Legal Writing and Legal Method (2d ed. 1994).

form surgery to arrest a degenerative disease that has now left Mallard paralyzed. The trial court found that Harkin breached his duty of reasonable care but that his actions did not proximately cause Mallard's condition. Only the latter ruling has been appealed. We agree with the trial court and affirm.

We held in *Moulton v. Ginocchio* (1966) that a doctor is liable when his negligence "prevents a substantial possibility of survival" for the decedent. In that case, there was testimony that the decedent would have survived. Traditional standards of proximate cause similarly require evidence that the result was more likely than not caused by the act. Mallard does not meet that standard. Mallard's expert witness testified that prompt surgery would have given Mallard "a possibility" of recovery but that she "probably would not have recovered."

It is an attractive and emotionally appealing idea that a physician should be held liable for the loss of even a remote chance of full recovery from a debilitating disease or injury. But such a rule would result in an unjust situation in which the physician would be held accountable for harm that he did not cause and may not have been able to prevent. We refuse, as a matter of public policy, to hold a physician liable on a mere possibility.

## Problem 3[2]

Bradley Greenleaf just finished renovating an old house located on a busy street in Porterville. The house, which is now the office for his twelve-person architectural firm, cost $145,000. The renovations, including retrofitting the house with solar panels, cost an additional $195,000. The solar panels provide heating and cooling for the air and water in the building, but they do not provide electricity. His firm, Greenleaf Associates, which specializes in solar design for residences, uses the building as a model for persons who are interested in constructing or retrofitting homes with solar panels. Its extensive "You can do it" promotional campaign relies heavily on the building for that purpose.

Peter Elliot owns the property just west of Greenleaf's office. Recently, Elliot erected two large billboards that shield the sun's rays from the panels by early afternoon and force Greenleaf to rely on conventional energy sources. As a result, Greenleaf is paying substantially more than before in utility bills (about $400 per month, he estimates), and his promotional appeal is less attractive. What good is solar energy, some potential customers ask, if it can be blocked? Greenleaf talked to Elliot about this problem. Elliot apologized for any inconvenience but refused to remove the billboards because he would lose too much money.

Greenleaf has asked you if he has a basis for a lawsuit against Elliot. You have determined that there are no relevant statutes, easements, or zoning provisions. There are, however, three relevant cases from this state.

**2.** Reproduced with permission from John C. Dernbach, Richard V. Singleton II, Cathleen S. Wharton & John M. Ruhtenberg, A Practical Guide to Legal Writing and Legal Method (2d ed. 1994).

### *Scott v. Shover* (1889)

Larry Shover brought an action against Wayne Scott, an adjoining landowner, for damage caused by Scott's excavation of adjacent land. The trial court found that the excavation caused Shover's land to cave in, destroyed a barn and some fences, and greatly devalued Shover's property. It ordered judgment for Shover. We affirm.

The maxim that landowners must so enjoy their property as not to injure the property of another has been interpreted in this state to mean that they must enjoy their property without injuring a legal right in the property of another. A landowner has the legal right to lateral support of his lot from the adjoining land. If the support is removed, the owner has a right of action against the person removing the support for the amount of the damages sustained to the land.

### *Horton v. Eicher* (1959)

Stephen Eicher, who owns 200 acres of growing honeydew melons, used a small airplane to dust his melons with calcium arsenate. The compound is toxic to a number of agricultural pests; it is also toxic to bees. John Horton owns sixty-five hives of bees on a parcel of land near Eicher's land. The bees were important to the pollination of Horton's plants and thus contributed to his livelihood. Horton brought this action for nuisance after the spray from Eicher's plane drifted over the hives and killed all of the bees. The trial court awarded $450 in damages, and we affirm. A property owner is entitled to the peaceful enjoyment of his property, free from unreasonable interference by others. This incident unmistakably interfered with Horton's use of his property.

### *Blum v. Disposal Systems, Inc.* (1987)

Disposal Systems, Inc. (DSI) operates a landfill adjacent to Loretta Blum's hog farm. Blum brought a nuisance action against DSI, alleging that noise and vibrations generated by DSI's trash-hauling trucks caused the conception rate of Blum's sows to decrease from 80% to 30%. The trial court found that the alleged facts were true but nevertheless entered judgment for DSI, holding that its use of the land was reasonable and therefore not a nuisance. We reverse.

In private nuisance actions, we must balance the interests of the respective landowners. Whether one's use of property is reasonable is determined by the effect such use has on the neighboring property. Although mere annoyance or inconvenience will not support an action for nuisance, a use of property that essentially confiscates or destroys the neighboring property is unreasonable and constitutes a private nuisance. The landfill operation has had that effect on Blum's hog farm.

The following case is from another state:

### Cassells International v. Avery Resorts (1959)

Cassells International, which owns a large resort hotel on an ocean beach, brought suit against Avery Resorts, a neighboring hotel owner, to prevent construction of a ten-story addition to Avery's existing hotel. Cassells claims that the addition will cast a shadow on its beaches and other sunbathing areas and will render these areas unfit for the use and enjoyment of its guests. The trial court refused to enjoin construction of the addition. We agree.

The doctrine of nuisance does not mean that a property owner must never use the property to the injury of another, but rather that the owner may not use the property to injure the legal rights of another. We have found no American case establishing—in the absence of a contractual or statutory obligation—that a property owner has a right to the free flow of light. Affirmed.

\* \* \*

## Problem 4

You are a law clerk to Judge Celia Taylor of the United States Court of Appeals for the Fourteenth Circuit. Judge Taylor has been assigned to the panel that will hear defendants' appeal in *United States v. Walker and Powell*. Below are the pertinent facts regarding the trial and the district court's determination.

In 1992, Florenz Walker and Tanya Powell were indicted and tried for a variety of federal drug-related offenses, including the illicit importation of heroin. A number of government witnesses agreed to testify only if they could remain overseas. As a result, the government deposed these witnesses on video, and offered the videotapes as evidence. Walker and Powell objected to major portions of the tapes, and the Court ruled that much of the tapes had to be edited as a result. Written transcripts of the videotapes were prepared, in which the deleted taped portions were highlighted. During the trial, the jury viewed the edited tapes, but the written transcripts were not entered as an exhibit.

Nonetheless, the transcripts were inadvertently included with the exhibits that the jurors asked to review during their deliberations. As a result, the jurors discovered the transcripts, highlighting and all. The jury, unaware of the mistake, asked District Judge Lorne Sossin if they could make use of the highlighted portions of the transcripts, to which they had not been exposed during the trial. Up to this point, the jurors had not carefully read the transcripts, but had skimmed their contents, including the highlighted portions. Walker and Powell immediately moved for a mistrial on the basis of juror bias due to the inadvertent disclosure of the transcripts.

The district judge conducted a hearing at which he questioned each of the jurors. Defense counsel and the prosecution were present at this hearing, and also questioned the jurors on their state of mind. Based on this investigation, the district judge ruled that there was "a good probability that none of the jurors had actually read the highlighted portions," but rather, "had only read far enough to recognize it as forbidden fruit." The district judge therefore denied the motion for a mistrial, instead instructing the jury to disregard the transcripts and to rely only on what they had seen and heard during the trial.

The jury convicted both defendants. Both have appealed to this court. They contend that the government should have borne the burden of disproving that juror bias resulted from the disclosure of the transcripts. Judge Taylor informs you that the sole relevant authority consists of four decisions (following): the United States' Supreme Court's decisions in *Remmer v. United States* and *Smith v. Phillips,* and two decisions from the Ninth and Sixth Circuits, respectively, *United States v. Littlefield,* and *United States v. Pennell.* No court in the 14th Circuit (apart from the district court here) has yet addressed this issue.

Judge Taylor asks, first, that you articulate all the methods of allocating the burdens that the opinions of these courts suggest. Second, she asks that you determine which of these methods of allocation this Circuit should apply here in light of the facts of this case. Please be sure to explain fully the analysis leading to your conclusion.

## Remmer v. United States

United States Supreme Court, 1954.
347 U.S. 227, 74 S.Ct. 450, 98 L.Ed. 654.

■ MR. JUSTICE MINTON delivered the opinion of the Court.

The petitioner was convicted by a jury on several counts charging willful evasion of the payment of federal income taxes. A matter admitted by the Government to have been handled by the trial court in a manner that may have been prejudicial to the petitioner, and therefore confessed as error, is presented at the threshold and must be disposed of first.

After the jury had returned its verdict, the petitioner learned for the first time that during the trial a person unnamed had communicated with a certain juror, who afterwards became the jury foreman, and remarked to him that he could profit by bringing in a verdict favorable to the petitioner. The juror reported the incident to the judge, who informed the prosecuting attorneys and advised with them. As a result, the Federal Bureau of Investigation was requested to make an investigation and report, which was accordingly done. The F.B.I. report was considered by the judge and prosecutors alone, and they apparently concluded that the statement to the juror was made in jest, and nothing further was done or said about the matter. Neither the judge nor the prosecutors informed the petitioner of the incident, and he and his counsel first learned of the matter by reading of it in the newspapers after the verdict.

The above-stated facts were alleged in a motion for a new trial, together with an allegation that the petitioner was substantially prejudiced, thereby depriving him of a fair trial, and a request for a hearing to determine the circumstances surrounding the incident and its effect on the jury. A supporting affidavit of the petitioner's attorneys recited the alleged occurrences and stated that if they had known of the incident they would have moved for a mistrial and requested that the juror in question be replaced by an alternate juror. Two newspaper articles reporting the incident were attached to the affidavit. The Government did not file answering affidavits. The District Court, without holding the requested hearing, denied the motion for a new trial. The Court of Appeals held that the District Court had not abused its discretion, since the petitioner had shown no prejudice to him. 205 F.2d 277, 291. The case is here on writ of certiorari. 346 U.S. 884.

In a criminal case, any private communication, contact, or tampering directly or indirectly, with a juror during a trial about the matter pending before the jury is, for obvious reasons, deemed presumptively prejudicial, if not made in pursuance of known rules of the court and the instructions and directions of the court made during the trial, with full knowledge of the parties. The presumption is not conclusive, but the burden rests heavily upon the Government to establish, after notice to and hearing of the defendant, that such contact with the juror was harmless to the defendant. Mattox v. United States, 146 U.S. 140, 148–150; Wheaton v. United States, 133 F.2d 522, 527.

We do not know from this record, nor does the petitioner know, what actually transpired, or whether the incidents that may have occurred were harmful or harmless. The sending of an F.B.I. agent in the midst of a trial to investigate a juror as to his conduct is bound to impress the juror and is very apt to do so unduly. A juror must feel free to exercise his functions without the F.B.I. or anyone else looking over his shoulder. The integrity of jury proceedings must not be jeopardized by unauthorized invasions. The trial court should not decide and take final action ex parte on information such as was received in this case, but should determine the circumstances, the impact thereof upon the juror, and whether or not it was prejudicial, in a hearing with all interested parties permitted to participate.

We therefore vacate the judgment of the Court of Appeals and remand the case to the District Court with directions to hold a hearing to determine whether the incident complained of was harmful to the petitioner, and if after hearing it is found to have been harmful, to grant a new trial.

Judgment vacated.

## Smith v. Phillips

United States Supreme Court, 1982.
455 U.S. 209, 102 S.Ct. 940, 71 L.Ed.2d 78.

■ JUSTICE REHNQUIST delivered the opinion of the Court.

Respondent was convicted in November 1974 by a New York state-court jury on two counts of murder and one count of attempted murder. After trial, respondent moved to vacate his conviction, and a hearing on his motion was held. The hearing was held before the justice who presided at respondent's trial, and the motion to vacate was denied by him in an opinion concluding that the events giving rise to the motion did not influence the verdict. People v. Phillips, 87 Misc.2d 613, 614, 630 (1975). The Appellate Division of the Supreme Court, First Judicial Department, affirmed the conviction without opinion. 52 App.Div.2d 758 (1976). The New York Court of Appeals denied leave to appeal. 39 N.Y.2d 949 (1976).

Respondent subsequently sought relief in the United States District Court for the Southern District of New York on the same ground which had been asserted in the state post-trial hearing. The District Court granted the writ, 485 F.Supp. 1365 (1980), and the United States Court of Appeals for the Second Circuit affirmed on a somewhat different ground. 632 F.2d 1019 (1980). We granted certiorari and now reverse.

# I

## A

Respondent's original motion to vacate his conviction was based on the fact that a juror in respondent's case, one John Dana Smith, submitted during the trial an application for employment as a major felony investigator in the District Attorney's Office.[3] Smith had learned of the position from a friend who had contacts within the office and who had inquired on Smith's behalf without mentioning Smith's name or the fact that he was a juror in respondent's trial. When Smith's application was received by the office, his name was placed on a list of applicants but he was not then contacted and was not known by the office to be a juror in respondent's trial.

During later inquiry about the status of Smith's application, the friend mentioned that Smith was a juror in respondent's case. The attorney to whom the friend disclosed this fact promptly informed his superior, and his superior in turn informed the Assistant District Attorney in charge of hiring investigators. The following day, more than one week before the end of respondent's trial, the assistant informed the two attorneys actually prosecuting respondent that one of the jurors had applied to the office for employment as an investigator.

The two prosecuting attorneys conferred about the application but concluded that, in view of Smith's statements during *voir dire* [the jury selection process],[4] there was no need to inform the trial court or defense

---

**3.** Smith's letter of application was addressed to the District Attorney and stated:

"I understand that a federally funded investigative unit is being formed in your office to investigate major felonies. I wish to apply for a position as an investigator."

The letter did not mention that Smith was a juror in respondent's trial. Appended to the letter was a resume containing biographical information about Smith. People v. Phillips, 87 Misc.2d 613, 616 (1975).

**4.** The trial judge described the jury selection process in respondent's case as "ten days of meticulous examination." Id., at 614. During his jury selection, Smith stated that he intended to pursue a career in law enforcement and that he had applied for employment with a federal drug enforcement agency. He also disclosed that his wife was interested in law enforcement, an interest which arose out of an incident in which she was assaulted and seriously injured. Smith stated that he had previously worked as a

counsel of the application. They did instruct attorneys in the office not to contact Smith until after the trial had ended, and took steps to insure that they would learn no information about Smith that had not been revealed during the jury selection process. When the jury retired to deliberate on November 20th, three alternate jurors were available to substitute for Smith, and neither the trial court nor the defense counsel knew of his application. The jury returned its verdict on November 21st.

The District Attorney first learned of Smith's application on December 4th. Five days later, after an investigation to verify the information, he informed the trial court and defense counsel of the application and the fact that its existence was known to attorneys in his office at some time before the conclusion of the trial. Respondent's attorney then moved to set aside the verdict.

At the hearing before the trial judge, Justice Harold Birns, the prosecuting attorneys explained their decision not to disclose the application and Smith explained that he had seen nothing improper in submitting the application during the trial. Justice Birns, from all the evidence adduced at the hearing, found that Smith's letter was indeed an indiscretion but that it in no way reflected a premature conclusion as to the respondent's guilt, or prejudice against the respondent, or an inability to consider the guilt or innocence of the respondent solely on the evidence. Id., at 627. With respect to the conduct of the prosecuting attorneys, Justice Birns found "no evidence" suggesting "a sinister or dishonest motive with respect to Mr. Smith's letter of application." Id., at 618–619.

### B

In his application for federal relief, respondent contended that he had been denied due process of law under the Fourteenth Amendment to the United States Constitution by Smith's conduct. The District Court found insufficient evidence to demonstrate that Smith was actually biased. 485 F.Supp., at 1371. Nonetheless, the court imputed bias to Smith because "the average man in Smith's position would believe that the verdict of the jury would directly affect the evaluation of his job application." Id., at 1371–1372. Accordingly, the court ordered respondent released unless the State granted him a new trial within 90 days.

The United States Court of Appeals for the Second Circuit affirmed by a divided vote. The court noted that "it is at best difficult and perhaps impossible to learn from a juror's own testimony after the verdict whether he was in fact 'impartial,'" but the court did not consider whether Smith was actually or impliedly biased. 632 F.2d, at 1022. Rather, the Court of Appeals affirmed respondent's release simply because "the failure of the

store detective for Bloomingdale's Department Store, and, in that capacity, had made several arrests which led to contact with the District Attorney's Office. In response to close inquiry by defense counsel, Smith declared his belief that he could be a fair and impartial juror in the case. This assurance apparently satisfied defense counsel, for Smith was permitted to take his seat among the jurors even though the defense could have removed him.

prosecutors to disclose their knowledge denied [respondent] due process." Ibid. The court explained: "To condone the withholding by the prosecutor of information casting substantial doubt as to the impartiality of a juror, such as the fact that he has applied to the prosecutor for employment, would not be fair to a defendant and would ill serve to maintain public confidence in the judicial process." Id., at 1023.

## II

This Court has long held that the remedy for allegations of juror partiality is a hearing in which the defendant has the opportunity to prove actual bias. For example, in Remmer v. United States, 347 U.S. 227 (1954), a juror in a federal criminal trial was approached by someone offering money in exchange for a favorable verdict. An FBI agent was assigned to investigate the attempted bribe, and the agent's report was reviewed by the trial judge and the prosecutor without disclosure to defense counsel. When they learned of the incident after trial, the defense attorneys moved that the verdict be vacated, alleging that "they would have moved for a mistrial and requested that the juror in question be replaced by an alternate juror" had the incident been disclosed to them during trial. Id., at 229.

This Court recognized the seriousness not only of the attempted bribe, which it characterized as "presumptively prejudicial," but also of the undisclosed investigation, which was "bound to impress the juror and [was] very apt to do so unduly." Ibid. Despite this recognition, and a conviction that "[the] integrity of jury proceedings must not be jeopardized by unauthorized invasions," ibid., the Court did not require a new trial like that ordered in this case. Rather, the Court instructed the trial judge to "determine the circumstances, the impact thereof upon the juror, and whether or not [they were] prejudicial, in a hearing with all interested parties permitted to participate." Id., at 230. In other words, the Court ordered precisely the remedy which was accorded by Justice Birns in this case.

This case demonstrates that due process does not require a new trial every time a juror has been placed in a potentially compromising situation. Were that the rule, few trials would be constitutionally acceptable. The safeguards of juror impartiality are not infallible; it is virtually impossible to shield jurors from every contact or influence that might theoretically affect their vote. Due process means a jury capable and willing to decide the case solely on the evidence before it, and a trial judge ever watchful to prevent prejudicial occurrences and to determine the effect of such occurrences when they happen. Such determinations may properly be made at a hearing like that ordered in Remmer and held in this case.

Therefore, the prosecutors' failure to disclose Smith's job application, although requiring a post-trial hearing on juror bias, did not deprive respondent of the fair trial guaranteed by the Due Process Clause. Accordingly, the judgment of the Court of Appeals is reversed.

■ Justice Marshall, with whom Justice Brennan and Justice Stevens join, dissenting.

Juror John Smith vigorously pursued employment with the office of the prosecutor throughout the course of his jury service in respondent's state criminal trial. The prosecutors learned of Smith's efforts during the trial, but improperly failed to disclose this information until after the jury had returned a verdict of guilty against respondent. The state court conducted a post-trial evidentiary hearing and determined that the juror was not actually biased. Thus, it ruled that respondent was not prejudiced, and refused to set aside the conviction. Respondent subsequently filed for relief in the United States District Court for the Southern District of New York, claiming that he was denied his constitutional right to an impartial jury. The District Court ruled that the conviction should be set aside, and the United States Court of Appeals for the Second Circuit affirmed. A majority of this Court now reverses, holding that the post-trial evidentiary hearing provided sufficient protection to respondent's right to an impartial jury. Because I find the majority's analysis completely unpersuasive, I dissent.

The majority concedes the importance of the right to a trial by an impartial jury. It claims, however, that respondent's right was adequately protected here, because the state trial judge conducted a postverdict evidentiary hearing and concluded that Smith was not actually biased. According to the majority, the Constitution requires only that the defendant be given an opportunity to prove actual bias. Indeed, it would apparently insist on proof of actual bias, not only when a juror had applied for employment with the prosecutor's office, but also when the juror was already employed in the prosecutor's office, or when he served as a prosecuting attorney. The majority relies on the premise that an evidentiary hearing provides adequate assurance that prejudice does not exist. This premise, however, ignores basic human psychology. In cases like this one, an evidentiary hearing can never adequately protect the right to an impartial jury.

Despite the majority's suggestions to the contrary, juror Smith was not a passive, indifferent job applicant.[5] He began pursuing employment as an investigator in the Office of the District Attorney on September 23, 1974, the same day he was sworn in. He asked a friend, Criminal Court Officer Rudolph Fontaine, to determine the proper method of applying for employment. Once he had completed his application, he gave it to Fontaine for hand delivery to the District Attorney's Office, apparently because he assumed that the court officer had a personal contact in the office. In addition, after the application had been filed, he met regularly with Fontaine and Jury Warden Mario Piazza in order to determine the progress of his application. On November 21, 1974, the jury returned a verdict of guilt and the trial ended. The very next day, Smith phoned the District Attorney's Office to check on the status of his application. When he was

---

5. The majority notes that during jury selection, the defense chose not to challenge Smith, even though he had stated that he had a strong interest in a law enforcement career. However, since the defendant was himself a law enforcement officer, such an interest would not necessarily have been unfavorable to the defense. I think it clear that a general career interest in law enforcement is very different from an application for a job with the prosecutor in a particular case.

unable to get in touch with anyone who knew about his application, he asked his former supervisor to make inquiries in his behalf.

When a juror vigorously and actively pursues employment in the prosecutor's office throughout the course of a trial, the probability of bias is substantial. This bias may be conscious, part of a calculated effort to obtain a job. The juror may believe that his application will be viewed favorably if the defendant is found guilty. Thus, he may decide to vote for a verdict of guilty regardless of the evidence, and he may attempt to persuade the other jurors that acquittal is not justified. There is also a very serious danger of unconscious bias. Only individuals of extraordinary character would not be affected in some way by their interest in future employment. Subconsciously, the juror may tend to favor the prosecutor simply because he feels some affinity with his potential employer. Indeed, the juror may make a sincere effort to remain impartial, and yet be unable to do so.

Not only is the probability of bias high, it is also unlikely that a post-trial evidentiary hearing would reveal this bias. As the Court of Appeals stated, given the human propensity for self-justification, it is very difficult "to learn from a juror's own testimony after the verdict whether he was in fact 'impartial.'" 632 F.2d 1019, 1022 (CA2 1980). Certainly, a juror is unlikely to admit that he had consciously plotted against the defendant during the course of the trial. Such an admission would have subjected juror Smith to criminal sanctions. It would also have damaged his prospects for a career in law enforcement. A law enforcement agency is unlikely to hire an investigator whose credibility could always be impeached by an admission that he had disregarded his juror's oath in a criminal trial.

Even when the bias was not part of an affirmative course of misconduct, however, but was unconscious, a juror is unlikely to admit that he had been unable to weigh the evidence fairly. If he honestly believes that he remained impartial throughout the trial, no amount of questioning will lead to an admission. Rather the juror will vehemently deny any accusation of bias.[7]

In the past, the Court has recognized that the question whether a juror is prejudiced poses substantial problems of proof.

> "Bias or prejudice is such an elusive condition of the mind that it is most difficult, if not impossible, to always recognize its existence, and it might exist in the mind of one (on account of his relations with one of the parties) who was quite positive that he had no bias, and said that he was perfectly able to decide the question wholly uninfluenced by anything but the evidence." Crawford v. United States, 212 U.S. 183, 196 (1909).

---

**7.** The petitioner emphasizes that during the hearing, the trial judge had an opportunity to observe the juror's demeanor. Thus, argues the petitioner, even where the juror denies that he was biased, the trial judge will be able to measure the juror's integrity, and decide whether to credit his claim that he fairly weighed the evidence. It may be true that the opportunity to observe the juror will be of assistance in some cases. However, it will be of little value where the juror honestly but falsely believes that he was impartial.

I believe that in cases like this one, where the probability of bias is very high, and where the evidence adduced at a hearing can offer little assurance that prejudice does not exist, the juror should be deemed biased as a matter of law. Specifically, where a juror pursues employment with the office of the prosecutor, under circumstances highly suggestive of misconduct or conflict of interest, bias should be "implied," and he should be automatically disqualified, despite the absence of proof of actual bias. If the juror's efforts to secure employment are not revealed until after the trial, the conviction must be set aside. The right to a trial by an impartial jury is too important, and the threat to that right too great, to justify rigid insistence on actual proof of bias. Such a requirement blinks reality.

The majority adopts a completely unrealistic view of the efficacy of a post-trial hearing, and thus fails to accord any meaningful protection to the right to an impartial jury, one of the most valuable rights possessed by criminal defendants. I would affirm the judgment of the Court of Appeals on the ground that a juror who applies for employment with the office of the prosecutor and vigorously pursues that employment throughout the course of the trial is impliedly biased.

## United States v. Littlefield

United States Court of Appeals for the Ninth Circuit, 1985.
752 F.2d 1429.

■ Goodwin, Circuit Judge:

Littlefield, Nicoladze, and Solomon appeal their convictions for conspiracy to violate the tax laws and for various tax-related criminal offenses arising from tax shelter activities. We remand for a new trial because a Time magazine article on similarly fraudulent tax shelters was carried by one of the jurors into the jury room during deliberations and was read and discussed by one or more of the other jurors.

The district judge determined that it could be concluded that the extrinsic evidence did not influence the verdict. We reverse because this finding fails to satisfy the standard of proof required to show lack of jury bias.

The government argues that defendants rather than the government bear the burden of proving jury partiality in a hearing on the matter. We believe that this argument misinterprets the meaning of Smith v. Phillips, 455 U.S. 209 (1982).

In Remmer v. United States, 347 U.S. 227 (1954), the Supreme Court placed the burden of proof on the government to overcome a presumption of prejudice where there is "any private communication, contact or tampering directly or indirectly with a juror during a trial about the matter pending before the jury." 347 U.S. at 229. In a hearing to determine whether contact with a juror was harmless, "the burden rests heavily upon the Government to establish ... that such contact with the juror was harmless to the defendant." Id. The government maintains that *Phillips* overruled *Remmer* by holding that the remedy for allegations of juror partiality is a hearing "in which the defendant has the opportunity to prove actual bias." 455 U.S. at 215. Quite simply, the government misread the *Phillips* "opportunity to prove actual bias" as a shifting of the burden of proof to the defendant.

The *Phillips* case did not confront the issue of burden or proof but rather concerned the necessity for a hearing on the issue of jury partiality. It was on that issue that the Court discussed the relevance of *Remmer*; its conclusion that the state hearing was constitutionally adequate did not even address the burden of proof issue. *Phillips*, 455 U.S. at 215–18.

In light of *Phillips*, therefore, we reject the government's assertion that Remmer is no longer good law. The government had an obligation here to prove beyond a reasonable doubt that the juror's reading of the Time magazine article was harmless.

Vacated and remanded.

■ WALLACE, CIRCUIT JUDGE, dissenting:

The district judge held a hearing to determine whether the Time magazine article influenced the jury's verdict.

The Court has stated "that due process does not require a new trial every time a juror has been placed in a potentially compromising situation. Were that the rule, few trials would be constitutionally acceptable." Smith v. Phillips, 455 U.S. 209, 217, (1982). The Court suggested that the government meets its burden of proof in a partiality hearing if it shows that the "jury [was] capable and willing to decide the case solely on the evidence before it, and [the] trial judge [was] ever watchful to prevent prejudicial occurrences and to determine the effect of such occurrences when they happen." Id.

I believe the majority fails to follow this sound advice. In this case at least, I would defer to the district judge's conclusion that the magazine did not influence the jury's verdict.

## United States v. Pennell
United States Court of Appeals for the Sixth Circuit, 1984.
737 F.2d 521.

■ CONTIE, CIRCUIT JUDGE:

Gordon Pennell, the defendant, appeals from jury convictions for one count of conspiracy to possess with intent to distribute cocaine, and one count of attempt to possess with intent to distribute cocaine. For the reasons set forth below, we affirm.

Pennell contends that the district court should have declared a mistrial after five jurors were contacted at their homes by an anonymous telephone caller. Jury deliberations began on Friday, January 28, 1983. Between 1:00 A.M. and 1:30 A.M. on Sunday, January 30, five jurors received anonymous telephone calls. Juror Larson was told, "Urness Larson, you had better find him guilty." Juror Page's daughter answered her father's telephone and was told, "tell Charles [Page] he better vote guilty." Juror Burgess was told, "Mrs. Burgess, find him guilty or you will wish you had." The caller told Juror Saveski, "is this Janet? You had better find him guilty." Finally, the caller instructed Juror Wilcox, "Ms. Wilcox, find him guilty." In all five instances, the caller urged the juror to convict and then quickly hung up.[9]

On the morning of Monday, January 31, the five jurors informed their counterparts of what had happened and then notified the court. The court proceeded individually to question the five who had received calls out of the presence of the other jurors. Juror Wilcox stated that her impartiality had not been compromised and that she did not feel intimidated. She indicated that the call could have been a prank by a young person attending the school at which she taught. Juror Burgess also assured the court that her impartiality had not been affected, but indicated that Juror Saveski had exhibited apprehension and nervousness about the telephone call. Burgess also stated that Saveski had not said "one way or the other whether the (telephone call) would have anything to do with her decision."

When asked if the telephone call would impair his ability to render a fair verdict, Juror Page responded, "I don't believe it is impaired in the least." Page did indicate, however, that Juror Saveski was "disturbed" about the matter and was "unsure" of herself. The court next questioned Saveski. During the ensuing discussion, Saveski stated four times in response to different questions that the telephone call had not affected her impartiality or her ability to decide the case on the basis of the testimony and exhibits. Finally, Juror Larson assured the court three times that she would exclude the telephone calls from consideration during deliberations.

With the concurrence of counsel for both parties, the court then summoned the entire jury and asked a series of questions designed to elicit whether any juror's impartiality had been compromised and whether any juror would find it difficult to render a verdict based upon the evidence and the court's instructions. When no juror responded, the court ordered the jury to resume deliberations. Defense counsel then moved for a mistrial.

After the jury resumed deliberations, the forewoman sent a note to the court which read in its entirety:

> Attention Honorable John Cook. We do have a juror Linda Lorenz, that does feel that the phone calls will influence her judgment in this case. Forewoman Darlene Patterson.

The court immediately summoned Juror Lorenz, who had not received a telephone call, back to the courtroom. In response to questions, Lorenz stated that listening to the other jurors had made her nervous and that she did not wish to receive a telephone call. Nevertheless, she twice indicated that the calls received by the others would not affect her verdict.

After Juror Lorenz returned to the jury room, the court denied the motion for mistrial. As to Juror Lorenz, the court found:

---

**9.** Although the government contends that the caller's statements should not be regarded as threats, similar statements were so regarded in United States v. Brown, 571 F.2d 980, 987 (6th Cir.1978).

After examining Ms. Lorenz in the presence of counsel and on the record, this Court believes that Ms. Lorenz, while nervous and apprehensive about potential harm to herself, that she is nevertheless able and willing to continue as a juror and, moreover, that I am satisfied that Ms. Lorenz, being aware of her responsibilities as a juror, will confine her assessment of the facts in this case to the testimony of the witnesses, the exhibits that have been received into evidence and the instructions that were presented to the Jury by the Court. Moreover, the last juror, Linda Lorenz, advised the Court that she could confine her evaluations to those three categories that I have just mentioned.

Regarding the jury as a whole, the court found:

It is my personal opinion, in speaking with the jurors prior to the—to this session and during the session that they were resolute in their belief that their opinion would not be swayed one way or the other by the telephone call. More specifically, I am satisfied that the jurors, in responding to my questions, were desirous of continuing in their roles as jurors and that the telephone calls would not play any part in their decision. Thus, I am satisfied that a verdict from the Jury, whether it is guilty or not guilty, will not be tainted or affected in any way by the telephone calls that were received by them on Sunday morning, between the hours of 1:00 and 1:30.

The court did offer the jury the opportunity to be sequestered. The jury declined this offer and deliberated for three more days without incident before rendering its verdict.

Remmer v. United States, 347 U.S. 227 (1954), has generally been regarded as the leading case on the issue of how a district court should treat unauthorized communications with jurors. The Supreme Court in Remmer fashioned the following rule:

In a criminal case, any private communication, contact, or tampering, directly or indirectly, with a juror during a trial about the matter pending before the jury is, for obvious reasons, *deemed presumptively prejudicial,* if not made in pursuance of known rules of the court and the instructions and directions of the court made during the trial, with full knowledge of the parties. *The presumption is not conclusive, but the burden rests heavily upon the Government to establish, after notice to and hearing of the defendant, that such contact with the juror was harmless to the defendant.* [Emphasis supplied.]

Id. at 229.

The Supreme Court, has more recently filed an opinion that is relevant to the case at hand. Smith v. Phillips, 455 U.S. 209 (1982). Thus, the question is whether *Phillips* has so changed the rules relating to unauthorized communications with jurors that the presumptive prejudice standard no longer governs. We conclude that *Phillips* has indeed altered the law concerning unauthorized communications with jurors.

Although *Phillips* involved bias resulting from a juror's potential employment relationship with a law enforcement agency, the principles set forth in the opinion apply to allegations of jury partiality generally. In essence, *Phillips* reinterpreted *Remmer*. Although the Court in *Phillips* referred to the *Remmer* presumptive prejudice standard, the Court nevertheless stated:

> This court has long held that the remedy for allegations of juror partiality is a *hearing* in which the defendant has the opportunity to prove actual bias. [Emphasis supplied.]

455 U.S. at 215. Thus, the Court held that *Remmer* does not govern the question of the burden of proof where potential jury partiality is alleged. Instead, *Remmer* only controls the question of how the district court should proceed where such allegations are made, i.e., a hearing must be held during which the defendant is entitled to be heard. 455 U.S. at 216. In light of *Phillips*, the burden of proof rests upon a defendant to demonstrate that unauthorized communications with jurors resulted in actual juror partiality. Prejudice is not to be presumed.[10]

Moreover, the Court in *Phillips* implied that deference should be accorded a district court's findings made after a properly conducted hearing. Accordingly, we hold that if a district court views juror assurances of continued impartiality to be credible, the court may rely upon such assurances in deciding whether a defendant has satisfied the burden of proving actual prejudice.

The judgment of the district court is Affirmed.

■ CELEBREZZE, SENIOR CIRCUIT JUDGE, dissenting.

The majority holds that a presumption of prejudice should not be applied in a hearing to determine juror bias when five jurors receive late night threatening phone calls, the entire jury discussed the phone calls during deliberations, and one juror expresses privately doubts as to whether she can render an objective decision based solely on the evidence. Respectfully, I dissent.

Generally, the remedy for allegations of juror bias is a hearing to determine whether actual bias exists. E.g., Smith v. Phillips, 455 U.S. 209 (1982).

In *Phillips*, the issue was whether a conclusive presumption of prejudice should apply. The issue of a conclusive presumption, more often termed the doctrine of "implied bias," involves a different line of cases than those which address a presumption of prejudice.[1] *Phillips* is merely another case which rejects the use of a conclusive presumption of prejudice under circumstances which are not extreme. In less extreme cases, such as

---

**10.** We read *Remmer* as requiring the government to do more than come forward with evidence that unauthorized communications with jurors were harmless. As the quotation cited supra, indicates, *Remmer* placed a heavy burden of proof upon the government. Accordingly, *Phillips* worked a substantive change in the law.

**1.** In extreme cases, such as when a juror is involved in serious misconduct, bias is to be presumed conclusively. Under less serious circumstances, such as when a jury might be affected by the misconduct of a third party, a *Remmer* type hearing safeguards adequately a defendant's right to an impartial jury.

those in *Phillips* and the case at bar, a post-conviction hearing, where the defendant is aided by the presumption of prejudice, will suffice to determine whether juror bias exists.

There is no precedent in support of the majority's conclusion that the Supreme Court has abandoned the application of the presumption of prejudice when unauthorized contacts are made with jurors.

There is no evidence in the record to suggest that the trial court applied the presumption of prejudice at the hearing to determine whether the improper jury contact was prejudicial. Because the court did not apply a presumption required by the law, the hearing was defective. In my view, the conviction should be reversed and the case remanded for a new trial.

\* \* \*

\*

# PART III

# THE INTERPRETATION OF STATUTES

## A. STATING AND RESOLVING STATUTORY ISSUES

### 1. FINDING AND STATING ISSUES OF STATUTE LAW

To interpret and apply a statute, you must work with its precise language. This proposition may seem obvious, but it marks an essential change of emphasis as the beginning law student moves from legal method in the use of case law to legal method in the use of statutes. After even a few weeks of case law analysis and synthesis, the first year law student has discovered that the rule of law derived from a case or from a line of cases can be stated in many different forms of language, each of which may constitute an acceptable statement. But a statutory rule of law is cast in an exclusive textual form. The beginning law student finds it difficult, as, for that matter, do many members of the profession, to work comfortably with a legal principle of which there is only one authorized version. Inevitably the beginner wants to handle statutes with the freedom of paraphrase that he has found permissible in the statement of case law principles.

The Problem Cases in this Section are designed to give you practice in statutory analysis and in the statement of statutory issues. The vital lesson to derive from the preparation and discussion of these Problem Cases is this: *The issue in a case of statutory interpretation must be so stated as to include an exact quotation of the precise term of the statute with respect to which the question of statutory applicability arises.*—DO NOT PARA-PHRASE THE STATUTE! As to each Problem Case—and, later, as to each judicial opinion in this Part—you must be prepared to give an accurate and precise answer to the question: "What does the statute *say,* exactly, with respect to the legal problem at hand?" Accordingly, you should analyze and discuss the following Problem Cases solely on the basis of the words of the statutes in point. Practice reading and rereading the text of the statute itself. Only after you have become used to examining the precise statutory language on its own terms should you turn to its judicial exposition.

**Some Problem Cases**

**Problem Case No. 1**

Humphrey Hume was born in England of English parents in 1940 and came to the United States in 1960. He has never become a naturalized citizen of the United States.

In 1969, Hume was indicted on a charge of wilfully destroying valuable federal property (Selective Service files) earlier in that year in the course of militant anti-war protest activity. He was tried shortly afterward and found guilty by a jury and then sentenced to imprisonment for a year and a day. He served his sentence as required.

Two and a half years ago, Hume drove a motor vehicle on behalf of a labor union engaged in demonstrations against certain West Coast grape growers. In the course of one demonstration his vehicle struck and killed a bystander. Hume was thereafter indicted for manslaughter, based on negligent and reckless operation (without intent to injure the victim) of a motor vehicle in violation of state law. On his plea of guilty he was sentenced to imprisonment by state authorities for a term of two years. He served his sentence and was recently released from the penitentiary. Thereupon deportation proceedings were commenced against him under Section 241(a) of the Immigration and Nationality Act of 1952, 66 Stat. 204, 8 U.S.C.A. Sec. 1251(a).

Section 241(a) of the Immigration and Nationality Act of 1952 (as modified for the purpose of this Problem Case) provides as follows:

(a) Any alien in the United States shall, upon the order of the Attorney General, be deported who—

* * *

> (4) is hereafter convicted of a crime involving moral turpitude committed within five years after entry and either sentenced to confinement or confined therefor in a prison or corrective institution for a year or more, or who hereafter at any time after entry is more than once convicted of a crime involving moral turpitude.

After a procedurally correct deportation hearing, Hume has now been ordered deported and taken into custody for that purpose. He seeks *habeas corpus* in a District Court of the United States on the ground that Section 241(a) does not authorize his deportation.

State the issue or issues of statutory interpretation raised by this case, noting as to each issue the precise language of the statute with respect to which the question of statutory applicability arises.

## Problem Case No. 2

Prior to 1949, no anti-discrimination legislation had ever been enacted in State X. During its 1949 session, the State Legislature passed the following statute, which was approved by the Governor and became effective June 1, 1949:

An Act to protect all citizens in the enjoyment of their civil rights.

*Be it enacted by the Legislature of the State of X:*

Section 1: This statute may be cited as "The Anti–Discrimination Act of 1949."

Section 2: All persons within the jurisdiction of this State shall be entitled to the full and equal accommodations, advantages, facilities and privileges of inns, restaurants, hotels, eating-houses, bath-houses, barber shops, theatres, music halls, public conveyances on land and water, and all other places of public accommodation or amusement, subject only to conditions and limitations applicable alike to all citizens.

Section 3: Any person who shall violate any of the provisions of the foregoing section by denying to any citizen, except for reasons applicable alike to all citizens of every race, creed or color, and regardless of race, creed or color, the full enjoyment of any of the accommodations, advantages, facilities or privileges in said section enumerated, or by aiding or inciting such denial, shall for every such offense be subject to a fine of not more than $5,000, or to imprisonment for not more than one year, or to both such fine and such imprisonment.

The facts of this Problem Case are as follows: Dr. Claudius Smythe, a retired physician, is the sole owner of a rest home for persons recovering from major operations or from severe illnesses. The rest home is situated in one of the rural counties of State X, and there are usually about fifteen convalescents in residence there. For some time, all financial and other business details have been handled by Rufus DeLong, who serves as the rest home's resident manager. Recently, DeLong wrote and had printed certain circulars describing the rest home, copies of which circulars were sent to all physicians in State X. At the specific direction of Dr. Smythe, DeLong included in the printed circulars the following statement:

*Admission Policy:* It is the policy of the Smythe Rest Home to admit *white* patients only. Applications from Negroes and other non-white persons will not be considered.

No Negro or other non-white person was ever actually turned away by the Smythe Rest Home; in fact, there is no record of any application to the rest home ever having been received from a Negro or other non-white person.

Early this year, copies of the Smythe Rest Home's circular were called to the attention of the prosecuting attorney of the county in which the rest home is situated. Dr. Smythe was promptly indicted for violation of the Anti–Discrimination Act of 1949. After trial before a jury, Dr. Smythe was convicted and fined $1,500. He appeals to the appropriate appellate court of State X.

State the issue or issues of statutory interpretation raised by Dr. Smythe's appeal, noting as to each issue the *precise language* of the statute with respect to which the question of statutory applicability arises.

**Problem Case No. 3**

The Growers' Irrigation Company (hereinafter called the "Company") owns, maintains and operates within State X an irrigation system consisting of four large storage reservoirs and 400 miles of irrigation canals. More than 100,000 acres of State X farm land, owned by many different farmers, are irrigated with water furnished by the Company. The water distributed by the Company is diverted from streams in State X during the non-irrigation season and runs through canals into the Company's reservoirs. During the irrigation season, this water is released from the reservoirs, carried through the Company's canals, and delivered to the lateral irrigation ditches of the farmers.

Sugar beets, corn, peas and beans are grown on the land irrigated. Virtually all of the sugar beets are processed into refined sugar in plants operated within State X, and large amounts of the corn, peas, and beans are canned in factories within State X. More than 75% of the refined sugar and canned vegetables is shipped in interstate commerce to purchasers outside State X.

There are 1,000 shares of authorized capital stock in the Company, all of which shares are owned by farmers in the irrigation area of State X. Each share of stock entitles the owner thereof to a $\frac{1}{1},000$th share of the property of the Company and of the total supply of water available during the irrigation season. The expenses necessary to the operation of the irrigation system are borne by annual assessments levied on the Company's stockholders, and the proceeds of the assessments constitute the Company's sole source of income. Payment of the assessment on his shares of stock is a condition precedent to the right of a stockholder to receive water for his farm during the irrigation season. The Company does not sell water to persons other than stockholders.

The Company employs 16 reservoir tenders, who take care of the diverting and storage of water during the non-irrigation season and attend the conduct of water through the Company's canals and into the lateral ditches of the farmers during the irrigation season. These reservoir tenders do not look after the lateral ditches of the farmers; in fact, they do not go at all on to the farmers' property. The Company pays its reservoir tenders a flat wage rate of $3 per hour, irrespective of the number of hours worked during any week. During the irrigation season, the 16 reservoir tenders work considerably more than 40 hours a week.

The Administrator of the Wage and Hour Division of the Department of Labor has now filed a complaint in the United States District Court for State X, charging that the Company is violating the federal Fair Labor Standards Act by failing to pay the 16 reservoir tenders time-and-a-half for overtime. The Administrator's complaint asks that the District Court issue an injunction against the Company restraining continued violation of the Act.

The Fair Labor Standards Act (as modified and renumbered for the purposes of this Problem Case) provides, in pertinent part, as follows:

Section 1: *Declaration of Policy.* The Congress finds that the existence, in industries engaged in commerce, of labor conditions detrimental to the maintenance of minimum standards of living causes commerce and the channels of commerce to be used to spread such detrimental labor conditions among the workers of the several States.

Section 2: No employer shall employ any employee who is engaged in commerce or in the production of goods for commerce for a workweek longer than 40 hours unless such employee receives compensation for his employment in excess of the hours above specified at a rate not less than one and one-half times the regular pay rate at which he is employed.

Section 3: The provisions of Section 2 of this Act shall not apply with respect to: (1) any employee employed in a bona fide executive, administrative, or professional capacity; (2) any employee engaged in any retail or service establishment the greater part of whose selling or servicing is done within the State; (3) any employee employed in agriculture; or (4) any individual employed in handling, packing, storing, or canning agricultural commodities for market.

Section 4: *Definitions.*

(a) "Commerce" means trade, commerce, transportation, transmission, or communication among the several States or from any State to any place outside thereof.

(b) "Employer" includes any person acting directly or indirectly in the interest of an employer in relation to an employee but shall not include the United States or any State or political subdivision of a State.

(c) "Employee" includes any individual employed by an employer.

(d) "Agriculture" includes farming and all its branches and includes any practices performed by a farmer or on a farm as incident to or in conjunction with farming operations, including preparation for market and delivery to storage or to market.

(e) "Goods" means wares, products, commodities, merchandise or articles or subjects of commerce of any character whatsoever.

(f) "Produced" means produced, manufactured, mined, handled, or in any other manner worked on in any State; and for the purposes of this Act an employee shall be deemed to have been engaged in the production of goods if such employee was employed in any process or occupation necessary to the production of goods in any State.

The Growers' Irrigation Company moves to dismiss the Administrator's injunction action on the ground that the Company's activities are not within the area of coverage of the Fair Labor Standards Act.

State the issues of statutory interpretation raised by this case, noting as to each issue the *precise language* of the statute with respect to which the question of statutory applicability arises.

**Note**

The importance to lawyers of the disciplines of statutory analysis here proposed, including finding and precisely stating the issues, is underlined by the remarks of Erwin N. Griswold, then Solicitor General of the United States, in his discussion of "Appellate Advocacy" at 26 The Record of the Association of the Bar of the City of New York 342 (1971). Solicitor General Griswold urged that advocates "orient the court" at the beginning of any oral argument on appeal. As a part of "orienting" the court, he recommended that counsel focus the issue for the judges, commenting as follows:

[L]et the court see—and I mean "see"—the exact language with which they have to deal. Tell them, right at the beginning: "The statutory language involved appears at page 4 of my brief. Though the clause is a somewhat long one, the issue turns, I believe, on the proper construction or effect of words in two lines near the top of the page." Give the court time to find the two lines, and then read the words to them. At this point, the eye can be as important as the ear in oral argument, and the court will follow all of the rest of your argument much better if you have taken pains to tell them exactly what it is about, and where to find the words if they want to look at them again.

In the years when I was a law teacher, I suppose that my most famous classroom remark was "Look at the statute"—or "What does the statute say?" Over the years, I have had literally hundreds of my former students write me and say that this was the most important thing they learned in law school. There is something about the student, and some oral advocates, too, which leads them to think great thoughts without ever taking the time and care to see just exactly what they are thinking about. Now I would not suggest that the court would make such a mistake. But courts are accustomed to think in terms of concrete, rather specific cases. The oral advocate takes a great step in advancing his cause, I think, if, right at the beginning of his argument, after the procedural setting has been established, he tells the court exactly what the case is about, including specific reference to any statutory language which must be construed or evaluated in bringing the case to a decision. With orientation, the court finds moorings. It is no longer cast adrift on the great sea of all the law. If you can get the court moored to the question as you see it, and so that they see it clearly and distinctly, you may be off to a good start towards leading them to decide the case your way.

## The Problem of Drafting Unambiguous Rules

Following is an extract from the Minutes of an English Borough Council Meeting[1]:

Councillor Trafford took exception to the proposed notice at the entrance of South Park: "No dogs must be brought to this Park except on a lead." He pointed out that this order would not prevent an owner from releasing his pets, or pet, from a lead when once safely inside the Park.

*The Chairman* (Colonel Vine): What alternative wording would you propose, Councillor?

*Councillor Trafford:* "Dogs are not allowed in this Park without leads."

---

1.  Reprinted by permission of Random House, Inc. from The Reader Over Your Shoulder by Robert Graves and Alan Hodge. Copyright 1943 by Robert Graves and Alan Hodge.

*Councillor Hogg:* Mr. Chairman, I object. The order should be addressed to the owners, not to the dogs.

*Councillor Trafford:* That is a nice point. Very well then: "Owners of dogs are not allowed in this Park unless they keep them on leads."

*Councillor Hogg:* Mr. Chairman, I object. Strictly speaking, this would prevent me as a dog-owner from leaving my dog in the back-garden at home and walking with Mrs. Hogg across the Park.

*Councillor Trafford:* Mr. Chairman, I suggest that our legalistic friend be asked to redraft the notice himself.

*Councillor Hogg:* Mr. Chairman, since Councillor Trafford finds it so difficult to improve on my original wording, I accept. "Nobody without his dog on a lead is allowed in this Park."

*Councillor Trafford:* Mr. Chairman, I object. Strictly speaking, this notice would prevent me, as a citizen who owns no dog, from walking in the Park without first acquiring one.

*Councillor Hogg* (with some warmth): Very simply, then: "Dogs must be led in this Park."

*Councillor Trafford:* Mr. Chairman, I object: this reads as if it were a general injunction to the Borough to lead their dogs into the Park.

Councillor Hogg interposed a remark for which he was called to order; upon his withdrawing it, it was directed to be expunged from the Minutes.

*The Chairman:* Councillor Trafford, Councillor Hogg has had three tries; you have had only two * * *.

*Councillor Trafford:* "All dogs must be kept on leads in the Park."

*The Chairman:* I see Councillor Hogg rising quite rightly to raise another objection. May I anticipate him with another amendment: "All dogs in this Park must be kept on the lead."

This draft was put to the vote and carried unanimously, with two abstentions.

* * *

Having seen the travails of the English Borough Council, try your hand at drafting a municipal ordinance:

At a recent city council meeting of Metropolis, in the state of New Hazard, numerous residents of the city complained bitterly about the proliferation of aggressive and harassing panhandlers on the subway platforms in all sectors of the city. They demanded an outright ban on soliciting money on subway property. Some of the specific concerns raised were:

1) People soliciting money on subway platforms are often perceived as threatening to subway patrons, either in their appearance or in their behavior.

2) Some panhandlers will not leave a customer alone if the customer refuses to give money.

3) The overall appearance of the subway and desirability of using the subway are diminished by the presence of panhandlers.

Countering the complaints of those citizens opposed to panhandlers are several important constituencies whose views must also be addressed in resolving this problem. First, there are a number of "legitimate" charities, such as the Salvation Army, who solicit donations on subway platforms. Without this source of income, their ability to feed and shelter the homeless would be severely curtailed. Second, there are the musicians and other artists who perform on subway platforms. For many, this is their sole source of income, and customers of the subway enjoy the range and diversity of talent these artists bring to the underground. Lastly, there are several groups who advocate on behalf of the homeless who argue that most panhandlers in the subway have nowhere else to go, that many patrons of the subway do voluntarily agree to give them money, and to that turn them out simply on esthetic grounds would be unfair and unjust.

Council Representative Compassion, Transit President Law and Mayor Order have asked you, a legislative aide, to draft an ordinance addressing the concerns of the subway patrons and community interests of Metropolis. Keep in mind not only the definition of the conduct you determine to regulate, but the means of enforcement of the ordinance.

Metropolis has a long-standing reputation of drafting legislation in plain English. Therefore, you know that any ordinance you draft on the Council's behalf must address the issues completely, but should be as clear and simple as possible.

## 2.  RESOLVING STATUTORY ISSUES—A GENERAL VIEW

In applying statutes, courts have traditionally assumed that doubts as to the meaning or legal effect of statutory language are to be resolved in accordance with "the intention of the legislature." In your study of the cases in this Chapter, you will find that the establishment of "legislative intention" is, on many occasions at least, quite as difficult and subtle an operation as is the parallel case law job of arriving at the "holding" of a case.

Consider the range of problems involved in the decision of particular cases by reference to the general commands of the statute law. A legislative direction must be expressed in words, and words are notoriously inexact and imperfect symbols for the communication of ideas. In addition, one must reckon with the inexhaustible variety of the facts to which such words must be applied. To determine from the language of an enactment the "legislative intention," in the sense of a pre-existing understanding of the law-makers as to the statute's construction in relation to a particular issue, may involve semantic problems of very great difficulty.

Even more difficult are the cases in which the interpretative issue before the court is one which was not, and perhaps could not have been, foreseen, even in the most general outline, by the legislators responsible for the enactment. In such cases, the "interpreting" judge must perform the originative function of assigning to the statute a meaning or legal effect which it did not possess before his action. Cardozo saw this with his characteristic clarity when he wrote:[3]

Interpretation is often spoken of as if it were nothing but the search and the discovery of a meaning which, however obscure and latent, had none the less a real and ascertainable pre-existence in the legislator's mind. The process is, indeed, that at times, but it is often something more.

Note that the traditional term "legislative intention" may be taken to signify at least two rather different concepts—either the more immediate concept of *specific intent* or the teleological concept of *purpose*.[4]

The principle that courts are bound to follow "the intention of the legislature" would normally require in relation to a demonstrated specific intent—i.e., a showing that Congress foresaw the issue presented and meant to resolve it in a particular way—that such a specific intent be given effect by the courts. In the latter or "purpose" signification of legislative intention, it would demand that the interpretive issues unforeseen specifically by the legislators be resolved in such a way as to advance rather than to retard the attainment of the objectives which the legislators sought to achieve by the enactment of the legislation.

As you study the cases in this Section, keep in mind this possible double signification of "legislative intention"—"intention" as specific intent, and "intention" as purpose. You will find it helpful in your analysis to ask yourself, each time you encounter a reference to "legislative intention" in a judicial opinion, "Is this court using 'intention' in the sense of what the legislators specifically thought the statute provided on this issue, or is the court using 'intention' in the sense of the purpose the legislators sought to accomplish by enactment of the statute?"

There are a number of other questions or considerations which should be kept in mind in analyzing the materials to come. What light does this case or other material shed on the nature and application of legislative intent or other basic approaches to interpretation? What, if anything, does this case or material reveal as to the types and causes of statutory ambiguity? What, if any, intrinsic and extrinsic aids to interpretation, or interpretative rules or maxims, are employed in this case and what conclusions may be drawn as to their value and use? What lessons emerge from these materials for purposes of advocacy in statutory cases? Note, incidentally, that the materials provide many illustrations of the different types of statutory enactments one may expect to encounter in law practice.

\* \* \*

**3.** The Nature of the Judicial Process 14 (1921).

**4.** Landis, A Note on Statutory Interpretation, 43 Harv.L.Rev. 886 (1930).

The opinions rendered in the appellate and Supreme Court decisions in *Johnson v. Southern Pacific Co.* expose many different varieties of statutory interpretation. As you study the opinions, try to identify the different interpretive techniques and devices employed.

BUT, before you read any of the judicial analysis, concentrate first on the facts of the case and on the language of the statute:

— What happened in this case?

— What does the statute say (verbatim)?

— How does the statute apply to these facts?

Consider how *you* would rule on Johnson's claim under the statute. Only then should you turn to the courts' treatment of his claim.

## Johnson v. Southern Pacific Co.

Circuit Court of Appeals, Eighth Circuit, 1902.
117 Fed. 462, reversed 196 U.S. 1, 25 S.Ct. 158, 49 L.Ed. 363 (1904).

The Southern Pacific Co. was operating passenger trains between San Francisco and Ogden, Utah. It habitually drew a dining car in these trains. Such a car formed a part of a train leaving San Francisco, and ran through to Ogden, where it was ordinarily turned and put into a train going west to San Francisco. On August 5, 1900, the east-bound train was so late that it was not practicable to get the dining car into Ogden in time to place it in the next west-bound train, and it was therefore left on a side track at Promontory, Utah, to be picked up by the west-bound train when it arrived. While it was standing on this track the conductor of an interstate freight train which arrived there was directed to take this dining car to a turntable, turn it, and place it back upon the side track so that it would be ready to return to San Francisco. The conductor instructed his crew to carry out this direction. The plaintiff, Johnson, the head brakeman, undertook to couple the freight engine to the dining car for the purpose of carrying out the conductor's order. The freight engine and the eight-wheel dining car involved were the property of defendant railroad company. The freight engine, regularly used in interstate hauling of standard eight-wheel freight cars, was equipped with a Janney coupler, which would couple automatically with another Janney coupler, and the dining car was provided with a Miller automatic hook; but the Miller hook would not couple automatically with the Janney coupler, because it was on the same side, and would pass over it. Johnson knew this, and undertook to make the coupling by means of a link and pin. He knew that it was a difficult coupling to make, and that it was necessary to go between the engine and the car to accomplish it, and that it was dangerous to do so. Nevertheless, he went in between the engine and the car without objection or protest and tried three times to make the coupling. He failed twice; the third time his hand was caught and crushed so that it became necessary to amputate his hand above the wrist.

Johnson brought an action for damages for personal injury against the railroad. The case was tried in the Circuit Court of the United States for the District of Utah. At the trial, Southern Pacific, after the plaintiff had rested, moved the court to instruct the jury to find in defendant's favor. The motion was granted and the jury found a verdict accordingly on which judgment was entered. Plaintiff carried the case to the Circuit Court of Appeals for the Eighth Circuit.

Defendant contended in the district and circuit courts that it was not liable for the injury on the ground that plaintiff, under the rules of the common law, had "assumed the risk" involved in coupling the dining car and locomotive. Plaintiff Johnson, on the other hand, contended that at the time of the injury defendant was violating a federal statute (infra) in respect to the dining car and locomotive concerned, and that by reason of such violation plaintiff, under this statute, was not to be deemed to have assumed the risk. It was acknowledged that the locomotive possessed a power driving-wheel brake, that there were train brakes and appliances for operating a train brake system as required and that there was no failure, as to either vehicle, to provide the requisite grab irons or drawbars.

The text of the federal statute relied on by plaintiff, which was in effect at the time of the injury and at all times pertinent to this problem, is set out herewith as it appears in the Statutes at Large (27 Stat. 531):

Chap. 196.—An act to promote the safety of employees and travelers upon railroads by compelling common carriers engaged in interstate commerce to equip their cars with automatic couplers and continuous brakes and their locomotives with driving-wheel brakes, and for other purposes.

Sec. 1. *Be it enacted by the Senate and House of Representatives of the United States of America in Congress assembled,* That from and after the first day of January, eighteen hundred and ninety-eight, it shall be unlawful for any common carrier engaged in interstate commerce by railroad to use on its line any locomotive engine in moving interstate traffic not equipped with a power driving-wheel brake and appliances for operating the train-brake system, or to run any train in such traffic after said date that has not a sufficient number of cars in it so equipped with power or train brakes that the engineer on the locomotive drawing such train can control its speed without requiring brakemen to use the common hand brake for that purpose.

Sec. 2. That on and after the first day of January, eighteen hundred and ninety-eight, it shall be unlawful for any such common carrier to haul or permit to be hauled or used on its line any car used in moving interstate traffic not equipped with couplers coupling automatically by impact, and which can be uncoupled without the necessity of men going between the ends of the cars.

Sec. 3. That when any person, firm, company, or corporation engaged in interstate commerce by railroad shall have equipped a sufficient number of its cars so as to comply with the provisions of section one of this act, it may lawfully refuse to receive from connecting lines of road or shippers any cars not equipped sufficiently, in accordance with the first section of this act, with such power or train brakes as will work and readily interchange with the brakes in use on its own cars, as required by this act.

Sec. 4. That from and after the first day of July, eighteen hundred and ninety-five, until otherwise ordered by the Interstate Commerce Commission, it shall be unlawful for any railroad company to use any car in interstate commerce that is not provided with secure grab irons or handholds in the ends and sides of each car for greater security to men in coupling and uncoupling cars.

Sec. 5. That within ninety days from the passage of this act the American Railway Association is authorized hereby to designate to the Interstate Commerce Commission the standard height of drawbars for freight cars, measured perpendicular from the level of the tops of the rails to the centers of the drawbars, for each of the several gauges of railroads in use in the United States, and shall fix a maximum variation from such standard height to be allowed between the drawbars of empty and loaded cars. Upon their determination being certified to the Interstate Commerce Commission, said Commission shall at once give notice of the standard fixed upon to all common carriers, owners, or lessees engaged in interstate commerce in the United States by such means as the Commission may deem proper. But should said association fail to determine a standard as above provided, it shall be the duty of the Interstate Commerce Commission to do so, before July first, eighteen hundred and ninety-four, and immediately to give notice thereof as aforesaid. And after July first, eighteen hundred and ninety-five, no cars, either loaded or unloaded, shall be used in interstate traffic which do not comply with the standard above provided for.

Sec. 6. That any such common carrier using any locomotive engine, running any train, or hauling or permitting to be hauled or used on its line any car in violation of any of the provisions of this act, shall be liable to a penalty of one hundred dollars for each and every such violation, to be recovered in a suit or suits to be brought by the United States district attorney in the district court of the United States having jurisdiction in the locality where such violation shall have been committed, and it shall be the duty of such district attorney to bring such suits upon duly verified information being lodged with him of such violation having occurred. And it shall also be the duty of the Interstate Commerce Commission to lodge with the proper district attorneys information of any such violations as may come to its knowledge: *Provided,* that nothing in this act contained shall apply to trains composed of four-wheel cars or to locomotives used in hauling such trains.

Sec. 7. That the Interstate Commerce Commission may from time to time upon full hearing and for good cause extend the period within which any common carrier shall comply with the provisions of this act.

Sec. 8. That any employee of any such common carrier who may be injured by any locomotive, car, or train in use contrary to the provision of this act shall not be deemed thereby to have assumed the risk thereby occasioned, although continuing in the employment of such carrier after the unlawful use of such locomotive, car, or train had been brought to his knowledge.

Approved, March 2, 1893.

■ SANBORN, CIRCUIT JUDGE, after stating the case

Under the common law the plaintiff assumed the risks and dangers of the coupling which he endeavored to make, and for that reason he is estopped from recovering the damages which resulted from his undertaking. He was an intelligent and experienced brakeman, familiar with the couplers he sought to join, and with their condition, and well aware of the difficulty and danger of his undertaking, so that he falls far within the familiar rules that the servant assumes the ordinary risks and dangers of the employment upon which he enters, so far as they are known to him, and so far as they would have been known to one of his age, experience, and capacity by the use of ordinary care, and that the risks and dangers of coupling cars provided with different kinds of well-known couplers, bumpers, brakeheads and deadwoods are the ordinary risks and dangers of a brakeman's service. [Citations omitted].

This proposition is not seriously challenged, but counsel base their claim for a reversal of the judgment below upon the position that the plaintiff was relieved of this assumption of risk, and of its consequences, by the provisions of the act of Congress of March 2, 1893 (27 Stat. c. 196, p. 531). The title of that act, and the parts of it that are material to the consideration of this contention are these: [see supra]

The first thought that suggests itself to the mind upon a perusal of this law, and a comparison of it with the facts of this case, is that this statute has no application here, because both the dining car and the engine were equipped as this act directs. The car was equipped with Miller couplers which would couple automatically with couplers of the same construction upon cars in the train in which it was used to carry on interstate commerce, and the engine was equipped with a power driving wheel brake such as this statute prescribes. To overcome this difficulty, counsel for the plaintiff persuasively argues that this is a remedial statute; that laws for the prevention of fraud, the suppression of a public wrong, and the bestowal of a public good are remedial in their nature, and should be liberally construed, to prevent the mischief and to advance the remedy, notwithstanding the fact that they may impose a penalty for their violation; and that this statute should be so construed as to forbid the use of a locomotive as well as a car which is not equipped with an automatic coupler. In support of this contention he cites Suth. St. Const. § 360; Wall v. Platt, 169 Mass. 398, 48 N.E. 270; Taylor v. U.S., 3 How. 197, 11 L.Ed. 559; and other cases of like character. The general propositions which counsel quote may be found in the opinions in these cases, and in some of them they were applied to the particular facts which those actions presented. But the interpolation in this act of Congress by construction of an ex post facto provision that it is, and ever since January 1, 1898, has been unlawful for any common carrier to use any engine in interstate traffic that is or was not equipped with couplers coupling automatically, and that any carrier that has used or shall use an engine not so equipped has been and shall be liable to a penalty of $100 for every violation of this provision, is too abhorrent to the sense of justice and fairness, too rank and radical a piece of judicial legislation, and in violation of too many established and salutary rules of construction, to commend itself to the judicial reason or conscience. The primary rule for the interpretation of a statute or a contract is to ascertain, if possible, and enforce, the intention which the legislative body that enacted the law, or the parties who made the agreement, have expressed therein. But it is the intention expressed in the law or contract, and that only, that the courts may give effect to. They cannot lawfully assume or presume secret purposes that are not indicated or expressed by the statute itself and then enact provisions to accomplish these supposed intentions. While ambiguous terms and doubtful expressions may be interpreted to carry out the intention of a legislative body which a statute fairly evidences, a secret intention cannot be interpreted into a statute which is plain and unambiguous, and which does not express it. The legal presumption is that the legislative body expressed its intention, that it intended what it expressed, and that it intended nothing more. U.S. v. Wiltberger, 5 Wheat. 76, 5 L.Ed. 37 * * *. Construction and interpretation have no place or office where the terms of a statute are clear and certain, and its meaning is plain. In such a case they serve only to create doubt and to confuse the judgment. When the language of a statute is unambiguous, and its meaning evident, it must be held to mean what it plainly expresses, and no room is left for construction. * * *

This statute clearly prohibits the use of any engine in moving interstate commerce not equipped with a power driving wheel brake, and the use of any car not equipped with automatic couplers, under a penalty of $100 for each offense; and it just as plainly omits to forbid, under that or any penalty, the use of any car which is not equipped with a power driving wheel brake, and the use of any engine that is not equipped with automatic couplers. This striking omission to express any intention to prohibit the use of engines unequipped with automatic couplers raises the legal presumption that no such intention existed, and prohibits the courts from importing such a purpose into the act, and enacting provisions to give it effect. The familiar rule that the expression of one thing is the exclusion of others points to the same conclusion. Section 2 of the act does not declare that it shall be unlawful to use any engine or car not equipped with automatic couplers, but that it shall be unlawful only to use any car lacking this equipment. This clear and concise definition of the unlawful act is a cogent and persuasive argument against the contention that the use without couplers of locomotives, hand cars, or other means of conducting interstate traffic, was made a misdemeanor by this act. Where the statute enumerates the persons, things, or acts affected by it, there is an implied exclusion of all others. Suth. St. Const. § 227. And when the title of this statute and its first section are again read; when it is perceived that it was not from inattention, thoughtlessness, or forgetfulness; that it was not because locomotives were overlooked or out of mind, but that it was advisedly and after careful consideration of the equipment which they should have, that Congress forbade the use of cars alone without automatic couplers; when it is seen that the title of the act is to compel common carriers to "equip their cars with automatic couplers * * * and their locomotives with driving wheel brakes"; that the first section makes it unlawful to use locomotives not equipped with such brakes, and the second section declares it to be illegal to use cars without automatic couplers,—the argument becomes unanswerable and conclusive.

Again, this act of Congress changes the common law. Before its enactment, servants coupling cars used in interstate commerce without automatic couplers assumed the risk and danger of that employment, and carriers were not liable for injuries which the employés suffered in the discharge of this duty. Since its passage the employés no longer assume this risk, and, if they are free from contributory negligence, they may recover for the damages they sustain in this work. A statute which thus changes the common law must be strictly construed. The common or the general law is not further abrogated by such a statute than the clear import of its language necessarily requires. Shaw v. Railroad Co., 101 U.S. 557, 565, 25 L.Ed. 892; Fitzgerald v. Quann, 109 N.Y. 441, 445, 17 N.E. 354; Brown v. Barry, 3 Dall. 365, 367, 1 L.Ed. 638. The language of this statute does not require the abrogation of the common law that the servant assumes the risk of coupling a locomotive without automatic couplers with a car which is provided with them.

Moreover, this is a penal statute, and it may not be so broadened by judicial construction as to make it cover and permit the punishment of an act which is not denounced by the fair import of its terms. The acts which this statute declares to be unlawful, and for the commission of which it imposes a penalty, were lawful before its enactment, and their performance subjected to no penalty or liability. It makes that unlawful which was lawful before its passage, and it imposes a penalty for its performance. Nor is this penalty a mere forfeiture for the benefit of the party aggrieved or injured. It is a penalty prescribed by the statute, and recoverable by the government. It is, therefore, under every definition of the term, a penal statute. The act which lies at the foundation of this suit—the use of a locomotive which was not equipped with a Miller hook to turn a car which was duly equipped with automatic couplers—was therefore unlawful or lawful as it was or was not forbidden by this statute. That act has been done. When it was done it was neither forbidden nor declared to be unlawful by the express terms of this law. There is no language in it which makes it unlawful to use in interstate commerce a locomotive engine which is not equipped with automatic couplers. The argument of counsel for the plaintiff is, however, that the statute should be construed to make this act unlawful because it falls within the mischief which congress was seeking to remedy, and hence it should be presumed that the legislative body intended to denounce this act as much as that which it forbade by the terms of the law. An ex post facto statute which would make such an innocent act a crime would be violative of the basic principles of Anglo–Saxon jurisprudence. An ex post facto construction which has the same effect is equally abhorrent to the sense of justice and of reason. The mischief at which a statute was leveled, and the fact that other acts which it does not denounce are within the mischief, and of equal atrocity with those which it forbids, do not raise the presumption that the legislative body which enacted it had the intention, which the law does not express, to prohibit the performance of the acts which it does not forbid. Nor will they warrant a construction which imports into the statute such a prohibition. The intention of the legislature and the meaning of a penal statute must be found in the language actually used, interpreted according to its fair and usual meaning, and not in the evils which it was intended to remedy, nor in the assumed secret intention of the lawmakers to accomplish that which they did not express. * * * The decision and opinion of the Supreme Court in U.S. v. Harris, 177 U.S. 305, 309, 20 S.Ct. 609, 44 L.Ed. 780, is persuasive—nay, it is decisive—in the case before us. The question there presented was analogous to that here in issue. It was whether Congress intended to include receivers managing a railroad among those who were prohibited from confining cattle, sheep, and other animals in cars more than 28 consecutive hours without unloading them for rest, water, and feeding, under "An act to prevent cruelty to animals while in transit by railroad or other means of transportation," approved March 3, 1873, and published in the Revised Statutes as sections 4386, 4387, 4388, and 4389. This statute forbids the confinement of stock in cars by any railroad company engaged in interstate commerce more than 28 consecutive hours, and prescribes a penalty of $500 for a violation of its provisions. The plain purpose of the act was to prohibit the confinement of stock while in transit for an unreasonable length of time. The confinement of cattle by receivers operating a railroad was as injurious as their confinement by a railroad company, and the argument for the United States was that, as such acts committed by receivers were plainly within the mischief Congress was seeking to remedy, the conclusion should be that it intended to prohibit receivers, as well as railroad companies, from the commission of the forbidden acts, and hence that receivers were subject to the provisions of the law. The Supreme Court conceded that the confinement of stock in transit was within the mischief that Congress sought to remedy. But it held that as the act did not, by its terms, forbid such acts when committed by receivers, it could not presume the intention of Congress to do so, and import such a provision into the plain terms of the law. Mr. Justice Shiras, who delivered the unanimous opinion of the court, said:

> "Giving all proper force to the contention of the counsel for the government, that there has been some relaxation on the part of the courts in applying the rule of strict construction to such statutes, it still remains that the intention of a penal statute must be found in the language actually used, interpreted according to its fair and obvious meaning. It is not permitted to courts, in this class of cases, to attribute inadvertence or oversight to the legislature when enumerating the classes of persons who are subjected to a penal enactment, nor to depart from the settled meaning of words or phrases in order to

bring persons not named or distinctly described within the supposed purpose of the statute."

He cited with approval the decision of the Supreme Court in Sarlis v. U.S., 152 U.S. 570, 575, 14 S.Ct. 720, 38 L.Ed. 556, to the effect that lager beer was not included within the meaning of the term "spirituous liquors" in the penal statute found in section 2139 of the Revised Statutes, and closed the discussion with the following quotation from the opinion of Chief Justice Marshall in U.S. v. Wiltberger, 5 Wheat. 76, 5 L.Ed. 37:

"The rule that penal statutes are to be construed strictly is perhaps not much less old than construction itself. It is founded on the tenderness of the law for the rights of individuals, and on the plain principle that the power of punishment is vested in the legislative, and not in the judicial, department. It is the legislature, not the court, which is to define a crime and ordain its punishment. It is said that, notwithstanding this rule, the intention of the lawmaker must govern in the construction of penal as well as other statutes. But this is not a new, independent rule, which subverts the old. It is a modification of the ancient maxim, and amounts to this: that, though penal statutes are to be construed strictly, they are not to be construed so strictly as to defeat the obvious intention of the legislature. The maxim is not to be applied so as to narrow the words of the statute, to the exclusion of cases which those words, in their ordinary acceptation, or in that sense in which the legislature ordinarily used them, would comprehend. The intention of the legislature is to be collected from the words they employ. Where there is no ambiguity in the words, there is no room for construction. The case must be a strong one, indeed, which would justify a court in departing from the plain meaning of words,— especially in a penal act,—in search of an intention which the words themselves did not suggest. To determine that a case is within the intention of a statute, its language must authorize us to say so. It would be dangerous, indeed, to carry the principle that a case which is within the reason or mischief of a statute is within its provisions, so far as to punish a crime not enumerated in the statute, because it is of equal atrocity or of a kindred character with those which are enumerated. If this principle has ever been recognized in expounding criminal law, it has been in cases of considerable irritation, which it would be unsafe to consider as precedents forming a general rule in other cases."

The act of March 2, 1893, is a penal statute, and it changes the common law. It makes that unlawful which was innocent before its enactment, and imposes a penalty, recoverable by the government. Its terms are plain and free from doubt, and its meaning is clear. It declares that it is unlawful for a common carrier to use in interstate commerce a car which is not equipped with automatic couplers, and it omits to declare that it is illegal for a common carrier to use a locomotive that is not so equipped. As Congress expressed in this statute no intention to forbid the use of locomotives which were not provided with automatic couplers, the legal presumption is that it had no such intention, and provisions to import such an intention into the law and to effectuate it may not be lawfully enacted by judicial construction. The statute does not make it unlawful to use locomotives that are not equipped with automatic couplers in interstate commerce, and it did not modify the rule of the common law under which the plaintiff assumed the known risk of coupling such an engine to the dining car.

There are other considerations which lead to the same result. If we are in error in the conclusion already expressed, and if the word "car," in the second section of this statute, means locomotive, still this case does not fall under the law, (1) because both the locomotive and the dining car were equipped with automatic couplers; and (2) because at the time of the accident they were not "used in moving interstate traffic."

For the reasons which have been stated, this statute may not be lawfully extended by judicial construction beyond the fair meaning of its language. There is nothing in it which requires a common carrier engaged in interstate commerce to have every car on its railroad equipped with the same kind of coupling, or which requires it to have every car equipped with a coupler which will couple automatically with every other coupler with which it may be brought into contact in the usual course of business upon a great transcontinental system of railroads. If the lawmakers had intended to require such an equipment, it would have been easy for them to have said so, and the fact that they made no such requirement raises the legal presumption that they intended to make none. Nor is the reason for their omission to do so far to seek or difficult to perceive. There are several kinds or makes of practical and efficient automatic couplers. Some railroad companies use one kind; others have adopted other kinds. Couplers of each kind will couple automatically with others of the same kind or construction. But some couplers will not couple automatically with couplers of different construction. Railroad companies engaged in interstate commerce are required to haul over their roads cars equipped with all these couplers. They cannot relieve themselves from this obligation or renounce this public duty for the simple reason that their cars or locomotives are not equipped with automatic couplers which will couple with those with which the cars of other roads are provided, and which will couple with equal facility with those of their kind. These facts and this situation were patent to the congress when it enacted this statute. It must have known the impracticability of providing every car with as many different couplers as it might meet upon a great system of railroads, and it made no such requirement. It doubtless knew the monopoly it would create by requiring every railroad company to use the same coupler, and it did not create this monopoly. The prohibition of the statute goes no farther than to bar the handling of a car "not equipped with couplers coupling automatically by impact and which can be uncoupled without the necessity of men going between the ends of the car." It does not bar the handling and use of a car which will couple automatically with couplers of its kind because it will not also couple automatically with couplers of all kinds, and it would be an unwarrantable extension of the terms of this law to import into it a provision to this effect.

A car equipped with practical and efficient automatic couplers, such as the Janney couplers or the Miller hooks, which will couple automatically with those of their kind, fully and literally complies with the terms of the law, although these couplers will not couple automatically with automatic couplers of all kinds or constructions. The dining car and the locomotive were both so equipped. Each was provided with an automatic coupler which would couple with those of its kind, as provided by the statute, although they would not couple with each other. Each was accordingly equipped as the statute directs, and the defendant was guilty of no violation of it by their use.

Again, the statute declares it to be unlawful for a carrier "to haul or permit to be hauled or used on its line any car used in moving interstate traffic not equipped," etc. It is not, then, unlawful, under this statute, for a carrier to haul a car not so equipped which is either used in intrastate traffic solely, or which is not used in any traffic at all. It would be no violation of the statute for a carrier to haul an empty car not used to move any interstate traffic from one end of its railroad to the other. It would be no violation of the law for it to haul such a car in its yards, on its side track, to put it into its trains, to move it in any manner it chose. It is only when a car is "used in moving interstate traffic" that it becomes unlawful to haul it unless it is equipped as the statute prescribes. On the day of this accident the dining car in this case was standing empty on the side track. The defendant drew it to a turntable, turned it, and placed it back upon the side track. The accident occurred during the performance of this act. The car was vacant when it went to the turntable, and vacant when it returned. It moved no traffic on its way. How could it be said to have been "used in moving interstate traffic" either while it was standing on the side track, or while it was going to and returning from the turntable? * * * [In a part of the opinion omitted here, the court argues that its conclusion that the dining car was not "used in moving interstate traffic" is dictated not only by rules of construction earlier referred to, but by limitations on the power of Congress.]

* * * The fact that such cars have been or will be so used does not constitute their use in moving interstate traffic, because the prohibition is not of the hauling of cars that have been or will be used in such traffic, but only of those used in moving that traffic. * * * Neither the empty dining car standing upon the side track, nor the freight engine which was used to turn it at the little station in Utah, was then used in moving interstate traffic, within the meaning of this statute, and this case did not fall within the provisions of this law.

The judgment below must accordingly be affirmed, and it is so ordered.

■ THAYER, CIRCUIT JUDGE, concurring. I am unable to concur in the conclusion, announced by the majority of the court, that the act of Congress of March 2, 1893 (27 Stat. 531, c. 196), does not require locomotive engines to be equipped with automatic couplers; and I am equally unable to concur in the other conclusion announced by my associates that the dining car in question at the time of the accident was not engaged or being used in moving interstate traffic.

In my judgment, it is a very technical interpretation of the provisions of the act in question, and one which is neither in accord with its spirit nor with the obvious purpose of the lawmaker, to say that Congress did not intend to require engines to be equipped with automatic couplers. The statute is remedial in its nature; it was passed for the protection of human life; and there was certainly as much, if not greater, need that engines should be equipped to couple automatically, as that ordinary cars should be so equipped, since engines have occasion to make couplings more frequently. In my opinion, the true view is that engines are included by the words "any car," as used in the second section of the act. The word "car" is generic, and may well be held to comprehend a locomotive or any other similar vehicle which moves on wheels; and especially should it be so held in a case like the one now in hand, where no satisfactory reason has been assigned or can be given which would probably have influenced Congress to permit locomotives to be used without automatic coupling appliances.

I am also of opinion that, within the fair intent and import of the act, the dining car in question at the time of the accident was being hauled or used in interstate traffic. The reasoning by which a contrary conclusion is reached seems to me to be altogether too refined and unsatisfactory to be of any practical value. It was a car which at the time was employed in no other service than to furnish meals to passengers between Ogden and San Francisco. It had not been taken out of that service, even for repairs or for any other use, when the accident occurred, but was engaged therein to the same extent that it would have been if it had been hauled through to Ogden, and if the accident had there occurred while it was being turned to make the return trip to San Francisco. The cars composing a train which is regularly employed in interstate traffic ought to be regarded as used in that traffic while the train is being made up with a view to an immediate departure on an interstate journey as well as after the journey has actually begun. I accordingly dissent from the conclusion of the majority of the court on this point.

While I dissent on the foregoing propositions, I concur in the other view which is expressed in the opinion of the majority, to the effect that the case discloses no substantial violation of the provisions of the act of Congress, because both the engine and the dining car were equipped with automatic coupling appliances. In this respect the case discloses a compliance with the law, and the ordinary rule governing the liability of the defendant company should be applied. The difficulty was that the car and engine were equipped with couplers of a different pattern, which would not couple, for that reason, without a link. Janney couplers and Miller couplers are in common use on the leading railroads of the country, and Congress did not see fit to command the use of either style of automatic coupler to the exclusion of the other, while it must have foreseen that, owing to the manner in which cars were ordinarily handled and exchanged, it would sometimes happen, as in the case at bar, that cars having different styles of automatic couplers would necessarily be brought in contact in the same train. It made no express provision for such an emergency, but declared generally that, after a certain date, cars should be provided with couplers coupling automatically. The engine and dining car were so equipped in the present instance, and there was no such violation of the provisions of the statute as should render the defendant company liable to the plaintiff by virtue of the provisions contained in the eighth section of the act. In other words, the plaintiff assumed the risk of making the coupling in the course of which he sustained the injury. On this ground I concur in the order affirming the judgment below.

## Johnson v. Southern Pacific Co.

Supreme Court of the United States, 1904.
196 U.S. 1, 25 S.Ct. 158, 49 L.Ed. 363.

Certiorari and error to the United States Circuit Court of Appeals for the Eighth Circuit.

Statement by Mr. Chief Justice Fuller:

Johnson brought this action in the district court of the first judicial district of Utah against the Southern Pacific Company to recover damages for injuries received while employed by that company as a brakeman. The case was removed to the circuit court of the United States for the district of Utah by defendant on the ground of diversity of citizenship.

The facts were briefly these: August 5, 1900, Johnson was acting as head brakeman on a freight train of the Southern Pacific Company, which was making its regular trip between San Francisco, California, and Ogden, Utah. On reaching the town of Promontory, Utah, Johnson was directed to uncouple the engine from the train and couple it to a dining car, belonging to the company, which was standing on a side track, for the purpose of turning the car around preparatory to its being picked up and put on the next westbound passenger train. The engine and the dining car were equipped, respectively, with the Janney coupler and the Miller hook, so called, which would not couple together automatically by impact, and it was, therefore, necessary for Johnson, and he was ordered, to go between the engine and the dining car, to accomplish the coupling. In so doing Johnson's hand was caught between the engine bumper and the dining car bumper, and crushed, which necessitated amputation of the hand above the wrist.

On the trial of the case, defendant, after plaintiff had rested, moved the court to instruct the jury to find in its favor, which motion was granted, and the jury found a verdict accordingly, on which judgment was entered. Plaintiff carried the case to the circuit court of appeals for the eighth circuit, and the judgment was affirmed. 54 C.C.A. 508, 117 Fed. 462.

■ Mr. Chief Justice Fuller delivered the opinion of the court:

The plaintiff claimed that he was relieved of assumption of risk under common-law rules by the act of Congress of March 2, 1893 (27 Stat. at L. 531, chap. 196, U.S.Comp.Stat.1901, p. 3174), entitled "An Act to Promote the Safety of Employees and Travelers upon Railroads by Compelling Common Carriers Engaged in Interstate Commerce to Equip their Cars with Automatic Couplers and Continuous Brakes and their Locomotives with Driving–Wheel Brakes, and for Other Purposes."

The issues involved questions deemed of such general importance that the government was permitted to file a brief and be heard at the bar.

The act of 1893 provided: [see supra]

The circuit court of appeals held, in substance, Sanborn, J., delivering the opinion and Lochren, J., concurring, that the locomotive and car were both equipped as required by the act, as the one had a power driving-wheel brake and the other a coupler; that § 2 did not apply to locomotives; that at the time of the accident the dining car was not "used in moving interstate traffic;" and, moreover, that the locomotive, as well as the dining car, was furnished with an automatic coupler, so that each was equipped as the statute required if § 2 applied to both. Thayer, J., concurred in the judgment on the latter ground, but was of opinion that locomotives were included by the words "any car" in the 2d section, and that the dining car was being "used in moving interstate traffic."

We are unable to accept these conclusions, notwithstanding the able opinion of the majority, as they appear to us to be inconsistent with the plain intention of Congress, to defeat the object of the legislation, and to be arrived at by an inadmissible narrowness of construction.

The intention of Congress, declared in the preamble and in §§ 1 and 2 of the act, was "to promote the safety of employees and travelers upon railroads by compelling common carriers engaged in interstate commerce to equip their cars with automatic couplers and continuous brakes and their locomotives with driving-wheel brakes," those brakes to be accompanied with "appliances for operating the train-brake system;" and every car to be "equipped with couplers coupling automatically by impact, and which can be uncoupled without the necessity of men going between the ends of the cars," whereby the danger and risk consequent on the existing system was averted as far as possible.

The present case is that of an injured employee, and involves the application of the act in respect of automatic couplers, the preliminary question being whether locomotives are required to be equipped with such couplers. And it is not to be successfully denied that they are so required if the words "any car" of the 2d section were intended to embrace, and do embrace, locomotives. But it is said that this cannot be so because locomotives were elsewhere, in terms, required to be equipped with power driving-wheel brakes, and that the rule that the expression of one thing excludes another applies. That, however, is a question of intention, and as there was special reason for requiring locomotives to be equipped with power driving-wheel brakes, if it were also necessary that locomotives should be equipped with automatic couplers, and the word "car" would cover locomotives, then the intention to limit the equipment of locomotives to power driving-wheel brakes, because they were separately mentioned, could not be imputed.

Now it was as necessary for the safety of employees in coupling and uncoupling that locomotives should be equipped with automatic couplers as it was that freight and passenger and dining cars should be; perhaps more so, as Judge Thayer suggests, "since engines have occasion to make couplings more frequently."

And manifestly the word "car" was used in its generic sense. There is nothing to indicate that any particular kind of car was meant. Tested by context, subject-matter, and object, "any car" meant all kinds of cars running on the rails, including locomotives. And this view is supported by the dictionary definitions and by many judicial decisions, some of them having been rendered in construction of this act. [Citing cases.]

The result is that if the locomotive in question was not equipped with automatic couplers, the company failed to comply with the provisions of the act. It appears, however, that this locomotive was in fact equipped with automatic couplers, as well as the dining car; but that the couplers on each, which were of different types, would not couple with each other automatically, by impact, so as to render it unnecessary for men to go between the cars to couple and uncouple.

Nevertheless, the circuit court of appeals was of opinion that it would be an unwarrantable extension of the terms of the law to hold that where the couplers would couple automatically with couplers of their own kind, the couplers must so couple with couplers of different kinds. But we think that what the act plainly forbade was the use of cars which could not be coupled together automatically by impact, by means of the couplers actually used on the cars to be coupled. The object was to protect the lives and limbs of railroad employees by rendering it unnecessary for a man operating the couplers to go between the ends of the cars; and that object would be defeated, not necessarily by the use of automatic couplers of different kinds, but if those different kinds would not automatically couple with each other. The point was that the railroad companies should be compelled, respectively, to adopt devices, whatever they were, which would act so far uniformly as to eliminate the danger consequent on men going between the cars.

If the language used were open to construction, we are constrained to say that the construction put upon the act by the circuit court of appeals was altogether too narrow.

This strictness was thought to be required because the common-law rule as to the assumption of risk was changed by the act, and because the act was penal.

The dogma as to the strict construction of statutes in derogation of the common law only amounts to the recognition of a presumption against an intention to change existing law; and as there is no doubt of that intention here, the extent of the application of the change demands at least no more rigorous construction than would be applied to penal laws. And, as Chief Justice Parker remarked, conceding that statutes in derogation of the common law are to be construed strictly, "They are also to be construed sensibly, and with a view to the object aimed at by the legislature." Gibson v. Jenney, 15 Mass. 205.

The primary object of the act was to promote the public welfare by securing the safety of employees and travelers; and it was in that aspect remedial; while for violations a penalty of $100, recoverable in a civil action, was provided for, and in that aspect it was penal. But the design to give relief was more dominant than to inflict punishment, and the act might well be held to fall within the rule applicable to statutes to prevent fraud upon the revenue, and for the collection of customs,—that rule not requiring absolute strictness of construction. Taylor v. United States, 3 How. 197, 11 L.Ed. 559; United States v. Stowell, 133 U.S. 1, 12, 33 L.Ed. 555, 558, 10 Sup.Ct.Rep. 244, and cases cited. And see Farmers' & M. Nat. Bank v. Dearing, 91 U.S. 29, 35, 23 L.Ed. 196, 199; Gray v. Bennett, 3 Met. 529.

Moreover, it is settled that "though penal laws are to be construed strictly, yet the intention of the legislature must govern in the construction of penal as well as other statutes; and they are not to be construed so strictly as to defeat the obvious intention of the legislature." United States v. Lacher, 134 U.S. 624, 33 L.Ed. 1080, 10 Sup.Ct.Rep. 625. * * *

Tested by these principles, we think the view of the circuit court of appeals, which limits the 2d section to merely providing automatic couplers, does not give due effect to the words "coupling automatically by impact, and which can be uncoupled without the necessity of men going between the cars," and cannot be sustained.

We dismiss, as without merit, the suggestion which has been made, that the words "without the necessity of men going between the ends of the cars," which are the test of compliance with § 2, apply only to the act of uncoupling. The phrase literally covers both coupling and uncoupling; and if read, as it should be, with a comma after the word "uncoupled," this becomes entirely clear. Chicago, M. & St. P.R. Co. v. Voelker, 129 Fed. 522; United States v. Lacher, 134 U.S. 624, 33 L.Ed. 1080, 10 Sup.Ct.Rep. 625.

The risk in coupling and uncoupling was the evil sought to be remedied, and that risk was to be obviated by the use of couplers actually coupling automatically. True, no particular design was required, but, whatever the devices used, they were to be effectively interchangeable. Congress was not paltering in a double sense. And its intention is found "in the language actually used, interpreted according to its fair and obvious meaning." United States v. Harris, 177 U.S. 309, 44 L.Ed. 782, 20 Sup.Ct.Rep. 609.

That this was the scope of the statute is confirmed by the circumstances surrounding its enactment, as exhibited in public documents to which we are at liberty to refer. Binns v. United States, 194 U.S. 486, 495, 48 L.Ed. 1087, 1091, 24 Sup.Ct.Rep. 816; Church of Holy Trinity v. United States, 143 U.S. 457, 463, 36 L.Ed. 226, 229, 12 Sup.Ct.Rep. 511.

President Harrison, in his annual messages of 1889, 1890, 1891, and 1892, earnestly urged upon Congress the necessity of legislation to obviate and reduce the loss of life and the injuries due to the prevailing method of coupling and braking. In his first message he said: "It is competent, I think, for Congress to require uniformity in the construction of cars used in interstate commerce, and the use of improved safety appliances upon such trains. Time will be necessary to make the needed changes, but an earnest and intelligent beginning should be made at once. It is a reproach to our civilization that any class of American workmen should, in the pursuit of a necessary and useful vocation, be subjected to a peril of life and limb as great as that of a soldier in time of war."

And he reiterated his recommendation in succeeding messages, saying in that for 1892: "Statistics furnished by the Interstate Commerce Commission show that during the year ending June 30, 1891, there were forty-seven different styles of car couplers reported to be in use, and that during the same period there were 2,660 employees killed and 26,140 injured. Nearly 16 per cent of the deaths occurred in the coupling and uncoupling of cars, and over 36 per cent of the injuries had the same origin."

The Senate report of the first session of the Fifty-second Congress (No. 1049) and the House report of the same session (No. 1678) set out the numerous and increasing casualties due to coupling, the demand for protection, and the necessity of automatic couplers, coupling interchangeably. The difficulties in the case were fully expounded and the result reached to require an automatic coupling by impact so as to render it unnecessary for men to go between the cars; while no particular device or type was adopted, the railroad companies being left free to work out the details for themselves, ample time being given for that purpose. The law gave five years, and that was enlarged, by the Interstate Commerce Commission as authorized by law, two years, and subsequently seven months, making seven years and seven months in all.

The diligence of counsel has called our attention to changes made in the bill in the course of its passage, and to the debates in the Senate on the report of its committee. 24 Cong.Rec., pt. 2, pp. 1246, 1273 et seq. These demonstrate that the difficulty as to interchangeability was fully in the mind of Congress, and was assumed to be met by the language which was used. The essential degree of uniformity was secured by providing that the couplings must couple automatically by impact without the necessity of men going between the ends of the cars.

In the present case the couplings would not work together; Johnson was obliged to go between the cars; and the law was not complied with.

March 2, 1903, 32 Stat. 943, c. 976, an act in amendment of the act of 1893 was approved, which provided, among other things, that the provisions and requirements of the former act "shall be held to apply to common carriers by railroads in the Territories and the District of Columbia and shall apply in all cases, whether or not the couplers brought together are of the same kind, make, or type;" and "shall be held to apply to all trains, locomotives, tenders, cars, and similar vehicles used on any railroad engaged in interstate commerce."

This act was to take effect September first, nineteen hundred and three, and nothing in it was to be held or construed to relieve any common carrier "from any of the provisions, powers, duties, liabilities, or requirements" of the act of 1893, all of which should apply except as specifically amended.

As we have no doubt of the meaning of the prior law, the subsequent legislation cannot be regarded as intended to operate to destroy it. Indeed, the latter act is affirmative, and declaratory, and, in effect, only construed and applied the former act. Bailey v. Clark, 21 Wall. 284; United States v. Freeman, 3 How. 556; Cope v. Cope, 137 U.S. 682; Wetmore v. Markoe, post, p. 68. This legislative recognition of the scope of the prior law fortifies and does not weaken the conclusion at which we have arrived.

Another ground on which the decision of the circuit court of appeals was rested remains to be noticed. That court held by a majority that, as the dining car was empty and had not actually entered upon its trip, it was not used in moving interstate traffic, and hence was not within the act. The dining car had been constantly used for several years to furnish meals to passengers between San Francisco and Ogden, and for no other purpose. On the day of the accident the eastbound train was so late that it was found that the car could not reach Ogden in time to return on the next westbound train according to intention, and it was therefore dropped off at Promontory, to be picked up by that train as it came along that evening.

\* \* \*

Confessedly this dining car was under the control of Congress while in the act of making its interstate journey, and in our judgment it was equally so when waiting for the train to be made up for the next trip. It was being regularly used in the movement of interstate traffic, and so within the law.

Finally, it is argued that Johnson was guilty of such contributory negligence as to defeat recovery, and that, therefore, the judgment should be affirmed. But the circuit court of appeals did not consider this question, nor apparently did the circuit court, and we do not feel constrained to inquire whether it could have been open under § 8, or, if so, whether it should have been left to the jury, under proper instructions.

The judgment of the Circuit Court of Appeals is reversed; the judgment of the Circuit Court is also reversed, and the cause remanded to that court with instructions to set aside the verdict, and award a new trial.

## Notes and Questions

**1.**   Review the Eighth Circuit and Supreme Court opinions: identify the different kinds of statutory interpretation techniques there employed. What can you infer about the consequences of resort to some techniques, as opposed to others? Do you find some interpretive devices more persuasive than others?

**2.**   While the *Johnson* case arose at the beginning of the 20th century, the same statutory provisions there at issue continue to demand judicial construction. Consider the following more recent decision:

**Porter v. Bangor & Aroostook Railroad Co.**, 75 F.3d 70 (1st Cir.1996)

■ ALDRICH, SENIOR CIRCUIT JUDGE.

Mark J. Porter, an experienced brakeman employed by defendant Bangor & Aroostook Railroad Co., injured his back on October 1, 1992, while adjusting a rusty car coupler device that had previously failed to couple automatically with another car. He seeks recovery under the Federal Safety Appliance Act (FSAA), 45 U.S.C. § 2,[1] a statute that has been ruled to impose liability without fault, San Antonio & Aransas Pass Railway Company v. Wagner, 241 U.S. 476, 36 S.Ct. 626, 60 L.Ed. 1110 (1916), when a violation contributed in any degree to an employee's injuries. Carter v. Atlantic & St. Andrews Bay Ry. Co., 338 U.S. 430, 434–35, 70 S.Ct. 226, 94 L.Ed. 236 (1949).... In response to special questions the jury found that defendant had violated the FSAA but that the failure was not a cause of plaintiff's injury.... After denial of plaintiff's motion for new trial ... , the court entered judgment for defendant. Plaintiff appeals. We affirm.

Plaintiff ... faces the substantial obstacle of a jury finding of no causal connection between the violation and the injury. Recognizing this burden, he takes the bull by the horns and argues that, the violation and injury having been established, the jury not merely should have found, but was required to find a causal connection between them as matter of law.

Plaintiff's contention takes two forms. First, he says the jury's finding that defendant violated the FSAA means that the coupling equipment was defective. Thus plaintiff strained his back working on defective coupler equipment; hence he was within the statute. We do not agree. There is nothing especially dangerous in coupling devices themselves, the statutory reach is the coupling maneuver. As the Court said in the early case of Johnson v. Southern Pacific Co., 196 U.S. 1, 19, 25 S.Ct. 158, 49 L.Ed. 363 (1904), "The risk in coupling and uncoupling was the evil sought to be remedied.... " Although plaintiff speaks about having to go between the ends of the cars, it was not for coupling, but in preparation for coupling. One must go behind, viz., between the cars, to align the drawbars before commencing the coupling operation.[2] If, as here, the cars are safely separated and not in motion, readying is not coupling, and does not involve the special coupling risks. What could be the reason, or purpose, for requiring special protection for this

---

**1.** "It shall be unlawful for any common carrier engaged in interstate commerce by railroad to haul or permit to be hauled or used on its line any car ... not equipped with couplers coupling automatically by impact, and which can be uncoupled without the necessity of men going between the ends of the cars." 45 U.S.C. § 2 (1893) (repealed 1994) (current version at 49 U.S.C. § 20302).

**2.** Plaintiff himself testified that the drawbars can swing, and must sometimes be lined up in order to meet, a procedure he performed routinely every day. See Goedel v. Norfolk & Western Railway Co., 13 F.3d 807, 809 (4th Cir.1994).

isolated activity? It is true that other circuits appear to have read the FSAA more broadly, see Clark v. Kentucky & Indiana Terminal Railroad, 728 F.2d 307 (6th Cir.1984) (collecting cases), but they give no answer to our question. We can think of none. Plaintiff had no FSAA case.

In light of *Johnson,* is the First Circuit's analysis persuasive? Is the court's distinction between going between railroad cars in order to couple them, and going between the cars in order to *prepare* to couple them, a convincing interpretation of the statutory language? Of the statute's "intent"?

**3.**   Note that the previous question asked if, *in light of a prior decision,* a subsequent court (bound by the prior court's authority) correctly interpreted the statute. While in this Part of the casebook we address statutory interpretation, you should recall that the interpreters of statutes are often courts. (For the interpretations of administrative agencies, see *infra,* Part III.D.2.) As a result, many of the concepts you learned in Part II (Analysis and Synthesis of Judicial Decisions) continue to apply. For example, under the doctrine of precedent, when a court has interpreted a statute, it and dependent lower courts are bound by that interpretation. Hence, should a case like *Johnson* arise in a federal district court after the Supreme Court's decision, the judge would not be free to rule that the statute tolerates equipment of cars with automatic couplers that do not in fact couple automatically to each other. By the same token, distinguishing cases on their facts—another technique with which you became familiar in the common law context—remains a tool in analyzing whether a prior judicial interpretation of a statute determines the case at hand. Thus, the First Circuit was able to rule that *Johnson* did not control the application of the FSAA to brakeman Porter, because *Johnson* involved an injury sustained in the act of coupling; by contrast, Porter was hurt not while coupling railroad cars, but merely while preparing to engage in the act of coupling railroad cars.

The materials in later subsections of Part III will afford you further opportunity to consider statutory interpretation in the context of prior judicial decisions.

**4.**   For another controversy involving application of the Federal Safety Appliance Act to an accident involving misaligned drawbars, see Goedel v. Norfolk & Western Railway Co., 13 F.3d 807 (4th Cir.1994). The report of the decision also contains a pictorial catalogue of automatic couplers.

**Note: Canons of Statutory Construction**

Both the Eighth Circuit and the Supreme Court invoked a variety of maxims to aid their interpretation of the Railway Safety Appliance Act. Sometimes these maxims, or "canons" appear to be opposed, such as the canon favoring narrow interpretation of a "penal" statute, and the canon counseling expansive interpretation of a "remedial" statute, when both canons are brought to bear on a statute designed to remedy a problem by imposing sanctions on those who violate the new norm. Sometimes different courts appear to apply the *same* canon of construction, yet reach different conclusions.

How helpful *are* canons of construction? What is their relationship to statutory text? Should we assume that legislatures enact statutes against the backdrop of the canons, and thus take into account, or are at least aware of, the interpretive lenses through which judges will study the statutory language? Is there an accepted repertory of canons?* Is there an accepted hierarchy of canons? Do we need an answer to both those questions before we can attribute to a legislature an understanding or an expectation of how courts will interpret the language it enacts? Does it make any difference whether canons of construction are implicitly part of the legislative package, or whether they are simply imposed by judges at a loss to understand the language? In the latter event, are canons any more reliable or useful than other extra-textual aids to interpretation? Consider the following discussion of the role of canons of construction:

> Karl Llewellyn largely persuaded two generations of academics that the canons of construction were not to be taken seriously. His point was simple: The canons are indeterminate, and judges use them to justify reasoning by other means.... [But] a large and growing number of academics (and academics-turned-judges) now believe in the utility of canons of construction.... Modern textualists, who tend to be formalist in orientation, understandably favor the use of canons, particularly the traditional linguistic canons. Justice Scalia, for instance, argues that many such canons are 'so commonsensical that, were [they] not couched in Latin, you would find it hard to believe that anyone could criticize them.' And Judge Easterbrook, a formalist with a law and economics twist, defends canons 'as off-the-rack provisions that spare legislators the costs of anticipating all possible interpretive problems and legislating solutions for them.' ... [T]hese scholars ... have sought to revive ... the idea that a system of established rules of construction might make the process of statutory interpretation more predictable, effective, and even legitimate.

> This intellectual development raises two questions. First, why have canons of construction recently gone from laughingstock to the subject of serious academic inquiry? And why do textualists and pragmatists, who think so differently about most questions of statutory interpretation, now share enthusiasm for the once maligned idea of such canons of construction? ... Although he is not usually identified with this trend, Llewellyn's view of the canons nicely complemented an emerging scholarly consensus that, contrary to prior realist scholarship, judges could meaningfully resolve textual ambiguity by consulting the

---

* Professors William Eskridge and Philip Frickey have catalogued canons of construction extracted from Supreme Court decisions from the 1986 through 1993 Terms. Their illuminating listing is set out in *Appendix: The Rehnquist Court's Canons of Statutory Construction*, in William N. Eskridge, Jr., Philip P. Frickey and Elizabeth Garrett, Legislation and Statutory Interpretation, 375–83 (Foundation Press, Concepts and Insights series, 2000).

legislature's intent or purpose, to be derived in no small part from legislative history. Conversely, his impact began to wane in the 1980s, when influential textualist and pragmatist scholars revived (for quite different reasons) broader realist claims about the inaccessibility and unreliability of legislative intent and purpose as organizing principles in statutory construction. . . .

In economists' terms, canons of construction and intent or purpose are substitutes, rather than complements. . . . Textualists believe that the statutory text will often be determinate and decisive, and that intent or purpose derived from the legislative history are unreliable guides for resolving statutory doubts. They want clearly established background rules of construction to guide legislators and interpreters in decoding textual commands. Pragmatists have less faith in the statutory text, but also question whether intent and purpose can effectively address its deficiencies. They favor the rationalization and harmonization of rules of construction to provide judges with guidelines for addressing indeterminacy and for doing so in ways that promote socially and institutionally beneficial outcomes. . . . In short, the canons' revival may be the flip side of a growing perception that the early realists were correct in arguing that it is hard to get inside "Congress's mind."

John F. Manning, Legal Realism & the Canons' Revival, 5 Green Bag 283, 283–85 (2002).

### Approaches to Statutory Interpretation: A View From the Bench

Professor Manning endorses application of the canons of statutory construction as a means to illuminate ambiguous text without recourse to the extra-textual aid of legislative history. Dictionaries offer another preferred "textualist" interpretative aid. (Several of the decisions you will soon encounter in the casebook make varying use of the dictionary.) As the *Johnson* case itself illustrates, however, strict textualism risks producing robotic results that rankle common sense (at least the common sense that some judges intuit, and that they, perhaps wishfully, attribute to legislators). Second Circuit judge Pierre N. Leval has endeavored to identify what kinds of statutes properly call for purely textualist interpretations, and which demand a more wide ranging analysis. In his view, textual ambiguity need not be seen as a shortcoming to be overcome by reference to static text-fillers, whether lexicographic or drawn from legislative history. Rather, ill-defined terms might instead be deemed invitations to judicial elaboration, in a dynamic process of partnership between legislators who design the frame, and judges who fill in the picture.

How should . . . statutes be understood? How far reaching are the rights they establish? To answer those questions, it is useful to divide statutes into two crude groups.

(1) *Micromanager.* One category is what I shall call a Micromanager Statute. The best example is the Internal Revenue Code. In passing a Micromanager Statute, the legislature undertakes not only to

set policies, but to answer all the questions that will arise. Such statutes are generally quite lengthy and detailed.

It is fashionable in speaking of statutory interpretation to say that the only interpretive source a court should use is a dictionary. That maxim is highly appropriate for micromanager statutes, because, at least in theory, the text contains the answers to all the questions.

(2) *Delegating Statutes.* The other category is what I shall call a Delegating Statute. The legislature states its policy in generalized terms, but intentionally delegates to the courts a considerable interpretive role. Delegating statutes divide into two subclasses.

(a) *Statutes Adopting Common Law.* One is a statute which adopts in statutory form a body of law previously developed by the courts. Such statutes may be highly circumspect. A single word—murder or larceny—may stand for the full complexity of the doctrine's development. When such a statute is passed, it is generally understood that the court's dynamic function, by which it previously created and shaped the law, will continue to operate, notwithstanding that the law is now expressed in statutory form.

(b) *New Policy.* In the second, of which a paradigm example is the Sherman Act, the legislature enacts a new policy, but does so in imprecise terms, recognizing that innumerable questions of interpretation will arise as experience unfolds. It delegates to the courts the task of answering the questions, as they arise, in the light of experience and common sense.

The proposition that courts should approach the task of interpretation armed only with a dictionary is wholly inappropriate to statutes in the Delegating classes. The words of the statute simply will not provide the answers, and were not intended by the legislature to do so. In passing Delegating statutes, legislatures recognize that they function together with courts in a law-making partnership—each having its proper role. The legislature sets the essential policy; but relies on the courts, as experience unfolds, to use their good judgment to do the fine-tuning, to establish contours, and boundaries. The courts' interpretive rulings, of course, are always subject to legislative correction.

Pierre N. Leval, Trademark: Champion of Free Speech, 27 Colum J. L. & The Arts (forthcoming 2003).

### Questions

**1.** Consider the *Johnson* case: Would you call the Federal Railway Safety Appliance Act a "Micromanager" or a "Delegating" statute? Some of both? Which, if any, portions call for development of judge-made standards in tandem with the statutory rules? As you work through the statutory language in the other cases in this section of the casebook, consider the extent to which the micromanager/delegating distinction helps you analyze the statute's application to the controversy at hand.

**2.** Are Prof. Manning's and Judge Leval's approaches to statutory interpretation reconcilable? How would a strict textualist interpret a "delegation statute" adopting the common law? One adopting a new policy?

## Problems

**1.** Brutus Forte is a musician who, under the pseudonym Brute Force, is an extremely popular entertainer, performing in the "heavy metal" genre of rock music. Brute Force has a distinctive vocal style, consisting in part of grunts and squawks that evoke a variety of barnyard fauna, principally pigs and turkeys. Perhaps not surprisingly, the song with which Brute Force opens and closes his live performances is his own, rather violent and idiosyncratic, version of "Old MacDonald Had A Farm." Brute Force often appears on stage, in music videos, and on album covers dressed in a turkey suit.

Brute Force has become a pop culture icon, and advertisers have sought to take advantage of his popularity by soliciting his participation in a variety of commercials. However, seeking to maintain his artistic purity, Brute Force has refused to perform in or to authorize any commercials incorporating sounds or images from his live or recorded performances.

Tina's Turkeys is a successful poultry producer in the State of New Hazard. Tina's has just aired a commercial on a local New Hazard television station that depicts a person in a turkey suit, striking an aggressive attitude. The turkey suit completely encloses its wearer. Next to the individual in the turkey suit is a roast turkey attractively arranged on a serving platter. The sound track plays "Old Mac Donald's Farm" in a traditional arrangement, but accompanied by sounds of squawking turkeys and grunting pigs. These sounds were taken from a sound effects recording. A voice-over declares "As tough as this turkey is (close up of the person in the turkey suit), that's how tender our's is (close up of the roast turkey). You don't have to be a brute to enjoy a good turkey ... Tina's Turkeys."

Mr. Forte asks you, his lawyer, whether he has a valid claim against Tina's Turkeys. In the State of New Hazard, there is a potentially applicable statute, reproduced below. Assume that there is no legislative history to this statute.

Were Mr. Forte to bring a claim under the statute, it would present a case of first instance for the New Hazard courts. Nor is there any common law case law on point. Basing your analysis solely on the text of the statute, advise Mr. Forte whether he has a claim under the statute; what arguments he should expect to encounter from Tina's Turkeys in opposition to his claim; how he should respond to these arguments; and how you think the court would resolve the issue. Mr. Forte is highly argumentative, and likes to have things clearly spelled out, so make sure you state your points clearly, and supply well elaborated rationales for your conclusions.

## New Hazard Collected Statutes, section 1995

a.   Any person who uses for advertising purposes, or for purposes of trade, the name, picture or likeness of any person, without first having obtained the written consent of such person, shall be liable in a civil action to such person.

b.   Any person who, in connection with any goods or services, uses any word, term, name, symbol or device, or any combination thereof, which is likely to cause confusion, or to cause mistake, or to deceive as to the affiliation, connection, or association of such person with another person, or as to the origin, sponsorship, or approval of his or her goods, services, or commercial activities by another person, shall be liable in a civil action by any person who believes that he or she is or is likely to be damaged by such act.

**2.**   In July of 2003, lured by end of season specials, Judy Church journeyed to a used car dealership outside of the city of Cacophony, serving the tri-state area of New Hazard (the state in which Cacophony is located), Harmony and North Bedlam. There she found the Trans Am of her dreams—black with tinted windows. The man with the loud tie informed her that with her purchase she was entitled to a pair of fuzzy dice, a set of beer mugs and a free car alarm.

Church bought the car, hung up the dice, put the mugs in the trunk and glanced briefly at the sticker on the back of the alarm. The alarm was capable of being operated by remote or activated on contact. According to the sticker, at least two pounds of direct pressure is necessary to activate the alarm, and there is a one-minute lag time between the activating of the alarm and its sounding "to allow the owner to de-activate the alarm before causing an inconvenience to others should the alarm be accidentally activated." Once the alarm sounds, it does so continuously for three minutes before ceasing. It then remains silent for three minutes, and if it is not deactivated, it resets and begins again.

Church was told she could trade in the alarm for a set of second-hand mag tires, which was tempting, but Church had fallen in love with her Trans Am and knew it would be the envy of the whole neighborhood—she decided she would feel more secure having the alarm. Church left the car at the dealer for a few days to have the alarm installed. This was done off the premises.

Church picked up the car and drove it for a month or two without incident. Then one day during a storm she parked it on the street in front of a friend's apartment building in Cacophony. She went inside and listened to the new Megadeath CD a few times while chatting with her friend. Later, she glanced out the window and spied a police cruiser along side her cherished black Trans Am. When she arrived at the scene, the police officer said, "the alarm on your car has been going off every few minutes for over an hour. Four residents of the building called to complain. One of them saw a branch from the tree fall onto your car during the storm, which apparently set it off, though it did not begin to sound until after a short delay." The officer gave Church a $100.00 ticket, explaining that she was in violation of a statute dealing with motor vehicle alarms. The statute is set forth below.

Church asks you, her lawyer, whether she may successfully contest the ticket. Assume that there is no legislative history and that this is a case of first impression. Your discussion must therefore be based solely on the text of the statute.

**NEW HAZARD STATUTES**

**GENERAL BUSINESS LAW**

**ARTICLE 26. MISCELLANEOUS**

**§ 369** *Motor Vehicle Alarms*

1. On and after the effective date of this section, all devices offered for sale or installed in the state as alarms for motor vehicles shall be so equipped and shall function so that the audible portion of the alarm resets and ceases to sound not more than three minutes after it is activated and commences sounding. No audible burglar alarm in a motor vehicle shall be capable of being activated except by:

a) direct physical contact with that motor vehicle; or

b) through the use of an individual remote activation that is designed to be used with the motor vehicle alarm so long as the alarm activated by such device ceases to sound within not more than three minutes

2. This Act shall take effect immediately.

3. A violation of the provisions of this section shall constitute an offense punishable by a fine of not more than one hundred dollars for the first offense and not more than two hundred fifty dollars for a second and subsequent offense.

Approved July 26, 2003.

---

# B. "PLAIN MEANING RULE"

## 1. ONCE IN DISFAVOR

### a. THE WORDS OF THE STATUTE

In applying statutory language, courts seek to give effect to "the intention of the legislature." Just how—and from what sources—that intention is to be discerned, however, provokes continuing controversy. The Johnson v. Southern Pacific case, as we have seen, presented a cross-section of interpretive devices, both intrinsic and extrinsic to the text of the statute.

The predominant judicial approach today to discerning legislative intent has sought guidance from extrinsic as well intrinsic sources of interpretation. For example, courts often consult legislative history and inquire into the social context in which the legislation was enacted. Some of the older cases—and a strain of more recent decisions as well, however, reject resort to extratextual aids to interpretation. These decisions generally omit reference to the understanding or purpose of the enacting legislature. Rather the "plain meaning" of the words alone suffices. It is not necessary to look beyond the words to ascertain what the legislature "intended": For all intents and purposes the legislature "meant what [it] said, and said what [it] meant."[1] (And—as some of the more recent decisions imply—if the legislature did not mean what it said, it is for the legislature, and not the courts, to correct its misstatement.)

The Plain Meaning Rule has venerable roots, and variable applications. The following two oft-cited judicial statements, indicate the function and effect of this approach to statutory interpretation:

> The general rule is perfectly well settled that, where a statute is of doubtful meaning and susceptible upon its face of two constructions, the court may look into prior and contemporaneous acts, the reasons which induced the act in question, the mischiefs intended to be remedied, the extraneous circumstances, and the purpose intended to be accomplished by it, to determine its proper construction. But where the act is clear upon its face, and when standing alone it is fairly susceptible of but one construction, that construction must be given to it. * * * The whole doctrine applicable to the subject may be summed up in the single observation that prior acts may be referred to *solve* but not to *create* an ambiguity.

Brown, J., in Hamilton v. Rathbone, 175 U.S. 414 (1899).

> Where words conflict with each other, where the different clauses of an instrument bear upon each other, and would be inconsistent unless the natural and common import of words be varied, construction becomes necessary, and a departure from the obvious meaning of words is justifiable. But if, in any case, the plain meaning of a provision, not contradicted by any other provision in the same instrument, is to be disregarded, because we believe the framers of that instrument could not intend what they say, it must be one in which the absurdity and injustice of applying the provision to the case would be so monstrous that all mankind would, without hesitation, unite in rejecting the application.

Marshall, Ch. J., in Sturges v. Crowninshield, 4 Wheat. 122, 202, 4 L.Ed. 529, 550 (1819).

In the statutes addressed in the following decisions, consider whether the meaning urged upon the statutory text is indeed "plain," and if you think it is, whether its application in the given case would in fact meet Chief Justice Marshall's absurdity test.

**1.**  Theodor Seuss Geisel (Dr. Seuss), Horton Hatches the Egg (1940)

# United States v. Church of the Holy Trinity

United States Circuit Court, Southern District of New York, 1888.
36 Fed. 303, reversed 143 U.S. 457, 12 S.Ct. 511, 36 L.Ed. 226 (1892).

■ WALLACE, J. This suit is brought to recover a penalty of $1,000 imposed by the act of congress of February 26, 1885, (23 St. at Large, 332,) upon every person or corporation offending against its provisions by knowingly encouraging the migration of any alien into the United States "to perform labor or service of any kind under contract or agreement, express or implied," previously made with such alien. The defendant, a religious corporation, engaged one Warren, an alien residing in England, to come here and take charge of its church as a pastor. The act makes it the duty of the United States district attorney to bring suit to enforce the penalty prescribed. The demurrer interposed to the complaint raises the single question whether such a contract as was made in this case is within the terms of the act. In other words, the question is whether congress intended to prohibit the migration here of an alien who comes pursuant to a contract with a religious society to perform the functions of a minister of the gospel, and to subject to the penalty the religious society making the contract and encouraging the migration of the alien minister. The act is entitled "An act to prohibit the importation and migration of foreigners and aliens under contract or agreement to perform labor in the United States." It was, no doubt, primarily the object of the act to prohibit the introduction of assisted immigrants, brought here under contracts previously made by corporations and capitalists to prepay their passage and obtain their services at low wages for limited periods of time. It was a measure introduced and advocated by the trades union and labor associations, designed to shield the interests represented by such organizations from the effects of the competition in the labor market of foreigners brought here under contracts having a tendency to stimulate immigration and reduce the rates of wages. Except from the language of the statute there is no reason to suppose a contract like the present to be within the evils which the law was designed to suppress; and, indeed, it would not be indulging a violent supposition to assume that no legislative body in this country would have advisedly enacted a law framed so as to cover a case like the present. Nevertheless, where the terms of a statute are plain, unambiguous, and explicit, the courts are not at liberty to go outside of the language to search for a meaning which it does not reasonably bear in the effort to ascertain and give effect to what may be imagined to have been or not to have been the intention of congress. Whenever the will of congress is declared in ample and unequivocal language, that will must be absolutely followed, and it is not admissible to resort to speculations of policy, nor even to the views of members of congress in debate, to find reasons to control or modify the statute. U.S. v. Railroad Co., 91 U.S. 72. If it were permissible to narrow the provisions of the act to correspond with the purport of the title, and restrain its operation to cases in which the alien is assisted to come here under contract "to perform labor," there might be room for interpretation; and the restricted meaning might possibly be given to the word "labor" which signifies the manual work of the laborer, as distinguished from the work of the skilled artisan, or the professional man. But no rule in the construction of statutes is more familiar than the one to the effect that the title cannot be used to extend or restrain positive provisions in the body of the act. In Hadden v. Collector, 5 Wall. 107, it is said: "The title of an act furnishes little aid in the construction of its provisions." The encouragement of migration prohibited by the first section is of aliens under contract or agreement previously made "to perform labor or service of any kind in the United States." The contracts which are declared to be void by the second section are contracts "having reference to the performance of labor or service by any person in the United States" previous to the migration of the alien. The penalty imposed by the third section is imposed on the person or corporation encouraging the migration of the alien under a contract or agreement previously made "to perform labor or service of any kind." No more comprehensive terms could have been employed to include every conceivable kind of labor or avocation, whether of the hand or brain, in the class of prohibited contracts; and, as if to emphasize and make more explicit the intention that the words "labor or service" should not be taken in any restricted sense, they are followed by the words "of any kind." Every kind of industry, and every employment, manual or intellectual, is embraced within the language used. If it were possible to import a narrower meaning than the natural and ordinary one to the language of these sections, the terms of the fifth section would forbid the attempt. That section is a proviso withdrawing from the operation of the act several classes of persons and contracts. Foreigners residing here temporarily, who may engage private secretaries; persons desirous of establishing a new industry not then existing in the United States, who employ skilled workmen therein; domestic servants; and a limited professional class, are thereby exempted from its provisions. The last clause of the proviso is: "Nor shall the provisions of this act apply to professional actors, artists, lecturers, or singers, nor to persons employed strictly as personal or domestic servants." If, without this exemption, the act would apply to this class of persons, because such persons come here under contracts for labor or service, then clearly it must apply to ministers, lawyers, surgeons, architects, and all others who labor in any professional calling. Unless congress supposed the act to apply to the excepted classes, there was no necessity for the proviso. The office of a proviso is generally to restrain an enacting clause, and to except something which would otherwise have been within it. Wayman v. Southard, 10 Wheat. 30; Minis v. U.S., 15 Pet. 423. In the language of the authorities: "A proviso carves special exemptions only out of the enacting clauses." U.S. v. Dickson, 15 Pet. 165; Ryan v. Carter, 93 U.S. 83. Giving effect to this well-settled rule of statutory interpretation, the proviso is equivalent to a declaration that contracts to perform professional services except those of actors, artists, lecturers, or singers, are within the prohibition of the preceding sections.

The argument based upon the fourth section of the act has not been overlooked. That section subjects to fine and imprisonment any master of a vessel who knowingly brings within the United States any alien "laborer, mechanic, or artisan," who has previously entered into any contract to perform labor or service in the United States. This section is wholly independent of the others, and the difference in the persons described may reasonably be referred to an intention to mitigate the severity of the act in its application to masters of vessels. The demurrer is overruled.

# Holy Trinity Church v. United States

Supreme Court of the United States, 1892.
143 U.S. 457, 12 S.Ct. 511, 36 L.Ed. 226.

In error to the circuit court of the United States for the southern district of New York.

■ MR. JUSTICE BREWER delivered the opinion of the court.

Plaintiff in error is a corporation duly organized and incorporated as a religious society under the laws of the state of New York. E. Walpole Warren was, prior to September, 1887, an alien residing in England. In that month the plaintiff in error made a contract with him, by which he was to remove to the city of New York, and enter into its service as rector and pastor; and, in pursuance of such contract, Warren did so remove and enter upon such service. It is claimed by the United States that this contract on the part of the plaintiff in error was forbidden by chapter 164, 23 St. p. 332; and an action was commenced to recover the penalty prescribed by that act. The circuit court held that the contract was within the prohibition of the statute, and rendered judgment accordingly, (36 Fed.Rep. 303,) and the single question presented for our determination is whether it erred in that conclusion.

The first section describes the act forbidden, and is in these words:

"*Be it enacted by the senate and house of representatives of the United States of America, in congress assembled,* that from and after the passage of this act it shall be unlawful for any person, company, partnership, or corporation, in any manner whatsoever, to prepay the transportation, or in any way assist or encourage the importation or migration, of any alien or aliens, any foreigner or foreigners, into the United States, its territories, or the District of Columbia, under contract or agreement, parol or special, express or implied, made previous to the importation or migration of such alien or aliens, foreigner or foreigners, to perform labor or service of any kind in the United States, its territories, or the District of Columbia.*"*

It must be conceded that the act of the corporation is within the letter of this section, for the relation of rector to his church is one of service, and implies labor on the one side with compensation on the other. Not only are the general words "labor" and "service" both used, but also, as it were to guard against any narrow interpretation and emphasize a breadth of meaning, to them is added "of any kind;" and, further, as noticed by the circuit judge in his opinion, the fifth section, which makes specific exceptions, among them professional actors, artists, lecturers, singers, and domestic servants, strengthens the idea that every other kind of labor and service was intended to be reached by the first section. While there is great force to this reasoning, we cannot think congress intended to denounce with penalties a transaction like that in the present case. It is a familiar rule that a thing may be within the letter of the statute and yet not within the statute, because not within its spirit nor within the intention of its makers. This has been often asserted, and the Reports are full of cases illustrating its application. This is not the substitution of the will of the judge for that of the legislator; for frequently words of general meaning are used in a statute, words broad enough to include an act in question, and yet a consideration of the whole legislation, or of the circumstances surrounding its enactment, or of the absurd results which follow from giving such broad meaning to the words, makes it unreasonable to believe that the legislator intended to include the particular act. * * *

* * * In U.S. v. Kirby, 7 Wall. 482, 486, the defendants were indicted for the violation of an act of congress providing "that if any person shall knowingly and willfully obstruct or retard the passage of the mail, or of any driver or carrier, or of any horse or carriage carrying the same, he shall, upon conviction, for every such offense, pay a fine not exceeding one hundred dollars." The specific charge was that the defendants knowingly and willfully retarded the passage of one Farris, a carrier of the mail, while engaged in the performance of his duty, and also in like manner retarded the steam-boat Gen. Buell, at that time engaged in carrying the mail. To this indictment the defendants pleaded specially that Farris had been indicted for murder by a court of competent authority in Kentucky; that a bench-warrant had been issued and placed in the hands of the defendant Kirby, the sheriff of the county, commanding him to arrest Farris, and bring him before the court to answer to the indictment; and that, in obedience to this warrant, he and the other defendants, as his posse, entered upon the steam-boat Gen. Buell and arrested Farris, and used only such force as was necessary to accomplish that arrest. The question as to the sufficiency of this plea was certified to this court, and it was held that the arrest of Farris upon the warrant from the state court was not an obstruction of the mail, or the retarding of the passage of a carrier of the mail, within the meaning of the act. In its opinion the court says: "All laws should receive a sensible construction. General terms should be so limited in their application as not to lead to injustice, oppression, or an absurd consequence. It will always, therefore, be presumed that the legislature intended exceptions to its language which would avoid results of this character. The reason of the law in such cases should prevail over its letter. The common sense of man approves the judgment mentioned by Puffendorf, that the Bolognian law which enacted 'that whoever drew blood in the streets should be punished with the utmost severity,' did not extend to the surgeon who opened the vein of a person that fell down in the street in a fit. The same common sense accepts the ruling, cited by Plowden, that the statute of 1 Edw. II., which enacts that a prisoner who breaks prison shall be guilty of felony, does not extend to a prisoner who breaks out when the prison is on fire, 'for he is not to be hanged because he would not stay to be burnt.' And we think that a like common sense will sanction the ruling we make, that the act of congress which punishes the obstruction or retarding

of the passage of the mail, or of its carrier, does not apply to a case of temporary detention of the mail caused by the arrest of the carrier upon an indictment for murder." * * *

Among other things which may be considered in determining the intent of the legislature is the title of the act. We do not mean that it may be used to add to or take from the body of the statute, (Hadden v. Collector, 5 Wall. 107,) but it may help to interpret its meaning. In the case of U.S. v. Fisher, 2 Cranch 358, 386, Chief Justice MARSHALL said: "On the influence which the title ought to have in construing the enacting clauses, much has been said, and yet it is not easy to discern the point of difference between the opposing counsel in this respect. Neither party contends that the title of an act can control plain words in the body of the statute; and neither denies that, taken with other parts, it may assist in removing ambiguities. Where the intent is plain, nothing is left to construction. Where the mind labors to discover the design of the legislature, it seizes everything from which aid can be derived; and in such case the title claims a degree of notice, and will have its due share of consideration." * * *

It will be seen that words as general as those used in the first section of this act were by that decision limited, and the intent of congress with respect to the act was gathered partially, at least, from its title. Now, the title of this act is, "An act to prohibit the importation and migration of foreigners and aliens under contract or agreement to perform labor in the United States, its territories, and the District of Columbia." Obviously the thought expressed in this reaches only to the work of the manual laborer, as distinguished from that of the professional man. No one reading such a title would suppose that congress had in its mind any purpose of staying the coming into this country of ministers of the gospel, or, indeed, of any class whose toil is that of the brain. The common understanding of the terms "labor" and "laborers" does not include preaching and preachers, and it is to be assumed that words and phrases are used in their ordinary meaning. So whatever of light is thrown upon the statute by the language of the title indicates an exclusion from its penal provisions of all contracts for the employment of ministers, rectors, and pastors.

Again, another guide to the meaning of a statute is found in the evil which it is designed to remedy; and for this the court properly looks at contemporaneous events, the situation as it existed, and as it was pressed upon the attention of the legislative body. U.S. v. Railroad Co., 91 U.S. 72, 79. The situation which called for this statute was briefly but fully stated by Mr. Justice Brown when, as district judge, he decided the case of U.S. v. Craig, 28 Fed.Rep. 795, 798: "The motives and history of the act are matters of common knowledge. It had become the practice for large capitalists in this country to contract with their agents abroad for the shipment of great numbers of an ignorant and servile class of foreign laborers, under contracts by which the employer agreed, upon the one hand, to prepay their passage, while, upon the other hand, the laborers agreed to work after their arrival for a certain time at a low rate of wages. The effect of this was to break down the labor market, and to reduce other laborers engaged in like occupations to the level of the assisted immigrant. The evil finally became so flagrant that an appeal was made to congress for relief by the passage of the act in question, the design of which was to raise the standard of foreign immigrants, and to discountenance the migration of those who had not sufficient means in their own hands, or those of their friends, to pay their passage."

It appears, also, from the petitions, and in the testimony presented before the committees of congress, that it was this cheap, unskilled labor which was making the trouble, and the influx of which congress sought to prevent. It was never suggested that we had in this country a surplus of brain toilers, and, least of all, that the market for the services of Christian ministers was depressed by foreign competition. Those were matters to which the attention of congress, or of the people, was not directed. So far, then, as the evil which was sought to be remedied interprets the statute, it also guides to an exclusion of this contract from the penalties of the act.

A singular circumstance, throwing light upon the intent of congress, is found in this extract from the report of the senate committee on education and labor, recommending the passage of the bill: "The general facts and considerations which induce the committee to recommend the passage of this bill are set forth in the report of the committee of the house. The committee report the bill back without amendment, although there are certain features thereof which might well be changed or modified, in the hope that the bill may not fail of passage during the present session. Especially would the committee have otherwise recommended amendments, substituting for the expression, 'labor and service,' whenever it occurs in the body of the bill, the words 'manual labor' or 'manual service,' as sufficiently broad to accomplish the purposes of the bill, and that such amendments would remove objections which a sharp and perhaps unfriendly criticism may urge to the proposed legislation. The committee, however, believing that the bill in its present form will be construed as including only those whose labor or service is manual in character, and being very desirous that the bill become a law before the adjournment, have reported the bill without change." Page 6059, Congressional Record, 48th Cong. And, referring back to the report of the committee of the house, there appears this language: "It seeks to restrain and prohibit the immigration or importation of laborers who would have never seen our shores but for the inducements and allurements of men whose only object is to obtain labor at the lowest possible rate, regardless of the social and material well-being of our own citizens, and regardless of the evil consequences which result to American laborers from such immigration. This class of immigrants care nothing about our institutions, and in many instances never even heard of them. They are men whose passage is paid by the importers. They come here under contract to labor for a certain number of years. They are ignorant of our social condition, and, that they may remain so, they are isolated and prevented from coming into contact with Americans. They are generally from the lowest social stratum, and live upon the coarsest food, and in hovels of a character before unknown to American workmen. They, as a rule, do not become citizens, and are certainly not a desirable acquisition to the body politic. The inevitable tendency of their presence among us is to degrade American labor, and to reduce it to the level of the imported pauper labor." Page 5359, Congressional Record, 48th Cong.

We find, therefore, that the title of the act, the evil which was intended to be remedied, the circumstances surrounding the appeal to congress, the reports of the committee of each house, all concur in affirming that the intent of congress was simply to stay the influx of this cheap, unskilled labor.

\* \* \*

The judgment will be reversed, and the case remanded for further proceedings in accordance with this opinion.

### Notes and Questions

**1.** How clear was it that the words of the statute encompassed the services of the Rev. E. Walpole Warren? Consider that, when the contract labor statute was enacted, in 1885, the predominant meaning of the word "labor" was "physical toil," and "service" generally was understood to mean "domestic service," rather than professional services (referred to in the plural). On the other hand, contemporary dictionaries also included broader meanings for these terms. See William N. Eskridge, Jr., *Textualism: The Unknown Ideal?*, 96 MICH. L. REV. 1509, 1518, 1533 (1998). Does the exemption clause's coverage of "persons employed strictly as personal or domestic servants" suggest what meaning should apply to "service of any kind"?

**2.** Is it relevant that the meaning of the word "lecturer" has evolved from its 16th-century meaning of "preacher" to its current secular connotations?\* If, as the Oxford English Dictionary suggests, both meanings were still current in the late 19th century, how should we interpret the contract labor statute's clause excluding "lecturers" from the statute's coverage? As a general matter, if judges are to consult dictionaries in aid of interpretation, should they not ensure that the dictionary they peruse offers definitions contemporaneous with the statute under scrutiny?

**3.** For an account of the history of the contract labor statute and the prosecution of the Holy Trinity Church under it, as well as different approaches to the Supreme Court's use of legislative history, *compare* Carol Chomsky, *Unlocking the Mysteries of Holy Trinity: Spirit, Letter, and History in Statutory Interpretation*, 100 COLUM. L. REV. 901 (2000) *with* Adrian Vermeule, *Legislative History and the Limits of Judicial Competence: the Story of* Holy Trinity Church, 50 STAN. L. REV. 1833 (1998).

**4.** Contrast the nature of the problem posed for the Court in the principal case with that posed in United States v. Kirby (discussed in the *Holy Trinity Church* case supra) and consider the result reached in the *Kirby* decision and the quoted justifications offered for that result. What other

---

\* Thanks to Prof. William Eskridge and to Josephine Coakley, Columbia JD 2004, for directing me to the etymology of the words "lecturer," "lectureship," and "lecture."

reasonable justifications, if any, might have been given? What are the implications of Kirby for the judicial function in interpretation? Compare Riggs v. Palmer, 115 N.Y. 506, 22 N.E. 188 (1889). In that case, the beneficiary under a will had murdered the testator and then claimed the property pursuant to the will's provisions. The question was whether the beneficiary could have the property in such circumstances. It was acknowledged that the statutes regulating the making, proof and effect of wills and the devolution of property (which statutes did not in terms deal with "murdering heirs") would if literally construed give the property to the murderer. The Court however ruled that the murderer was not entitled to the property. Inter alia, the Court stated:

> The purpose of [the statutes concerned] was to enable testators to dispose of their estates to the objects of their bounty at death, and to carry into effect their final wishes legally expressed; and in considering and giving effect to them this purpose must be kept in view. It was the intention of the law-makers that the donees in a will should have the property given to them. But it never could have been their intention that a donee who murdered the testator to make the will operative should have any benefit under it. * * *

* * *

> What could be more unreasonable than to suppose that it was the legislative intention in the general laws passed for the orderly, peaceable and just devolution of property, that they should have operation in favor of one who murdered his ancestor that he might speedily come into the possession of his estate? Such an intention is inconceivable. We need not, therefore, be much troubled by the general language contained in the laws.

> Besides, all laws as well as all contracts may be controlled in their operation and effect by general, fundamental maxims of the common law. No one shall be permitted to profit by his own fraud, or to take advantage of his own wrong, or to found any claim upon his own iniquity, or to acquire property by his own crime. These maxims are dictated by public policy, have their foundation in universal law administered in all civilized countries, and have nowhere been superseded by statutes.

Compare, in addition, Glus v. Brooklyn Eastern Dist. Terminal, 359 U.S. 231, 79 S.Ct. 760, 3 L.Ed.2d 770 (1959), where, notwithstanding the existence of an express three-year statute of limitations, the Supreme Court held that an FELA action brought after more than three years was not barred where defendant misled the plaintiff into believing he had more than three years in which to sue. The Court relied on the principle that no man may take advantage of his own wrong, noting that it had been shown nothing in the language or history of the Federal Employers' Liability Act to indicate a contrary result.

**5.** In United States v. American Trucking Ass'n, 310 U.S. 534 (1940) Justice Reed described the role he saw for plain meaning in statutory interpretation:

> There is, of course, no more persuasive evidence of the purpose of a statute than the words by which the legislature undertook to give expression to its wishes. Often these words are sufficient in and of themselves to determine the purpose of the legislation. In such cases we have followed their plain meaning. When that meaning has led to absurd or futile results, however, this Court has looked beyond the words to the purpose of the act. Frequently, however, even when the plain meaning did not produce absurd results but merely an unreasonable one "plainly at variance with the policy of the legislation as a whole" this Court has followed that purpose, rather than the literal words. When aid to construction of the meaning of words, as used in the statute, is available, there certainly can be no "rule of law" which forbids its use, however clear the words may appear on "superficial examination." The interpretation of the meaning of statutes, as applied to justiciable controversies, is exclusively a judicial function. This duty requires one body of public servants, the judges, to construe the meaning of what another body, the legislators, has said. Obviously there is danger that the courts' conclusion as to legislative purpose will be unconsciously influenced by the judges' own views or by factors not considered by the enacting body. A lively appreciation of the danger is the best assurance of escape from its threat but hardly justifies an acceptance of a literal interpretation dogma which withholds from the courts available information for reaching a correct conclusion. Emphasis should be laid, too, upon the necessity for appraisal of the purposes as a whole of Congress in analyzing the meaning of clauses or sections of general acts. A few words of general connotation appearing in the text of statutes should not be given a wide meaning, contrary to a settled policy, "excepting as a different purpose is plainly shown."

Contrast Justice Reed's view with that of the four dissenting Justices, quoting the District Court's opinion in the case:

> If the words are clear, there is no room for construction.

> To search elsewhere for a meaning either beyond or short of that which they disclose is to invite the danger, in the one case, of converting what was meant to be open and precise, into a concealed trap for the unsuspecting, or, in the other, of relieving from the grasp of the statute some whom the Legislature definitely meant to include. Van Camp & Sons Co. v. American Can Co., 278 U.S. 245 (1929).

> \* \* \*

> In the view we take, the language of the disputed section is so plain as to permit only one interpretation, and we find nothing in the Act as a whole which can with any assurance be said to lead to a different result. The circumstances under which the section was placed in the bill may possibly have created a situation not contemplated by its

sponsors, but to say that this is true would be pure speculation, in which we have no right to indulge and upon which we can base no conclusion.

The Supreme Court in EEOC v. Commercial Office Products, 486 U.S. 107, 120–21 (1988) cited *American Trucking* as support for the proposition that

> [T]his severe consequence ... demonstrates that respondent's interpretation of the language of § 706 leads to "absurd or futile results ... 'plainly at variance with the policy of the legislation as a whole,'" which this Court need not and should not countenance.

If the meaning is indeed "plain," why *shouldn't* a court "countenance" its application when that application leads to "absurd or futile results plainly at variance with the policy of the legislation as a whole"? How does a court know what is "the policy of the legislation as a whole," and what is "plainly at variance" with that policy?

**6.** The Plain Meaning Rule rests on the premise that the meaning is indeed "plain." But plainness may be in the eye of the beholder; one reader's certainty may be another's ambiguity. Consider the following examples:

**Q.:** "Do you have the time?"

This statement poses at least two problems: 1. What does it mean? 2. What is the proper response? First, taken literally, the statement advances a rather metaphysical proposition: does anyone (other than a Diety) possess time? Assuming the questioner sought more down-to-earth information, the inquiry could mean either: "What time is it?" or "Do you have time to do something/go somewhere ... ?" The meaning of the statement, and thus, the proper response, depend on the context in which the inquiry was made. The words alone do not convey enough information (or, rather, the information they convey is insufficiently specific). Here, context supplies a necessary element of meaning.

Let us assume the questioner meant to inquire what time it was. Consider the following response:

**A.:** "It's two o'clock."

Here, the interlocutor has not in fact answered the question. She has collapsed her response and its anticipated rejoinder. Had she answered the question, she would have said: "Yes, I have the time" (or, "Yes, I can tell you what time it is" ...). She anticipates that her questioner would follow up her response with a question such as "What time is it, then?" In other words, she understands that the question "really" means "tell me what time it is, if you can." Here, custom tells us the true meaning of the question: had the speaker followed the "plain meaning" of the words, her questioner would probably have found her answer non-responsive (or impudent).

Consider another example: in some parts of the English speaking world, when people meet, they simply say:

**Q.:** "How are you?"

**A.:** "How are you?"

and they will leave it at that. They do not expect an answer. The words, through custom, have lost their plain meaning and are now used as greetings. The same question asked by a physician will get a different answer. Once again, custom and context supply the "meaning".

**7.** Sometimes "clear" statements include lacunae: they in fact leave much to assumption. For example, if one office-worker asks another to borrow a stapler, he also assumes that the loaned stapler will include staples. To supply an empty stapler would respond literally to the request, but would "clearly" not offer what the borrower sought.

In order to understand a statement, we often need to know its purpose. Consider a sign posted in a classroom: "NO COFFEE." What is this supposed to mean? If a student brings in a sealed can of ground coffee, has she violated the rule indicated by the sign? What if she brings in a cup of tea? What do we know about this rule? Is it intended to keep classrooms clean? If so, one can infer that it prohibits bringing in cups of the coffee beverage. If that is the purpose of the rule, should one infer by extension a prohibition on other beverages? All other beverages? What about other potential sources of classroom untidiness, such as candy bars? Newspapers? Loose notebook paper? Eraser shavings—erasers?

What if the classroom at issue were located in the Macrobiotic Institute of America, an institution whose creed bans artificial stimulants, such as caffeine? Does the prohibition take on a different meaning now? What purpose do you now infer? What meaning follows from it?

As you look back on the statutory materials already studied, and as you encounter new issues of statutory interpretation, think about when a law's meaning is truly "plain." If so, what makes it so?

On the other hand, it is not your task to torture an understandable rule into ambiguity. The point is that what makes a rule understandable may include more than the words themselves.

b. INTERPRETING A PREEXISTING STATUTE IN LIGHT OF NEW CIRCUMSTANCES FALLING WITHIN THE STATUTE'S LITERAL PURVIEW—THE JURY DUTY CASES

# Commonwealth v. Maxwell

Supreme Court of Pennsylvania, 1921.
271 Pa. 378, 114 A. 825.

■ Opinion by MR. JUSTICE SCHAFFER. In this case, the court below quashed an indictment, charging the defendants with murder, because a woman served on the grand jury which found the bill. The Commonwealth has appealed; and this brings before us the important question whether women are eligible as jurors in Pennsylvania.

It is conceded that, under the 19th Amendment to the Constitution of the United States, women are given the right to vote, and are therefore electors; but the oyer and terminer held that the provision of our Constitution (article I, section 6),—"Trial by jury shall be as heretofore and the right thereof remain inviolate,"—preserves in this State trial by jury as it existed at common law, and that neither the federal amendment nor its effect upon the Act of April 10, 1867, P.L. 62, providing for the selection of jurors, alters the ancient rule that men only may serve.

Let it be noted that what we are called upon to determine is the composition of juries, so far as the qualifications of jurors are concerned, not the conduct of trials before such a body nor the kinds of cases which under the Constitution must be decided by that character of tribunal.

At the time the provision we are considering was placed in Pennsylvania's first Constitution, in 1776, justice had been administered in the Commonwealth according to English forms for about a century. Does the word "heretofore" refer to jury trials as conducted in England or in Pennsylvania? We find the method of selecting juries and the qualifications of jurors, at the time of the promulgation of this Constitution, September 28, 1776, was regulated in Pennsylvania and in England by legislation and not by the common law, in the latter country by the Act of 3 George II, c. 25; 3 Blackstone 361.

* * *

Under the Act of April 10, 1867, P.L. 62, section 2, (2 Purdon 2062, placitum 2), which expressly applies to each of the counties in the Commonwealth, except Philadelphia, the jury commissioners are required to select "from the *whole qualified electors* of the respective county, at large, a number," such as shall be designated by the court of common pleas, "of sober, intelligent and judicious persons, to serve as jurors in the several courts of such county during that year." The seventh section of this act exempts Philadelphia from its provisions. The statutory enactment which covers Philadelphia is section 2 of the Act of April 20, 1858, P.L. 354 (2 Purdon 2077, placitum 94); it sets forth: "That prior to the first day of December in each and every year, the receiver of public taxes of the said city shall lodge with the said sheriff, for the use of the said board [of judges], a duly certified list of *all taxable inhabitants of the said city,* setting out their names, places of residence and occupation; and, prior to the tenth day of December in each and every year, it shall be the duty of the said board, or a quorum thereof, to assemble together and select from the said list of taxables a sufficient number of sober, healthy and discreet citizens, to constitute the several panels of jurors, grand and petit, that may be required for service in the several courts for the next ensuing year, in due proportion from the several wards of the said city and the principal avocations."

It will thus be seen that since 1805, when the Constitution of 1790 was in force, the persons charged with the duty of jury service have been fixed, from time to time, by the legislature and have been "taxable citizens," "white male taxable citizens," "male taxable citizens," "taxable inhabitants" and "qualified electors."

\* \* \*

Without feeling called upon to determine what other matters the word "heretofore" in the Constitution of 1873 refers to, we do say that when that instrument was adopted the uniform method of selecting jurors and determining their qualification was by legislation, both here and in England. This was known to the framers of the first and all succeeding Constitutions, in the first being specifically recognized, and, in guaranteeing the right of trial by jury, it and all the others did not in any way limit the legislature from determining from time to time how juries should be composed.

We have then the Act of 1867, constitutionally providing that the jury commissioners are required to select "from the *whole qualified electors* of the respective county \* \* \* persons to serve as jurors in the several courts of such county," and the 19th Amendment to the federal Constitution putting women in the body of electors. "The term 'elector' is a technical, generic term, descriptive of a citizen having constitutional and statutory qualifications that enable him to vote, and including not only those who vote, but also those who are qualified yet fail to exercise the right of franchise": 20 Corpus Juris 58. If the Act of 1867 is prospective in operation, and takes in new classes of electors as they come to the voting privilege from time to time, then necessarily women being electors are eligible to jury service. That the Act of 1867 does cover those who at any time shall come within the designation of electors there can be no question. "Statutes framed in general terms apply to new cases that arise, and to new subjects that are created from time to time, and which come within their general scope and policy. It is a rule of statutory construction that legislative enactments in general and comprehensive terms, prospective in operation, apply alike to all persons, subjects and business within their general purview and scope coming into existence subsequent to their passage": 25 Ruling Case Law 778.

Summing up, we conclude, (1) there was no absolute and fixed qualification of jurors at common law, and from very ancient times their qualifications were fixed by act of parliament; (2) the qualification of jurors was not the thing spoken of by the section of the Constitution under consideration; (3) the words "as heretofore" in that section refer to the kinds of cases triable before juries and the trial, not the qualifications of the jurors; (4) the designation "qualified elector" embraces all electors at the time jurors are selected from the body of electors; (5) the term "electors" embraces those who may be added to the electorate from time to time.

\* \* \*

The pending case calls for the immediate decision only of the right of women to serve as jurors in those counties which are covered by the Act of 1867. We entertain no doubt, however, that women are eligible to serve as jurors in all the Commonwealth's courts.

The order quashing the indictment is reversed, and the indictment is reinstated with direction to the court below to proceed with the trial of the defendants in due course.

# Commonwealth v. Welosky

Supreme Court of Massachusetts, 1931.
276 Mass. 398, 177 N.E. 656.

Complaint, received and sworn to in the District Court of Chelsea on July 9, 1930, charging the defendant with keeping and exposing intoxicating liquor with intent unlawfully to sell the same.

Upon appeal to the Superior Court, the complaint was tried before *Hayes, J.*, a judge of a district court sitting in the Superior Court under statutory provisions. The defendant's challenge to the array is described in the opinion. The judge sustained a replication by the Commonwealth thereto. The defendant was found guilty and alleged exceptions.

■ Rugg, C.J. As the jurors were about to be empaneled for the trial of this complaint, the defendant filed a challenge to the array. Issue of law was joined thereon. The ground on which that challenge rests is that there were no women on the lists from which the jurors were drawn.

**1.** The first question to be decided is whether the statutes of this Commonwealth require that the names of women otherwise qualified be placed upon jury lists so that they may be drawn for service as jurors.

It is plain that women could not rightly serve as jurors, save in the rare instances where a jury of matrons was called, under the Constitution and laws of this Commonwealth prior to the adoption of the Nineteenth Amendment to the Constitution of the United States. The terms of the statute, in the light of the Constitution, express decisions, universal understanding, and unbroken practice, forbid any other view. The trial by jury of the common law and that contemplated by both the Constitution of this Commonwealth and that of the United States were by a jury of twelve composed exclusively of men. [citations omitted].

The statute to be interpreted is G.L. c. 234, § 1. Its relevant language is: "A person qualified to vote for representatives to the general court shall be liable to serve as a juror," with exceptions not here material.

The words of a statute are the main source for the ascertainment of a legislative purpose. They are to be construed according to their natural import in common and approved usage. The imperfections of language to express intent often render necessary further inquiry. Statutes are to be interpreted, not alone according to their simple, literal or strict verbal meaning, but in connection with their development, their progression through the legislative body, the history of the times, prior legislation, contemporary customs and conditions and the system of positive law of which they are part, and in the light of the Constitution and of the common law, to the end that they be held to cover the subjects presumably within the vision of the Legislature and, on the one hand, be not unduly constricted so as to exclude matters fairly within their scope, and, on the other hand, be not stretched by enlargement of signification to comprehend matters not within the principle and purview on which they were founded when originally framed and their words chosen. General expressions may be restrained by relevant circumstances showing a legislative intent that they be narrowed and used in a particular sense. [citations omitted].

It is clear beyond peradventure that the words of G.L. c. 234, § 1, when originally enacted could not by any possibility have included or been intended by the General Court to include women among those liable to jury duty. The Constitution forbade the words, "A person qualified to vote for representatives to the general court," to comprehend women. Women have been qualified to vote in this Commonwealth only since the adoption of the Nineteenth Amendment to the Constitution of the United States. It is not argued in behalf of the defendant that the terms of the statutes preceding G.L. c. 234, § 1, that is to say of R.L. c. 176, § 1, and its predecessors in substantially the same words since a time before the adoption of the Constitution, could possibly have imposed jury duty upon women. The argument on this point is twofold: (A) that the phrase of the statute is general and therefore was intended automatically to include women if their constitutional inhibitions were ever removed; and (B) that, since the General Laws were enacted in December, 1920, after the ratification of the Nineteenth Amendment, the statute was intended to include women. These arguments will be considered in turn.

A.  The Nineteenth Amendment was, on August 26, 1920, proclaimed to have been duly ratified. That amendment declared that "The right of citizens of the United States to vote shall not be denied or abridged by the United States or by any state on account of sex." It became forthwith binding upon the people and the several departments of this Commonwealth. By its own self-executing force it struck from the Constitution of this Commonwealth the word "male" wherever it occurred as a limitation upon the right to vote.

Statutes framed in general terms commonly look to the future and may include conditions as they arise from time to time not even known at the time of enactment, provided they are fairly within the sweep and the meaning of the words and falling within their obvious scope and purpose. But statutes do not govern situations not within the reason of their enactment and giving rise to radically diverse circumstances presumably not within the dominating purpose of those who framed and enacted them. [citations omitted].

As matter of strict and abstract verbal interpretation, apart from context, circumstances, and contemporary and antecedent history, the language of G.L. c. 234, § 1, is broad enough to comprise women. The word "person" when used in an unrestricted sense includes a woman. It has been said that "The word 'persons,' in its natural and usual signification, includes women as well as men." *Opinion of the Justices,* 136 Mass. 578, 580. Binney v. Globe National Bank, 150 Mass. 574. "The natural and obvious meaning of the word 'person' is a living human being." Sawyer v. Mackie, 149 Mass. 269, 270. Madden v. Election Commissioners of Boston,

251 Mass. 95, 98. The word "person," like many other words, has no fixed and rigid signification, but has different meanings dependent upon contemporary conditions, the connection in which it is used, and the result intended to be accomplished. It has been said to be "an ambiguous word" and may refer to those of either or both sexes. Nairn v. University of St. Andrews, [1909] A.C. 147, 162.... Yet it was held not to include corporations upon the facts in Commonwealth v. Phoenix Bank, 11 Met. 129, 149. Notwithstanding Pub.Sts. c. 3, § 3, Sixteenth, (G.L. c. 4, § 7, Twenty-third) to the effect that the word "person" in construing statutes shall include corporations, it was held not thus inclusive in Steel Edge Stamping & Retinning Co. v. Manchester Savings Bank, 163 Mass. 252. It has also been held not to include a woman. Mashburn v. State, 65 Fla. 470, 474. Several cases have arisen where the question was whether the word "person," when used respecting the right to hold office or to exercise the franchise, included women. In Nairn v. University of St. Andrews, [1909] A.C. 147, it appeared that, by Acts of Parliament of 1868 and 1881, the university franchise was conferred upon "every person" whose name was on the register and on whom degrees had been conferred. At that time women were not admitted to graduation and could not receive degrees. In 1889, a further act was passed for the appointment of commissioners with extensive regulatory powers over universities. These commissioners adopted an ordinance enabling the universities to confer degrees on women for satisfactory academic accomplishments. The appellants, having received degrees upon graduation, contended that they had the right to vote. In rejecting that contention, it was said by Lord Loreburn, at page 161: "It proceeds upon the supposition that the word 'person' in the Act of 1868 did include women, though not then giving them the vote, so that at some later date an Act purporting to deal only with education might enable commissioners to admit them to the degree, and thereby also indirectly confer upon them the franchise. It would require a convincing demonstration to satisfy me that Parliament intended to effect a constitutional change so momentous and far-reaching by so furtive a process. It is a dangerous assumption to suppose that the Legislature foresees every possible result that may ensue from the unguarded use of a single word, or that the language used in statutes is so precisely accurate that you can pick out from various Acts this and that expression and, skillfully piecing them together, lay a safe foundation for some remote inference." It was held that the statutory word "person" did not in these circumstances include women. It was held in *Viscountess Rhondda's Claim,* [1922] 2 A.C. 339, that an Act of Parliament passed in 1919, providing that "A person shall not be disqualified by sex or marriage from the exercise of any public function," did not entitle a peeress of the United Kingdom in her own right to receive the writ of summons to Parliament. Doubtless, as an abstract conception, it is a public function to sit in the House of Lords and to exercise the prerogatives of a member. But it was held by ten out of twelve law lords sitting in the case, among whom were the most eminent judges of the day, that the word "person" as used in the act could not rightly be interpreted to include women in those entitled to sit in the House of Lords. It was said by Lord Birkenhead in the

course of an exhaustive statement reviewing many decisions, at page 369: " . . . a long stream of cases has established that general words are to be construed so as, in an old phrase, 'to pursue the intent of the makers of statutes' . . . and so as to import all those implied exceptions which arise from a close consideration of the mischiefs sought to be remedied and of the state of the law at the moment, when the statute was passed." At pages 372–373, the words of Lord Loreburn in Nairn v. University of St. Andrews, [1909] A.C. 147, at pages 160, 161, to which reference has already been made, were quoted with high commendation.

This brief review of authorities demonstrates that "person" by itself is an equivocal word. Its meaning in a statute requires interpretation. The statute here under examination (G.L. c. 234, § 1) is a reenactment of a long line of statutes of the Commonwealth running back to a time shortly after the adoption of the Constitution as well as through all intermediate revisions dealing with qualifications for jury service. Laws of the Colony and of the Province are in effect the same. In the earlier and later statutes, the same essential and almost the identical words have been employed. The word "person" occurs in them all. The selection of jurors has constantly been required to be from those qualified to vote. Qualifications for voting have been continuously established by the Constitution. By the words of that instrument and its amendments (apart from the effect of the Nineteenth Amendment to the Federal Constitution) the right to vote was confined to male inhabitants, male persons, and finally to male citizens, until the word "male" was stricken out in 1924 by Amendment 68. See c. 1, § 2, art. 2; c. 1, § 3, art. 4; arts. 3 and 32 of the Amendments. Manifestly, therefore, the intent of the Legislature must have been, in using the word "person" in statutes concerning jurors and jury lists, to confine its meaning to men.

Possession of property of specified value and payment of taxes, as qualifications for voters, were required in earlier days and from time to time, but these were gradually eliminated by amendments to the Constitution until the last of such limitations disappeared with the approval of Amendment 32 in 1891. When the suffrage has been thus widened among male citizens, there has followed, without further legislation and without change in the phrase of the statute, a like extension of citizens liable to service as jurors. These concurring enlargements of those liable to jury service were simply an extension to larger numbers of the same classification of persons. Since the word "person" in the statutes respecting jurors meant men, when there was an extension of the right to vote to other men previously disqualified, the jury statutes by specific definition included them. No amendment to the statute can be conceived which could have made that meaning more clear.

Changes in suffrage and in liability for jury service in the past differ in kind from the change here urged.

The Nineteenth Amendment to the Federal Constitution conferred the suffrage upon an entirely new class of human beings. It did not extend the right to vote to members of an existing classification theretofore disqualified, but created a new class. It added to qualified voters those who did not fall within the meaning of the word "person" in the jury statutes. No member of the class thus added to the body of voters had ever theretofore in this Commonwealth had the right to vote for candidates for offices created by the Constitution. The change in the legal status of women wrought by the Nineteenth Amendment was radical, drastic and unprecedented. While it is to be given full effect in its field, it is not to be extended by implication. It is unthinkable that those who first framed and selected the words for the statute now embodied in G.L. c. 234, § 1, had any design that it should ever include women within its scope. It is equally inconceivable that those who from time to time have reenacted that statute had any such design. When they used the word "person" in connection with those qualified to vote for members of the more numerous branch of the General Court, to describe those liable to jury service, no one contemplated the possibility of women becoming so qualified. The same is true in general of those who from time to time reenacted the statute in substantially the same words. No intention to include women can be deduced from the omission of the word male. That word was imbedded in the Constitution of the Commonwealth as a limitation upon those citizens who might become voters and thereby members of a class from which jurors might be drawn. It would have been superfluous also to insert that word in the statute. The words of Chief Justice Gray in *Robinson's Case,* 131 Mass. 376, at pages 380, 381, are equally pertinent to the case at bar: "Whenever the Legislature has intended to make a change in the legal rights or capacities of women, it has used words clearly manifesting its intent and the extent of the change intended.... In making innovations upon the long-established system of law on this subject, the Legislature appears to have proceeded with great caution, one step at a time; and the whole course of legislation precludes the inference that any change in the legal rights or capacities of women is to be implied, which has not been clearly expressed."

The conclusion is irresistible that, according to sound principles of statutory construction, it cannot rightly be held that the scope of R.L. c. 176, § 1, the statute in force on August 26, 1920, now G.L. c. 234, § 1, was extended by the ratification of the Nineteenth Amendment so as to render women liable to jury duty. To reach that result would be directly contrary to every purpose and intent of the General Court in enacting that law.

### Questions

**1.** The statutory text construed in *Maxwell* directed that jurors were to be drawn "from the whole qualified electors ... " In *Welosky,* the statute designated "persons qualified to vote ... " Does the different language explain the different outcomes in the two cases?

**2.** *Maxwell*'s approach to statutory interpretation seems consistent with the "plain meaning rule," while *Welosky*'s interpretive techniques recall a variety of other devices to ascertain legislative intent. Do those devices seem more problematic here than, for example, in Johnson v. Southern Pacific, *supra?*

**3.** Is it relevant that the different outcomes on the composition of juries permitted the convictions in both cases to be sustained?

c. INTERPRETING A STATUTE'S INADVERTENT REPEAL

# In re Adamo

United States Court of Appeals, Second Circuit, 1980.
619 F.2d 216.

■ BARTELS, DISTRICT JUDGE:

This is an appeal from a judgment of the United States District Court for the Western District of New York, Burke, J., affirming the discharge by the Bankruptcy Court of certain student loan obligations in proceedings brought on by twenty-one voluntary petitions in bankruptcy. The sole question for review is the effect of the repeal by Congress of Section 439A of the Higher Education Act of 1965, as amended, 20 U.S.C. § 1087–3, pertaining to dischargeability of student loans, on petitions in bankruptcy commenced but not disposed of prior to the date of such repeal.

The pertinent facts are undisputed. Each of the loans here involved is either owed to or guaranteed by appellant New York State Higher Education Services Corporation ("NYSHESC"), and each was reinsured to appellant by the United States Office of Education by agreements entered into pursuant to the Higher Education Act of 1965, as amended, 20 U.S.C. §§ 1071 et seq. At the time the twenty-one voluntary petitions in bankruptcy were filed, § 1087–3 of Title 20 provided, in part, as follows:

(a) A debt which is a loan insured or guaranteed under the authority of this part may be released by a discharge in bankruptcy under the Bankruptcy Act only if such discharge is granted after the five-year period ... beginning on the date of commencement of the repayment period of such loan, except that prior to the expiration of that five-year period, such loan may be released only if the court in which the proceeding is pending determines that payment from future income or other wealth will impose an undue hardship on the debtor or his dependents.

(b) Subsection (a) of this section shall be effective with respect to any proceedings begun under the Bankruptcy Act on or after September 30, 1977.

This provision was subsequently repealed effective November 6, 1978, however, by Section 317 of the Bankruptcy Reform Act of 1978 ("BRA"), Pub.L. 95–598,[3] and was replaced by Section 523(a)(8), as amended by Pub.L. 96–56, which provides:

---

**3.** Section 317 of the Bankruptcy Reform Act of 1978 ("BRA") provides that "Section 439A of part B of title IV of the Higher Education Act of 1965 (20 U.S.C. § 1087–3) is repealed." The effective date of this section appears in section 402(d) of the BRA, which provides that "(t)he amendments made by sections 217, 218, 230, 247, 302, 314(j), 317, 327, 328, 338, and 411 of this Act

(a) A discharge under section 727, 1141, or 1328(b) of this title does not discharge an individual debtor from any debt . . .

(8) for an educational loan made, insured, or guaranteed by a governmental unit, or made under any program funded in whole or in part by a governmental unit or a nonprofit institution of higher education, unless—

(A) such loan first became due before five years . . . before the date of the filing of the petition; or

(B) excepting such debt from discharge under this paragraph will impose an undue hardship on the debtor and the debtor's dependents;

. . .

Under section 402(a) of the BRA, this replacement provision did not become effective until October 1, 1979, approximately eleven months after the effective date of the repeal of its predecessor, 20 U.S.C. § 1087–3.[4] According to appellant, this interruption in the rule of nondischargeability of student loans constitutes a loophole through which certain student loan debtors now attempt to escape their repayment obligations.

The Bankruptcy Court disposed of all of the twenty-one petitions by two identical memorandum decisions and orders dated March 16 and April 5, 1979, respectively, holding that because the petitions were considered and resolved after the repeal of 20 U.S.C. § 1087–3 but before the effective date of 11 U.S.C. § 523(a)(8), the Bankruptcy Court no longer had jurisdiction "to determine that the subject bankrupts are not entitled to a discharge, since the law which exists at the time of this decision has no provision for the denial of the discharge of student loans." Accordingly, Bankruptcy Judge Hayes ordered that the student loan debts in question be discharged. His decision was affirmed by the district court in a brief order on September 27, 1979, and this appeal followed.

\* \* \*

We conclude that the hiatus between the repeal of section 1087–3 of Title 20 and the effective date of its successor provision, 11 U.S.C. § 523(a)(8), was purely a manifestation of congressional inadvertence and that to follow blindly the plain meaning of the statute without regard to the obvious intention of Congress would create an absurd result in accord with neither established principles of statutory construction nor common sense. Accordingly, the decisions of the district court and the bankruptcy court below must be reversed.

Analysis of the legislative history of the BRA supports appellant's contention that the failure of the effective dates of the repeal and replacement statutes to coincide resulted from a mistake of Congress. Section 1087–3 of Title 20 of the United States Code was enacted in 1976 to

shall take effect on the date of enactment of this Act."

**4.** Section 402(a) of the BRA provides that "(e)xcept as otherwise provided in this title, this Act shall take effect on October 1, 1979."

prevent abuse of the bankruptcy laws by students petitioning for bankruptcy immediately upon graduation without attempting to realize the potential increased earning capacity which education may provide. [citations omitted]. By creating a special exception from discharge for education loans, Congress hoped to insure a more realistic view of a student's ability to repay the debt.

During the 95th Congress, however, bankruptcy reform legislation was introduced in the House of Representatives which included the repeal of section 1087–3 in order to "restore the law to where it had been before the 1976 amendment . . . " *H.Rep. 95–595,* 95th Cong., 1st Sess., 132, *reprinted in* [1978] U.S.Code Cong. & Admin.News, pp. 5787, 6093. This repeal provision, which was to take effect on the date of enactment of the legislation, was predicated upon the view that student abuses were not as widespread as had been thought and, therefore, did not warrant special treatment under the bankruptcy laws. This sentiment did not prevail, however, and when the legislation H.R. 8200 was reintroduced for further consideration in early 1978, the House, by amendment to section 523(a)(8) of the bill, adopted a replacement provision making nondischargeable educational loans insured or guaranteed under Part B of Title IV of the Higher Education Act of 1965, *supra.*

Similar bankruptcy reform legislation was introduced in the Senate in October 1977 as S. 2266. While § 317 of S. 2266 also provided for the repeal of 20 U.S.C. § 1087–3, the bill contained a more comprehensive replacement provision in section 523(a)(8) excepting from discharge any debt for an educational loan. The effective date of both sections 317 and 523(a)(8) was October 1, 1979. The differences between the House and Senate versions of the relevant provisions were resolved by the conference committee in September 1978. Because the Senate members would not acquiesce to the limited nondischargeability provision contained in H.R. 8200, the committee amended the House bill by broadening the scope of section 523(a)(8) to make nondischargeable all educational loans owing to or insured or guaranteed by a governmental unit or a nonprofit institution of higher education. The committee failed, however, to notice that the section repealing 20 U.S.C. § 1087–3 as of the date of enactment remained in the House bill. Thus, as subsequently approved by Congress and signed into law by the President, the BRA contained the House repeal provision and, due to the insistence of the Senate conferees, a broad replacement provision, the effective dates of which did not coincide. There is no indication in the history of the BRA that Congress intended to legislate such an inconsistency or that it sought for some unexpressed reason to create an approximately eleven-month hiatus for the benefit of student loan debtors.

The inadvertence of this action was subsequently acknowledged by the Senate Committee on the Judiciary . . . :

> The gap in coverage of a prohibition on the discharge in bankruptcy of loans made under the Guaranteed Student Loan Program resulting from the early repeal of section 349A (sic) is very undesirable and

totally inadvertent.... [An] inadvertent "gap" [was] created when the applicable section of the Higher Education Act of 1965 prohibiting discharge of student loans was repealed as of November 6, 1978, and its replacement section in Title II was not made effective until October 1, 1979. Congress obviously did not mean to create a gap and at all times held to the principle of nondischargeability of student loans ...[7]

Although such an interpretation by a subsequent Congress is not necessarily controlling, it may be useful in determining the intention of an earlier Congress. [citations omitted].

The language of the BRA gives further credence to this interpretation. In addition to the obvious significance of the inclusion of a more comprehensive exception provision in section 523(a)(8) of the BRA than had existed previously in section 1087–3 of Title 20 U.S.C., the BRA also includes a "savings" provision in section 403(a) which preserves the substantive rights of the parties to actions commenced prior to the effective date of the BRA. Section 403(a) provides as follows:

> A case commenced under the Bankruptcy Act, and all matters and proceedings in or relating to any such case, shall be conducted and determined under such Act as if this Act had not been enacted, and the substantive rights of parties in connection with any such bankruptcy case, matter or proceeding shall continue to be governed by the law applicable to such case, matter or proceeding as if the Act had not been enacted.

Because this section, together with the BRA as a whole, did not become effective until October 1, 1979, it is not dispositive of this appeal. However, we consider it persuasive evidence of Congress' desire not to impair the rights of parties to actions commenced under the old Bankruptcy Act.

Finally, we note the apparent absurdity of a construction of the BRA which, for no discernible reason, would permit the discharge of student loans by debtors who, by sheer chance, have their bankruptcy petitions adjudicated during the eleven-month gap. Both before and after this period, nondischargeability has been and will continue to be the rule; absent an explicit statement of intent by Congress to provide a period of "amnesty" for student loan debtors, to recognize the repeal of section 1087–3 before giving effect to either section 523(a)(8) of the BRA or the savings provision

---

**7.** ... The remarks of various members of Congress ... confirm the conclusion of the Senate Judiciary Committee quoted above. Senator DeConcini (D.Ariz.), principal sponsor and floor manager for the BRA in the Senate, explained the intent of Congress with respect to ... the BRA:

> [T]he Bankruptcy Reform Act ... inadvertently created a "gap" in provisions of existing law concerning nondischargeability of student loans in a bankruptcy case. Public Law 95–598 repealed provisions in the Higher Education Act mak-

ing student loans nondischargeable. It was the intent to merely shift the location of the nondischargeability provision from the Higher Education Act to the Bankruptcy Code, 11 U.S.C. However, ... a "gap" was created between November 6, 1978, and October 1, 1979, when it can be argued that there is no nondischargeability provision in the law although it clearly was not the intent of Congress to have created such a gap.

125 *Cong.Rec.* S.9160 (daily ed. July 11, 1979)....

in section 403(a) would, it seems to us, effectuate a legislative mistake prejudicial to the substantive rights of appellant.

The result of an obvious mistake should not be enforced, particularly when it "overrides common sense and evident statutory purpose." *United States v. Babcock,* 530 F.2d 1051, 1053 (D.C.Cir.1976); ... It is a well established principle of statutory construction that a statute should not be applied strictly in accord with its literal meaning where to do so would pervert its manifest purpose. Nowhere has this principle been expressed more eloquently than by Judge Learned Hand in his concurring opinion in *Guiseppi v. Walling,* 144 F.2d 608, 624 (2d Cir.1944), where he stated:

> There is no surer way to misread any document than to read it literally; in every interpretation we must pass between Scylla and Charybdis; and I certainly do not wish to add to the barrels of ink that have been spent in logging the route. As nearly as we can, we must put ourselves in the place of those who uttered the words, and try to divine how they would have dealt with the unforeseen situation; and, although their words are by far the most decisive evidence of what they would have done, they are by no means final....

In this case, a literal application of the effective date of section 317 of the BRA, repealing 20 U.S.C. § 1087–3, would require us to disregard its intended purpose.[9] We hold, therefore, that the premature repeal of section 1087–3 is of no effect with respect to proceedings commenced prior to the effective date of the BRA on October 1, 1979. Accordingly, the decision of the district court is hereby reversed, and the petitions at bar are remanded to the bankruptcy court for further proceedings in accordance with this opinion.

## Notes and Questions

**1.** Independent Ins. Agents v. Clarke, 955 F.2d 731 (D.C.Cir.1992) involved the inadvertent repeal of § 92 of the National Bank Act. Section 92 permitted any national bank, or its branch, located in a community of not more than 5,000 inhabitants to sell insurance to customers outside that community. Although early provisions of Title 12 of the United States Code included § 92, the 1952 U.S.C. and subsequent editions omitted it, with a note indicating that Congress had repealed the section in 1918. The parties in the case did not raise the issue of the validity of § 92, but, assuming the section to be applicable, differed as to its interpretation.

The Court of Appeals, acting *sua sponte,* held that § 92 had been repealed in 1918, notwithstanding the perception of Congress, other courts, and the Comptroller of the Currency that the section remained in effect. The court rejected arguments that the deletion of § 92 was the result of mistake in punctuation (in this case, the misplacement of quotation marks around restated text of the statute, which excluded the language at issue) and that its repeal should therefore be ignored. The Court stated (p. 739):

**9.** "[F]or the letter killeth but the spirit giveth life." 2 Corinthians 3.6.

We recognize that, in order to give effect to a clear congressional intent, federal courts have assumed a rather broad responsibility for correcting flaws in the language and punctuation of federal statutes. There is a point, however, beyond which a court cannot go without trespassing on the exclusive prerogatives of the legislative branch.

We believe we are at that point. It is one thing for a court to bend statutory language to make it achieve a clearly stated congressional purpose; it is quite another for a court to reinstate a law that, intentionally or unintentionally, Congress has stricken from the statute books. If the deletion of section 92 was a mistake, it is one for Congress to correct, not the courts.

The Supreme Court reversed, holding that § 92 was not repealed in 1918. Writing for a unanimous Court, Justice Souter concluded that the deletion of the section "was a simple scrivener's error, a mistake made by someone unfamiliar with the law's object and design.... The true meaning of the ... Act is clear beyond question, and so we repunctuate." United States National Bank of Oregon v. Independent Ins. Agents, 508 U.S. 439, 113 S.Ct. 2173, 2186 (1993).

**2.**   Can you reconcile the different approaches of the Second Circuit and the D.C. Circuit in In re Adamo and Independent Insurance Agents v. Clarke?

**3.**   Should a court correct inadvertent errors in a law in accordance with congressional intent, or should it apply the law as enacted by Congress? Which approach shows more deference to Congress?

**4.**   Note: France, Cassation Chambre Criminelle, decision of March 8, 1930, D.1930.I.101, note Voirin

The law in question forbade descending from a train *"when* it has completely stopped" (emphasis supplied). Apparently, the legislature intended to forbid descending from a train before it has completely stopped. The defendant descended from a still-moving train, and was fined for this conduct. He claimed that he had not violated the law, but had in fact obeyed it to the letter (though it is doubtful he knew of the drafting error in the penal code at the time he got off the train). The Cour de cassation rejected the appeal from the lower court's decision upholding the fine, on the ground that the lower court was entitled to interpret the text as forbidding defendant's act.

The commentary of Professor Pierre Voirin justifies the result on the ground that there was evidence "intrinsic" to the text of the law to indicate that the legislature intended to prohibit descent from still-moving trains. (It appears that other provisions of the same law must have supported that interpretation, though he does not quote them.) He distinguishes judicial error-correction based on "intrinsic" evidence of statutory intent from "extrinsic" evidence of legislative error. He finds the latter illegitimate.

He evokes a then-recent High Court decision in which the Cour de cassation ruled as if a provision of the civil code concerning the guardians of minors had not been repealed, when in fact it had: "Even if it occurred unintentionally and unbeknown to the legislature, the repeal nonetheless occurred in fact, and nothing in the current text of the civil code permits one to avoid that result, for the general principle, from which the repealed provision derogated, remaining in effect, barred any room for interpretation." (This is indeed *Adamo* "avant la lettre," for the repealed provision in *Adamo* created an exception from normal bankruptcy rules; in the absence of that exception, the general rules remaining in the statute would apply to permit the student filings.)

Professor Voirin then explores the consequences of allowing "extrinsic" considerations, such as the judges' conviction that the legislature made a mistake, to justify courts' error-correction:

> If the interpreter could correct texts that are enacted, promulgated, and published in the regular fashion, on the pretext of giving effect to the true will of the legislature, when this intent is discerned exclusively by extrinsic information, that would be the end of the guarantees that the formalities of legislative or administrative procedure assure to citizens. And once embarked on this slope, no doubt we will manage to declare without effect the formulation of some laws whose terms each Assembly will have voted, by giving a very different meaning to those words, for in fact there will have been no "legislative intent."

Do these criticisms sound familiar? Should it make a difference to the defendant's criminal liability in the train case that the textual error could be corrected based on other provisions of the same statute, even though defendant's conduct comported perfectly with the precisely applicable provision? Would your answer be the same if defendant faced only civil liability?

## 2. Now Resurgent?

## Bailey v. United States

Supreme Court of the United States, 1995.
516 U.S. 137, 116 S.Ct. 501, 133 L.Ed.2d 472.

■ Justice O'Connor delivered the opinion of the Court.

These consolidated petitions each challenge a conviction under 18 U.S.C. § 924(c)(1). In relevant part, that section imposes a 5–year minimum term of imprisonment upon a person who "during and in relation to any crime of violence or drug trafficking crime ... uses or carries a firearm." We are asked to decide whether evidence of the proximity and accessibility of a firearm to drugs or drug proceeds is alone sufficient to support a conviction for "use" of a firearm during and in relation to a drug trafficking offense under 18 U.S.C. § 924(c)(1).

### I

In May 1989, petitioner Roland Bailey was stopped by police officers after they noticed that his car lacked a front license plate and an inspection sticker. When Bailey failed to produce a driver's license, the officers ordered him out of the car. As he stepped out, the officers saw Bailey push something between the seat and the front console. A search of the passenger compartment revealed one round of ammunition and 27 plastic bags containing a total of 30 grams of cocaine. After arresting Bailey, the officers searched the trunk of his car where they found, among a number of items, a large amount of cash and a bag containing a loaded 9–mm. pistol.

Bailey was charged on several counts, including using and carrying a firearm in violation of 18 U.S.C. § 924(c)(1). A prosecution expert testified at trial that drug dealers frequently carry a firearm to protect their drugs and money as well as themselves. Bailey was convicted by the jury on all charges, and his sentence included a consecutive 60–month term of imprisonment on the § 924(c)(1) conviction.

The Court of Appeals for the District of Columbia Circuit rejected Bailey's claim that the evidence was insufficient to support his conviction under § 924(c)(1). *United States v. Bailey,* 995 F.2d 1113 (C.A.D.C.1993). The court held that Bailey could be convicted for "using" a firearm during and in relation to a drug trafficking crime if the jury could reasonably infer that the gun facilitated Bailey's commission of a drug offense. *Id.,* at 1119. In Bailey's case, the court explained, the trier of fact could reasonably infer that Bailey had used the gun in the trunk to protect his drugs and drug proceeds and to facilitate sales. Judge Douglas H. Ginsburg, dissenting in part, argued that prior circuit precedent required reversal of Bailey's conviction.

In June 1991, an undercover officer made a controlled buy of crack cocaine from petitioner Candisha Robinson. The officer observed Robinson retrieve the drugs from the bedroom of her one-bedroom apartment. After a second controlled buy, the police executed a search warrant of the apartment. Inside a locked trunk in the bedroom closet, the police found, among other things, an unloaded, holstered .22–caliber Derringer, papers and a tax return belonging to Robinson, 10.88 grams of crack cocaine, and a marked $20 bill from the first controlled buy.

Robinson was indicted on a number of counts, including using or carrying a firearm in violation of § 924(c)(1). A prosecution expert testified that the Derringer was a "second gun," *i.e.,* a type of gun a drug dealer might hide on his or her person for use until reaching a "real gun." The expert also testified that drug dealers generally use guns to protect themselves from other dealers, the police, and their own employees. Robinson was convicted on all counts, including the § 924(c)(1) count, for which she received a 60–month term of imprisonment. The District Court denied Robinson's motion for a judgment of acquittal with respect to the "using or carrying" conviction and ruled that the evidence was sufficient to establish a violation of § 924(c)(1).

A divided panel of the Court of Appeals reversed Robinson's conviction on the § 924(c)(1) count. *United States v. Robinson,* 997 F.2d 884 (C.A.D.C. 1993). The court determined, "[g]iven the way section 924(c)(1) is drafted, even if an individual intends to use a firearm in connection with a drug trafficking offense, the conduct of that individual is not reached by the statute unless the individual actually uses the firearm for that purpose." *Id.,* at 887. The court held that Robinson's possession of an unloaded .22–caliber Derringer in a locked trunk in a bedroom closet fell significantly short of the type of evidence the court had previously held necessary to establish actual use under § 924(c)(1). The mere proximity of the gun to the drugs was held insufficient to support the conviction. Judge Henderson dissented, arguing among other things that the firearm facilitated Robinson's distribution of drugs because it protected Robinson and the drugs during sales.

In order to resolve the apparent inconsistencies in its decisions applying § 924(c)(1), the Court of Appeals for the District of Columbia Circuit consolidated the two cases and reheard them en banc. In a divided opinion, a majority of the court held that the evidence was sufficient to establish that each defendant had used a firearm in relation to a drug trafficking offense and affirmed the § 924(c)(1) conviction in each case. 36 F.3d 106 (C.A.D.C.1994) (en banc).

The majority ... "[held] that one uses a gun, i.e., avails oneself of a gun, and therefore violates [§ 924(c)(1) ], whenever one puts or keeps the gun in a particular place from which one (or one's agent) can gain access to it if and when needed to facilitate a drug crime." *Id.,* at 115. The court applied this new standard and affirmed the convictions of both Bailey and Robinson. In both cases, the court determined that the gun was sufficiently accessible and proximate to the drugs or drug proceeds that the jury could properly infer that the defendant had placed the gun in order to further the drug offenses or to protect the possession of the drugs.

Judge Wald, [dissented].... Judge Williams, joined by Judges Silberman and Buckley, also dissented. He explained his understanding that "use" under § 924(c)(1) denoted active employment of the firearm "rather than possession with a contingent intent to use." *Id.,* at 121. "[B]y articulating a 'proximity' plus 'accessibility' test, however, the court has in effect diluted 'use' to mean simply possession with a floating intent to use." *Ibid.*

As the debate within the District of Columbia Circuit illustrates, § 924(c)(1) has been the source of much perplexity in the courts. The Circuits are in conflict both in the standards they have articulated, compare *United States* v. *Torres–Rodriguez,* 930 F.2d 1375, 1385 (C.A.9 1991) (mere possession sufficient to satisfy § 924(c)) with *United States* v. *Castro–Lara,* 970 F.2d 976, 983 (C.A.1 1992), cert. denied, 508 U.S. 962 (1993) (mere possession insufficient); and in the results they have reached, compare *United States* v. *Feliz–Cordero,* 859 F.2d 250, 254 (C.A.2 1988) (presence of gun in dresser drawer in apartment with drugs, drug proceeds, and paraphernalia insufficient to meet § 924(c)(1)) with *United States* v. *McFadden,* 13 F.3d 463, 465 (C.A.1 1994) (evidence of gun hidden under mattress with money, near drugs, was sufficient to show "use") and *United States* v. *Hager,* 969 F.2d 883, 889 (C.A.10), cert. denied, 506 U.S. 964 (1992) (gun in boots in living room near drugs was "used"). We granted certiorari to clarify the meaning of "use" under § 924(c)(1). 514 U.S. 1062 (1995).

## II

Section 924(c)(1) requires the imposition of specified penalties if the defendant, "during and in relation to any crime of violence or drug trafficking crime ... uses or carries a firearm." Petitioners argue that "use" signifies active employment of a firearm. Respondent opposes that definition and defends the proximity and accessibility test adopted by the Court of Appeals. We agree with petitioners, and hold that § 924(c)(1) requires evidence sufficient to show an *active employment* of the firearm by the defendant, a use that makes the firearm an operative factor in relation to the predicate offense.

This case is not the first one in which the Court has grappled with the proper understanding of "use" in § 924(c)(1). In *Smith,* we faced the question whether the barter of a gun for drugs was a "use," and concluded that it was. Smith v. United States, 508 U.S. 223 (1993). As the debate in *Smith* illustrated, the word "use" poses some interpretational difficulties because of the different meanings attributable to it. Consider the paradoxical statement: "I *use* a gun to protect my house, but I've never had to *use* it." "Use" draws meaning from its context, and we will look not only to the word itself, but also to the statute and the sentencing scheme, to determine the meaning Congress intended.

We agree with the majority below that "use" must connote more than mere possession of a firearm by a person who commits a drug offense. See 36 F.3d, at 109; accord, United States v. Castro–Lara, *supra,* at 983; United States v. Theodoropoulos, 866 F.2d 587, 597–598 (C.A.3 1989); United States v. Wilson, 884 F.2d 174, 177 (C.A.5 1989). Had Congress intended possession alone to trigger liability under § 924(c)(1), it easily could have so provided. This obvious conclusion is supported by the frequent use of the term "possess" in the gun-crime statutes to describe prohibited gun-related conduct. See, *e.g.,* §§ 922(g), 922(j), 922(k), 922(o)(1), 930(a), 930(b).

Where the Court of Appeals erred was not in its conclusion that "use" means more than mere possession, but in its standard for evaluating whether the involvement of a firearm amounted to something more than mere possession. Its proximity and accessibility standard provides almost no limitation on the kind of possession that would be criminalized; in practice, nearly every possession of a firearm by a person engaged in drug trafficking would satisfy the standard, "thereby eras[ing] the line that the statutes, and the courts, have tried to draw." *United States* v. *McFadden, supra,* at 469 (Breyer, C.J., dissenting). Rather than requiring actual use, the District of Columbia Circuit would criminalize "simpl[e] possession with a floating intent to use." 36 F.3d, at 121 (Williams, J., dissenting). The shortcomings of this test are succinctly explained in Judge Williams' dissent:

"While the majority attempts to fine-tune the concept of facilitation (and thereby, use) through its twin guideposts of proximity and accessibility, the ultimate result is that possession amounts to 'use' because possession enhances the defendant's confidence. Had Congress intended that, all it need have mentioned is possession. In this regard, the majority's test is either so broad as to assure automatic affirmance of any jury conviction or, if not so broad, is unlikely to produce a clear guideline." *Id.,* at 124–125 (citations omitted).

An evidentiary standard for finding "use" that is satisfied in almost every case by evidence of mere possession does not adhere to the obvious congressional intent to require more than possession to trigger the statute's application.

This conclusion—that a conviction for "use" of a firearm under § 924(c)(1) requires more than a showing of mere possession—requires us to answer a more difficult question. What must the Government show, beyond mere possession, to establish "use" for the purposes of the statute? We conclude that the language, context, and history of § 924(c)(1) indicate that the Government must show active employment of the firearm.

We start, as we must, with the language of the statute. See United States v. Ron Pair Enterprises, Inc., 489 U.S. 235, 241 (1989). The word "use" in the statute must be given its "ordinary or natural" meaning, a meaning variously defined as "[t]o convert to one's service," "to employ," "to avail oneself of," and "to carry out a purpose or action by means of." *Smith, supra,* at ___ (slip op., at 5) (internal quotation marks omitted) (citing Webster's New International Dictionary of English Language 2806 (2d ed. 1949) and Black's Law Dictionary 1541 (6th ed. 1990)). These various definitions of "use" imply action and implementation. See also *McFadden,* 13 F.3d, at 467 (Breyer, C.J., dissenting) ("the ordinary meanings of the words 'use and carry' ... connote activity beyond simple possession").

We consider not only the bare meaning of the word but also its placement and purpose in the statutory scheme. " '[T]he meaning of statutory language, plain or not, depends on context.' " Brown v. Gardner, 513 U.S. 115 (1994) (slip op., at 3) (citing King v. St. Vincent's Hosp., 502 U.S. 215, 221 (1991)). Looking past the word "use" itself, we read § 924(c)(1) with the assumption that Congress intended each of its terms to have meaning. "Judges should hesitate ... to treat [as surplusage] statutory terms in any setting, and resistance should be heightened when the words describe an element of a criminal offense." Ratzlaf v. United States, 510 U.S. 135 (1994) (slip op., at 5–6). Here, Congress has specified two types of conduct with a firearm: "uses" or "carries."

Under the Government's reading of § 924(c)(1), "use" includes even the action of a defendant who puts a gun into place to protect drugs or to embolden himself. This reading is of such breadth that no role remains for "carry." The Government admits that the meanings of "use" and "carry" converge under its interpretation, but maintains that this overlap is a product of the particular history of § 924(c)(1). Therefore, the Government argues, the canon of construction that instructs that "a legislature is presumed to have used no superfluous words," Platt v. Union Pacific R.

Co., 99 U.S. 48, 58 (1879), is inapplicable. Brief for United States 24–25. We disagree. Nothing here indicates that Congress, when it provided these two terms, intended that they be understood to be redundant.

We assume that Congress used two terms because it intended each term to have a particular, nonsuperfluous meaning. While a broad reading of "use" undermines virtually any function for "carry," a more limited, active interpretation of "use" preserves a meaningful role for "carries" as an alternative basis for a charge. Under the interpretation we enunciate today, a firearm can be used without being carried, *e.g.,* when an offender has a gun on display during a transaction, or barters with a firearm without handling it; and a firearm can be carried without being used, *e.g.,* when an offender keeps a gun hidden in his clothing throughout a drug transaction.

This reading receives further support from the context of § 924(c)(1). As we observed in *Smith,* "using a firearm" should not have a "different meaning in § 924(c)(1) than it does in § 924(d)." 508 U.S., at 235(slip op., at 11). See also *United Savings Assn.* v. *Timbers of Inwood Forest Assocs., Ltd.,* 484 U.S. 365, 371 (1988) ("A provision that may seem ambiguous in isolation is often clarified by the remainder of the statutory scheme"). Section 924(d)(1) provides for the forfeiture of any firearm that is "used" or "intended to be used" in certain crimes. In that provision, Congress recognized a distinction between firearms "used" in commission of a crime and those "intended to be used," and provided for forfeiture of a weapon even before it had been "used." In § 924(c)(1), however, liability attaches only to cases of actual use, not intended use, as when an offender places a firearm with the intent to use it later if necessary. The difference between the two provisions demonstrates that, had Congress meant to broaden application of the statute beyond actual "use," Congress could and would have so specified, as it did in § 924(d)(1).

The amendment history of § 924(c) casts further light on Congress' intended meaning. The original version, passed in 1968, read:

"(c) Whoever—

"(1) uses a firearm to commit any felony which may be prosecuted in a court of the United States, or

"(2) carries a firearm unlawfully during the commission of any felony which may be prosecuted in a court of the United States, shall be sentenced to a term of imprisonment for not less than one year nor more than 10 years." § 102, 82 Stat. 1224.

The phrase "uses to commit" indicates that Congress originally intended to reach the situation where the firearm was actively employed during commission of the crime. This original language would not have stretched so far as to cover a firearm that played no detectable role in the crime's commission. For example, a defendant who stored a gun in a nearby closet for retrieval in case the deal went sour would not have "use[d] a firearm to commit" a crime. This version also shows that "use" and "carry" were employed with distinctly different meanings.

Congress' 1984 amendment to § 924(c) altered the scope of predicate offenses from "any felony" to "any crime of violence," removed the "unlawfully" requirement, merged the "uses" and "carries" prongs, substituted "during and in relation to" the predicate crimes for the earlier provisions linking the firearm to the predicate crimes, and raised the minimum sentence to five years. § 1005(a), 98 Stat. 2138–2139. The Government argues that this amendment stripped "uses" and "carries" of the qualifications ("to commit" and "unlawfully during") that originally gave them distinct meanings, so that the terms should now be understood to overlap. Of course, in *Smith* we recognized that Congress' subsequent amendments to § 924(c) employed "use" expansively, to cover both use as a weapon and use as an item of barter. See *Smith, supra,* at ___ (slip op., at 12–13). But there is no evidence to indicate that Congress intended to expand the meaning of "use" so far as to swallow up any significance for "carry." If Congress had intended to deprive "use" of its active connotations, it could have simply substituted a more appropriate term—"possession"—to cover the conduct it wished to reach.

The Government nonetheless argues that our observation in *Smith* that "§ 924(c)(1)'s language sweeps broadly," 508 U.S. at 229 (slip op., at 5), precludes limiting "use" to active employment. But our decision today is not inconsistent with *Smith.* Although there we declined to limit "use" to the meaning "use as a weapon," our interpretation of § 924(c)(1) nonetheless adhered to an active meaning of the term. In *Smith,* it was clear that the defendant had "used" the gun; the question was whether that particular use (bartering) came within the meaning of § 924(c)(1). *Smith* did not address the question we face today of what evidence is required to permit a jury to find that a firearm had been used at all.

To illustrate the activities that fall within the definition of "use" provided here, we briefly describe some of the activities that fall within "active employment" of a firearm, and those that do not.

The active-employment understanding of "use" certainly includes brandishing, displaying, bartering, striking with, and most obviously, firing or attempting to fire, a firearm. We note that this reading compels the conclusion that even an offender's reference to a firearm in his possession could satisfy § 924(c)(1). Thus, a reference to a firearm calculated to bring about a change in the circumstances of the predicate offense is a "use," just as the silent but obvious and forceful presence of a gun on a table can be a "use."

The example given above—"I *use* a gun to protect my house, but I've never had to *use* it"—shows that "use" takes on different meanings depending on context. In the first phrase of the example, "use" refers to an ongoing, inactive function fulfilled by a firearm. It is this sense of "use" that underlies the Government's contention that "placement for protection"—*i.e.,* placement of a firearm to provide a sense of security or to embolden—constitutes a "use." It follows, according to this argument, that a gun placed in a closet is "used," because its mere presence emboldens or protects its owner. We disagree. Under this reading, mere possession of a firearm by a drug offender, at or near the site of a drug crime or its proceeds or paraphernalia, is a "use" by the offender, because its availability for intimidation, attack, or defense would always, presumably, embolden or comfort the offender. But the inert presence of a firearm, without more, is not enough to trigger § 924(c)(1). Perhaps the nonactive nature of this asserted "use" is clearer if a synonym is used: storage. A defendant cannot be charged under § 924(c)(1) merely for storing a weapon near drugs or drug proceeds. Storage of a firearm, without its more active employment, is not reasonably distinguishable from possession.

A possibly more difficult question arises where an offender conceals a gun nearby to be at the ready for an imminent confrontation. Cf. 36 F.3d, at 119 (Wald, J., dissenting) (discussing distinction between firearm's accessibility to drugs or drug proceeds, and its accessibility to defendant). Some might argue that the offender has "actively employed" the gun by hiding it where he can grab and use it if necessary. In our view, "use" cannot extend to encompass this action. If the gun is not disclosed or mentioned by the offender, it is not actively employed, and it is not "used." To conclude otherwise would distort the language of the statute as well as create an impossible line-drawing problem. How "at the ready" was the firearm? Within arm's reach? In the room? In the house? How long before the confrontation did he place it there? Five minutes or 24 hours? Placement for later active use does not constitute "use." An alternative rationale for why "placement at the ready" is a "use"—that such placement is made with the intent to put the firearm to a future active use—also fails. As discussed above, § 924(d)(1) demonstrates that Congress knew how to draft a statute to reach a firearm that was "intended to be used." In § 924(c)(1), it chose not to include that term, but instead established the five-year mandatory minimum only for those defendants who actually "use" the firearm.

While it is undeniable that the active-employment reading of "use" restricts the scope of § 924(c)(1), the Government often has other means available to charge offenders who mix guns and drugs. The "carry" prong of § 924(c)(1), for example, brings some offenders who would not satisfy the "use" prong within the reach of the statute. And Sentencing Guidelines § 2D1.1(b)(1) provides an enhancement for a person convicted of certain drug-trafficking offenses if a firearm was possessed during the offense. United States Sentencing Commission, Guidelines Manual § 2D1.1(b)(1) (Nov. 1994). But the word "use" in § 924(c)(1) cannot support the extended applications that prosecutors have sometimes placed on it, in order to penalize drug-trafficking offenders for firearms possession.

The test set forth by the Court of Appeals renders "use" virtually synonymous with "possession" and makes any role for "carry" superfluous. The language of § 924(c)(1), supported by its history and context, compels the conclusion that Congress intended "use" in the active sense of "to avail oneself of." To sustain a conviction under the "use" prong of § 924(c)(1), the Government must show that the defendant actively employed the firearm during and in relation to the predicate crime.

## III

Having determined that "use" denotes active employment, we must conclude that the evidence was insufficient to support either Bailey's or Robinson's conviction for "use" under § 924(c)(1).

The police stopped Bailey for a traffic offense and arrested him after finding cocaine in the driver's compartment of his car. The police then found a firearm inside a bag in the locked car trunk. There was no evidence that Bailey actively employed the firearm in any way. In Robinson's case, the unloaded, holstered firearm that provided the basis for her § 924(c)(1) conviction was found locked in a footlocker in a bedroom closet. No evidence showed that Robinson had actively employed the firearm. We reverse both judgments.

Bailey and Robinson were each charged under both the "use" and "carry" prongs of § 924(c)(1). Because the Court of Appeals did not consider liability under the "carry" prong of § 924(c)(1) for Bailey or Robinson, we remand for consideration of that basis for upholding the convictions.

*It is so ordered.*

### Notes and Questions

**1.** Do you understand why the term "use" as used in 18 U.S.C. § 924(c)(1) does not encompass all the meanings the term used to have?

**2.** 15 U.S.C. § 1644(a) imposes criminal liability on any person who:

knowingly in a transaction affecting interstate or foreign commerce, uses or attempts or conspires to use any counterfeit, fictitious, altered, forged, lost, stolen, or fraudulently obtained credit card to obtain money, goods, services, or anything else of value which within any one-year period has an aggregating value of $1,000 or more.

"Credit card" is defined as "any card, plate, coupon book or other credit device existing for the purpose of obtaining money, property, labor, or services on credit." 15 U.S.C. § 1702(k). Can a person be convicted under this statute if the government can show that the defendant made use of a credit card number, but not the credit card itself? See United States v. Bice-Bey, 701 F.2d 1086 (4th Cir.1983).

## Muscarello v. United States

Supreme Court of the United States, 1998.
524 U.S. 125, 118 S.Ct. 1911, 141 L.Ed.2d 111.

■ Justice Breyer delivered the opinion of the Court.

A provision in the firearms chapter of the federal criminal code imposes a 5–year mandatory prison term upon a person who "uses or carries a firearm" "during and in relation to" a "drug trafficking crime." 18 U.S.C. § 924(c)(1). The question before us is whether the phrase "carries a firearm" is limited to the carrying of firearms on the person. We hold that it is not so limited. Rather, it also applies to a person who knowingly possesses and conveys firearms in a vehicle, including in the locked glove compartment or trunk of a car, which the person accompanies.

The question arises in two cases, which we have consolidated for argument. The defendant in the first case, Frank J. Muscarello, unlawfully sold marijuana, which he carried in his truck to the place of sale. Police officers found a handgun locked in the truck's glove compartment. During plea proceedings, Muscarello admitted that he had "carried" the gun "for protection in relation" to the drug offense, though he later claimed to the contrary, and added that, in any event, his "carrying" of the gun in the glove compartment did not fall within the scope of the statutory word "carries."

The defendants in the second case, Donald Cleveland and Enrique Gray–Santana, placed several guns in a bag, put the bag in the trunk of a car, and then traveled by car to a proposed drug-sale point, where they intended to steal drugs from the sellers. Federal agents at the scene stopped them, searched the cars, found the guns and drugs, and arrested them.

In both cases the Courts of Appeals found that the defendants had "carried" the guns during and in relation to a drug trafficking offense. 106 F.3d 636, 639 (C.A.5 1997); 106 F.3d 1056, 1068 (C.A.1 1997). We granted certiorari to determine whether the fact that the guns were found in the locked glove compartment, or the trunk, of a car, precludes application of § 924(c)(1). We conclude that it does not.

## A.

We begin with the statute's language. The parties vigorously contest the ordinary English meaning of the phrase "carries a firearm." Because they essentially agree that Congress intended the phrase to convey its ordinary, and not some special legal, meaning, and because they argue the linguistic point at length, we too have looked into the matter in more than usual depth. Although the word "carry" has many different meanings, only two are relevant here. When one uses the word in the first, or primary, meaning, one can, as a matter of ordinary English, "carry firearms" in a wagon, car, truck, or other vehicle that one accompanies. When one uses the word in a different, rather special, way, to mean, for example, "bearing" or (in slang) "packing" (as in "packing a gun"), the matter is less clear. But, for reasons we shall set out below, we believe Congress intended to use the word in its primary sense and not in this latter, special way.

Consider first the word's primary meaning. The Oxford English Dictionary gives as its first definition "convey, originally by cart or wagon, hence in any vehicle, by ship, on horseback, etc." 2 Oxford English Dictionary 919 (2d ed. 1989); see also Webster's Third New International Dictionary 343 (1986) (first definition: "move while supporting (as in a vehicle or in one's hands or arms)"); The Random House Dictionary of the English Language Unabridged 319 (2d ed. 1987) (first definition: "to take or support from one place to another; convey; transport").

The origin of the word "carries" explains why the first, or basic, meaning of the word "carry" includes conveyance in a vehicle. See The Barnhart Dictionary of Etymology 146 (1988) (tracing the word from Latin "carum," which means "car" or "cart"); 2 Oxford English Dictionary, supra, at 919 (tracing the word from Old French "carier" and the late Latin "carricare," which meant to "convey in a car"); The Oxford Dictionary of English Etymology 148 (C. Onions ed.1966) (same); The Barnhart Dictionary of Etymology, supra, at 143 (explaining that the term "car" has been used to refer to the automobile since 1896).

The greatest of writers have used the word with this meaning. See, e.g., the King James Bible, 2 Kings 9:28 ("His servants carried him in a chariot to Jerusalem"); id., Isaiah 30:6 ("They will carry their riches upon the shoulders of young asses"). Robinson Crusoe says, "with my boat, I carry'd away every Thing." D. Defoe, Robinson Crusoe 174 (J. Crowley ed. 1972). And the owners of Queequeg's ship, Melville writes, "had lent him a [wheelbarrow], in which to carry his heavy chest to his boarding-house." H. Melville, Moby Dick 43 (U. Chicago 1952). This Court, too, has spoken of the "carrying" of drugs in a car or in its "trunk." California v. Acevedo, 500 U.S. 565, 572–573, 114 L. Ed. 2d 619, 111 S. Ct. 1982 (1991); Florida v. Jimeno, 500 U.S. 248, 249, 114 L. Ed. 2d 297, 111 S. Ct. 1801 (1991).

These examples do not speak directly about carrying guns. But there is nothing linguistically special about the fact that weapons, rather than drugs, are being carried. Robinson Crusoe might have carried a gun in his boat; Queequeg might have borrowed a wheelbarrow in which to carry, not a chest, but a harpoon. And, to make certain that there is no special ordinary English restriction (unmentioned in dictionaries) upon the use of "carry" in respect to guns, we have surveyed modern press usage, albeit crudely, by searching computerized newspaper databases—both the New York Times database in Lexis/Nexis, and the "US News" database in Westlaw. We looked for sentences in which the words "carry," "vehicle," and "weapon" (or variations thereof) all appear. We found thousands of such sentences, and random sampling suggests that many, perhaps more than one third, are sentences used to convey the meaning at issue here, i.e., the carrying of guns in a car.

Now consider a different, somewhat special meaning of the word "carry"—a meaning upon which the linguistic arguments of petitioners and the dissent must rest. The Oxford English Dictionary's twenty-sixth definition of "carry" is "bear, wear, hold up, or sustain, as one moves about; habitually to bear about with one." 2 Oxford English Dictionary, supra, at 921. Webster's defines "carry" as "to move while supporting," not just in a vehicle, but also "in one's hands or arms." Webster's Third New International Dictionary, supra, at 343. And Black's Law Dictionary defines the entire phrase "carry arms or weapons" as

> "To wear, bear or carry them upon the person or in the clothing or in a pocket, for the purpose of use, or for the purpose of being armed and ready for offensive or defensive action in case of a conflict with another person." Black's Law Dictionary 214 (6th ed. 1990).

These special definitions, however, do not purport to limit the "carrying of arms" to the circumstances they describe. No one doubts that one who bears arms on his person "carries a weapon." But to say that is not to deny that one may also "carry a weapon" tied to the saddle of a horse or placed in a bag in a car.

Nor is there any linguistic reason to think that Congress intended to limit the word "carries" in the statute to any of these special definitions. To the contrary, all these special definitions embody a form of an important, but secondary, meaning of "carry," a meaning that suggests support rather than movement or transportation, as when, for example, a column "carries" the weight of an arch. 2 Oxford English Dictionary, supra, at 919, 921. In this sense a gangster might "carry" a gun (in colloquial language, he might "pack a gun") even though he does not move from his chair. It is difficult to believe, however, that Congress intended to limit the statutory word to this definition—imposing special punishment upon the comatose gangster while ignoring drug lords who drive to a sale carrying an arsenal of weapons in their van.

We recognize, as the dissent emphasizes, that the word "carry" has other meanings as well. But those other meanings, (e.g., "carry all he knew," "carries no colours"), see post, at 6, are not relevant here. And the fact that speakers often do not add to the phrase "carry a gun" the words "in a car" is of no greater relevance here than the fact that millions of Americans did not see Muscarello carry a gun in his car. The relevant linguistic facts are that the word "carry" in its ordinary sense includes carrying in a car and that the word, used in its ordinary sense, keeps the same meaning whether one carries a gun, a suitcase, or a banana.

Given the ordinary meaning of the word "carry," it is not surprising to find that the Federal Circuit Courts of Appeals have unanimously concluded that "carry" is not limited to the carrying of weapons directly on the person but can include their carriage in a car. United States v. Toms, 136 F.3d 176, 181 (C.A.D.C.1998); United States v. Foster, 133 F.3d 704, 708 (C.A.9 1998); United States v. Eyer, 113 F.3d 470, 476 (C.A.3 1997); 106 F.3d at 1066 *(case below)*; 106 F.3d at 639 *(case below)*; United States v. Malcuit, 104 F.3d 880, 885, *rehearing en banc granted,* 116 F.3d 163 (C.A.6 1997), United States v. Mitchell, 104 F.3d 649, 653–654 (C.A.4 1997); United States v. Molina, 102 F.3d 928, 932 (C.A.7 1996); United States v. Willis, 89 F.3d 1371, 1379 (C.A.8 1996); United States v. Miller, 84 F.3d 1244, 1259–1260 (1996), *overruled on other grounds,* United States v. Holland, 116 F.3d 1353 (C.A.10 1997); United States v. Giraldo, 80 F.3d 667, 676–677 (C.A.2 1996); United States v. Farris, 77 F.3d 391, 395–396 (C.A.11 1996).

**B.**

We now explore more deeply the purely legal question of whether Congress intended to use the word "carry" in its ordinary sense, or whether it intended to limit the scope of the phrase to instances in which a gun is carried "on the person." We conclude that neither the statute's basic purpose nor its legislative history support circumscribing the scope of the word "carry" by applying an "on the person" limitation.

This Court has described the statute's basic purpose broadly, as an effort to combat the "dangerous combination" of "drugs and guns." Smith v. United States, 508 U.S. 223, 240, 124 L. Ed. 2d 138, 113 S. Ct. 2050 (1993). And the provision's chief legislative sponsor has said that the provision seeks "to persuade the man who is tempted to commit a Federal felony to leave his gun at home." 114 Cong. Rec. 22231 (1968) (Rep. Poff).

. . .

From the perspective of any such purpose (persuading a criminal "to leave his gun at home") what sense would it make for this statute to penalize one who walks with a gun in a bag to the site of a drug sale, but to ignore a similar individual who, like defendant Gray–Santana, travels to a similar site with a similar gun in a similar bag, but instead of walking, drives there with the gun in his car? How persuasive is a punishment that is without effect until a drug dealer who has brought his gun to a sale (indeed has it available for use) actually takes it from the trunk (or unlocks the glove compartment) of his car? It is difficult to say that, considered as a class, those who prepare, say, to sell drugs by placing guns in their cars are less dangerous, or less deserving of punishment, than those who carry handguns on their person.

We have found no significant indication elsewhere in the legislative history of any more narrowly focused relevant purpose. We have found an instance in which a legislator referred to the statute as applicable when an individual "has a firearm on his person," Ibid. (Rep. Meskill); an instance in which a legislator speaks of "a criminal who takes a gun in his hand," id., at 22239 (Rep. Pucinski); and a reference in the Senate Report to a "gun carried in a pocket." S. Rep No. 98–225, p. 314, n. 10 (1983); see also 114 Cong. Rec. 21788, 21789 (1968) (references to gun "carrying" without more). But in these instances no one purports to define the scope of the term "carries": and the examples of guns carried on the person are not used to illustrate the reach of the term "carries" but to illustrate, or to criticize, a different aspect of the statute.

Regardless, in other instances, legislators suggest that the word "carries" has a broader scope. One legislator indicates that the statute responds in part to the concerns of law enforcement personnel, who had urged that "carrying short firearms in motor vehicles be classified as carrying such weapons concealed." Id., at 22242 (Rep. May). Another criticizes a version of the proposed statute by suggesting it might apply to drunken driving, and gives as an example a drunken driver who has a "gun in his car." Id., at 21792 (Rep. Yates). Others describe the statute as criminalizing gun "possession"—a term that could stretch beyond both the "use" of a gun and the carrying of a gun on the person. . . .

## C.

We are not convinced by petitioners' remaining arguments to the contrary. First, they say that our definition of "carry" makes it the equivalent of "transport." Yet, Congress elsewhere in related statutes used the word "transport" deliberately to signify a different, and broader, statutory coverage. The immediately preceding statutory subsection, for example, imposes a different set of penalties on one who, with an intent to commit a crime, "ships, transports, or receives a firearm" in interstate commerce. 18 U.S.C. § 924(b). Moreover, § 926A specifically "entitles" a person "not otherwise prohibited ... from transporting, shipping, or receiving a firearm" to "transport a firearm ... from any place where he may lawfully possess and carry" it to "any other place" where he may do so. Why, petitioners ask, would Congress have used the word "transport," or used both "carry" and "transport" in the same provision, if it had intended to obliterate the distinction between the two?

The short answer is that our definition does not equate "carry" and "transport." "Carry" implies personal agency and some degree of possession, whereas "transport" does not have such a limited connotation and, in addition, implies the movement of goods in bulk over great distances. ... If Smith, for example, calls a parcel delivery service, which sends a truck to Smith's house to pick up Smith's package and take it to Los Angeles, one might say that Smith has shipped the package and the parcel delivery service has transported the package. But only the truck driver has "carried" the package in the sense of "carry" that we believe Congress intended. Therefore, "transport" is a broader category that includes "carry" but also encompasses other activity.

The dissent refers to § 926A and to another statute where Congress used the word "transport" rather than "carry" to describe the movement of firearms. 18 U.S.C. §§ 925(a)(2)(B); post, at 8–9. According to the dissent, had Congress intended "carry" to have the meaning we give it, Congress would not have needed to use a different word in these provisions. But as we have discussed above, we believe the word "transport" is broader than the word "carry."

And, if Congress intended "carry" to have the limited definition the dissent contends, it would have been quite unnecessary to add the proviso in § 926A requiring a person, to be exempt from penalties, to store her firearm in a locked container not immediately accessible. See § 926A (quoted in full at post, 8–9) (exempting from criminal penalties one who transports a firearm from a place where "he may lawfully possess and carry such firearm" but not exempting the "transportation" of a firearm if it is "readily accessible or is directly accessible from the passenger compartment of transporting vehicle"). The statute simply could have said that such a person may not "carry" a firearm. But, of course, Congress did not say this because that is not what "carry" means.

As we interpret the statutory scheme, it makes sense. Congress has imposed a variable penalty with no mandatory minimum sentence upon a person who "transports" (or "ships" or "receives") a firearm knowing it will be used to commit any "offense punishable by imprisonment for [more than] ... one year," § 924(b), and it has imposed a 5–year mandatory minimum sentence upon one who "carries" a firearm "during and in relation to" a "drug trafficking crime," § 924(c). The first subsection imposes a less strict sentencing regime upon one who, say, ships firearms by mail for use in a crime elsewhere; the latter subsection imposes a mandatory sentence upon one who, say, brings a weapon with him (on his person or in his car) to the site of a drug sale.

Second, petitioners point out that, in Bailey v. United States, 516 U.S. 137, 133 L. Ed. 2d 472, 116 S. Ct. 501 (1995), we considered the related phrase "uses ... a firearm" found in the same statutory provision now before us. See 18 U.S.C. § 924(c)(1) ("uses or carries a firearm"). We construed the term "use" narrowly, limiting its application to the "active employment" of a firearm. *Bailey*, 516 U.S. at 144. Petitioners argue that it would be anomalous to construe broadly the word "carries," its statutory next-door neighbor.

In Bailey, however, we limited "use" of a firearm to "active employment" in part because we assumed "that Congress ... intended each term to have a particular, non-superfluous meaning." *Id.*, at 146. A broader interpretation of "use," we said, would have swallowed up the term "carry." Ibid. But "carry" as we interpret that word does not swallow up the term "use." "Use" retains the same independent meaning we found for it in Bailey, where we provided examples involving the displaying or the bartering of a gun. Ibid. "Carry" also retains an independent meaning, for, under Bailey, carrying a gun in a car does not necessarily involve the gun's "active employment." More importantly, having construed "use" narrowly in Bailey, we cannot also construe "carry" narrowly without undercutting the statute's basic objective. For the narrow interpretation would remove the act of carrying a gun in a car entirely from the statute's reach, leaving a gap in coverage that we do not believe Congress intended.

Third, petitioners say that our reading of the statute would extend its coverage to passengers on buses, trains, or ships, who have placed a firearm, say, in checked luggage. To extend this statute so far, they argue, is unfair, going well beyond what Congress likely would have thought possible. They add that some lower courts, thinking approximately the same, have limited the scope of "carries" to instances where a gun in a car is immediately accessible, thereby most likely excluding from coverage a gun carried in a car's trunk or locked glove compartment. See, e.g., *Foster*, 133 F.3d at 708 (concluding that person "carries" a firearm in a car only if the firearm is immediately accessible); *Giraldo*, 80 F.3d at 676 (same).

In our view, this argument does not take adequate account of other limiting words in the statute—words that make the statute applicable only where a defendant "carries" a gun *both* "during *and* in relation to" a drug crime. § 924(c)(1) (emphasis added). Congress added these words in part to prevent prosecution where guns"played" no part in the crime. See S. Rep. No. 98–225, at 314, n. 10; cf. United States v. Stewart, 779 F.2d 538, 539 (C.A.9 1985) (Kennedy, J.) (observing that " 'in relation to' " was "added to allay explicitly the concern that a person could be prosecuted ... for committing an entirely unrelated crime while in possession of a firearm"), overruled in part on other grounds, United States v. Hernandez, 80 F.3d 1253, 1257 (C.A.9 1996).

Once one takes account of the words "during" and "in relation to," it no longer seems beyond Congress' likely intent, or otherwise unfair, to interpret the statute as we have done. If one carries a gun in a car "during" and "in relation to" a drug sale, for example, the fact that the gun is carried in the car's trunk or locked glove compartment seems not only logically difficult to distinguish from the immediately accessible gun, but also beside the point.

At the same time, the narrow interpretation creates its own anomalies. The statute, for example, defines "firearm" to include a "bomb," "grenade," "rocket having a propellant charge of more than four ounces," or "missile having an explosive or incendiary charge of more than one-quarter ounce," where such device is "explosive," "incendiary," or delivers "poison gas." 18 U.S.C. § 921(a)(4)(A). On petitioners' reading, the "carry" provision would not apply to instances where drug lords, engaged in a major transaction, took with them "firearms" such as these, which most likely could not be carried on the person.

Fourth, petitioners argue that we should construe the word "carry" to mean "immediately accessible." And, as we have said, they point out that several Circuit Courts of Appeals have limited the statute's scope in this way. See, e.g., *Foster, supra*, at 708; *Giraldo, supra*, at 676. That interpretation, however, is difficult to square with the statute's language, for one "carries" a gun in the glove compartment whether or not that glove compartment is locked. Nothing in the statute's history suggests that Congress intended that limitation. And, for reasons pointed out above, see supra, at 11, we believe that the words "during" and "in relation to" will limit the statute's application to the harms that Congress foresaw.

Finally, petitioners and the dissent invoke the "rule of lenity." The simple existence of some statutory ambiguity, however, is not sufficient to warrant application of that rule, for most statutes are ambiguous to some degree. Cf. *Smith*, 508 U.S. at 239 ("The mere possibility of articulating a narrower construction ... does not by itself make the rule of lenity applicable"). " 'The rule of lenity applies only if, "after seizing everything from which aid can be derived," ... we can make "no more than a guess as to what Congress intended." ... To invoke the rule, we must conclude that there is a " 'grievous ambiguity or uncertainty' in the statute." Staples v. United States, 511 U.S. 600, 619, n. 17, 128 L. Ed. 2d 608, 114 S. Ct. 1793 (1994) (*quoting* Chapman v. United States, 500 U.S. 453, 463, 114 L. Ed. 2d 524, 111 S. Ct. 1919 (1991)). Certainly, our decision today is based on much more than a "guess as to what Congress intended," and there is no "grievous ambiguity" here. The problem of statutory interpretation in this case is indeed no different from that in many of the criminal cases that confront us. Yet, this Court has never held that the rule of lenity automatically permits a defendant to win.' "

In sum, the "generally accepted contemporary meaning" of the word "carry" includes the carrying of a firearm in a vehicle. The purpose of this statute warrants its application in such circumstances. The limiting phrase "during and in relation to" should prevent misuse of the statute to penalize those whose conduct does not create the risks of harm at which the statute aims.

For these reasons, we conclude that the petitioners' conduct falls within the scope of the phrase "carries a firearm." The decisions of the Courts of Appeals are affirmed.

It is so ordered.

■ JUSTICE GINSBURG, with whom THE CHIEF JUSTICE, JUSTICE SCALIA, and JUSTICE SOUTER join, dissenting.

Section 924(c)(1) of Title 18, United States Code, is a punishment-enhancing provision; it imposes a mandatory five-year prison term when the defendant "during and in relation to any crime of violence or drug trafficking ... uses or carries a firearm." In Bailey v. United States, 516 U.S. 137, 133 L. Ed. 2d 472, 116 S. Ct. 501 (1995), this Court held that the term "uses," in the context of § 924(c)(1), means "active employment" of the firearm. In today's cases we confront a related question: What does the term "carries" mean in the context of § 924(c)(1), the enhanced punishment prescription again at issue.

It is uncontested that § 924(c)(1) applies when the defendant bears a firearm, i.e., carries the weapon on or about his person "for the purpose of being armed and ready for offensive or defensive action in case of a conflict." Black's Law Dictionary 214 (6th ed. 1990) (defining the phrase "carry arms or weapons"); see ante, at 5. The Court holds that, in addition, "carries a firearm," in the context of § 924(c)(1), means personally transporting, possessing, or keeping a firearm in a vehicle, anyplace in a vehicle.

Without doubt, "carries" is a word of many meanings, definable to mean or include carting about in a vehicle. But that encompassing definition is not a ubiquitously necessary one. Nor, in my judgment, is it a proper construction of "carries" as the term appears in § 924(c)(1). In line with Bailey and the principle of lenity the Court has long followed, I would confine "carries a firearm," for § 924(c)(1) purposes, to the undoubted meaning of that expression in the relevant context. I would read the words to indicate not merely keeping arms on one's premises or in one's vehicle, but bearing them in such manner as to be ready for use as a weapon.

# I

## A

I note first what is at stake for petitioners. The question before the Court "is not whether possession of a gun [on the drug offender's premises or in his car, during and in relation to commission of the offense,] means a longer sentence for a convicted drug dealer. It most certainly does.... Rather, the question concerns which sentencing statute governs the precise length of the extra term of punishment," § 924(c)(1)'s "blunt 'mandatory minimum'" five-year sentence, or the more finely tuned "sentencing guideline statutes, under which extra punishment for drug-related gun possession varies with the seriousness of the drug crime." United States v. McFadden, 13 F.3d 463, 466 (C.A.1 1994) (Breyer, C. J., dissenting).

Accordingly, there would be no "gap," see ante, at 12, no relevant conduct "ignored," see ante, at 8, were the Court to reject the Government's broad reading of § 924(c)(1). To be more specific, as cogently explained on another day by today's opinion writer:

"The special 'mandatory minimum' sentencing statute says that anyone who 'uses or carries' a gun 'during and in relation to any ... drug trafficking crime' must receive a mandatory five-year prison term added on to his drug crime sentence. 18 U.S.C. § 924(c). At the same time, the Sentencing Guidelines, promulgated under the authority of a different statute, 28 U.S.C. § 994, provide for a two-level (i.e., a 30% to 40%) sentence enhancement where a 'firearm ... was possessed' by a drug offender, U.S. S. G. § 2D1.1(b)(1), unless the possession clearly was not 'connected with the [drug] offense.' " McFadden, 13 F.3d at 467 (Breyer, C. J., dissenting).

In Muscarello's case, for example, the underlying drug crimes involved the distribution of 3.6 kilograms of marijuana, and therefore carried a base offense level of 12. See United States Sentencing Commission, Guidelines Manual § 2D1.1(a)(3) (Nov. 1995). After adjusting for Muscarello's acceptance of responsibility, see id., § 3E1.1(a), his final offense level was 10, placing him in the 6–to–12 month sentencing range. See id., ch. 5, pt. A. The two-level enhancement for possessing a firearm, id., § 2D1.1(b)(1), would have increased his final offense level to 12 (a sentencing range of 10 to 16 months). In other words, the less rigid (tailored to "the seriousness of the drug crime," McFadden, 13 F.3d at 466) Guidelines regime would have added four months to Muscarello's prison time, in contrast to the five-year minimum addition the Court's reading of § 924(c)(1) mandates.

In sum, drug traffickers will receive significantly longer sentences if they are caught travelling in vehicles in which they have placed firearms. The question that divides the Court concerns the proper reference for enhancement in the cases at hand, the Guidelines or § 924(c)(1).

## B

Unlike the Court, I do not think dictionaries,[2] surveys of press reports,[3]

---

**2.**  I note, however, that the only legal dictionary the Court cites, Black's Law Dictionary, defines "carry arms or weapons" restrictively.

**3.**  Many newspapers, the New York Times among them, have published stories using "transport," rather than "carry," to describe gun placements resembling petitioners'. See, e.g., Atlanta Constitution, Feb. 27, 1998, p. 9D, col. 2 ("House members last week expanded gun laws by allowing weapons to be *carried into restaurants or transported*

*anywhere in cars*."); Chicago Tribune, June 12, 1997, sports section, p. 13 ("Disabled hunters with permission to hunt from a standing vehicle would be able to *transport a shotgun in an all-terrain vehicle* as long as the gun is unloaded and the breech is open."); Colorado Springs Gazette Telegraph, Aug. 4, 1996, p. C10 (British gun laws require "locked steel cases bolted onto a car for *transporting guns from home to shooting range*."); Detroit News, Oct. 26, 1997, p. D14 ("It is unlawful to *carry afield or transport a*

or the Bible[4] tell us, dispositively, what "carries" means embedded in § 924(c)(1). On definitions, "carry" in legal formulations could mean, inter alia, transport, possess, have in stock, prolong (carry over), be infectious, or wear or bear on one's person.[5] At issue here is not "carries" at large but "carries a firearm." The Court's computer search of newspapers is revealing in this light. Carrying guns in a car showed up as the meaning "perhaps more than one third" of the time. Ante, at 4. One is left to wonder what meaning showed up some two thirds of the time. Surely a most familiar meaning is, as the Constitution's Second Amendment ("keep and *bear* Arms") (emphasis added) and Black's Law Dictionary, at 214, indicate: "wear, bear, or carry ... upon the person or in the clothing or in a pocket, for the purpose ... of being armed and ready for offensive or defensive action in a case of conflict with another person."

On lessons from literature, a scan of Bartlett's and other quotation collections shows how highly selective the Court's choices are. See ante, at 3–4. If "the greatest of writers" have used "carry" to mean convey or transport in a vehicle, so have they used the hydra-headed word to mean, inter alia, carry in one's hand, arms, head, heart, or soul, sans vehicle. Consider, among countless examples:

> "He shall gather the lambs with his arm, and carry them in his bosom." The King James Bible, Isaiah 40:11.

> "And still they gaz'd, and still the wonder grew, That one small head could carry all he knew." O. Goldsmith, The Deserted Village, ll. 215–216, in The Poetical Works of Oliver Goldsmith 30 (A. Dobson ed. 1949).

> "There's a Legion that never was 'listed, That carries no colours or crest." R. Kipling, The Lost Legion, st. 1, in Rudyard Kipling's Verse, 1885–1918, p. 222 (1920).

*rifle* ... or shotgun if you have buckshot, slug, ball loads, or cut shells in possession except while traveling directly to deer camp or target range with firearm not readily available to vehicle occupants."); N. Y. Times, July 4, 1993, p. A21, col. 2 ("The gun is supposed to be *transported unloaded*, in a locked box in the trunk."); Santa Rosa Press Democrat, Sept. 28, 1996, p. B1 ("Police and volunteers ask that participants ... *transport [their guns] to the fairgrounds* in the trunks of their cars."); Worcester Telegram & Gazette, July 16, 1996, p. B3 ("Only one gun can be turned in per person. *Guns transported in a vehicle* should be locked in the trunk.") (emphasis added in all quotations).

**4.** The translator of the Good Book, it appears, bore responsibility for determining whether the servants of Ahaziah "carried" his corpse to Jerusalem. Compare ante, at 3–4, with, e.g., The New English Bible, 2 Kings 9:28 ("His servants *conveyed* his body to Jerusalem."); Saint Joseph Edition of the New American Bible ("His servants *brought* him in a chariot to Jerusalem."); Tanakh: The Holy Scriptures ("His servants *conveyed* him in a chariot to Jerusalem."); see also id., Isaiah 30:6 ("They *convey* their wealth on the backs of asses."); The New Jerusalem Bible ("They *bear* their riches on donkeys' backs.") (emphasis added in all quotations).

**5.** The dictionary to which this Court referred in Bailey v. United States, 516 U.S. 137, 145, 133 L. Ed. 2d 472, 116 S. Ct. 501 (1995), contains 32 discrete definitions of "carry," including "to make good or valid," "to bear the aspect of," and even "to bear (a hawk) on the fist." See Webster's New International Dictionary of English Language 412 (2d ed. 1949).

"There is a homely adage which runs, 'Speak softly and carry a big stick; you will go far.'" T. Roosevelt, Speech at Minnesota State Fair, Sept. 2, 1901, in J. Bartlett, Familiar Quotations 575:16 (J. Kaplan ed. 1992).[6]

These and the Court's lexicological sources demonstrate vividly that "carry" is a word commonly used to convey various messages. Such references, given their variety, are not reliable indicators of what Congress meant, in § 924(c)(1), by "carries a firearm."

## C

Noting the paradoxical statement, "'I use a gun to protect my house, but I've never had to use it,'" the Court in *Bailey*, 516 U.S. at 143, emphasized the importance of context—the statutory context. Just as "uses" was read to mean not simply "possession," but "active employment," so "carries," correspondingly, is properly read to signal the most dangerous cases—the gun at hand, ready for use as a weapon.[7] It is reasonable to comprehend Congress as having provided mandatory minimums for the most life-jeopardizing gun-connection cases (guns in or at the defendant's hand when committing an offense), leaving other, less imminently threatening, situations for the more flexible guidelines regime.[8] As the Ninth Circuit suggested, it is not apparent why possession of a gun in a drug dealer's moving vehicle would be thought more dangerous than gun possession on premises where drugs are sold: "A drug dealer who packs heat is more likely to hurt someone or provoke someone else to violence. A gun in a bag under a tarp in a truck bed [or in a bedroom closet] poses substantially less risk." United States v. Foster, 133 F.3d 704, 707 (C.A.9 1998) (en banc).[9]

---

**6.** Popular films and television productions provide corroborative illustrations. In "The Magnificent Seven," for example, O'Reilly (played by Charles Bronson) says: "You think I am brave because I carry a gun; well, your fathers are much braver because they carry responsibility, for you, your brothers, your sisters, and your mothers." See http://us.imdb.com/M/search_quotes?for=carry. And in the television series "M * A * S * H," Hawkeye Pierce (played by Alan Alda) presciently proclaims: "I will not carry a gun.... I'll carry your books, I'll carry a torch, I'll carry a tune, I'll carry on, carry over, carry forward, Cary Grant, cash and carry, carry me back to Old Virginia, I'll even 'hari-kari' if you show me how, but I will not carry a gun!" See http://www.geocities.com/Hollywood/8915/mashquotes.html.

**7.** In my view, the Government would carry its burden by proving a firearm was kept so close to the person as to approximate placement in a pocket or holster, e.g., guns carried at one's side in a briefcase or handbag, or strapped to the saddle of a horse.

**8.** The Court reports that the Courts of Appeals "have unanimously concluded that 'carry' is not limited to the carrying of weapons directly on the person." Ante, at 6–7. In Bailey, however, the Government's argument based on a similar observation did not carry the day....

**9.** The "Firearms" statutes indicate that Congress, unlike the Court, ante, at 8, recognizes that a gun in the hand is indeed more dangerous than a gun in the trunk. See, e.g., 18 U.S.C. § 926A (permitting the transportation of firearms in a vehicle, but only if "neither the firearm nor any ammunition being transported is readily accessible or is directly accessible from the passenger compartment of such transporting vehicle")

For indicators from Congress itself, it is appropriate to consider word usage in other provisions of Title 18's chapter on "Firearms." See *Bailey*, 516 U.S. at 143, 146 (interpreting § 924(c)(1) in light of 18 U.S.C. §§ 922(g), 922(j), 922(k), 922(*o*)(1), 924(d)(1), 930(a), 930(b)). The Court, however, does not derive from the statutory complex at issue its thesis that " 'carry' implies personal agency and some degree of possession, whereas 'transport' does not have such a limited connotation and, in addition, implies the movement of goods in bulk over great distances." Ante, at 9. Looking to provisions Congress enacted, one finds that the Legislature did not acknowledge or routinely adhere to the distinction the Court advances today; instead, Congress sometimes employed "transports" when, according to the Court, "carries" was the right word to use.

Section 925(a)(2)(B), for example, provides that no criminal sanction shall attend "the transportation of [a] firearm or ammunition carried out to enable a person, who lawfully received such firearm or ammunition from the Secretary of the Army, to engage in military training or in competitions." The full text of § 926A, rather than the truncated version the Court presents, see ante, at 9, is also telling:

"Notwithstanding any other provision of any or any rule or regulation of a State or any political subdivision thereof, any person who is not otherwise prohibited by this chapter from transporting, shipping, or receiving a firearm shall be entitled to transport a firearm for any lawful purpose from any place where he may lawfully possess and carry such firearm to any other place where he may lawfully possess and carry such firearm if, during such transportation the firearm is unloaded, and neither the firearm nor any ammunition being transported is readily accessible or is directly accessible from the passenger compartment of such transporting vehicle: Provided, That in the case of a vehicle without a compartment separate from the driver's compartment the firearm or ammunition shall be contained in a locked container other than the glove compartment or console."

In describing when and how a person may travel in a vehicle that contains his firearm without violating the law, §§ 925(a)(2)(B) and 926A use "transport," not "carry," to "imply personal agency and some degree of possession."[10] Reading "carries" in § 924(c)(1) to mean "on or about [one's]

---

**10.** The Court asserts that " 'transport' is a broader category that includes 'carry' but encompasses other activity." Ante, at 10. "Carry," however, is not merely a subset of "transport" A person seated at a desk with a gun in hand or pocket is carrying the gun, but is not transporting it. Yes, the words "carry" and "transport" often can be employed interchangeably, as can the words "carry" and "use." But in Bailey, this Court settled on constructions that gave "carry" and "use" independent meanings. See Bailey, 516 U.S. at 145–146. Without doubt, Congress is alert to the discrete meanings of "transport" and "carry" in the context of vehicles, as the Legislature's placement of each word in § 926A illustrates. The narrower reading of "carry" preserves discrete meanings for the two words, while in the context of vehicles the Court's interpretation of "carry" is altogether synonymous with "transport." Tellingly, when referring to firearms traveling in vehicles, the "Firearms" statutes routinely use a form of "transport"; they never use a form of "carry."

person" is fully compatible with these and other "Firearms" statutes.[11] For example, under § 925(a)(2)(B), one could carry his gun to a car, transport it to the shooting competition, and use it to shoot targets. Under the conditions of § 926A, one could transport her gun in a car, but under no circumstances could the gun be readily accessible while she travels in the car. "Courts normally try to read language in different, but related, statutes, so as best to reconcile those statutes, in light of their purposes and of common sense." *McFadden*, 13 F.3d at 467 (Breyer, C. J., dissenting). So reading the "Firearms" statutes, I would not extend the word "carries" in § 924(c)(1) to mean transports out of hand's reach in a vehicle.[12]

## II

Section 924(c)(1), as the foregoing discussion details, is not decisively clear one way or another. The sharp division in the Court on the proper reading of the measure confirms, "at the very least, . . . that the issue is subject to some doubt. Under these circumstances, we adhere to the familiar rule that, 'where there is ambiguity in a criminal statute, doubts are resolved in favor of the defendant.'" Adamo Wrecking Co. v. United States, 434 U.S. 275, 284–285, 54 L. Ed. 2d538, 98 S. Ct. 566 (1978) (citation omitted). . . . "Carry" bears many meanings, as the Court and the "Firearms" statutes demonstrate.[13] The narrower "on or about [one's]

---

**11.** See infra, at 11–12, nn. 13, 14. The Government points to numerous federal statutes that authorize law enforcement officers to "carry firearms" and notes that, in those authorizing provisions, "carry" of course means "both on the person and in a vehicle." Brief for United States 31–32, and n. 18. Quite right. But as viewers of "Sesame Street" will quickly recognize, "one of these things [a statute *authorizing* conduct] is not like the other [a statute *criminalizing* conduct]." The authorizing statutes in question are properly accorded a construction compatible with the clear purpose of the legislation to aid federal law enforcers in the performance of their official duties. It is fundamental, however, that a penal statute is not to be construed generously in the Government's favor. See, e.g., United States v. Bass, 404 U.S. 336, 348, 30 L. Ed. 2d 488, 92 S. Ct. 515 (1971).

**12.** The Court places undue reliance on Representative Poff's statement that § 924(c)(1) seeks " 'to persuade the man who is tempted to commit a Federal felony to leave his gun at home.'" See ante, at 7 (quoting 114 Cong. Rec. 22231 (1968)). As the Government argued in its brief to this Court in Bailey:

"In making that statement, Representative Poff was not referring to the 'carries' prong of the original Section 924(c). As originally enacted, the 'carries' prong of the statute prohibited only the 'unlawful' carrying of a firearm while committing an offense. The statute would thus not have applied to an individual who, for instance, had a permit for carrying a gun and carried it with him when committing an offense, and it would have had no force in 'persuading' such an individual 'to leave his gun at home.' Instead, Representative Poff was referring to the 'uses' prong of the original Section 924(c)." Brief for United States in Bailey v. United States, 516 U.S.137, 116 S. Ct. 501, 133 L. Ed. 2d 472 p. 28.

Representative Poff's next sentence confirms that he was speaking of "uses," not "carries": "Any person should understand that if he *uses* his gun and is caught and convicted, he is going to jail." 114 Cong. Rec., at 22231 (emphasis added).

**13.** Any doubt on that score is dispelled by examining the provisions in the "Firearms" chapter, in addition to § 924(c)(1), that include a form of the word "carry": 18 U.S.C. § 922(a)(5) (*"carry out* a bequest");

person" interpretation is hardly implausible nor at odds with an accepted meaning of "carries a firearm."

Overlooking that there will be an enhanced sentence for the gun-possessing drug dealer in any event, see supra, at 2–4, the Court asks rhetorically: "How persuasive is a punishment that is without effect until a drug dealer who has brought his gun to a sale (indeed has it available for use) actually takes it from the trunk (or unlocks the glove compartment) of his car?" Ante, at 8. Correspondingly, the Court defines "carries a firearm" to cover "a person who knowingly possesses and conveys firearms [anyplace] in a vehicle ... which the person accompanies." Ante, at 1. Congress, however, hardly lacks competence to select the words "possesses" or "conveys" when that is what the Legislature means.[14] Notably in view of the Legislature's capacity to speak plainly, and of overriding concern, the Court's inquiry pays scant attention to a core reason for the rule of lenity: "Because of the seriousness of criminal penalties, and because criminal punishment usually represents the moral condemnation of the community, legislatures and not courts should define criminal activity. This policy embodies 'the instinctive distaste against men languishing in prison unless the lawmaker has clearly said they should.'" United States v. Bass, 404 U.S. 336, 348, 30 L. Ed. 2d 488, 92 S. Ct. 515 (1971) (quoting H. Friendly, Mr. Justice Frankfurter and the Reading of Statutes, in Benchmarks 196, 209 (1967)).

* * *

The narrower "on or about [one's] person" construction of "carries a firearm" is consistent with the Court's construction of "uses" in Bailey to entail an immediacy element. It respects the Guidelines system by resisting overbroad readings of statutes that deviate from that system. See *McFadden*, 13 F.3d at 468 (Breyer, C. J., dissenting). It fits plausibly with other provisions of the "Firearms" chapter, and it adheres to the principle that, given two readings of a penal provision, both consistent with the statutory text, we do not choose the harsher construction. The Court, in my view, should leave it to Congress to speak " 'in language that is clear and

---

§§ 922(s)(6)(B)(ii), (iii) ("carry out this subsection"); § 922(u) ("*carry away* [a firearm]"); 18 U.S.C. A. § 924(a)(6)(B)(ii) (Supp. 1998) ("*carry* or otherwise possess or discharge or otherwise use [a] handgun"); 18 U.S.C. § 924(e)(2)(B) ("*carrying* of a firearm"); § 925(a)(2) ("carried out to enable a person"); § 926(a) ("*carry out* the provisions of this chapter"); § 926A ("lawfully possess and *carry* such firearm to any other place where he may lawfully possess and *carry* such firearm"); § 929(a)(1) ("uses or *carries* a firearm and is in possession of armor piercing ammunition"); § 930(d)(3) ("lawful *carrying* of firearms ... in a Federal facility incident to hunting or other lawful purposes") (emphasis added in all quotations).

14. See, e.g., 18 U.S.C. A. § 924(a)(6)(B)(ii) (Supp. 1998) ("if the person sold ... a handgun ... to a juvenile knowing ... that the juvenile intended to *carry or otherwise possess* ... the handgun ... in the commission of a crime of violence"); 18 U.S.C. § 926A ("may lawfully *possess and carry* such firearm to any other place where he may lawfully *possess and carry* such firearm"); § 929(a)(1) ("uses or *carries a firearm and is in possession* of armor piercing ammunition"); § 2277 ("brings, *carries, or possesses* any dangerous weapon") (emphasis added in all quotations).

definite' " if the Legislature wishes to impose the sterner penalty. Bass, 404 U.S. at 347 (quoting United States v. Universal C. I. T. Credit Corp., 344 U.S. 218, 222, 97 L. Ed. 260, 73 S. Ct. 227 (1952)). Accordingly, I would reverse the judgments of the First and Fifth Circuits.

## Questions

1.   Do you agree with the majority that the "primary" meaning of the "carry" means to " 'carry ...' in a wagon, car, truck, or other vehicle"? Should the "primary" meaning be dispositive if there are alternative meanings? How do we know which, if any, is the "plain" meaning? To be "plain" must the word's meaning be "ubiquitously necessary"? What difference does/should the "rule of lenity" make?

2.   Should the Oxford English Dictionary play a pivotal role in the interpretation of statutes? Do you think that lawmakers consulted the OED while writing or voting on the Bill? Is it significant that Congress could have cited to the OED in the "definitions" section of the bill had it so desired?

3.   The dissent points out that "Congress ... hardly lacks the competence to select the words 'possess' or 'conveys' when that is what the legislature means." What inference should one draw from Congress' use of a different term?

## Buckhannon Board and Care Home, Inc. v. West Virginia Department of Health and Human Resources

Supreme Court of the United States, 2001.
532 U.S. 598, 121 S.Ct. 1835, 149 L.Ed.2d 855.

■ CHIEF JUSTICE REHNQUIST delivered the opinion of the Court.

Numerous federal statutes allow courts to award attorney's fees and costs to the "prevailing party." The question presented here is whether this term includes a party that has failed to secure a judgment on the merits or a court-ordered consent decree, but has nonetheless achieved the desired result because the lawsuit brought about a voluntary change in the defendant's conduct. We hold that it does not.

Buckhannon Board and Care Home, Inc., which operates care homes that provide assisted living to their residents, failed an inspection by the West Virginia Office of the State Fire Marshal because some of the residents were incapable of "self-preservation" as defined under state law. See W. Va. Code § § 16–5H–1, 16–5H–2 (1998) (requiring that all residents of residential board and care homes be capable of "self-preservation," or capable of moving themselves "from situations involving imminent danger, such as fire"); W. Va. Code of State Rules, tit. 87, ser. 1, § 14.07(1) (1995) (same). On October 28, 1997, after receiving cease and desist orders requiring the closure of its residential care facilities within 30 days, Buckhannon Board and Care Home, Inc., on behalf of itself and other similarly situated homes and residents (hereinafter petitioners), brought suit in the United States District Court for the Northern District of West

Virginia against the State of West Virginia, two of its agencies, and 18 individuals (hereinafter respondents), seeking declaratory and injunctive relief that the "self-preservation" requirement violated the Fair Housing Amendments Act of 1988 (FHAA), 102 Stat. 1619, 42 U.S.C. § 3601 *et seq.*, and the Americans with Disabilities Act of 1990 (ADA), 104 Stat. 327, 42 U.S.C. § 12101 *et seq*. . . .

Respondents agreed to stay enforcement of the cease and desist orders pending resolution of the case and the parties began discovery. In 1998, the West Virginia Legislature enacted two bills eliminating the "self-preservation" requirement, see H. R. 4200, I 1998 W. Va. Acts 983–986 (amending regulations); S. 627, II 1998 W. Va. Acts 1198–1199 (amending statute), and respondents moved to dismiss the case as moot. The District Court granted the motion, finding that the 1998 legislation had eliminated the allegedly offensive provisions and that there was no indication that the West Virginia Legislature would repeal the amendments.

. . .

Petitioners requested attorney's fees as the "prevailing party" under the FHAA, 42 U.S.C. § 3613(c)(2) ("The court, in its discretion, may allow the prevailing party . . . a reasonable attorney's fee and costs"), and ADA, 42 U.S.C. § 12205 ("The court . . . , in its discretion, may allow the prevailing party . . . a reasonable attorney's fee, including litigation expenses, and costs"). Petitioners argued that they were entitled to attorney's fees under the "catalyst theory," which posits that a plaintiff is a "prevailing party" if it achieves the desired result because the lawsuit brought about a voluntary change in the defendant's conduct. Although most Courts of Appeals recognize the "catalyst theory," the Court of Appeals for the Fourth Circuit rejected it in S–1 and S–2 v. State Bd. of Ed. of N. C., 21 F.3d 49, 51 (1994) (en banc) ("A person may not be a 'prevailing party' . . . except by virtue of having obtained an enforceable judgment, consent decree, or settlement giving some of the legal relief sought"). The District Court accordingly denied the motion and, for the same reason, the Court of Appeals affirmed in an unpublished, *per curiam* opinion. Judgt. order reported at 203 F.3d 819 (C.A.4 2000). . . .

To resolve the disagreement amongst the Courts of Appeals, we granted certiorari, 530 U.S. 1304 (2000), and now affirm.

In the United States, parties are ordinarily required to bear their own attorney's fees—the prevailing party is not entitled to collect from the loser. . . . Under this "American Rule," we follow "a general practice of not awarding fees to a prevailing party absent explicit statutory authority." Key Tronic Corp. v. United States, 511 U.S. 809, 819, 128 L. Ed. 2d 797, 114 S. Ct. 1960 (1994). Congress, however, has authorized the award of attorney's fees to the "prevailing party" in numerous statutes in addition to those at issue here, such as the Civil Rights Act of 1964, 78 Stat. 259, 42 U.S.C. § 2000e–5(k), the Voting Rights Act Amendments of 1975, 89 Stat. 402, 42 U.S.C. § 1973l(e), and the Civil Rights Attorney's Fees Awards Act of 1976, 90 Stat. 2641, 42 U.S.C. § 1988. . . .

In designating those parties eligible for an award of litigation costs, Congress employed the term "prevailing party," a legal term of art. Black's Law Dictionary 1145 (7th ed. 1999) defines "prevailing party" as "[a] party in whose favor a judgment is rendered, regardless of the amount of damages awarded (in certain cases, the court will award attorney's fees to the prevailing party).—Also termed *successful party*." This view that a "prevailing party" is one who has been awarded some relief by the court can be distilled from our prior cases.[5]

In Hanrahan v. Hampton, 446 U.S. 754, 758, 64 L. Ed. 2d 670, 100 S. Ct. 1987 (1980) *(per curiam)*, we reviewed the legislative history of § 1988 and found that "Congress intended to permit the interim award of counsel fees only when a party has prevailed on the merits of at least some of his claims." Our "respect for ordinary language requires that a plaintiff receive at least some relief on the merits of his claim before he can be said to prevail." Hewitt v. Helms, 482 U.S. 755, 760, 96 L. Ed. 2d 654, 107 S. Ct. 2672 (1987). We have held that even an award of nominal damages suffices under this test. See Farrar v. Hobby, 506 U.S. 103, 121 L. Ed. 2d 494, 113 S. Ct. 566 (1992). . . .

In addition to judgments on the merits, we have held that settlement agreements enforced through a consent decree may serve as the basis for an award of attorney's fees. See Maher v. Gagne, 448 U.S. 122, 65 L. Ed. 2d 653, 100 S. Ct. 2570 (1980). Although a consent decree does not always include an admission of liability by the defendant, see, *e.g., id.* at 126, n. 8, it nonetheless is a court-ordered "change [in] the legal relationship between [the plaintiff] and the defendant." Texas State Teachers Assn. v. Garland Independent School Dist., 489 U.S. 782, 792, 103 L. Ed. 2d 866, 109 S. Ct. 1486 (1989) (citing *Hewitt, supra,* at 760–761, and Rhodes v. Stewart, 488 U.S. 1, 3–4, 102 L. Ed. 2d 1, 109 S. Ct. 202 (1988) *(per curiam)).*[7] These decisions, taken together, establish that enforceable judg-

**5.** We have never had occasion to decide whether the term "prevailing party" allows an award of fees under the "catalyst theory" described above. Dicta in Hewitt v. Helms, 482 U.S. 755, 760, 96 L. Ed. 2d 654, 107 S. Ct. 2672 (1987), alluded to the possibility of attorney's fees where "voluntary action by the defendant . . . affords the plaintiff all or some of the relief . . . sought," but we expressly reserved the question, see *id.* at 763 ("We need not decide the circumstances, if any, under which this 'catalyst' theory could justify a fee award"). And though the Court of Appeals for the Fourth Circuit relied upon our decision in Farrar v. Hobby, 506 U.S. 103, 121 L. Ed. 2d 494, 113 S. Ct. 566 (1992), in rejecting the "catalyst theory," *Farrar* "involved no catalytic effect." Friends of Earth, Inc. v. Laidlaw Environmental Services (TOC), Inc., 528 U.S. 167, 194, 145 L. Ed. 2d 610, 120 S. Ct. 693 (2000). Thus, there is language in our cases supporting both petitioners and respondents, and last Term we observed that it was an open question here. See *ibid.*

**7.** We have subsequently characterized the *Maher* opinion as also allowing for an award of attorney's fees for private settlements. See Farrar v. Hobby, *supra,* at 111; Hewitt v. Helms, *supra,* at 760. But this dicta ignores that *Maher* only "held that fees *may* be assessed . . . after a case has been settled by the entry of a consent decree." Evans v. Jeff D., 475 U.S. 717, 720, 89 L. Ed. 2d 747, 106 S. Ct. 1531 (1986). Private settlements do not entail the judicial approval and oversight involved in consent decrees. And federal jurisdiction to enforce a private contractual settlement will often be lacking unless the terms of the agreement are incorporated into the order of dismissal. See Kokkonen v.

ments on the merits and court-ordered consent decrees create the "material alteration of the legal relationship of the parties" necessary to permit an award of attorney's fees. 489 U.S. at 792–793; see also *Hanrahan, supra*, at 757 ("It seems clearly to have been the intent of Congress to permit . . . an interlocutory award only to a party who has established his entitlement to some relief on the merits of his claims, either in the *trial court* or *on appeal*" (emphasis added)).

We think, however, the "catalyst theory" falls on the other side of the line from these examples. It allows an award where there is no judicially sanctioned change in the legal relationship of the parties. Even under a limited form of the "catalyst theory," a plaintiff could recover attorney's fees if it established that the "complaint had sufficient merit to withstand a motion to dismiss for lack of jurisdiction or failure to state a claim on which relief may be granted." Brief for United States as *Amicus Curiae* 27. This is not the type of legal merit that our prior decisions, based upon plain language and congressional intent, have found necessary. Indeed, we held in *Hewitt* that an interlocutory ruling that reverses a dismissal for failure to state a claim "is not the stuff of which legal victories are made." 482 U.S. at 760. See also *Hanrahan, supra,* at 754 (reversal of a directed verdict for defendant does not make plaintiff a "prevailing party"). A defendant's voluntary change in conduct, although perhaps accomplishing what the plaintiff sought to achieve by the lawsuit, lacks the necessary judicial *imprimatur* on the change. Our precedents thus counsel against holding that the term "prevailing party" authorizes an award of attorney's fees *without* a corresponding alteration in the legal relationship of the parties.

The dissenters chide us for upsetting "long-prevailing *Circuit* precedent." (emphasis added). But, as JUSTICE SCALIA points out in his concurrence, several Courts of Appeals have relied upon dicta in our prior cases in approving the "catalyst theory." Now that the issue is squarely presented, it behooves us to reconcile the plain language of the statutes with our prior *holdings*. We have only awarded attorney's fees where the plaintiff has received a judgment on the merits, see, *e.g., Farrar, supra*, at 112, or obtained a court-ordered consent decree, *Maher, supra,* at 129–130—we have not awarded attorney's fees where the plaintiff has secured the reversal of a directed verdict, see *Hanrahan, supra*, at 759, or acquired a judicial pronouncement that the defendant has violated the Constitution unaccompanied by "*judicial* relief," *Hewitt, supra,* at 760 (emphasis added). Never have we awarded attorney's fees for a nonjudicial "alteration of actual circumstances." While urging an expansion of our precedents on this front, the dissenters would simultaneously abrogate the "merit" requirement of our prior cases and award attorney's fees where the plaintiff's claim "was at least colorable" and "not . . . groundless." (internal quotation marks and citation omitted). We cannot agree that the term "prevailing party" authorizes federal courts to award attorney's fees to a plaintiff

Guardian Life Ins. Co. of America, 511 U.S.
375, 128 L. Ed. 2d 391, 114 S. Ct. 1673
(1994).

who, by simply filing a nonfrivolous but nonetheless potentially meritless lawsuit (it will never be determined), has reached the "sought-after destination" without obtaining any judicial relief. . . .

Petitioners nonetheless argue that the legislative history of the Civil Rights Attorney's Fees Awards Act supports a broad reading of "prevailing party" which includes the "catalyst theory." We doubt that legislative history could overcome what we think is the rather clear meaning of "prevailing party"—the term actually used in the statute. Since we resorted to such history in *Garland,* 489 U.S. at 790, *Maher,* 448 U.S. at 129, and *Hanrahan*, 446 U.S. at 756–757, however, we do likewise here.

The House Report to § 1988 states that "the phrase 'prevailing party' is not intended to be limited to the victor only after entry of a final judgment following a full trial on the merits, "H. R. Rep. No. 94–1558, p. 7 (1976), while the Senate Report explains that "parties may be considered to have prevailed when they vindicate rights through a consent judgment or without formally obtaining relief," S. Rep. No. 94–1011, p. 5 (1976). Petitioners argue that these Reports and their reference to a 1970 decision from the Court of Appeals for the Eighth Circuit, Parham v. Southwestern Bell Telephone Co., 433 F.2d 421 (1970), indicate Congress' intent to adopt the "catalyst theory."[9] We think the legislative history cited by petitioners is at best ambiguous as to the availability of the "catalyst theory" for awarding attorney's fees. Particularly in view of the "American Rule" that attorney's fees will not be awarded absent "explicit statutory authority," such legislative history is clearly insufficient to alter the accepted meaning of the statutory term. *Key Tronic*, 511 U.S. at 819; see also *Hanrahan, supra*, at 758 ("Only when a party has prevailed on the merits of at least some of his claims . . . has there been a determination of the 'substantial rights of the parties,' which Congress determined was a necessary foundation for departing from the usual rule in this country that each party is to bear the expense of his own attorney" (quoting H. R. Rep. No. 94–1558, at 8)).

Petitioners finally assert that the "catalyst theory" is necessary to prevent defendants from unilaterally mooting an action before judgment in an effort to avoid an award of attorney's fees. They also claim that the rejection of the "catalyst theory" will deter plaintiffs with meritorious but

---

**9.** Although the Court of Appeals in *Parham* awarded attorney's fees to the plaintiff because his "lawsuit acted as a catalyst which prompted the [defendant] to take action . . . seeking compliance with the requirements of Title VII," 433 F.2d at 429–430, it did so only after finding that the defendant had acted unlawfully, see *id.* at 426 ("We hold as a matter of law that [plaintiff's evidence] established a violation of Title VII"). Thus, consistent with our holding in *Farrar*, *Parham* stands for the proposition that an enforceable judgment permits an award of attorney's fees. And like the consent decree in Maher v. Gagne, 448 U.S. 122, 65 L. Ed. 2d 653, 100 S. Ct. 2570 (1980), the Court of Appeals in *Parham* ordered the District Court to "retain jurisdiction over the matter for a reasonable period of time to insure the continued implementation of the appellee's policy of equal employment opportunities." 433 F.2d at 429. Clearly *Parham* does not support a theory of fee shifting untethered to a material alteration in the legal relationship of the parties as defined by our precedents.

expensive cases from bringing suit. We are skeptical of these assertions, which are entirely speculative and unsupported by any empirical evidence (*e.g.*, whether the number of suits brought in the Fourth Circuit has declined, in relation to other Circuits, since the decision in *S–1 and S–2*).

Petitioners discount the disincentive that the "catalyst theory" may have upon a defendant's decision to voluntarily change its conduct, conduct that may not be illegal. "The defendants' potential liability for fees in this kind of litigation can be as significant as, and sometimes even more significant than, their potential liability on the merits," Evans v. Jeff D., 475 U.S. 717, 734, 89 L. Ed. 2d 747, 106 S. Ct. 1531 (1986), and the possibility of being assessed attorney's fees may well deter a defendant from altering its conduct.

And petitioners' fear of mischievous defendants only materializes in claims for equitable relief, for so long as the plaintiff has a cause of action for damages, a defendant's change in conduct will not moot the case. Even then, it is not clear how often courts will find a case mooted: "It is well settled that a defendant's voluntary cessation of a challenged practice does not deprive a federal court of its power to determine the legality of the practice" unless it is "absolutely clear that the allegedly wrongful behavior could not reasonably be expected to recur." Friends of Earth, Inc. v. Laidlaw Environmental Services (TOC), Inc., 528 U.S. 167, 189, 145 L. Ed. 2d 610, 120 S. Ct. 693 (2000) (internal quotation marks and citations omitted). If a case is not found to be moot, and the plaintiff later procures an enforceable judgment, the court may of course award attorney's fees. Given this possibility, a defendant has a strong incentive to enter a settlement agreement, where it can negotiate attorney's fees and costs. Cf. Marek v. Chesny, 473 U.S. at 7 ("Many a defendant would be unwilling to make a binding settlement offer on terms that left it exposed to liability for attorney's fees in whatever amount the court might fix on motion of the plaintiff" (internal quotation marks and citation omitted)) . . . .

We have also stated that "[a] request for attorney's fees should not result in a second major litigation," Hensley v. Eckerhart, 461 U.S. 424, 437, 76 L. Ed. 2d 40, 103 S. Ct. 1933 (1983), and have accordingly avoided an interpretation of the fee-shifting statutes that would have "spawned a second litigation of significant dimension," *Garland*, 489 U.S. at 791. Among other things, a "catalyst theory" hearing would require analysis of the defendant's subjective motivations in changing its conduct, an analysis that "will likely depend on a highly factbound inquiry and may turn on reasonable inferences from the nature and timing of the defendant's change in conduct." Brief for United States as *Amicus Curiae* 28. Although we do not doubt the ability of district courts to perform the nuanced "three thresholds" test required by the "catalyst theory"—whether the claim was colorable rather than groundless; whether the lawsuit was a substantial rather than an insubstantial cause of the defendant's change in conduct; whether the defendant's change in conduct was motivated by the plaintiff's threat of victory rather than threat of expense, see *post*, at 6–7—it is clearly not a formula for "ready administrability." Burlington v. Dague, 505 U.S. 557, 566, 120 L. Ed. 2d 449, 112 S. Ct. 2638 (1992).

Given the clear meaning of "prevailing party" in the fee-shifting statutes, we need not determine which way these various policy arguments cut. In *Alyeska*, 421 U.S. at 260, we said that Congress had not "extended any roving authority to the Judiciary to allow counsel fees as costs or otherwise whenever the courts might deem them warranted." To disregard the clear legislative language and the holdings of our prior cases on the basis of such policy arguments would be a similar assumption of a "roving authority." For the reasons stated above, we hold that the "catalyst theory" is not a permissible basis for the award of attorney's fees under the FHAA, 42 U.S.C. § 3613(c)(2), and ADA, 42 U.S.C. § 12205.

The judgment of the Court of Appeals is

Affirmed.

■ JUSTICE SCALIA, with whom JUSTICE THOMAS joined, issued a separate, concurring opinion.

[omitted]

■ JUSTICE GINSBURG, with whom JUSTICE STEVENS, JUSTICE SOUTER, and JUSTICE BREYER join, dissenting.

The Court today holds that a plaintiff whose suit prompts the precise relief she seeks does not "prevail," and hence cannot obtain an award of attorney's fees, unless she also secures a court entry memorializing her victory. The entry need not be a judgment on the merits. Nor need there be any finding of wrongdoing. A court-approved settlement will do.

The Court's insistence that there be a document filed in court—a litigated judgment or court-endorsed settlement—upsets long-prevailing Circuit precedent applicable to scores of federal fee-shifting statutes. The decision allows a defendant to escape a statutory obligation to pay a plaintiff's counsel fees, even though the suit's merit led the defendant to abandon the fray, to switch rather than fight on, to accord plaintiff sooner rather than later the principal redress sought in the complaint. Concomitantly, the Court's constricted definition of "prevailing party," and consequent rejection of the "catalyst theory," impede access to court for the less well-heeled, and shrink the incentive Congress created for the enforcement of federal law by private attorneys general.

In my view, the "catalyst rule," as applied by the clear majority of Federal Circuits, is a key component of the fee-shifting statutes Congress adopted to advance enforcement of civil rights. Nothing in history, precedent, or plain English warrants the anemic construction of the term "prevailing party" the Court today imposes.

## I

\* \* \*

Prior to 1994, every Federal Court of Appeals (except the Federal Circuit, which had not addressed the issue) concluded that plaintiffs in situations like Buckhannon's and Pierce's could obtain a fee award if their suit acted as a "catalyst" for the change they sought, even if they did not obtain a judgment or consent decree.[4] The Courts of Appeals found it "clear that a party may be considered to have prevailed even when the legal action stops short of final . . . judgment due to . . . intervening mootness." Grano v. Barry, 251 U.S. App. D.C. 289, 783 F.2d 1104, 1108 (C.A.D.C.1986). Interpreting the term "prevailing party" in "a practical sense," Stewart v. Hannon, 675 F.2d 846, 851 (C.A.7 1982) (citation omitted), federal courts across the country held that a party "prevails" for fee-shifting purposes when "its ends are accomplished as a result of the litigation," Associated Builders & Contractors v. Orleans Parish School Bd., 919 F.2d 374, 378 (C.A.5 1990) (citation and internal quotation marks omitted).

In 1994, the Fourth Circuit en banc, dividing 6–to–5, broke ranks with its sister courts. The court declared that, in light of Farrar v. Hobby, 506 U.S. 103, 121 L. Ed. 2d 494, 113 S. Ct. 566 (1992), a plaintiff could not become a "prevailing party" without "an enforceable judgment, consent decree, or settlement." S–1 and S–2 v. State Bd. of Ed. of N. C., 21 F.3d 49, 51 (1994). As the Court today acknowledges, and as we have previously observed, the language on which the Fourth Circuit relied was dictum: Farrar "involved no catalytic effect"; the issue plainly "was not presented for this Court's decision in Farrar." Friends of Earth, Inc. v. Laidlaw Environmental Services (TOC), Inc., 528 U.S. 167, 194, 145 L. Ed. 2d 610, 120 S. Ct. 693 (2000).

After the Fourth Circuit's en banc ruling, nine Courts of Appeals reaffirmed their own consistently held interpretation of the term "prevail."[5] On this predominant view, "securing an enforceable decree or

---

**4.** Nadeau v. Helgemoe, 581 F.2d 275, 279–281 (C.A.1 1978); Gerena-Valentin v. Koch, 739 F.2d 755, 758–759 (C.A.2 1984); Institutionalized Juveniles v. Secretary of Pub. Welfare, 758 F.2d 897, 910–917 (C.A.3 1985); Bonnes v. Long, 599 F.2d 1316, 1319 (C.A.4 1979); Robinson v. Kimbrough, 652 F.2d 458, 465–467 (C.A.5 1981); Citizens Against Tax Waste v. Westerville City School Dist. Bd. of Ed., 985 F.2d 255, 257–258 (C.A.6 1993); Stewart v. Hannon, 675 F.2d 846, 851 (C.A.7 1982); Williams v. Miller, 620 F.2d 199, 202 (C.A.8 1980); American Constitutional Party v. Munro, 650 F.2d 184, 187–188 (C.A.9 1981); J & J Anderson, Inc. v. Erie, 767 F.2d 1469, 1474–1475 (C.A.10 1985); Doe v. Busbee, 684 F.2d 1375, 1379 (C.A.11 1982); Grano v. Barry, 251 U.S. App. D.C. 289, 783 F.2d 1104, 1108–1110 (C.A.D.C.1986). All *twelve* of these decisions antedate Hewitt v. Helms, 482 U.S. 755, 96 L. Ed. 2d 654, 107 S. Ct. 2672 (1987). But cf. *ante*, at 12, and n. 5

(SCALIA, J., concurring) (maintaining that this Court's decision in Hewitt "improvidently suggested" the catalyst rule, and asserting that only "a few cases adopting the catalyst theory predate Hewitt"). Hewitt said it was "settled law" that when a lawsuit prompts a defendant's "voluntary action . . . that redresses the plaintiff's grievances," the plaintiff "is deemed to have prevailed despite the absence of a formal judgment in his favor." 482 U.S. at 760–761. That statement accurately conveyed the unanimous view then held by the Federal Circuits.

**5.** Stanton v. Southern Berkshire Regional School Dist., 197 F.3d 574, 577, n. 2 (C.A.1 1999); Marbley v. Bane, 57 F.3d 224, 234 (C.A.2 1995); Baumgartner v. Harrisburg Housing Auth., 21 F.3d 541, 546–550 (C.A.3 1994); Payne v. Board of Ed., 88 F.3d 392, 397 (C.A.6 1996); Zinn v. Shalala, 35 F.3d 273, 276 (C.A.7 1994); Little Rock School Dist. v. Pulaski Cty. School Dist., #1, 17 F.3d

agreement may evidence prevailing party status, but the judgment or agreement simply embodies and enforces what is sought in bringing the lawsuit. . . . Victory can be achieved well short of a final judgment (or its equivalent). . . ." Marbley v. Bane, 57 F.3d 224, 234 (C.A.2 1995) (Jacobs, J.).

The array of federal court decisions applying the catalyst rule suggested three conditions necessary to a party's qualification as "prevailing" short of a favorable final judgment or consent decree. A plaintiff first had to show that the defendant provided "some of the benefit sought" by the lawsuit. Wheeler v. Towanda Area School Dist., 950 F.2d 128, 131 (C.A.3 1991). Under most Circuits' precedents, a plaintiff had to demonstrate as well that the suit stated a genuine claim, *i.e.*, one that was at least "colorable," not "frivolous, unreasonable, or groundless." *Grano*, 783 F.2d at 1110 (internal quotation marks and citation omitted). Plaintiff finally had to establish that her suit was a "substantial" or "significant" cause of defendant's action providing relief. Williams v. Leatherbury, 672 F.2d 549, 551 (C.A.5 1982). In some Circuits, to make this causation showing, plaintiff had to satisfy the trial court that the suit achieved results "by threat of victory," not "by dint of nuisance and threat of expense." *Marbley*, 57 F.3d at 234–235; see also Hooper v. Demco, Inc., 37 F.3d 287, 293 (C.A.7 1994) (to render plaintiff "prevailing party," suit "must have prompted the defendant . . . to act or cease its behavior based on the strength of the case, not 'wholly gratuitously' "). One who crossed these three thresholds would be recognized as a "prevailing party" to whom the district court, "in its discretion," *supra*, at 3–4, n. 1, could award attorney's fees.

Developed over decades and in legions of federal-court decisions, the catalyst rule and these implementing standards deserve this Court's respect and approbation.

## II

### A

The Court today detects a "clear meaning" of the term prevailing party, that has heretofore eluded the large majority of courts construing those words. "Prevailing party," today's opinion announces, means "one who has been awarded some relief by the court". The Court derives this "clear meaning" principally from Black's Law Dictionary, which defines a "prevailing party," in critical part, as one "in whose favor a judgment is rendered," (quoting Black's Law Dictionary 1145 (7th ed. 1999)).

One can entirely agree with Black's Law Dictionary that a party "in whose favor a judgment is rendered" prevails, and at the same time resist, as most Courts of Appeals have, any implication that *only* such a party may prevail. In prior cases, we have not treated Black's Law Dictionary as

260, 263, n. 2 (C.A.8 1994); Kilgour v. Pasadena, 53 F.3d 1007, 1010 (C.A.9 1995); Beard v. Teska, 31 F.3d 942, 951–952 (C.A.10 1994);     Morris v. West Palm Beach, 194 F.3d 1203, 1207 (C.A.11 1999).

preclusively definitive; instead, we have accorded statutory terms, including legal "terms of art," a contextual reading. See, *e.g.*, Pioneer Investment Services Co. v. Brunswick Associates Ltd. Partnership, 507 U.S. 380, 395–396, n. 14, 123 L. Ed. 2d 74, 113 S. Ct. 1489 (1993) (defining "excusable neglect," as used in Federal Rule of Bankruptcy Procedure 9006(b)(1), more broadly than Black's defines that term); United States v. Rodgers, 466 U.S. 475, 479–480, 80 L. Ed. 2d 492, 104 S. Ct. 1942 (1984) (adopting "natural, nontechnical" definition of word "jurisdiction," as that term is used in 18 U.S.C. § 1001, and declining to confine definition to "narrower, more technical meanings," citing Black's). Notably, this Court did not refer to Black's Law Dictionary in Maher v. Gagne, 448 U.S. 122, 65 L. Ed. 2d 653, 100 S. Ct. 2570 (1980), which held that a consent decree could qualify a plaintiff as "prevailing." The Court explained:

> "The fact that [plaintiff] prevailed through a settlement rather than through litigation does not weaken her claim to fees. Nothing in the language of [42 U.S.C.] § 1988 conditions the District Court's power to award fees on full litigation of the issues or on a judicial determination that the plaintiff's rights have been violated." *Id.* at 129.

The spare "prevailing party" language of the fee-shifting provision applicable in *Maher,* and the similar wording of the fee-shifting provisions now before the Court, contrast with prescriptions that so tightly bind fees to judgments as to exclude the application of a catalyst concept. The Prison Litigation Reform Act of 1995, for example, directs that fee awards to prisoners under § 1988 be "proportionately related to the *court ordered relief* for the violation." 110 Stat. 1321–72, as amended, 42 U.S.C. § 1997e(d)(1)(B)(i) (1994 ed., Supp. IV) (emphasis added). That statute, by its express terms, forecloses an award to a prisoner on a catalyst theory. But the FHAA and ADA fee-shifting prescriptions, modeled on 42 U.S.C. § 1988 unmodified, do not similarly staple fee awards to "court ordered relief." Their very terms do not foreclose a catalyst theory. . . .

## C

Recognizing that no practice set in stone, statute, rule, or precedent dictates the proper construction of modern civil rights fee-shifting prescriptions, I would "assume . . . that Congress intends the words in its enactments to carry 'their ordinary, contemporary, common meaning.'" *Pioneer,* 507 U.S. at 388 (defining "excusable neglect") (quoting Perrin v. United States, 444 U.S. 37, 42, 62 L. Ed. 2d 199, 100 S. Ct. 311 (1979) (defining "bribery")); see also, *e.g.*, Sutton v. United Air Lines, Inc., 527 U.S. 471, 491, 144 L. Ed. 2d 450, 119 S. Ct. 2139 (1999) (defining "substantially" in light of ordinary usage); Rutledge v. United States, 517 U.S. 292, 299–300, n. 10, 134 L. Ed. 2d 419, 116 S. Ct. 1241 (1996) (similarly defining "in concert"). In everyday use, "prevail" means "gain victory by virtue of strength or superiority: win mastery: triumph." Webster's Third New International Dictionary 1797 (1976). There are undoubtedly situations in which an individual's goal is to obtain approval of a judge, and in those situations, one cannot "prevail" short of a judge's formal declaration. In a piano competition or a figure skating contest, for example, the person who prevails is the person declared winner by the judges. However, where the ultimate goal is not an arbiter's approval, but a favorable alteration of actual circumstances, a formal declaration is not essential. Western democracies, for instance, "prevailed" in the Cold War even though the Soviet Union never formally surrendered. Among television viewers, John F. Kennedy "prevailed" in the first debate with Richard M. Nixon during the 1960 Presidential contest, even though moderator Howard K. Smith never declared a winner. See T. White, The Making of the President 1960, pp. 293–294 (1961).

A lawsuit's ultimate purpose is to achieve actual relief from an opponent. Favorable judgment may be instrumental in gaining that relief. Generally, however, "the judicial decree is not the end but the means. At the end of the rainbow lies not a judgment, but some action (or cessation of action) by the defendant...." Hewitt v. Helms, 482 U.S. 755, 761, 96 L. Ed. 2d 654, 107 S. Ct. 2672 (1987). On this common understanding, if a party reaches the "sought-after destination," then the party "prevails" regardless of the "route taken." Hennigan v. Ouachita Parish School Bd., 749 F.2d 1148, 1153 (C.A.5 1985).

Under a fair reading of the FHAA and ADA provisions in point, I would hold that a party "prevails" in "a true and proper sense," *Mansfield*, 111 U.S. at 388, when she achieves, by instituting litigation, the practical relief sought in her complaint. The Court misreads Congress, as I see it, by insisting that, invariably, relief must be displayed in a judgment, and correspondingly that a defendant's voluntary action never suffices. In this case, Buckhannon's purpose in suing West Virginia officials was not narrowly to obtain a judge's approbation. The plaintiffs' objective was to stop enforcement of a rule requiring Buckhannon to evict residents like centenarian Dorsey Pierce as the price of remaining in business. If Buckhannon achieved that objective on account of the strength of its case—if it succeeded in keeping its doors open while housing and caring for Ms. Pierce and others similarly situated—then Buckhannon is properly judged a party who prevailed.

## III

As the Courts of Appeals have long recognized, the catalyst rule suitably advances Congress' endeavor to place private actions, in civil rights and other legislatively defined areas, securely within the federal law enforcement arsenal.

The catalyst rule stemmed from modern legislation extending civil rights protections and enforcement measures. The Civil Rights Act of 1964 included provisions for fee awards to "prevailing parties" in Title II (public accommodations), 42 U.S.C. § 2000a–3(b), and Title VII (employment), 42 U.S.C. § 2000e–5(k), but not in Title VI (federal programs). The provisions' central purpose was "to promote vigorous enforcement" of the laws by private plaintiffs; although using the two-way term "prevailing party," Congress did not make fees available to plaintiffs and defendants on equal terms. Christiansburg Garment Co. v. EEOC, 434 U.S. 412, 417, 421, 54 L. Ed. 2d 648, 98 S. Ct. 694 (1978) (under Title VII, prevailing plaintiff qualifies for fee award absent "special circumstances," but prevailing defendant may obtain fee award only if plaintiff's suit is "frivolous, unreasonable, or without foundation")....

As explained in the Reports supporting § 1988, civil rights statutes vindicate public policies "of the highest priority," S. Rep. No. 94–1011, p. 3 (1976) (quoting Newman v. Piggie Park Enterprises, Inc., 390 U.S. 400, 402, 19 L. Ed. 2d 1263, 88 S. Ct. 964 (1968) (per curiam)), yet "depend heavily on private enforcement," S. Rep. No. 94–1011, at 2. Persons who bring meritorious civil rights claims, in this light, serve as "private attorneys general." Id. at 5; H. R. Rep. No. 94–1558, p. 2 (1976). Such suitors, Congress recognized, often "cannot afford legal counsel." Id. at 1. They therefore experience "severe hardship" under the "American Rule." Id. at 2. Congress enacted § 1988 to ensure that nonaffluent plaintiffs would have "effective access" to the Nation's courts to enforce civil rights laws. Id. at 1.[9] That objective accounts for the fee-shifting provisions before the Court in this case, prescriptions of the FHAA and the ADA modeled on § 1988.

Under the catalyst rule that held sway until today, plaintiffs who obtained the relief they sought through suit on genuine claims ordinarily qualified as "prevailing parties," so that courts had discretion to award them their costs and fees. Persons with limited resources were not impelled to "wage total law" in order to assure that their counsel fees would be paid. They could accept relief, in money or of another kind, voluntarily proffered by a defendant who sought to avoid a recorded decree. And they could rely on a judge then to determine, in her equitable discretion, whether counsel fees were warranted and, if so, in what amount.[10]

**9.** See H. R. Rep. No. 94–1558, at 1 ("Because a vast majority of the victims of civil rights violations cannot afford legal counsel, they are unable to present their cases to the courts.... [This statute] is designed to give such persons effective access to the judicial process...."); S. Rep. No. 94–1011, at 2 ("If private citizens are to be able to assert their civil rights, and if those who violate the Nation's fundamental laws are not to proceed with impunity, then citizens must have the opportunity to recover what it costs them to vindicate these rights in court."), quoted in part in Kay v. Ehrler, 499 U.S. 432, 436, n. 8, 113 L. Ed. 2d 486, 111 S. Ct. 1435 (1991). See also Newman v. Piggie Park Enterprises, Inc., 390 U.S. 400, 401–402, 19 L. Ed. 2d 1263, 88 S. Ct. 964 (1968) (per curiam) ("When the Civil Rights Act of 1964 was passed, it was evident that enforcement would prove difficult and that the Nation would have to rely in part upon private

litigation as a means of securing broad compliance with the law.... [Congress] enacted the provision for counsel fees ... to encourage individuals injured by racial discrimination to seek judicial relief....").

**10.** Given the protection furnished by the catalyst rule, aggrieved individuals were not left to worry, and wrongdoers were not led to believe, that strategic maneuvers by defendants might succeed in averting a fee award. Apt here is Judge Friendly's observation construing a fee-shifting statute kin to the provisions before us: "Congress clearly did not mean that where a [Freedom of Information Act] suit had gone to trial and developments have made it apparent that the judge was about to rule for the plaintiff, the Government could abort any award of attorney fees by an eleventh hour tender of information." Vermont Low Income Advocacy Council v. Usery, 546 F.2d 509, 513 (C.A.2 1976) (interpreting 5 U.S.C. § 552(a)(4)(E),

Congress appears to have envisioned that very prospect. The Senate Report on the 1976 Civil Rights Attorney's Fees Awards Act states: "For purposes of the award of counsel fees, parties may be considered to have prevailed when they vindicate rights through a consent judgment *or without formally obtaining relief.*" S. Rep. No. 94–1011, at 5 (emphasis added). In support, the Report cites cases in which parties recovered fees in the absence of any court-conferred relief.[11] The House Report corroborates: "After a complaint is filed, a defendant might voluntarily cease the unlawful practice. *A court should still award fees* even though it might conclude, as a matter of equity, that *no formal relief*, such as an injunction, is needed." H. R. Rep. No. 94–1558, at 7 (emphases added). These Reports, Courts of Appeals have observed, are hardly ambiguous. Compare *ante*, at 9 ("legislative history ... is at best ambiguous"), with, *e.g.*, Dunn v. The Florida Bar, 889 F.2d 1010, 1013 (C.A.11 1989) (legislative history "evinces a clear Congressional intent" to permit award "even when no formal judicial relief is obtained" (internal quotation marks omitted)); Robinson v. Kimbrough, 652 F.2d 458, 465 (C.A.5 1981) (same); American Constitutional Party v. Munro, 650 F.2d 184, 187 (C.A.9 1981) (Senate Report "directs" fee award under catalyst rule). Congress, I am convinced, understood that " 'victory' in a civil rights suit is typically a practical, rather than a strictly legal matter." Exeter-West Greenwich Regional School Dist. v. Pontarelli, 788 F.2d 47, 51 (C.A.1 1986) (citation omitted).

## IV

The Court identifies several "policy arguments" that might warrant rejection of the catalyst rule. A defendant might refrain from altering its conduct, fearing liability for fees as the price of voluntary action. Moreover, rejection of the catalyst rule has limited impact: Desisting from the chal-

---

allowing a complainant who "substantially prevails" to earn an attorney's fee); accord, Cuneo v. Rumsfeld, 180 U.S. App. D.C. 184, 553 F.2d 1360, 1364 (C.A.D.C.1977).

**11.** See S. Rep. No. 94–1011, at 5 (citing Kopet v. Esquire Realty Co., 523 F.2d 1005, 1008–1009 (C.A.2 1975) (partner sued his firm for release of documents, firm released the documents, court awarded fees because of the release, even though the partner's claims were "dismissed for lack of subject matter jurisdiction"), and Thomas v. Honeybrook Mines, Inc., 428 F.2d 981, 984, 985 (C.A.3 1970) (union committee twice commenced suit for pension fund payments, suits prompted recovery, and court awarded fees even though the first suit had been dismissed and the second had not yet been adjudicated)).

The Court features a case cited by the House as well as the Senate in the Reports on § 1988, Parham v. Southwestern Bell Tel. Co., 433 F.2d 421 (C.A.8 1970). The Court deems *Parham* consistent with its rejection of the catalyst rule, alternately because the Eighth Circuit made a "finding that the defendant had acted unlawfully," and because that court ordered the District Court to " 'retain jurisdiction over the matter ... to insure the continued implementation of the [defendant's] policy of equal employment opportunities.' " (quoting 433 F.2d at 429). Congress did not fix on those factors, however: Nothing in either Report suggests that judicial findings or retention of jurisdiction is essential to an award of fees. The courts in *Kopet* and *Thomas* awarded fees based on claims as to which they neither made "a finding" nor "retained jurisdiction." (It nonetheless bears attention that, in line with the Court's description of *Parham*, a plaintiff could qualify as the "prevailing party" based on a finding or retention of jurisdiction.)

lenged conduct will not render a case moot where damages are sought, and even when the plaintiff seeks only equitable relief, a defendant's voluntary cessation of a challenged practice does not render the case moot "unless it is 'absolutely clear that the allegedly wrongful behavior could not reasonably be expected to recur.' " (quoting *Friends of Earth, Inc.*, 528 U.S. at 189). Because a mootness dismissal is not easily achieved, the defendant may be impelled to settle, negotiating fees less generous than a court might award. Finally, a catalyst rule would "require analysis of the defendant's subjective motivations," and thus protract the litigation.

The Court declines to look beneath the surface of these arguments, placing its reliance, instead, on a meaning of "prevailing party" that other jurists would scarcely recognize as plain. Had the Court inspected the "policy arguments" listed in its opinion, I doubt it would have found them impressive.

In opposition to the argument that defendants will resist change in order to stave off an award of fees, one could urge that the catalyst rule may lead defendants promptly to comply with the law's requirements: the longer the litigation, the larger the fees. Indeed, one who knows noncompliance will be expensive might be encouraged to conform his conduct to the legal requirements before litigation is threatened. Cf. Hylton, Fee Shifting and Incentives to Comply with the Law, 46 Vand. L. Rev. 1069, 1121 (1993) ("fee shifting in favor of prevailing plaintiffs enhances both incentives to comply with legal rules *and* incentives to settle disputes"). No doubt, a mootness dismissal is unlikely when recurrence of the controversy is under the defendant's control. But, as earlier observed, why should this Court's fee-shifting rulings drive a plaintiff prepared to accept adequate relief, though out-of-court and unrecorded, to litigate on and on? And if the catalyst rule leads defendants to negotiate not only settlement terms but also allied counsel fees, is that not a consummation to applaud, not deplore?

As to the burden on the court, is it not the norm for the judge to whom the case has been assigned to resolve fee disputes (deciding whether an award is in order, and if it is, the amount due), thereby clearing the case from the calendar? If factfinding becomes necessary under the catalyst rule, is it not the sort that "the district courts, in their factfinding expertise, deal with on a regular basis"? Baumgartner v. Harrisburg Housing Auth., 21 F.3d 541, 548 (C.A.3 1994). Might not one conclude overall, as Courts of Appeals have suggested, that the catalyst rule "saves judicial resources," Paris v. Department of Housing and Urban Development, 988 F.2d 236, 240 (C.A.1 1993), by encouraging "plaintiffs to discontinue litigation after receiving through the defendant's acquiescence the remedy initially sought"? Morris v. West Palm Beach, 194 F.3d 1203, 1207 (C.A.11 1999).

* * * The Court states that the term "prevailing party" in fee-shifting statutes has an "accepted meaning." If that is so, the "accepted meaning" is not the one the Court today announces. It is, instead, the meaning accepted by every Court of Appeals to address the catalyst issue before our 1987 decision in *Hewitt*, and disavowed since then only by the Fourth

Circuit. A plaintiff prevails, federal judges have overwhelmingly agreed, when a litigated judgment, consent decree, out-of-court settlement, or the defendant's voluntary, postcomplaint payment or change in conduct in fact affords redress for the plaintiff's substantial grievances.

When this Court rejects the considered judgment prevailing in the Circuits, respect for our colleagues demands a cogent explanation. Today's decision does not provide one. The Court's narrow construction of the words "prevailing party" is unsupported by precedent and unaided by history or logic. Congress prescribed fee-shifting provisions like those included in the FHAA and ADA to encourage private enforcement of laws designed to advance civil rights. Fidelity to that purpose calls for court-awarded fees when a private party's lawsuit, whether or not its settlement is registered in court, vindicates rights Congress sought to secure. I would so hold and therefore dissent from the judgment and opinion of the Court.

## Questions

**1.** Both the *Buckhannon* majority and the dissent perceive a plain or "accepted" meaning to the term "prevailing party." But the two meanings are plainly not the same. What sources and arguments support the opposing meanings?

**2.** Compare the use of dictionaries in *Muscarello* and *Buckhannon*. To what extent is the plain meaning of a term determined by which dictionary the interpreter chooses as his reference? Is the plain meaning rule thus applied more or less deferential to the legislature?

**3.** Why do you think the *Buckhannon* majority "doubt[s] that legislative history could overcome what we think is the rather clear meaning of . . . the term actually used in that statute." What policies undergird this stance? What reasons can you think of for adopting the opposite rule?

## 3.   Focusing on Issues Raised by Criminal Statutes

There are no common law crimes in the United States. Instead, all crimes are defined by statute in order to provide notice to individuals. Due process requires adequate notice because the police power wielded by the state to enforce criminal penalties is a great one. As you have seen in the cases above, interpreting plain meaning in the criminal context raises specific issues of construction. The following cases explore this idea further.

## McBoyle v. United States

Supreme Court of the United States, 1931.
283 U.S. 25, 51 S.Ct. 340, 75 L.Ed. 816.

■ Mr. Justice Holmes delivered the opinion of the Court.

The petitioner was convicted of transporting from Ottawa, Illinois, to Guymon, Oklahoma, an airplane that he knew to have been stolen, and was sentenced to serve three years' imprisonment and to pay a fine of $2,000. The judgment was affirmed by the Circuit Court of Appeals for the Tenth

Circuit. 43 F.(2d) 273. A writ of certiorari was granted by this Court on the question whether the National Motor Vehicle Theft Act applies to aircraft. Act of October 29, 1919, c. 89; 41 Stat. 324; U.S.Code, Title 18, § 408. That Act provides: "Sec. 2. That when used in this Act: (a) The term 'motor vehicle' shall include an automobile, automobile truck, automobile wagon, motor cycle, or any other self-propelled vehicle not designed for running on rails; ... Sec. 3. That whoever shall transport or cause to be transported in interstate or foreign commerce a motor vehicle, knowing the same to have been stolen, shall be punished by a fine of not more than $5,000, or by imprisonment of not more than five years, or both."

Section 2 defines the motor vehicles of which the transportation in interstate commerce is punished in § 3. The question is the meaning of the word 'vehicle' in the phrase "any other self-propelled vehicle not designed for running on rails." No doubt etymologically it is possible to use the word to signify a conveyance working on land, water or air, and sometimes legislation extends the use in that direction, e.g., land and air, water being separately provided for, in the Tariff Act, September 22, 1922, c. 356, § 401(b), 42 Stat. 858, 948. But in everyday speech 'vehicle' calls up the picture of a thing moving on land. Thus in Rev.Stats. § 4, intended, the Government suggests, rather to enlarge than to restrict the definition, vehicle includes every contrivance capable of being used "as a means of transportation on land." And this is repeated, expressly excluding aircraft, in the Tariff Act, June 17, 1930, c. 997, § 401(b); 46 Stat. 590, 708. So here, the phrase under discussion calls up the popular picture. For after including automobile truck, automobile wagon and motor cycle, the words "any other self-propelled vehicle not designed for running on rails" still indicate that a vehicle in the popular sense, that is a vehicle running on land, is the theme. It is a vehicle that runs, not something, not commonly called a vehicle, that flies. Airplanes were well known in 1919, when this statute was passed; but it is admitted that they were not mentioned in the reports or in the debates in Congress. It is impossible to read words that so carefully enumerate the different forms of motor vehicles and have no reference of any kind to aircraft, as including airplanes under a term that usage more and more precisely confines to a different class. The counsel for the petitioner have shown that the phraseology of the statute as to motor vehicles follows that of earlier statutes of Connecticut, Delaware, Ohio, Michigan and Missouri, not to mention the late Regulations of Traffic for the District of Columbia, Title 6, c. 9, § 242, none of which can be supposed to leave the earth.

Although it is not likely that a criminal will carefully consider the text of the law before he murders or steals, it is reasonable that a fair warning should be given to the world in language that the common world will understand, of what the law intends to do if a certain line is passed. To make the warning fair, so far as possible the line should be clear. When a rule of conduct is laid down in words that evoke in the common mind only the picture of vehicles moving on land, the statute should not be extended to aircraft, simply because it may seem to us that a similar policy applies, or upon the speculation that, if the legislature had thought of it, very likely broader words would have been used. United States v. Thind, 261 U.S. 204, 209.

*Judgment reversed.*

## United States v. Reid

United States District Court for the District of Massachusetts, 2002.
206 F.Supp.2d 132.

■ YOUNG, CHIEF JUDGE.

### I.   Introduction

Is an airplane a "mass transportation vehicle" as that phrase is used in section 801 of the USA PATRIOT Act of 2001, Pub.L. No. 107–56, 115 Stat. 272, 374–76 (codified at 18 U.S.C. § 1993) ("section 1993"), a comprehensive anti-terrorism law enacted in the wake of September 11. That is the question raised by Richard C. Reid ("Reid"), who is accused of attempting to detonate an explosive device in his shoe while aboard an international flight from Paris to Miami that was diverted to Boston after his attempt was foiled by the flight crew and other passengers. If the answer to this question is no, as Reid suggests, then Count Nine of the indictment against him, which alleges that he attempted to "wreck, set fire to, and disable a mass transportation vehicle," in violation of section 1993, see Indictment at 11, must be dismissed.

### II.   Background

The charges against Reid arise out of an incident on December 22, 2001, on American Airlines Flight 63 ("Flight 63"). According to Magistrate Judge Dein's Memorandum and Order dated December 28, 2001 [Docket No. 3] regarding probable cause and the government's motion to detain Reid, there is probable cause to believe the following facts:

Flight 63 was en route from Paris to Miami until Reid created a disturbance on board that caused the aircraft to be diverted to Boston. After one of the flight attendants smelled what she thought was a match, she observed Reid place a match in his mouth. She alerted the captain over the intercom system to what she had seen, and when she returned a few moments later, she saw Reid light another match. According to the flight attendant, Reid appeared to be trying to light the inner tongue of his sneaker, from which a wire was protruding. The attendant tried to stop Reid from lighting his sneaker, but he shoved her into the bulkhead and pushed her to the floor. She got up and ran to get water, at which point a second flight attendant tried to stop Reid. Reid bit the second attendant on the thumb. Shortly thereafter, the first flight attendant returned and threw water in Reid's face. At this point, several passengers came to the aid of the flight attendants and restrained Reid for the duration of the flight. They also injected him with sedatives that were on board the aircraft.

Preliminary laboratory analysis has revealed that both of Reid's sneakers contained "a 'functioning improvised explosive device,' i.e., 'a home-made bomb.' " Dein Order at 4. Had the sneakers been placed against the wall of the aircraft and detonated, they might have been able to blow a hole in the fuselage, potentially causing the aircraft to crash.

### III.   Discussion

In relevant parts, section 1993 states: "whoever willfully wrecks, derails, sets fire to, or disables a mass transportation vehicle ... [or] attempts, threatens, or conspires to do any of the aforesaid acts, shall be fined under this title or imprisoned not more than twenty years, or both." 18 U.S.C. § 1993(a)(1), (a)(8). The phrase "mass transportation" is defined by a cross-reference to section 5302(a)(7) of Title 49 of the United States Code ("section 5302"), "except that the term shall include schoolbus, charter, and sightseeing transportation." 18 U.S.C. § 1993(c)(5). Section 5302 defines "mass transportation" as "transportation by a conveyance that provides regular and continuing general or special transportation to the public." 49 U.S.C. § 5302(a)(7). In contrast to the phrase "mass transportation," the word "vehicle" is given no explicit definition in section 1993, nor is it defined in section 5302.

Reid argues that an airplane is neither a "vehicle" nor engaged in "mass transportation," as those words are used in section 1993. The Court addresses these arguments in turn, but first it considers an argument made by Reid that section 1993 does not provide a punishment for attempt offenses.

* * *

### C.   Is an Aircraft a "Vehicle"?

Finally, Reid argues that an airplane is not a "vehicle." He points to a number of dictionaries that define the word vehicle in a way that could not be read to include aircraft. The second edition of the Random House Dictionary of the English Language (1987), for instance, defines vehicle as "a conveyance moving on wheels, runners, tracks, or the like, as a cart, sled, automobile, or tractor, etc." Def.'s Mot. at 3. The government responds with some dictionary definitions of its own, definitions that are broad enough to include aircraft. An example is found in the seventh edition of Black's Law Dictionary (1999), which defines vehicle as "any conveyance used in transporting passengers or merchandise by land, water, or air." Gov't's Opp'n at 9.

It is not entirely surprising that the parties resort to a battle of dictionaries to resolve the issue, as section 1993 itself provides no definition of the word "vehicle" the way it does for the phrase "mass transportation," and the Supreme Court has on occasion resorted to dictionaries to define words that are not otherwise defined in a statute. E.g., Toyota Motor Mfg. v. Williams, 534 U.S. 184, 122 S.Ct. 681, 691, 151 L.Ed.2d 615 (2002); Tyler v. Cain, 533 U.S. 656, 662, 121 S.Ct. 2478, 150 L.Ed.2d 632 (2001). It is surprising, however, that the parties neglect to include in their litanies of definitions the definition given to the word "vehicle" by Congress.

The Dictionary Act of the United States Code, 1 U.S.C. § 1 et seq., provides general definitions for a handful of words appearing within the code, along with general rules of construction, that apply to the entire code in the absence of a more specific indication within the statute being analyzed. See Rowland v. Cal. Men's Colony, 506 U.S. 194, 200, 113 S.Ct. 716, 121 L.Ed.2d 656 (1993) ("[C]ourts would hardly need direction [from the Dictionary Act] where Congress had thought to include an express, specialized definition for the purpose of a particular Act; ordinary rules of statutory construction would prefer the specific definition over the Dictionary Act's general one."). Although the Dictionary Act defines but a few words appearing in the code, the word "vehicle" is one of them. It states that "[t]he word 'vehicle' includes every description of carriage or other artificial contrivance used, or capable of being used, as a means of transportation *on land*." 1 U.S.C. § 4 (emphasis added).

In a Supreme Court case of some vintage, McBoyle v. United States, 283 U.S. 25, 51 S.Ct. 340, 75 L.Ed. 816 (1931), Justice Holmes wrote for the court that an individual could not be punished for stealing an airplane under a statute that prohibited stealing any "self-propelled vehicle not designed for running on rails." Id. at 26, 51 S.Ct. 340. In so holding, the Supreme Court observed that the definition of "vehicle" supplied by the Dictionary Act did not include an aircraft. Id.

In the seventy-one years since McBoyle, Congress has never amended the Dictionary Act to give the word "vehicle" a broader meaning. Congress has, however, amended the Dictionary Act recently, e.g., Defense of Marriage Act, Pub.L. No. 104–199, § 3(a), 110 Stat. 2419 (1996) (creating 1 U.S.C. § 7, which defines "marriage" and "spouse"), which suggests that the Dictionary Act is not an obscure, forgotten portion of the United States Code, but instead remains vital to the process of interpreting the rest of the code.

The narrow definition of the word "vehicle" set out in the Dictionary Act and clarified by the Supreme Court in McBoyle is consistent with the general structure of the United States Code, which distinguishes among three types of conveyances: vessels, which provide transportation on water, 1 U.S.C. § 3; vehicles, which provide transportation on land, id. § 4; and aircraft, which provide transportation through the air, 49 U.S.C. § 40102(a)(6). A number of statutory provisions recognize this distinction. For example, a provision of the immigration laws makes inadmissible to the United States any alien who engages in terrorist activities, defined to include "[t]he highjacking or sabotage of any conveyance (including an aircraft, vessel, or vehicle)." 8 U.S.C. § 1182(a)(3)(B)(iii)(I). A customs law provides definitions of several words, including vessel and vehicle, and in both of these definitions expressly excludes aircraft. 19 U.S.C. § 1401(a), (b). A criminal law makes it illegal to import or export a "motor vehicle . . . , vessel, [or] aircraft" known to have been stolen. 18 U.S.C. § 553(a)(1). An armed forces provision authorizes the Secretary of Defense to institute a system of reporting to Congress on the readiness of the armed forces, including a measurement of "the extent to which units of the armed forces remove serviceable parts, supplies, or equipment from one vehicle, vessel, or aircraft in order to render a different vehicle, vessel, or aircraft operational." 10 U.S.C. § 117(c)(7). A conservation law states that any individual who traffics in fish, wildlife, or plants in criminal violation of the endangered species laws is subject to forfeiture of "[a]ll vessels, vehicles, aircraft, and other equipment used to aid" in the trafficking of the endangered species. 16 U.S.C. § 3374. These are but a few examples of a pattern that recurs throughout the code. See also, e.g., 8 U.S.C. § 1225(d)(1); id. § 1324(b)(1); id. § 1357(a)(3); 10 U.S.C. § 2401a(b); 16 U.S.C. § 19jj-1(b); id. § 668b(b); id. § 2403(a)(8); id. § 2409(d)(2); 18 U.S.C. § 659; id. § 682(a)(6)(A)(i); id. § 1956(c)(4); 19 U.S.C. § 1433; id. § 1459(a); id. § 1594(a).

Indeed, Title 18 of the code contains a separate provision making illegal the same acts proscribed in section 1993, but with respect to aircraft in particular. Section 32 of Title 18 subjects to the same punishment as section 1993 any individual who "willfully sets fire to, damages, destroys, disables, or wrecks any aircraft in the special aircraft jurisdiction of the United States," 18 U.S.C. § 32(a)(1), and any individual who "attempts or conspires" to do the same, id. § 32(a)(7).] In the Court's view, the structure of the United States Code provides compelling evidence that the word "vehicle" is used in a very particular manner within the code, a manner separate and distinct from the word "aircraft."

In the event that any doubt remains about the fact that the word "vehicle" does not comprise aircraft, the Court notes that the legislative history of the USA PATRIOT Act further supports the notion that airplanes are not within the ambit of section 1993. Senator Leahy, one of the sponsors of the bill, made the following remarks during his presentation of the bill to the Senate for final vote:

> Just last week, a Greyhound bus crashed in Tennessee after a deranged passenger slit the driver's throat and then grabbed the steering wheel, forc[ing] the bus into oncoming traffic. Six people were killed in the crash. *Because there are currently no federal law[s] addressing terrorism of mass transportation systems, however, there may be no federal jurisdiction over such a case*, even if it were committed by suspected terrorists. Clearly, there is an urgent need for strong criminal legislation to deter attacks against mass transportation systems. Section 801 [section 1993] will fill this gap.

147 Cong. Rec. S10,551 (daily ed. Oct. 11, 2001) (statement of Sen. Leahy) (emphasis added). Senator Leahy's comments suggest that section 1993 was intended not to provide additional punishment for destruction or attempted destruction of aircraft, but rather to ensure that other modes of transportation, vulnerable to terrorist attack but believed to be outside the reach of the federal criminal laws, come within the reach of those laws. This legislation was intended to "fill in the gaps" and address modes of transportation that Congress had not already specifically protected.

There were existing federal laws addressing terrorist acts against airplanes before September 11, 2001, and Reid has been charged under these laws. As mentioned earlier, Count Seven of the indictment charges Reid with attempted destruction of an aircraft, in violation of 18 U.S.C. § 32. Indictment at 8. In addition, Count Three of the indictment charges Reid with violating 49 U.S.C. § 46505(b)(3) and (c), which makes it illegal to place or attempt to place an explosive device on board an aircraft. Indictment at 4. Counts Five and Six of the indictment allege that Reid interfered with flight crew members during the performance of the crew members' duties by assaulting or intimidating them, in violation of 49 U.S.C. § 46504. Indictment at 6–7. As the indictment against Reid illustrates, a comprehensive patchwork of laws existed prior to the enactment of the USA PATRIOT Act that address acts of terrorism against aircraft.

The government argues that the legislative history mentioned above suggests that what motivated Congress in passing section 1993 was to ensure that acts of terrorism against mass transportation systems, including aircraft, were criminalized. In other words, Senator Leahy's comments reflect concern that acts of terrorism generally might not be federal crimes, not that attacks against Greyhound buses, for example, were not federal crimes. The Court finds this argument unpersuasive. The government's argument does not square with the language of section 1993, particularly as it relates to section 32, which proscribes similar acts against aircraft. A comparison of these two statutes reveals that there is no difference in the two provisions in terms of the acts that are proscribed, except in ways that are not relevant here. Section 1993, for instance, makes it unlawful to "derail" a mass transportation vehicle, but that would appear to apply only to trains. There is no new proscription of acts of terrorism, however defined, in section 1993 that is not also found in section 32. Instead, the key distinction between section 1993 and section 32 lies in the type of conveyance that is protected by the provision.

According to the government, this form of reasoning does not advance Reid's cause, because section 1993 is necessarily duplicative no matter how it is read. The government contends that destruction of a subway train or bus is already addressed in separate statutes, just as is destroying an airplane, and thus construing section 1993 to cover only buses and trains renders the statute entirely gratuitous, as it would proscribe no new conduct. The government points to the phrase "motor vehicle"—defined as "every description of carriage or other contrivance propelled or drawn by mechanical power and used for commercial purposes on the highways in the transportation of passengers," 18 U.S.C. § 31(a)(6)—as evidence that much of what Congress sought to cover in section 1993 was already covered elsewhere. The Court agrees that this definition almost certainly encompasses buses, although it is an open question whether it covers trains, subway systems, and other forms of mass transportation.

The Court disagrees, however, that this argument compels the Court to include aircraft within the definition of "vehicle." It may be true that the one form of transportation (buses) that motivated Congress (or at least one of its members) to pass the law in the first place was already covered by pre-existing law. It may also be true that the outer limits of the word "vehicle" are fuzzy and imprecise. These factors do not dissuade the Court from its ultimate conclusion. The clear distinction within the United States Code between vehicles and aircraft, the legislative history of section 1993 suggesting a concern with attacks on buses or similar conveyances, and the variety of pre-existing criminal laws addressing attacks against aircraft, outweigh countervailing factors and lead the Court to conclude that "vehicle," as it is used in section 1993, does not comprise aircraft.

## IV. Conclusion

Reid's motion to dismiss Count Nine of the indictment against him [Docket No. 32] is ALLOWED because Reid's alleged actions are not within the scope of conduct prohibited by section 1993. While section 1993 does proscribe attempts, and the airplane that Reid allegedly attempted to destroy was engaged in "mass transportation," it is not a "vehicle" as that word is used by Congress.

It is important to note that the result the Court reaches here can have no effect at all on the sentence ultimately to be visited on Reid were he to be convicted. Even had this Court denied the motion to dismiss Count Nine and . . . were Reid convicted on this count as well, under the United States Sentencing Guidelines he cannot be made to serve one more day in prison due to this violation. See U.S. Sentencing Guidelines Manual §§ 3D1.2, 3D1.3(a). Nor, however, ought the government here be considered to have "overcharged" to obtain some sort of litigation advantage, e.g., piling on redundant charges just to afford the jury separate opportunities to convict. To the contrary, section 1993 is new legislation, its contours not yet fully explored. Both the defense and the government are to be commended for ably briefing and presenting this issue. Its prompt resolution by the Court now will allow the government, should it wish, to appeal this Court's interpretation without disturbing the November 4, 2002 trial date.

SO ORDERED.

## United States v. Marshall

United States Court of Appeals for Seventh Circuit, 1990.
908 F.2d 1312.

aff'd *sub nom* Chapman v. U.S., 500 U.S. 453, 111 S.Ct. 1919, 114 L.Ed.2d 524 (1991).

■ EASTERBROOK, J.

\* \* \*

. . . [W]e must resolve . . . [w]hether 21 U.S.C. § 841(b)(1)(A)(v) and (B)(v), which set mandatory minimum terms of imprisonment—five years for selling more than one gram of a "mixture or substance containing a detectable amount" of LSD, ten years for more than ten grams—exclude the weight of a carrier medium. \* \* \*

### I

According to the Sentencing Commission, the LSD in an average dose weighs 0.05 milligrams. Twenty thousand pure doses are a gram. But 0.05 mg is almost invisible, so LSD is distributed to retail customers in a carrier. Pure LSD is dissolved in a solvent such as alcohol and sprayed on paper or gelatin; alternatively the paper may be dipped in the solution. After the solvent evaporates, the paper or gel is cut into one-dose squares and sold by the square. Users swallow the squares or may drop them into a beverage, releasing the drug. Although the gelatin and paper are light, they weigh much more than the drug. Marshall's 11,751 doses weighed 113.32 grams; the LSD accounted for only 670.72 mg of this, not enough to activate the five-year mandatory minimum sentence, let alone the ten-year minimum. The ten sheets of blotter paper carrying the 1,000 doses Chapman and confederates sold weighed 5.7 grams; the LSD in the paper did not approach the one-gram threshold for a mandatory minimum sentence. This disparity between the weight of the pure LSD and the weight of LSD-plus-carrier underlies the defendants' arguments.

### A

If the carrier counts in the weight of the "mixture or substance containing a detectable amount" of LSD, some odd things may happen. Weight in the hands of distributors may exceed that of manufacturers and wholesalers. Big fish then could receive paltry sentences or small fish draconian ones. Someone who sold 19,999 doses of pure LSD (at 0.05 mg per dose) would escape the five-year mandatory minimum of § 841(b)(1)(B)(v) and be covered by § 841(b)(1)(C), which lacks a minimum term and has a maximum of "only" 20 years. Someone who sold a single hit of LSD dissolved in a tumbler of orange juice could be exposed to a ten-year mandatory minimum. Retailers could fall in or out of the mandatory terms depending not on the number of doses but on the medium: sugar cubes weigh more than paper, which weighs more than gelatin. One way to eliminate the possibility of such consequences is to say that the carrier is not a "mixture or substance containing a detectable amount" of the drug. Defendants ask us to do this.

\* \* \*

[The 7th Circuit *en banc* majority concluded that despite these arguably anomalous results, the LSD carrier came within the statutory term "mixture or substance containing a detectable amount."]

■ POSNER, J., dissenting.

\* \* \*

LSD is a potentially dangerous drug, especially for psychotics (whom it can drive to suicide). Hoffman, LSD: My Problem Child 67–71 (1983). But many things are dangerous for psychotics. No one believes that LSD is a more dangerous drug than heroin or cocaine (particularly crack cocaine). The general view is that it is *much* less dangerous. Cox, *et al.*, Drugs and Drug Abuse: A Reference Text 313–15 (1983). There is no indication that

Congress believes it to be more dangerous, or more difficult to control. The heavy sentences that the law commands for minor traffickers in LSD are the inadvertent result of the interaction among a statutory procedure for measuring weight, adopted without understanding how LSD is sold; a decision to specify harsh mandatory minimum sentences for drug traffickers, based on the weight of the drug sold; and a decision (gratuitous and unreflective, as far as I can see) by the framers of the Guidelines to key punishment to the statutory measure of weight, thereby amplifying Congress's initial error and ensuring that the big dealer who makes or ships the pure drug will indeed receive a shorter sentence than the small dealer who handles the stuff in its street form. As the wholesale value of LSD may be as little as 35 cents a dose (Report 1988: The Supply of Illicit Drugs to the United States 52 (National Narcotics Intelligence Consumers Comm. 1989)), a seller of five sugar cubes could be subject to a mandatory minimum prison term of ten years for selling $2 worth of illegal drugs. Dean received six years (no parole, remember) for selling $73 worth. The irrationality is quite bad enough if we confine our attention to LSD sold on blotter paper, since the weight of blotter paper varies considerably, making punishment turn on a factor that has no relation to the dosages or market values of LSD.

Well, what if anything can we judges do about this mess? The answer lies in the shadow of a jurisprudential disagreement that is not less important by virtue of being unavowed by most judges. It is the disagreement between the severely positivistic view that the content of law is exhausted in clear, explicit, and definite enactments by or under express delegation from legislatures, and the natural lawyer's or legal pragmatist's view that the practice of interpretation and the general terms of the Constitution (such as "equal protection of the laws") authorize judges to enrich positive law with the moral values and practical concerns of civilized society. Judges who in other respects have seemed quite similar, such as Holmes and Cardozo, have taken opposite sides of this issue. Neither approach is entirely satisfactory. The first buys political neutrality and a type of objectivity at the price of substantive injustice, while the second buys justice in the individual case at the price of considerable uncertainty and, not infrequently, judicial willfulness. It is no wonder that our legal system oscillates between the approaches. The positivist view, applied unflinchingly to this case, commands the affirmance of prison sentences that are exceptionally harsh by the standards of the modern Western world, dictated by an accidental, unintended scheme of punishment nevertheless implied by the words (taken one by one) of the relevant enactments. The natural law or pragmatist view leads to a freer interpretation, one influenced by norms of equal treatment; and let us explore the interpretive possibilities here. One is to interpret "mixture or substance containing a detectable amount of [LSD]" to exclude the carrier medium—the blotter paper, sugar or gelatin cubes, and orange juice or other beverage. That is the course we rejected in *United States v. Rose, supra,* 881 F.2d at 388, as have the other circuits. I wrote *Rose,* but I am no longer confident that its literal interpretation of the statute, under which the blotter paper, cubes, etc. are "substances" that "contain" LSD, is inevitable. The blotter paper, etc. are better viewed, I now think, as carriers, like the package in which a kilo of cocaine comes wrapped or the bottle in which a fifth of liquor is sold.

Interpreted to exclude the carrier, the punishment schedule for LSD would make perfectly good sense; it would not warp the statutory design. The comparison with heroin and cocaine is again illuminating. The statute imposes the five-year mandatory minimum sentence on anyone who sells a substance or mixture containing a hundred grams of heroin, equal to 10,000 to 20,000 doses. One gram of pure LSD, which also would trigger the five-year minimum, yields 20,000 doses. The comparable figures for cocaine are 3250 to 50,000 doses, placing LSD in about the middle. So Congress may have wanted to base punishment for the sale of LSD on the weight of the pure drug after all, using one and ten grams of the pure drug to trigger the five-year and ten-year minima (and corresponding maxima— twenty years and forty years). This interpretation leaves "substance or mixture containing" without a referent, so far as LSD is concerned. But we must remember that Congress used the identical term in each subsection that specifies the quantity of a drug that subjects the seller to the designated minimum and maximum punishments. In thus automatically including the same term in each subsection, Congress did not necessarily affirm that, for each and every drug covered by the statute, a substance or mixture containing the drug *must* be found.

## Notes and Questions

1. In Chapman v. United States, 500 U.S. 453 (1991), the Supreme Court adopted the position of the Seventh Circuit majority in *Marshall* that the mandatory minimum prison term statute should be interpreted to include the weight of the LSD carrier in calculating the weight of the "mixture or substance containing a detectable amount" of the drug.

2. The two broad trends in statutory interpretation that Judge Posner recognizes in United States v. Marshall are by no means limited to the construction of criminal statutes. The sequence of decisions in this book, from Johnson v. Southern Pacific to *Holy Trinity,* and onward also demonstrate courts' "jurisprudential disagreement" over the interpretation of statutes.

3. How do the interpretive techniques employed in *Marshall* differ from those used in *McBoyle* and *Reid*?

## Review Problem

Recall the Metropolis municipal ordinance on panhandling that you drafted in response to an exercise at the beginning of Part III. Assume that your ordinance is now in effect. The following events have transpired since.

a. It is rush hour in August, and the subway platform in the heart of Metropolis is packed. Hot and sticky commuters wait for a train that has been delayed. In the middle of the subway platform, a reasonably well-dressed, slightly disheveled looking woman named Billie removes a deformed horn from her bag. She places it to her lips, and a sudden, piercing din begins to emanate from the instrument. Everyone immediately looks up. Most of the people near Billie start to edge away, although two or three jazz-punk-heavy-metal fusion fans converge and urge her to continue the performance.

Billie tosses her hat upturned onto the ground and shouts the following words to the crowded platform:

EXCUSE ME LADIES AND GENTLEMEN. I APOLOGIZE FOR THE INTERRUPTION. I AM HOMELESS. I AM HUNGRY. I CANNOT AFFORD TO REPAIR MY HORN WITHOUT YOUR HELP. IF YOU GIVE GENEROUSLY, I PROMISE TO PLAY MY HORN SOMEWHERE ELSE.

A few tentative hands toss quarters and bills into the hat. However, Billie is disappointed with the response, and she lifts the horn threateningly to her mouth. Suddenly, two transit officers arrive and escort Billie away. She is charged under your new ordinance.

Disillusioned with the political process, you have quit your job as a legislative aide, and you now work at a Legal Aid Clinic. Billie has hired you to defend her. Based on the ordinance you have drafted, what do you think Billie's best arguments would be? Would she be convicted? On the basis of Billie's case, is there any provision of the ordinance you would amend?

b. The Metropolis Transit Authority has given permission to the Metropolis Animal Shelter to set up a booth where uniformed volunteers may accept donations. On a slow evening not long ago, Don, one of the Shelter's volunteers, was told to find some way to solicit donations more actively. Having little experience in such matters, Don decided to buy a cup of coffee and hope an idea would occur to him. Suddenly, an older woman walked by Don, who was decked out in a distinctive Animal Shelter uniform, and dropped two dimes into his coffee. The dimes sank to the bottom of Don's cup, still half-filled with coffee. Other subway patrons followed suit, though Don did not say a word. Delighted, Don walked back and forth on the platform, until the cup was about to burst. As he returned to the Shelter's booth, two transit officers detained him. Don has been charged under your ordinance.

This time you are no longer a legislative aide, nor a Legal Aid attorney; you have now moved on to greener, private practice pastures. The Metropolis Animal Shelter has hired you to defend Don. Based on the ordinance you have drafted, what would Don's best arguments be? Would he be convicted? On the basis of the Animal Shelter's case, is there any provision of the ordinance you would amend?

---

## C. THE CONTEXTS OF STATUTES AND THEIR INTERPRETATION

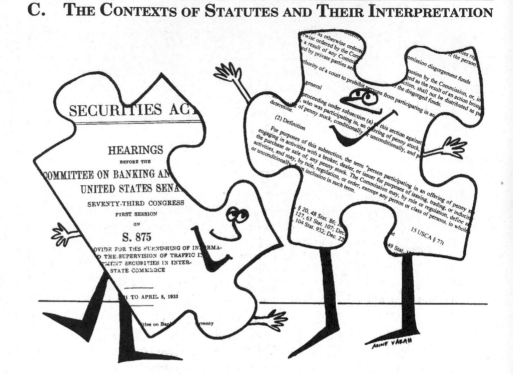

## 1. INTERPRETING STATUTES BY REFERENCE TO THE PRIOR STATE OF THE LAW

### Johnson v. Southern Pacific

(U.S. 1904).

[Reread the Supreme Court's opinion, *supra*, analyzing particularly the nature of the evidence of legislative intent and the Supreme Court's treatment of it]

### Heydon's Case

3 Coke 7a, 76 Eng.Rep. 637 (Court of Exchequer 1584).

[The technique of "purpose interpretation," of which the U.S. Supreme Court's opinion in the *Johnson* case is a good example, is usually traced back to this case. The much-quoted "Doctrine of Heydon's Case" was stated by the reporter as follows:]

And it was resolved by them [the judges], that for the sure and true interpretation of all statutes in general (be they penal or beneficial, restrictive or enlarging of the common law) four things are to be discerned and considered—

1st. What was the common law before the making of the Act.

2nd. What was the mischief and defect for which the common law did not provide.

3rd. What remedy the Parliament hath resolved and appointed to cure the disease of the commonwealth.

And 4th. The true reason of the remedy; and then the office of all the Judges is always to make such construction as shall suppress the mischief, and *pro privato commodo,* and to add force and life to the cure and remedy, according to the true intent of the makers of the Act, *pro bono publico.*

## Question

What assumptions about sources of law underlie the "Doctrine of Heydon's Case"? How valid are these assumptions today?

## Peacock v. Lubbock Compress Company

United States Court of Appeals for the Fifth Circuit, 1958.
252 F.2d 892.

■ John R. Brown, Circuit Judge.

This whole case turns on one word. Does the word 'and' mean *and?* Does it mean *or?* May it have been primarily used as a comma?

The question arises in connection with an FLSA [Fair Labor Standards Act] suit for overtime wages brought by three night watchmen against the Compress Company who, admittedly, was subject to the Act, and had employed them for eighty-four hours each week at a wage in excess of the minimum hourly rate (75 cents) but without payment of overtime. The dispute narrows down to Section 207(c) with emphasis on the few words italicized:

"In the case of an employer engaged in the first processing of milk, buttermilk, whey, skimmed milk, or cream into dairy products, *or in the ginning and compressing of cotton,* or in the processing of cottonseed, or in the processing of sugar beets, sugar-beet molasses, sugarcane, or maple sap, into sugar * * * the provisions of subsection (a) * * *(29 U.S.C.A. § 207(a) requiring overtime) shall not apply to his employees in any place of employment where he is so engaged * * *." 29 U.S.C.A. § 207(c), Section 7 of the Act.

The statute, of course, says "ginning and compressing of cotton." If it is conjunctive, the watchmen are right, the Compress is wrong, and the cause must be reversed. This is so because it is admitted that the Compress Company is engaged exclusively in compressing cotton and never has engaged in the activity of ginning cotton or a combination of ginning and compressing. Actually, it cuts much deeper since it is an acknowledged undisputed fact of the cotton industry that compressing is an operation entirely removed from ginning and that the two are never carried on together. To read it literally here is to read it out of the statute.

But the word "and" is not a word with a single meaning, for chameleonlike, it takes its color from its surroundings. Nor has the law looked upon it as such. It is ancient learning, recorded authoritatively for us nearly one hundred years ago, echoing that which had accumulated in the previous years and forecasting that which was to come,[1] that, "In the construction of statutes, it is the duty of the Court to ascertain the clear intention of the legislature. In order to do this, Courts are often compelled to construe 'or' as meaning 'and,' and again 'and' as meaning 'or.'" United States v. Fisk, 70 U.S. 445, 448 (1866), and see Heydon's Case, 3 Co. 7a (1584).

In searching then for the Congressional purpose, there appears to be no basis for concluding that the exemption was to be confined to those engaging in *both* ginning and compressing. Indeed, the contrary appears. The great concern of Congress was to exempt agriculture as such from the Act. Maneja v. Waialua Agricultural Co., 349 U.S. 254. Once it set out to shore up that basic exclusion, certain operation such as those defined in Section 207(c) were specifically removed so far as *hours* were concerned, and other operations of the kind described in 213(a)(10) within the area of production to be defined administratively were taken[2] out from the Act as to both *hours* and *wages*. The latter, Section 213(a)(10), note 2, supra, was to make certain that for services described in it, the small farms forced to use nearby independent contractors, or the like, would not be worse off than larger integrated farms equipped with their own facilities.[3] In that Section, Congress did not even find it necessary to use the descriptive term "cotton." So long as the operation is within the area of production as promulgated, the 213(a)(10) exemption applies to ginning of cotton, the compressing of cotton, or either one or both of them.

Of course the two sections, 207(c) and 213(a)(10) are not complementary and are intended to, and do, accomplish different objectives. Maneja v. Waialua Agricultural Co., supra. But if either of the two activities, ginning *or* compressing, was such as to warrant exemption within the geographical-population limits of the area of production, Mitchell v. Budd, 350 U.S. 473,

---

**1.** Hundreds of cases are conveniently collected in Vol. 3, Words and Phrases, under the title word "And," at page 569, and see especially pages 583–593 under the heading of "Civil Statutes." Whatever the particular meaning attributed to the word or words may be in each of these collected cases, the universal test may be summarized. The words "and" and "or" when used in a statute are convertible, as the sense may require. A substitution of one for the other is frequently resorted to in the interpretation of statutes, when the evident intention of the lawmaker requires it.

**2.** 29 U.S.C.A. § 213(a)(10): "The provisions of sections 206 and 207 * * * (29 U.S.C.A. §§ 206, 207) shall not apply with respect to * * * (10) any individual employed within the area of production (as defined by the Administrator), engaged in handling, packing, storing, *ginning, compressing*, pasteurizing, drying, preparing in their raw or natural state, or canning of agricultural or horticultural commodities for market, or in making cheese or butter or other dairy products." (Emphasis supplied.)

**3.** Maneja v. Waialua Agricultural Co., 349 U.S. 254, 268,: "Thus, for example, the cotton farmer without a gin was placed on an equal footing with farms who ginning their own cotton, since each could have their cotton ginned by employees who were covered by neither the wage nor the hour provisions of the Act."

from the whole Act, it seems highly improbable[4] that Congress in mentioning the two again deliberately set out to prescribe a standard impossible to meet as to the hours-overtime exemption of 207(c).

If Congress did not intend the Section 207(c) exemption to apply to those same operations described in 213(a)(10) "ginning, compressing," all it had to do was to omit altogether any reference to this activity in 207(c). To accomplish any such assumed objective, it was not necessary for Congress to go at it by the roundabout method of appearing to grant it only to take it away by the prerequisite of a dual combination of "ginning and compressing" of cotton.[5]

For us to conclude that Congress meant "and" in a literal conjunctive sense is to determine that Congress meant in fact to grant no relief. To do this is to ignore realities, for Congress has long been acutely aware of the manifold problems of the production, marketing and distribution of cotton. The commodity is one of the most important in the complex pattern of farm parity and production control legislation. It is inconceivable that Congress legislated in ignorance of the distinctive nature of the physical operations of ginning of cotton as compared to the compressing of cotton, or that, with full consciousness of these practicable considerations, it meant to lay down a standard which could not be met in fact.

Literalism gives way in the face of such considerations. [Citations omitted]. Under Section 207(c), the ginning of cotton, the compressing of cotton, the performance of either or both is exempt from the overtime provisions of the Act.

Affirmed.

## Question

A literal reading of the relevant provision of the Fair Labor Standards Act would have exempted from an obligation to pay overtime only employers of workers engaged in the combined activity of both ginning and compressing cotton; it would have required payment of overtime of workers engaged separately in either of those activities. The employer's preferred construction of the statute, reading "and" as "or," thus substantially

---

**4.**  Maneja v. Waialua Agricultural Co., 349 U.S. 254, 267: That case involved the processing of sugar cane into sugar. The Court's reference to "cotton ginning" alone and not in conjunction with compressing indicates, however, that it saw no decisive significance in the coupling word "and". To the suggested argument that the express exemption in 207(c) from overtime liabilities was a deliberate choice by Congress to limit relief to overtime, the Court said: "But we cannot be sure of this, because § 7(c) (207(c)) includes similar exemptions for operations like cotton ginning, which also come within the agricultural exemption if performed by the farmer on his own crops. More significant is the omission of sugar milling from the exemption provided by § 13(a)(10) § 213(a)(10) from various processing operations performed within the area of production."

**5.**  The sparse legislative history on the point as set forth in the briefs is unilluminating. Apparently in its original form, Senate Bill 2475, 75th Congress, granted the overtime exemption for "the ginning and bailing of cotton." The "bailing" is an integral part of the "ginning" process. In Committee "compressing and storing" of cotton was added.

broadened the scope of the employers' exemption. Given the significantly different meanings and effects of "and" and "or," as well as the overall purpose of the FLSA to improve workers' conditions, why was it appropriate for the court to substitute "or" for "and"? Is the court's interpretation any more or less problematic than interpolating a comma in *Johnson v. Southern Pacific*, or than ignoring the repeal of the bankruptcy provisions in *Adamo*?

## 2.  INTERPRETING A STATUTE IN LIGHT OF RELATED STATUTES OR PROVISIONS

### Alaska Steamship Co. v. United States

Supreme Court of the United States, 1933.
290 U.S. 256, 54 S.Ct. 159, 78 L.Ed. 302.

Certiorari to review the affirmance of a judgment dismissing a suit against the United States under the Tucker Act.

■ MR. JUSTICE STONE delivered the opinion of the Court.

In this suit, brought under the Tucker Act, 24 Stat. 505, in the District Court for Western Washington, petitioner sought compensation at an agreed rate for the transportation of certain destitute seamen from Ketchikan, Alaska, to Seattle, under the provisions of § 4578 R.S., as amended, 46 U.S.C.A. § 679. That section imposes on masters of United States vessels homeward bound the duty, upon request of consular officers, to receive and carry destitute seamen to the port of destination at such compensation not exceeding a specified amount as may be agreed upon by the master with a consular officer, and authorizes the consular officer to issue certificates for such transportation, "which shall be assignable for collection." By § 4526 R.S., 17 Stat. 269, as amended December 21, 1898, 30 Stat. 755, 46 U.S.C.A. § 593, seamen, whose term of service is terminated by loss or wreck of their vessel, are "destitute seamen," and are required to be transported as provided in § 4578.

The demand in the present case was for compensation for the transportation of the crew of the S.S. Depere, owned by petitioner, which had been wrecked on the Alaska coast and for that reason had been unable to complete her voyage. The crew was received and carried to Seattle on petitioner's S.S. Yukon, on certificate of the deputy customs collector of Alaska that he had agreed with the master for their transportation at a specified rate. The Comptroller General refused payment upon the certificate on the sole ground that it was the duty of petitioner to transport to the United States the crew of its own wrecked vessel, and that the Congressional appropriation for the relief of American seamen was not available to compensate the owner for performing that duty. Judgment of the district court dismissing the complaint, 60 F.2d 135, was affirmed by the Court of Appeals for the Ninth Circuit, on the ground that the certificate of the deputy collector authorizing the transportation did not satisfy the requirement of the statute that the certificate should be that of a consular officer. 63 F.2d 398. This court granted certiorari.

The government, conceding that the statute by long administrative practice has been construed as authorizing payment for transportation of seamen from Alaska on the certificate of deputy customs collectors, insists that it does not authorize payment to the owner for the transportation of the crew of his own wrecked vessel and that such has been its administrative construction.

1.  If the statutory language is to be taken literally, the certificate, which by R.S. § 4578 is authority for the transportation and evidence of the right of the vessel to compensation, must be that of a consular officer. Deputy collectors of customs are not consular officers and there are no consular officers in Alaska. If the right to compensation is dependent upon certification by a consular officer the statutes providing for transportation of destitute seamen can be given no effect in Alaska. But the meaning of this provision must be ascertained by reading it with related statutes and in the light of a long and consistent administrative practice.

Since 1792 the statutes of the United States have made provision for the return of destitute seamen to this country upon suitable action taken by consular officers of the United States. And since 1803 the government has undertaken to compensate for their transportation. Beginning in 1896, Congress has made provision for the relief of American seamen shipwrecked in Alaska in annual appropriation bills for the maintenance of the diplomatic and consular service. The appropriation bill for that year, 29 Stat. 186, and every later one has extended the benefits of the appropriation for the relief of American seamen in foreign countries to "American seamen shipwrecked in Alaska." The appropriation for 1922 and 1923, c. 204, 42 Stat. 599, 603; c. 21, 42 Stat. 1068, 1072, contained the proviso, not appearing in previous acts, that no part of the appropriation should be available for payment for transportation in excess of a specified rate agreed upon by a consular officer and the master of the vessel. The proviso did not appear in subsequent appropriation acts, but by Act of January 3, 1923, 43 Stat. 1072, it was transferred to its proper place in the shipping laws, where it now appears in § 680 of Title 46 of the United States Code. The Act of 1929, 45 Stat. 1098, applicable when the seamen in the present case were transported, appropriated $70,000 "for relief, protection and burial of American seamen in foreign countries, in the Panama Canal Zone, and in the Philippine Islands, and shipwrecked American seamen in the Territory of Alaska, in the Hawaiian Islands, in Porto Rico and in the Virgin Islands." By the amendment of R.S. § 5226 of December 21, 1898, 30 Stat. 755, 46 U.S.C.A., § 593, it was provided that where the service of a seaman terminates by reason of the loss or wreck of the vessel, "he shall not be entitled to wages for any period beyond such termination of the service and shall be considered as a destitute seaman, and shall be treated and transported to port of shipment," as provided in R.S. § 4578. No exception is made in the case of transportation of seamen from Alaska or other dependencies of the United States.

Thus, from 1896 to the present time, there has been a definite obligation on the part of the government to provide transportation for shipwrecked seamen without reference to the place where shipwrecked, and funds have been annually appropriated for the purpose of carrying out that obligation in the case of seamen shipwrecked in Alaska. As appears from the findings of the trial court, not challenged here, the appropriations have been expended for the transportation of shipwrecked seamen from Alaska, in conformity to a practice established and consistently followed at least since 1900. Certificates for the transportation of shipwrecked seamen have been regularly signed and issued by the collector of customs or the deputy collector in Alaska upon forms provided by the Bureau of Navigation of the Department of Commerce. That Bureau, which has a general superintendence over merchant seamen of the United States, 46 U.S.C.A., §§ 1 and 2, has regularly supplied its customs officials and its agents in Alaska with these forms, with instructions that they were to be used in arranging transportation of shipwrecked seamen to the United States, as provided by the sections of the statute to which reference has been made. The stipulated amounts due for the transportation, as certified, have been regularly paid without objection upon presentation of the certificate to the disbursing officer of the United States.

Courts are slow to disturb the settled administrative construction of a statute long and consistently adhered to. Brown v. United States, 113 U.S. 568, 571, 5 S.Ct. 648, 28 L.Ed. 1079; United States v. Philbrick, 120 U.S. 52, 59, 7 S.Ct. 413, 30 L.Ed. 559; United States v. G. Falk & Bro., 204 U.S. 143, 151, 27 S.Ct. 191, 51 L.Ed. 411. This is especially the case where, as here, the declared will of the legislative body could not be carried out without the construction adopted. That construction must be accepted and applied by the courts when, as in the present case, it has received Congressional approval, implicit in the annual appropriations over a period of thirty-five years, the expenditure of which was effected by resort to the administrative practice, and in amendments by Congress to the statutes relating to transportation of destitute seamen without modification of that practice. United States v. G. Falk & Bro., supra; compare United States v. Missouri Pacific R. Co., 278 U.S. 269, 49 S.Ct. 133, 73 L.Ed. 322.

2.  The rejection of petitioner's claim by the Comptroller General rests upon the supposed duty of the owner to transport to the home port the seamen of its own wrecked vessel. Diligent search by counsel of the ancient learning of the admiralty has failed to disclose the existence of any such duty.

* * *

The rulings of the Comptroller General rest upon a proposition so plainly contrary to law and so plainly in conflict with the statute as to leave them without weight as administrative constructions of it. United States v. Missouri Pacific R. Co., supra.

Reversed.

## Question

Recall the Supreme Court's use of legislative history in *Holy Trinity:* the Court there relied on a Committee Report to hold that Congress never intended to bring "brain toilers" within the scope of the immigration prohibition on contract labor. The Committee recognized that the statute, as written, would cover "brain toilers," but feared that time constraints would prevent redrafting the bill. Under these circumstances, the Court's application of the Committee's unenacted clarification may seem troublesome. In *Alaska Steamship,* the Court relied on subsequent legislation to clarify the meaning of the destitute seaman statute, in so far as it applied to repatriations from Alaska. Is the Court on firmer ground when it interprets a statute in light of *subsequent* legislation, as opposed to interpreting a statute in light of legislative information contemporaneous with the bill's passage?

## United States v. Hutcheson

Supreme Court of the United States, 1941.
312 U.S. 219, 61 S.Ct. 463, 85 L.Ed. 788.

■ MR. JUSTICE FRANKFURTER delivered the opinion of the Court.

Whether the use of conventional, peaceful activities by a union in controversy with a rival union over certain jobs is a violation of the Sherman Law, Act of July 2, 1890, 26 Stat. 209, as amended, 15 U.S.C. § 1, is the question. It is sharply presented in this case because it arises in a criminal prosecution. Concededly an injunction either at the suit of the Government or of the employer could not issue.

Summarizing the long indictment, these are the facts. Anheuser–Busch, Inc., operating a large plant in St. Louis, contracted with Borsari Tank Corporation for the erection of an additional facility. The Gaylord Container Corporation, a lessee of adjacent property from Anheuser–Busch, made a similar contract for a new building with the Stocker Company. Anheuser–Busch obtained the materials for its brewing and other operations and sold its finished products largely through interstate shipments. The Gaylord Corporation was equally dependent on interstate commerce for marketing its goods, as were the construction companies for their building materials. Among the employees of Anheuser–Busch were members of the United Brotherhood of Carpenters and Joiners of America and of the International Association of Machinists. The conflicting claims of these two organizations, affiliated with the American Federation of Labor, in regard to the erection and dismantling of machinery had long been a source of controversy between them. Anheuser–Busch had had agreements with both organizations whereby the Machinists were given the disputed jobs and the Carpenters agreed to submit all disputes to arbitration. But in 1939 the president of the Carpenters, their general representative, and two officials of the Carpenters' local organization, the four men under indictment, stood on the claims of the Carpenters for the jobs. Rejection by the employer of the Carpenters' demand and the refusal of the latter to submit to arbitration were followed by a strike of the Carpenters, called by the defendants against Anheuser–Busch and the construction companies, a picketing of Anheuser–Busch and its tenant, and a request through circular letters and the official publication of the Carpenters that union members and their friends refrain from buying Anheuser–Busch beer.

These activities on behalf of the Carpenters formed the charge of the indictment as a criminal combination and conspiracy in violation of the Sherman Law. Demurrers denying that what was charged constituted a violation of the laws of the United States were sustained, 32 F.Supp. 600, and the case came here under the Criminal Appeals Act. Act of March 2, 1907, 34 Stat. 1246, 18 U.S.C. § 682; Judicial Code § 238, 28 U.S.C. § 345.

In order to determine whether an indictment charges an offense against the United States, designation by the pleader of the statute under which he purported to lay the charge is immaterial. He may have conceived the charge under one statute which would not sustain the indictment but it may nevertheless come within the terms of another statute. See *Williams v. United States,* 168 U.S. 382. On the other hand, an indictment may validly satisfy the statute under which the pleader proceeded, but other statutes not referred to by him may draw the sting of criminality from the allegations. Here we must consider not merely the Sherman Law but the related enactments which entered into the decision of the district court.

Section 1 of the Sherman Law on which the indictment rested is as follows: "Every contract, combination in the form of trust or otherwise, or conspiracy, in restraint of trade or commerce among the several States, or with foreign nations, is hereby declared to be illegal." The controversies engendered by its application to trade union activities and the efforts to secure legislative relief from its consequences are familiar history. The Clayton Act of 1914 was the result. Act of October 15, 1914, 38 Stat. 730. "This statute was the fruit of unceasing agitation, which extended over more than twenty years and was designed to equalize before the law the position of workingmen and employer as industrial combatants." *Duplex Co. v. Deering,* 254 U.S. 443, 484. Section 20 of that Act, which is set out in the margin in full,[1] withdrew from the general interdict of the Sherman

---

1.  38 Stat. 738, 29 U.S.C. § 52: "No restraining order or injunction shall be granted by any court of the United States, or a judge or the judges thereof, in any case between an employer and employees, or between employers and employees, or between employees, or between persons employed and persons seeking employment, involving, or growing out of, a dispute concerning terms or conditions of employment, unless necessary to prevent irreparable injury to property, or to a property right, of the party making the application, for which injury there is no adequate remedy at law, and such property or property right must be described with particularity in the application, which must be in writing and sworn to by the applicant or by his agent or attorney.

"And no such restraining order or injunction shall prohibit any person or persons, whether singly or in concert, from terminating any relation of employment, or from ceasing to perform any work or labor, or from recommending, advising, or persuading others by peaceful means so to do; or from attending at any place where any such person or persons may lawfully be, for the purpose of peacefully obtaining or communicating information, or from peacefully persuading any person to work or to abstain from working; or from ceasing to patronize or to employ any party to such dispute, or from recommending,

Law specifically enumerated practices of labor unions by prohibiting injunctions against them—since the use of the injunction had been the major source of dissatisfaction—and also relieved such practices of all illegal taint by the catch-all provision, "nor shall any of the acts specified in this paragraph be considered or held to be violations of any law of the United States." The Clayton Act gave rise to new litigation and to renewed controversy in and out of Congress regarding the status of trade unions. By the generality of its terms the Sherman Law had necessarily compelled the courts to work out its meaning from case to case. It was widely believed that into the Clayton Act courts read the very beliefs which that Act was designed to remove. Specifically the courts restricted the scope of § 20 to trade union activities directed against an employer by his own employees. *Duplex Co. v. Deering, supra.* Such a view it was urged, both by powerful judicial dissents and informed lay opinion, misconceived the area of economic conflict that had best be left to economic forces and the pressure of public opinion and not subjected to the judgment of courts. *Ibid.*, p. 485–486. Agitation again led to legislation and in 1932 Congress wrote the Norris–LaGuardia Act. Act of March 23, 1932, 47 Stat. 70, 29 U.S.C. §§ 101–115.

The Norris–LaGuardia Act removed the fetters upon trade union activities, which according to judicial construction § 20 of the Clayton Act had left untouched, by still further narrowing the circumstances under which the federal courts could grant injunctions in labor disputes. More especially, the Act explicitly formulated the "public policy of the United States" in regard to the industrial conflict,[2] and by its light established that the allowable area of union activity was not to be restricted, as it had been in the *Duplex* case, to an immediate employer-employee relation. Therefore, whether trade union conduct constitutes a violation of the Sherman Law is to be determined only by reading the Sherman Law and § 20 of the Clayton Act and the Norris–LaGuardia Act as a harmonizing text of outlawry of labor conduct.

advising, or persuading others by peaceful and lawful means so to do; or from paying or giving to, or withholding from, any person engaged in such dispute, any strike benefits or other moneys or things of value; or from peaceably assembling in a lawful manner, and for lawful purposes; or from doing any act or thing which might lawfully be done in the absence of such dispute by any party thereto; nor shall any of the acts specified in this paragraph be considered or held to be violations of any law of the United States."

**2.** "Whereas under prevailing economic conditions, developed with the aid of governmental authority for owners of property to organize in the corporate and other forms of ownership association, the individual unorganized worker is commonly helpless to exercise actual liberty of contract and to protect his freedom of labor, and thereby to obtain acceptable terms and conditions of employment, wherefore, though he should be free to decline to associate with his fellows, it is necessary that he have full freedom of association, self-organization, and designation of representatives of his own choosing, to negotiate the terms and conditions of his employment, and that he shall be free from the interference, restraint, or coercion of employers of labor, or their agents, in the designation of such representatives or in self-organization or in other concerted activities for the purpose of collective bargaining or other mutual aid or protection."

Were, then, the acts charged against the defendants prohibited, or permitted, by these three interlacing statutes? If the facts laid in the indictment come within the conduct enumerated in § 20 of the Clayton Act they do not constitute a crime within the general terms of the Sherman Law because of the explicit command of that section that such conduct shall not be "considered or held to be violations of any law of the United States." So long as a union acts in its self-interest and does not combine with non-labor groups, the licit and the illicit under § 20 are not to be distinguished by any judgment regarding the wisdom or unwisdom, the rightness or wrongness, the selfishness or unselfishness of the end of which the particular union activities are the means. There is nothing remotely within the terms of § 20 that differentiates between trade union conduct directed against an employer because of a controversy arising in the relation between employer and employee, as such, and conduct similarly directed but ultimately due to an internecine struggle between two unions seeking the favor of the same employer. Such strife between competing unions has been an obdurate conflict in the evolution of so-called craft unionism and has undoubtedly been one of the potent forces in the modern development of industrial unions. These conflicts have intensified industrial tension but there is not the slightest warrant for saying that Congress has made § 20 inapplicable to trade union conduct resulting from them.

In so far as the Clayton Act is concerned, we must therefore dispose of this case as though we had before us precisely the same conduct on the part of the defendants in pressing claims against Anheuser–Busch for increased wages, or shorter hours, or other elements of what are called working conditions. The fact that what was done was done in a competition for jobs against the Machinists rather than against, let us say, a company union is a differentiation which Congress has not put into the federal legislation and which therefore we cannot write into it.

It is at once apparent that the acts with which the defendants are charged are the kind of acts protected by § 20 of the Clayton Act.... But to argue, as it was urged before us, that the *Duplex* case still governs for purposes of a criminal prosecution is to say that that which on the equity side of the court is allowable conduct may in a criminal proceeding become the road to prison. It would be strange indeed that although neither the Government nor Anheuser–Busch could have sought an injunction against the acts here challenged, the elaborate efforts to permit such conduct failed to prevent criminal liability punishable with imprisonment and heavy fines. That is not the way to read the will of Congress, particularly when expressed by a statute which, as we have already indicated, is practically and historically one of a series of enactments touching one of the most sensitive national problems. Such legislation must not be read in a spirit of mutilating narrowness. On matters far less vital and far less interrelated we have had occasion to point out the importance of giving "hospitable scope" to Congressional purpose even when meticulous words are lacking. *Keifer & Keifer v. Reconstruction Finance Corp.,* 306 U.S. 381, 391, and authorities there cited. The appropriate way to read legislation in a situation like the one before us, was indicated by Mr. Justice Holmes on circuit: "A statute may indicate or require as its justification a change in the policy of the law, although it expresses that change only in the specific cases most likely to occur in the mind. The Legislature has the power to decide what the policy of the law shall be, and if it has intimated its will, however indirectly, that will should be recognized and obeyed. The major premise of the conclusion expressed in a statute, the change of policy that induces the enactment, may not be set out in terms, but it is not an adequate discharge of duty for the courts to say: We see what you are driving at, but you have not said it, and therefore we shall go on as before." *Johnson v. United States* 163 F. 30, 32.

The relation of the Norris–LaGuardia Act to the Clayton Act is not that of a tightly drawn amendment to a technically phrased tax provision. The underlying aim of the Norris–LaGuardia Act was to restore the broad purpose which Congress thought it had formulated in the Clayton Act but which was frustrated, so Congress believed, by unduly restrictive judicial construction. This was authoritatively stated by the House Committee on the Judiciary. "The purpose of the bill is to protect the rights of labor in the same manner the Congress intended when it enacted the Clayton Act, October 15, 1914 (38 Stat.L., 738), which act, by reason of its construction and application by the Federal courts, is ineffectual to accomplish the congressional intent." H.Rep. No. 669, 72d Congress, 1st Session, p. 3. The Norris–LaGuardia Act was a disapproval of *Duplex Printing Press Co. v. Deering, supra,* and *Bedford Cut Stone Co. v. Journeymen Stone Cutters' Assn.,* 274 U.S. 37, as the authoritative interpretation of § 20 of the Clayton Act, for Congress now placed its own meaning upon that section. The Norris–LaGuardia Act reasserted the original purpose of the Clayton Act by infusing into it the immunized trade union activities as redefined by the later Act. In this light § 20 removes all such allowable conduct from the taint of being a "violation of any law of the United States," including the Sherman Law. It was precisely in order to minimize the difficulties to which the general language of the Sherman Law in its application to workers had given rise, that Congress cut through all the tangled verbalisms and enumerated concretely the types of activities which had become familiar incidents of union procedure.

*Affirmed.*

■ Mr. Justice Murphy took no part in the disposition of this case.

[The concurring opinion of Mr. Justice Stone is omitted.]

■ Mr. Justice Roberts, dissenting.

I am of [the] opinion that the judgment should be reversed.

The indictment adequately charges a conspiracy to restrain trade and commerce with the specific purpose of preventing Anheuser–Busch from receiving in interstate commerce commodities and materials intended for use in its plant; of preventing the Borsari Corporation from obtaining materials in interstate commerce for use in performing a contract for Anheuser–Busch, and of preventing the Stocker Company from receiving materials in like manner for the construction of a building for the Gaylord

Corporation. The indictment further charges that the conspiracy was to restrain interstate commerce flowing from Missouri into other states of products of Anheuser–Busch and generally to restrain the interstate trade and commerce of the three corporations named.

Without detailing the allegations of the indictment, it is sufficient to say that they undeniably charge a secondary boycott, affecting interstate commerce.

[Discussion of prior decisions under the Clayton Act omitted.]

This court also unanimously held that a conspiracy such as is charged in the instant case renders the conspirators liable to criminal prosecution by the United States under the anti-trust acts.

It is common knowledge that the agitation for complete exemption of labor unions from the provisions of the anti-trust laws persisted. Instead of granting the complete exemption desired, Congress adopted, March 23, 1932, the Norris–LaGuardia Act. The title and the contents of that Act, as well as its legislative history, demonstrate beyond question that its purpose was to define and to limit the jurisdiction of federal courts sitting in equity. The Act broadens the scope of labor disputes as theretofore understood, that is, disputes between an employer and his employees with respect to wages, hours, and working conditions, and provides that before a federal court can enter an injunction to restrain illegal acts certain preliminary findings, based on evidence, must be made. The Act further deprives the courts of the right to issue an injunction against the doing of certain acts by labor organizations or their members. It is unnecessary to detail the acts as to which the jurisdiction of a court of equity is abolished. It is sufficient to say, what a reading of the Act makes letter clear, that the jurisdiction of actions for damages authorized by the Sherman Act, and of the criminal offenses denounced by that Act, are not touched by the Norris–LaGuardia Act.

By a process of construction never, as I think, heretofore indulged by this court, it is now found that, because Congress forbade the issuing of injunctions to restrain certain conduct, it intended to repeal the provisions of the Sherman Act authorizing actions at law and criminal prosecutions for the commission of torts and crimes defined by the anti-trust laws. The doctrine now announced seems to be that an indication of a change of policy in an Act as respects one specific item in a general field of the law, covered by an earlier Act, justifies this court in spelling out an implied repeal of the whole of the earlier statute as applied to conduct of the sort here involved. I venture to say that no court has ever undertaken so radically to legislate where Congress has refused so to do.

The construction of the act now adopted is the more clearly inadmissible when we remember that the scope of proposed amendments and repeals of the anti-trust laws in respect of labor organizations has been the subject of constant controversy and consideration in Congress. In the light of this history, to attribute to Congress an intent to repeal legislation which has had a definite and well understood scope and effect for decades past, by resurrecting a rejected construction of the Clayton Act and extending a policy strictly limited by the Congress itself in the Norris–LaGuardia Act, seems to me a usurpation by the courts of the function of the Congress not only novel but fraught, as well, with the most serious dangers to our constitutional system of division of powers.

■ The CHIEF JUSTICE joins in this opinion.

### Question

United States v. Hutcheson presents another example of the Supreme Court's reference to a legislative scheme consisting of a series or sequence of enactments in order to elucidate the disputed text. What, if any, are the differences in the Court's use of this technique in *Hutcheson* and *Alaska Steamship?* Is its use any more or less (or not at all) problematic in either case?

## 3.   INTERPRETING A STATUTE IN LIGHT OF THE LEGISLATIVE HISTORY

## Securities and Exchange Commission v. Robert Collier & Co.

United States Court of Appeals, Second Circuit, 1935.
76 F.2d 939.

Appeal from the District Court of the United States for the Southern District of New York.

Suit by the Securities & Exchange Commission against Robert Collier & Co., Inc., and others, to enjoin the defendants under the Securities Act of 1933. From a decree dismissing the bill (10 F.Supp. 95), plaintiff appeals.

Before L. Hand, Swan, and Augustus N. Hand, Circuit Judges.

■ L. HAND, CIRCUIT JUDGE. The single question presented by this appeal is whether the Securities and Exchange Commission, created under section 4(a) of title 1 of the Securities Exchange Act of 1934, section 78d, tit. 15, U.S.Code, 15 U.S.C.A. § 78d, may appear in the District Court by its own solicitor and file a bill under section 20(b) of the Securities Act (15 U.S.C.A. § 77t, subd. (b)), or whether it must appear by the Attorney General, or a district attorney. The defendants and the judge thought that the situation fell within our decision in Sutherland v. International Insurance Co., 43 F.2d 969; the Commission insists that section 20(b) is an exception to the general rule. Though we had before us section 20(b) without any knowledge of its amendments in committee, we might still have held that the contrast between the diction of the two clauses was enough to turn the scale against a tradition of even such long standing as that on which the defendants rely. There would have been strong reasons for supposing that so striking a change in expression could only have proceeded from a deliberate difference of intent, no matter how inveterate the contrary usage. But if that be doubtful, the change in the section on its way through Congress makes the intent entirely plain. When first introduced, the two clauses were in identical language. "Whenever it shall appear to the Commission" (at that time the Federal Trade Commission), "that the practices investigated constitute a fraud . . . it shall transmit such evidence as may be available" to "the Attorney General who may in his discretion bring an action. . . . The Commission may transmit such evidence as may be available concerning such acts and practices to the Attorney General who may, in his discretion institute the necessary criminal proceedings under this subchapter." Hearings on H.R. 4314, 73d Congress, 1st Session, p. 6; Hearings on S.R. 875, p. 7. As the bill then stood, its intent was therefore to follow the ancient custom and deny to the Commission control over civil, as well as criminal, prosecutions. During the hearings before the committees, the chief counsel of the Federal Trade Commission, Robert E. Healey, testified; we quote the relevant passages in the margin.* It was after this that the first clause was changed to its present form. We cannot see how any one can doubt what was the purpose of both committees in this amendment, though it is quite true that they said nothing about it in their reports. Healey was not a casual interloper; he was the person chiefly responsible for the prosecution of the new functions about to be conferred, at least so far as they touched legal questions. There cannot be the least question that in fact it was at his suggestion that the change was made and that it was intended to allow the Commission complete autonomy in civil prosecutions. The committees' intent may be irrelevant in construing the section, but the evidence of it as a fact is incontrovertible.

* "This bill provides that if the Commission discovers fraud and misrepresentation in connection with the sale of securities, it shall bring that information to the attention of the Attorney General, who shall proceed by injunction to stop that fraud and also to prosecute the guilty person criminally. My suggestion is where there is such a condition existing that Congress by this bill should say to the Attorney General, 'Punish them,' and then say to the Federal Trade Commission, 'Stop them.' I would amend this bill to provide for giving the power to apply for injunctions to the Commission. It is not wise to leave it to us to submit the information to the Attorney General. If we get the information why should we not use it and go after the fellow right then and there and get the injunction against him continuing to sell the stock? Why should we tell the Attorney General about it so he can seek the injunction? We should tell the Attorney General about it so that he can punish them, but why divide the responsibility? Why create such a magnificent buck-passing opportunity as that?

"Now if this Commission is competent to go out and get these facts,—and I will tell you I think that we are,—and if not, there are two vacancies down there, two vacancies that are just yearning to be filled, by some deserving Democrats,—I tell you I believe that we should be allowed to stop the practice. I submit to you gentlemen, first, if this Commission is on to its job and it finds these fellows selling stock by fraud or misrepresentation, we should be given the power to apply to the courts for an injunction and the prosecuting power should be left to the Attorney General where it belongs." [Hearings on H.R. 4312, 73rd Cong., 1st Sess. pp. 240, 241].

"I wish to offer the suggestion that in the section of this bill which provides that the power of injunction shall be given, that provision be made that if the Commission which is charged with the administration of the bill finds people acting contrary to law or in defiance of the Act, that Commission and not the Attorney General will proceed to ask for an injunction. I would suggest that it is unwise to divide the responsibility and to encounter the delay that would come if we have to send our stuff to the Attorney General. Let him prosecute criminally, let us proceed to stop them." [Hearings on S. 875, 73rd Cong., 1st Sess. p. 226.]

The defendants suggest that the purpose may have been limited to giving power to the Commission to decide when suits should be begun, but yet to require district attorneys to conduct them. Congress has indeed done just that on occasion. Section 12(1) tit. 49, U.S.Code, 49 U.S.C.A. § 12(1); section 413, tit. 33, U.S.Code (33 U.S.C.A. § 413); section 486, tit. 28, U.S.Code (28 U.S.C.A. § 486). But the resulting situation is certainly undesirable administratively, and whenever it has been prescribed, the language has been express. It is extremely unlikely that such a halfway measure should have been here intended. The original bill gave power to the Attorney General not only to decide when to sue, but necessarily to conduct the suit. The amendment was in form at least a transfer of the total power; unless some good reason to the contrary appears, it ought to be construed as total, not as leaving the Commission subject to a public officer whom they could not control. * * *

Finally, it is said that we should not regard the testimony of a witness before the committees; that it is not even as relevant as speeches on the floor of either house, which courts will not consider at all. United States v. Trans–Missouri Freight Association, 166 U.S. 290, 317, 318, 17 S.Ct. 540, 41 L.Ed. 1007; Duplex, etc., Co. v. Deering, 254 U.S. 443, 474, 41 S.Ct. 172, 65 L.Ed. 349, 16 A.L.R. 196; McCaughn v. Hershey Chocolate Co., 283 U.S. 488, 493, 494, 51 S.Ct. 510, 75 L.Ed. 1183. It would indeed be absurd to suppose that the testimony of a witness by itself could be used to interpret an act of Congress; we are not so using it. The bill was changed in a most significant way; we are concerned to learn why this was done; we find that it can most readily be explained, and indeed cannot naturally be explained on any other assumption than by supposing that the committees assented to a request from the very agency to whom the new functions were to be committed. To close our eyes to this patent and compelling argument would be the last measure of arid formalism. The amendments of a bill in committee are fertile sources of interpretation, Pennsylvania R. Co. v. International Coal Co., 230 U.S. 184, 198, 199, 33 S.Ct. 893, 57 L.Ed. 1446, Ann.Cas. 1915A, 315. It is of course true that members who vote upon a bill do not all know, probably very few of them know, what has taken place in committee. On the most rigid theory possibly we ought to assume that they accept the words just as the words read, without any background of amendment or other evidence as to their meaning. But courts have come to treat the facts more really; they recognize that while members deliberately express their personal position upon the general purposes of the legislation, as to the details of its articulation they accept the work of the committees; so much they delegate because legislation could not go on in any other way.

Decree reversed.

### Notes and Questions

**1.** How did the change in the Section in the course of its enactment make the Congressional intent "entirely plain"?

**2.** In what respect does the contrast in diction of the two clauses indicate a deliberate difference of intent?

**3.** Under what theory did the court solve the problem of the transference of the committee intent to Congress?

**4.** In Zuber v. Allen, 396 U.S. 168, 90 S.Ct. 314, 24 L.Ed.2d 345 (1969), quoted favorably in Garcia v. United States, 469 U.S. 70, 76 (1984), the Supreme Court stated, per Justice Harlan: "We consider our conclusions in no way undermined by the colloquy on the floor between Senator Copeland and Senator Murphy upon which the dissent places such emphasis. A committee report represents the considered and collective understanding of those Congressmen involved in drafting and studying proposed legislation. Floor debates reflect at best the understanding of individual Congressmen. It would take extensive and thoughtful debate to detract from the plain thrust of a committee report in this instance." 396 U.S. at 186, 90 S.Ct. at 324. In a dissenting opinion, Justice Black took issue with the majority's treatment of the floor debates, observing that "anyone acquainted with the realities of the United States Senate knows that the remarks of the floor manager [Senator Murphy] are taken by other Senators as reflecting the views of the committee itself." Justice Rehnquist, dissenting in the case of Simpson v. United States, 435 U.S. 6, 17–18, 98 S.Ct. 909, 915, 55 L.Ed.2d 70, 80 (1978), made the following statements:

> The decisions of this Court have established that some types of legislative history are substantially more reliable than others. The report of a joint conference committee of both Houses of Congress, for example, or the report of a Senate or a House committee, is accorded a good deal more weight than the remarks even of the sponsor of a particular portion of a bill on the floor of the chamber. (Citations omitted.) It is a matter of common knowledge that at any given time during the debate, particularly a prolonged debate, of a bill the members of either House in attendance on the Floor may not be great, and it is only these members or those who later read the remarks in the Congressional Record, who will have the benefit of the Floor remarks. In the last analysis, it is the statutory language embodied in the enrolled bill which Congress enacts, and that must be our first reference point in interpreting its meaning.

The Court has also noted that "oral testimony of . . . individual Congressmen, unless very precisely directed to the intended meaning of particular words in a statute, can seldom be expected to be as precise as the enacted language itself." Regan v. Wald, 468 U.S. 222, 237 (1984).

In Chrysler Corp. v. Brown, 441 U.S. 281, 311, 99 S.Ct. 1705, 1722, 60 L.Ed.2d 208, 231 (1979), Justice Rehnquist's opinion for a virtually unanimous Court went still further, arguing that "[t]he remarks of a single legislator, even the sponsor, are not controlling in analyzing legislative history . . . [such remarks] must be considered with the Reports of both Houses and the statements of other Congressmen" as well as with the statute in question.

More recently, in Barnhart v. Sigmon Coal Company, 534 U.S. 438 (2002), Justice Thomas writing for a majority of six Justices wrote:

Floor statements from two Senators cannot amend the clear and unambiguous language of a statute. We see no reason to give greater weight to the views of two Senators than to the collective votes of both Houses, which are memorialized in the unambiguous statutory text. Moreover, were we to adopt this form of statutory interpretation, we would be placing an obligation on Members of Congress not only to monitor their colleague's floor statements but to read every word of the Congressional Record including written explanations inserted into the record. This we will not do. The only "evidence" that we need rely on is the clear statutory text.

In contrast, Justice Stevens, writing in dissent, argued that ignoring Floor Statements that provide convincing evidence of Congressional intent leads to arbitrary results:

This case raises the question whether clear evidence of coherent congressional intent should inform the Court's construction of a statutory provision that seems, at first blush, to convey an incoherent message. Today a majority of the Court chooses to disregard that evidence and instead, adheres to an interpretation of the statute that produces absurd results. Two Members of Congress—both sponsors of the legislation at issue—have explained that the statute does not mandate such results, and the agency charged with administering the statute agrees. As a partner of the other two branches of Government, we should heed their more reasonable interpretation of Congress' objectives.

Note that Justice Stevens' dissent refers to the Court's role in interpreting legislation as one of "partnership" with the other branches of government. Based on the decisions you have studied so far, does this characterization accurately capture the approach of the current Supreme Court? Of its predecessors? How would you describe the Court's role? Keep these inquiries in mind as you work through the other materials in this part of the Casebook.

The Supreme Court has not always viewed floor statements so skeptically. See Chicago, Milwaukee, St. Paul & Pacific Railroad Co. v. Acme Fast Freight, Inc., 336 U.S. 465, 69 S.Ct. 692, 93 L.Ed. 817 (1949) where statements made in debate on the House floor by Representative Wolverton, ranking minority member of the standing committee, were given greater weight in interpretation than contrary statements contained in the committee's own formal report on the bill concerned. It appeared from the Representative's statements that, due to limitations of time, the formal report had not been submitted to committee or subcommittee members for their approval before issuance. The Supreme Court (per Vinson, C.J.) commented as follows (336 U.S. at 472–76, 69 S.Ct. at 695–98):

In weighing the relative importance of [the Congressman's] statement and the committee report, a number of additional facts assume importance. The bill under consideration was reported unanimously by the House Committee on Interstate and Foreign Commerce. Congressman Wolverton, who was the ranking minority member of the committee, spoke on behalf of the bill and presented the only extended exposition of its provisions. His explanation of its meaning was not challenged or contradicted by any member of the committee. On the contrary, his part in its drafting was recognized by the chairman of the committee, and his remarks have been quoted as authority by the Interstate Commerce Commission.

In this posture of events, the committee report can be given little weight. A report not previously submitted to members of the committee and expressly contradicted without challenge on the floor of the House by a ranking member of the committee can hardly be considered authoritative. The Committee of Conference of which Representative Wolverton was a member, adopted § 1013 exactly as it appeared in the House amendment. It bore, at that time, the gloss placed upon it on the floor of the House. [In the Congressional Record's report of debate on the bill as it emerged from conference, Representative Wolverton had indicated that his earlier floor remarks on the provisions in question remained applicable to the conference bill—Ed.] Under those circumstances we cannot construe the statute [in the manner called for by the committee report].

**5.** An article by a Member of Congress has called attention to the emergence of the "planned colloquy" as an element of the legislative process in Congress. See Moorehead, A Congressman Looks at the Planned Colloquy and Its Effect in the Interpretation of Statutes, 45 A.B.A .. J. 1314 (1959). The "planned colloquy" is described as "a friendly exchange of questions and answers about the pending legislation between members, one of whom is usually a member of the committee from which the legislation emanated ... [the exchange having been] carefully planned by the parties for the express purpose of providing a legislative interpretation of a statutory provision which might otherwise be differently interpreted."

Such a colloquy may be designed on the one hand simply to explain the impact of particular provisions. Or it may be aimed, on the other hand, at circumventing parliamentary rules barring amendment or, perhaps, at establishing a policy which it is feared would raise serious political opposition if stated explicitly in the bill concerned.

In Regan v. Wald, 468 U.S. 222, 237 (1984), the Supreme Court noted that "[t]o permit what we regard as clear statutory language to be materially altered by such colloquies, which often take place before the bill has achieved its final form, would open the door to the inadvertent, or perhaps even planned, undermining of the language actually voted on by Congress and signed into law by the President." What is the significance of this development for the appraisal and use of floor debate materials as aids to construction?

In State of R.I. v. Narragansett Indian Tribe, 19 F.3d 685, 699–700 (1st Cir.1994) the court refused to give weight to the comments of individual legislators when they contradicted the plain meaning of the statute:

Once Congress has spoken, it is bound by what it has plainly said, notwithstanding the nods and winks that may have been exchanged in floor debates and committee hearings. After all, it is not the proper role of legislators to use unwritten assurances or side arrangements to alter the clear meaning of agreed language. And the judiciary must stand as the ultimate guarantor of the integrity of an enacted statute's text.

For a summary of the use of legislative intent in statutory interpretation and a discussion of what weight to give floor statements in particular, see Lori L. Outz, *A Principled Use of Congressional Floor Speeches in Statutory Interpretation*, 28 Colum. J.L. & Soc. Probs. 297 (1995).

**6.**  Foti v. Immigration and Naturalization Service, 375 U.S. 217, 84 S.Ct. 306, 11 L.Ed.2d 281 (1963) involved interpretation of "§ 106(a) of the Immigration and Nationality Act, 8 U.S.C.A. § 1105a(a) . . . as added by § 5(a) of Public Law 87–301, approved September 26, 1961, 75 Stat. 651, 8 U.S.C.A. (Supp. IV, 1962) § 1105a." The Supreme Court based its reading on the "historical background of the Immigration and Nationality Act, the manifest purpose of Congress in enacting § 106(a), and the context of the statutory language when viewed against the prevailing administrative practices and procedures, and pertinent legislative history of § 106(a)." After discussing the development of administrative practice on the subject at hand, the Court stated (375 U.S. at 223–24, 84 S.Ct. at 310–11):

It must be concluded that Congress knew of this familiar administrative practice and had it in mind when it enacted § 106(a). These usages and procedures, which were actually followed when the provision was enacted, must reasonably be regarded as composing the context of the legislation. A colloquy between Congressmen Walter, Lindsay and Moore, all knowledgeable in deportation matters, is definitely corroborative of this view. This colloquy occurred during the House debates on the predecessor to the bill which was enacted in 1961 and contained § 106(a). . . . With the dissenters below, we feel that the court's speculation that few congressmen were present at the time of this exchange was unwarranted and probably immaterial.

In an accompanying footnote, the Court observed that

Representative Walter was the chairman of a subcommittee of the House Judiciary Committee responsible for immigration and nationality matters, author and chief sponsor of the measure under consideration, and a respected congressional leader in the whole area of immigration law. Representative Lindsay was thoroughly familiar with the problems in this area and the role of discretionary determinations denying suspension in the deportation process, as a result of having represented the Government, three years earlier, in Jay v. Boyd, 351 U.S. 345, 76 S.Ct. 919, 100 L.Ed. 1242 (1956). Representative Moore was a co-sponsor of the bill under discussion and a member of the House Judiciary Committee from which the bill containing § 106(a) was reported out.

Does this suggest that the views of particularly knowledgeable legislators are entitled to special weight, even if they seem to diverge from the text? Does it matter if the knowledgeable legislator expresses her view in the legislative history (for example, by opportunistic insertion into the Congressional Record), as opposed to some other forum, such as a newspaper or a law review?

## Bank One Chicago, N.A. v. Midwest Bank & Trust Company

Supreme Court of the United States, 1996.
516 U.S. 264, 116 S.Ct. 637, 133 L.Ed.2d 635.

[This case involved the Expedited Funds Availability Act, a 1987 law designed to improve the Nation's check payment system. The Supreme Court analyzed the statute's jurisdictional provisions to determine the forum in which disputes between banks governed by the Act are to be aired in the first instance—in federal court or before an administrative adjudicator.

The Act requires banks to make deposited funds available for withdrawal within specified time periods. It grants the Board of Governors of the Federal Reserve System broad authority to prescribe rules controlling the collection and return of checks. The Supreme Court construed a section of the Act titled "Civil liability." That section authorizes claims for relief, enforceable in federal court, for violations of the Act.

Petitioner Bank One sued respondent Midwest Bank in Federal District Court for dishonoring a check. Bank One alleged that Midwest failed to meet its obligations under a Federal Reserve Board regulation issued pursuant to the Act. The District Court entered summary judgment for Bank One, but the Court of Appeals for the Seventh Circuit vacated that judgment and ordered the action dismissed for lack of subject-matter jurisdiction. The Seventh Circuit held that the Act provides for federal-court jurisdiction only in disputes between banks and customers. Disputes between two banks, such as the dispute at issue here, the Court of Appeals concluded, are to be adjudicated in a different forum: either in administrative proceedings before the Federal Reserve Board, or perhaps in state court.

The Supreme Court held that the Court of Appeals misread the law when it ordered the action dismissed for lack of subject-matter jurisdiction. The language of the Act's civil liability provision, reinforced by the provision's title ("Civil liability") and its drafting history indicated that Congress meant to provide a federal-court forum for resolution of disputes between two banks, as well as for disputes between banks and customers. According to the Supreme Court, nothing in the Act supported the Court of Appeals' view that Congress meant the Federal Reserve Board to function as an adjudicator of interbank controversies.

Although the judgment was unanimous, Justice Scalia wrote separately to disapprove the Court's reference to "drafting history." Justice Stevens responded in defense of legislative history as an aid to statutory interpretation.

The portion of the Court's opinion addressing "drafting history," and the separate opinions of Justice Scalia and of Justice Stevens, follow.]

■ JUSTICE GINSBURG delivered the opinion of the Court.

\* \* \*

## IV

Section 4010 is entitled Civil liability; its purpose is to afford private parties a claim for relief based on violations of the statute and its implementing regulations. Subsection (a) affords a claim for relief by making banks liable to "any person other than another depository institution."\* It refers to both individual and class actions, and specifies the measure of damages recoverable in such actions. All agree that suits described in subsection (a) may be brought in federal court under § 4010(d).\*\*

Subsection (f) governs the area of liability not covered by subsection (a): banks' liability inter se.\*\*\* It authorizes the Federal Reserve Board to "impose on or allocate among depository institutions the risks of loss and liability in connection with any aspect of the [check] payment system," and states that "liability under this subsection" shall be limited to the amount of the check, except in cases involving bad faith. In our view, subsection (f), like subsection (a), provides a statutory basis for claims for relief cognizable in federal court under § 4010(d). Both subsections impose civil liability for violation of the EFA Act and its implementing regulations. Though the two prescriptions are not parallel—most prominently, subsection (f) vests the Board with authority to establish the governing liability standards—they serve the same key purpose: both permit recovery of damages caused by a regulated party's failure to comply with the Act.

* [Ed.'s note—Subsection 4010(a) addresses a bank's liability to persons other than another depository institution. It provides, in pertinent part:

> Except as otherwise provided in this section, any depository institution which fails to comply with any requirement imposed under this chapter or any regulation prescribed under this chapter with respect to any person other than another depository institution is liable to such person in an amount equal to the sum of [a specified measure of damages].]

** [Ed.'s note—Subsection 4010(d) provides for concurrent federal and state court jurisdiction over civil liability suits:

> Any action under this section may be brought in any United States district court, or in any other court of competent jurisdiction, within one year after the date of the occurrence of the violation involved.]

*** [Ed.'s note—Subsection 4010(f) governs a bank's liability to another bank for violation of the Act's provisions. It states:

> The Board is authorized to impose on or allocate among depository institutions the risks of loss and liability in connection with any aspect of the [check] payment system.... Liability under this subsection shall not exceed the amount of the check giving rise to the loss or liability, and, where there is bad faith, other damages, if any, suffered as a proximate consequence of any act or omission giving rise to the loss or liability.]

The drafting history of § 4010 casts some light on the discrete composition and separate placement of subsections (a) and (f). Under the versions of the statute originally passed by each House of Congress, subsection (a) encompassed actions between banks and persons other than banks, as well as interbank actions. The Conference Committee narrowed subsection (a) by excluding interbank actions, but simultaneously inserted, still under the section heading "Civil liability," a new subsection (f). Compare H.R.Rep. No. 100–52, p. 10 (1987), and S. 790, 100th Cong., 1st Sess., § 609(a) (1987), with H.R.Conf.Rep. No. 100–261, pp. 105–106 (1987).

These changes reflect recognition that interbank disputes arising out of the check payment system may be more complex than those involving banks and depositors; such disputes, therefore, may warrant regulatory standards, set by an expert agency, to fill statutory interstices. Thus, in subsection (f), Congress delegated to the Federal Reserve Board authority to establish rules allocating among depository institutions "the risks of loss and liability" relating to the payment and collection of checks. 12 U.S.C. § 4010(f). Having conferred this authority on the Board, Congress sensibly consolidated in subsection (f) aspects of § 4010 that relate to interbank disputes—liability limits as well as rulemaking authority.

Congress no doubt intended rules regarding interbank losses and liability to be developed administratively. But nothing in § 4010(f)'s text suggests that Congress meant the Federal Reserve Board to function as both regulator and adjudicator in interbank controversies. Rather, subsections (f) and (d) fit a familiar pattern: agency regulates, court adjudicates. See, e.g., Securities Act of 1933, 15 U.S.C. § 77j(c) (mandating compliance with disclosure requirements established by Securities and Exchange Commission); § 77k (creating right of action in "any court of competent jurisdiction" for violation of those requirements). As the United States persuasively contends: "Congress left it to the Board to determine the liability standards for losses in the inter-bank payment system because of the greater complexity of that subject, and not because Congress intended to create remedies that would be adjudicated in different fora. Brief for United States as Amicus Curiae 13."

\* \* \*

■ JUSTICE SCALIA, concurring in part and concurring in the judgment.

I agree with the Court's opinion, except that portion of it which enters into a discussion of the drafting history of § 4010. In my view a law means what its text most appropriately conveys, whatever the Congress that enacted it might have "intended." The law is what the law says, and we should content ourselves with reading it rather than psychoanalyzing those who enacted it. See United States v. Public Util. Comm'n of Cal., 345 U.S. 295, 319, 97 L.Ed. 1020, 73 S.Ct. 706 (1953) (Jackson, J., concurring). Moreover, even if subjective intent rather than textually expressed intent were the touchstone, it is a fiction of Jack-and-the-Beanstalk proportions to assume that more than a handful of those Senators and Members of the House who voted for the final version of the Expedited Funds Availability Act, and the President who signed it, were, when they took those actions, aware of the drafting evolution that the Court describes; and if they were, that their actions in voting for or signing the final bill show that they had the same "intent" which that evolution suggests was in the minds of the drafters.

Justice Stevens acknowledges that this is so, but asserts that the intent of a few committee members is nonetheless dispositive because legislators are "busy people," and "most members [of Congress] are content to endorse the views of the responsible committees." I do not know the factual basis for that assurance. Many congressional committees tend not to be representative of the full house, but are disproportionately populated by Members whose constituents have a particular stake in the subject matter—agriculture, merchant marine and fisheries, science and technology, etc. I think it quite unlikely that the House of Representatives would be "content to endorse the views" that its Agriculture Committee would come up with if that committee knew (as it knows in drafting Committee Reports) that those views need not be moderated to survive a floor vote. And even more unlikely that the Senate would be "content to endorse the views" of the House Agriculture Committee. But assuming Justice Stevens is right about this desire to leave details to the committees, the very first provision of the Constitution forbids it. Article I, Section 1 provides that "all legislative Powers herein granted shall be vested in a Congress of the United States, which shall consist of a Senate and a House of Representatives." It has always been assumed that these powers are nondelegable—or, as John Locke put it, that legislative power consists of the power "to make laws, ... not to make legislators." J. Locke, Second Treatise of Government 87 (R. Cox ed. 1982). No one would think that the House of Representatives could operate in such fashion that only the broad outlines of bills would be adopted by vote of the full House, leaving minor details to be written, adopted, and voted upon, only by the cognizant committees. Thus, if legislation consists of forming an "intent" rather than adopting a text (a proposition with which I do not agree), Congress cannot leave the formation of that intent to a small band of its number, but must, as the Constitution says, form an intent of the Congress. There is no escaping the point: Legislative history that does not represent the intent of the whole Congress is nonprobative; and legislative history that does represent the intent of the whole Congress is fanciful.

Our opinions using legislative history are often curiously casual, sometimes even careless, in their analysis of what "intent" the legislative history shows. See Wisconsin Public Intervenor v. Mortier, 501 U.S. 597, 617–620, 115 L.Ed.2d 532, 111 S.Ct. 2476 (1991) (Scalia, J., concurring). Perhaps that is because legislative history is in any event a make-weight; the Court really makes up its mind on the basis of other factors. Or perhaps it is simply hard to maintain a rigorously analytical attitude, when the point of departure for the inquiry is the fairyland in which legislative history reflects what was in "the Congress's mind."

In any case, it seems to me that if legislative history is capable of injecting into a statute an "intent" that its text alone does not express, the drafting history alluded to in today's opinion should have sufficed to win this case for respondent. It shows that interbank liability was not merely omitted from subsection (a), entitled "Civil liability." It was removed from that subsection, simultaneously with the addition of subsection (f), 12 U.S.C. § 4010(f), which gave the Federal Reserve Board power to "impose on or allocate among depository institutions the risks of loss and liability in connection with any aspect of the payment system" (language that is at least as compatible with adjudication as with rulemaking). Now if the only function of this new subsection (f) had been to give the Board rulemaking power, there would have been no logical reason to eliminate interbank disputes from the "Civil liability" subsection, whose basic prescription (banks are civilly liable for violations of the statute or of rules issued under the statute)[1] applies no less in the interbank than in the bank-customer context. Nor can the removal of interbank disputes from subsection (a) be explained on the ground that Congress had decided to apply different damages limits to those disputes. The former subsection (a), in both House and Senate versions, already provided varying damages limits for individual suits and class actions, see S. 790, 100th Cong., 1st Sess., § 609(a) (1987); H.R.Rep. No. 100–52, pp. 10–11 (1987), and it would have been logical to set forth the newly desired interbank variation there as well, leaving to the new subsection (f) only the conferral of rulemaking authority. Or, if it were thought essential to "consolidate" all the details of interbank disputes in subsection (f), it would still not have been necessary to specifically exclude interbank disputes from the general "civil liability" pronouncement of subsection (a). The prologue of that subsection, "except as otherwise provided in this section," would have made it clear that interbank civil liability was limited as set forth in subsection (f). The most plausible explanation for specifically excluding interbank disputes from the "Civil liability" subsection when subsection (f) was added—and for avoiding any reference to "civil liability" in subsection (f) itself—is an intent to commit those disputes to a totally different regime, i.e., to Board adjudication rather than the normal civil-liability regime of the law courts.[2]

---

**1.**  The Senate version of subsection (a) did not refer to violations of rules, see S. 790, 100th Cong., 1st Sess., § 609(a) (1987), but it was the House version of subsection (a), see H.R.Rep. No. 100–52, p. 10 (1987), which did specifically mention rules, that was retained.

**2.**  I have explained why the "consolidation" explanation developed by Justice Stevens, ante, at 2, does not ring true. Even if it did, however, it would not be accurate to say that the legislative history thus provides "the answer to an otherwise puzzling aspect of the statutory text," ibid. What JUSTICE STEVENS calls "the answer" (viz., the wish to consolidate all the interbank provisions in one section) is no more evident from the legislative history than it is from the face of the statute itself. Nothing in the legislative history says "we will consolidate interbank matters in a new subsection (f)"; Justice Stevens simply surmises, from the fact that the final text contains such consolidation, that consolidation was the reason for excluding interbank disputes from subsection (a). What investigation of legislative history has produced, in other words, is not an answer (that, if there is one, is in the text), but rather the puzzlement to which an answer is necessary: why were interbank disputes eliminated from subsection (a) when subsection (f) was adopted? Being innocent of legislative history, I would not have known of that curious excision if the Court's opinion had not told me. Thus, legislative history has produced what it usually produces: more questions rather than more answers.

Today's opinion does not consider this argument, but nonetheless refutes it (in my view) conclusively. After recounting the drafting history, the Court states that *"nothing in § 4010(f)'s text* suggests that Congress meant the Federal Reserve Board to function as both regulator and adjudicator in interbank controversies." Ante, at 9 (emphasis added). Quite so. The text's the thing. We should therefore ignore drafting history without discussing it, instead of after discussing it.

■ JUSTICE STEVENS, concurring.

Given the fact that the Expedited Funds Availability Act was a measure that easily passed both houses of Congress, Justice Scalia is quite right that it is unlikely that more than a handful of legislators were aware of the Act's drafting history. He is quite wrong, however, to conclude from that observation that the drafting history is not useful to conscientious and disinterested judges trying to understand the statute's meaning.

Legislators, like other busy people, often depend on the judgment of trusted colleagues when discharging their official responsibilities. If a statute such as the Funds Availability Act has bipartisan support and has been carefully considered by committees familiar with the subject matter, Representatives and Senators may appropriately rely on the views of the committee members in casting their votes. In such circumstances, since most members are content to endorse the views of the responsible committees, the intent of those involved in the drafting process is properly regarded as the intent of the entire Congress.

In this case, as the Court and Justice Scalia agree, the statutory text of § 4010 supports petitioner's construction of the Act. However, the placement of the authorization for interbank litigation in subsection (f) rather than subsection (a) lends some support to the Court of Appeals' interpretation. When Congress creates a cause of action, the provisions describing the new substantive rights and liabilities typically precede the provisions describing enforcement procedures; subsection (f) does not conform to this pattern. The drafting history, however, provides a completely satisfactory explanation for this apparent anomaly in the text.

Justice Scalia nevertheless views the Court's reference to this history as unwise. As he correctly notes, the simultaneous removal of the provision for interbank liability from subsection (a) and the addition of a new subsection (f) support another inference favoring the Court of Appeals' construction of the statute: that the drafters intended to relegate the resolution of interbank disputes to a different tribunal. Justice Scalia is mistaken, however, in believing that this inference provides the "most plausible explanation" for the change, post, at 4. In my judgment the Court has correctly concluded that the most logical explanation for the change is a decision to consolidate the aspects of § 4010 that relate to interbank disputes—liability limits and rulemaking authority—in the same subsection. Thus, the net result of the inquiry into drafting history is to find the answer to an otherwise puzzling aspect of the statutory text.

I must also take exception to Justice Scalia's psychoanalysis of judges who examine legislative history when construing statutes. He confidently asserts that we use such history as a make-weight after reaching a conclusion on the basis of other factors. I have been performing this type of work for more than 25 years and have never proceeded in the manner JUSTICE SCALIA suggests. It is quite true that I have often formed a tentative opinion about the meaning of a statute and thereafter examined the statute's drafting history to see whether the history supported my provisional conclusion or provided a basis for revising it. In my judgment, a reference to history in the Court's opinion in such a case cannot properly be described as a "make-weight." That the history could have altered my opinion is evidenced by the fact that there are significant cases, such as Green v. Bock Laundry Machine Co., 490 U.S. 504, 104 L.Ed.2d 557, 109 S.Ct. 1981 (1989), in which the study of history did alter my original analysis. In any event, I see no reason why conscientious judges should not feel free to examine all public records that may shed light on the meaning of a statute.

Finally, I would like to suggest that JUSTICE SCALIA may be guilty of the transgression that he ascribes to the Court. He has confidently asserted that the legislative history in this case and in Wisconsin Public Intervenor v. Mortier, 501 U.S. 597, 115 L.Ed.2d 532, 111 S.Ct. 2476 (1991), supports a result opposite to that reached by the Court. While I do not wish to reargue the *Mortier* case, I will say that I remain convinced that a disinterested study of the entire legislative history supports the conclusion reached by the eight-member majority of the Court. Even if his analysis in both cases is plausible, it is possible that Justice Scalia's review of the history in *Mortier* and in this case may have been influenced by his zealous opposition to any reliance on legislative history in any case. In this case, as in *Mortier*, his opinion is a fine example of the work product of a brilliant advocate.[2] It is the Court's opinion, however, that best sets forth the reasons for reversing the judgment of the Court of Appeals.

Justice Breyer has authorized me to say that he agrees with the foregoing views.

## Questions

**1.** If you were drafting § 4010, how would you have exhibited—solely through the statutory text—Congress' intention that the Federal Reserve Board establish standards for interbank liability, but not adjudicate disputes between banks? How would you draft the section to express Congress intent that the Board do both?

**2.** Justice Jackson, whose opinion in United States v. Public Util. Comm'n of Cal., 345 U.S. 295, 97 L.Ed. 1020, 73 S.Ct. 706 (1953), Justice Scalia cites, was also a brilliant advocate. Like Justice Scalia, he recognized the danger of indiscriminate use of legislative history, but unlike Justice Scalia he also recognized that it can be helpful in appropriate cases. See Schwegmann Brothers v. Calvert Distillers Corp., 341 U.S. 384, 395–396, 95 L.Ed. 1035, 71 S.Ct. 745 (1951).

**2.**  § 4010(d) states that "any action under this *section* may be brought in any United States district court ..." (emphasis supplied). Since § 4010(f) is part of § 4010, why is there any doubt that federal courts have jurisdiction over interbank disputes?

**3.**  Recall Question 3 following S.E.C. v. Collier, *supra*, asking you to articulate the theory underlying Judge Hand's transference of the House Committee's intent to the entire enacting Congress. What are the views of the opinion writers in *Bank One* concerning transference of intent? Whose views do you find most persuasive?

**4.**  As with most questions worthy of adjudication before a court, the inquiry into legislative history is usually not clear-cut but requires balancing the evidence in support of conflicting interpretations. In Justice Scalia's view, one can characterize "the use of legislative history as the equivalent of entering a crowded cocktail party and looking over the heads of the guests for one's friends.... The legislative history of [the Act in question] contains a variety of diverse personages, a selected few of whom—its 'friends'—the Court has introduced to us in support of its result. But there are many other faces in the crowd, most of which, I think, are set against today's result." Conroy v. Aniskoff, 507 U.S. 511 (1993) (Scalia, J., concurring in the judgment). Does this critique discredit legislative history *per se*, or simply its selective citation? Is there a difference?

## 4.  STATUTORY GUIDES TO STATUTORY INTERPRETATION

Given the difficulties you have now seen courts confront, might legislatures make the task of interpretation easier if they simply enacted a general statute *telling* courts how to interpret their enactments? To a very limited extent, Congress has done that, by passing the "Dictionary Act," a statute you encountered in the U.S. v. Reid decision, *supra*, Part III.B.3. Many federal statutes also contain their own definition sections, as well as purpose clauses. But these are far from full guides to statutory interpretation. Similarly, as discussed earlier, Part III.A.2, legislatures may pass laws against a backdrop of canons of construction, but these are judge-made devices (and are susceptible of varied application); they are not legislated codes of construction. How advisable might such a code be? Consider the following:

### Note: Acts Interpretation Acts[1]

The interpretative status quo is cacophonous. Every judge and scholar has his own theory of how best to interpret statutes, and this diversity renders the interpretative project unpredictable. Each theory may have its own merits, and some may be better than others, but these differences ultimately may matter less than a central imperative of

---

**1.**  Thanks to Daniel Kalderimis, Associate-in-Law, Columbia University, LLB (Hons)    Victoria University of Wellington, N.Z.

statutory interpretation: a single, predictable, coherent set of rules. The Supreme Court, with its nine competing perspectives and its jurisdictional restriction to cases and controversies, will never be able to achieve this coherence alone.

Nicholas Quinn Rosenkrantz, *Federal Rules of Statutory Interpretation*, 115 Harv. L. Rev. 2085, 2088 (2002)

Acts Interpretations Acts are statutes that codify rules for interpreting statutes. The pre-eminent example of such codification is the Vienna Convention on the Law of Treaties, which in Article 31.1 sets out a general rule for the interpretation of treaties between states: "A treaty shall be interpreted in good faith in accordance with the ordinary meaning given to the terms of the treaty in context and in light of its object and purpose." Article 32 authorizes recourse to extrinsic information in certain circumstances.

As you have seen, in common law systems, interpretation rules have traditionally evolved through judge-made canons of construction. Where they exist, interpretation statutes displace the canons. In practice, however, the canons interplay with the statutory rules by filling any gaps left open. In this way, interpretation statutes can sometimes expand, rather than restrict, debate as to the proper meaning of legislation. Although many federal statutes contain definition sections and sometimes also purpose clauses to aid interpretation, there is no overall US federal interpretation act. By contrast, all fifty states and the District of Columbia have interpretative codes which, while not fully-blown interpretation acts, provide more detailed instructions on interpretation than anything appearing in the United States Code.[2] The reason these interpretative codes are not "fully-blown" is that, instead of general interpretative rules (such as those found in the Vienna Convention), the state codes tend to provide only technical guidance for the interpretation of particular terms.[3] For instance, the Michigan code provides a rule for the computation of time under any statute or administrative rule.[4] Even more specifically, the Florida code defines the word "writing" to include "handwriting, printing, typewriting, and all other methods and means of forming letters and characters upon paper, stone, wood, or other materials."[5]

Unlike judicial canons of construction, interpretation statutes dictate the rules for constructing the legislature's own enactments. Rather than

---

**2.** *See* the legislation cited in Nicholas Quinn Rosenkrantz, *Federal Rules of Statutory Interpretation*, 115 HARV. L. REV. 2085, 2089 n.10 (2002).

**3.** The comprehensive New York code is an exception to this principle and does contain some general guidance. *See for instance* N.Y. Stat. Law § 76 (McKinney 1971 & Supp. 2001–2002): "Where words of a statute are free from ambiguity and express plainly, clearly and distinctly the legislative intent, resort may not be had to other means of interpretation." *See generally* §§ 71—424.

**4.** Mich. Comp. Laws § 8.6 (1979). The rule is that the first day of the period is excluded and the last day is included, unless the last day of the period is a Saturday, Sunday or legal holiday (in which case the period is extended to include the next working day).

**5.** Fla. Stat. ch. 1.01 (2001).

leaving it to courts to devise an interpretive methodology, the legislature tells the court how to undertake the interpretive task. This element of control appealed to the British Empire, which enacted interpretation statutes for its colonies but not for England. (Apparently, English courts could be entrusted with unassisted interpretation of English laws, but the same could not be assumed of colonial jurists.) To this day, both Australia and New Zealand have legislation providing explicit direction on statutory interpretation: the Australian Acts Interpretation Act 1901 (Cth)[6] (the "Australian Act"), and the New Zealand Interpretation Act 1999 (the "New Zealand Act"), which recently replaced its 1924 predecessor. After reviewing the scope and purpose of these two statutes, consider the following questions from a US perspective:

(1) Does legislative direction to the courts on how to interpret legislation improperly interfere with the judicial function and breach the separation of powers?

(2) Might any statutory interpretation controversies that you have already encountered, or that you will yet study in this casebook have been decided differently under either of the Interpretations Acts excerpted below? What difference would either (or both) of these Interpretation Acts have made?

### Acts Interpretation Act 1901 (Australia)

The key provisions of the Australian Act are found in Part IV, which is headed "General Provisions". These broadly reflect Articles 31 and 32 of the Vienna Convention. Section 15AA is perhaps the central provision of the Act and bears setting out in full:

15AA Regard to be had to purpose or object of Act

(1) In the interpretation of a provision of an Act, a construction that would promote the purpose or object underlying the Act (whether that purpose or object is expressly stated in the Act or not) shall be preferred to a construction that would not promote that purpose or object.

This mandates the so-called "purposive" approach to interpretation. Many would argue that the choice before courts is rarely as stark at the section suggests–between an interpretation that promotes the purpose or object of an Act and an interpretation that does not.[7] This may be correct; certainly § 15AA is not a magic solution for thorny interpretative problems. Nevertheless, the purposive approach is a specific interpretative technique inconsistent with some other interpretative techniques, such as a strictly literalist approach. In practice, many well-known Australian deci-

---

**6.** Note that this Act is Commonwealth (or federal) legislation. At least one Australian State, New South Wales, has its own interpretation act also: the Interpretation Act 1987 (N.S.W.).

**7.** See e.g., J.J. Spigelman A.C., *The Poet's Rich Resource: Issues in Statutory Interpretation*, 21 Australian BarRev. 14, 4 (2001).

sions have rejected literalist or "plain-meaning" interpretations in favor of the purposive approach.[8]

Closely related to purpose is the notion that words must be read in their context–that is, in light of the surrounding words and the statutory scheme. It is now well accepted that reading words in context is an important first step to interpretation.[9] Although the "plain meaning" rule is still applied in Australia, it may not be a reliable guide to legislative purpose if applied to words in isolation.[10]

A second important provision is § 15AB, which governs when resort may be made to extrinsic material to assist interpretation. Resort may be made in three situations:

1.  to confirm the ordinary meaning of the provision, in context and with regard to the Act's purpose and object;

2.  to determine meaning where the provision is ambiguous or obscure; or

3.  to determine meaning when the ordinary meaning (again derived in context and with regard to the Act's purpose and object), would lead to absurdity.

The width of the first situation in particular allows the courts much scope for resort to extrinsic materials. Extrinsic materials are defined, in a non-exhaustive list, in § 15AB.2. They include, for example, any parliamentary committee or external commission report, any explanatory memorandum to legislation and floor debates. Finally, § 15AB.3 cautions against excessive reliance on extrinsic material, requiring courts to have regard to "the desirability of persons being able to rely on the ordinary meaning conveyed by the text of a provision..." and to "the need to avoid prolonging legal or other proceedings without compensating advantage".

In addition to these two general provisions, the Australian Act contains a host of more specific rules—similar to those contained in many US state interpretative codes—on the meaning of terms such as "individual", "month" and "land" as they appear in legislation (§ 22). The Act also provides that, unless the contrary intention appears, words importing one gender include every other gender (§ 23). To this extent, the Act functions as a "backstop" provision for interpreting terms which are not explicitly defined in other legislation. This system can save time for legislative drafters by providing a dictionary of settled terms on which they can rely when creating new legislation.

**8.**  See e.g., Mills v. Meeking (1990) 169 C.L.R. 214 (H.C.A.1990); Cooper Brookes (Woolongong) Pty. Ltd. v. Federal Commissioner of Taxation, 147 C.L.R. 297 (H.C.A. 1981); and The King v. Wilson; Ex parte Kisch, 52 C.L.R. 234 (H.C.A. 1934).

**9.**  See e.g., CIC Insurance v. Bankstown Football Club Ltd., 141 A.L.R. 618, 630 (H.C.A. 1997); K & S Lakes City Freighters Pty. Ltd. v. Gordon & Gotch Ltd., 157 C.L.R. 309, 315 (H.C.A. 1985).

**10.**  See, e.g., *CIC Insurance*, 141 A.L.R. at 630; Isherwood v. Bulter Pollnow Pty. Ltd., 6 N.S.W.L.R. 363, 388 (N.S.W.S.C. 1986).

### *Interpretation Act 1999 (New Zealand)*

The 1999 New Zealand Act replaces the prior 1924 Interpretation Act. Its modernity can be seen in the conscious attempt to draft the statute in clear, ordinary language and by its relaxation of certain rules vis-à-vis its Australian counterpart. The key provision is § 5:

5 Ascertaining meaning of legislation

(1) The meaning of an enactment must be ascertained from its text and in the light of its purpose.

(2) The matters that may be considered in ascertaining the meaning of an enactment include the indications provided in the enactment.

(3) Examples of those indications are preambles, the analysis, a table of contents, headings to Parts and sections, marginal notes, diagrams, examples and explanatory material, and the organisation and format of the enactment.

Although there is notably no direction to the courts to consider the context of an enactment in ascertaining its meaning, it has been held that "[b]oth the text and the purpose of the Act must be read in context".[11] The reference to both "text" and "purpose" in § 5.1 is intended to promote a measured purposive approach that does not torture the statutory words to give effect to an unexpressed legislative intent. Section 5.1 prevails over common law canons of construction to the extent of any inconsistency.[12] Subsections 2 and 3 are notable in that they require the courts to take account of all clues an Act might provide as to its meaning, including marginal notes, examples and section headings. In contrast, § 13.1 of the Australian Act provides that an Act does not include marginal notes, footnotes, or section headings.

Other key provisions in the New Zealand Act address retrospectivity (§ 7); the calculation of references to time or distance (§§ 35 and 36); and the date enactments come into effect (§ 8). As with the Australian Act, there is also a general definitions section, defining such words as "person" (to cover both genders), "repeal" and "working day" (§ 29).

---

11.  R. v. Pora, [2001] 2 NZLR 37, 43 (N.Z.C.A.)

12.  Id. at 48.

## D.  WEIGHT OF PRIOR INTERPRETATIONS

### 1.  BORROWED STATUTES—THE WEIGHT OF THE ORIGINATING JURISDICTION'S INTERPRETATIONS

**Donahue v. Warner Brothers, 272 P.2d 177 (Utah 1954).** The case arose out of the exhibition, for profit, of the movie "Look for the Silver Lining," a musical show, which incidentally portrayed the life of Jack Donahue, a famous singer, dancer and comedian. Plaintiffs in the case, the widow and daughters of Donahue, sued for compensation and exemplary damages and an injunction, relying on the following Utah statutory provisions, adopted in 1909, which were modeled, with minor modifications, on an earlier New York statute:

> U.C.A.1953, Sec. 76–4–8. Any person who uses for advertising purposes or for purposes of trade, or upon any postal card, the name, portrait or picture of any person, if such person is living, without first having

obtained the written consent of such person, or if a minor, of his parent or guardian, or, if such person is dead, without the written consent of his heirs or personal representatives, is guilty of a misdemeanor.

Sec. 9. Any living person, or the heirs or personal representatives of any deceased person, whose name, portrait or picture is used within this state for advertising purposes or for purposes of trade, without the written consent first obtained as provided in the next preceding section may maintain an action against such person so using his name, picture or portrait to prevent and restrain the use thereof; and may in the same action recover damages for any injuries sustained by reason of such use, and, if the defendant shall have knowingly used such person's name, portrait or picture in such manner as is declared to be unlawful, the jury or court, if tried without a jury, in its discretion, may award exemplary damages.

Plaintiffs contended that the use of a person's name or picture in any manner involving the profit motive was a use "for purposes of trade" forbidden by these provisions. Defendants argued that the provisions were meant to apply only to actual advertising or to promotion of sales of a collateral commodity. The Supreme Court of Utah decided in favor of the defendants, concluding that the showing was not for "purposes of trade" under the Act. *Inter alia,* various New York cases under the original New York statute were urged upon the Utah court. One such case was Rhodes v. Sperry & Hutchinson & Co., 193 N.Y. 223, 85 N.E. 1097, 34 L.R.A.N.S. 1143 (1908), affirmed 220 U.S. 502, 31 S.Ct. 490, 55 L.Ed. 561 (1911), which was said to have interpreted the New York statute as addressed to advertising and sales promotion. Other New York cases urged on the court, decided in 1913 and later years, extended the New York act to other situations. In regard to the New York cases the Utah court observed:

It is well settled that 'when the legislature of a state has used a statute of another state or country as a guide for the preparation and enactment of a statute, the courts of the adopting state will usually adopt the construction placed on the statute in the jurisdiction of its inception.' Thus the enactment of the Utah statute at a time when the language of the Rhodes case above ... [cited] was the declared law of New York seems to indicate that the intent of the Utah Legislature was to give a right of action only when the name was used in advertising or sales promotion schemes. It is here pertinent to observe, however, in view of later New York decisions, that although our Legislature may be assumed to have been aware of the construction of the statute by the courts of the state of its origin at the time of our enactment, that principle does not apply to decisions of the state of origin handed down after the time the legislation was adopted, as it would not have been known to, and could not have been in the contemplation of our Legislature. While such later cases may be helpful and in some instances persuasive, we are of course not obliged to follow the subsequent New York decisions, which have given a broader scope to the operation of their statute than we believe was intended for our enactment....

*Donahue,* 272 P.2d at 180–81.

On examination, the court refused to follow the later New York cases in extending the statute as sought by the plaintiff. It grounded this refusal on the "difficulties and uncertainties" found to ensue from extension, posing substantial problems for the courts and for the practical operations of publishers and other purveyors of public information, as well as raising serious constitutional questions. In this area the public interest in free expression in the channels of public information was to be preferred to the right of privacy. Besides such considerations, the text of the statute itself (particularly the narrowing effect of the "any postcard" phrase) and its title (referring only to advertising) were found by the court to demand a restrictive reading. And the same result was said to be called for by legislative history, the court noting that:

> Near the beginning of the 1909 legislative session Governor Spry, in his message, recommended legislation "to prevent the use of the name of any public institution of the state, or the official title of any of its officers, *for the purpose of advertising or promoting the sale of any article of merchandise* or stock in any corporation" (emphasis added).

Id. at 183.

### Questions

**1.** In the interest of uniformity, *shouldn't* Utah continue to follow New York?

**2.** Suppose another state, subsequent to *Donahue,* enacts a statute virtually identical to New York's and Utah's. Which state's statute did the newly enacting state "borrow"?

## Shannon v. United States

Supreme Court of the United States, 1994.
512 U.S. 573, 114 S.Ct. 2419, 129 L.Ed.2d 459.

■ JUSTICE THOMAS delivered the opinion of the Court.

In this case, we consider whether a federal district court is required to instruct the jury regarding the consequences to the defendant of a verdict of "not guilty by reason of insanity," either under the Insanity Defense Reform Act of 1984 or as a matter of general federal practice. We conclude that such an instruction is not required, and therefore affirm.

I

A

Prior to the enactment of the Insanity Defense Reform Act of 1984 (IDRA or Act), 98 Stat. 2057, as amended, 18 U.S.C. §§ 17, 4241–4247, federal courts generally did not recognize a verdict of "not guilty by reason of insanity" (NGI). Defendants who mounted a successful insanity defense—that is, those who raised a reasonable doubt as to their sanity at the time of the offense—were simply found "not guilty." See, e.g., United States v. McCracken, 488 F.2d 406, 409, 418 (C.A.5 1974); Evalt v. United States, 359 F.2d 534, 537 (C.A.9 1966). In addition, there was no general federal civil commitment procedure available to ensure that an insanity acquittee would receive proper care and treatment. Only in the District of Columbia was a defendant who successfully presented an insanity defense to a federal criminal charge subject to a federal commitment process—a process governed by a 1955 congressional enactment. See 69 Stat. 609, as amended, D.C.Code Ann. § 24–301 (1981). Elsewhere, federal authorities were forced to rely on the willingness of state authorities to institute civil commitment proceedings. Reliance on state cooperation was "at best a partial solution to a serious problem," however, and federal courts "time and again ... decried this gaping statutory hole." McCracken, supra, at 417.

\* \* \*

The acquittal of John Hinckley on all charges stemming from his attempt on President Reagan's life, coupled with the ensuing public focus on the insanity defense, prompted Congress to undertake a comprehensive overhaul of the insanity defense as it operated in the federal courts. The result of this effort was the IDRA. In the IDRA, Congress made insanity an affirmative defense to be proved by the defendant by clear and convincing evidence, and created a special verdict of "not guilty only by reason of insanity." 18 U.S.C. §§ 17 and 4242(b). In addition, Congress filled the "statutory hole" that had been identified by federal courts, see McCracken, supra, by creating a comprehensive civil commitment procedure. § 4243. Under that procedure, a defendant found NGI is held in custody pending a court hearing, which must occur within 40 days of the verdict. § 4243(c). At the conclusion of the hearing, the court determines whether the defendant should be hospitalized or released. § 4243(d), (e).

### B

At about 4 a.m. on August 25, 1990, a police officer stopped petitioner Terry Lee Shannon, a convicted felon, on a street in Tupelo, Mississippi. For reasons not explained in the record before us, the officer asked Shannon to accompany him to the station house to speak with a detective. After telling the officer that he did not want to live anymore, Shannon walked across the street, pulled a pistol from his coat, and shot himself in the chest.

Shannon survived his suicide attempt and was indicted for unlawful possession of a firearm by a felon in violation of 18 U.S.C. § 922(g)(1). At trial, he raised the insanity defense, and asked the District Court to instruct the jury that he would be involuntarily committed if the jury returned an NGI verdict.[2] The District Court refused to give Shannon's proposed charge. Instead, it instructed the jury "to apply the law as

---

**2.** Shannon asked the court to give either of the two following instructions: (1)  " 'In the event it is your verdict that [Shannon] is not guilty only by reason of insanity, [instructed] regardless of the consequence," and that "punishment ... should not enter your consideration or discussion." The jury returned a guilty verdict.

The Court of Appeals for the Fifth Circuit affirmed Shannon's conviction. 981 F.2d 759 (1993). The court noted that under its pre-IDRA precedent, juries were not to be instructed concerning the consequences of an insanity acquittal. Id., at 761–762 (discussing McCracken, supra). Turning to the text of the IDRA, the court observed that Congress had "said nothing about informing juries of the consequences" of an NGI verdict. 981 F.2d, at 764. Because there was no "statutory requirement" to the contrary, the court "adhered to the established axiom that it is inappropriate for a jury to consider or be informed about the consequences of its verdict." Ibid.

We granted certiorari, 510 U.S. 943 (1993), in order to consider whether federal district courts are required to instruct juries with regard to the consequences of an NGI verdict.

## II

It is well established that when a jury has no sentencing function, it should be admonished to "reach its verdict without regard to what sentence might be imposed." Rogers v. United States, 422 U.S. 35, 40, 45 L.Ed.2d 1, 95 S.Ct. 2091 (1975). The principle that juries are not to consider the consequences of their verdicts is a reflection of the basic division of labor in our legal system between judge and jury. The jury's function is to find the facts and to decide whether, on those facts, the defendant is guilty of the crime charged. The judge, by contrast, imposes sentence on the defendant after the jury has arrived at a guilty verdict. Information regarding the consequences of a verdict is therefore irrelevant to the jury's task. Moreover, providing jurors sentencing information invites them to ponder matters that are not within their province, distracts them from their factfinding responsibilities, and creates a strong possibility of confusion. See Pope v. United States, 298 F.2d 507, 508 (GA5 1962); cf. Rogers, supra, at 40.

Despite these familiar precepts, Shannon contends that an instruction informing the jury of the consequences of an NGI verdict is required under the IDRA whenever requested by the defendant.

* * *

## A

To determine whether Congress intended courts to depart from the principle that jurors are not to be informed of the consequences of their verdicts, we turn first, as always, to the text of the statute. The IDRA refers to the subject of jury instructions only once, and that reference occurs in its description of the possible verdicts a jury may return. Under

it is required that the Court commit [him]' ''; or (2) '' 'You should know that it is required that the Court commit [Shannon] to a suitable hospital facility until such time as [he] does not pose a substantial risk of bodily injury to another or serious damage to the property of another.' '' App. A–22.

the Act, "the jury shall be instructed to find ... the defendant—(1) guilty; (2) not guilty; or (3) not guilty only by reason of insanity." 18 U.S.C. § 4242(b). The text of the Act gives no indication that jurors are to be instructed regarding the consequences of an NGI verdict. As the court below observed, the Act "leaves the jury solely with its customary determination of guilt or innocence." 981 F.2d, at 763. The Act's text thus gives no support to Shannon's contention that an instruction informing the jury of the consequences of an NGI verdict is required.

Shannon asserts, however, that an express statutory directive is not necessary because, by modeling the IDRA on D.C.Code Ann. § 24–301 (1981), Congress impliedly adopted the D.C. Circuit's decision in Lyles v. United States, 103 U.S.App.D.C. 22, 254 F.2d 725 (1957) and the practice endorsed by that decision of instructing the jury as to the consequences of an NGI verdict. For this argument he relies on Capital Traction Co. v. Hof, 174 U.S. 1, 36, 43 L.Ed. 873, 19 S.Ct. 580 (1899), in which we stated:

> "By a familiar canon of interpretation, heretofore applied by this court whenever Congress ... has borrowed from the statutes of a State provisions which had received in that State a known and settled construction before their enactment by Congress, that construction must be deemed to have been adopted by Congress together with the text which it expounded, and the provisions must be construed as they were understood at the time in the State."

See also Carolene Products Co. v. United States, 323 U.S. 18, 26, 89 L.Ed. 15, 65 S.Ct. 1 (1944) ("The general rule [is] that adoption of the wording of a statute from another legislative jurisdiction carries with it the previous judicial interpretations of the wording"); Cathcart v. Robinson, 5 Pet. 264, 280 (1831). The canon of interpretation upon which Shannon relies, however, is merely a "presumption of legislative intention" to be invoked only "under suitable conditions." Carolene Products, supra, at 26. We believe that the "conditions" are not "suitable" in this case. Indeed, although Congress may have had the D.C.Code in mind when it passed the IDRA, see United States v. Crutchfield, 282 U.S.App.D.C. 169, 893 F.2d 376, 378 (C.A.D.C.1990), it did not, in the language of Hof, "borrow" the terms of the IDRA from the D.C.Code. Rather, Congress departed from the scheme embodied in D.C.Code Ann. § 24–301 in several significant ways.

The IDRA, for example, requires a defendant at trial to prove insanity by clear and convincing evidence, 18 U.S.C. § 17(b); the D.C. statute, by contrast, employs a preponderance standard. D.C.Code Ann. § 24–301(j). A commitment hearing must be held under the IDRA within 40 days of an NGI verdict, 18 U.S.C. § 4243(c); the period is 50 days under the D.C. scheme. D.C.Code Ann. § 24–301(d)(2)(A). Under the IDRA, a defendant whose offense involved bodily injury to another or serious damage to another's property, or the substantial risk thereof, must demonstrate at the hearing by clear and convincing evidence that he is entitled to release, 18 U.S.C. § 4243(d); under the D.C. scheme, an acquittee, regardless of the character of his offense, need only meet the preponderance standard. D.C.Code Ann. § 24–301(k)(3). The IDRA provides that an acquittee, once committed, may be released when he no longer presents a substantial risk of harm to others or to their property, 18 U.S.C. § 4243(f); an acquittee under the D.C. system may be released from commitment when he "will not in the reasonable future be dangerous to himself or others." D.C.Code Ann. § 24–301(e). Finally, in the IDRA, Congress rejected the broad test for insanity that had been utilized under the District of Columbia provision[7], and instead adopted a more restrictive formulation under which a person is deemed insane if he is unable "to appreciate the nature and quality or the wrongfulness of his acts." 18 U.S.C. § 17(a). We believe that these significant differences between the IDRA and D.C.Code Ann. § 24–301 render the canon upon which Shannon relies inapplicable in this case.[8]

* * *

### Questions

1.  Does *Shannon* stand for the proposition that a statute must be "borrowed" verbatim? Does the spirit or intent of the legislation carry any interpretative weight?

2.  The *Shannon* court held that D.C.Circuit's interpretation of the original statute was not applicable because "Congress departed from the scheme * * * in several significant ways." In this case, the federal statute created a stricter standard of liability. Would the court have held differently if the borrowing jurisdiction's version of the statute was more lenient than the original?

## 2.  Statutes Implemented by Administrative Agencies

[Re-read Part I. C. Administrative Law.]

## Chevron, U.S.A., Inc. v. Natural Resources Defense Council, Inc.

Supreme Court of the United States, 1984.
467 U.S. 837, 104 S.Ct. 2778, 81 L.Ed.2d 694.

■ Justice Stevens delivered the opinion of the Court.

In the Clean Air Act Amendments of 1977, Pub.L. 95–95, 91 Stat. 685, Congress enacted certain requirements applicable to States that had not

---

7.  Under the D.C. system, the courts had defined insanity as either the lack of substantial capacity to conform one's conduct to the requirements of the law or the lack of substantial capacity to appreciate the wrongfullness of one's acts. See *Brawner*, 471 F.2d, at 973–995.

8.  In addition, we note that the canon upon which Shannon relies is a canon of statutory construction. It stems from the notion that a court, in interpreting "borrowed" statutory language, should apply the same construction to that language that was placed upon it by the courts in the jurisdiction from which it was borrowed. In this case, however, the court in the jurisdiction from which the statutory text was supposedly borrowed— that is, the *Lyles* court—did not purport to construe the language of the D.C.Code provision; rather, in holding that jurors should be informed of the consequences of an NGI verdict, the court appears to have relied on its supervisory power over the Federal District Courts in the District of Columbia. Cf. infra, at 11. Thus, we conclude that the canon is also inapplicable in this case because there was no "known and settled construction," *Capital Traction Co. v. Hof*, 174 U.S. 1, 36, 43 L.Ed. 873, 19 S.Ct. 580 (1899), of the statute that Congress could have adopted by virtue of borrowing language from the D.C. statutory scheme.

achieved the national air quality standards established by the Environmental Protection Agency (EPA) pursuant to earlier legislation. The amended Clean Air Act required these "nonattainment" States to establish a permit program regulating "new or modified major stationary sources" of air pollution. Generally, a permit may not be issued for a new or modified major stationary source unless several stringent conditions are met. The EPA regulation promulgated to implement this permit requirement allows a State to adopt a plantwide definition of the term "stationary source." Under this definition, an existing plant that contains several pollution-emitting devices may install or modify one piece of equipment without meeting the permit conditions if the alteration will not increase the total emissions from the plant. The question presented by these cases is whether EPA's decision to allow States to treat all of the pollution-emitting devices within the same industrial grouping as though they were encased within a single "bubble" is based on a reasonable construction of the statutory term "stationary source."

## I

The EPA regulations containing the plantwide definition of the term stationary source were promulgated on October 14, 1981. 46 Fed.Reg. 50766. Respondents filed a timely petition for review in the United States Court of Appeals for the District of Columbia Circuit pursuant to 42 U.S.C. § 7607(b)(1). The Court of Appeals set aside the regulations. National Resources Defense Council, Inc. v. Gorsuch, 685 F.2d 718 (D.C.Cir.1982).

The court observed that the relevant part of the amended Clean Air Act "does not explicitly define what Congress envisioned as a 'stationary source,' to which the permit program ... should apply," and further stated that the precise issue was not "squarely addressed in the legislative history." Id., at 273, 685 F.2d, at 723. In light of its conclusion that the legislative history bearing on the question was "at best contradictory," it reasoned that "the purposes of the nonattainment program should guide our decision here." Id., at 276, n. 39, 685 F.2d, at 726, n. 39.[5] Based on two of its precedents concerning the applicability of the bubble concept to certain Clean Air Act programs, the court stated that the bubble concept was "mandatory" in programs designed merely to maintain existing air quality, but held that it was "inappropriate" in programs enacted to improve air quality. Id., at 276, 685 F.2d, at 726. Since the purpose of the permit program—its "raison d'être," in the court's view—was to improve air quality, the court held that the bubble concept was inapplicable in these

---

**5.** The court remarked in this regard: "We regret, of course, that Congress did not advert specifically to the bubble concept's application to various Clean Air Act programs, and note that a further clarifying statutory directive would facilitate the work of the agency and of the court in their endeavors to serve the legislators' will." 685 F.2d at 726 n.39.

cases under its prior precedents. Ibid. It therefore set aside the regulations embodying the bubble concept as contrary to law. We ... now reverse.

The basic legal error of the Court of Appeals was to adopt a static judicial definition of the term "stationary source" when it had decided that Congress itself had not commanded that definition....

## II

When a court reviews an agency's construction of the statute which it administers, it is confronted with two questions. First, always, is the question whether Congress has directly spoken to the precise question at issue. If the intent of Congress is clear, that is the end of the matter; for the court, as well as the agency, must give effect to the unambiguously expressed intent of Congress.[9] If, however, the court determines Congress has not directly addressed the precise question at issue, the court does not simply impose its own construction on the statute, as would be necessary in the absence of an administrative interpretation. Rather, if the statute is silent or ambiguous with respect to the specific issue, the question for the court is whether the agency's answer is based on a permissible construction of the statute.

The power of an administrative agency to administer a congressionally created ... program necessarily requires the formulation of policy and the making of rules to fill any gap left, implicitly or explicitly, by Congress. Morton v. Ruiz, 415 U.S. 199, 231 (1974). If Congress has explicitly left a gap for the agency to fill, there is an express delegation of authority to the agency to elucidate a specific provision of the statute by regulation. Such legislative regulations are given controlling weight unless they are arbitrary, capricious, or manifestly contrary to the statute. Sometimes the legislative delegation to an agency on a particular question is implicit rather than explicit. In such a case, a court may not substitute its own construction of a statutory provision for a reasonable interpretation made by the administrator of an agency.

We have long recognized that considerable weight should be accorded to an executive department's construction of a statutory scheme it is entrusted to administer, and the principle of deference to administrative interpretations "has been consistently followed by this Court whenever decision as to the meaning or reach of a statute has involved reconciling conflicting policies, and a full understanding of the force of the statutory policy in the given situation has depended upon more than ordinary knowledge respecting the matters subjected to agency regulations.["] [sic] See, e.g., National Broadcasting Co. v. United States, 319 U.S. 190; Labor Board v. Hearst Publications, Inc., 322 U.S. 111; Republic Aviation Corp. v.

---

**9.** The judiciary is the final authority on issues of statutory construction and must reject administrative constructions which are contrary to clear congressional intent. See, e.g., FEC v. Democratic Senatorial Campaign Committee, 454 U.S. 27, 32 (1981) [further citations omitted]. If a court, employing traditional tools of statutory construction, ascertains that Congress had an intention on the precise question at issue, that intention is the law and must be given effect.

Labor Board, 324 U.S. 793; Securities & Exchange Comm'n v. Chenery Corp., 322 U.S. 194; Labor Board v. Seven–Up Bottling Co., 344 U.S. 344.

". . . If this choice represents a reasonable accommodation of conflicting policies that were committed to the agency's care by the statute, we should not disturb it unless it appears from the statute or its legislative history that the accommodation is not one that Congress would have sanctioned." United States v. Shimer, 367 U.S. 374, 382, 383 (1961). Accord Capital Cities Cable, Inc. v. Crisp, 467 U.S. 691, 699–700 (1984).

In light of these well-settled principles it is clear that the Court of Appeals misconceived the nature of its role in reviewing the regulations at issue. Once it determined, after its own examination of the legislation, that Congress did not actually have an intent regarding the applicability of the bubble concept to the permit program, the question before it was not whether in its view the concept is "inappropriate" in the general context of a program designed to improve air quality, but whether the Administrator's view that it is appropriate in the context of this particular program is a reasonable one. Based on the examination of the legislation and its history which follows, we agree with the Court of Appeals that Congress did not have a specific intention on the applicability of the bubble concept in these cases, and conclude that the EPA's use of that concept here is a reasonable policy choice for the agency to make.

### III

[The Court then reviewed the legislative history at length, remarking that the issue before it concerned "one phase" of a "small portion" of "a lengthy, detailed, technical, complex, and comprehensive response to a major social issue," the Clean Air Act Amendments of 1977, that in turn was only part of a much larger statutory scheme under EPA's administration. "The legislative history of the portion of the 1977 Amendments dealing with nonattainment areas," it remarked, "does not contain any specific comment on the 'bubble concept' or the question whether a plantwide definition of a stationary source is permissible under the permit program. It does, however, plainly disclose that in the permit program Congress sought to accommodate the conflict between the economic interest in permitting capital improvements to continue and the environmental interest in improving air quality."

[Turning to the administrative history of implementation, the Court noted that EPA had at first proposed interpretations like that under challenge.]

\* \* \*

### VI

\* \* \*

In August 1980, however, the EPA adopted a regulation that, in essence, applied the basic reasoning of the Court of Appeals in these cases. The EPA took particular note of the two then-recent Court of Appeals decisions, which had created the bright-line rule that the "bubble concept" should be employed in a program designed to maintain air quality but not in one designed to enhance air quality. Relying heavily on those cases, EPA adopted a dual definition of "source" for nonattainment areas that required a permit whenever a change in either the entire plant, or one of its components, would result in a significant increase in emissions even if the increase was completely offset by reductions elsewhere in the plant. . . .

In 1981 a new administration took office and initiated a "Government-wide reexamination of regulatory burdens and complexities." 46 Fed.Reg. 16281. In the context of that review, the EPA reevaluated the various arguments that had been advanced in connection with the proper definition of the term "source" and concluded that the term should be given the same definition in both nonattainment areas and PSD areas.

In explaining its conclusion, the EPA first noted that the definitional issue was not squarely addressed in either the statute or its legislative history and therefore that the issue involved an agency "judgment as how to best carry out the Act." Ibid. It then set forth several reasons for concluding that the plantwide definition was more appropriate. . . .

## VII

\* \* \*

Based on our examination of the legislative history, we agree with the Court of Appeals that it is unilluminating. The general remarks pointed to by respondents "were obviously not made with this narrow issue in mind and they cannot be said to demonstrate a Congressional desire. . . . " Jewell Ridge Coal Corp. v. Mine Workers, 325 U.S. 161, 168–169 (1945). . . . We find that the legislative history as a whole is silent on the precise issue before us. It is, however, consistent with the view that the EPA should have broad discretion in implementing the policies of the 1977 Amendments.

More importantly, that history plainly identifies the policy concerns that motivated the enactment; the plantwide definition is fully consistent with one of those concerns—the allowance of reasonable economic growth—and, whether or not we believe it most effectively implements the other, we must recognize that the EPA has advanced a reasonable explanation for its conclusion that the regulations serve the environmental objectives as well. See supra, at 2789–2790, and n. 29; see also supra, at 2788, n. 27. Indeed, its reasoning is supported by the public record developed in the rulemaking process, as well as by certain private studies.[37]

**37.** "Economists have proposed that economic incentives be substituted for the cumbersome administrative-legal framework. The objective is to make the profit and cost incentives that work so well in the marketplace work for pollution control. . . . [The 'bubble' or 'netting' concept] is a first attempt in this direction. By giving a plant manager flexibility to find the places and processes within a plant that control emissions most cheaply, pollution control can be achieved more quickly and cheaply." L. Lave & G. Omenn, Cleaning Air: Reforming the Clean Air Act 28 (1981) (footnote omitted).

Our review of the EPA's varying interpretations of the word "source"—both before and after the 1977 Amendments—convinces us that the agency primarily responsible for administering this important legislation has consistently interpreted it flexibly—not in a sterile textual vacuum, but in the context of implementing policy decisions in a technical and complex arena. The fact that the agency has from time to time changed its interpretation of the term "source" does not, as respondents argue, lead us to conclude that no deference should be accorded the agency's interpretation of the statute. An initial agency interpretation is not instantly carved in stone. On the contrary, the agency, to engage in informed rulemaking, must consider varying interpretations and the wisdom of its policy on a continuing basis. Moreover, the fact that the agency has adopted different definitions in different contexts adds force to the argument that the definition itself is flexible, particularly since Congress has never indicated any disapproval of a flexible reading of the statute.

Significantly, it was not the agency in 1980, but rather the Court of Appeals that read the statute inflexibly to command a plantwide definition for programs designed to maintain clean air and to forbid such a definition for programs designed to improve air quality. The distinction the court drew may well be a sensible one, but our labored review of the problem has surely disclosed that it is not a distinction that Congress ever articulated itself, or one that the EPA found in the statute before the courts began to review the legislative work product. We conclude that it was the Court of Appeals, rather than Congress or any of the decisionmakers who are authorized by Congress to administer this legislation, that was primarily responsible for the 1980 position taken by the agency.

Policy

\* \* \*

In these cases, the Administrator's interpretation represents a reasonable accommodation of manifestly competing interests and is entitled to deference: the regulatory scheme is technical and complex, the agency considered the matter in a detailed and reasoned fashion, and the decision involves reconciling conflicting policies. Congress intended to accommodate both interests, but did not do so itself on the level of specificity presented by these cases. Perhaps that body consciously desired the Administrator to strike the balance at this level, thinking that those with great expertise and charged with responsibility for administering the provision would be in a better position to do so; perhaps it simply did not consider the question at this level; and perhaps Congress was unable to forge a coalition on either side of the question, and those on each side decided to take their chances with the scheme devised by the agency. For judicial purposes, it matters not which of these things occurred.

Judges are not experts in the field, and are not part of either political branch of the Government. Courts must, in some cases, reconcile competing political interests, but not on the basis of the judges' personal policy preferences. In contrast, an agency to which Congress has delegated policymaking responsibilities may, within the limits of that delegation, properly rely upon the incumbent administration's views of wise policy to inform its judgments. While agencies are not directly accountable to the people, the Chief Executive is, and it is entirely appropriate for this political branch of the Government to make such policy choices—resolving the competing interests which Congress itself either inadvertently did not resolve, or intentionally left to be resolved by the agency charged with the administration of the statute in light of everyday realities.

When a challenge to an agency construction of a statutory provision, fairly conceptualized, really centers on the wisdom of the agency's policy, rather than whether it is a reasonable choice within a gap left open by Congress, the challenge must fail. In such a case, federal judges—who have no constituency—have a duty to respect legitimate policy choices made by those who do. The responsibilities for assessing the wisdom of such policy choices and resolving the struggle between competing views of the public interest are not judicial ones: "Our Constitution vests such responsibilities in the political branches." TVA v. Hill, 437 U.S. 153, 195 (1978).

. . . [R]eversed.

It is so ordered.

■ JUSTICE MARSHALL and JUSTICE REHNQUIST took no part in the consideration or decision of these cases.

■ JUSTICE O'CONNOR took no part in the decision of these cases.

## Richard J. Pierce, Chevron and Its Aftermath: Judicial Review of Agency Interpretations of Statutory Provisions

41 Vand.L.Rev. 301, 304–08 (1988)(excerpt).

In determining whether an agency's interpretation of a statute involves an issue of law or policy, it is useful to analyze and characterize the issue prior to Congress' enactment of the statute in question. For example, in *Chevron* most would agree that, prior to the enactment of the Clean Air Act, the question of whether to limit emissions at the plant level or the level of each piece of combustion equipment is a pure question of policy. This question is but one of hundreds of policy issues that some institution of government must resolve in order to implement any regulatory program to reduce air pollution. In the process of enacting the Clean Air Act, or any other regulatory statute, Congress invariably resolves some policy issues but leaves to some other institution of government the task of resolving many other policy issues.

As the Court recognized in *Chevron*, Congress declines to resolve policy issues for many different reasons: Congress simply may have neglected to consider the issue; Congress may have believed that the agency was in a better position to resolve the issue; or finally, Congress may not have been able to forge a coalition or simply may have lacked the political courage necessary to resolve the issue, given that a resolution either way might damage the political future of many members of Congress. The general proposition that Congress cannot and does not resolve all the policy issues raised by its creation of a regulatory scheme probably is not at all controversial.

A more controversial point, however, may be that Congress resolves very few issues when it enacts a statute empowering an agency to regulate. Rather, Congress typically leaves the vast majority of policy issues, including many of the most important issues, for. resolution by some other institution of government. Congress accomplishes this through several different statutory drafting techniques, including the use of empty standards, lists of unranked decisional goals, and contradictory standards. Thus, Congress declines to resolve many policy issues by using statutory language that is incapable of meaningful definition and application.

\* \* \*

Once a court realizes that it is reviewing an agency's resolution of a policy issue, rather than an issue of law, comparative institutional analysis demonstrates that the agency is a more appropriate institution than a court to resolve the controversy. Because agencies are more accountable to the electorate than courts, agencies should have the dominant role in policy making when the choice is between agencies and courts. A court's function in reviewing a policy decision made by an agency should be the same whether the agency policy decision is made by interpreting an ambiguous statutory provision or by any other means of agency policy making. The court should affirm the agency's policy decision, and hence its statutory interpretation, if the policy is "reasonable." The court should reverse the agency's policy decision if the policy is arbitrary and capricious. Of course, in deciding whether the agency's policy decision is "reasonable," the court should review the agency's decision making process by which the agency determined that its choice of policy was consistent with statutory goals and the contextual facts of the controversy in question.

## Public Citizen v. Young

United States Court of Appeals, District of Columbia Circuit, 1987.
831 F.2d 1108.

■ WILLIAMS, CIRCUIT JUDGE:

The Color Additive Amendments of 1960, Pub.L. No. 86–618, 74 Stat. 397 (codified at 21 U.S.C. § 376 (1982)), part of the Food, Drug and Cosmetic Act (the "Act"), establish an elaborate system for regulation of color additives in the interests of safety. A color additive may be used only after the Food and Drug Administration ("FDA") has published a regulation listing the additive for such uses as are safe. Such listing may occur only if the color additive in question satisfies (among other things) the requirements of the applicable "Delaney Clause," § 706(b)(5)(B) of the Act, 21 U.S.C. § 376(b)(5)(B), one of three such clauses in the total system for regulation of color additives, food and animal food and drugs.[1] The Clause prohibits the listing of any color additive "found ... to induce cancer in man or animal."

In No. 86–1548, Public Citizen and certain individuals challenge the decision of the FDA to list two color additives, Orange No. 17 and Red No. 19, based on quantitative risk assessments indicating that the cancer risks presented by these dyes were trivial. This case thus requires us to determine whether the Delaney Clause for color additives is subject to an implicit "*de minimis*" exception. We conclude, with some reluctance, that the Clause lacks such an exception.

\* \* \*

## I.   THE DELANEY CLAUSE AND "DE MINIMIS" EXCEPTIONS

### A.   Factual Background

The FDA listed Orange No. 17 and Red No. 19 for use in externally applied cosmetics on August 7, 1986. *See* 21 C.F.R. §§ 74.1267, 74.2267 (1987) (Orange No. 17); *id.* §§ 74.1319, 74.2319 (Red No. 19). In the listing notices, it ... specifically rejected industry arguments that the Delaney Clause did not apply because the tests were inappropriate for evaluation of the dyes. 51 Fed.Reg. at 28,342; *id.* at 28,358–59. It thus concluded that the studies established that the substances caused cancer in the test animals. *Id.* at 28,334–36, 28,341 ...; *id.* at 28,349–52, 28,357....

The notices then went on to describe two quantitative risk assessments of the dyes, one by the Cosmetic, Toiletry and Fragrance Association ("CTFA," an intervenor here and the industry proponent of both dyes) and one by a special scientific review panel made up of Public Health Service scientists. Such assessments seek to define the extent of health effects of exposures to particular hazards.... All agree that gaps exist in the available information and that the risk estimator must use assumptions to fill those gaps. See, e.g., Report of the Color Additive Scientific Review Panel (Sept. 1985), Joint Appendix ("J.A.") in No. 86–1548, at 139–40, 167. The choice among possible assumptions is inevitably a matter of policy to some degree.... *See* [National Research Council], *Risk Assessment [in the Federal Government: Managing the Process]* 3 [National Academy Press 1983].

The assessments considered the risk to humans from the substances when used in various cosmetics—lipsticks, face powders and rouges, hair cosmetics, nail products, bathwater products, and wash-off products. The scientific review panel found the lifetime cancer risks of the substances extremely small: for Orange No. 17, it calculated them as one in 19 billion at worst, and for Red No. 19 one in nine million at worst. The FDA explained that the panel had used conservative assumptions in deriving these figures, and it characterized the risks as "so trivial as to be effectively no risk." It concluded that the two dyes were safe. 51 Fed.Reg. at 28,344, 28,360.

---

**1.**  The other clauses relate to food additives, 21 U.S.C. s 348(c)(3)(A), and to animal drugs, *id.* s 306b(d)(1)(H). All clauses prohibit carcinogens....

The FDA candidly acknowledged that its safety findings represented a departure from past agency practice: "In the past, because the data and information show that D & C Orange No. 17 is a carcinogen when ingested by laboratory animals, FDA in all likelihood would have terminated the provisional listing and denied CTFA's petition for the externally applied uses ... without any further discussion." *Id.* at 28,341; *accord id.* at 28,357 (same for Red No. 19). It also acknowledged that "[a] strictly literal application of the Delaney Clause would prohibit FDA from finding [both dyes] safe, and therefore, prohibit FDA from permanently listing [them].... " *Id.* at 28,341; *id.* at 28,356. Because the risks presented by these dyes were so small, however, the agency declared that it had "inherent authority" under the *de minimis* doctrine to list them for use in spite of this language. *Id.* at 28,341; *id.* at 28,358. It indicated that as a general matter any risk lower than a one-in-one-million lifetime risk would meet the requirements for a *de minimis* exception to the Delaney Clause. *Id.* at 28,344; *id.* at 28,362.

Assuming that the quantitative risk assessments are accurate, as we do for these purposes, it seems altogether correct to characterize these risks as trivial. For example, CTFA notes that a consumer would run a one-in-a-million lifetime risk of cancer if he or she ate *one* peanut with the FDA-permitted level of aflatoxins once every *250* days (liver cancer). [citation omitted] Another activity posing a one-in-a-million lifetime risk is spending 1,000 minutes (less than 17 hours) every year in the city of Denver—with its high elevation and cosmic radiation levels—rather than in the District of Columbia.... Most of us would not regard these as high-risk activities. Those who indulge in them can hardly be thought of as living dangerously. Indeed, they are risks taken without a second thought by persons whose economic position allows them a broad range of choice.

According to the risk assessments here, the riskier dye poses one ninth as much risk as the peanut or Colorado hypothetical; the less risky one poses only one 19,000th as much.

It may help put the one-in-a-million lifetime risk in perspective to compare it with a concededly dangerous activity, in which millions nonetheless engage, cigarette smoking. Each one-in-a-million risk amounts to less than one *200,000th* the lifetime risk incurred by the average male smoker. [citation omitted] Thus, a person would have to be exposed to more than 2,000 chemicals bearing the one-in-a-million lifetime risk, at the rates assumed in the risk assessment, in order to reach 100th the risk involved in smoking. To reach that level of risk with chemicals equivalent to the less risky dye (Orange No. 17), he would have to be exposed to more than 40 million such chemicals.

B.   Plain Language and the de Minimis Doctrine

The Delaney Clause of the Color Additive Amendments provides as follows:

> a color additive ... (ii) shall be deemed unsafe, and shall not be listed, for any use which will not result in ingestion of any part of

such additive, if, after tests which are appropriate for the evalua-tion of the safety of additives for such use, or after other relevant exposure of man or animal to such additive, it is found by the Secretary to induce cancer in man or animal....

21 U.S.C. § 376(b)(5)(B).

The natural—almost inescapable—reading of this language is that if the Secretary finds the additive to "induce" cancer in animals, he must deny listing. Here, of course, the agency made precisely the finding that Orange No. 17 and Red No. 19 "induce[ ] cancer when tested in laboratory animals." ...

The setting of the clause supports this strict reading. Adjacent to it is a section governing safety generally and directing the FDA to consider a variety of factors, including probable exposure, cumulative effects, and detection difficulties. 21 U.S.C. § 376(b)(5)(A). The contrast in approach seems to us significant. For all safety hazards other than carcinogens, Congress made safety the issue, and authorized the agency to pursue a multifaceted inquiry in arriving at an evaluation. For carcinogens, however, it framed the issue in the simple form, "If A [finding that cancer is induced in man or animals], then B [no listing]." There is language inviting administrative discretion, but it relates only to the process leading to the finding of carcinogenicity: "appropriate" tests or "other relevant expo-sure," and the agency's "evaluation" of such data. Once the finding is made, the dye "shall be deemed unsafe, and shall not be listed." 21 U.S.C. § 367(b)(5)(B).

Courts (and agencies) are not, of course, helpless slaves to literalism. One escape hatch, invoked by the government and CTFA here, is the *de minimis* doctrine, shorthand for *de minimis non curat lex* ("the law does not concern itself with trifles"). The doctrine—articulated in recent times in a series of decisions by Judge Leventhal—serves a number of purposes. One ... [derives from] the concept that "notwithstanding the 'plain meaning' of a statute, a court must look beyond the words to the purpose of the act where its literal terms lead to 'absurd or futile results.'" Alabama Power v. Costle, 636 F.2d 323, 360 n. 89 (D.C.Cir.1979) (quoting United States v. American Trucking Ass'ns, 310 U.S. 534, 543, 60 S.Ct. 1059, 1063, 84 L.Ed. 1345 (1939)). Imposition of pointless burdens on regulated entities is obviously to be avoided if possible, *see Alabama Power,* 636 F.2d at 360–61, especially as burdens on them almost invariably entail losses for their customers: here, obviously, loss of access to the colors made possible by a broad range of dyes.

We have employed the concept in construing the Clean Air Act's mandate to the Environmental Protection Agency to set standards provid-ing "an ample margin of safety to protect the public health," 42 U.S.C. § 7412(b)(1) (1982). That does not, we said, require limits assuring a "risk-free" environment. Rather, the agency must decide "what risks are accept-able in the world in which we live" and set limits accordingly. *See* Natural Resources Defense Council, Inc. v. EPA, 824 F.2d 1146, 1164–65 (D.C.Cir. 1987) (citing Industrial Union Dep't, AFL–CIO v. American Petroleum

Inst., 448 U.S. 607, 642, 100 S.Ct. 2844, 2864, 65 L.Ed.2d 1010 (1980)). Assuming as always the validity of the risk assessments, we believe that the risks posed by the two dyes would have to be characterized as "acceptable." Accordingly, if the statute were to permit a *de minimis* exception, this would appear to be a case for its application.[4]

Moreover, failure to employ a *de minimis* doctrine may lead to regulation that not only is "absurd or futile" in some general cost-benefit sense but also is directly contrary to the *primary* legislative goal. . . . In a certain sense, precisely that may be the effect here. The primary goal of the Act is human safety, but literal application of the Delaney Clause may in some instances increase risk. No one contends that the Color Additive Amendments impose a zero-risk standard for non-carcinogenic substances; if they did, the number of dyes passing muster might prove miniscule. As a result, makers of drugs and cosmetics who are barred from using a carcinogenic dye carrying a one–in–20–million lifetime risk may use instead a non-carcinogenic, but toxic, dye carrying, say, a one–in–10–million lifetime risk. The substitution appears to be a clear loss for safety.

Judge Leventhal articulated the standard for application of *de minimis* as virtually a presumption in its favor: "Unless Congress has been extraordinarily rigid, there is likely a basis for an implication of *de minimis* authority to provide [an] exemption when the burdens of regulation yield a gain of trivial or no value." *Alabama Power*, 636 F.2d at 360–61. But the doctrine obviously is not available to thwart a statutory command; it must be interpreted with a view to "implementing the legislative design." *Id.* at 360. Nor is an agency to apply it on a finding merely that regulatory costs exceed regulatory benefits. *Id.* at 361.

Here, we cannot find that exemption of exceedingly small (but measurable) risks tends to implement the legislative design of the color additive Delaney Clause. The language itself is rigid; the context—an alternative design admitting administrative discretion for all risks other than carcinogens—tends to confirm that rigidity. Below we consider first the legislative history; rather than offering any hint of softening, this only strengthens the inference. Second, we consider a number of factors that make Congress's apparent decision at least a comprehensible policy choice.

## 1. *Legislative History*

The Delaney Clause arose in the House bill and was, indeed, what principally distinguished the House from the Senate bill. The House included it in H.R. 7624, 106 Cong.Rec. 14,353–56, and the Senate accepted the language without debate, 106 Cong.Rec. 15,133 (1960). The House committee gave considerable attention to the degree of discretion permitted under the provision. The discussion points powerfully against any *de*

---

**4.** We do not, of course, purport to decide the appropriate dividing point between *de minimis* and other risks. FDA's proposed one-in-one-million dividing point has been used by EPA to distinguish acceptable and unacceptable risks. . . . FDA has used the same break point to determine whether the general safety clause of the Act applies. 47 Fed.Reg. 14,138 (1982).

*minimis* exception, and is not contradicted either by consideration on the House floor or by a post-enactment colloquy in the Senate.

*House Committee.* The House Report on the Color Additive Amendments is the most detailed evidence as to Congress's intentions on this issue. H.R.Rep. No. 1761, 86th Cong., 2d Sess. (1960), U.S.Code Cong. & Admin.News p. 2887 (hereinafter the *"House Report"*). In discussing the Clause, the report first explains the source of concern: "[T]oday cancer is second only to heart disease as a cause of death among the American people. Every year, approximately 250,000 people die of cancer in this country. Approximately 450,000 new cases of cancer are discovered each year." *Id.* at 11, U.S.Code Cong. & Admin.News 1960, p. 2893. The report reflects intense congressional concern over cancer risks from man-made substances.

The report acknowledged the "many unknowns about cancer," but highlighted certain areas of general agreement: "Laboratory experiments have shown that a number of substances when added to the diet of test animals have produced cancers of various kinds in the test animals. It is this fact—namely, that small quantities of certain materials over a period of time will cause abnormal cell growth in animals—that gave rise to the Delaney anticancer clause.... " *Id.* The report quoted at length from the hearing testimony of Arthur S. Flemming, Secretary of Health, Education, and Welfare (the parent agency of the FDA and the predecessor of Health and Human Services). The Secretary took a very strong line on the absence of a basis for finding "threshold" levels below which carcinogens would not be dangerous:

> We have no basis for asking Congress to give us discretion to establish a safe tolerance for a substance which definitely has been shown to produce cancer when added to the diet of test animals. We simply have no basis on which such discretion could be exercised because no one can tell us with any assurance at all how to establish a safe dose of any cancer-producing substance.

*Id.* at 13, U.S.Code Cong. & Admin.News 1960, p. 2894.[6]

Secretary Flemming also developed the theme that, with many cancer risks inescapably present in the environment, it made sense to remove unnecessary ones:

> ... The population is inadvertently exposed to certain carcinogens.... In view of these facts, it becomes all the more imperative to protect the

---

**6.** In fact the existence of a threshold for chemical carcinogens, below which their use would have no ill effect, appears to depend on whether one is speaking of an "initiating" agent, a "promoting" agent, or a "complete carcinogen." (The latter both initiates and promotes.) Both activities are necessary for the production of tumors. Both the theory of the operation of initiating agents and the empirical data support the belief that for them no threshold applies. Equally, the theory and data as to promoting agents support the view that there is a "no-effect" threshold level. [citation omitted].

public from deliberate introduction of additional carcinogenic materials into the human environment.

\* \* \*

It is clear that if we include in our diet substances that induce cancer when included in the diet of test animals, we are taking a risk. In light of the rising number of cases of cancer, why should we take that risk?

*Id.* at 12–13, U.S.Code Cong. & Admin.News 1960, p. 2894.

Before adopting Flemming's no-threshold premise the House committee heard many witnesses on the opposite side of the debate, and its *Report* acknowledges their contentions. *Id.* at 13 (witnesses stated that it was "possible to establish safe tolerance levels"). It also notes that some took the position that the ban should "apply only to colors that induce cancer when ingested in an amount and under conditions reasonably related to their intended use." *Id.* Similarly, it notes support for making carcinogenicity simply one of the factors for the Secretary to consider in determining safety. *Id.*[8] Finally, it mentions a position taken by some scientific witnesses strikingly similar to that taken by FDA here. These experts suggested that, in spite of the difficulties in designing and evaluating tests for carcinogenicity, the Secretary "should have the authority to decide that a minute amount of a cancer-producing chemical may be added to man's food after a group of scientists consider all the facts and conclude that the quantity to be tolerated is probably without hazard." *Id.* at 13–14, U.S.Code Cong. & Admin.News 1960, p. 2895.

The committee rejected all these positions on the grounds that they would "weaken the present anticancer clause." *Id.* at 13. The report responded to them with another quote from Secretary Flemming's hearing testimony, reflecting the view that agency discretion should cease once "a substance has been shown to produce cancer when added to the diet of test animals":

... [T]he clause allows the exercise of all the judgment that can safely be exercised on the basis of our present knowledge.... It allows the Department and its scientific people full discretion and judgment in deciding whether a substance has been shown to produce cancer when added to the diet of test animals. But once this decision is made, the limits of judgment have been reached and there is no reliable basis on which discretion could be exercised in determining a safe threshold dose for the established carcinogen.

*Id.* at 14, U.S.Code Cong. & Admin.News 1960, pp. 2895–96.

Beyond this delineation of the intended scope of discretion, the *House Report* also addressed the possibility that its scientific premise—the absence of a threshold—might prove false. Its evident solution was that *Congress,* not the FDA, should examine the evidence and find a solution.

---

**8.** Several industry representatives and other experts testified that the Delaney Clause was too inflexible as written and should be modified to permit greater administrative discretion. [citations omitted].

The *House Report* at 12, U.S.Code Cong. & Admin.News 1960, p. 2894 quotes Secretary Flemming to precisely this effect:

> Whenever a sound scientific basis is developed for the establishment of tolerances for carcinogens, we will request the Congress to give us that authority. We believe, however, that the issue is so important that the elected representatives of the people should have the opportunity of examining the evidence and determining whether or not the authority should be granted. . . .

The government and CFTA note that exempting substances shown by quantitative risk assessment to carry only trivial risks rests on a quite different foundation from establishing threshold levels below which no cancer is thought to occur. We agree that the two are distinguishable, but do not find the distinctions between them to cut in favor of a *de minimis* exception. If it is correct to read the statute as barring tolerances based on an assumed threshold, it follows a *fortiori* that the agency must ban color additives with real but negligible cancer risks.

*House floor.* In the House debate, little of substance occurred. Congressman Delaney contended that the anticancer provision was essential "if the public health is to be adequately protected," 106 Cong.Rec. at 14,350, and asserted in conclusory terms the inability to establish a safe dose or tolerance, *id.* Congressman Rogers, describing the anticancer clause (which he supported), observed that "[t]he 'safe for use' principle does not apply to situations where carcinogenicity is at issue." *Id.* at 14,371. One participant, Congressman Allen, expressed the view that the anticancer clause was "unnecessary and restrictive," and that the "decision on safety [should] be determined by the Secretary of Health, Education and Welfare rather than . . . determined by law." *Id.* at 14,351. Accordingly, he urged passage of the Senate bill instead. Although Congressman Allen's view of the bill was negative, his interpretation seems to accord with that of its proponents: a ban follows automatically from a finding of carcinogenicity in man or animal.

*Post-enactment Senate colloquy.* The inferences of rigidity supported by the above remarks are drawn slightly in question—but ultimately, we think, not much—by an exchange that occurred the day *after* the Senate took final action on the final version of the Act. Senator Javits politely complained about the Senate's acting on this legislation in his absence. He secured unanimous consent for including in the Record the conclusions of a then-recent Report of the Panel on Food Additives of the President's Advisory Committee (the "Kistiakowsky Report"). He characterized the Report as stating that "authority such as that conferred by the amendment [the Report was addressed to the food additive Delaney Clause] should be used and applied within the 'rule of reason.'" 106 Cong.Rec. at 15,381. After Senators Dirksen and Hill assented to this proposition, Javits agreed to lay on the table a motion to reconsider the vote of the previous day. *Id.*

Appellees interpret the rule-of-reason colloquy as squarely supporting their *de minimis* approach, but in fact it is ambiguous. The Kistiakowsky Report defined "rule of reason" by a quotation from *Rathbun v. United*

*States,* 355 U.S. 107, 109, 78 S.Ct. 161, 162, 2 L.Ed.2d 134 (1957): "Every statute must be interpreted in the light of reason and common understanding to reach the results intended by the legislature." The proposition accords exactly with the way in which Judge Leventhal formulated the test for application of the *de minimis* doctrine: would the doctrine "implement[ ] the legislative design"? *Alabama Power,* 636 F.2d at 360. But that is the question, not the answer. Thus the exchange invoking the rule of reason appears to do no more than exhort us to pursue the inquiry we've been pursuing. . . .

Taken as a whole, the remarks do not seem strong enough to undermine the inference we have drawn that the clause was to operate automatically once the FDA squeezed the scientific trigger. This is so even without regard to the usual hazards of post-enactment legislative history, which ordinarily lead to its being disregarded altogether. *See Regional Rail Reorganization Act Cases,* 419 U.S. 102, 132, 95 S.Ct. 335, 352, 42 L.Ed.2d 320 (1974) ("post-passage remarks of legislators, however explicit, cannot serve to change the legislative intent of Congress expressed before the Act's passage").

### 2. *Possible Explanations for an Absolute Rule*

Like all legislative history, this is hardly conclusive. But short of an explicit declaration in the statute barring use of a *de minimis* exception, this is perhaps as strong as it is likely to get. Facing the explicit claim that the Clause was "extraordinarily rigid," a claim well supported by the Clause's language in contrast with the bill's grants of discretion elsewhere, Congress persevered.

Moreover, our reading of the legislative history suggests some possible explanations for Congress's apparent rigidity. One is that Congress, and the nation in general (at least as perceived by Congress), appear to have been truly alarmed about the risks of cancer. *House Report* at . . . 491 (statement of Dr. Zavon) (Delaney Clause "tends to highlight the current hysteria regarding cancer"). This concern resulted in a close focus on substances increasing cancer threats and a willingness to take extreme steps to lessen even small risks. Congress hoped to reduce the incidence of cancer by banning carcinogenic dyes, and may also have hoped to lessen public fears by demonstrating strong resolve.

A second possible explanation for Congress's failure to authorize greater administrative discretion is that it perceived color additives as lacking any great value. For example, Congressman Delaney remarked, "Some food additives serve a useful purpose. . . . However, color additives provide no nutrient value. They have no value at all, except so-called eye appeal." *Color Additives Hearings* at 108. Representative Sullivan said, "we like the bright and light [lipstick] shades but if they cannot safely be produced, then we prefer to do without these particular shades." *Id.* at 114. . . .

So far as we can determine, no one drew the legislators' attention to the way in which the Delaney Clause, interacting with the flexible standard for determining safety of non-carcinogens, might cause manufacturers to substitute more dangerous toxic chemicals for less dangerous carcinogens. . . . But the obviously more stringent standard for carcinogens may rest on a view that cancer deaths are in some way more to be feared than others.

Finally, as we have already noted, the House committee (or its amanuenses) considered the possibility that its no-threshold assumption might prove false and contemplated a solution: renewed consideration by Congress.

Considering these circumstances—great concern over a specific health risk, the apparently low cost of protection, and the possibility of remedying any mistakes—Congress's enactment of an absolute rule seems less surprising.

\* \* \*

D.   The Meaning of "[I]nduce Cancer"

After Public Citizen initiated the litigation in No. 86–5150, the FDA published a notice embellishing the preamble to its initial safety determinations. 52 Fed.Reg. at 5081 (Orange No. 17); *id.* at 5083 (Red No. 19). These notices effectively apply quantitative risk assessment at the stage of determining whether a substance "induce[s] cancer in man or animal." They assert that even where a substance does cause cancer in animals in the conventional sense of the term, the FDA may find that it does not "induce cancer in man or animal" within the meaning of 21 U.S.C. § 376(b)(5)(B). It is not crystal clear whether such a negative finding would flow simply from a quantitative risk assessment finding the risk to be trivial for humans under conditions of intended use, or whether it would require a projection back to the laboratory animals: *i.e.,* an assessment that the risk would be trivial for animals exposed to the substance in quantities proportional to the exposure hypothesized for human risk assessment purposes. (Perhaps the distinction is without a difference.) In any event, the notices argued:

> The words "induce cancer in man or animal" as used in the Delaney Clause are terms of art intended to convey a regulatory judgment that is something more than a scientific observation that an additive is carcinogenic in laboratory animals. To limit this judgment to such a simple observation would be to arbitrarily exclude from FDA's consideration developing sophisticated testing and analytical methodologies, leaving FDA with only the most primitive techniques for its use in this important endeavor to protect public health. Certainly the language of the Delaney Clause itself cannot be read to mandate such a counterproductive limit on FDA's discharge of its responsibilities.

*Id.* at 5082; *id.* at 5084.

The notices acknowledged that the words "to induce cancer" had not been "rigorously and unambiguously" so limited in the previous notices. *Id.* at 5082; *id.* at 5084. This is a considerable understatement. The original determinations were quite unambiguous in concluding that the colors induced cancer in animals in valid tests; the explanations went to some trouble to rebut industry arguments to the contrary. Despite these arguments, FDA concluded that the tests demonstrated that the dyes were responsible for increases in animal tumors.

The plain language of the Delaney Clause covers all animals exposed to color additives, including laboratory animals exposed to high doses. It would be surprising if it did not. High-dose exposures are standard testing procedure, today just as in 1960; such high doses are justified to offset practical limitations on such tests: compared to expected exposure of millions of humans over long periods, the time periods are short and the animals few. Many references in the legislative history reflect awareness of reliance on animal testing, and at least the more sophisticated participants must have been aware that this meant high-dose testing. A few so specified.

All this indicates to us that Congress did not intend the FDA to be able to take a finding that a substance causes only trivial risk in humans and work back from that to a finding that the substance does not "induce cancer in ... animals." This is simply the basic question—is the operation of the clause automatic once the FDA makes a finding of carcinogenicity in animals?—in a new guise. The only new argument offered in the notices is that, without the new interpretation, only "primitive techniques" could be used. In fact, of course, the agency is clearly free to incorporate the latest breakthroughs in animal testing; indeed, here it touted the most recent animal tests as "state of the art." The limitation on techniques is only that the agency may not, once a color additive is found to induce cancer in test animals in the conventional sense of the term, undercut the statutory consequence. As we find the FDA's construction "contrary to clear congressional intent," Chevron U.S.A. v. Natural Resources Defense Council, Inc., 467 U.S. 837, 843 n. 9, 104 S.Ct. 2778, 2781 n. 9, 81 L.Ed.2d 694 (1984), we need not defer to it.

\* \* \*

In sum, we hold that the Delaney Clause of the Color Additive Amendments does not contain an implicit *de minimis* exception for carcinogenic dyes with trivial risks to humans. We based this decision on our understanding that Congress adopted an "extraordinarily rigid" position, denying the FDA authority to list a dye once it found it to "induce cancer in ... animals" in the conventional sense of the term. We believe that, in the color additive context, Congress intended that if this rule produced unexpected or undesirable consequences, the agency should come to it for relief. That moment may well have arrived, but we cannot provide the desired escape.

\* \* \*

CONCLUSION

... [T]he agency's *de minimis* interpretation of the Delaney Clause of the Color Additive Amendments is contrary to law. The listing decisions for Orange No. 17 and Red No. 19 based on that interpretation must therefore be corrected.

So ordered.

## Question

As the court points out, strict interpretation of the "Delaney Clause" could lead to the result that color additives will be *more* toxic (albeit non-carcinogenic) than they would be were a "de minimis" exception admitted. Is this not an absurd result that courts should strive to avoid by departing from the text's "plain meaning"?

---

*Chevron* introduced a two-stage analysis: (1) has Congress remitted the issue to agency discretion?; (2) if so, is the agency's interpretation a permissible construction of the statute. If Congress has not left the issue to agency discretion, there is no place for a "stage two" inquiry.

The preceding decision, Public Citizen v. Young, offered a clear-cut *Chevron* stage one controversy. Other decisions, including the two presented here after *Public Citizen,* however, are harder to classify. As you read Rust v. Sullivan, Babbitt v. Sweet Home, and FDA v. Brown & Williamson consider whether the majority and dissenting opinions are debating whether the agency's interpretation was unreasonable, or whether Congress foreclosed any agency discretion with respect to the disputed issue.

## Rust v. Sullivan

Supreme Court of the United States, 1991.
500 U.S. 173, 111 S.Ct. 1759, 114 L.Ed.2d 233.

■ Rehnquist, C.J., delivered the opinion of the Court, in which White, Kennedy, Scalia, and Souter, JJ., joined. Blackmun, J., filed a dissenting opinion, in which Marshall, J., joined; in Part I of which O'Connor, J., joined; and in Parts II and III of which Stevens, J., joined. Stevens, J., and O'Connor, J., filed dissenting opinions.

■ Chief Justice Rehnquist delivered the opinion of the Court.

These cases concern a facial challenge to Department of Health and Human Services (HHS) regulations which limit the ability of Title X fund recipients to engage in abortion-related activities. The United States Court of Appeals for the Second Circuit upheld the regulations, finding them to be a permissible construction of the statute as well as consistent with the First and Fifth Amendments of the Constitution. We granted certiorari to resolve a split among the Courts of Appeals. We affirm.

### I

### A

In 1970, Congress enacted Title X of the Public Health Service Act (Act), 84 stat. 1506, as amended, 42 U.S.C. §§ 300–300a–6, which provides federal funding for family-planning services. The Act authorizes the Secretary to "make grants to and enter into contracts with public or nonprofit private entities to assist in the establishment and operation of voluntary family planning projects which shall offer a broad range of acceptable and effective family planning methods and services." 42 U.S.C. § 300(a). Grants and contracts under Title X must "be made in accordance with such regulations as the Secretary may promulgate." 42 U.S.C. § 300a–4. Section 1008 of the Act, however, provides that "[n]one of the funds appropriated under this subchapter shall be used in programs where abortion is a method of family planning." 42 U.S.C. § 300a–6. That restriction was intended to ensure that Title X funds would "be used only to support preventive family planning services, population research, infertility services, and other related medical, informational, and educational activities." H.R.Conf.Rep. No. 91–1667, p. 8 (1970), U.S. Code Cong. & Admin.News 1970, pp. 5068, 5081–82.

In 1988, the Secretary promulgated new regulations designed to provide " 'clear and operational guidance' to grantees about how to preserve the distinction between Title X programs and abortion as a method of family planning." 53 Fed.Reg. 2923–2924 (1988). The regulations clarify, through the definition of the term "family planning," that Congress intended Title X funds "to be used only to support *preventive* family planning services." H.R.Conf.Rep. No. 91–1667, p. 8, U.S. Code Cong. & Admin.News 1970, p. 5081 (emphasis added). Accordingly, Title X services are limited to "preconceptual counseling, education, and general reproductive health care," and expressly exclude "pregnancy care (including obstetric or prenatal care)." 42 CFR § 59.2 (1989). The regulations "focus the emphasis of the Title X program on its traditional mission: The provision of preventive family planning services specifically designed to enable individuals to determine the number and spacing of their children, while clarifying that pregnant women must be referred to appropriate prenatal care services." 53 Fed.Reg. 2925 (1988).

The regulations attach three principal conditions on the grant of federal funds for Title X projects. First, the regulations specify that a "Title X project may not provide counseling concerning the use of abortion as a method of family planning or provide referral for abortion as a method of family planning." 42 CFR § 59.8(a)(1)(1989).... Title X projects must refer every pregnant client "for appropriate prenatal and/or social services by furnishing a list of available providers that promote the welfare of the mother and the unborn child." *Ibid.* The list may not be used indirectly to encourage or promote abortion, "such as by weighing the list of referrals in favor of health care providers which perform abortions, by including on the list of referral providers health care providers whose principal business is the provision of abortions, by excluding available providers who do not provide abortions, or by 'steering' clients to providers who offer abortion as a method of family planning." § 59.8(a)(3). The Title X project is expressly prohibited from referring a pregnant woman to an abortion provider, even upon specific request. One permissible response to such an inquiry is that "the project does not consider abortion an appropriate method of family planning and therefore does not counsel or refer for abortion." § 59.8(b)(5).

Second, the regulations broadly prohibit a Title X project from engaging in activities that "encourage, promote or advocate abortion as a method of family planning." § 59.10(a). Forbidden activities include lobbying for legislation that would increase the availability of abortion as a method of family planning, developing or disseminating materials advocating abortion as a method of family planning, providing speakers to promote abortion as a method of family planning, using legal action to make abortion available in any way as a method of family planning, and paying dues to any group that advocates abortion as a method of family planning as a substantial part of its activities. *Ibid.* Third, the regulations require that Title X projects be organized so that they are "physically and financially separate" from prohibited abortion activities. § 59.9. To be deemed physically and financially separate, "a Title X project must have an objective integrity and independence from prohibited activities. Mere bookkeeping separation of Title X funds from other monies is not sufficient." *Ibid....*

\* \* \*

## II

We turn first to petitioners' contention that the regulations exceed the Secretary's authority under Title X and are arbitrary and capricious....

## A

We need not dwell on the plain language of the statute because we agree with every court to have addressed the issue that the language is ambiguous. The language of § 1008—that "[n]one of the funds appropriated under this subchapter shall be used in programs where abortion is a method of family planning"—does not speak directly to the issues of counseling, referral, advocacy, or program integrity. If a statute is "silent or ambiguous with respect to the specific issue, the question for the court is whether the agency's answer is based on a permissible construction of the statute." Chevron U.S.A. v. NRDC, Inc., 467 U.S. 837, 842–843 (1984).

The Secretary's construction of Title X may not be disturbed as an abuse of discretion if it reflects a plausible construction of the plain language of the statute and does not otherwise conflict with Congress' expressed intent. *Ibid....*

The broad language of Title X plainly allows the Secretary's construction of the statute. By its own terms, § 1008 prohibits the use of Title X funds "in programs where abortion is a method of family planning." Title X does not define the term "method of family planning," nor does it enumerate what types of medical and counseling services are entitled to Title X funding. Based on the broad directives provided by Congress in Title X in general and § 1008 in particular, we are unable to say that the Secretary's construction of the prohibition in § 1008 to require a ban on counseling, referral, and advocacy within the Title X project, is impermissible.

The District Courts and Courts of Appeals that have examined the legislative history have all found, at least with regard to the Act's counseling, referral, and advocacy provisions, that the legislative history is ambiguous with respect to Congress' intent in enacting Title X and the prohibition of § 1008. [citations omitted]. We join these courts in holding that the legislative history is ambiguous and fails to shed light on relevant congressional intent. At no time did Congress directly address the issues of abortion counseling, referral, or advocacy....

\* \* \*

... Having concluded that the plain language and legislative history are ambiguous as to Congress' intent in enacting Title X, we must defer to the Secretary's permissible construction of the statute.

\* \* \*

Petitioners ... contend that the regulations must be invalidated because they raise serious questions of constitutional law. They rely on Edward J. Debartolo Corp. v. Florida Gulf Coast Building and Construction Trades Council, 485 U.S. 568 (1988), ... which [held] that "an Act of Congress ought not to be construed to violate the Constitution if any other possible construction remains available". Under this canon of statutory construction, "[t]he elementary rule is that every reasonable construction must be resorted to in order to *save* a *statute* from unconstitutionality." *Id.* at 575 (emphasis added), quoting Hooper v. California, 155 U.S. 648, 657 (1895).

The principle enunciated in *Hooper v. California, supra,* and subsequent cases, is a categorical one: "as between two possible interpretations of a statute, but one of which it would be unconstitutional and by the other valid, our plain duty is to adopt that which will save the Act." Blodgett v. Holden, 275 U.S. 142, 148 (1927) (opinion of Holmes, J.). This principle is based at least in part on the fact that a decision to declare an act of Congress unconstitutional "is the gravest and most delicate duty that this Court is called on to perform." *Id.* Following *Hooper, supra,* cases ... developed the corollary doctrine that "[a] statute must be construed, if fairly possible, so as to avoid not only the conclusion that it is unconstitutional but also grave doubts upon that score." United States v. Jin Fuey Moy, 241 U.S. 394, 401 (1916). This canon is followed out of respect for Congress, which we assume legislates in the light of constitutional limitations. FTC v. American Tobacco Co., 264 U.S. 298, 305–307 (1924)....

Here Congress forbade the use of appropriated funds in programs where abortion is a method of family planning. It authorized the Secretary to promulgate regulations implementing this provision. The extensive litigation regarding governmental restrictions on abortion since our decision in Roe v. Wade, 410 U.S. 113 (1973), suggests that it was likely that any set of regulations promulgated by the Secretary—other than the ones in force prior to 1988 and found by him to be relatively toothless and ineffectual— would be challenged on constitutional grounds. While we do not think that the constitutional arguments made by petitioners in this case are without some force, in Part III, infra, we hold that they do not carry the day. Applying the canon of construction under discussion as best we can, we hold that the regulations promulgated by the Secretary do not raise the sort of "grave and doubtful constitutional questions," United States v. Delaware and Hudson Co., 213 U.S. 366 (1909), that would lead us to assume Congress did not intend to authorize their issuance. Therefore, we need not invalidate the regulations in order to save the statute from unconstitutionality.

## III

[The majority held that the regulations do not violate the First Amendment free speech rights of Title X fund recipients, their staffs, or their patients by imposing viewpoint-discriminatory conditions on government subsidies. Citing earlier cases, the Court held that the government may make a value judgment favoring childbirth over abortion and may implement that judgment through the allocation of public funds. "In so doing," Chief Justice Rehnquist wrote, "the government has not discriminated on the basis of viewpoint; it has merely chosen to fund one activity to the exclusion of another." Furthermore, according to the Supreme Court majority, "a legislature's decision not to subsidize the exercise of a fundamental right does not infringe the right." The majority also rejected petitioners' argument that the regulations unconstitutionally condition the receipt of a benefit, Title X funding, on the relinquishment of a constitutional right, the First Amendment right to engage in abortion advocacy and counseling. Finding that the doctor-patient relationship established by Title X is not "all-encompassing," the Court determined that the regulations do not force a Title X grantee, or its employees, to give up abortion-related speech; rather, they require that such speech be kept "separate and distinct from Title X activities."

The majority then held that the regulations do not violate a woman's Fifth Amendment right to choose whether to terminate her pregnancy because under Webster v. Reproductive Health Services, 492 U.S. 490 (1989), the government has no duty to subsidize a constitutionally protected activity and may validly choose to allocate public funds for medical services relating to childbirth but not to abortion. Such allocation places no government obstacle in the path of a woman wishing to terminate her pregnancy; instead, it "leaves her with the same choices as if the government had chosen not to fund family-planning services at all." The majority also rejected petitioners' argument that the regulations violate a woman's Fifth Amendment right to medical self-determination by infringing on the doctor-patient relationship. Chief Justice Rehnquist distinguished cases in which the Supreme Court invalidated laws requiring all doctors to provide pregnant woman with specific anti-abortion information. Unlike those laws, he argued, the regulations at issue do not restrict a doctor's ability to provide, and a woman's right to receive, abortion-related information outside the context of the Title X program. The majority acknowledged that poverty may preclude most Title X clients from seeing a health-care provider for abortion-related services; however, that did not affect the outcome of the case, since "the financial constraints that restrict an indigent woman's ability to enjoy the full range of constitutionally protected freedom of choice are the product not of governmental restrictions . . . but rather of her indigency.''']

The Secretary's regulations are a permissible construction of Title X and do not violate either the First or Fifth Amendments to the Constitution. Accordingly, the judgment of the Court of Appeals is

*Affirmed.*

■ Justice Blackmun, with whom Justice Marshall joins, with whom Justice Stevens joins as to Parts II and III, and with whom Justice O'Connor joins as to Part I, dissenting.

Casting aside established principles of statutory construction and administrative jurisprudence, the majority in these cases today unnecessarily passes upon important questions of constitutional law. In so doing, the Court, for the first time, upholds viewpoint-based suppression of speech solely because it is imposed on those dependent upon the Government for economic support. Under essentially the same rationale, the majority upholds direct regulation of dialogue between a pregnant woman and her physician when that regulation has both the purpose and the effect of manipulating her decision as to the continuance of her pregnancy. I conclude that the Secretary's regulation of referral, advocacy, and counseling activities exceeds his statutory authority, and, also, that the Regulations violate the First and Fifth Amendments of our Constitution. Accordingly, I dissent and would reverse the divided-vote judgment of the Court of Appeals.

## I

The majority does not dispute that "[f]ederal statutes are to be so construed as to avoid serious doubt of their constitutionality." Machinists v. Street, 367 U.S. 740, 749 (1961). . . . Nor does the majority deny that this principle is fully applicable to cases such as the instant one, in which a plausible but constitutionally suspect statutory interpretation is embodied in an administrative regulation. [citations omitted]. Rather, in its zeal to address the constitutional issues, the majority sidesteps this established canon of construction with the feeble excuse that the challenged Regulations "do not raise the sort of 'grave and doubtful constitutional questions,' . . . that would lead us to assume Congress did not intend to authorize their issuance."

This facile response to the intractable problem the Court addresses today is disingenuous at best. Whether or not one believes that these Regulations are valid, it avoids reality to contend that they do not give rise to serious constitutional questions. The canon is applicable to this case not because "it was likely that [the Regulations] . . . would be challenged on constitutional grounds," but because the question squarely presented by the Regulations—the extent to which the Government may attach an otherwise unconstitutional condition to the receipt of a public benefit— implicates a troubled area of our jurisprudence in which a court ought not entangle itself unnecessarily. [citations omitted].

... [T]he Regulations impose viewpoint-based restrictions upon protected speech and are aimed at a woman's decision whether to continue or terminate her pregnancy. In both respects, they implicate core constitutional values. This verity is evidenced by the fact that two of the three Courts of Appeals that have entertained challenges to the Regulations have invalidated them on constitutional grounds. [citations omitted].

... That a bare majority of this Court today reaches a different result does not change the fact that the constitutional questions raised by the Regulations are both grave and doubtful.

Nor is this a case in which the statutory language itself requires us to address a constitutional question. Section 1008 of the Public Health Service Act, 84 Stat. 1508, 42 U.S.C. § 300a–6, provides simply: "None of the funds appropriated under this title shall be used in programs where abortion is a method of family planning." The majority concedes that this language "does not speak directly to the issues of counseling, referral, advocacy, or program integrity," and that "the legislative history is ambiguous" in this respect. Consequently, the language of § 1008 easily sustains a constitutionally trouble-free interpretation.[1]

... Indeed, it would appear that our duty to avoid passing unnecessarily upon important constitutional questions is strongest where, as here, the language of the statute is decidedly ambiguous. It is both logical and eminently prudent to assume that when Congress intends to press the limits of constitutionality in its enactments, it will express that intent in explicit and unambiguous terms....

Because I conclude that a plainly constitutional construction of § 1008 "is not only 'fairly possible' but entirely reasonable," *Machinists,* 367 U.S. at 750, I would reverse the judgment of the Court of Appeals on this ground without deciding the constitutionality of the Secretary's Regulations.

## II

I also strongly disagree with the majority's disposition of petitioners' constitutional claims ...

[Justice Blackmun argued that the regulations prohibiting abortion counseling and referral violate the First Amendment free speech rights of Title X fund recipients because they discriminate on the basis of viewpoint. "While suppressing speech favorable to abortion with one hand," he wrote,

---

1. The majority states: "There is no question but that the statutory prohibition contained in § 1008 is constitutional." Ante, at 1772. This statement simply begs the question. Were the Court to read § 1008 to prohibit only the actual performance of abortions with Title X funds—as, indeed, the Secretary did until February 2, 1988, see 53 Fed.Reg. 2923 (1988)—the provision would fall within the category of restrictions that the Court upheld in Harris v. McRae, 448 U.S. 297 (1980), and Maher v. Roe, 432 U.S. 464 (1977). By interpreting the statute to authorize the regulation of abortion-related speech between physician and patient, however, the Secretary, and now the Court, have rejected a constitutionally sound construction in favor of one that is by no means clearly constitutional.

"the Secretary compels anti-abortion speech with the other" by requiring Title X projects to refer pregnant patients to prenatal care and adoption services. The advocacy regulations, Justice Blackmun continued, clearly discriminate on the basis of viewpoint because they prohibit pro-abortion advocacy but do not proscribe or even regulate anti-abortion advocacy. Justice Blackmun disagreed with the majority's conclusion that the regulations merely limit a Title X grantee's speech to preventive family planning services, noting that Title X recipients may provide physical examinations, screening for breast cancer, and treatment of gynecological problems, all of which, he argued, are non-preventive services. He also argued that the regulations prohibiting abortion counseling and referral violate the First Amendment rights of Title X staff members, citing cases holding that restrictions on speech in the workplace require courts to balance the speaker's interests against those of the government. In the instant case, he reasoned, the interest of physicians and counselors in providing patients with information regarding their health and reproductive freedom outweigh the government's articulated interest in suppressing such information. He concluded, "By failing to balance or even to consider the free speech interests claimed by Title X physicians against the Government's asserted interest in suppressing the speech, the Court falters in its duty to implement the protection that the First Amendment clearly provides for this important message."

Justice Blackmun then argued that the regulations violate a woman's Fifth Amendment right to choose whether to terminate her pregnancy. In his view, the regulations interfere in a pregnant woman's decision by suppressing medically pertinent information. "The undeniable message conveyed by this forced speech ... is that abortion nearly always is an improper medical option." Such a message, Justice Blackmun wrote, would compel many women to carry their pregnancy to term and would prevent others from having abortions during the period in which the procedure is medically safe and constitutionally protected. "For these women," he concluded, "the Government will have obliterated the freedom to choose as surely as if it had banned abortions outright. The denial of this freedom is not a consequence of poverty but of the Government's ill-intentioned distortion of information it has chosen to provide." Finally, Justice Blackmun argued that the regulations violate a woman's Fifth Amendment right to medical self-determination by infringing on the doctor-patient relationship. He disagreed with the majority's reasoning that the regulations are permissible because they do not apply to doctors and patients outside the context of the Title X program. "The rights protected by the Constitution are personal rights," he wrote. "[F]or the individual woman, the deprivation of liberty by the Government is no less substantial because it affects few rather than many. It cannot be that an otherwise unconstitutional infringement of choice is made lawful because it touches only some of the Nation's pregnant women and not all of them."]

■ JUSTICE STEVENS, dissenting.

In my opinion, the Court has not paid sufficient attention to the language of the controlling statute or to the consistent interpretation accorded the statute by the responsible cabinet officers during four different Presidencies and 18 years.

\* \* \*

The entirely new approach adopted by the Secretary in 1988 was not, in my view, authorized by the statute. The new regulations did not merely reflect a change in a policy determination that the Secretary had been authorized by Congress to make. Cf. Chevron U.S.A. Inc. v. NRDC, Inc., 467 U.S. 837, 865 (1984). Rather, they represented an assumption of policymaking responsibility that Congress had not delegated to the Secretary.... In a society that abhors censorship and in which policymakers have traditionally placed the highest value on the freedom to communicate, it is unrealistic to conclude that statutory authority to regulate conduct implicitly authorized the Executive to regulate speech.

Because I am convinced that the 1970 Act did not authorize the Secretary to censor the speech of grant recipients or their employees, I would hold the challenged regulations invalid and reverse the judgment of the Court of Appeals.

Even if I thought the statute were ambiguous, however, I would reach the same result for the reasons stated in Justice O'Connor's dissenting opinion....

■ JUSTICE O'CONNOR, dissenting.

\* \* \*

This Court acts at the limits of its power when it invalidates a law on constitutional grounds. In recognition of our place in the constitutional scheme, we must act with "great gravity and delicacy" when telling a coordinate branch that its actions are absolutely prohibited absent constitutional amendment. Adkins v. Children's Hospital of District of Columbia, 261 U.S. 525, 544 (1923).... In this case, we need only tell the Secretary that his regulations are not a reasonable interpretation of the statute; we need not tell Congress that it cannot pass such legislation. If we rule solely on statutory grounds, Congress retains the power to force the constitutional question by legislating more explicitly. It may instead choose to do nothing. That decision should be left to Congress; we should not tell Congress what it cannot do before it has chosen to do it. It is enough in this case to conclude that neither the language nor the history of § 1008 compels the Secretary's interpretation, and that the interpretation raises serious First Amendment concerns. On this basis alone, I would reverse the judgment of the Court of Appeals and invalidate the challenged regulations.

### Questions

**1.** Recall the canon of interpretation that urges against ruling on a constitutional issue if the case can be resolved on a statutory ground without implicating the constitution. What role does that canon play when an agency's interpretation of a statute is at issue?

**2.**   Is this a *Chevron* stage I or a stage II controversy?

**Note**

On January 22, 1993, President Clinton signed an executive order directing the Secretary of Health and Human Services to suspend the rule prohibiting Title X projects from providing abortion counseling and referrals. In the order he also directed the Secretary to promulgate new regulations to formally rescind the rule.

## Babbitt v. Sweet Home Chapter of Communities for a Great Oregon

Supreme Court of the United States, 1995.
515 U.S. 687, 115 S.Ct. 2407, 132 L.Ed.2d 597.

■ JUSTICE STEVENS delivered the opinion of the Court.

The Endangered Species Act of 1973 ... makes it unlawful for any person to "take" any endangered or threatened species. The Secretary has promulgated a regulation that defines the statute's prohibition on takings to include "significant habitat modification or degradation where it actually kills or injures wildlife." This case presents the question whether the Secretary exceeded his authority under the Act by promulgating that regulation.

### I

\* \* \*

Section 3(19) of the [Endangered Species] Act defines the statutory term "take":

"The term 'take' means to harass, harm, pursue, hunt, shoot, wound, kill, trap, capture, or collect, or to attempt to engage in any such conduct." 16 U.S.C. § 1532(19).

The Act does not further define the terms it uses to define "take." The Interior Department regulations that implement the statute, however, define the statutory term "harm":

"*Harm* in the definition of 'take' in the Act means an act which actually kills or injures wildlife. Such act may include significant habitat modification or degradation where it actually kills or injures wildlife by significantly impairing essential behavioral patterns, including breeding, feeding, or sheltering." 50 CFR § 17.3 (1994).

This regulation has been in place since 1975.[2]

---

**2.** The Secretary, through the Director of the Fish and Wildlife Service, originally promulgated the regulation in 1975 and amended it in 1981 to emphasize that actual death or injury of a protected animal is necessary for a violation. See 40 Fed.Reg. 44412, 44416 (1975); 46 Fed.Reg. 54748, 54750 (1981).

A limitation on the § 9 "take" prohibition appears in § 10(a)(1)(B) of the Act, which Congress added by amendment in 1982. That section authorizes the Secretary to grant a permit for any taking otherwise prohibited by § 9(a)(1)(B) "if such taking is incidental to, and not the purpose of, the carrying out of an otherwise lawful activity." 16 U.S.C. § 1539(a)(1)(B).

Respondents in this action are small landowners, logging companies, and families dependent on the forest products industries in the Pacific Northwest and in the Southeast, and organizations that represent their interests. They brought this declaratory judgment action against petitioners, the Secretary of the Interior and the Director of the Fish and Wildlife Service, in the United States District Court for the District of Columbia to challenge the statutory validity of the Secretary's regulation defining "harm," particularly the inclusion of habitat modification and degradation in the definition. Respondents challenged the regulation on its face. Their complaint alleged that application of the "harm" regulation to the redcockaded woodpecker, an endangered species, and the northern spotted owl, a threatened species, had injured them economically.

Respondents advanced three arguments to support their submission that Congress did not intend the word "take" in § 9 to include habitat modification, as the Secretary's "harm" regulation provides. First, they correctly noted that language in the Senate's original version of the ESA would have defined "take" to include "destruction, modification, or curtailment of [the] habitat or range" of fish or wildlife, but the Senate deleted that language from the bill before enacting it. Second, respondents argued that Congress intended the Act's express authorization for the Federal Government to buy private land in order to prevent habitat degradation in § 5 to be the exclusive check against habitat modification on private property. Third, because the Senate added the term "harm" to the definition of "take" in a floor amendment without debate, respondents argued that the court should not interpret the term so expansively as to include habitat modification.

The District Court considered and rejected each of respondents' arguments, finding "that Congress intended an expansive interpretation of the word 'take,' an interpretation that encompasses habitat modification." 806 F.Supp. 279, 285 (1992). The court noted that in 1982, when Congress was aware of a judicial decision that had applied the Secretary's regulation, see Palila v. Hawaii Dept. of Land and Natural Resources, 639 F.2d 495 (C.A.9 1981) (Palila I), it amended the Act without using the opportunity to change the definition of "take." 806 F.Supp., at 284. The court stated that, even had it found the ESA " 'silent or ambiguous' " as to the authority for the Secretary's definition of "harm," it would nevertheless have upheld the regulation as a reasonable interpretation of the statute. Id., at 285 (quoting Chevron U.S.A. Inc. v. Natural Resources Defense Council, Inc., 467 U.S. 837, 843, 104 S.Ct. 2778, 2782, 81 L.Ed.2d 694 (1984)). The District Court therefore entered summary judgment for petitioners and dismissed respondents' complaint.

A divided panel of the Court of Appeals initially affirmed the judgment of the District Court. 1 F.3d 1 (C.A.D.C.1993). After granting a petition for rehearing, however, the panel reversed. 17 F.3d 1463 (C.A.D.C.1994). Although acknowledging that "[t]he potential breadth of the word 'harm' is indisputable," *id.,* at 1464, the majority concluded that the immediate statutory context in which "harm" appeared counseled against a broad reading; like the other words in the definition of "take," the word "harm" should be read as applying only to "the perpetrator's direct application of force against the animal taken.... The forbidden acts fit, in ordinary language, the basic model 'A hit B.' " *Id.,* at 1465. The majority based its reasoning on a canon of statutory construction called *noscitur a sociis,* which holds that a word is known by the company it keeps.

... The Court performed a lengthy analysis of the 1982 amendment to § 10 that provided for "incidental take permits" and concluded that the amendment did not change the meaning of the term "take" as defined in the 1973 statute.

Chief Judge Mikva, who had announced the panel's original decision, dissented. See 17 F.3d, at 1473. In his view, a proper application of *Chevron* indicated that the Secretary had reasonably defined "harm," because respondents had failed to show that Congress unambiguously manifested its intent to exclude habitat modification from the ambit of "take." Chief Judge Mikva found the majority's reliance on *noscitur a sociis* inappropriate in light of the statutory language and unnecessary in light of the strong support in the legislative history for the Secretary's interpretation. He did not find the 1982 "incidental take permit" amendment alone sufficient to vindicate the Secretary's definition of "harm," but he believed the amendment provided additional support for that definition because it reflected Congress' view in 1982 that the definition was reasonable.

The Court of Appeals' decision created a square conflict with a 1988 decision of the Ninth Circuit that had upheld the Secretary's definition of "harm." See Palila v. Hawaii Dept. of Land and Natural Resources, 852 F.2d 1106 (1988) (Palila II). The Court of Appeals neither cited nor distinguished *Palila II,* despite the stark contrast between the Ninth Circuit's holding and its own. We granted certiorari to resolve the conflict. 513 U.S. 1072, 115 S.Ct. 714, 130 L.Ed.2d 621 (1995). Our consideration of the text and structure of the Act, its legislative history, and the significance of the 1982 amendment persuades us that the Court of Appeals' judgment should be reversed.

## II

Because this case was decided on motions for summary judgment, we may appropriately make certain factual assumptions in order to frame the legal issue. First, we assume respondents have no desire to harm either the red-cockaded woodpecker or the spotted owl; they merely wish to continue logging activities that would be entirely proper if not prohibited by the

ESA. On the other hand, we must assume *arguendo* that those activities will have the effect, even though unintended, of detrimentally changing the natural habitat of both listed species and that, as a consequence, members of those species will be killed or injured. Under respondents' view of the law, the Secretary's only means of forestalling that grave result—even when the actor knows it is certain to occur—is to use his § 5 authority to purchase the lands on which the survival of the species depends. The Secretary, on the other hand, submits that the § 9 prohibition on takings, which Congress defined to include "harm," places on respondents a duty to avoid harm that habitat alteration will cause the birds unless respondents first obtain a permit pursuant to § 10.

The text of the Act provides three reasons for concluding that the Secretary's interpretation is reasonable. First, an ordinary understanding of the word "harm" supports it. The dictionary definition of the verb form of "harm" is "to cause hurt or damage to: injure." Webster's Third New International Dictionary 1034 (1966). In the context of the ESA, that definition naturally encompasses habitat modification that results in actual injury or death to members of an endangered or threatened species.

Respondents argue that the Secretary should have limited the purview of "harm" to direct applications of force against protected species, but the dictionary definition does not include the word "directly" or suggest in any way that only direct or willful action that leads to injury constitutes "harm."[10] Moreover, unless the statutory term "harm" encompasses indirect as well as direct injuries, the word has no meaning that does not duplicate the meaning of other words that § 3 uses to define "take." A reluctance to treat statutory terms as surplusage supports the reasonableness of the Secretary's interpretation.[11]

---

**10.** Respondents and the dissent emphasize what they portray as the "established meaning" of "take" in the sense of a "wildlife take," a meaning respondents argue extends only to "the effort to exercise dominion over some creature, and the concrete effect of [*sic* ] that creature." ... This limitation ill serves the statutory text, which forbids not taking "some creature" but "tak[ing] any [endangered] *species* "—a formidable task for even the most rapacious feudal lord. More importantly, Congress explicitly defined the operative term "take" in the ESA, no matter how much the dissent wishes otherwise ... thereby obviating the need for us to probe its meaning as we must probe the meaning of the undefined subsidiary term "harm." Finally, Congress' definition of "take" includes several words—most obviously "harass," "pursue," and "wound," in addition to "harm" itself—that fit respondents' and the dissent's definition of "take" no better than does "significant habitat modification or degradation."

**11.** In contrast, if the statutory term "harm" encompasses such indirect means of killing and injuring wildlife as habitat modification, the other terms listed in § 3—"harass," "pursue," "hunt," "shoot," "wound," "kill," "trap," "capture," and "collect"—generally retain independent meanings. Most of those terms refer to deliberate actions more frequently than does "harm," and they therefore do not duplicate the sense of indirect causation that "harm" adds to the statute. In addition, most of the other words in the definition describe either actions from which habitat modification does not usually result (*e.g.,* "pursue," "harass") or effects to which activities that modify habitat do not usually lead (*e.g.,* "trap," "collect"). To the extent the Secretary's definition of "harm" may have applications that overlap with other words in the definition, that overlap reflects the broad purpose of the Act.

Second, the broad purpose of the ESA supports the Secretary's decision to extend protection against activities that cause the precise harms Congress enacted the statute to avoid. In TVA v. Hill, 437 U.S. 153, 98 S.Ct. 2279, 57 L.Ed.2d 117 (1978), we described the Act as "the most comprehensive legislation for the preservation of endangered species ever enacted by any nation." *Id.,* at 180, 98 S.Ct., at 2294. Whereas predecessor statutes enacted in 1966 and 1969 had not contained any sweeping prohibition against the taking of endangered species except on federal lands, see *id.,* at 175, 98 S.Ct., at 2292, the 1973 Act applied to all land in the United States and to the Nation's territorial seas. As stated in § 2 of the Act, among its central purposes is "to provide a means whereby the ecosystems upon which endangered species and threatened species depend may be conserved.... " 16 U.S.C. § 1531(b).

... Congress' intent to provide comprehensive protection for endangered and threatened species supports the permissibility of the Secretary's "harm" regulation.

Respondents advance strong arguments that activities that cause minimal or unforeseeable harm will not violate the Act as construed in the "harm" regulation. Respondents, however, present a facial challenge to the regulation.... Thus, they ask us to invalidate the Secretary's understanding of "harm" in every circumstance, even when an actor knows that an activity, such as draining a pond, would actually result in the extinction of a listed species by destroying its habitat. Given Congress' clear expression of the ESA's broad purpose to protect endangered and threatened wildlife, the Secretary's definition of "harm" is reasonable.

Third, the fact that Congress in 1982 authorized the Secretary to issue permits for takings that § 9(a)(1)(B) would otherwise prohibit, "if such taking is incidental to, and not the purpose of, the carrying out of an otherwise lawful activity," 16 U.S.C. § 1539(a)(1)(B), strongly suggests that Congress understood § 9(a)(1)(B) to prohibit indirect as well as deliberate takings. ... The permit process requires the applicant to prepare a "conservation plan" that specifies how he intends to "minimize and mitigate" the "impact" of his activity on endangered and threatened species, 16 U.S.C. § 1539(a)(2)(A), making clear that Congress had in mind foreseeable rather than merely accidental effects on listed species. No one could seriously request an "incidental" take permit to avert § 9 liability for direct, deliberate action against a member of an endangered or threatened species, but respondents would read "harm" so narrowly that the permit procedure would have little more than that absurd purpose. "When Congress acts to amend a statute, we presume it intends its amendment to have real and substantial effect." Stone v. INS, 514 U.S. 386, 397, 115 S.Ct. 1537, 1545, 131 L.Ed.2d 465 (1995). Congress' addition of the § 10 permit provision supports the Secretary's conclusion that activities not intended to harm an endangered species, such as habitat modification, may constitute unlawful takings under the ESA unless the Secretary permits them.

The Court of Appeals made three errors in asserting that "harm" must refer to a direct application of force because the words around it do. First, the court's premise was flawed. Several of the words that accompany "harm" in the § 3 definition of "take," especially "harass," "pursue," "wound," and "kill," refer to actions or effects that do not require direct applications of force. Second, to the extent the court read a requirement of intent or purpose into the words used to define "take," it ignored § 9's express provision that a "knowing" action is enough to violate the Act. Third, the court employed *noscitur a sociis* to give "harm" essentially the same function as other words in the definition, thereby denying its independent meaning. The canon, to the contrary, counsels that a word "gathers meaning from the words around it." Jarecki v. G.D. Searle & Co., 367 U.S. 303, 307, 81 S.Ct. 1579, 1582, 6 L.Ed.2d 859 (1961). The statutory context of "harm" suggests that Congress meant that term to serve a particular function in the ESA, consistent with but distinct from the functions of the other verbs used to define "take." The Secretary's interpretation of "harm" to include indirectly injuring endangered animals through habitat modification permissibly interprets "harm" to have "a character of its own not to be submerged by its association." Russell Motor Car Co. v. United States, 261 U.S. 514, 519, 43 S.Ct. 428, 430, 67 L.Ed. 778 (1923).

. . . Respondents' argument that the Government lacks any incentive to purchase land under § 5 when it can simply prohibit takings under § 9 ignores the practical considerations that attend enforcement of the ESA. Purchasing habitat lands may well cost the Government less in many circumstances than pursuing civil or criminal penalties. In addition, the § 5 procedure allows for protection of habitat before the seller's activity has harmed any endangered animal, whereas the Government cannot enforce the § 9 prohibition until an animal has actually been killed or injured. The Secretary may also find the § 5 authority useful for preventing modification of land that is not yet but may in the future become habitat for an endangered or threatened species. . . .

We need not decide whether the statutory definition of "take" compels the Secretary's interpretation of "harm," because our conclusions that Congress did not unambiguously manifest its intent to adopt respondents' view and that the Secretary's interpretation is reasonable suffice to decide this case. See generally Chevron U.S.A. Inc. v. Natural Resources Defense Council, Inc., 467 U.S. 837, 104 S.Ct. 2778, 81 L.Ed.2d 694 (1984). The latitude the ESA gives the Secretary in enforcing the statute, together with the degree of regulatory expertise necessary to its enforcement, establishes that we owe some degree of deference to the Secretary's reasonable interpretation. . . .

### III

Our conclusion that the Secretary's definition of "harm" rests on a permissible construction of the ESA gains further support from the legislative history of the statute. The Committee Reports accompanying the bills that became the ESA do not specifically discuss the meaning of "harm," but they make clear that Congress intended "take" to apply broadly to cover indirect as well as purposeful actions. The Senate Report stressed that " '[t]ake' is defined ... in the broadest possible manner to include every conceivable way in which a person can 'take' or attempt to 'take' any fish or wildlife." S.Rep. No. 93–307, p. 7 (1973). U.S.Code Cong. & Admin.News 1973, pp. 2989, 2995. The House Report stated that "the broadest possible terms" were used to define restrictions on takings. H.R.Rep. No. 93–412, p. 15 (1973). The House Report underscored the breadth of the "take" definition by noting that it included "harassment, *whether intentional or not.*" *Id.,* at 11 (emphasis added). The Report explained that the definition "would allow, for example, the Secretary to regulate or prohibit the activities of bird-watchers where the effect of those activities might disturb the birds and make it difficult for them to hatch or raise their young." *Ibid.* These comments, ignored in the dissent's welcome but selective foray into legislative history, *see* post, at 2427, support the Secretary's interpretation that the term "take" in § 9 reached far more than the deliberate actions of hunters and trappers.

Two endangered species bills, S. 1502 and S. 1983, were introduced in the Senate and referred to the Commerce Committee. Neither bill included the word "harm" in its definition of "take," although the definitions otherwise closely resembled the one that appeared in the bill as ultimately enacted. See Hearings on S. 1592 and S. 1983 before the Subcommittee on Environment of the Senate Committee on Commerce, 93d Cong., 1st Sess., pp. 7, 27 (1973) (hereinafter Hearings). Senator Tunney, the floor manager of the bill in the Senate, subsequently introduced a floor amendment that added "harm" to the definition, noting that this and accompanying amendments would "help to achieve the purposes of the bill." 119 Cong.Rec. 25683 (July 24, 1973). Respondents argue that the lack of debate about the amendment that added "harm" counsels in favor of a narrow interpretation. We disagree. An obviously broad word that the Senate went out of its way to add to an important statutory definition is precisely the sort of provision that deserves a respectful reading.

The definition of "take" that originally appeared in S. 1983 differed from the definition as ultimately enacted in one other significant respect: It included "the destruction, modification, or curtailment of [the] habitat or range" of fish and wildlife. Hearings, at 27. Respondents make much of the fact that the Commerce Committee removed this phrase from the "take" definition before S. 1983 went to the floor. See 119 Cong.Rec. 25663 (1973). We do not find that fact especially significant. The legislative materials contain no indication why the habitat protection provision was deleted. That provision differed greatly from the regulation at issue today. Most notably, the habitat protection in S. 1983 would have applied far more broadly than the regulation does because it made adverse habitat modification a categorical violation of the "take" prohibition, unbounded by the regulation's limitation to habitat modifications that actually kill or injure wildlife. The S. 1983 language also failed to qualify "modification" with the regulation's limiting adjective "significant." We do not believe the Senate's unelaborated disavowal of the provision in S. 1983 undermines the reasonableness of the more moderate habitat protection in the Secretary's "harm" regulation.

The history of the 1982 amendment that gave the Secretary authority to grant permits for "incidental" takings provides further support for his reading of the Act. The House Report expressly states that "[b]y use of the word 'incidental' the Committee intends to cover situations in which it is known that a taking will occur if the other activity is engaged in but such taking is incidental to, and not the purpose of, the activity." H.R.Rep. No. 97–567, p. 31 (1982). U.S.Code Cong. & Admin.News 1982, pp. 2807, 2831. This reference to the foreseeability of incidental takings undermines respondents' argument that the 1982 amendment covered only accidental killings of endangered and threatened animals that might occur in the course of hunting or trapping other animals. Indeed, Congress had habitat modification directly in mind: both the Senate Report and the House Conference Report identified as the model for the permit process a cooperative state-federal response to a case in California where a development project threatened incidental harm to a species of endangered butterfly by modification of its habitat. *See* S.Rep. No. 97–418, p. 10 (1982): H.R.Conf. Rep. No. 97–835, pp. 30–32 (1982). Thus, Congress in 1982 focused squarely on the aspect of the "harm" regulation at issue in this litigation. Congress' implementation of a permit program is consistent with the Secretary's interpretation of the term "harm."

## IV

When it enacted the ESA, Congress delegated broad administrative and interpretive power to the Secretary. See 16 U.S.C. §§ 1533, 1540(f). The task of defining and listing endangered and threatened species requires an expertise and attention to detail that exceeds the normal province of Congress. Fashioning appropriate standards for issuing permits under § 10 for takings that would otherwise violate § 9 necessarily requires the exercise of broad discretion. The proper interpretation of a term such as "harm" involves a complex policy choice. When Congress has entrusted the Secretary with broad discretion, we are especially reluctant to substitute our views of wise policy for his. See *Chevron,* 467 U.S., at 865–866, 104 S.Ct., at 2793. In this case, that reluctance accords with our conclusion, based on the text, structure, and legislative history of the ESA, that the Secretary reasonably construed the intent of Congress when he defined "harm" to include "significant habitat modification or degradation that actually kills or injures wildlife."

\* \* \*

The judgment of the Court of Appeals is reversed.

*It is so ordered.*

[The concurring opinion of Justice O'Connor is omitted.]

■ JUSTICE SCALIA, with whom THE CHIEF JUSTICE and JUSTICE THOMAS join, dissenting.

I think it unmistakably clear that the legislation at issue here (1) forbade the hunting and killing of endangered animals, and (2) provided federal lands and federal funds *for the acquisition of private lands,* to preserve the habitat of endangered animals. The Court's holding that the hunting and killing prohibition incidentally preserves habitat on private lands imposes unfairness to the point of financial ruin—not just upon the rich, but upon the simplest farmer who finds his land conscripted to national zoological use. I respectfully dissent.

# I

\* \* \*

In my view petitioners must lose—the regulation must fall—even under the test of Chevron U.S.A. Inc. v. Natural Resources Defense Council, Inc., 467 U.S. 837, 843, 104 S.Ct. 2778, 2782, 81 L.Ed.2d 694 (1984)....

The regulation has three features which, for reasons I shall discuss at length below, do not comport with the statute. First, it interprets the statute to prohibit habitat modification that is no more than the cause-in-fact of death or injury to wildlife. *Any* "significant habitat modification" that in fact produces that result by "impairing essential behavioral patterns" is made unlawful, regardless of whether that result is intended or even foreseeable, and no matter how long the chain of causality between modification and injury....

\* \* \*

Second, the regulation does not require an "act"; the Secretary's officially stated position is that an *omission* will do....

The third and most important unlawful feature of the regulation is that it encompasses injury inflicted, not only upon individual animals, but upon populations of the protected species. "Injury" in the regulation includes "significantly impairing essential behavioral patterns, including *breeding,*" 50 CFR § 17.3 (1994) (emphasis added). Impairment of breeding does not "injure" living creatures; it prevents them from propagating, thus "injuring" *a population* of animals which would otherwise have maintained or increased its numbers. What the face of the regulation shows, the Secretary's official pronouncements confirm. The Final Redefinition of "Harm" accompanying publication of the regulation said that "harm" is not limited to "direct physical injury to an individual member of the wildlife species," 46 Fed.Reg. 54748 (1981), and refers to "injury *to a population,*" *id.,* at 54749 (emphasis added)....

*None* of these three features of the regulation can be found in the statutory provisions supposed to authorize it. The term "harm" in § 1532(19) has no legal force of its own. An indictment or civil complaint that charged the defendant with "harming" an animal protected under the Act would be dismissed as defective, for the only *operative* term in the statute is to "take." If "take" were not elsewhere defined in the Act, none could dispute what it means, for the term is as old as the law itself. To "take," when applied to wild animals, means to reduce those animals, by killing or capturing, to human control. See, *e.g.,* 11 Oxford English Dictionary (1933) ("Take ... To catch, capture (a wild beast, bird, fish, etc.)"); Webster's New International Dictionary of the English Language (2d ed. 1949) (take defined as "to catch or capture by trapping, snaring, etc., or as prey"); Geer v. Connecticut, 161 U.S. 519, 523, 16 S.Ct. 600, 602, 40 L.Ed. 793 (1896) ("[A]ll the animals which can be taken upon the earth, in the sea, or in the air, that is to say, wild animals, belong to those who take them") (quoting the Digest of Justinian); 2 W. Blackstone, Commentaries 411 (1766) ("Every man ... has an equal right of pursuing and taking to his own use all such creatures as are *ferae naturae*"). This is just the sense in which "take" is used elsewhere in federal legislation and treaty. See, *e.g.,* Migratory Bird Treaty Act, 16 U.S.C. § 703 (1988 ed., Supp. V) (no person may "pursue, hunt, take, capture, kill, [or] attempt to take, capture, or kill" any migratory bird); Agreement on the Conservation of Polar Bears, Nov. 15, 1973, Art. I, 27 U.S.T. 3918, 3921, T.I.A.S. No. 8409 (defining "taking" as "hunting, killing and capturing"). And that meaning fits neatly with the rest of § 1538(a)(1), which makes it unlawful not only to take protected species, but also to import or export them (§ 1538(a)(1)(A)); to possess, sell, deliver, carry, transport, or ship any taken species (§ 1538(a)(1)(D)); and to transport, sell, or offer to sell them in interstate or foreign commerce (§§ 1538(a)(1)(E)(F)). The taking prohibition, in other words, is only part of the regulatory plan of § 1538(a)(1), which covers all the stages of the process by which protected wildlife is reduced to man's dominion and made the object of profit. It is obvious that "take" in this sense—a term of art deeply embedded in the statutory and common law concerning wildlife—describes a class of acts (not omissions) done directly and intentionally (not indirectly and by accident) to particular animals (not populations of animals).

The Act's definition of "take" does expand the word slightly (and not unusually), so as to make clear that it includes not just a completed taking, but the process of taking, and all of the acts that are customarily identified with or accompany that process ("to harass, harm, pursue, hunt, shoot, wound, kill, trap, capture, or collect"); and so as to include attempts. § 1532(19). The tempting fallacy—which the Court commits with abandon, see *ante,* at 2413, n. 10—is to assume that *once defined,* "take" loses any significance, and it is only the definition that matters. The Court treats the statute as though Congress had directly enacted the § 1532(19) definition as a self-executing prohibition, and had not enacted § 1538(a)(1)(B) at all. But § 1538(a)(1)(B) *is* there, and if the terms contained in the definitional section are susceptible of two readings, one of which comports with the standard meaning of "take" as used in application to wildlife, and one of which does not, an agency regulation that adopts the latter reading is necessarily unreasonable, for it reads the defined term "take"—the only operative term—out of the statute altogether.[2]

**2.** The Court suggests halfheartedly that "take" cannot refer to the taking of    particular animals, because § 1538(a)(1)(B) prohibits "tak[ing] any [endangered] *spe-*

That is what has occurred here. The verb "harm" has a *range* of meaning: "to cause injury" at its broadest, "to do hurt or damage" in a narrower and more direct sense. See, *e.g.,* 1 N. Webster, An American Dictionary of the English Language (1828) ("Harm, *v.t.* To hurt; to injure; to damage; *to impair soundness of body, either animal* or vegetable") (emphasis added); American College Dictionary 551 (1970) ("harm ... *n.* injury; damage; hurt: *to do him bodily harm* "). In fact the more directed sense of "harm" is a somewhat more common and preferred usage; "*harm* has in it a little of the idea of specifically focused hurt or injury, as if a personal injury has been anticipated and intended." J. Opdycke, Mark My Words: A Guide to Modern Usage and Expression 330 (1949). See also American Heritage Dictionary of the English Language (1981) ("*Injure* has the widest range.... *Harm* and *hurt* refer principally to what causes physical or mental distress to living things"). To define "harm" as an act or omission that, however remotely, "actually kills or injures" a population of wildlife through habitat modification, is to choose a meaning that makes nonsense of the word that "harm" defines—requiring us to accept that a farmer who tills his field and causes erosion that makes silt run into a nearby river which depletes oxygen and thereby "impairs [the] breeding" of protected fish, has "taken" or "attempted to take" the fish. It should take the strongest evidence to make us believe that Congress has defined a term in a manner repugnant to its ordinary and traditional sense.

Here the evidence shows the opposite. "Harm" is merely one of 10 prohibitory words in § 1532(19), and the other 9 fit the ordinary meaning of "take" perfectly. To "harass, pursue, hunt, shoot, wound, kill, trap, capture, or collect" are all affirmative acts (the provision itself describes them as "conduct," see § 1532(19)) which are directed immediately and intentionally against a particular animal—not acts or omissions that indirectly and accidentally cause injury to a population of animals....

I am not the first to notice this fact, or to draw the conclusion that it compels. In 1981 the Solicitor of the Fish and Wildlife Service delivered a legal opinion on § 1532(19) that is in complete agreement with my reading:

"The Act's definition of 'take' contains a list of actions that illustrate the intended scope of the term.... With the possible exception of 'harm,' these terms all represent forms of conduct that are directed against and likely to injure or kill *individual* wildlife. Under the principle of statutory construction, *ejusdem generis,* ... the term 'harm' should be interpreted to include only those actions that are directed against, and likely to injure or kill, individual wildlife." Memorandum of April 17, 1981, reprinted in 46 Fed.Reg. 29490, 29491 (emphasis in original).

I would call it *noscitur a sociis,* but the principle is much the same: the fact that "several items in a list share an attribute counsels in favor of

---

*cies.*" The suggestion is halfhearted because that reading obviously contradicts the statutory intent. It would mean no violation in the intentional shooting of a single bald eagle— or, for that matter, the intentional shooting of 1,000 bald eagles out of the extant 1,001. The phrasing of § 1538(a)(1)(B), as the Court recognizes elsewhere, is shorthand for "take any *member of* [an endangered] species."

interpreting the other items as possessing that attribute as well," *Beecham v. United States*, 511 U.S. 368, 368, 114 S.Ct. 1669, 1671, 128 L.Ed.2d 383 (1994). The Court contends that the canon cannot be applied to deprive a word of all its "independent meaning," *ante,* at 2415. That proposition is questionable to begin with, especially as applied to long lawyers' listings such as this. If it were true, we ought to give the word "trap" in the definition its rare meaning of "to clothe" (whence "trappings")—since otherwise it adds nothing to the word "capture." See *Moskal v. United States*, 498 U.S. 103, 120, 111 S.Ct. 461, 471, 112 L.Ed.2d 449 (1990) (Scalia, J., dissenting)....

The penalty provisions of the Act counsel this interpretation as well. Any person who "knowingly" violates § 1538(a)(1)(B) is subject to criminal penalties under § 1540(b)(1) and civil penalties under § 1540(a)(1); moreover, under the latter section, any person "who otherwise violates" the taking prohibition (*i.e.,* violates it *un* knowingly) may be assessed a civil penalty of $500 for each violation, with the stricture that "[e]ach such violation shall be a separate offense." This last provision should be clear warning that the regulation is in error, for when combined with the regulation it produces a result that no legislature could reasonably be thought to have intended: A large number of routine private activities—farming, for example, ranching, roadbuilding, construction and logging—are subjected to strict-liability penalties when they fortuitously injure protected wildlife, no matter how remote the chain of causation and no matter how difficult to foresee (or to disprove) the "injury" may be (*e.g.,* an "impairment" of breeding).

\* \* \*

The broader structure of the Act confirms the unreasonableness of the regulation. Section 1536 provides:

> "Each Federal agency shall ... insure that any action authorized, funded, or carried out by such agency ... is not likely to jeopardize the continued existence of any endangered species or threatened species or *result in the destruction or adverse modification of habitat* of such species which is determined by the Secretary ... to be critical." 16 U.S.C. § 1536(a)(2) (emphasis added).

> The Act defines "critical habitat" as habitat that is "essential to the conservation of the species," §§ 1532(5)(A)(i), (A)(ii), with "conservation" in turn defined as the use of methods necessary to bring listed species "to the point at which the measures provided pursuant to this chapter are no longer necessary." § 1532(3).

These provisions have a double significance. Even if §§ 1536(a)(2) and 1538(a)(1)(B) were totally independent prohibitions—the former applying only to federal agencies and their licensees, the latter only to private parties—Congress's explicit prohibition of habitat modification in the one section would bar the inference of an implicit prohibition of habitat modification in the other section....

In fact, however, §§ 1536(a)(2) and 1538(a)(1)(B) do *not* operate in separate realms; federal agencies are subject to *both,* because the "person[s]" forbidden to take protected species under § 1538 include agencies and departments of the Federal Government. See § 1532(13). This means that the "harm" regulation also contradicts another principle of interpretation: that statutes should be read so far as possible to give independent effect to all their provisions. See Ratzlaf v. United States, 510 U.S. 135, 155, 114 S.Ct. 655, 666–667, 126 L.Ed.2d 615. By defining "harm" in the definition of "take" in § 1538(a)(1)(B) to include significant habitat modification that injures populations of wildlife, the regulation makes the habitat-modification restriction in § 1536(a)(2) almost wholly superfluous. . . .

## II

The Court makes four other arguments. First, "the broad purpose of the [Act] supports the Secretary's decision to extend protection against activities that cause the precise harms Congress enacted the statute to avoid." I thought we had renounced the vice of "simplistically . . . assum[ing] that *whatever* furthers the statute's primary objective must be the law." Rodriguez v. United States, 480 U.S. 522, 526, 107 S.Ct. 1391, 1393, 94 L.Ed.2d 533 (1987) (*per curiam* ) (emphasis in original). Deduction from the "broad purpose" of a statute begs the question if it is used to decide by what *means* (and hence to what *length* ) Congress pursued that purpose; to get the right answer to that question there is no substitute for the hard job (or in this case, the quite simple one) of reading the whole text. "The Act must do everything necessary to achieve its broad purpose" is the slogan of the enthusiast, not the analytical tool of the arbiter.

* * *

## III

In response to the points made in this dissent, the Court's opinion stresses two points, neither of which is supported by the regulation, and so cannot validly be used to uphold it. First, the Court and the concurrence suggest that the regulation should be read to contain a requirement of proximate causation or foreseeability, principally *because the statute does—* and "[n]othing in the regulation purports to weaken those requirements [of the statute]." I quite agree that the statute contains such a limitation, because the verbs of purpose in § 1538(a)(1)(B) denote action directed at animals. *But the Court has rejected that reading.* The critical premise on which it has upheld the regulation is that, despite the weight of the other words in § 1538(a)(1)(B), "the statutory term 'harm' encompasses indirect as well as direct injuries," (describing "the sense of indirect causation that 'harm' adds to the statute"); (stating that the Secretary permissibly interprets " 'harm' " to include "indirectly injuring endangered animals"). Consequently, unless there is some strange category of causation that is indirect and yet also proximate, the Court has already rejected its own basis for finding a proximate-cause limitation in the regulation. In fact "proximate" causation simply *means* "direct" causation. . . .

The only other reason given for finding a proximate-cause limitation in the regulation is that "by use of the word 'actually,' " the regulation clearly rejects speculative or conjectural effects, and thus itself involves principles of proximate causation. . . . "actually" defines the requisite *injury,* not the requisite *causality.*

The regulation says (it is worth repeating) that "harm" means (1) an act which (2) actually kills or injures wildlife. If that does not dispense with a proximate cause requirement, I do not know what language would. And changing the regulation by judicial invention, even to achieve compliance with the statute, is not permissible. Perhaps the agency itself would prefer to achieve compliance in some other fashion. We defer to reasonable agency interpretations of ambiguous statutes precisely in order that agencies, rather than courts, may exercise policymaking discretion in the interstices of statutes. See *Chevron,* 407 U.S., at 843–845, 104 S.Ct., at 2782. Just as courts may not exercise an agency's power to adjudicate, and so may not affirm an agency order on discretionary grounds the agency has not advanced, see SEC v. Chenery Corp., 318 U.S. 80, 63 S.Ct. 454, 87 L.Ed. 626 (1943), so also this Court may not exercise the Secretary's power to regulate, and so may not uphold a regulation by adding to it even the most reasonable of elements it does not contain.

The second point the Court stresses in its response seems to me a belated mending of its holding. It apparently *concedes* that the statute requires injury *to particular animals* rather than merely to populations of animals (referring to killing or injuring *"members of* [listed] species" (emphasis added)). The Court then rejects my contention that the regulation ignores this requirement, since, it says, "every term in the regulation's definition of 'harm' is subservient to the phrase 'an act which actually kills or injures wildlife.' " As I have pointed out, this reading is incompatible with the regulation's specification of impairment of "breeding" as one of the *modes* of "kill[ing] or injur[ing] wildlife." . . .

But since the Court is reading the regulation and the statute incorrectly in other respects, it may as well introduce this novelty as well—law à la carte. As I understand the regulation that the Court has created and held consistent with the statute that it has also created, habitat modification can constitute a "taking," but only if it results in the killing or harming of *individual animals,* and only if that consequence is the direct result of the modification. This means that the destruction of privately owned habitat that is essential, not for the feeding or nesting, but for the *breeding,* of butterflies, would not violate the Act, since it would not harm or kill any living butterfly. I, too, think it would not violate the Act—not for the utterly unsupported reason that habitat modifications fall outside the regulation if they happen not to kill or injure a living animal, but for the textual reason that only action directed at living animals constitutes a "take."

\* \* \*

The Endangered Species Act is a carefully considered piece of legislation that forbids all persons to hunt or harm endangered animals, but places upon the public at large, rather than upon fortuitously accountable individual landowners, the cost of preserving the habitat of endangered species. There is neither textual support for, nor even evidence of congressional consideration of, the radically different disposition contained in the regulation that the Court sustains. For these reasons, I respectfully dissent.

## Question

The *Babbitt v. Sweet Home* dissent quarrels with, among other things, reference to the purpose of the statute to clarify the meaning of the contentious word or phrase. Does this lead to undue literalism? Consider the following example, proposed by Professor Eskridge in *Textualism: The Unknown Ideal?*, 96 MICH. L. REV. 1509, 1549 (1998):

> Scalia, a hotel manager, tells me, his employee, to "gather all of the ashtrays in the public areas of the hotel and put them in my office by 2:00 p.m., *today*," while he is dining. I diligently collect the ashtrays until I come to an elevator bank, where a metal ashtray is bolted onto the wall. Should I rip it off? A pragmatic agent would leave it on the wall, construing "all ashtrays" to exclude those whose removal would be unduly costly, a judgment call.

A judgment against ripping off the ashtray takes account of the perceived reason for the command, implicitly attributing sensible goals to the commander. By contrast, an "honest textualist" in Professor Eskridge's phrase, would be a "crummy agent" and would rip out the ashtrays, because that is what the order *said*, whether or not it made any sense. Should a court limit itself to narrowly construing statutes, even in a way that may contradict perceived legislative intent, in order to force Congress to amend the statute explicitly? For the view that the Court should construe statutes in the face of ambiguity in order to provoke legislative amendment, see Einer Elhauge, Preference–Eliciting Statutory Default Rules, 102 Colum. L. Rev. 2162 (2002).

## FDA v. Brown & Williamson Tobacco Corp.

Supreme Court of the United States, 2000.
529 U.S. 120, 120 S.Ct. 1291, 146 L.Ed.2d 121.

■ JUSTICE O'CONNOR delivered the opinion of the Court.

This case involves one of the most troubling public health problems facing our Nation today: the thousands of premature deaths that occur each year because of tobacco use. In 1996, the Food and Drug Administration (FDA), after having expressly disavowed any such authority since its inception, asserted jurisdiction to regulate tobacco products. See 61 Fed. Reg. 44619–45318. The FDA concluded that nicotine is a drug within the meaning of the Food, Drug, and Cosmetic Act (FDCA or Act), 52 Stat. 1040, as amended, 21 U.S.C. § 301 et seq., and that cigarettes and smokeless tobacco are combination products that deliver nicotine to the body. 61 Fed.Reg. 44397 (1996). Pursuant to this authority, it promulgated regulations intended to reduce tobacco consumption among children and adolescents. Id., at 44615–44618. The agency believed that, because most tobacco consumers begin their use before reaching the age of 18, curbing tobacco use by minors could substantially reduce the prevalence of addiction in future generations and thus the incidence of tobacco-related death and disease. Id., at 44398–44399.

Regardless of how serious the problem an administrative agency seeks to address, however, it may not exercise its authority in a manner that is inconsistent with the administrative structure that Congress enacted into law. ETSI Pipeline Project v. Missouri, 484 U.S. 495, 517 (1988). And although agencies are generally entitled to deference in the interpretation of statutes that they administer, a reviewing court, as well as the agency, must give effect to the unambiguously expressed intent of Congress. Chevron U.S.A. Inc. v. Natural Resources Defense Council, Inc., 467 U.S. 837, 842–843 (1984). In this case, we believe that Congress has clearly precluded the FDA from asserting jurisdiction to regulate tobacco products. Such authority is inconsistent with the intent that Congress has expressed in the FDCA's overall regulatory scheme and in the tobacco-specific legislation that it has enacted subsequent to the FDCA. In light of this clear intent, the FDA's assertion of jurisdiction is impermissible.

I

The FDCA grants the FDA, as the designee of the Secretary of Health and Human Services, the authority to regulate, among other items, drugs and devices. See 21 U.S.C. §§ 321(g)-(h), 393 (1994 ed. and Supp. III). The Act defines drug to include articles (other than food) intended to affect the structure or any function of the body. 21 U.S.C. § 321(g)(1)(C). It defines device, in part, as an instrument, apparatus, implement, machine, contrivance, ... or other similar or related article, including any component, part, or accessory, which is ... intended to affect the structure or any function of the body. § 321(h). The Act also grants the FDA the authority to regulate so-called combination products, which constitute a combination of a drug, device, or biologic product. § 353(g)(1). The FDA has construed this provision as giving it the discretion to regulate combination products as drugs, as devices, or as both. See 61 Fed.Reg. 44400 (1996)....

Based on [its] findings [regarding the dangerousness of tobacco], the FDA promulgated regulations concerning tobacco products' promotion, labeling, and accessibility to children and adolescents. See id., at 44615–44618....

The FDA promulgated these regulations pursuant to its authority to regulate restricted devices. See 21 U.S.C. § 360j(e). The FDA construed § 353(g)(1) as giving it the discretion to regulate combination products using the Act's drug authorities, device authorities, or both, depending on how the public health goals of the act can be best accomplished. 61 Fed.Reg. 44403 (1996). Given the greater flexibility in the FDCA for the regulation of devices, the FDA determined that the device authorities provide the most appropriate basis for regulating cigarettes and smokeless tobacco. Id., at 44404. Under 21 U.S.C. § 360j(e), the agency may require that a device be restricted to sale, distribution, or use ... upon such other conditions as [the FDA] may prescribe in such regulation, if, because of its potentiality for harmful effect or the collateral measures necessary to its use, [the FDA] determines that there cannot otherwise be reasonable assurance of its safety and effectiveness. The FDA reasoned that its regulations fell within the authority granted by § 360j(e) because they related to the sale or distribution of tobacco products and were necessary for providing a reasonable assurance of safety. 61 Fed.Reg. 44405–44407 (1996).

Respondents, a group of tobacco manufacturers, retailers, and advertisers, filed suit in United States District Court for the Middle District of North Carolina challenging the regulations. See Coyne Beahm, Inc. v. FDA, 966 F.Supp. 1374 (1997). They moved for summary judgment on the grounds that the FDA lacked jurisdiction to regulate tobacco products as customarily marketed, the regulations exceeded the FDA's authority under 21 U.S.C. § 360j(e).... The District Court granted respondents' motion in part and denied it in part. 966 F.Supp., at 1400. The court held that the FDCA authorizes the FDA to regulate tobacco products as customarily marketed and that the FDA's access and labeling regulations are permissible, but it also found that the agency's advertising and promotion restrictions exceed its authority under § 360j(e). Id., at 1380–1400....

The Court of Appeals for the Fourth Circuit reversed, holding that Congress has not granted the FDA jurisdiction to regulate tobacco products. See 153 F.3d 155 (1998)....

We granted the Government's petition for certiorari, 526 U.S. 1086 (1999), to determine whether the FDA has authority under the FDCA to regulate tobacco products as customarily marketed.

## II

The FDA's assertion of jurisdiction to regulate tobacco products is founded on its conclusions that nicotine is a drug and that cigarettes and smokeless tobacco are drug delivery devices....

A threshold issue is the appropriate framework for analyzing the FDA's assertion of authority to regulate tobacco products. Because this case involves an administrative agency's construction of a statute that it administers, our analysis is governed by Chevron U.S.A. Inc. v. Natural Resources Defense Council, Inc., 467 U.S. 837 (1984). Under Chevron, a reviewing court must first ask whether Congress has directly spoken to the precise question at issue. Id., at 842. If Congress has done so, the inquiry is at an end; the court must give effect to the unambiguously expressed intent of Congress. Id., at 843 [other citations omitted]. But if Congress has not specifically addressed the question, a reviewing court must respect the agency's construction of the statute so long as it is permissible. [citations omitted]. Such deference is justified because [t]he responsibilities for assessing the wisdom of such policy choices and resolving the struggle between competing views of the public interest are not judicial ones,

Chevron, supra, at 866, 104 S.Ct. 2778, and because of the agency's greater familiarity with the ever-changing facts and circumstances surrounding the subjects regulated [citation omitted].

In determining whether Congress has specifically addressed the question at issue, a reviewing court should not confine itself to examining a particular statutory provision in isolation. The meaning—or ambiguity—of certain words or phrases may only become evident when placed in context. See Brown v. Gardner, 513 U.S. 115, 118 (1994) (Ambiguity is a creature not of definitional possibilities but of statutory context). It is a fundamental canon of statutory construction that the words of a statute must be read in their context and with a view to their place in the overall statutory scheme. Davis v. Michigan Dept. of Treasury, 489 U.S. 803, 809 (1989). A court must therefore interpret the statute as a symmetrical and coherent regulatory scheme, Gustafson v. Alloyd Co., 513 U.S. 561, 569 (1995), and fit, if possible, all parts into an harmonious whole, FTC v. Mandel Brothers, Inc., 359 U.S. 385, 389 (1959). Similarly, the meaning of one statute may be affected by other Acts, particularly where Congress has spoken subsequently and more specifically to the topic at hand. [citations omitted]. In addition, we must be guided to a degree by common sense as to the manner in which Congress is likely to delegate a policy decision of such economic and political magnitude to an administrative agency. [citations omitted].

With these principles in mind, we find that Congress has directly spoken to the issue here and precluded the FDA's jurisdiction to regulate tobacco products.

## A

Viewing the FDCA as a whole, it is evident that one of the Act's core objectives is to ensure that any product regulated by the FDA is safe and effective for its intended use. See 21 U.S.C. § 393(b)(2) (1994 ed., Supp. III) (defining the FDA's mission).... This essential purpose pervades the FDCA. For instance, 21 U.S.C. § 393(b)(2) (1994 ed., Supp. III) defines the FDA's mission to include protect [ing] the public health by ensuring that ... drugs are safe and effective and that there is reasonable assurance of the safety and effectiveness of devices intended for human use. The FDCA requires premarket approval of any new drug, with some limited exceptions, and states that the FDA shall issue an order refusing to approve the application of a new drug if it is not safe and effective for its intended purpose. §§ 355(d)(1)-(2), (4)-(5). If the FDA discovers after approval that a drug is unsafe or ineffective, it shall, after due notice and opportunity for hearing to the applicant, withdraw approval of the drug. 21 U.S.C. §§ 355(e)(1)-(3). The Act also requires the FDA to classify all devices into one of three categories. § 360c(b)(1). Regardless of which category the FDA chooses, there must be a reasonable assurance of the safety and effectiveness of the device. 21 U.S.C. §§ 360c(a)(1)(A)(i), (B), (C) (1994 ed. and Supp. III); 61 Fed.Reg. 44412 (1996). Even the restricted device provision pursuant to which the FDA promulgated the regulations at issue here authorizes the agency to place conditions on the sale or distribution of a device specifically when there cannot otherwise be reasonable assurance of its safety and effectiveness. 21 U.S.C. § 360j(e). Thus, the Act generally requires the FDA to prevent the marketing of any drug or device where the potential for inflicting death or physical injury is not offset by the possibility of therapeutic benefit. United States v. Rutherford, 442 U.S. 544, 556 (1979).

In its rulemaking proceeding, the FDA quite exhaustively documented that tobacco products are unsafe, dangerous, and cause great pain and suffering from illness. 61 Fed.Reg. 44412 (1996). . . . These findings logically imply that, if tobacco products were devices under the FDCA, the FDA would be required to remove them from the market. Consider, first, the FDCA's provisions concerning the misbranding of drugs or devices. The Act prohibits [t]he introduction or delivery for introduction into interstate commerce of any food, drug, device, or cosmetic that is adultered or misbranded. 21 U.S.C. § 331(a). . . . Thus, were tobacco products within the FDA's jurisdiction, the Act would deem them misbranded devices that could not be introduced into interstate commerce. . . .

Congress, however, has foreclosed the removal of tobacco products from the market. A provision of the United States Code currently in force states that [t]he marketing of tobacco constitutes one of the greatest basic industries of the United States with ramifying activities which directly affect interstate and foreign commerce at every point, and stable conditions therein are necessary to the general welfare. 7 U.S.C. § 1311(a). More importantly, Congress has directly addressed the problem of tobacco and health through legislation on six occasions since 1965. . . . Nonetheless, Congress stopped well short of ordering a ban. Instead, it has generally regulated the labeling and advertisement of tobacco products, expressly providing that it is the policy of Congress that commerce and the national economy may be . . . protected to the maximum extent consistent with consumers be[ing] adequately informed about any adverse health effects. 15 U.S.C. § 1331. Congress' decisions to regulate labeling and advertising and to adopt the express policy of protecting commerce and the national economy . . . to the maximum extent reveal its intent that tobacco products remain on the market. Indeed, the collective premise of these statutes is that cigarettes and smokeless tobacco will continue to be sold in the United States. A ban of tobacco products by the FDA would therefore plainly contradict congressional policy. . . .

The dissent contends that our conclusion means that the FDCA requires the FDA to ban outright 'dangerous' drugs or devices, and that this is a perverse reading of the statute. This misunderstands our holding. The FDA, consistent with the FDCA, may clearly regulate many dangerous products without banning them. Indeed, virtually every drug or device poses dangers under certain conditions. What the FDA may not do is conclude that a drug or device cannot be used safely for any therapeutic purpose and yet, at the same time, allow that product to remain on the market. Such regulation is incompatible with the FDCA's core objective of ensuring that every drug or device is safe and effective.

Considering the FDCA as a whole, it is clear that Congress intended to exclude tobacco products from the FDA's jurisdiction.... [I]f tobacco products were within the FDA's jurisdiction, the Act would require the FDA to remove them from the market entirely. But a ban would contradict Congress' clear intent as expressed in its more recent, tobacco-specific legislation. The inescapable conclusion is that there is no room for tobacco products within the FDCA's regulatory scheme. If they cannot be used safely for any therapeutic purpose, and yet they cannot be banned, they simply do not fit.

### B

In determining whether Congress has spoken directly to the FDA's authority to regulate tobacco, we must also consider in greater detail the tobacco-specific legislation that Congress has enacted over the past 35 years. At the time a statute is enacted, it may have a range of plausible meanings. Over time, however, subsequent acts can shape or focus those meanings. The classic judicial task of reconciling many laws enacted over time, and getting them to "make sense" in combination, necessarily assumes that the implications of a statute may be altered by the implications of a later statute. United States v. Fausto, 484 U.S., at 453. This is particularly so where the scope of the earlier statute is broad but the subsequent statutes more specifically address the topic at hand. As we recognized recently in United States v. Estate of Romani, a specific policy embodied in a later federal statute should control our construction of the [earlier] statute, even though it ha[s] not been expressly amended. 523 U.S., at 530–531.

Congress has enacted six separate pieces of legislation since 1965 addressing the problem of tobacco use and human health. See supra, at 1322. Those statutes, among other things, require that health warnings appear on all packaging and in all print and outdoor advertisements, see 15 U.S.C. §§ 1331, 1333, 4402; prohibit the advertisement of tobacco products through any medium of electronic communication subject to regulation by the Federal Communications Commission (FCC), see §§ 1335, 4402(f); require the Secretary of Health and Human Services (HHS) to report every three years to Congress on research findings concerning the addictive property of tobacco, 42 U.S.C. § 290aa–2(b)(2); and make States' receipt of certain federal block grants contingent on their making it unlawful for any manufacturer, retailer, or distributor of tobacco products to sell or distribute any such product to any individual under the age of 18, § 300x–26(a)(1).

In adopting each statute, Congress has acted against the backdrop of the FDA's consistent and repeated statements that it lacked authority under the FDCA to regulate tobacco absent claims of therapeutic benefit by the manufacturer. In fact, on several occasions over this period, and after the health consequences of tobacco use and nicotine's pharmacological effects had become well known, Congress considered and rejected bills that would have granted the FDA such jurisdiction. Under these circumstances, it is evident that Congress' tobacco-specific statutes have effectively ratified the FDA's long-held position that it lacks jurisdiction under the FDCA to regulate tobacco products. Congress has created a distinct regulatory scheme to address the problem of tobacco and health, and that scheme, as presently constructed, precludes any role for the FDA. . . .

Taken together, these actions by Congress over the past 35 years preclude an interpretation of the FDCA that grants the FDA jurisdiction to regulate tobacco products. We do not rely on Congress' failure to act—its consideration and rejection of bills that would have given the FDA this authority—in reaching this conclusion. Indeed, this is not a case of simple inaction by Congress that purportedly represents its acquiescence in an agency's position. To the contrary, Congress has enacted several statutes addressing the particular subject of tobacco and health, creating a distinct regulatory scheme for cigarettes and smokeless tobacco. In doing so, Congress has been aware of tobacco's health hazards and its pharmacological effects. It has also enacted this legislation against the background of the FDA repeatedly and consistently asserting that it lacks jurisdiction under the FDCA to regulate tobacco products as customarily marketed. Further, Congress has persistently acted to preclude a meaningful role for any administrative agency in making policy on the subject of tobacco and health. Moreover, the substance of Congress' regulatory scheme is, in an important respect, incompatible with FDA jurisdiction. Although the supervision of product labeling to protect consumer health is a substantial component of the FDA's regulation of drugs and devices, see 21 U.S.C. § 352 (1994 ed. and Supp. III), the FCLAA and the CSTHEA explicitly prohibit any federal agency from imposing any health-related labeling requirements on cigarettes or smokeless tobacco products, see 15 U.S.C. §§ 1334(a), 4406(a).

Under these circumstances, it is clear that Congress' tobacco-specific legislation has effectively ratified the FDA's previous position that it lacks jurisdiction to regulate tobacco. . . .

It is hardly conceivable that Congress—and in this setting, any Member of Congress—was not abundantly aware of what was going on. Congress has affirmatively acted to address the issue of tobacco and health, relying on the representations of the FDA that it had no authority to regulate tobacco. It has created a distinct scheme to regulate the sale of tobacco products, focused on labeling and advertising, and premised on the belief that the FDA lacks such jurisdiction under the FDCA. As a result, Congress' tobacco-specific statutes preclude the FDA from regulating tobacco products as customarily marketed. . . .

[O]ur conclusion does not rely on the fact that the FDA's assertion of jurisdiction represents a sharp break with its prior interpretation of the FDCA. Certainly, an agency's initial interpretation of a statute that it is charged with administering is not carved in stone. Chevron, 467 U.S., at 863 [other citations omitted]. As we recognized in Motor Vehicle Mfrs. Assn. of United States, Inc. v. State Farm Mut. Automobile Ins. Co., 463 U.S. 29 (1983), agencies must be given ample latitude to "adapt their rules and policies to the demands of changing circumstances." Id., at 42. The consistency of the FDA's prior position is significant in this case for a different reason: it provides important context to Congress' enactment of its tobacco-specific legislation. When the FDA repeatedly informed Congress that the FDCA does not grant it the authority to regulate tobacco products, its statements were consistent with the agency's unwavering position since its inception, and with the position that its predecessor agency had first taken in 1914. Although not crucial, the consistency of the FDA's prior position bolsters the conclusion that when Congress created a distinct regulatory scheme addressing the subject of tobacco and health, it understood that the FDA is without jurisdiction to regulate tobacco products and ratified that position.

The dissent also argues that the proper inference to be drawn from Congress' tobacco-specific legislation is critically ambivalent. We disagree. In that series of statutes, Congress crafted a specific legislative response to the problem of tobacco and health, and it did so with the understanding, based on repeated assertions by the FDA, that the agency has no authority under the FDCA to regulate tobacco products. Moreover, Congress expressly preempted any other regulation of the labeling of tobacco products concerning their health consequences, even though the oversight of labeling is central to the FDCA's regulatory scheme. And in addressing the subject, Congress consistently evidenced its intent to preclude any federal agency from exercising significant policymaking authority in the area. Under these circumstances, we believe the appropriate inference—that Congress intended to ratify the FDA's prior position that it lacks jurisdiction—is unmistakable.

The dissent alternatively argues that, even if Congress' subsequent tobacco-specific legislation did, in fact, ratify the FDA's position, that position was merely a contingent disavowal of jurisdiction. Specifically, the dissent contends that the FDA's traditional view was largely premised on a perceived inability to prove the necessary statutory "intent" requirement. A fair reading of the FDA's representations prior to 1995, however, demonstrates that the agency's position was essentially unconditional.... To the extent the agency's position could be characterized as equivocal, it was only with respect to the well-established exception of when the manufacturer makes express claims of therapeutic benefit.... Thus, what Congress ratified was the FDA's plain and resolute position that the FDCA gives the agency no authority to regulate tobacco products as customarily marketed....

\* \* \*

Reading the FDCA as a whole, as well as in conjunction with Congress' subsequent tobacco-specific legislation, it is plain that Congress has not given the FDA the authority that it seeks to exercise here. For these reasons, the judgment of the Court of Appeals for the Fourth Circuit is affirmed.

It is so ordered.

■ JUSTICE BREYER, with whom JUSTICE STEVENS, JUSTICE SOUTER, and JUSTICE GINSBURG join, dissenting.

The Food and Drug Administration (FDA) has the authority to regulate articles (other than food) intended to affect the structure or any function of the body. . . . Federal Food, Drug and Cosmetic Act (FDCA), 21 U.S.C. § 321(g)(1)(C). Unlike the majority, I believe that tobacco products fit within this statutory language.

In its own interpretation, the majority nowhere denies the following two salient points. First, tobacco products (including cigarettes) fall within the scope of this statutory definition, read literally. Cigarettes achieve their mood-stabilizing effects through the interaction of the chemical nicotine and the cells of the central nervous system. Both cigarette manufacturers and smokers alike know of, and desire, that chemically induced result. Hence, cigarettes are intended to affect the body's structure and function, in the literal sense of these words.

Second, the statute's basic purpose—the protection of public health—supports the inclusion of cigarettes within its scope. See United States v. Article of Drug . . . Bacto–Unidisk, 394 U.S. 784, 798 (1969) (FDCA is to be given *a liberal construction consistent with [its] overriding purpose to protect the public health* (emphasis added)). Unregulated tobacco use causes [m]ore than 400,000 people [to] die each year from tobacco-related illnesses, such as cancer, respiratory illnesses, and heart disease. 61 Fed.Reg. 44398 (1996). Indeed, tobacco products kill more people in this country every year than . . . AIDS, car accidents, alcohol, homicides, illegal drugs, suicides, and fires, *combined*. Ibid. (emphasis added).

Despite the FDCA's literal language and general purpose (both of which support the FDA's finding that cigarettes come within its statutory authority), the majority nonetheless reads the statute as excluding tobacco products for two basic reasons:

(1) the FDCA does not fit the case of tobacco because the statute requires the FDA to prohibit dangerous drugs or devices (like cigarettes) outright, and the agency concedes that simply banning the sale of cigarettes is not a proper remedy, ante, at 1306; and

(2) Congress has enacted other statutes, which, when viewed in light of the FDA's long history of denying tobacco-related jurisdiction and considered together with Congress' failure explicitly to grant the agency tobacco-specific authority, demonstrate that Congress did not intend for the FDA to exercise jurisdiction over tobacco.

In my view, neither of these propositions is valid. Rather, the FDCA does not significantly limit the FDA's remedial alternatives. And the later statutes do not tell the FDA it cannot exercise jurisdiction, but simply leave FDA jurisdictional law where Congress found it. . . .

The bulk of the opinion that follows will explain the basis for these latter conclusions. In short, I believe that the most important indicia of statutory meaning—language and purpose—along with the FDCA's legislative history (described briefly in Part I) are sufficient to establish that the FDA has authority to regulate tobacco....

## I

Before 1938, the federal Pure Food and Drug Act contained only two jurisdictional definitions of drug:

> [1]   medicines and preparations recognized in the United States Pharmacopoeia or National Formulary ... and [2] any substance or mixture of substances intended to be used for the cure, mitigation, or prevention of disease. Act of June 30, 1906, ch. 3915, § 6, 34 Stat. 769.

In 1938, Congress added a third definition, relevant here:

> (3) articles (other than food) intended to affect the structure or any function of the body.... Act of June 25, 1938, ch. 675, § 201(g), 52 Stat. 1041 (codified at 21 U.S.C. § 321(g)(1)(C)).

It also added a similar definition in respect to a device. See § 201(h), 52 Stat. 1041 (codified at 21 U.S.C. § 321(h)). As I have mentioned, the literal language of the third definition and the FDCA's general purpose both strongly support a projurisdiction reading of the statute. See supra, at 1316.

The statute's history offers further support. The FDA drafted the new language, and it testified before Congress that the third definition would expand the FDCA's jurisdictional scope significantly....

That Congress would grant the FDA such broad jurisdictional authority should surprise no one. In 1938, the President and much of Congress believed that federal administrative agencies needed broad authority and would exercise that authority wisely—a view embodied in much Second New Deal legislation.... Thus, at around the same time that it added the relevant language to the FDCA, Congress enacted laws granting other administrative agencies even broader powers to regulate much of the Nation's transportation and communication.... Why would the 1938 New Deal Congress suddenly have hesitated to delegate to so well established an agency as the FDA all of the discretionary authority that a straightforward reading of the relevant statutory language implies?

Nor is it surprising that such a statutory delegation of power could lead after many years to an assertion of jurisdiction that the 1938 legislators might not have expected. Such a possibility is inherent in the very nature of a broad delegation. In 1938, it may well have seemed unlikely that the FDA would ever bring cigarette manufacturers within the FDCA's statutory language by proving that cigarettes produce chemical changes in the body and that the makers intended their product chemically to affect the body's structure or function. Or, back then, it may have seemed unlikely that, even assuming such proof, the FDA actually would exercise its discretion to regulate so popular a product. See R. Kluger, Ashes to Ashes 105 (1997) (in the 1930's Americans were in love with smoking ... ).

But it should not have seemed unlikely that, assuming the FDA decided to regulate and proved the particular jurisdictional prerequisites, the courts would rule such a jurisdictional assertion fully authorized. Cf. United States v. Southwestern Cable Co., 392 U.S. 157, 172 (1968) (reading Federal Communications Act as authorizing FCC jurisdiction to regulate cable systems while noting that Congress could not in 1934 have foreseen the development of advanced communications systems). After all, this Court has read more narrowly phrased statutes to grant what might have seemed even more unlikely assertions of agency jurisdiction. See, e.g., Permian Basin Area Rate Cases, 390 U.S. 747, 774–777 (1968) (statutory authority to regulate interstate transportation of natural gas includes authority to regulate prices charged by field producers); Phillips Petroleum Co. v. Wisconsin, 347 U.S. 672, 677–684 (1954) (independent gas producer subject to regulation despite Natural Gas Act's express exemption of gathering and production facilities).

I shall not pursue these general matters further, for neither the companies nor the majority denies that the FDCA's literal language, its general purpose, and its particular legislative history favor the FDA's present jurisdictional view. Rather, they have made several specific arguments in support of one basic contention: even if the statutory delegation is broad, it is not broad enough to include tobacco. I now turn to each of those arguments.

## II

## A

The tobacco companies contend that the FDCA's words cannot possibly be read to mean what they literally say. The statute defines device, for example, as an instrument, apparatus, implement, machine, contrivance, implant, in vitro reagent, or other similar or related article ... intended to affect the structure or any function of the body.... 21 U.S.C. § 321(h). Taken literally, this definition might include everything from room air conditioners to thermal pajamas. The companies argue that, to avoid such a result, the meaning of drug or device should be confined to medical or therapeutic products, narrowly defined.

The companies may well be right that the statute should not be read to cover room air conditioners and winter underwear. But I do not agree that we must accept their proposed limitation. For one thing, such a cramped reading contravenes the established purpose of the statutory language. See *Bacto-Unidisk*, 394 U.S., at 798 (third definition is clearly, broader than any strict medical definition); 1 Leg. Hist. 108 (definition covers products that cannot be alleged to be treatments for diseased conditions). For another, the companies' restriction would render the other two drug definitions superfluous. See 21 U.S.C. §§ 321(g)(1)(A), (g)(1)(B) (covering articles in the leading pharmacology compendia and those intended for use in the diagnosis, cure, mitigation, treatment, or prevention of disease).

Most importantly, the statute's language itself supplies a different, more suitable, limitation: that a drug must be a *chemical* agent. The

FDCA's device definition states that an article which affects the structure or function of the body is a device only if it does *not* achieve its primary intended purposes through chemical action within ... the body, and is *not* dependent upon being metabolized for the achievement of its primary intended purposes. § 321(h) (emphasis added). One can readily infer from this language that at least an article that *does* achieve its primary purpose through chemical action within the body and that *is* dependent upon being metabolized is a drug, provided that it otherwise falls within the scope of the drug definition. And one need not hypothesize about air conditioners or thermal pajamas to recognize that the chemical nicotine, an important tobacco ingredient, meets this test. . . .

## B

The tobacco companies' principal definitional argument focuses upon the statutory word intended. See 21 U.S.C. § 321(g)(1)(C). The companies say that intended in this context is a term of art. See Brief for Respondent Brown & Williamson Tobacco Corp. 2. They assert that the statutory word intended means that the product's maker has made an express claim about the effect that its product will have on the body. Ibid. Indeed, according to the companies, the FDA's inability to prove that cigarette manufacturers make such claims is precisely why that agency historically has said it lacked the statutory power to regulate tobacco. See id., at 19–20.

The FDCA, however, does not use the word claimed; it uses the word intended. And the FDA long ago issued regulations that say the relevant intent can be shown not only by a manufacturer's expressions, but also by the circumstances surrounding the distribution of the article. 41 Fed.Reg. 6896 (1976) (codified at 21 CFR § 801.4 (1999)); see also 41 Fed.Reg. 6896 (1976) (objective intent shown if article is, with the knowledge [of its makers], offered and used for a particular purpose). Thus, even in the absence of express claims, the FDA has regulated products that affect the body if the manufacturer wants, and knows, that consumers so use the product. See, e.g., 60 Fed.Reg. 41527–41531 (1995) (describing agency's regulation of topical hormones, sunscreens, fluoride, tanning lamps, thyroid in food supplements, novelty condoms—all marketed without express claims); see also O'Reilly, Food and Drug Administration § 13.04, at 13–15 (Sometimes the very nature of the material makes it a drug ...).

Courts ordinarily reverse an agency interpretation of this kind only if Congress has clearly answered the interpretive question or if the agency's interpretation is unreasonable. Chevron U.S.A. Inc. v. Natural Resources Defense Council, Inc., 467 U.S. 837, 842–843 (1984). The companies, in an effort to argue the former, point to language in the legislative history tying the word intended to a technical concept called intended use. But nothing in Congress' discussion either of intended or intended use suggests that an express claim (which often shows intent) is always necessary. Indeed, the primary statement to which the companies direct our attention says only that a manufacturer can determine what kind of regulation applies—food or drug—because, through his representations in connection with its sale, [the manufacturer] can determine whether an article is to be used as a food, as a drug, or as both. S.Rep. No. 361, 74th Cong., 1st Sess., 4 (1935), reprinted in 3 Leg. Hist. 696.

Nor is the FDA's objective intent interpretation unreasonable. It falls well within the established scope of the ordinary meaning of the word intended. See Agnew v. United States, 165 U.S. 36, 53 (1897) (intent encompasses the known consequences of an act). And the companies acknowledge that the FDA can regulate a drug-like substance in the ordinary circumstance, i.e., where the manufacturer makes an express claim, so it is not unreasonable to conclude that the agency retains such power where a product's effects on the body are so well known (say, like those of aspirin or calamine lotion), that there is no need for express representations because the product speaks for itself.

The companies also cannot deny that the evidence of their intent is sufficient to satisfy the statutory word intended as the FDA long has interpreted it. . . . With such evidence, the FDA has more than sufficiently established that the companies intend their products to affect the body within the meaning of the FDCA.

C

The majority nonetheless reaches the inescapable conclusion that the language and structure of the FDCA as a whole simply do not fit the kind of public health problem that tobacco creates. Ante, at 1306. That is because, in the majority's view, the FDCA requires the FDA to ban outright dangerous drugs or devices (such as cigarettes); yet, the FDA concedes that an immediate and total cigarette-sale ban is inappropriate. Ibid.

This argument is curious because it leads with similarly inescapable force to precisely the opposite conclusion, namely, that the FDA does have jurisdiction but that it must ban cigarettes. More importantly, the argument fails to take into account the fact that a statute interpreted as requiring the FDA to pick a more dangerous over a less dangerous remedy would be a perverse statute, causing, rather than preventing, unnecessary harm whenever a total ban is likely the more dangerous response. And one can at least imagine such circumstances.

Suppose, for example, that a commonly used, mildly addictive sleeping pill (or, say, a kind of popular contact lens), plainly within the FDA's jurisdiction, turned out to pose serious health risks for certain consumers. Suppose further that many of those addicted consumers would ignore an immediate total ban, turning to a potentially more dangerous black-market substitute, while a less draconian remedy (say, adequate notice) would wean them gradually away to a safer product. Would the FDCA still force the FDA to impose the more dangerous remedy? For the following reasons, I think not.

First, the statute's language does not restrict the FDA's remedial powers in this way. The FDCA permits the FDA to regulate a combination product—i.e., a device (such as a cigarette) that contains a drug (such as nicotine)—under its device provisions. 21 U.S.C. § 353(g)(1). And the FDCA's device provisions explicitly grant the FDA wide remedial discretion. For example, where the FDA cannot otherwise obtain reasonable assurance of a device's safety and effectiveness, the agency may restrict by regulation a product's sale, distribution, or use upon *such ... conditions as the Secretary may prescribe.* § 360j(e)(1) (emphasis added). And the statutory section that most clearly addresses the FDA's power to ban (entitled Banned devices) says that, where a device presents an unreasonable and substantial risk of illness or injury, the Secretary *may*—not *must*—initiate a proceeding ... to make such device a banned device. § 360f(a) (emphasis added).

The tobacco companies point to another statutory provision which says that if a device would cause serious, adverse health consequences or death, the Secretary *shall* issue a cease distribution order. 21 U.S.C. § 360h(e)(1) (emphasis added). But that word shall in this context cannot mean that the Secretary must resort to the recall remedy *whenever* a device would have serious, adverse health effects. Rather, that language must mean that the Secretary shall issue a cease distribution order in compliance with the section's procedural requirements if the Secretary chooses *in her discretion* to use that particular subsection's recall remedy. Otherwise, the subsection would trump and make meaningless the same section's provision of other lesser remedies such as simple notice (which the Secretary similarly can impose if, but only if, she finds that the device presents an unreasonable risk of substantial harm to the public). § 360h(a)(1). And reading the statute to compel the FDA to recall every dangerous device likewise would conflict with that same subsection's statement that the recall remedy shall be *in addition to* [the other] remedies provided in the statute. § 360h(e)(3) (emphasis added).

The statute's language, then, permits the agency to choose remedies consistent with its basic purpose—the overall protection of public health.

The second reason the FDCA does not require the FDA to select the more dangerous remedy, is that, despite the majority's assertions to the contrary, the statute does not distinguish among the kinds of health effects that the agency may take into account when assessing safety. The Court insists that the statute only permits the agency to take into account the health risks and benefits of the product itself as used by individual consumers, ante, at 1304, and, thus, that the FDA is prohibited from considering that a ban on smoking would lead many smokers to suffer severe withdrawal symptoms or to buy possibly stronger, more dangerous, black market cigarettes—considerations that the majority calls the aggregate health effects of alternative administrative actions. Ibid. But the FDCA expressly permits the FDA to take account of comparative safety in precisely this manner. See, e.g., 21 U.S.C. § 360h(e)(2)(B)(i)(II) (no device recall if risk of recall[] presents a greater health risk than no recall); § 360h(a) (notification unless notification would present a greater danger than no such notification). . . .

I concede that, as a matter of logic, one could consider the FDA's safety evaluation to be different from its choice of remedies. But to read the statute to forbid the agency from taking account of the realities of consumer behavior either in assessing safety or in choosing a remedy could increase the risks of harm—doubling the risk of death to each individual user in my example above. Why would Congress insist that the FDA ignore such realities, even if the consequent harm would occur only unusually, say, where the FDA evaluates a product (a sleeping pill; a cigarette; a contact lens) that is already on the market, potentially habit forming, or popular? I can find no satisfactory answer to this question. And that, I imagine, is why the statute itself says nothing about any of the distinctions that the Court has tried to draw. See 21 U.S.C. § 360c(a)(2) (instructing FDA to determine the safety and effectiveness of a device in part by weighing any probable benefit to health ... against *any* probable risk of injury or illness ... ) (emphasis added).

In my view, where linguistically permissible, we should interpret the FDCA in light of Congress' overall desire to protect health. That purpose requires a flexible interpretation that both permits the FDA to take into account the realities of human behavior and allows it, in appropriate cases, to choose from its arsenal of statutory remedies. A statute so interpreted easily fit[s] this, and other, drug-and device-related health problems.

### III

In the majority's view, laws enacted since 1965 require us to deny jurisdiction, whatever the FDCA might mean in their absence. But why? Do those laws contain language barring FDA jurisdiction? The majority must concede that they do not. Do they contain provisions that are inconsistent with the FDA's exercise of jurisdiction? With one exception, see infra, at 1327, the majority points to no such provision. Do they somehow repeal the principles of law (discussed in Part II, supra) that otherwise would lead to the conclusion that the FDA has jurisdiction in this area? The companies themselves deny making any such claim. See Tr. of Oral Arg. 27 (denying reliance on doctrine of partial repeal). Perhaps the later laws shape and focus what the 1938 Congress meant a generation earlier. Ante, at 1306. But this Court has warned against using the views of a later Congress to construe a statute enacted many years before. See Pension Benefit Guaranty Corporation v. LTV Corp., 496 U.S. 633, 650 (1990) (later history is "a hazardous basis for inferring the intent of an earlier" Congress (quoting United States v. Price, 361 U.S. 304, 313 (1960))). And, while the majority suggests that the subsequent history control[s] our construction of the FDCA, see ante, at 1306 (citation and internal quotation marks omitted), this Court expressly has held that such subsequent views are not controlling. Haynes v. United States, 390 U.S. 85, 87–88, n. 4 (1968); accord, Southwestern Cable Co., 392 U.S., at 170 (such views have "very little, if any, significance"); see also Sullivan v. Finkelstein, 496 U.S. 617, 632 (1990) (SCALIA, J., concurring) (Arguments based on subsequent legislative history ... should not be taken seriously, not even in a footnote.).

Regardless, the later statutes do not support the majority's conclusion. That is because, whatever individual Members of Congress after 1964 may have assumed about the FDA's jurisdiction, the laws they enacted did not embody any such no jurisdiction assumption. And one cannot automatically infer an antijurisdiction intent, as the majority does, for the later statutes are both (and similarly) consistent with quite a different congressional desire, namely, the intent to proceed without interfering with whatever authority the FDA otherwise may have possessed. See, e.g., Cigarette Labeling and Advertising—1965: Hearings on H.R. 2248 et al. before the House Committee on Interstate and Foreign Commerce, 89th Cong., 1st Sess., 19 (1965) (hereinafter 1965 Hearings) (statement of Rep. Fino that the proposed legislation would not erode agency authority).... [Indeed], the subsequent legislative history is critically ambivalent, for it can be read either as (a) ratif[ying] a no-jurisdiction assumption, see ante, at 1313, or as (b) leaving the jurisdictional question just where Congress found it. And the fact that both inferences are equally tenable, *Pension Benefit Guaranty Corp., supra*, at 650 (citation and internal quotation marks omitted); Johnson v. Transportation Agency, Santa Clara Cty., 480 U.S. 616, 672 (1987) (SCALIA, J., dissenting), prevents the majority from drawing from the later statutes the firm, antijurisdiction implication that it needs....

IV

I now turn to the final historical fact that the majority views as a factor in its interpretation of the subsequent legislative history: the FDA's former denials of its tobacco-related authority.

Until the early 1990's, the FDA expressly maintained that the 1938 statute did not give it the power that it now seeks to assert. It then changed its mind. The majority agrees with me that the FDA's change of positions does not make a significant legal difference. see also *Chevron*, 467 U.S., at 863 (An initial agency interpretation is not instantly carved in stone); accord, Smiley v. Citibank (South Dakota), N. A., 517 U.S. 735, 742 (1996) ([C]hange is not invalidating). Nevertheless, it labels those denials important context for drawing an inference about Congress' intent. In my view, the FDA's change of policy, like the subsequent statutes themselves, does nothing to advance the majority's position.

When it denied jurisdiction to regulate cigarettes, the FDA consistently stated why that was so. In 1963, for example, FDA administrators wrote that cigarettes did not satisfy the relevant FDCA definitions—in particular, the intent requirement—because cigarette makers did not sell their product with accompanying therapeutic claims. Letter to Directors of Bureaus, Divisions and Directors of Districts from FDA Bureau of Enforcement (May 24, 1963), in Public Health Cigarette Amendments of 1971: Hearings on S. 1454 before the Consumer Subcommittee of the Senate Committee on Commerce, 92d Cong., 2d Sess., 240 (1972) (hereinafter FDA Enforcement Letter). And subsequent FDA Commissioners made roughly the same assertion....

[A] fair reading of the FDA's denials suggests that the overwhelming problem was one of proving the requisite manufacturer intent. See Action on Smoking and Health v. Harris, 655 F.2d 236, 238–239 (C.A.D.C.1980) (FDA comments reveal its understanding that the crux of FDA jurisdiction over drugs lay in manufacturers' representations as revelatory of their intent).

What changed? For one thing, the FDA obtained evidence sufficient to prove the necessary intent despite the absence of specific claims. This evidence, which first became available in the early 1990's, permitted the agency to demonstrate that the tobacco companies knew nicotine achieved appetite-suppressing, mood-stabilizing, and habituating effects through chemical (not psychological) means, even at a time when the companies were publicly denying such knowledge.

Moreover, scientific evidence of adverse health effects mounted, until, in the late 1980's, a consensus on the seriousness of the matter became firm....

Finally, administration policy changed. Earlier administrations may have hesitated to assert jurisdiction for the reasons prior Commissioners expressed. Commissioners of the current administration simply took a different regulatory attitude.

Nothing in the law prevents the FDA from changing its policy for such reasons....

The upshot is that the Court today holds that a regulatory statute aimed at unsafe drugs and devices does not authorize regulation of a drug (nicotine) and a device (a cigarette) that the Court itself finds unsafe. Far more than most, this particular drug and device risks the life-threatening harms that administrative regulation seeks to rectify. The majority's conclusion is counter-intuitive. And, for the reasons set forth, I believe that the law does not require it.

Consequently, I dissent.

## Questions

**1.** The majority suggests that the FDA's current determination to regulate tobacco products is illegitimate in light of the agency's prior disavowals of authority. Is this consistent with the *Chevron* approach to agency policy changes?

**2.** The majority contends that, if the FDA has jurisdiction to regulate tobacco products at all, the FDA must ban them, it may not take lesser measures. As Congress has given no indication that it wished tobacco products banned, it would follow that the FDA lacks jurisdiction over tobacco products. More typically, however, if a legislature grants authority to take "greater" actions (such as totally prohibiting), it also implicitly authorizes "lesser" responses (such as regulation). Should a "greater/lesser" argument prevail here? Why or why not?

## 3. INTERPRETING LEGISLATIVE RESPONSE TO PRIOR JUDICIAL INTERPRETATIONS:

### a. WHEN CONGRESS DECLINES, OR FAILS, TO RESPOND

## Girouard v. United States

Supreme Court of the United States, 1946.
328 U.S. 61, 66 S.Ct. 826, 90 L.Ed. 1084.

Certiorari to the United States Circuit Court of Appeals for the First Circuit.

■ MR. JUSTICE DOUGLAS delivered the opinion of the Court.

In 1943 petitioner, a native of Canada, filed his petition for naturalization in the District Court of Massachusetts. He stated in his application that he understood the principles of the government of the United States, believed in its form of government, and was willing to take the oath of allegiance (54 Stat. 1157, 8 U.S.C.A. § 735(b)), which reads as follows:

"I hereby declare, on oath, that I absolutely and entirely renounce and abjure all allegiance and fidelity to any foreign prince, potentate, state, or sovereignty of whom or which I have heretofore been a subject or citizen; that I will support and defend the Constitution and laws of the United States of America against all enemies, foreign and domestic; that I will bear true faith and allegiance to the same; and that I take this obligation freely without any mental reservation or purpose of evasion: So help me God."

To the question in the application "If necessary, are you willing to take up arms in defense of this country?" he replied, "No (Noncombatant) Seventh Day Adventist." He explained that answer before the examiner by saying "it is a purely religious matter with me, I have no political or personal reasons other than that." He did not claim before his Selective Service board exemption from all military service, but only from combatant military duty. At the hearing in the District Court petitioner testified that he was a member of the Seventh Day Adventist denomination, of whom approximately 10,000 were then serving in the armed forces of the United States as non-combatants, especially in the medical corps; and that he was willing to serve in the army but would not bear arms. The District Court admitted him to citizenship. The Circuit Court of Appeals reversed, one judge dissenting. 1 Cir., 149 F.2d 760. It took that action on the authority of United States v. Schwimmer, 279 U.S. 644, 49 S.Ct. 448, 73 L.Ed. 889; United States v. Macintosh, 283 U.S. 605, 51 S.Ct. 570, 75 L.Ed. 1302, and United States v. Bland, 283 U.S. 636, 51 S.Ct. 569, 75 L.Ed. 1319, saying that the facts of the present case brought it squarely within the principles of those cases. The case is here on a petition for a writ of certiorari which we granted so that those authorities might be re-examined.

The *Schwimmer, Macintosh* and *Bland* cases involved, as does the present one, a question of statutory construction. At the time of those cases, Congress required an alien, before admission to citizenship, to declare on oath in open court that "he will support and defend the Constitution and laws of the United States against all enemies, foreign and domestic, and bear true faith and allegiance to the same." It also required the court to be satisfied that the alien had during the five year period immediately preceding the date of his application "behaved as a man of good moral character, attached to the principles of the Constitution of the United States, and well disposed to the good order and happiness of the same." Those provisions were reenacted into the present law in substantially the same form.

While there are some factual distinctions between this case and the *Schwimmer* and *Macintosh* cases, the *Bland* case on its facts is indistinguishable. But the principle emerging from the three cases obliterates any factual distinction among them. As we recognized in In re Summers, 325 U.S. 561, 572, 577, 65 S.Ct. 1307, 1313, 1316, they stand for the same general rule—that an alien who refuses to bear arms will not be admitted to citizenship. As an original proposition, we could not agree with that rule. The fallacies underlying it were, we think, demonstrated in the dissents of Mr. Justice Holmes in the *Schwimmer* case and of Mr. Chief Justice Hughes in the *Macintosh* case.

The oath required of aliens does not in terms require that they promise to bear arms. Nor has Congress expressly made any such finding a prerequisite to citizenship. To hold that it is required is to read it into the Act by implication. But we could not assume that Congress intended to make such an abrupt and radical departure from our traditions unless it spoke in unequivocal terms.

The bearing of arms, important as it is, is not the only way in which our institutions may be supported and defended, even in times of great peril. Total war in its modern form dramatizes as never before the great cooperative effort necessary for victory. The nuclear physicists who developed the atomic bomb, the worker at his lathe, the seaman on cargo vessels, construction battalions, nurses, engineers, litter bearers, doctors, chaplains—these, too, made essential contributions. And many of them made the supreme sacrifice. Mr. Justice Holmes stated in the *Schwimmer* case, 279 U.S. at page 655, 49 S.Ct. at page 451, 73 L.Ed. 889, that "the Quakers have done their share to make the country what it is." And the annals of the recent war show that many whose religious scruples prevented them from bearing arms, nevertheless were unselfish participants in the war effort. Refusal to bear arms is not necessarily a sign of disloyalty or a lack of attachment to our institutions. One may serve his country faithfully and devotedly though his religious scruples make it impossible for him to shoulder a rifle. Devotion to one's country can be as real and as enduring among non-combatants as among combatants. One may adhere to what he deems to be his obligation to God and yet assume all military risks to secure victory. The effort of war is indivisible; and those whose religious scruples prevent them from killing are no less patriots than those whose special traits or handicaps result in their assignment to duties far behind the fighting front. Each is making the utmost contribution according to his capacity. The fact that his role may be limited by religious convictions rather than by physical characteristics has no necessary bearing on his attachment to his country or on his willingness to support and defend it to his utmost.

Petitioner's religious scruples would not disqualify him from becoming a member of Congress or holding other public offices. While Article VI, Clause 3 of the Constitution provides that such officials, both of the United States and the several States, "shall be bound by Oath or Affirmation, to support this Constitution," it significantly adds that "no religious Test shall ever be required as a Qualification to any Office or public Trust under the United States." The oath required is in no material respect different from that prescribed for aliens under the Naturalization Act. It has long contained the provision "that I will support and defend the Constitution of the United States against all enemies, foreign and domestic; that I will bear true faith and allegiance to the same; that I take this obligation freely, without any mental reservation or purpose of evasion." R.S. § 1757, 5 U.S.C.A. § 16. As Mr. Chief Justice Hughes stated in his dissent in the *Macintosh* case, 283 U.S. at page 631, 51 S.Ct. at page 577, 75 L.Ed. 1302, "the history of the struggle for religious liberty, the large number of citizens of our country from the very beginning who have been unwilling to sacrifice their religious convictions, and in particular, those who have been conscientiously opposed to war and who would not yield what they sincerely believed to be their allegiance to the will of God"—these considerations make it impossible to conclude "that such persons are to be deemed disqualified for public office in this country because of the requirement of the oath which must be taken before they enter upon their duties."

There is not the slightest suggestion that Congress set a stricter standard for aliens seeking admission to citizenship than it did for officials who make and enforce the laws of the nation and administer its affairs. It is hard to believe that one need forsake his religious scruples to become a citizen but not to sit in the high councils of state.

As Mr. Chief Justice Hughes pointed out (United States v. Macintosh, supra, 283 U.S. at page 633, 51 S.Ct. at page 578, 75 L.Ed. 1302), religious scruples against bearing arms have been recognized by Congress in the various draft laws. This is true of the Selective Training and Service Act of 1940, 54 Stat. 889, 50 U.S.C.A. Appendix, § 305(g), as it was of earlier acts. He who is inducted into the armed services takes an oath which includes the provision "that I will bear true faith and allegiance to the United States of America; that I will serve them honestly and faithfully against all their enemies whomsoever." 41 Stat. 809, 10 U.S.C.A. § 1581. Congress has thus recognized that one may adequately discharge his obligations as a citizen by rendering non-combatant as well as combatant services. This respect by Congress over the years for the conscience of those having religious scruples against bearing arms is cogent evidence of the meaning of the oath. It is recognition by Congress that even in time of war one may truly support and defend our institutions though he stops short of using weapons of war.

That construction of the naturalization oath received new support in 1942. In the Second War Powers Act, 56 Stat. 176, 182, 8 U.S.C.A. § 1001, Congress relaxed certain of the requirements for aliens who served honorably in the armed forces of the United States during World War II and provided machinery to expedite their naturalization. Residence requirements were relaxed, educational tests were eliminated, and no fees were required. But no change in the oath was made; nor was any change made in the requirement that the alien be attached to the principles of the Constitution. Yet it is clear that these new provisions cover non-combatants as well as combatants. If petitioner had served as a non-combatant (as he was willing to do), he could have been admitted to citizenship by taking the identical oath which he is willing to take. Can it be that the oath means one thing to one who has served to the extent permitted by his religious scruples and another thing to one equally willing to serve but who has not had the opportunity? It is not enough to say that petitioner is not entitled to the benefits of the new Act since he did not serve in the armed forces. He is not seeking the benefits of the expedited procedure and the relaxed requirements. The oath which he must take is identical with the oath which both non-combatants and combatants must take. It would, indeed, be a strange construction to say that "support and defend the Constitution and laws of the United States of America against all enemies, foreign and domestic" demands something more from some than it does from others. That oath can hardly be adequate for one who is unwilling to bear arms because of religious scruples and yet exact from another a promise to bear arms despite religious scruples.

Mr. Justice Holmes stated in the *Schwimmer* case, 279 U.S. at pages 654, 655, 49 S.Ct. at page 451, 73 L.Ed. 889: "if there is any principle of the Constitution that more imperatively calls for attachment than any other it is the principle of free thought—not free thought for those who agree with us but freedom for the thought that we hate. I think that we should adhere to that principle with regard to admission into, as well as to life within this country." The struggle for religious liberty has through the centuries been an effort to accommodate the demands of the State to the conscience of the individual. The victory for freedom of thought recorded in our Bill of Rights recognizes that in the domain of conscience there is a moral power higher than the State. Throughout the ages men have suffered death rather than subordinate their allegiance to God to the authority of the State. Freedom of religion guaranteed by the First Amendment is the product of that struggle. As we recently stated in United States v. Ballard, 322 U.S. 78, 86, 64 S.Ct. 882, 886, 88 L.Ed. 1148, "Freedom of thought, which includes freedom of religious belief, is basic in a society of free men. West Virginia State Board of Education v. Barnette, 319 U.S. 624, 63 S.Ct. 1178, 87 L.Ed. 1628, 147 A.L.R. 674." The test oath is abhorrent to our tradition. Over the years Congress has meticulously respected that tradition and even in time of war has sought to accommodate the military requirements to the religious scruples of the individual. We do not believe that Congress intended to reverse that policy when it came to draft the naturalization oath. Such an abrupt and radical departure from our traditions should not be implied. See Schneiderman v. United States, 320 U.S. 118, 132, 63 S.Ct. 1333, 1340, 87 L.Ed. 1796. Cogent evidence would be necessary to convince us that Congress took that course.

We conclude that the *Schwimmer, Macintosh* and *Bland* cases do not state the correct rule of law.

We are met, however, with the argument that even though those cases were wrongly decided, Congress has adopted the rule which they announced. The argument runs as follows: Many efforts were made to amend the law so as to change the rule announced by those cases; but in every instance the bill died in committee. Moreover, in 1940 when the new Naturalization Act was passed, Congress reenacted the oath in its pre-existing form, though at the same time it made extensive changes in the requirements and procedure for naturalization. From this it is argued that Congress adopted and reenacted the rule of the *Schwimmer, Macintosh,* and *Bland* cases. Cf. Apex Hosiery Co. v. Leader, 310 U.S. 469, 488, 489, 60 S.Ct. 982, 989, 990, 84 L.Ed. 1311, 128 A.L.R. 1044.

We stated in Helvering v. Hallock, 309 U.S. 106, 119, 60 S.Ct. 444, 451, 84 L.Ed. 604, 125 A.L.R. 1368, that "It would require very persuasive circumstances enveloping Congressional silence to debar this Court from re-examining its own doctrines." It is at best treacherous to find in Congressional silence alone the adoption of a controlling rule of law. We do not think under the circumstances of this legislative history that we can properly place on the shoulders of Congress the burden of the Court's own error. The history of the 1940 Act is at most equivocal. It contains no affirmative recognition of the rule of the *Schwimmer, Macintosh* and *Bland* cases. The silence of Congress and its inaction are as consistent with a desire to leave the problem fluid as they are with an adoption by silence of the rule of those cases. But for us, it is enough to say that since the date of those cases Congress never acted affirmatively on this question but once and that was in 1942. At that time, as we have noted, Congress specifically granted naturalization privileges to noncombatants who like petitioner were prevented from bearing arms by their religious scruples. That was affirmative recognition that one could be attached to the principles of our government and could support and defend it even though his religious convictions prevented him from bearing arms. And, as we have said, we cannot believe that the oath was designed to exact something more from one person than from another. Thus the affirmative action taken by Congress in 1942 negatives any inference that otherwise might be drawn from its silence when it re-enacted the oath in 1940.

Reversed.

■ MR. JUSTICE JACKSON took no part in the consideration or decision of this case.

■ MR. CHIEF JUSTICE STONE dissenting.

I think the judgment should be affirmed, for the reason that the court below, in applying the controlling provisions of the naturalization statutes, correctly applied them as earlier construed by this Court, whose construction Congress has adopted and confirmed.

In three cases decided more than fifteen years ago, this Court denied citizenship to applicants for naturalization who had announced that they proposed to take the prescribed oath of allegiance with the reservation or qualification that they would not, as naturalized citizens, assist in the defense of this country by force of arms or give their moral support to the government in any war which they did not believe to be morally justified or in the best interests of the country. See United States v. Schwimmer, 279 U.S. 644, 49 S.Ct. 448, 73 L.Ed. 889; United States v. Macintosh, 283 U.S. 605, 51 S.Ct. 570, 75 L.Ed. 1302; United States v. Bland, 283 U.S. 636, 51 S.Ct. 569, 75 L.Ed. 1319.

In each of these cases this Court held that the applicant had failed to meet the conditions which Congress had made prerequisite to naturalization by § 4 of the Naturalization Act of June 29, 1906, c. 3592, 34 Stat. 596, the provisions of which, here relevant, were enacted in the Nationality Act of October 14, 1940. See c. 876, 54 Stat. 1137, as amended by the Act of March 27, 1942, c. 199, 56 Stat. 176, 182, 183, and by the Act of December 7, 1942, c. 690, 56 Stat. 1041, 8 U.S.C.A. §§ 707, 723a, 735, 1001 et seq. Section 4 of the Naturalization Act of 1906, paragraph "Third", provided that before the admission to citizenship the applicant should declare on oath in open court that "he will support and defend the Constitution and laws of the United States against all enemies, foreign and domestic, and bear true faith and allegiance to the same." And paragraph "Fourth" required that before admission it be made to appear "to the satisfaction of the court admitting any alien to citizenship" that at least for a period of five years immediately preceding his application the applicant "has behaved as a man of good moral character, attached to the principles of the Constitution of the United States, and well disposed to the good order and happiness of the same." In applying these provisions in the cases mentioned, this Court held only that an applicant who is unable to take the oath of allegiance without the reservations or qualifications insisted upon by the applicants in those cases manifests his want of attachment to the principles of the Constitution and his unwillingness to meet the requirements of the oath, that he will support and defend the Constitution of the United States and bear true faith and allegiance to the same, and so does not comply with the statutory conditions of his naturalization. No question of the constitutional power of Congress to withhold citizenship on these grounds was involved. That power was not doubted. See Selective Draft Law Cases [(Arver v. United States)], 245 U.S. 366[, 38 S.Ct. 159, 62 L.Ed. 349, L.R.A.1918C, 361, Ann.Cas.1918B, 856]; Hamilton v. Regents, 293 U.S. 245[, 55 S.Ct. 197, 79 L.Ed. 343]. The only question was of construction of the statute which Congress at all times has been free to amend if dissatisfied with the construction adopted by the Court.

With three other Justices of the Court I dissented in the *Macintosh* and *Bland* cases, for reasons which the Court now adopts as ground for overruling them. Since this Court in three considered earlier opinions has rejected the construction of the statute for which the dissenting Justices contended, the question, which for me is decisive of the present case, is whether Congress has likewise rejected that construction by its subsequent legislative action, and has adopted and confirmed the Court's earlier construction of the statutes in question. A study of Congressional action taken with respect to proposals for amendment of the naturalization laws since the decision in the *Schwimmer* case, leads me to conclude that Congress has adopted and confirmed this Court's earlier construction of the naturalization laws. For that reason alone I think that the judgment should be affirmed.

The construction of the naturalization statutes, adopted by this Court in the three cases mentioned, immediately became the target of an active, publicized legislative attack in Congress which persisted for a period of eleven years, until the adoption of the Nationality Act in 1940. Two days after the *Schwimmer* case was decided, a bill was introduced in the House, H.R. 3547, 71st Cong., 1st Sess., to give the Naturalization Act a construction contrary to that which had been given to it by this Court and which, if adopted, would have made the applicants rejected by this Court in the *Schwimmer, Macintosh* and *Bland* cases eligible for citizenship. This effort to establish by Congressional action that the construction which this Court had placed on the Naturalization Act was not one which Congress had adopted or intended, was renewed without success after the decision in the Macintosh and Bland cases, and was continued for a period of about ten years. All of these measures were of substantially the same pattern as H.R. 297, 72d Cong., 1st Sess., introduced December 8, 1931, at the first session of Congress, after the decision in the Macintosh case. It provided that no person otherwise qualified "shall be debarred from citizenship by reason of his or her religious views or philosophical opinions with respect to the lawfulness of war as a means of settling international disputes, but every alien admitted to citizenship shall be subject to the same obligation as the native-born citizen." H.R. 3547, 71st Cong., 1st Sess., introduced immediately after the decision in the *Schwimmer* case, had contained a like provision, but with the omission of the last clause beginning "but every alien." Hearings were had before the House Committee on Immigration and Naturalization on both bills at which their proponents had stated clearly their purpose to set aside the interpretation placed on the oath of allegiance by the *Schwimmer* and *Macintosh* cases. There was opposition on each occasion. Bills identical with H.R. 297 were introduced in three later Congresses. None of these bills were reported out of Committee. The other proposals, all of which failed of passage . . ., had the same purpose and differed only in phraseology.

Thus, for six successive Congresses, over a period of more than a decade, there were continuously pending before Congress in one form or another proposals to overturn the rulings in the three Supreme Court decisions in question. Congress declined to adopt these proposals after full hearings and after speeches on the floor advocating the change. 72 Cong. Rec. 6966–7; 75th Cong.Rec. 15354–7. In the meantime the decisions of this Court had been followed in Clarke's Case, 301 Pa. 321, 152 A. 92; Beale v. United States, 8 Cir., 71 F.2d 737; In re Warkentin, 7 Cir., 93 F.2d 42. In Beale v. United States, supra, [71 F.2d 737] the court pointed out that the proposed amendments affecting the provisions of the statutes relating to admission to citizenship had failed saying: "We must conclude, therefore, that these statutory requirements as construed by the Supreme Court have Congressional sanction and approval."

Any doubts that such were the purpose and will of Congress would seem to have been dissipated by the reenactment by Congress in 1940 of Paragraphs "Third" and "Fourth" of § 4 of the Naturalization Act of 1906, and by the incorporation in the Act of 1940 of the very form of oath which had been administratively prescribed for the applicants in the *Schwimmer, Macintosh* and *Bland* cases. See Rule 8(c), Naturalization Regulations of July 1, 1929.

The Nationality Act of 1940 was a comprehensive, slowly matured and carefully considered revision of the naturalization laws. The preparation of this measure was not only delegated to a Congressional Committee, but was considered by a committee of Cabinet members, one of whom was the Attorney General. Both were aware of our decisions in the *Schwimmer* and related cases and that no other question pertinent to the naturalization laws had been as persistently and continuously before Congress in the ten years following the decision in the *Schwimmer* case. The modifications in the provisions of Paragraphs "Third" and "Fourth" of § 4 of the 1906 Act show conclusively the careful attention which was given to them.

In the face of this legislative history the "failure of Congress to alter the Act after it had been judicially construed, and the enactment by Congress of legislation which implicitly recognizes the judicial construction as effective, is persuasive of legislative recognition that the judicial construction is the correct one. This is the more so where, as here, the application of the statute . . . has brought forth sharply conflicting views both on the Court and in Congress, and where after the matter has been fully brought to the attention of the public and the Congress, the latter has not seen fit to change the statute." Apex Hosiery Co. v. Leader, 310 U.S.

469, 488, 489, 60 S.Ct. 982, 989, 84 L.Ed. 1311, 128 A.L.R. 1044. And see to like effect United States v. Ryan, 284 U.S. 167–175, 52 S.Ct. 65–68, 76 L.Ed. 224; United States v. Elgin, J. & E.R. Co., 298 U.S. 492, 500, 56 S.Ct. 841, 843, 80 L.Ed. 1300; State of Missouri v. Ross, 299 U.S. 72, 75, 57 S.Ct. 60, 62, 81 L.Ed. 46; cf. Helvering v. Winmill, 305 U.S. 79, 82, 83, 59 S.Ct. 45, 46, 47, 83 L.Ed. 52. It is the responsibility of Congress, in reenacting a statute, to make known its purpose in a controversial matter of interpretation of its former language, at least when the matter has, for over a decade, been persistently brought to its attention. In the light of this legislative history, it is abundantly clear that Congress has performed that duty. In any case it is not lightly to be implied that Congress has failed to perform it and has delegated to this Court the responsibility of giving new content to language deliberately readopted after this Court has construed it. For us to make such an assumption is to discourage, if not to deny, legislative responsibility. By thus adopting and confirming this Court's construction of what Congress had enacted in the Naturalization Act of 1906 Congress gave that construction the same legal significance as though it had written the very words into the Act of 1940.

The only remaining question is whether Congress repealed this construction by enactment of the 1942 amendments of the Nationality Act. That Act extended special privileges to applicants for naturalization who were aliens and who have served in the armed forces of the United States in time of war, by dispensing with or modifying existing requirements, relating to declarations of intention, period of residence, education, and fees. It left unchanged the requirements that the applicant's behavior show his attachment to the principles of the Constitution and that he take the oath of allegiance. In adopting the 1942 amendments Congress did not have before it any question of the oath of allegiance with which it had been concerned when it adopted the 1940 Act. In 1942 it was concerned with the grant of special favors to those seeking naturalization who had worn the uniform and rendered military service in time of war and who could satisfy such naturalization requirements as had not been dispensed with by the amendments. In the case of those entitled to avail themselves of these privileges, Congress left it to the naturalization authorities, as in other cases, to determine whether, by their applications and their conduct in the military service they satisfy the requirements for naturalization which had not been waived.

It is pointed out that one of the 1942 amendments, 8 U.S.C.A. § 1004, provided that the provisions of the amendment should not apply to "any conscientious objector who performed no military duty whatever or refused to wear the uniform." It is said that the implication of this provision is that conscientious objectors who rendered noncombatant service and wore the uniform were, under the 1942 amendments, to be admitted to citizenship. From this it is argued that since the 1942 amendments apply to those who have been in noncombatant, as well as combatant, military service, the amendment must be taken to include some who have rendered noncombatant service who are also conscientious objectors and who would be admitted to citizenship under the 1942 amendments, even though they made the same reservations as to the oath of allegiance as did the applicants in the *Schwimmer, Macintosh* and *Bland* cases. And it is said that although the 1942 amendments are not applicable to petitioner, who has not been in military service, the oath cannot mean one thing as to him and another as to those who have been in the noncombatant service.

To these suggestions there are two answers. One is that if the 1942 amendment be construed as including noncombatants who are also conscientious objectors, who are unwilling to take the oath without the reservations made by the applicants in the *Schwimmer, Macintosh* and *Bland* cases, the only effect would be to exempt noncombatant conscientious objectors from the requirements of the oath, which had clearly been made applicable to all objectors, including petitioner, by the Nationality Act of 1940, and from which petitioner was not exempted by the 1942 amendments. If such is the construction of the 1942 Act, there is no constitutional or statutory obstacle to Congress' taking such action. Congress if it saw fit could have admitted to citizenship those who had rendered noncombatant service, with a modified oath or without any oath at all. Petitioner has not been so exempted.

Since petitioner was never in the military or naval forces of the United States, we need not decide whether the 1942 amendments authorized any different oath for those who had been in noncombatant service than for others. The amendments have been construed as requiring the same oath, without reservations, from conscientious objectors, as from others. In re Nielsen, D.C., 60 F.Supp. 240. Not all of those who rendered noncombatant service were conscientious objectors. Few were. There were others in the noncombatant service who had announced their conscientious objections to combatant service, who may have waived or abandoned their objections. Such was the experience in the First World War. See "Statement Concerning the Treatment of Conscientious Objectors in the Army", prepared and published by direction of the Secretary of War, June 18, 1919. All such could have taken the oath without the reservations made by the applicants in the *Schwimmer, Macintosh* and *Bland* cases and would have been entitled to the benefits of the 1942 amendments provided they had performed military duty and had not refused to wear the uniform. The fact that Congress recognized by indirection, in 8 U.S.C.A. § 1004, that those who had appeared in the role of conscientious objectors, might become citizens by taking the oath of allegiance and establishing their attachment to the principles of the Constitution, does not show that Congress dispensed with the requirements of the oath as construed by this Court and plainly confirmed by Congress in the Nationality Act of 1940. There is no necessary inconsistency in this respect between the 1940 Act and the 1942 amendments. Without it repeal by implication is not favored. United States v. Borden Co., 308 U.S. 188, 198, 199, 203–206, 60 S.Ct. 182, 188, 189, 190–192, 84 L.Ed. 181; State of Georgia v. Pennsylvania R. Co., 324 U.S. 439, 457, 65 S.Ct. 716, 726; United States Alkali Export Ass'n v. United States, 325 U.S. 196, 209, 65 S.Ct. 1120, 1128. The amendments and their legislative history give no hint of any purpose of Congress to relax, at least for persons who had rendered no military service, the requirements of the oath of allegiance and proof of attachment to the Constitution as this Court had interpreted them and as the Nationality Act of 1940 plainly required them to be interpreted. It is not the function of this Court to disregard the will of Congress in the exercise of its constitutional power.

■ MR. JUSTICE REED and MR. JUSTICE FRANKFURTER join in this opinion.

### Question

How pointed must Congress' non response to a controversial statutory interpretation be before Congress should be deemed to have "ratified" that interpretation? Would it matter if no bills to amend the statute to "overrule" the judicial interpretation were ever proposed? If bills were repeatedly submitted, but no action taken? Submitted and hearings held? Submitted and committee reports issued? Voted on but failed to pass? Is this kind of inquiry helpful at all?

### b.   WHEN CONGRESS DOES RESPOND

## Newport News Shipbuilding and Dry Dock Co. v. EEOC

Supreme Court of the United States, 1983.
462 U.S. 669, 103 S.Ct. 2622, 77 L.Ed.2d 89.

■ JUSTICE STEVENS delivered the opinion of the Court.

In 1978 Congress decided to overrule our decision in General Electric Co. v. Gilbert, 429 U.S. 125 (1976), by amending Title VII of the Civil Rights Act of 1964 "to prohibit sex discrimination on the basis of pregnancy."[1] On the effective date of the Act, petitioner amended its health insurance plan to provide its female employees with hospitalization benefits for pregnancy-related conditions to the same extent as for other medical conditions.[2] The plan continued, however, to provide less favorable pregnancy benefits for spouses of male employees. The question presented is whether the amended plan complies with the amended statute.

---

**1.**  Pub.L. 95–555, 92 Stat. 2076 (quoting title of 1978 Act). The new statute (the Pregnancy Discrimination Act) amended the "Definitions" section of Title VII, 42 U.S.C. § 2000e, to add a new subsection (k) reading in pertinent part as follows:

"The terms 'because of sex' or 'on the basis of sex' include, but are not limited to, because of or on the basis of pregnancy, childbirth, or related medical conditions; and women affected by pregnancy, childbirth, or related medical conditions shall be treated the same for all employment-related purposes, including receipt of benefits under fringe benefit programs, as other persons not so affected but similar in their ability or inability to work, and nothing in section 2000e–2(h) of this title shall be interpreted to permit otherwise...." § 2000e(k) (1976 ed., Supp. V).

**2.**  The amendment to Title VII became effective on the date of its enactment, October 31, 1978, but its requirements did not apply to any then-existing fringe benefit program until 180 days after enactment—April 29, 1979. 92 Stat. 2076. The amendment to petitioner's plan became effective on April 29, 1979.

Petitioner's plan provides hospitalization and medical-surgical coverage for a defined category of employees and a defined category of dependents. Dependents covered by the plan include employees' spouses, unmarried children between 14 days and 19 years of age, and some older dependent children. Prior to April 29, 1979, the scope of the plan's coverage for eligible dependents was identical to its coverage for employees. All covered males, whether employees or dependents, were treated alike for purposes of hospitalization coverage. All covered females, whether employees or dependents, also were treated alike. Moreover, with one relevant exception, the coverage for males and females was identical. The exception was a limitation on hospital coverage for pregnancy that did not apply to any other hospital confinement.

After the plan was amended in 1979, it provided the same hospitalization coverage for male and female employees themselves for all medical conditions, but it differentiated between female employees and spouses of male employees in its provision of pregnancy-related benefits.[7] In a booklet describing the plan, petitioner explained the amendment that gave rise to this litigation in this way:

"B. Effective April 29, 1979, maternity benefits for female employees will be paid the same as any other hospital confinement as described in question 16. This applies only to deliveries beginning on April 29, 1979 and thereafter.

"C. Maternity benefits for the wife of a male employee will continue to be paid as described in part 'A' of this question." App. to Pet. for Cert. 37a.

In turn, Part A stated: "The Basic Plan pays up to $500 of the hospital charges and 100% of reasonable and customary for delivery and anesthesiologist charges." *Ibid.* As the Court of Appeals observed: "To the extent that the hospital charges in connection with an uncomplicated delivery may exceed $500, therefore, a male employee receives less complete coverage of spousal disabilities than does a female employee." 667 F.2d 448, 449 (C.A.4 1982).

After the passage of the Pregnancy Discrimination Act, and before the amendment to petitioner's plan became effective, the Equal Employment Opportunity Commission issued "interpretive guidelines" in the form of questions and answers. Two of those questions, numbers 21 and 22, made it clear that the EEOC would consider petitioner's amended plan unlawful. Number 21 read as follows:

"21. Q. Must an employer provide health insurance coverage for the medical expenses of pregnancy-related conditions of the spouses of male employees? Of the dependents of all employees?

---

**7.** Thus, as the Equal Employment Opportunity Commission found after its investigation, "the record reveals that the present disparate impact on male employees had its genesis in the gender-based distinction accorded to female employees in the past." App. 37.

"A. Where an employer provides no coverage for dependents, the employer is not required to institute such coverage. However, if an employer's insurance program covers the medical expenses of spouses of female employees, then it must equally cover the medical expenses of spouses of male employees, including those arising from pregnancy-related conditions.

"But the insurance does not have to cover the pregnancy-related conditions of non-spouse dependents as long as it excludes the pregnancy-related conditions of such non-spouse dependents of male and female employees equally." 44 Fed.Reg. 23807 (Apr. 20, 1979).

On September 20, 1979, one of petitioner's male employees filed a charge with the EEOC alleging that petitioner had unlawfully refused to provide full insurance coverage for his wife's hospitalization caused by pregnancy; a month later the United Steelworkers filed a similar charge on behalf of other individuals. App. 15–18. Petitioner then commenced an action in the United States District Court for the Eastern District of Virginia, challenging the Commission's guidelines and seeking both declaratory and injunctive relief. The complaint named the EEOC, the male employee, and the United Steelworkers of America as defendants. *Id.*, at 5–14. Later the EEOC filed a civil action against petitioner alleging discrimination on the basis of sex against male employees in the company's provision of hospitalization benefits. *Id.*, at 28–31. Concluding that the benefits of the new Act extended only to female employees, and not to spouses of male employees, the District Court held that petitioner's plan was lawful and enjoined enforcement of the EEOC guidelines relating to pregnancy benefits for employees' spouses. 510 F.Supp. 66 (1981). It also dismissed the EEOC's complaint. App. to Pet. for Cert. 21a. The two cases were consolidated on appeal.

A divided panel of the United States Court of Appeals for the Fourth Circuit reversed, reasoning that since "the company's health insurance plan contains a distinction based on pregnancy that results in less complete medical coverage for male employees with spouses than for female employees with spouses, it is impermissible under the statute." 667 F.2d, at 451. After rehearing the case en banc, the court reaffirmed the conclusion of the panel over the dissent of three judges who believed the statute was intended to protect female employees "in their ability or inability to work," and not to protect spouses of male employees. 682 F.2d 113 (1982). Because the important question presented by the case had been decided differently by the United States Court of Appeals for the Ninth Circuit, EEOC v. Lockheed Missiles & Space Co., 680 F.2d 1243 (1982), we granted certiorari 459 U.S. 1069 (1982).

Ultimately the question we must decide is whether petitioner has discriminated against its male employees with respect to their compensation, terms, conditions, or privileges of employment because of their sex within the meaning of § 703(a)(1) of Title VII.[11] Although the Pregnancy

---

11. Section 703(a), 42 U.S.C. § 2000e–2(a), provides in pertinent part:

"It shall be an unlawful employment practice for an employer—

Discrimination Act has clarified the meaning of certain terms in this section, neither that Act nor the underlying statute contains a definition of the word "discriminate." In order to decide whether petitioner's plan discriminates against male employees because of *their* sex, we must therefore go beyond the bare statutory language. Accordingly, we shall consider whether Congress, by enacting the Pregnancy Discrimination Act, not only overturned the specific holding in General Electric Co. v. Gilbert, 429 U.S. 125 (1976), but also rejected the test of discrimination employed by the Court in that case. We believe it did. Under the proper test petitioner's plan is unlawful, because the protection it affords to married male employees is less comprehensive than the protection it affords to married female employees.

## I

At issue in *General Electric Co. v. Gilbert* was the legality of a disability plan that provided the company's employees with weekly compensation during periods of disability resulting from nonoccupational causes. Because the plan excluded disabilities arising from pregnancy, the District Court and the Court of Appeals concluded that it discriminated against female employees because of their sex. This Court reversed.

After noting that Title VII does not define the term "discrimination," the Court applied an analysis derived from cases construing the Equal Protection Clause of the Fourteenth Amendment to the Constitution. *Id.,* at 133. The *Gilbert* opinion quoted at length from a footnote in Geduldig v. Aiello, 417 U.S. 484 (1974), a case which had upheld the constitutionality of excluding pregnancy coverage under California's disability insurance plan.[12]

"(1) to fail or refuse to hire or discharge any individual, or otherwise to discriminate against any individual with respect to his compensation, terms, conditions, or privileges of employment, because of such individual's race, color, religion, sex, or national origin. . . ."

Although the 1978 Act makes clear that this language should be construed to prohibit discrimination against a female employee on the basis of her own pregnancy, it did not remove or limit Title VII's prohibition of discrimination on the basis of the sex of the employee—male or female—which was already present in the Act. As we explain *infra,* at 682–685, petitioner's plan discriminates against male employees on the basis of their sex.

12.  " 'While it is true that only women can become pregnant, it does not follow that every legislative classification concerning pregnancy is a sex-based classification like

those considered in *Reed* [*v. Reed,* 404 U.S. 71 (1971)], and *Frontiero* [*v. Richardson,* 411 U.S. 677 (1973)]. Normal pregnancy is an objectively identifiable physical condition with unique characteristics. Absent a showing that distinctions involving pregnancy are mere pretexts designed to effect an invidious discrimination against the members of one sex or the other, lawmakers are constitutionally free to include or exclude pregnancy from the coverage of legislation such as this on any reasonable basis, just as with respect to any other physical condition.

" 'The lack of identity between the excluded disability and gender as such under this insurance program becomes clear upon the most cursory analysis. The program divides potential recipients into two groups—pregnant women and nonpregnant persons. While the first group is exclusively female, the second includes members of both sexes.' [417 U.S.], at 496–497, n. 20." 429 U.S., at 134–135.

"Since it is a finding of sex-based discrimination that must trigger, in a case such as this, the finding of an unlawful employment practice under § 703(a)(1)," the Court added, "*Geduldig* is precisely in point in its holding that an exclusion of pregnancy from a disability-benefits plan providing general coverage is not a gender-based discrimination at all." 429 U.S., at 136.

The dissenters in *Gilbert* took issue with the majority's assumption "that the Fourteenth Amendment standard of discrimination is coterminous with that applicable to Title VII." *Id.*, at 154, n. 6 (Brennan, J., dissenting); *id.*, at 160–161 (Stevens, J., dissenting). As a matter of statutory interpretation, the dissenters rejected the Court's holding that the plan's exclusion of disabilities caused by pregnancy did not constitute discrimination based on sex. As Justice Brennan explained, it was facially discriminatory for the company to devise "a policy that, but for pregnancy, offers protection for all risks, even those that are 'unique to' men or heavily male dominated." *Id.*, at 160. It was inaccurate to describe the program as dividing potential recipients into two groups, pregnant women and non-pregnant persons, because insurance programs "deal with future *risks* rather than historic facts." Rather, the appropriate classification was "between persons who face a risk of pregnancy and those who do not." *Id.*, at 161–162, n. 5 (Stevens, J., dissenting). The company's plan, which was intended to provide employees with protection against the risk of uncompensated unemployment caused by physical disability, discriminated on the basis of sex by giving men protection for all categories of risk but giving women only partial protection. Thus, the dissenters asserted that the statute had been violated because conditions of employment for females were less favorable than for similarly situated males.

When Congress amended Title VII in 1978, it unambiguously expressed its disapproval of both the holding and the reasoning of the Court in the *Gilbert* decision. It incorporated a new subsection in the "definitions" applicable "[f]or the purposes of this subchapter." 42 U.S.C. § 2000e (1976 ed., Supp. V). The first clause of the Act states, quite simply: "The terms 'because of sex' or 'on the basis of sex' include, but are not limited to, because of or on the basis of pregnancy, childbirth, or related medical conditions." § 2000e(k).[14] The House Report stated: "It is the Committee's view that the dissenting Justices correctly interpreted the Act."[15] Similarly, the Senate Report quoted passages from the two dissenting opinions, stating that they "correctly express both the principle and the meaning of

---

The principal emphasis in the text of the *Geduldig* opinion, unlike the quoted footnote, was on the reasonableness of the State's cost justifications for the classification in its insurance program.

**14.** The meaning of the first clause is not limited by the specific language in the second clause, which explains the application of the general principle to women employees.

**15.** H.R.Rep. No. 95–948, p. 2 (1978), Legislative History of the Pregnancy Discrimination Act of 1978 (Committee Print prepared for the Senate Committee on Labor and Human Resources), p. 148 (1979) (hereinafter Leg. Hist.).

title VII."[16] Proponents of the bill repeatedly emphasized that the Supreme Court had erroneously interpreted congressional intent and that amending legislation was necessary to reestablish the principles of Title VII law as they had been understood prior to the *Gilbert* decision. Many of them expressly agreed with the views of the dissenting Justices.[17]

As petitioner argues, congressional discussion focused on the needs of female members of the work force rather than spouses of male employees. This does not create a "negative inference" limiting the scope of the Act to the specific problem that motivated its enactment. See United States v. Turkette, 452 U.S. 576, 591 (1981). Cf. McDonald v. Santa Fe Trail Transp. Co., 427 U.S. 273, 285–296 (1976).[18] Congress apparently assumed that existing plans that included benefits for dependents typically provided no less pregnancy-related coverage for the wives of male employees than they did for female employees.[19] When the question of differential coverage for

---

**16.** S.Rep. No. 95–331, pp. 2–3 (1977), Leg. Hist., at 39–40.e

**17.** *Id.,* at 7–8 ("the bill is merely reestablishing the law as it was understood prior to *Gilbert* by the EEOC and by the lower courts"); H.R.Rep. No. 95–948, *supra,* at 8 (same); 123 Cong.Rec. 10581 (1977) (remarks of Rep. Hawkins) ("H.R. 5055 does not really add anything to title VII as I and, I believe, most of my colleagues in Congress when title VII was enacted in 1964 and amended in 1972, understood the prohibition against sex discrimination in employment. For, it seems only commonsense, that since only women can become pregnant, discrimination against pregnant people is necessarily discrimination against women, and that forbidding discrimination based on sex therefore clearly forbids discrimination based on pregnancy"); *id.,* at 29387 (remarks of Sen. Javits) ("this bill is simply corrective legislation, designed to restore the law with respect to pregnant women employees to the point where it was last year, before the Supreme Court's decision in *Gilbert* ... "); *id.,* at 29647; *id.,* at 29655 (remarks of Sen. Javits) ("What we are doing is leaving the situation the way it was before the Supreme Court decided the Gilbert case last year"); 124 Cong.Rec. 21436 (1978) (remarks of Rep. Sarasin) ("This bill would restore the interpretation of title VII prior to that decision").

For statements expressly approving the views of the dissenting Justices that pregnancy discrimination is discrimination on the basis of sex, see Leg.Hist., at 18 (remarks of Sen. Bayh, Mar. 18, 1977, 123 Cong.Rec. 8144); 24 (remarks of Rep. Hawkins, Apr. 5,

1977, 123 Cong.Rec. 10582); 67 (remarks of Sen. Javits, Sept. 15, 1977, 123 Cong.Rec. 29387); 73 (remarks of Sen. Bayh, Sept. 16, 1977, 123 Cong.Rec. 29641); 134 (remarks of Sen. Mathias, Sept. 16, 1977, 123 Cong.Rec. 29663–29664); 168 (remarks of Rep. Sarasin, July 18, 1978, 124 Cong.Rec. 21436). See also Discrimination on the Basis of Pregnancy, 1977, Hearings on S. 995 before the Subcommittee on Labor of the Senate Committee on Human Resources, 95th Cong., 1st Sess., 13 (1977) (statement of Sen. Bayh); *id.,* at 37, 51 (statement of Assistant Attorney General for Civil Rights Drew S. Days).

**18.** In *McDonald,* the Court held that 42 U.S.C. § 1981, which gives "[a]ll persons within the jurisdiction of the United States ... the same right in every State and Territory to make and enforce contracts ... as is enjoyed by white citizens," protects whites against discrimination on the basis of race even though the "immediate impetus for the bill was the necessity for further relief of the constitutionally emancipated former Negro slaves." 427 U.S., at 289.

**19.** This, of course, was true of petitioner's plan prior to the enactment of the statute. See *supra,* at 672. See S.Rep. No. 95–331, *supra* n. 16, at 6, Leg.Hist., at 43 ("Presumably because plans which provide comprehensive medical coverage for spouses of women employees but not spouses of male employees are rare, we are not aware of any Title VII litigation concerning such plans. It is certainly not this committee's desire to encourage the institution of such plans"); 123 Cong.Rec. 29663 (1977) (remarks of Sen. Cranston); Brief for Respondent 31–33, n. 31.

dependents was addressed in the Senate Report, the Committee indicated that it should be resolved "on the basis of existing title VII principles."[20] The legislative context makes it clear that Congress was not thereby referring to the view of Title VII reflected in this Court's *Gilbert* opinion. Proponents of the legislation stressed throughout the debates that Congress had always intended to protect *all* individuals from sex discrimination in employment—including but not limited to pregnant women workers.[21] Against this background we review the terms of the amended statute to decide whether petitioner has unlawfully discriminated against its male employees.

**20.** "Questions were raised in the committee's deliberations regarding how this bill would affect medical coverage for dependents of employees, as opposed to employees themselves. In this context it must be remembered that the basic purpose of this bill is to protect women employees, it does not alter the basic principles of title VII law as regards sex discrimination. Rather, this legislation clarifies the definition of sex discrimination for title VII purposes. Therefore the question in regard to dependents' benefits would be determined on the basis of existing title VII principles." S.Rep. No. 95–331, *supra* n. 16, at 5–6, Leg.Hist., at 42–43.

This statement does not imply that the new statutory definition has no applicability; it merely acknowledges that the new definition does not itself resolve the question.

The dissent quotes extensive excerpts from an exchange on the Senate floor between Senators Hatch and Williams. *Post,* at 692–693. Taken in context, this colloquy clearly deals only with the second clause of the bill, see n. 14, *supra,* and Senator Williams, the principal sponsor of the legislation, addressed only the bill's effect on income maintenance plans. Leg.Hist., at 80. Senator Williams first stated, in response to Senator Hatch: "With regard to more maintenance plans for pregnancy-related disabilities, I do not see how this language could be misunderstood." Upon further inquiry from Senator Hatch, he replied: "If there is any ambiguity, with regard to income maintenance plans, I cannot see it." At the end of the same response, he stated: "It is narrowly drawn and would not give any employee the right to obtain income maintenance as a result of the pregnancy of someone who is not an employee." *Ibid.* These comments, which clearly limited the scope of Senator Williams' responses, are omitted from the dissent's lengthy quotation, *post,* at 692–693.

Other omitted portions of the colloquy make clear that it was logical to discuss the pregnancies of employees' spouses in connection with income maintenance plans. Senator Hatch asked, "what about the status of a woman coworker who is not pregnant but rides with a pregnant woman and cannot get to work once the pregnant female commences her maternity leave or the employed mother who stays home to nurse her pregnant daughter?" Leg.Hist., at 80. The reference to spouses of male employees must be understood in light of these hypothetical questions; it seems to address the situation in which a male employee wishes to take time off from work because his wife is pregnant.

**21.** See, *e.g.,* 123 Cong.Rec. 7539 (1977) (remarks of Sen. Williams) ("the Court has ignored the congressional intent in enacting title VII of the Civil Rights Act—that intent was to protect all individuals from unjust employment discrimination, including pregnant workers"); *id.,* at 29385, 29652. In light of statements such as these, it would be anomalous to hold that Congress provided that an employee's pregnancy is sex-based, while a spouse's pregnancy is gender-neutral.

During the course of the Senate debate on the Pregnancy Discrimination Act, Senator Bayh and Senator Cranston both expressed the belief that the new Act would prohibit the exclusion of pregnancy coverage for spouses if spouses were otherwise fully covered by an insurance plan. See *id.,* at 29642, 29663. Because our holding relies on the 1978 legislation only to the extent that it unequivocally rejected the *Gilbert* decision, and ultimately we rely on our understanding of general Title VII principles, we attach no more significance to these two statements than to the many other comments by both Senators and Congressmen disapproving the Court's reasoning and conclusion in *Gilbert.* See n. 17, *supra.*

## II

Section 703(a) makes it an unlawful employment practice for an employer to "discriminate against any individual with respect to his compensation, terms, conditions, or privileges of employment, because of such individual's race, color, religion, sex, or national origin...." 42 U.S.C. § 2000e–2(a)(1). Health insurance and other fringe benefits are "compensation, terms, conditions, or privileges of employment." Male as well as female employees are protected against discrimination. Thus, if a private employer were to provide complete health insurance coverage for the dependents of its female employees, and no coverage at all for the dependents of its male employees, it would violate Title VII. Such a practice would not pass the simple test of Title VII discrimination that we enunciated in Los Angeles Dept. of Water & Power v. Manhart, 435 U.S. 702, 711 (1978), for it would treat a male employee with dependents " 'in a manner which but for that person's sex would be different.' " The same result would be reached even if the magnitude of the discrimination were smaller. For example, a plan that provided complete hospitalization coverage for the spouses of female employees but did not cover spouses of male employees when they had broken bones would violate Title VII by discriminating against male employees.

Petitioner's practice is just as unlawful. Its plan provides limited pregnancy-related benefits for employees' wives, and affords more extensive coverage for employees' spouses for all other medical conditions requiring hospitalization. Thus the husbands of female employees receive a specified level of hospitalization coverage for all conditions; the wives of male employees receive such coverage except for pregnancy-related conditions. Although *Gilbert* concluded that an otherwise inclusive plan that singled out pregnancy-related benefits for exclusion was nondiscriminatory on its face, because only women can become pregnant, Congress has unequivocally rejected that reasoning. The 1978 Act makes clear that it is discriminatory to treat pregnancy-related conditions less favorably than other medical conditions. Thus petitioner's plan unlawfully gives married male employees a benefit package for their dependents that is less inclusive than the dependency coverage provided to married female employees.

There is no merit to petitioner's argument that the prohibitions of Title VII do not extend to discrimination against pregnant spouses because the statute applies only to discrimination in employment. A two-step analysis demonstrates the fallacy in this contention. The Pregnancy Discrimination Act has now made clear that, for all Title VII purposes, discrimination based on a woman's pregnancy is, on its face, discrimination because of her sex. And since the sex of the spouse is always the opposite of the sex of the employee, it follows inexorably that discrimination against female spouses in the provision of fringe benefits is also discrimination against male employees. Cf. Wengler v. Druggists Mutual Ins. Co., 446 U.S. 142, 147 (1980). By making clear that an employer could not discriminate on the basis of an employee's pregnancy, Congress did not erase the original prohibition against discrimination on the basis of an employee's sex.

In short, Congress' rejection of the premises of *General Electric Co. v. Gilbert* forecloses any claim that an insurance program excluding pregnancy coverage for female beneficiaries and providing complete coverage to similarly situated male beneficiaries does not discriminate on the basis of sex. Petitioner's plan is the mirror image of the plan at issue in *Gilbert*. The pregnancy limitation in this case violates Title VII by discriminating against male employees.

The judgment of the Court of Appeals is

*Affirmed.*

■ JUSTICE REHNQUIST, with whom JUSTICE POWELL joins, dissenting.

In *General Electric Co. v. Gilbert,* 429 U.S. 125 (1976), we held that an exclusion of pregnancy from a disability-benefits plan is not discrimination "because of [an] individual's . . . sex" within the meaning of Title VII of the Civil Rights Act of 1964, § 703(a)(1), 78 Stat. 255, 42 U.S.C. § 2000e–2(a)(1). In our view, therefore, Title VII was not violated by an employer's disability plan that provided all employees with nonoccupational sickness and accident benefits, but excluded from the plan's coverage disabilities arising from pregnancy. Under our decision in *Gilbert,* petitioner's otherwise inclusive benefits plan that excludes pregnancy benefits for a male employee's spouse clearly would not violate Title VII. For a different result to obtain, *Gilbert* would have to be judicially overruled by this Court or Congress would have to legislatively overrule our decision in its entirety by amending Title VII.

Today, the Court purports to find the latter by relying on the Pregnancy Discrimination Act of 1978, Pub.L. 95–555, 92 Stat. 2076, 42 U.S.C. § 2000e(k) (1976 ed., Supp. V), a statute that plainly speaks only of female employees affected by pregnancy and says nothing about spouses of male employees. Congress, of course, was free to legislatively overrule *Gilbert* in whole or in part, and there is no question but that the Pregnancy Discrimination Act manifests congressional dissatisfaction with the result we reached in *Gilbert*. But I think the Court reads far more into the Pregnancy Discrimination Act than Congress put there, and that therefore it is the Court, and not Congress, which is now overruling *Gilbert*.

In a case presenting a relatively simple question of statutory construction, the Court pays virtually no attention to the language of the Pregnancy Discrimination Act or the legislative history pertaining to that language. The Act provides in relevant part:

"The terms 'because of sex' or 'on the basis of sex' include, but are not limited to, because of or on the basis of pregnancy, childbirth, or related medical conditions; and women affected by pregnancy, childbirth, or related medical conditions shall be treated the same for all employment-related purposes, including receipt of benefits under fringe benefit programs, as other persons not so affected but similar in their ability or inability to work...." 42 U.S.C. § 2000e(k) (1976 ed., Supp. V).

The Court recognizes that this provision is merely definitional and that "[u]ltimately the question we must decide is whether petitioner has discriminated against its male employees ... because of their sex within the meaning of § 703(a)(1)" of Title VII. *Ante,* at 675. Section 703(a)(1) provides in part:

> "It shall be an unlawful employment practice for an employer ... to fail or refuse to hire or to discharge any individual, or otherwise to discriminate against any individual with respect to his compensation, terms, conditions, or privileges of employment, because of such individual's race, color, religion, sex, or national origin...." 42 U.S.C. § 2000e–2(a)(1).

It is undisputed that in § 703(a)(1) the word "individual" refers to an employee or applicant for employment. As modified by the first clause of the definitional provision of the Pregnancy Discrimination Act, the proscription in § 703(a)(1) is for discrimination "against any individual ... *because of such individual's ... pregnancy,* childbirth, or related medical conditions." This can only be read as referring to the pregnancy of an *employee.*

That this result was not inadvertent on the part of Congress is made very evident by the second clause of the Act, language that the Court essentially ignores in its opinion. When Congress in this clause further explained the proscription it was creating by saying that "women affected by pregnancy ... shall be treated the same ... as other persons not so affected but *similar in their ability or inability to work*" it could only have been referring to *female employees.* The Court of Appeals below stands alone in thinking otherwise.

The Court concedes that this is a correct reading of the second clause. *Ante,* at 678, n. 14. Then in an apparent effort to escape the impact of this provision, the Court asserts that "[t]he meaning of the first clause is not limited by the specific language in the second clause." *Ibid.* I do not disagree. But this conclusion does not help the Court, for as explained above, when the definitional provision of the first clause is inserted in § 703(a)(1), it says the very same thing: the proscription added to Title VII applies only to female employees.

The plain language of the Pregnancy Discrimination Act leaves little room for the Court's conclusion that the Act was intended to extend beyond female employees. The Court concedes that "congressional discussion focused on the needs of female members of the work force rather than spouses of male employees." In fact, the singular focus of discussion on the problems of the *pregnant worker* is striking.

When introducing the Senate Report on the bill that later became the Pregnancy Discrimination Act, its principal sponsor, Senator Williams, explained:

"Because of the Supreme Court's decision in the *Gilbert* case, this legislation is necessary to provide fundamental protection against sex discrimination for our Nation's 42 million *working women*. This protection will go a long way toward insuring that American women are permitted to assume their rightful place in our Nation's economy.

"In addition to providing protection to *working women* with regard to fringe benefit programs, such as health and disability insurance programs, this legislation will prohibit other employment policies which adversely affect *pregnant workers*." 124 Cong.Rec. 36817 (1978) (emphasis added).[4]

As indicated by the examples in the margin,[5] the Congressional Record is overflowing with similar statements by individual Members of Congress expressing their intention to ensure with the Pregnancy Discrimination Act

---

**4.** Reprinted in a Committee Print prepared for the Senate Committee on Labor and Human Resources, 96th Cong., 2d Sess., Legislative History of the Pregnancy Discrimination Act of 1978, pp. 200–201 (1979) (hereinafter referred to as Leg.Hist.). In the foreword to the official printing of the Act's legislative history, Senator Williams further described the purpose of the Act, saying:

"The Act provides an essential protection for working women. The number of women in the labor force has increased dramatically in recent years. Most of these women are working or seeking work because of the economic need to support themselves or their families. It is expected that this trend of increasing participation by women in the workforce will continue in the future and that an increasing proportion of working women will be those who are mothers. It is essential that these women and their children be fully protected against the harmful effects of unjust employment discrimination on the basis of pregnancy." *Id.*, at III.

**5.** See 123 Cong.Rec. 8145 (1977), Leg. Hist., at 21 (remarks of Sen. Bayh) (bill will "help provide true equality for working women of this Nation"); 123 Cong.Rec. 29385 (1977), Leg.Hist., at 62–63 (remarks of Sen. Williams) ("central purpose of the bill is to require that women workers be treated equally with other employees on the basis of their ability or inability to work"); 124 Cong. Rec. 36818 (1978), Leg.Hist., at 203 (remarks of Sen. Javits) ("bill represents only basic fairness for women employees"); 124 Cong. Rec. 36819 (1978), Leg.Hist., at 204 (remarks of Sen. Stafford) (bill will end "major source

of discrimination unjustly afflicting working women in America"); 124 Cong.Rec. 21437 (1978), Leg.Hist., at 172 (remarks of Rep. Green) (bill "will provide rights working women should have had years ago"); 124 Cong.Rec. 21439 (1978), Leg.Hist., at 177 (remarks of Rep. Quie) (bill is "necessary in order for women employees to enjoy equal treatment in fringe benefit programs"); 124 Cong.Rec. 21439 (1978), Leg.Hist., at 178 (remarks of Rep. Akaka) ("bill simply requires that pregnant workers be fairly and equally treated").

See also 123 Cong.Rec. 7541 (1977), Leg. Hist., at 7 (remarks of Sen. Brooke); 123 Cong.Rec. 7541, 29663 (1977), Leg.Hist., at 8, 134 (remarks of Sen. Mathias); 123 Cong.Rec. 29388 (1977), Leg.Hist., at 71 (remarks of Sen. Kennedy); 123 Cong.Rec. 29661 (1977), Leg.Hist., at 126 (remarks of Sen. Biden); 123 Cong.Rec. 29663 (1977), Leg.Hist., at 132 (remarks of Sen. Cranston); 123 Cong.Rec. 29663 (1977), Leg.Hist., at 132 (remarks of Sen. Culver); 124 Cong.Rec. 21439 (1978), Leg.Hist., at 178 (remarks of Rep. Corrada); 124 Cong.Rec. 21435, 38573 (1978), Leg. Hist., at 168, 207 (remarks of Rep. Hawkins); 124 Cong.Rec. 38574 (1978), Leg.Hist., at 208–209 (remarks of Rep. Sarasin); 124 Cong. Rec. 21440 (1978), Leg.Hist., at 180 (remarks of Rep. Chisholm); 124 Cong.Rec. 21440 (1978), Leg.Hist., at 181 (remarks of Rep. LaFalce); 124 Cong.Rec. 21441 (1978), Leg. Hist., at 182 (remarks of Rep. Collins); 124 Cong.Rec. 21441 (1978), Leg.Hist., at 184 (remarks of Rep. Whalen); 124 Cong.Rec. 21442 (1978), Leg.Hist., at 185 (remarks of Rep. Burke); 124 Cong.Rec. 21442 (1978), Leg. Hist., at 185 (remarks of Rep. Tsongas).

that working women are not treated differently because of pregnancy. Consistent with these views, all three Committee Reports on the bills that led to the Pregnancy Discrimination Act expressly state that the Act would require employers to treat pregnant employees the same as "other employees."[6]

The Court tr[ie]s to avoid the impact of this legislative history by saying that it "does not create a 'negative inference' limiting the scope of the Act to the specific problem that motivated its enactment." *Ante,* at 679. This reasoning might have some force if the legislative history was silent on an arguably related issue. But the legislative history is not silent. The Senate Report provides:

> "Questions were raised in the committee's deliberations regarding how this bill would affect medical coverage for dependents of employees, as opposed to employees themselves. In this context it must be remembered that the basic purpose of this bill is to protect women employees, it does not alter the basic principles of title VII law as regards sex discrimination.... [T]he question in regard to dependents' benefits would be determined on the basis of existing title VII principles.... *[T]he question of whether an employer who does cover dependents, either with or without additional cost to the employee, may exclude conditions related to pregnancy from that coverage is a different matter.* Presumably because plans which provide comprehensive medical coverage for spouses of women employees but not spouses of male employees are rare, we are not aware of any title VII litigation concerning such plans. It is certainly not this committee's desire to encourage the institution of such plans. If such plans should be instituted in the future, the question would remain whether, under title VII, the affected employees were discriminated against on the basis of their sex as regards the extent of coverage for their dependents." S.Rep. No. 95–331, pp. 5–6 (1977), Leg.Hist., at 42–43 (emphasis added).

This plainly disclaims any intention to deal with the issue presented in this case. Where Congress says that it would not want "to encourage" plans such as petitioner's, it cannot plausibly be argued that Congress has intended "to prohibit" such plans. Senator Williams was questioned on this point by Senator Hatch during discussions on the floor and his answers are to the same effect.

> "MR. HATCH: ... The phrase 'women affected by pregnancy, childbirth or related medical conditions,' ... appears to be overly broad, and is not limited in terms of employment. It does not even require that the person so affected be pregnant.
>
> *"Indeed under the present language of the bill, it is arguable that spouses of male employees are covered by this civil rights amendment....*

---

**6.** See Report of the Senate Committee on Human Resources, S.Rep. No. 95–331 (1977), Leg.Hist., at 38–53; Report of the House Committee on Education and Labor, H.R.Rep. No. 95–948 (1978), Leg.Hist., at 147–164; Report of the Committee of Conference, H.R.Conf.Rep. No. 95–1786 (1978), Leg. Hist., at 194–198.

"Could the sponsors clarify exactly whom that phrase intends to cover?

\* \* \*

"MR. WILLIAMS: ... I do not see how one can read into this any pregnancy other than that pregnancy that relates to the employee, and if there is any ambiguity, *let it be clear here now that this is very precise. It deals with a woman, a woman who is an employee,* an employee in a work situation where all disabilities are covered under a company plan that provides income maintenance in the event of medical disability; that her particular period of disability, when she cannot work because of childbirth or anything related to childbirth, is excluded. ...

\* \* \*

"MR. HATCH: So the Senator is satisfied that, though the committee language I brought up, 'woman affected by pregnancy' seems to be ambiguous, what it means is that *this act only applies to the particular woman who is actually pregnant, who is an employee and has become pregnant after her employment?*

\* \* \*

"MR. WILLIAMS: *Exactly.*" 123 Cong.Rec. 29643–29644 (1977), Leg. Hist., at 80 (emphasis added).[7]

It seems to me that analysis of this case should end here. Under our decision in *General Electric Co. v. Gilbert* petitioner's exclusion of pregnancy benefits for male employee's spouses would not offend Title VII. Nothing in the Pregnancy Discrimination Act was intended to reach beyond female employees. Thus, *Gilbert* controls and requires that we reverse the Court of

---

**7.** The Court suggests that in this exchange Senator Williams is explaining only that spouses of male employees will not be put on "income maintenance plans" while pregnant. *Ante,* at 680, n. 20. This is utterly illogical. Spouses of employees have no income from the relevant employer to be maintained. Senator Williams clearly says that the Act is limited to female employees and as to such employees it will ensure income maintenance where male employees would receive similar disability benefits. Senator Hatch's final question and Senator Williams' response could not be clearer. The Act was intended to affect *only* pregnant workers. This is exactly what the Senate Report said and Senator Williams confirmed that this is exactly what Congress intended.

The only indications arguably contrary to the views reflected in the Senate Report and the exchange between Senators Hatch and Williams are found in two isolated remarks by Senators Bayh and Cranston. 123 Cong.Rec. 29642, 29663 (1977), Leg.Hist., at 75, 131. These statements, however, concern these two Senators' views concerning Title VII sex discrimination as it existed prior to the Pregnancy Discrimination Act. Their conclusions are completely at odds with our decision in *General Electric Co. v. Gilbert,* 429 U.S. 125 (1976), and are not entitled to deference here. We have consistently said: "The views of members of a later Congress, concerning different [unamended] sections of Title VII ... are entitled to little if any weight. It is the intent of the Congress that enacted [Title VII] in 1964 ... that controls." Teamsters v. United States, 431 U.S. 324, 354, n. 39 (1977). See also Southeastern Community College v. Davis, 442 U.S. 397, 411, n. 11 (1979).

Appeals. But it is here, at what should be the stopping place, that the Court begins. The Court says:

"Although the Pregnancy Discrimination Act has clarified the meaning of certain terms in this section, neither that Act nor the underlying statute contains a definition of the word 'discriminate.' In order to decide whether petitioner's plan discriminates against male employees because of *their* sex, we must therefore go beyond the bare statutory language. Accordingly, we shall consider whether Congress, by enacting the Pregnancy Discrimination Act, not only overturned the specific holding in *General Electric v. Gilbert, supra,* but also rejected the test of discrimination employed by the Court in that case. We believe it did."

It would seem that the Court has refuted its own argument by recognizing that the Pregnancy Discrimination Act only clarifies the meaning of the phrases "because of sex" and "on the basis of sex," and says nothing concerning the definition of the word "discriminate."[8] Instead the Court proceeds to try to explain that while Congress said one thing, it did another.

The crux of the Court's reasoning is that even though the Pregnancy Discrimination Act redefines the phrases "because of sex" and "on the basis of sex" only to include discrimination against female employees affected by pregnancy, Congress also expressed its view that in *Gilbert* "the Supreme Court ... erroneously interpreted congressional intent." Somehow the Court then concludes that this renders all of *Gilbert* obsolete.

In support of its argument, the Court points to a few passages in congressional Reports and several statements by various Members of the 95th Congress to the effect that the Court in *Gilbert* had, when it construed Title VII, misperceived the intent of the 88th Congress. The Court also points out that "[m]any of [the Members of the 95th Congress] expressly agreed with the views of the dissenting Justices." Certainly *various Members of Congress* said as much. But the fact remains that *Congress as a body* has not expressed these sweeping views in the Pregnancy Discrimination Act.

Under our decision in *General Electric Co. v. Gilbert,* petitioner's exclusion of pregnancy benefits for male employees' spouses would not violate Title VII. Since nothing in the Pregnancy Discrimination Act even arguably reaches beyond female employees affected by pregnancy, *Gilbert* requires that we reverse the Court of Appeals. Because the Court concludes otherwise, I dissent.

## Questions

**1.** The *Newport News* majority held that Congress, in enacting the 1978 pregnancy discrimination amendments, rejected the rationale of the *Gilbert*

---

**8.** The Court also concedes at one point that the Senate Report on the Pregnancy Discrimination Act "acknowledges that the new definition [in the Act] does not itself resolve the question" presented in this case.

decision. There, Justice Rehnquist identified two classes of individuals, pregnant persons, and non-pregnant persons. This was not sex discrimination, according to the majority, because the second class consisted of both women and men. While the pregnancy discrimination amendments prohibited classifications based on pregnancy, by subsuming them under sex discrimination, do those amendments discredit other classification exercises of the *Gilbert* variety?

**2.**   In light of this decision, how should a court analyze a Title VII claim by a female worker concerning a company's health insurance plan that does not cover a spouse's prostate disease? How would the *Newport News* dissent analyze the claim?

# E.   RETROACTIVITY OF STATUTES

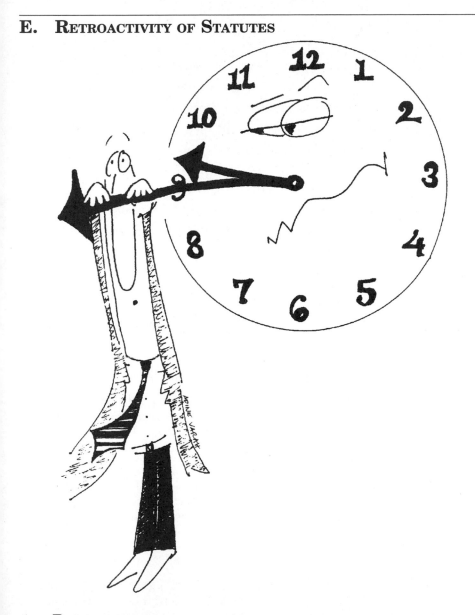

## 1.   PRESUMPTIONS

You have already encountered the problem of retroactivity in the context of judicial decisions announcing new rules or overruling old rules. Are the analysis and results different when the source of the new or changed rule is the legislature?

In the absence of specific legislative provision, which of the following variants would/should apply? Why?

The new statute governs:

1.   All situations arising after passage of the statute.

2.   All unadjudicated noncontractual situations arising before passage of the statute.

    a.   If the statute addresses procedural issues.

    b.   If the statute addresses substantive rights.

    c.   If the statute enacts criminal penalties.

3.   Rights and duties arising under preexisting contracts:

    a.   Does not affect preexisting contracts, even if these continue to be executed subsequent to the statute's enactment.

    b.   Governs only future effects of these contracts.

    c.   Also governs past transactions or effects of these contracts.

4.   Final decisions rendered pursuant to the law before the statute's enactment.

    a.   Not affected.

    b.   Can be reopened and readjudicated.

## Bradley v. School Board of the City of Richmond

Supreme Court of the United States, 1974.
416 U.S. 696, 94 S.Ct. 2006, 40 L.Ed.2d 476.

■ MR. JUSTICE BLACKMUN delivered the opinion of the Court.

In this protracted school desegregation litigation, the District Court awarded the plaintiff-petitioners expenses and attorneys' fees for services rendered from March 10, 1970, to January 29, 1971. The United States Court of Appeals for the Fourth Circuit, one judge dissenting, reversed.

We granted certiorari, to determine whether the allowance of attorneys' fees was proper. Pertinent to the resolution of the issue is the enactment in 1972 of § 718 of Title VII, the Emergency School Aid Act, 20 U.S.C. § 1617 (1970 ed., Supp. II), as part of the Education Amendments of 1972, Pub.L. 92–318, 86 Stat. 235, 369.

### I

The suit was instituted in 1961 by 11 Negro parents and guardians against the School Board of the city of Richmond, Virginia, as a class action under the Civil Rights Act of 1871, 42 U.S.C. § 1983, to desegregate the public schools.

\* \* \*

On January 10, 1972, the court ordered into effect a plan for the integration of the Richmond schools with those of Henrico and Chesterfield Counties.... The Court of Appeals' judgment was affirmed by an equally divided Court. Richmond School Board v. Board of Education, 412 U.S. 92 (1973).

## II

The petitioners' request for a significant award of attorneys' fees was included, as has been noted, in their pivotal motion of March 10, 1970. That application was renewed on July 2. The District Court first suggested, by letter to the parties, that they attempt to reach agreement as to fees. When agreement was not reached, the court called for supporting material and briefs. In due course the court awarded counsel fees in the amount of $43,355 for services rendered from March 10, 1970, to January 29, 1971, and expenses of $13,064.65.

\* \* \*

As an alternative basis for the award, the District Court observed that the circumstances that persuaded Congress to authorize by statute the payment of counsel fees under certain sections of the Civil Rights Act of 1964[11] were present in even greater degree in school desegregation litigation. In 1970–1971, cases of this kind were characterized by complex issues pressed on behalf of large classes and thus involved substantial expenditures of lawyers' time with little likelihood of compensation or award of monetary damages. If forced to bear the burden of attorneys' fees, few aggrieved persons would be in a position to secure their and the public's interests in a nondiscriminatory public school system. Reasoning from this Court's *per curiam* decision in Newman v. Piggie Park Enterprises, Inc., 390 U.S. 400, 402 (1968), the District Judge held that plaintiffs in actions of this kind were acting as private attorneys general in leading school boards into compliance with the law, thereby effectuating the constitutional guarantee of nondiscrimination and rendering appropriate the award of counsel fees. 53 F.R.D., at 41–42.

The Court of Appeals, in reversing, emphasized that the Board was not operating "in an area where the practical methods to be used were plainly illuminated or where prior decisions had not left a 'lingering doubt' as to the proper procedure to be followed," particularly in the light of uncertainties existing prior to this Court's then impending decision in Swann v. Charlotte–Mecklenburg Board of Education, 402 U.S. 1 (1971). 472 F.2d, at 327. It felt that by the failure of Congress to provide specifically for counsel fees "in a statutory scheme designed to further a public purpose, it may be fairly accepted that it did so purposefully," and that "if such awards are to be made to promote the public policy expressed in legislative action, they should be authorized by Congress and not by the courts." *Id.*, at 330–331.

After initial submission of the case to the Court of Appeals, but prior to its decision, the Education Amendments of 1972, of which § 718 of Title VII of the Emergency School Aid Act is a part, became law. Section 718, 20 U.S.C. § 1617 (1970 ed., Supp. II), grants authority to a federal court to

---

**11.** Title 42 U.S.C. § 2000a–3(b) authorizes an allowance of a reasonable attorney's fee to a prevailing party, other than the United States, in an action under the public accommodation subchapter of the Civil Rights Act of 1964. Similarly, 42 U.S.C. § 2000e– 5(k) authorizes an allowance of a reasonable attorney's fee to a prevailing party, other than the Equal Employment Opportunity Commission or the United States, in an action under the equal employment opportunity subchapter of that Act.

award a reasonable attorney's fee when appropriate in a school desegregation case.[12] The Court of Appeals, sitting en banc, then heard argument as to the applicability of § 718 to this and other litigation.[13] In the other cases it held that only legal services rendered after July 1, 1972, the effective date of § 718, see Pub.L. 92–318, § 2(c)(1), 86 Stat. 236, were compensable under that statute. Thompson v. School Board of the City of Newport News, 472 F.2d 177 (C.A.4 1972). In the instant case the court held that, because there were no orders pending or appealable on either May 26, 1971, when the District Court made its fee award, or on July 1, 1972, when the statute became effective, § 718 did not sustain the allowance of counsel fees.

## III

In Northcross v. Board of Education of the Memphis City Schools, 412 U.S. 427, 428 (1973), we held that under § 718 "the successful plaintiff 'should ordinarily recover an attorney's fee unless special circumstances would render such an award unjust.' " We decide today a question left open in *Northcross,* namely, "whether § 718 authorizes an award of attorneys' fees insofar as those expenses were incurred prior to the date that that section came into effect." *Id.,* at 429 n. 2.

The District Court in this case awarded counsel fees for services rendered from March 10, 1970, when petitioners filed their motion for further relief, to January 29, 1971, when the court declined to implement the plan proposed by the petitioners. It made its award on May 26, 1971, after it had ordered into effect the noninterim desegregation plan which it had approved. The Board appealed from that award, and its appeal was pending when Congress enacted § 718. The question, properly viewed, then, is not simply one relating to the propriety of retroactive application of § 718 to services rendered prior to its enactment, but rather, one relating to the applicability of that section to a situation where the propriety of a fee award was pending resolution on appeal when the statute became law.

\* \* \*

## A

We anchor our holding in this case on the principle that a court is to apply the law in effect at the time it renders its decision, unless doing so

---

**12.**  "§ 1617. Attorney fees.

"Upon the entry of a final order by a court of the United States against a local educational agency, a State (or any agency thereof), or the United States (or any agency thereof), for failure to comply with any provision of this chapter or for discrimination on the basis of race, color, or national origin in violation of title VI of the Civil Rights Act of 1964, or the fourteenth amendment to the Constitution of the United States as they pertain to elementary and secondary education, the court, in its discretion, upon a finding that the proceedings were necessary to bring about compliance, may allow the prevailing party, other than the United States, a reasonable attorney's fee as part of the costs."

**13.**  The fee issue had been argued in the Court of Appeals on March 7, 1972. The Education Amendments of 1972 were approved by the President on June 23. The argument before the en banc court took place on October 2.

would result in manifest injustice or there is statutory direction or legislative history to the contrary.

The origin and the justification for this rule are found in the words of Mr. Chief Justice Marshall in United States v. Schooner Peggy, 1 Cranch 103 (1801):

> "It is in the general true that the province of an appellate court is only to enquire whether a judgment when rendered was erroneous or not. But if subsequent to the judgment and before the decision of the appellate court, a law intervenes and positively changes the rule which governs, the law must be obeyed, or its obligation denied. If the law be constitutional ... I know of no court which can contest its obligation. It is true that in mere private cases between individuals, a court will and ought to struggle hard against a construction which will, by a retrospective operation, affect the rights of parties, but in great national concerns ... the court must decide according to existing laws, and if it be necessary to set aside a judgment, rightful when rendered, but which cannot be affirmed but in violation of law, the judgment must be set aside." *Id.,* at 110.[16]

In the wake of *Schooner Peggy,* however, it remained unclear whether a change in the law occurring while a case was pending on appeal was to be given effect only where, by its terms, the law was to apply to pending cases, as was true of the convention under consideration in *Schooner Peggy,* or, conversely, whether such a change in the law must be given effect *unless* there was clear indication that it was *not* to apply in pending cases. For a very long time the Court's decisions did little to clarify this issue.[17]

---

**16.** *Schooner Peggy* concerned a condemnation following the seizure of a French vessel by an American ship. The trial court found that the vessel was within French territorial waters at the time of seizure and, hence, was not a lawful prize. On appeal, the Circuit Court reversed, holding that the vessel in fact was on the high seas. A decree was entered accordingly. While the case was pending on appeal to this Court, a convention with France was entered into providing in part: "Property captured, and not yet *definitively* condemned, or which may be captured before the exchange of ratifications ... shall be mutually restored." 1 Cranch, at 107. This Court reversed, holding that it must apply the terms of the convention despite the propriety of the Circuit Court's decision when it was rendered, and that the vessel was to be restored since, by virtue of the pending appeal, it had not been *"definitively* condemned," *id.,* at 108.

**17.** In United States v. Chambers, 291 U.S. 217 (1934), the Court held that pending prosecutions, including those on appeal,

brought pursuant to the National Prohibition Act were to be dismissed in view of the interim ratification of the Twenty-first Amendment, absent inclusion of a saving clause. In Carpenter v. Wabash R. Co., 309 U.S. 23 (1940), the Court, in reliance on *Schooner Peggy,* held that an amendment to the Bankruptcy Act, effected while the case was pending on petition for writ of certiorari, was to be given effect. The amendment, however, provided explicitly that it was applicable to railroad receiverships then pending in any United States court. In Vandenbark v. Owens–Illinois Glass Co., 311 U.S. 538 (1941), again in reliance on *Schooner Peggy,* it was held that a federal appellate court, in diversity jurisdiction, must follow a state supreme court decision changing the applicable state law subsequent to the decision in the federal trial court. In Ziffrin, Inc. v. United States, 318 U.S. 73 (1943), the Court held that an amendment to the Interstate Commerce Act, made after the hearing upon an application for a permit to continue contract carrier operations, was to be given effect. "A change in

Ultimately, in Thorpe v. Housing Authority of the City of Durham, 393 U.S. 268 (1969), the broader reading of *Schooner Peggy* was adopted, and this Court ruled that "an appellate court must apply the law in effect at the time it renders its decision." *Id.,* at 281. In that case, after the plaintiff Housing Authority had secured a state court eviction order, and it had been affirmed by the Supreme Court of North Carolina, Housing Authority of the City of Durham v. Thorpe, 267 N.C. 431, 148 S.E.2d 290 (1966), and this Court had granted certiorari, 385 U.S. 967 (1966), the Department of Housing and Urban Development ordered a new procedural prerequisite for an eviction. Following remand by this Court for such further proceedings as might be appropriate in the light of the new directive, 386 U.S. 670 (1967), the state court adhered to its decision. 271 N.C. 468, 157 S.E.2d 147 (1967).[18] This Court again granted certiorari. 390 U.S. 942 (1968). Upon review, we held that, although the circular effecting the change did not indicate whether it was to be applied to pending cases or to events that had transpired prior to its issuance; it was, nonetheless, to be applied to anyone residing in the housing project on the date of its promulgation. The Court recited the language in *Schooner Peggy,* quoted above, and noted that that reasoning "has been applied where the change was constitutional, statutory, or judicial," 393 U.S., at 282 (footnotes omitted), and that it must apply "with equal force where the change is made by an administrative agency acting pursuant to legislative authorization." *Ibid. Thorpe* thus stands for the proposition that even where the intervening law does not explicitly recite that it is to be applied to pending cases, it is to be given recognition and effect.

the law between a nisi prius and an appellate decision requires the appellate court to apply the changed law." *Id.,* at 78. In United States v. Alabama, 362 U.S. 602 (1960), the District Court had dismissed an action under the Civil Rights Act of 1957, 42 U.S.C. § 1971(c), brought by the United States against the State of Alabama and others, and did so with respect to Alabama on the ground that the Act did not authorize the action against the State. While the case was pending after a grant of certiorari, the Civil Rights Act of 1960, 74 Stat. 86, was passed, expressly authorizing an action of that kind against a State. The Court applied the new statute without discussion of the legislative history and remanded the case with instructions to reinstate the action.

See also Freeborn v. Smith, 2 Wall. 160 (1865); Moores v. National Bank, 104 U.S. 625 (1882), where a state statute of limitations was construed by the State Supreme Court in a way contrary to the construction given theretofore by the lower federal court, and this Court followed the later construction; Stephens v. Cherokee Nation, 174 U.S. 445 (1899), where the Court upheld a federal statute, containing retrospectivity language and conferring jurisdiction upon this Court over cases on review of actions of the Dawes Commission, enacted after rulings below that decrees of the courts in the Indian territories were final; Dinsmore v. Southern Express Co., 183 U.S. 115 (1901), where the Court, relying upon *Schooner Peggy,* applied a statute, enacted while the case was pending on certiorari, to affirm the judgment of the lower court; Watts, Watts & Co. v. Unione Austriaca, 248 U.S. 9 (1918); Dorchy v. Kansas, 264 U.S. 286, 289 (1924); Missouri ex rel. Wabash R. Co. v. Public Service Comm'n, 273 U.S. 126 (1927); Sioux County v. National Surety Co., 276 U.S. 238, 240 (1928); Patterson v. Alabama, 294 U.S. 600, 607 (1935).

**18.** The Supreme Court of North Carolina held that since all "critical events" had occurred prior to the date of the circular, "[t]he rights of the parties had matured and had been determined before the directive was issued." 271 N.C., at 470, 157 S.E.2d, at 149.

Accordingly, we must reject the contention that a change in the law is to be given effect in a pending case only where that is the clear and stated intention of the legislature. While neither our decision in *Thorpe* nor our decision today purports to hold that courts must always thus apply new laws to pending cases in the absence of clear legislative direction to the contrary, we do note that insofar as the legislative history of § 718 is supportive of either position, it would seem to provide at least implicit support for the application of the statute to pending cases.[23]

### B

The Court in *Thorpe,* however, observed that exceptions to the general rule that a court is to apply a law in effect at the time it renders its decision "had been made to prevent manifest injustice," citing *Greene v. United States,* 376 U.S. 149 (1964). Although the precise category of cases to which this exception applies has not been clearly delineated, the Court in *Schooner Peggy* suggested that such injustice could result "in mere private cases between individuals," and implored the courts to "struggle hard against a construction which will, by a retrospective operation, affect the rights of parties." 1 Cranch, at 110. We perceive no such threat of manifest injustice present in this case. We decline, accordingly, to categorize it as an exception to *Thorpe's* general rule.

The concerns expressed by the Court in *Schooner Peggy* and in *Thorpe* relative to the possible working of an injustice center upon (a) the nature and identity of the parties, (b) the nature of their rights, and (c) the nature of the impact of the change in law upon those rights.

In this case the parties consist, on the one hand, of the School Board, a publicly funded governmental entity, and, on the other, a class of children whose constitutional right to a nondiscriminatory education has been advanced by this litigation. The District Court rather vividly described what it regarded as the disparity in the respective abilities of the parties adequately to present and protect their interests. Moreover, school desegregation litigation is of a kind different from "mere private cases between individuals." With the Board responsible for the education of the very students who brought suit against it to require that such education comport with constitutional standards, it is not appropriate to view the

---

**23.** The legislation that ultimately resulted in the passage of § 718 grew out of a bill that would have provided for the establishment of a $15 million federal fund from which successful litigants in school discrimination cases would be paid a reasonable fee "for services rendered, and costs incurred, *after the date of enactment of this Act.*" S. 683, § 11(a), 92d Cong., 1st Sess. (1971) (emphasis supplied). The bill was reported out of the Senate Committee on Labor and Public Welfare as S. 1557, with the relevant clause intact in § 11. See S.Rep. No. 92–61, pp. 55–

56 (1971). The section, however, was stricken in the Senate, 117 Cong.Rec. 11338–11345 (1971), and the present language of § 718 took its place. *Id.,* at 11521–11529 and 11724–11726. The House, among other amendments, deleted all mention of counsel fees. In conference, the fee provision was restored. S.Rep. No. 92–798, p. 143 (1972).

Thus, while there is no explicit statement that § 718 may be applied to services rendered prior to enactment, we are reluctant specifically to read into the statute the very fee limitation that Congress eliminated.

parties as engaged in a routine private lawsuit. In this litigation the plaintiffs may be recognized as having rendered substantial service both to the Board itself, by bringing it into compliance with its constitutional mandate, and to the community at large by securing for it the benefits assumed to flow from a nondiscriminatory educational system. Brown v. Board of Education, 347 U.S., at 494.

In *Northcross* we construed, as *in pari passu,* § 718 and § 204(b) of the Civil Rights Act of 1964, 42 U.S.C. § 2000a–3(b), providing for an award of counsel fees to a successful plaintiff under the public accommodation subchapter of that Act. Our discussion of the latter provision in *Piggie Park* is particularly apt in the context of school desegregation litigation:

"When the Civil Rights Act of 1964 was passed, it was evident that enforcement would prove difficult and that the Nation would have to rely in part upon private litigation as a means of securing broad compliance with the law. A Title II suit is thus private in form only. When a plaintiff brings an action under that Title, he cannot recover damages. If he obtains an injunction, he does so not for himself alone but also as a 'private attorney general,' vindicating a policy that Congress considered of the highest priority. If successful plaintiffs were routinely forced to bear their own attorneys' fees, few aggrieved parties would be in a position to advance the public interest by invoking the injunctive powers of the federal courts." 390 U.S., at 401–402 (footnotes omitted).

Application of § 718 to such litigation would thus appear to have been anticipated by Mr. Chief Justice Marshall in *Schooner Peggy* when he noted that in "great national concerns ... the court must decide according to existing laws." 1 Cranch, at 110. Indeed, the circumstances surrounding the passage of § 718, and the numerous expressions of congressional concern and intent with respect to the enactment of that statute, all proclaim its status as having to do with a "great national concern."[27]

The second aspect of the Court's concern that injustice may arise from retrospective application of a change in law relates to the nature of the rights affected by the change. The Court has refused to apply an intervening change to a pending action where it has concluded that to do so would infringe upon or deprive a person of a right that had matured or become unconditional. We find here no such matured or unconditional right affected by the application of § 718. It cannot be claimed that the publicly elected School Board had such a right in the funds allocated to it by the taxpayers. These funds were essentially held in trust for the public, and at all times the Board was subject to such conditions or instructions on the

---

**27.** It is particularly in the area of desegregation that this Court in *Newman* and in *Northcross* recognized that, by their suit, plaintiffs vindicated a national policy of high priority. Other courts have given explicit and implicit recognition to the priority placed on desegregation litigation by the Congress. See Knight v. Auciello, 453 F.2d 852, 853 (C.A.1 1972) and Lee v. Southern Home Sites Corp., 444 F.2d 143, 145 (C.A.5 1971) (housing); Johnson v. Combs, 471 F.2d, at 86 (schools); Miller v. Amusement Enterprises, Inc., 426 F.2d 534, 537–538 (C.A.5 1970) (public accommodation); Cooper v. Allen, 467 F.2d 836, 841 (C.A.5 1972) (employment).

use of the funds as the public wished to make through its duly elected representatives.

The third concern has to do with the nature of the impact of the change in law upon existing rights, or, to state it another way, stems from the possibility that new and unanticipated obligations may be imposed upon a party without notice or an opportunity to be heard. Here no increased burden was imposed since § 718 did not alter the Board's constitutional responsibility for providing pupils with a nondiscriminatory education. Also, there was no change in the substantive obligation of the parties. From the outset, upon the filing of the original complaint in 1961, the Board engaged in a conscious course of conduct with the knowledge that, under different theories, discussed by the District Court and the Court of Appeals, the board could have been required to pay attorney's fees. Even assuming a degree of uncertainty in the law at that time regarding the Board's constitutional obligations, there is no indication that the obligation under § 718, if known, rather than simply the common-law availability of an award, would have caused the Board to order its conduct so as to render this litigation unnecessary and thereby preclude the incurring of such costs.

The availability of § 718 to sustain the award of fees against the Board therefore merely serves to create an additional basis or source for the Board's potential obligation to pay attorney's fees. It does not impose an additional or unforeseeable obligation upon it.

Accordingly, upon considering the parties, the nature of the rights, and the impact of § 718 upon those rights, it cannot be said that the application of the statute to an award of fees for services rendered prior to its effective date, in an action pending on that date, would cause "manifest injustice," as that term is used in *Thorpe,* so as to compel an exception of the case from the rule of *Schooner Peggy.*

* * *

## Question

When Congress legislates retroactively, does not that mean that it is calling for the subsequent application of a rule that did not exist at the time that the disputed acts occurred? Do you see any problems with this? *Cf. In re Adamo, supra,* page 309.

## Bennett v. New Jersey

Supreme Court of the United States, 1985.
470 U.S. 632, 105 S.Ct. 1555, 84 L.Ed.2d 572.

■ O'CONNOR, J., delivered the opinion of the Court, in which BURGER, C.J., and BRENNAN, WHITE, BLACKMUN, and REHNQUIST, JJ., joined. STEVENS, J., filed a dissenting opinion, in which MARSHALL, J., joined POWELL, J., took no part in the consideration or decision of the case.

■ JUSTICE O'CONNOR delivered the opinion of the Court.

The issue presented is whether substantive provisions of the 1978 Amendments to Title I of the Elementary and Secondary Education Act apply retroactively for determining if Title I funds were misused during the years 1970–1972. This case was previously before the Court, and we then held that the Federal Government may recover misused funds from States that provided assurances that federal grants would be spent only on eligible programs.... We expressly declined, however, to address the retroactive effect of substantive provisions of the 1978 Amendments. On remand from our decision, the Court of Appeals for the Third Circuit held that the standards of the 1978 Amendments should apply to determine if funds were improperly expended in previous years....

## I

We hold that the substantive standards of the 1978 Amendments do not affect obligations under previously made grants, and we reverse....

## II

The Court of Appeals based its holding on a presumption that statutory amendments apply retroactively to pending cases. Relying on language from *Bradley v. Richmond School Board,* 416 U.S. 696 (1974), the Court of Appeals observed that "[a] federal court or administrative agency must 'apply the law in effect at the time it renders its decision, unless doing so would result in manifest injustice or there is statutory direction or legislative history to the contrary.'" 724 F.2d, at 36, quoting 416 U.S., at 711. We conclude, however, that reliance on such a presumption in this context is inappropriate. Both the nature of the obligations that arose under the Title I program and *Bradley* itself suggest that changes in substantive requirements for federal grants should not be presumed to operate retroactively. Moreover, practical considerations related to the administration of federal grant programs imply that obligations generally should be determined by reference to the law in effect when the grants were made.[3]

As we explained in our first decision in this case, "the pre–1978 version [of Title I] contemplated that States misusing federal funds would incur a debt to the Federal Government for the amount misused." 461 U.S., at 782. Although our conclusion was based on the statutory provisions, *id.,* at 782–790, we also acknowledged that Title I, like many other federal grant programs, was "much in the nature of a contract." "The State chose to participate in the Title I program and, as a condition of receiving the grant, freely gave its assurances that it would abide by the conditions of Title I." A State that failed to fulfill its assurances has no right to retain the federal funds, and the Federal Government is entitled to recover amounts spent contrary to terms of the grant agreement. In order to obtain the Title I

---

**3.** In determining compliance with federal grant programs, other Courts of Appeals have consistently applied the legal requirements in effect when the grants were made. See, *e.g., Indiana v. Bell,* 728 F.2d 938, 941, n. 6 (C.A.7 1984); *North Carolina Comm'n of Indian Affairs v. Department of Labor,* 725 F.2d 238, 239 (C.A.4 1984); *Woods v. United States,* 724 F.2d 1444, 1446 (C.A.9 1984); *West Virginia v. Secretary of Education,* 667 F.2d 417, 420 (C.A.4 1981).

funds involved here, New Jersey gave assurances that the money would be distributed to local education agencies for programs that qualified under the existing statute and regulations. Assuming that these assurances were not met for the years 1970–1972, see 461 U.S., at 791, the State became liable for the improper expenditures; as a correlative, the Federal Government had, before the 1978 Amendments, a pre-existing right of recovery.

The fact that the Government's right to recover any misused funds preceded the 1978 Amendments indicates that the presumption announced in *Bradley* does not apply here. *Bradley* held that a statutory provision for attorney's fees applied retroactively to a fee request that was pending when the statute was enacted. This holding rested on the general principle that a court must apply the law in effect at the time of its decision, see United States v. Schooner Peggy, 1 Cranch 103 (1801), which *Bradley* concluded holds true even if the intervening law does not expressly state that it applies to pending cases. 416 U.S., at 715. *Bradley,* however, expressly acknowledged limits to this principle. "The Court has refused to apply an intervening change to a pending action where it has concluded that to do so would infringe upon or deprive a person of a right that had matured or become unconditional." *Id.,* at 720. This limitation comports with another venerable rule of statutory interpretation, *i.e.,* that statutes affecting substantive rights and liabilities are presumed to have only prospective effect. See, *e.g.,* United States v. Security Industrial Bank, 459 U.S. 70, 79 (1982); Greene v. United States, 376 U.S. 149, 160 (1964). Cf. *Bradley, supra,* at 721 (noting that statutory change did not affect substantive obligations).

Practical considerations related to the enforcement of the requirements of grant-in-aid programs also suggest that expenditures must presumptively be evaluated by the law in effect when the grants were made. The federal auditors who completed their review of the disputed expenditures in 1975 could scarcely base their findings on the substantive standards adopted in the 1978 Amendments. Similarly, New Jersey when it applied for and received Title I funds for the years 1970–1972 had no basis to believe that the propriety of the expenditures would be judged by any standards other than the ones in effect at the time. Retroactive application of changes in the substantive requirements of a federal grant program would deny both federal auditors and grant recipients fixed, predictable standards for determining if expenditures are proper.

Requiring audits to be redetermined in response to every statutory change that occurs while review is pending would be unworkable and would unfairly make obligations depend on the fortuitous timing of completion of the review process. Moreover, the practical difficulties associated with retroactive application of substantive provisions in the 1978 Amendments would be particularly objectionable, because Congress expressly intended those Amendments to strengthen the auditing process by clarifying the Department's responsibilities and specifying the procedures to be followed. We conclude that absent a clear indication to the contrary in the relevant statutes or legislative history, changes in the substantive standards governing federal grant programs do not alter obligations and liabilities arising under earlier grants.

   *It is so ordered.*

■ JUSTICE POWELL took no part in the consideration or decision of this case.

■ [The dissenting opinion of JUSTICE STEVENS, with whom JUSTICE MARSHALL joins, is omitted.]

## Questions

**1.** Which party was seeking retrospective application of the 1978 amendments? Why?

**2.** Justice O'Connor states that "statutes affecting substantive rights and liabilities are presumed to have only prospective effect." Is this consistent with the presumption announced in *Bradley*? Can you reconcile the two presumptions?

## Bowen v. Georgetown Univ. Hospital

Supreme Court of the United States, 1988.
488 U.S. 204, 109 S.Ct. 468, 102 L.Ed.2d 493.

■ JUSTICE KENNEDY delivered the opinion of the Court.

Under the Medicare program, health care providers are reimbursed by the Government for expenses incurred in providing medical services to Medicare beneficiaries. See Title XVIII of the Social Security Act, 79 Stat. 291, as amended, 42 U.S.C. § 1395 et seq. (the Medicare Act). Congress has authorized the Secretary of Health and Human Services to promulgate regulations setting limits on the levels of Medicare costs that will be reimbursed. The question presented here is whether the Secretary may exercise this rulemaking authority to promulgate cost limits that are retroactive.

### I

The Secretary's authority to adopt cost-limit rules is established by § 223(b) of the Social Security Amendments of 1972, 86 Stat. 1393, amending 42 U.S.C. § 1395x(v)(1)(A). This authority was first implemented in 1974 by promulgation of a cost-limit schedule for hospital services; new cost-limit schedules were issued on an annual basis thereafter.

On June 30, 1981, the Secretary issued a cost-limit schedule that included technical changes in the methods for calculating cost limits. One of these changes affected the method for calculating the "wage index," a factor used to reflect the salary levels for hospital employees in different parts of the country. Under the prior rule, the wage index for a given geographic area was calculated by using the average salary levels for all hospitals in the area; the 1981 rule provided that wages paid by Federal Government hospitals would be excluded from that computation. 46 Fed. Reg. 33637, 33638–33639 (1981).

Various hospitals in the District of Columbia area brought suit in United States District Court seeking to have the 1981 schedule invalidated. On April 29, 1983, the District Court struck down the 1981 wage-index rule, concluding that the Secretary had violated the Administrative Procedure Act (APA), 5 U.S.C. § 551 et seq., by failing to provide notice and an opportunity for public comment before issuing the rule. See District of Columbia Hospital Assn. v. Heckler, No. 82–2520, App. to Pet. for Cert. 49a (hereinafter DCHA). The court did not enjoin enforcement of the rule, however, finding it lacked jurisdiction to do so because the hospitals had not yet exhausted their administrative reimbursement remedies. The court's order stated:

"If the Secretary wishes to put in place a valid prospective wage index, she should begin proper notice and comment proceedings; any wage index currently in place that has been promulgated without notice and comment is invalid as was the 1981 schedule." DCHA, App. to Pet. for Cert. 64a.

The Secretary did not pursue an appeal. Instead, after recognizing the invalidity of the rule, see 48 Fed.Reg. 39998 (1983), the Secretary settled the hospitals' cost reimbursement reports by applying the pre–1981 wage-index method.

In February 1984, the Secretary published a notice seeking public comment on a proposal to reissue the 1981 wage-index rule, retroactive to July 1, 1981. 49 Fed.Reg. 6175 (1984). Because Congress had subsequently amended the Medicare Act to require significantly different cost reimbursement procedures, the readoption of the modified wage-index method was to apply exclusively to a 15–month period commencing July 1, 1981. After considering the comments received, the Secretary reissued the 1981 schedule in final form on November 26, 1984, and proceeded to recoup sums previously paid as a result of the District Court's ruling in DCHA. 49 Fed.Reg. 46495 (1984). In effect, the Secretary had promulgated a rule retroactively, and the net result was as if the original rule had never been set aside.

Respondents, a group of seven hospitals who had benefited from the invalidation of the 1981 schedule, were required to return over $2 million in reimbursement payments. After exhausting administrative remedies, they sought judicial review under the applicable provisions of the APA, claiming that the retroactive schedule was invalid under both the APA and the Medicare Act.

The United States District Court for the District of Columbia granted summary judgment for respondents. Applying the balancing test enunciated in Retail, Wholesale and Department Store Union, AFL–CIO v. NLRB, 151 U.S.App.D.C. 209, 466 F.2d 380 (1972), the court held that retroactive application was not justified under the circumstances of the case.

The Secretary appealed to the United States Court of Appeals for the District of Columbia Circuit, which affirmed. 261 U.S.App.D.C. 262, 821 F.2d 750 (1987). The court based its holding on the alternative grounds that the APA, as a general matter, forbids retroactive rulemaking and the

Medicare Act, by specific terms, bars retroactive cost-limit rules. We granted certiorari, 485 U.S. 903, 99 L.Ed.2d 232, 108 S.Ct. 1073 (1988), and we now affirm.

## II

It is axiomatic that an administrative agency's power to promulgate legislative regulations is limited to the authority delegated by Congress. In determining the validity of the Secretary's retroactive cost-limit rule, the threshold question is whether the Medicare Act authorizes retroactive rulemaking.

Retroactivity is not favored in the law. Thus, congressional enactments and administrative rules will not be construed to have retroactive effect unless their language requires this result. E.g., Greene v. United States, 376 U.S. 149, 160, 11 L.Ed.2d 576, 84 S.Ct. 615 (1964); Claridge Apartments Co. v. Commissioner, 323 U.S. 141, 164, 89 L.Ed. 139, 65 S.Ct. 172 (1944); Miller v. United States, 294 U.S. 435, 439, 79 L.Ed. 977, 55 S.Ct. 440 (1935); United States v. Magnolia Petroleum Co., 276 U.S. 160, 162–163, 72 L.Ed. 509, 48 S.Ct. 236 (1928). By the same principle, a statutory grant of legislative rulemaking authority will not, as a general matter, be understood to encompass the power to promulgate retroactive rules unless that power is conveyed by Congress in express terms. See Brimstone R. Co. v. United States, 276 U.S. 104, 122, 72 L.Ed. 487, 48 S.Ct. 282 (1928) ("The power to require readjustments for the past is drastic. It ... ought not to be extended so as to permit unreasonably harsh action without very plain words"). Even where some substantial justification for retroactive rulemaking is presented, courts should be reluctant to find such authority absent an express statutory grant.

The Secretary contends that the Medicare Act provides the necessary authority to promulgate retroactive cost-limit rules in the unusual circumstances of this case. He rests on alternative grounds: first, the specific grant of authority to promulgate regulations to "provide for the making of suitable retroactive corrective adjustments," 42 U.S.C. § 1395x(v)(1)(A)(ii); and second, the general grant of authority to promulgate cost limit rules, §§ 1395x(v)(1)(A), 1395hh, 1395ii. We consider these alternatives in turn.

### A

The authority to promulgate cost reimbursement regulations is set forth in § 1395x(v)(1)(A). That subparagraph also provides that:

"Such regulations shall ... (ii) provide for the making of suitable retroactive corrective adjustments where, for a provider of services for any fiscal period, the aggregate reimbursement produced by the methods of determining costs proves to be either inadequate or excessive." Ibid.

This provision on its face, permits some form of retroactive action. We cannot accept the Secretary's argument, however, that it provides authority for the retroactive promulgation of cost-limit rules. To the contrary, we agree with the Court of Appeals that clause (ii) directs the Secretary to establish a procedure for making case-by-case adjustments to reimbursement payments where the regulations prescribing computation methods do not reach the correct result in individual cases. The structure and language of the statute require the conclusion that the retroactivity provision applies only to case-by-case adjudication, not to rulemaking.

Section 1395x(v)(1)(A), of which clause (ii) is a part, directs the Secretary to promulgate regulations (including cost-limit rules) establishing the methods to be used in determining reasonable costs for "institutions" and "providers" that participate in the Medicare program. Clause (i) of § 1395x(v)(1)(A) requires these cost-method regulations to take into account both direct and indirect costs incurred by "providers." Clause (ii) mandates that the cost-method regulations include a mechanism for making retroactive corrective adjustments. These adjustments are required when, for *"a provider,"* the "aggregate reimbursement produced by the methods of determining costs" is too low or too high. By its terms, then, clause (ii) contemplates a mechanism for adjusting the reimbursement received by a provider, while the remainder of § 1395x(v)(1)(A) speaks exclusively in the plural. The distinction suggests that clause (ii), rather than permitting modifications to the cost-method rules in their general formulation, is intended to authorize case-by-case inquiry into the accuracy of reimbursement determinations for individual providers. Indeed, it is difficult to see how a corrective adjustment could be made to the aggregate reimbursement paid "a provider" without performing an individual examination of the provider's expenditures in retrospect.

Our conclusion is buttressed by the statute's use of the term "adjustments." Clause (ii) states that the cost-method regulations shall "provide for the making of ... adjustments." In order to derive from this language the authority to promulgate cost-limit rules, the "adjustments" that the cost-method regulations must "provide for the making of" would themselves be additional cost-method regulations. Had Congress intended the Secretary to promulgate regulations providing for the issuance of further amendatory regulations, we think this intent would have been made explicit.

<h2 style="text-align:center">B</h2>

The statutory provisions establishing the Secretary's general rulemaking power contain no express authorization of retroactive rulemaking.[3] Any

**3.** Section 223(b) of the 1972 amendments amended the Medicare Act to state that the Secretary's regulations for computing reasonable costs may:

"provide for the establishment of limits on the direct or indirect overall incurred costs or incurred costs of specific items or services or groups of items or services to be recognized as reasonable based on estimates of the costs necessary in the efficient delivery of needed health services to individuals covered by the insurance programs established under this subchapter...." 42 U.S.C. § 1395x(v)(1)(A).

Section 1395hh provides that "[t]he Secretary shall prescribe such regulations as may be necessary to carry out the administration of the insurance programs under this subchapter." Finally, § 1395ii incorporates 42 U.S.C. § 405(a), which provides that

light that might be shed on this matter by suggestions of legislative intent also indicates that no such authority was contemplated. In the first place, where Congress intended to grant the Secretary the authority to act retroactively, it made that intent explicit. As discussed above, § 1395x(v)(1)(A)(ii) directs the Secretary to establish procedures for making retroactive corrective adjustments; in view of this indication that Congress considered the need for retroactive agency action, the absence of any express authorization for retroactive cost-limit rules weighs heavily against the Secretary's position.

The legislative history of the cost-limit provision directly addresses the issue of retroactivity. In discussing the authority granted by § 223(b) of the 1972 amendments, the House and Senate Committee Reports expressed a desire to forbid retroactive cost-limit rules: "The proposed new authority to set limits on costs ... would be exercised on a prospective, rather than retrospective, basis so that the provider would know in advance the limits to Government recognition of incurred costs and have the opportunity to act to avoid having costs that are not reimbursable." H.R.Rep. No. 92–231, p. 83 (1971); see S.Rep. No. 92–1230, p. 188 (1972).

[The concurring opinion of Justice Scalia is omitted.]

### Questions

**1.**  The unanimous *Bowen* court declared: "Retroactivity is not favored in the law. Thus, congressional enactments and administrative rules will not be construed to have retroactive effect unless their language requires this result." Is this consistent with *Bradley* (also a unanimous decision)? With *Bennett*? How would you reconcile the three decisions?

**2.**  What difference to the analysis might it make that *Bowen* involved an administrative interpretation of a statute, rather than a statute directly interpreted by courts?

## Kaiser Aluminum & Chem. Corp. v. Bonjorno

Supreme Court of the United States, 1990.
494 U.S. 827, 110 S.Ct. 1570, 108 L.Ed.2d 842.

■ JUSTICE O'CONNOR delivered the opinion of the Court.

We are called upon in these cases to decide the applicable rate of postjudgment interest and the date from which postjudgment interest should be calculated pursuant to the federal postjudgment interest statute. 28 U.S.C. § 1961 (1982 ed.) (amended).

### I

Respondents (Bonjorno) were the sole stockholders of now defunct Columbia Metal Culvert Co., Inc., which was at one time a fabricator of

"[t]he Secretary shall have full power and authority to make rules and regulations ... , not inconsistent with the provisions of this subchapter, which are necessary or appropriate to carry out such provisions. . . ."

aluminum drainage pipe in Vineland, New Jersey. Bonjorno brought suit against petitioners (Kaiser) in the United States District Court for the Eastern District of Pennsylvania on the theory that Kaiser had monopolized the market for aluminum drainage pipe in the Mid–Atlantic region of the United States in violation of the Sherman Act. 26 Stat. 209, as amended, 15 U.S.C. §§ 1 and 2.

At the first trial, the District Court entered a directed verdict for Kaiser. The Court of Appeals for the Third Circuit reversed, holding that there was sufficient evidence for the case to go to the jury. Columbia Metal Culvert Co. v. Kaiser Aluminum & Chemical Corp., 579 F.2d 20, 37 (1978).

On August 21, 1979, a second trial resulted in a jury verdict in Bonjorno's favor in the trebled amount of $5,445,000. The judgment was entered on August 22, 1979. The District Court held that the evidence did not support the jury's damages award and granted Kaiser's motion for a new trial as to damages only. Bonjorno v. Kaiser Aluminum & Chemical Corp., 518 F.Supp. 102, 109, 119 (E.D.Pa.1981). A limited retrial on damages resulted in a jury award on December 2, 1981, in the trebled amount of $9,567,939. Judgment was entered on December 4, 1981. On January 17, 1983, the District Court granted Kaiser's motion for judgment notwithstanding the verdict as to a portion of the damages awarded by the jury. Bonjorno v. Kaiser Aluminum & Chemical Corp., 559 F.Supp. 922 (E.D.Pa.1983). Bonjorno appealed the reduction in damages, and the Court of Appeals reversed the District Court's partial grant of Kaiser's motion for judgment notwithstanding the verdict as to damages, vacated the judgment, and reinstated and affirmed the judgment entered on December 4, 1981. Bonjorno v. Kaiser Aluminum & Chemical Corp., 752 F.2d 802, 815 (C.A.3 1984). Kaiser's petition for rehearing in banc was denied, 1985, 1 CCH Trade Cases ¶ 66,551 (CA3 1985), as was its subsequent petition for certiorari to this Court. Kaiser Aluminum & Chemical Corp. v. Bonjorno, 477 U.S. 908, 91 L.Ed.2d 572, 106 S.Ct. 3284 (1986).

The Court of Appeals did not refer in its opinion to the allowance of postjudgment interest; Bonjorno petitioned the Court of Appeals for instructions regarding interest to be included in the mandate pursuant to Federal Rule of Appellate Procedure 37, which permits courts of appeals to direct payment of interest commencing with the entry of judgment in the district court unless otherwise provided by law. Before the Court of Appeals could rule on the petition, the parties entered into a stipulation providing that the District Court first address all issues of interest allowable under 28 U.S.C. § 1961 and Federal Rule of Appellate Procedure 37. The Court of Appeals approved the stipulation and certified the judgment in lieu of a formal mandate. On July 1, 1986, the mandate of the Court of Appeals, stayed pending disposition of Kaiser's petition for a writ of certiorari with this Court, was issued to the District Court. On July 3, 1986, Kaiser paid Bonjorno $9,567,939, the trebled amount of damages awarded by the jury on December 2, 1981.

The federal statute governing awards of postjudgment interest in effect at the time Bonjorno filed the complaint on January 17, 1974, and until October 1, 1982, provided:

"Interest shall be allowed on any money judgment in a civil case recovered in a district court. Execution therefor may be levied by the marshal, in any case where, by the law of the State in which such court is held, execution may be levied from interest on judgments recovered in the courts of the State. Such interest shall be calculated from the date of the entry of judgment, at the rate allowed by State law." 28 U.S.C. § 1961 (1976 ed.).

On April 2, 1982, Congress passed the Federal Courts Improvement Act of 1982, Pub.L. 97–164, 96 Stat. 25, § 302 of which amended 28 U.S.C. § 1961. To permit courts and the bar to prepare themselves for the changes wrought by the Act, Congress delayed its effective date by six months to October 1, 1982. § 402, 96 Stat. 57. The amended version provides:

"(a) Interest shall be allowed on any money judgment in a civil case recovered in a district court. Execution therefor may be levied by the marshal, in any case where, by the law of the State in which such court is held, execution may be levied for interest on judgments recovered in the courts of the State. Such interest shall be calculated from the date of the entry of the judgment, at a rate equal to the coupon issue yield equivalent (as determined by the Secretary of the Treasury) of the average accepted auction price for the last auction of fifty-two week United States Treasury bills settled immediately prior to the date of the judgment. The Director of the Administrative Office of the United States Courts shall distribute notice of that rate and any changes in it to all Federal judges.

"(b) Interest shall be computed daily to the date of payment except as provided in section 2516(b) of this title and section 1304(b) of title 31, and shall be compounded annually." 28 U.S.C. § 1961 (1982 ed.).

The District Court held that 28 U.S.C. § 1961 required interest to be calculated from December 2, 1981, the date of the damages verdict on which the correct judgment would have been entered but for the District Court's erroneous partial grant of judgment notwithstanding the verdict. App. to Pet. for Cert. A–31, A–36 to A–41. See Poleto v. Consolidated Rail Corp., 826 F.2d 1270, 1280 (C.A.3 1987) (interest calculated from date of verdict rather than judgment); Institutionalized Juveniles v. Secretary of Public Welfare, 758 F.2d 897, 927 (C.A.3 1985) (interest calculated from date correct award would have been entered but for the District Court's error). The District Court rejected Bonjorno's argument that the amended version of § 1961 should be applied for the purpose of determining the applicable interest rate under Bradley v. Richmond School Bd., 416 U.S. 696, 40 L.Ed.2d 476, 94 S.Ct. 2006 (1974) (courts are to apply the law in effect at the time a court renders its decision unless such application results in manifest injustice or runs contrary to congressional intent), reasoning that application of amended § 1961 would result in manifest injustice. Thus, the District Court applied the earlier version of § 1961, which set the interest rate allowed by state law. App. to Pet. for Cert., at A–41 to A–50. At that time, Pennsylvania provided for a 6 percent rate of interest. 42 Pa.Cons.Stat. § 8101 (1988); Pa.Stat.Ann., Tit. 41, § 202 (Purdon Supp.1989).

The Court of Appeals affirmed the District Court's determination that interest should be calculated from December 2, 1981, but reversed the District Court on the issue of which version of § 1961 applied. The Court of Appeals invoked the rule in *Bradley, supra,* that a court should apply the law in effect at the time a court renders its decision, but noted that "the *Bradley* presumption of applying the law in effect at the time a court renders its decision in the absence of contrary legislative intent seems inconsistent with the longstanding rule of statutory construction that statutes are presumed to have only 'prospective' effect and will be given 'retroactive' effect only if there is affirmative legislative direction to do so." 865 F.2d 566, 573 (C.A.3 1989). Finding the legislative history unclear and that application of the amended § 1961 would not result in manifest injustice, the Court of Appeals held that the *Bradley* presumption required application of the amended § 1961 in effect at the time the District Court and the Court of Appeals reached their decisions.

<h2 style="text-align:center">III</h2>

The Court in Bradley v. Richmond School Bd., 416 U.S. 696, 40 L.Ed.2d 476, 94 S.Ct. 2006 (1974), faced the issue whether an attorney's fees statute that went into effect during the pendency of the appeal was to be applied by the appellate court. Relying on Thorpe v. Housing Authority of Durham, 393 U.S. 268, 21 L.Ed.2d 474, 89 S.Ct. 518 (1969), the Court held that "a court is to apply the law in effect at the time it renders its decision." 416 U.S., at 711, 40 L.Ed.2d 476, 94 S.Ct. 2006. The Court derived this holding from a broad reading of United States v. Schooner Peggy, 1 Cranch 103, 2 L.Ed. 49 (1801), in which the following principles were articulated:

> "[I]f subsequent to the judgment, and before the decision of the appellate court, a law intervenes and positively changes the rule which governs, the law must be obeyed.... It is true that in mere private cases between individuals, a court will and ought to struggle hard against a construction which will, by a retrospective operation, affect the rights of parties, but in great national concerns ... the court must decide according to existing laws." Id., at 110, 2 L.Ed. 49.

Under the rule set forth in *Schooner Peggy,* an amendment to the law while a case was pending should be applied by the appellate court only if, "by its terms," the law was to be applied to pending cases. See *Bradley, supra,* at 712, 40 L.Ed.2d 476, 94 S.Ct. 2006. In *Thorpe, supra,* the Court broadened the rule set forth in *Schooner Peggy*: "[E]ven where the intervening law does not explicitly recite that it is to be applied to pending cases, it is to be given recognition and effect." *Bradley, supra,* at 715, 40 L.Ed.2d 476, 94 S.Ct. 2006. As a means of softening the potentially harsh impact of this broadening retrospective application of congressional enactments, the

Court recognized two exceptions to the presumption that courts are to apply the law in effect at the time of decision. The presumption does not govern where retrospective application would result in manifest injustice to one of the parties or where there is clear congressional intent to the contrary. See 416 U.S., at 711, 40 L.Ed.2d 476, 94 S.Ct. 2006. The Court of Appeals applied the *Bradley* test and held that the legislative history was ambiguous and that retrospective application of amended § 1961 did not result in manifest injustice.

In apparent tension with the rule articulated in *Bradley, supra,* is our recent reaffirmation of the generally accepted axiom that "[r]etroactivity is not favored in the law. . . . [C]ongressional enactments and administrative rules will not be construed to have retroactive effect unless their language requires this result." Bowen v. Georgetown University Hospital, 488 U.S. 204, 208, 102 L.Ed.2d 493, 109 S.Ct. 468 (1988). In Georgetown University Hospital, we held that the Department of Health and Human Services did not have the power to promulgate retroactive cost-limit rules, because authority to issue retroactive rules was not authorized by Congress in the Medicare Act. Id., at 208–216, 102 L.Ed.2d 493, 109 S.Ct. 468.

We need not in this case, however, reconcile the two lines of precedent represented by *Bradley, supra,* and *Georgetown, supra,* because under either view, where the congressional intent is clear, it governs. See *Bradley, supra,* at 716–717, 40 L.Ed.2d 476, 94 S.Ct. 2006 (intervening statute applies retroactively unless a contrary intention appears); *Georgetown, supra,* at 208, 102 L.Ed.2d 493, 109 S.Ct. 468 (statute does not apply retroactively unless its language requires it). We conclude that the plain language of both the original and amended versions of § 1961 evidences clear congressional intent that amended § 1961 is not applicable to judgments entered before its effective date.

■ JUSTICE SCALIA, concurring.

I join the Court's opinion because I agree that this statute, 28 U.S.C. § 196 (1982 ed.), contains positive indication that its operation is to be prospective. In my view, however, that indication is unnecessary to our determination. I regret that the Court has chosen not to resolve the conflict between two relatively recent cases saying that unless there is specific indication to the contrary a new statute should be applied retroactively absent "manifest injustice," Bradley v. Richmond School Bd., 416 U.S. 696, 716, 40 L.Ed.2d 476, 94 S.Ct. 2006 (1974); Thorpe v. Housing Authority of Durham, 393 U.S. 268, 282, 21 L.Ed.2d 474, 89 S.Ct. 518 (1969), and the many cases, old and new, which have said that unless there is specific indication to the contrary a new statute should be applied only prospectively, e.g., Bowen v. Georgetown University Hospital, 488 U.S. 204, 208, 102 L.Ed.2d 493, 109 S.Ct. 468 (1988); United States v. American Sugar Refining Co., 202 U.S. 563, 577, 50 L.Ed. 1149, 26 S.Ct. 717 (1906). In the rules of construction that they announce, if not in the results they produce, these two lines of cases are not merely, as the Court confesses, in "apparent tension," ante, at 837, 108 L.Ed.2d, at 853; they are in irreconcilable contradiction, and have spawned Courts of Appeals opinions to match.

Compare, e.g., Davis v. Omitowoju, 883 F.2d 1155, 1170–1171 (C.A.3 1989), and Anderson v. USAIR, Inc., 260 U.S.App.D.C. 183, 187, 818 F.2d 49, 53 (1987), with United States v. R.W. Meyer, Inc., 889 F.2d 1497, 1505–1506 (C.A.6 1989), and United States v. Marengo County Comm'n, 731 F.2d 1546, 1553–1555 (C.A.11), appeal dism'd, 469 U.S. 976, 83 L.Ed.2d 311, 105 S.Ct. 375 (1984). Since the issue has been briefed and argued in this case, I would have taken the occasion to admit that the rule we expressed in *Thorpe* and *Bradley* was wrong.

■ JUSTICE WHITE, with whom JUSTICE BRENNAN, JUSTICE MARSHALL, and JUSTICE BLACKMUN join, dissenting.

The Court today holds that the amended version of the federal post-judgment interest statute, 28 U.S.C. § 1961 (1982 ed.), does not apply to a judgment entered before the effective date of the amendment, even though the litigation was still pending when the amendment took effect and the District Court calculated the amount of postjudgment interest long after the effective date. Because I cannot concur in the Court's decision denying effect to an important ameliorative federal statute in precisely the kind of situation demonstrating the need for the amendment, I respectfully dissent.

**Questions**

**1.** What do the dissenters mean when they object that the majority's decision "den[ies] effect to an important ameliorative federal statute in precisely the kind of situation demonstrating the need for the amendment?" What goals does a postjudgment interest rate promote? Given those goals, at what moment should a rate change attach? What difference does it make which rate applies?

**2.** How do the *Bradley*, *Bennett*, and *Bowen* presumptions fare under *Bonjorno*? Is it possible to reconcile all four decisions, or is the caselaw in "irreconcilable contradiction?" *Should* the *Bonjorno* court have endeavored to resolve the "tension" in its retroactivity jurisprudence?

## 2.   PROBLEM: RETROACTIVITY OF DAMAGES PROVISIONS OF THE 1991 CIVIL RIGHTS ACT

Do the compensatory and punitive damages provisions of the 1991 amendments to the 1964 Civil Rights Act apply to employment discrimination claims arising before the 1991 law's enactment?

To answer this question it is necessary, first, to work your way through the prior statutory regime, in order to understand what the law had been. In particular, what kinds of facts gave rise to a Title VII claim, and how was that claim pursued? Then, after analyzing the 1991 amendments, you should be able to perceive how the law changed.

As you review the following statutory text you should identify:

– What conduct does the statute prohibit?

– What, if any, defenses does the statute set out?

– When and where are claims filed? What administrative and/or judicial bodies address Title VII claims?

(It may be helpful to make a timetable to follow the steps of an enforcement proceeding.)

– What is the remedial scheme?

A related civil rights provision is the Reconstruction-era statute set out at 42 U.S.C. § 1981:

### § 1981.  Equal Rights Under The Law

(a) Statement of equal rights. All persons within the jurisdiction of the United States shall have the same right in every State and Territory to make and enforce contracts, to sue, be parties, give evidence, and to the full and equal benefit of all laws and proceedings for the security of persons and property as is enjoyed by white citizens, and shall be subject to like punishment, pains, penalties, taxes, licenses, and exactions of every kind, and to no other.

Beginning in 1976, the Supreme Court has construed § 1981's language to afford a tort claim against private actors who refused to contract with the plaintiff on grounds of race. See Runyon v. McCrary, 427 U.S. 160 (1976) (claim against private schools denying admission to African–American children). The right to "make and enforce contracts" has also been applied generally to race discrimination in employment, see, e.g., Carter v. Gallagher, 452 F.2d 315 (8th Cir.1971).

Section 1981 contained no provisions limiting the nature or amount of remedies afforded for its violation. As a result, claims under Section 1981 could supply additional remedies to Title VII plaintiffs who qualified under both statutes. See, e.g., Hernandez v. Hill Country Tel. Cooperative, Inc., 849 F.2d 139 (5th Cir.1988). The claimant overlap, however, extended only to plaintiffs alleging race discrimination; Section 1981 has not been construed to afford claims for refusal to contract on grounds of sex, religion or national origin.

a.  TITLE VII: STATUTORY TEXT

i.  *The State of the Law Before the 1991 Civil Rights Act*

## Civil Rights Act of 1964, Title VII (As Amended Through 1978)(Excerpts)

42 U.S.C. §§ 2000e–2–5

### § 2000e–2. Unlawful employment practices [Title VII, § 703]
### Employer practices

(a) It shall be an unlawful employment practice for an employer—

(1) to fail or refuse to hire or to discharge any individual, or otherwise to discriminate against any individual with respect to his compensation, terms, conditions, or privileges of employment, because of such individual's race, color, religion, sex, or national origin; or

(2) to limit, segregate, or classify his employees or applicants for employment in any way which would deprive or tend to deprive any individual of employment opportunities or otherwise adversely affect his status as an employee, because of such individual's race, color, religion, sex, or national origin.

\* \* \*

## Businesses or enterprises with personnel qualified on basis of religion, sex, or national origin; educational institutions with personnel of particular religion

(e) Notwithstanding any other provision of this subchapter, (1) it shall not be an unlawful employment practice for an employer to hire and employ employees, for an employment agency to classify or refer for employment any individual, for a labor organization to classify its membership or to classify or refer for employment any individual, or for an employer, labor organization, or joint labor-management committee controlling apprenticeship or other training or retraining programs to admit or employ any individual in any such program, on the basis of his religion, sex, or national origin in those certain instances where religion, sex, or national origin is a bona fide occupational qualification reasonably necessary to the normal operation of that particular business or enterprise, and (2) it shall not be an unlawful employment practice for a school, college, university, or other educational institution or institution of learning to hire and employ employees of a particular religion if such school, college, university, or other educational institution or institution of learning is, in whole or in substantial part, owned, supported, controlled, or managed by a particular religion or by a particular religious corporation, association, or society, or if the curriculum of such school, college, university, or other educational institution or institution of learning is directed toward the propagation of a particular religion.

\* \* \*

## Seniority or merit system; quantity or quality of production; ability tests; compensation based on sex and authorized by minimum wage provisions

(h) Notwithstanding any other provision of this subchapter, it shall not be an unlawful employment practice for an employer to apply different standards of compensation, or different terms, conditions, or privileges of employment pursuant to a bona fide seniority or merit system, or a system which measures earnings by quantity or quality of production or to employees who work in different locations, provided that such differences are not the result of an intention to discriminate because of race, color, religion, sex, or national origin, nor shall it be an unlawful employment practice for an employer to give and to act upon the results of any professionally developed ability test provided that such test, its administration or action upon the results is not designed, intended or used to discriminate because of race, color, religion, sex or national origin. It shall not be an unlawful employment practice under this subchapter for any employer to differentiate upon the basis of sex in determining the amount of the wages or compensation paid or to be paid to employees of such employer if such differentiation is authorized by the provisions of section 206(d) of Title 29.

* * *

### (k) Definitions

The terms "because of sex" or "on the basis of sex" include, but are not limited to, because of or on the basis of pregnancy, childbirth, or related medical conditions; and women affected by pregnancy, childbirth, or related medical conditions shall be treated the same for all employment-related purposes, including receipt of benefits under fringe benefit programs, as other persons not so affected but similar in their ability or inability to work, and nothing in section 2000e–2(h) of this title shall be interpreted to permit otherwise. . . .

* * *

### § 2000e–4. Equal Employment Opportunity Commission [Title VII, § 705]

### Creation; composition; political representation; appointment; term; vacancies; Chairman and Vice Chairman; duties of Chairman; appointment of personnel; compensation of personnel

(a) There is hereby created a Commission to be known as the Equal Employment Opportunity Commission, which shall be composed of five members, not more than three of whom shall be members of the same political party. Members of the Commission shall be appointed by the President by and with the advice and consent of the Senate for a term of five years. Any individual chosen to fill a vacancy shall be appointed only for the unexpired term of the member whom he shall succeed, and all members of the Commission shall continue to serve until their successors are appointed and qualified, except that no such member of the Commission shall continue to serve (1) for more than sixty days when the Congress is in session unless a nomination to fill such vacancy shall have been submitted to the Senate, or (2) after the adjournment sine die of the session of the Senate in which such nomination was submitted. The President shall designate one member to serve as Chairman of the Commission, and one member to serve as Vice Chairman. The Chairman shall be responsible on behalf of the Commission for the administrative operations of the Commission, and, except as provided in subsection (b) of this section, shall appoint, in accordance with the provisions of Title 5 governing appointments in the competitive service, such officers, agents, attorneys, administrative law judges, and employees as he deems necessary to assist it in the performance of its functions and to fix their compensation in accordance with the provisions of chapter 51 and subchapter III of chapter 53 of Title 5, relating to classification and General Schedule pay rates: *Provided,* That assignment, removal, and compensation of administrative law judges shall be in accordance with sections 3105, 3344, 5372, and 7521 of Title 5.

### General Counsel; appointment; term; duties; representation by attorneys and Attorney General

(b)(1) There shall be a General Counsel of the Commission appointed by the President, by and with the advice and consent of the Senate, for a term of four years. The General Counsel shall have responsibility for the conduct of litigation as provided in sections 2000e–5 and 2000e–6 of this title. The General Counsel shall have such other duties as the Commission may prescribe or as may be provided by law and shall concur with the Chairman of the Commission on the appointment and supervision of regional attorneys. The General Counsel of the Commission on the effective date of this Act shall continue in such position and perform the functions specified in this subsection until a successor is appointed and qualified.

(2) Attorneys appointed under this section may, at the direction of the Commission, appear for and represent the Commission in any case in court, provided that the Attorney General shall conduct all litigation to which the Commission is a party in the Supreme Court pursuant to this subchapter.

\* \* \*

### Powers of Commission

(g) The Commission shall have power—

(1) to cooperate with and, with their consent, utilize regional, State, local, and other agencies, both public and private, and individuals;

(2) to pay to witnesses whose depositions are taken or who are summoned before the Commission or any of its agents the same witness and mileage fees as are paid to witnesses in the courts of the United States;

(3) to furnish to persons subject to this subchapter such technical assistance as they may request to further their compliance with this subchapter or an order issued thereunder;

(4) upon the request of (i) any employer, whose employees or some of them, or (ii) any labor organization, whose members or some of them, refuse or threaten to refuse to cooperate in effectuating the provisions of this subchapter, to assist in such effectuation by conciliation or such other remedial action as is provided by this subchapter;

(5) to make such technical studies as are appropriate to effectuate the purposes and policies of this subchapter and to make the results of such studies available to the public;

(6) to intervene in a civil action brought under section 2000e–5 of this title by an aggrieved party against a respondent other than a government, governmental agency or political subdivision.

### Cooperation with other departments and agencies in performance of educational or promotional activities

(h) The Commission shall, in any of its educational or promotional activities, cooperate with other departments and agencies in the performance of such educational and promotional activities.

### Personnel subject to political activity restrictions

(i) All officers, agents, attorneys, and employees of the Commission shall be subject to the provisions of section 7324 of Title 5, notwithstanding any exemption contained in such section.

### § 2000e–5. Enforcement provisions [Title VII, § 706]

### Power of Commission to prevent unlawful employment practices

(a) The Commission is empowered, as hereinafter provided, to prevent any person from engaging in any unlawful employment practice as set forth in section 2000e–2 or 2000e–3 of this title.

### Charges by persons aggrieved or member of Commission of unlawful employment practices by employers, etc.; filing; allegations; notice to respondent; contents of notice; investigation by Commission; contents of charges; prohibition on disclosure of charges; determination of reasonable cause; conference, conciliation, and persuasion for elimination of unlawful practices; prohibition on disclosure of informal endeavors to end unlawful practices; use of evidence in subsequent proceedings; penalties for disclosure of information; time for determination of reasonable cause

(b) Whenever a charge is filed by or on behalf of a person claiming to be aggrieved, or by a member of the Commission, alleging that an employer, employment agency, labor organization, or joint labor-management committee controlling apprenticeship or other training or retraining, including on-the-job training programs, has engaged in an unlawful employment practice, the Commission shall serve a notice of the charge (including the date, place and circumstances of the alleged unlawful employment practice) on such employer, employment agency, labor organization, or joint labor-management committee (hereinafter referred to as the "respondent") within ten days, and shall make an investigation thereof. Charges shall be in writing under oath or affirmation and shall contain such information and be in such form as the Commission requires. Charges shall not be made public by the Commission. If the Commission determines after such investigation that there is not reasonable cause to believe that the charge is true, it shall dismiss the charge and promptly notify the person claiming to be aggrieved and the respondent of its action. In determining whether reasonable cause exists, the Commission shall accord substantial weight to final findings and orders made by State or local authorities in proceedings commenced under State or local law pursuant to the requirements of subsections (c) and (d) of this section. If the Commission determines after such investigation that there is reasonable cause to believe that the charge is true, the Commission shall endeavor to eliminate any such alleged unlawful employment practice by informal methods of conference, conciliation, and persuasion. Nothing said or done during and as a part of such informal endeavors may be made public by the Commission, its officers or employees, or used as evidence in a subsequent proceeding without the written consent of the persons concerned. Any person who makes public information in violation of this subsection shall be fined not more than $1,000 or imprisoned for not more than one year, or both. The Commission shall make its determination on reasonable cause as promptly as possible and, so far as practicable, not later than one hundred and twenty days from the filing of the charge or, where applicable under subsection (c) or (d) of this section, from the date upon which the Commission is authorized to take action with respect to the charge.

### State or local enforcement proceedings; notification of State or local authority; time for filing charges with Commission; commencement of proceedings

(c) In the case of an alleged unlawful employment practice occurring in a State, or political subdivision of a State, which has a State or local law prohibiting the unlawful employment practice alleged and establishing or authorizing a State or local authority to grant or seek relief from such practice or to institute criminal proceedings with respect thereto upon receiving notice thereof, no charge may be filed under subsection (b) of this section by the person aggrieved before the expiration of sixty days after proceedings have been commenced under the State or local law, unless such proceedings have been earlier terminated, provided that such sixty-day period shall be extended to one hundred and twenty days during the first year after the effective date of such State or local law. If any requirement for the commencement of such proceedings is imposed by a State or local authority other than a requirement of the filing of a written and signed statement of the facts upon which the proceeding is based, the proceeding shall be deemed to have been commenced for the purposes of this subsection at the time such statement is sent by registered mail to the appropriate State or local authority.

### State or local enforcement proceedings; notification of State or local authority; time for action on charges by Commission

(d) In the case of any charge filed by a member of the Commission alleging an unlawful employment practice occurring in a State or political subdivision of a State which has a State or local law prohibiting the practice alleged and establishing or authorizing a State or local authority to grant or seek relief from such practice or to institute criminal proceedings with respect thereto upon receiving notice thereof, the Commission shall, before taking any action with respect to such charge, notify the appropriate State or local officials and, upon request, afford them a reasonable time, but not less than sixty days (provided that such sixty-day period shall be extended to one hundred and twenty days during the first year after the effective [date] of such State or local law), unless a shorter period is requested, to act under such State or local law to remedy the practice alleged.

### Time for filing charges; time for service of notice of charge on respondent; filing of charge by Commission with State or local agency

(e) A charge under this section shall be filed within one hundred and eighty days after the alleged unlawful employment practice occurred and notice of the charge (including the date, place and circumstances of the alleged unlawful employment practice) shall be served upon the person against whom such charge is made within ten days thereafter, except that in a case of an unlawful employment practice with respect to which the person aggrieved has initially instituted proceedings with a State or local agency with authority to grant or seek relief from such practice or to institute criminal proceedings with respect thereto upon receiving notice thereof, such charge shall be filed by or on behalf of the person aggrieved within three hundred days after the alleged unlawful employment practice occurred, or within thirty days after receiving notice that the State or local agency has terminated the proceedings under the State or local law, whichever is earlier, and a copy of such charge shall be filed by the Commission with the State or local agency.

### Civil action by Commission, Attorney General, or person aggrieved; preconditions; procedure; appointment of attorney; payment of fees, costs, or security; intervention; stay of Federal Proceedings; action for appropriate temporary or preliminary relief pending final disposition of charge; jurisdiction and venue of United States courts; designation of judge to hear and determine case; assignment of case for hearing; expedition of case; appointment of master

(f)(1) If within thirty days after a charge is filed with the Commission or within thirty days after expiration of any period of reference under subsection (c) or (d) of this section, the Commission has been unable to secure from the respondent a conciliation agreement acceptable to the Commission, the Commission may bring a civil action against any respondent not a government, governmental agency, or political subdivision named in the charge. In the case of a respondent which is a government, governmental agency, or political subdivision, if the Commission has been unable to secure from the respondent a conciliation agreement acceptable to the Commission, the Commission shall take no further action and shall refer the case to the Attorney General who may bring a civil action against such respondent in the appropriate United States district court. The person or persons aggrieved shall have the right to intervene in a civil action brought by the Commission or the Attorney General in a case involving a government, governmental agency, or political subdivision. If a charge filed with the Commission pursuant to subsection (b) of this section is dismissed by the Commission, or if within one hundred and eighty days from the filing of such charge or the expiration of any period of reference under subsection (c) or (d) of this section, whichever is later, the Commission has not filed a civil action under this section or the Attorney General has not filed a civil action in a case involving a government, governmental agency, or political subdivision, or the Commission has not entered into a conciliation agreement to which the person aggrieved is a party, the Commission, or the Attorney General in a case involving a government, governmental agency, or political subdivision, shall so notify the person aggrieved and within ninety days after the giving of such notice a civil action may be brought against the respondent named in the charge (A) by the person claiming to be aggrieved or (B) if such charge was filed by a member of the Commission, by any person whom the charge alleges was aggrieved by the alleged unlawful employment practice. Upon application by the complainant and in such circumstances as the court may deem just, the court may appoint an attorney for such complainant, and may authorize the commencement of the action without the payment of fees, costs, or security. Upon timely application, the court may, in its discretion, permit the Commission, or the Attorney General in a case involving a government, governmental agency, or political subdivision, to intervene in such civil action upon certification that the case is of general public importance. Upon request, the court may, in its discretion, stay further proceedings for not more than sixty days pending the termination of State or local proceedings described in subsection (c) or (d) of this section or further efforts of the Commission to obtain voluntary compliance.

(2) Whenever a charge is filed with the Commission and the Commission concludes on the basis of a preliminary investigation that prompt judicial action is necessary to carry out the purposes of this Act, the Commission, or the Attorney General in a case involving a government, governmental agency, or political subdivision, may bring an action for appropriate temporary or preliminary relief pending final disposition of such charge. Any temporary restraining order or other order granting preliminary or temporary relief shall be issued in accordance with rule 65 of the Federal Rules of Civil Procedure. It shall be the duty of a court having jurisdiction over proceedings under this section to assign cases for hearing at the earliest practicable date and to cause such cases to be in every way expedited.

(3) Each United States district court and each United States court of a place subject to the jurisdiction of the United States shall have jurisdiction of actions brought under this subchapter. Such an action may be brought in any judicial district in the State in which the unlawful employment practice is alleged to have been committed, in the judicial district in which the employment records relevant to such practice are maintained and administered, or in the judicial district in which the aggrieved person would have worked but for the alleged unlawful employment practice, but if the

respondent is not found within any such district, such an action may be brought within the judicial district in which the respondent has his principal office. For purposes of sections 1404 and 1406 of Title 28, the judicial district in which the respondent has his principal office shall in all cases be considered a district in which the action might have been brought.

(4) It shall be the duty of the chief judge of the district (or in his absence, the acting chief judge) in which the case is pending immediately to designate a judge in such district to hear and determine the case. In the event that no judge in the district is available to hear and determine the case, the chief judge of the district, or the acting chief judge, as the case may be, shall certify this fact to the chief judge of the circuit (or in his absence, the acting chief judge) who shall then designate a district or circuit judge of the circuit to hear and determine the case.

(5) It shall be the duty of the judge designated pursuant to this subsection to assign the case for hearing at the earliest practicable date and to cause the case to be in every way expedited. If such judge has not scheduled the case for trial within one hundred and twenty days after issue has been joined, that judge may appoint a master pursuant to rule 53 of the Federal Rules of Civil Procedure.

### Injunctions; appropriate affirmative action; equitable relief; accrual of back pay; reduction of back pay; limitations on judicial orders

(g) If the court finds that the respondent has intentionally engaged in or is intentionally engaging in an unlawful employment practice charged in the complaint, the court may enjoin the respondent from engaging in such unlawful employment practice, and order such affirmative action as may be appropriate, which may include, but is not limited to, reinstatement or hiring of employees, with or without back pay (payable by the employer, employment agency, or labor organization, as the case may be, responsible for the unlawful employment practice), or any other equitable relief as the court deems appropriate. Back pay liability shall not accrue from a date more than two years prior to the filing of a charge with the Commission. Interim earnings or amounts earnable with reasonable diligence by the person or persons discriminated against shall operate to reduce the back pay otherwise allowable. No order of the court shall require the admission or reinstatement of an individual as a member of a union, or the hiring, reinstatement, or promotion of an individual as an employee, or the payment to him of any back pay, if such individual was refused admission, suspended, or expelled, or was refused employment or advancement or was suspended or discharged for any reason other than discrimination on account of race, color, religion, sex, or national origin or in violation of section 2000e–3(a) of this title.

. . .

### Proceedings by Commission to compel compliance with judicial orders

(i) In any case in which an employer, employment agency, or labor organization fails to comply with an order of a court issued in a civil action brought under this section, the Commission may commence proceedings to compel compliance with such order.

## Appeals

(j) Any civil action brought under this section and any proceedings brought under subsection (i) of this section shall be subject to appeal as provided in sections 1291 and 1292, Title 28.

## Attorney's fee; liability of Commission and United States for costs

(k) In any action or proceeding under this subchapter the court, in its discretion, may allow the prevailing party, other than the Commission or the United States, a reasonable attorney's fee as part of the costs, and the Commission and the United States shall be liable for costs the same as a private person.

## ii.   The Remedial Scheme Put in Place by the 1991 Amendments

### Civil Rights Act of 1991, Pub.l. 102–166, Nov. 21, 1991, 105 Stat. 1071 (excerpts)

### Sec. 2. Findings

The Congress finds that—

(1) additional remedies under Federal law are needed to deter unlawful harassment and intentional discrimination in the workplace . . .

### Sec. 3 Purposes

The purposes of this Act are—

(1) to provide appropriate remedies for intentional discrimination and unlawful harassment in the workplace . . .

### Sec. 102. Damages in cases of intentional discrimination

The Revised Statutes are amended by inserting after section 1977 (42 U.S.C. 1981) the following new section:

### Sec. 1977A. Damages in cases of intentional discrimination in employment

(a) Right of Recovery.—

(1) Civil Rights.—In an action brought by a complaining party under section 706 or 717 of the Civil Rights Act of 1964 (42 U.S.C. 2000e–5) against a respondent who engaged in unlawful intentional discrimination (not an employment practice that is unlawful because of its disparate impact) prohibited under section 704, 704, or 717 of the Act (42 U.S.C. 2000e–2 or 2000e–3), . . . the complaining party may recover compensatory and punitive damages as allowed in subsection (b), in addition to any relief authorized by section 706(g) of the Civil Rights Act of 1964, from the respondent.

(b) Compensatory and Punitive Damages.—

(1) Determination of Punitive Damages.—A complaining party may recover punitive damages under this section against a respondent (other than a government, governmental agency or political subdivision) if the complaining party demonstrates that the respondent engaged in a discriminatory practice or discriminatory practices with malice or with reckless indifference to the federally protected rights of an aggrieved individual.

(2) Exclusions from Compensatory Damages.—Compensatory damages awarded under this section shall not include backpay, interest on backpay, or any other type of relief authorized under section 706(g) of the Civil Rights Act of 1964.

(3) Limitations.—The sum of the amount of compensatory damages awarded under this section for future pecuniary losses, emotional pain, suffering, inconvenience, mental anguish, loss of enjoyment of life, and other nonpecuniary losses, and the amount of punitive damages awarded under this section, shall not exceed, for each complaining party—

(A) in the case of a respondent who has more than 14 and fewer than 101 employees in each of 20 or more calendar weeks in the current or preceding calendar year, $50,000; and

(B) in the case of a respondent who has more than 100 and fewer than 201 employees in each of 20 or more calendar weeks in the current or preceding calendar year, $100,000; and

(C) in the case of a respondent who has more than 200 and fewer than 501 employees in each of 20 or more calendar weeks in the current or preceding calendar year, $200,000; and

(D) in the case of a respondent who has more than 500 employees in each of 20 or more calendar weeks in the current or preceding calendar year, $300,000.

(4) Construction.—Nothing in this section shall be construed to limit the scope of, or the relief available under, section 1977 of the Revised Statutes (42 U.S.C. 1981).

## Question

What remedies do the 1991 amendments to Title VII afford, that prior Title VII did not? What is the highest damages figure available under Title VII? Under claims combining Title VII and § 1981?

## Provisions of the 1991 Act Addressing its Application over Time

## Sec. 402. Effective Date

(a) In General.—Except as otherwise specifically provided, this Act and the amendments made by this act shall take effect upon enactment.

(b) Certain Disparate Impact Cases.—Notwithstanding any other provision of this Act, nothing in this Act shall apply to any disparate impact cases for which a complaint was filed before March 1, 1975, and for which an initial decision was rendered after October 30, 1983.

### Sec. 109. Protection of extraterritorial employment

[setting forth circumstances in which a U.S. employer will be liable for discrimination against persons employed in a foreign country; this provision "overrules" a Supreme Court decision, *EEOC v. Aramco,* 499 U.S. 244 (1991), that had held that Title VII did not apply to U.S. companies discriminatory practices overseas.]

(c) Application of Amendments.—The amendments made by this section shall not apply with respect to conduct occurring before the date of the enactment of this Act.

### Question

Working only from the text of §§ 402 and 109, what do you understand by the phrase "take effect upon enactment"?

*iii.   Legislative History of the Remedies and Effective Date Provisions: Prior Versions*

### H.R. 1

## CIVIL RIGHTS AND WOMEN'S EQUITY IN EMPLOYMENT ACT OF 1991

§§ 206 (damages); 213 (application of amendments and transition rules)

### Sec. 206. Providing for Damages in Cases of Intentional Discrimination.

Section 706(g) of the Civil Rights Act of 1964 (42 U.S.C. 2000e–5(g)) is amended by inserting before the last sentence the following new sentences: "With respect to an unlawful employment practice (other than an unlawful employment practice established in accordance with section 703(k)) or in the case of an unlawful employment practice under the Americans with Disabilities Act of 1990 (other than an unlawful employment practice established in accordance with paragraph (3)(A) or paragraph (6) of section 102 of that Act) as it relates to standards and criteria that tend to screen out individuals with disabilities)—

"(A) compensatory damages may be awarded; and

"(B) if the respondent (other than a government, government agency, or a political subdivision) engaged in the unlawful employment practice with malice, or with reckless or callous indifference to the federally protected rights of others, punitive damages may be awarded against such respondent;

in addition to the relief authorized by the preceding sentences of this
subsection, except that compensatory damages shall not include backpay or
any interest thereon. Compensatory and punitive damages and jury trials
shall be available only for claims of intentional discrimination. If compensatory or punitive damages are sought with respect to a claim of intentional
discrimination arising under this title, any party may demand a trial by
jury.''

### Sec. 213. Application of Amendments and Transition Rules.*

(a) APPLICATION OF AMENDMENTS.—The amendments made by—

(1) section 202 shall apply to all proceedings pending on or commenced after June 5, 1989;

(2) section 203 shall apply to all proceedings pending on or commenced after May 1, 1989;

(3) section 204 shall apply to all proceedings pending on or commenced after June 12, 1989;

(4) sections 205(a)(1), 205(a)(3), 205(a)(4), 205(b), 206, 207, 208,
and 209 shall apply to all proceedings pending on or commenced
after the date of enactment of this Act;

(5) section 205(a)(2) shall apply to all proceedings pending on or
commenced after June 12, 1989; and

(6) section 210 shall apply to all proceedings pending on or commenced after June 15, 1989.

(b) TRANSITION RULES.—

(1) IN GENERAL.—Any orders entered by a court between the effective dates described in subsection (a) and the date of enactment of
this Act that are inconsistent with the amendments made by
section 202, 203, 205(a)(2), or 210, shall be vacated if, not later
than 1 year after such date of enactment, a request for such relief
is made.

(2) SECTION 204.—Any orders entered between June 12, 1989, and
the date of enactment of this Act, that permit a challenge to an
employment practice that implements a litigated or consent judgment or order and that is inconsistent with the amendment made
by section 204, shall be vacated if, not later than 6 months after
the date of enactment of this Act, a request for such relief is made.
For the 1-year period beginning on the date of enactment of this
Act, an individual whose challenge to an employment practice that
implements a litigated or consent judgment or order is denied
under the amendment made by section 204, or whose order or
relief obtained under such challenge is vacated under such section,

* Ed's note: The dates set out in this subsection correspond to the dates of a series of Supreme Court employment discrimination decisions whose results Congress "over-ruled" in the 1991 Civil Rights Act. The decisions are set out at n. 8 of the majority opinion in Landgraf v. USI Film Products, infra p. 522 of this Casebook.

shall have the same right of intervention in the case in which the challenged litigated or consent judgment or order was entered as that individual had on June 12, 1989.

## Congressional Record—Senate

Tuesday, March 12, 1991; (Legislative day of Wednesday, February 6, 1991)

102nd Cong. 1st Sess.

137 Cong. Rec. S 3021

[Bush Administration sponsored version of Civil Rights Bill]

## S.  611 / H.R. 1375

BE IT ENACTED BY THE SENATE AND HOUSE OF REPRESEN-TATIVES OF THE UNITED STATES OF AMERICA IN CONGRESS ASSEMBLED,

SECTION 1. SHORT TITLE.

This Act may be cited as the "Civil Rights Act of 1991".

\* \* \*

## SEC.  8.  PROVIDING FOR ADDITIONAL REMEDIES FOR HARASSMENT IN THE WORKPLACE BECAUSE OF RACE, COLOR, RELIGION, SEX, OR NATIONAL ORIGIN.

(a) Subsection 703(a) of the Civil Rights Act of 1964 (42 U.S.C. 2000e–2(a)) is amended by deleting the period at the end and inserting in lieu thereof "; or" and by adding at the end the following new paragraph:

"(3) to harass any employee or applicant for employment because of that individual's race, color, religion, sex, or national origin; provided, however, that no such unlawful employment practice shall be found to have occurred if the complaining party failed to avail himself or herself of a procedure, of which the complaining party was or should have been aware, established by the employer for resolving complaints of harassment in an effective fashion within a period not exceeding 90 days."

(b) Section 706 of the Civil Rights Act of 1964 (42 U.S.C. 2000e–5) is amended by adding at the end the following new subsections:

"(1) Emergency Relief in Harassment Cases.—An employee or other complaining party alleging a violation of section 703(a)(3) of this Title may petition the court for temporary or preliminary relief. If the complaining party establishes a substantial probability of success on the merits of such harassment claim, the continued submission to the harassment shall be deemed injury sufficiently irreparable to warrant the entry of temporary or preliminary relief. A court having jurisdiction over a request for temporary or preliminary relief pursuant to this paragraph shall assign the case for hearing at the earliest practicable date and cause such case to be expedited in every way practicable.

"(m) Equitable Monetary Awards in Harassment Cases.—

"(1) In ordering relief for a violation of section 703(a)(3) of this Title, the court may, in addition to ordering appropriate equitable relief under subsection (g) of this section, exercise its equitable discretion to require the employer to pay the complaining party an amount up to but not exceeding a total of $150,000.00, if the court finds that an additional equitable remedy beyond those available under subsection (g) of this section is justified by the equities, is consistent with the purposes of this Title, and is in the public interest. In weighing the equities and fixing the amount of any award under this paragraph, the court shall give due consideration, along with any other relevant equitable factors, to (i) the nature of compliance programs, if any, established by the employer to ensure that unlawful harassment does not occur in the workplace; (ii) the nature of procedures, if any, established by the employer for resolving complaints of harassment in an effective fashion; (iii) whether the employer took prompt and reasonable corrective action upon becoming aware of the conduct complained of; (iv) the employer's size and the effect of the award on its economic viability; (v) whether the harassment was willful or egregious; and (vi) the need, if any, to provide restitution for the complaining party.

"(2) All issues in cases arising under this Title, including cases arising under section 703(a)(3) of this Title, shall be heard and determined by a judge, as provided in subsection (f) of this section. If, however, the court holds that a monetary award pursuant to paragraph (1) of this subsection is sought by the complaining party and that such an award cannot constitutionally be granted unless a jury determines liability on one or more issues with respect to which such award is sought, a jury may be empaneled to hear and determine such liability issues and no others. In no case arising under this Title shall a jury consider, recommend, or determine the amount of any monetary award sought pursuant to paragraph (1) of this subsection."

(c) Subsection 706(e) of the Civil Rights Act of 1964 (42 U.S.C. 2000e–5(e)) (as amended by section 7 of this Act) is further amended by adding at the end the following sentence: "For purposes of actions involving harassment under section 703(a)(3) of this Title, the period of limitations established under this subsection shall be tolled during the time (not exceeding 90 days) that an employee avails himself or herself of a procedure established by the employer for resolving complaints of harassment."

\* \* \*

## SEC. 14. EFFECTIVE DATE.

This Act and the amendments made by this Act shall take effect upon enactment. The amendments made by this Act shall not apply to any claim arising before the effective date of this Act.

[The identical Administration Bill was introduced the same day in the House of Representatives as H.R. 1375, see 137 Cong. Rec. H 1662 (March 12, 1991).]

## b. THE SUPREME COURT DECISION ON RETROACTIVITY OF THE 1991 ACT'S REMEDIAL PROVISIONS

Prior to the Supreme Court's 1994 decision in *Landgraf v. USI Film Products et al.*, several circuit courts had already addressed the question whether the Civil Rights Act of 1991 should be applied to claims arising before the new law's enactment. The appellate courts offered a variety of divergent answers and analyses.

In Reynolds v. Martin, 985 F.2d 470 (9th Cir.1993), the United States Court of Appeals for the Ninth Circuit ruled that the 1991 Act should be applied retroactively. The court based its decision on the "plain language" of § 402(a), which states: "Except as otherwise specifically provided, this Act and the amendments made by this Act shall take effect upon enactment." The Court emphasized the canon of statutory interpretation that directs courts to avoid reading statutory language in a manner that creates redundancies; courts should seek to invest each phrase with independent meaning. Because two other sections—§§ 402(b) and 109(c)—specifically called for prospective application, the court argued that it could only give effect to the phrase "except as otherwise specifically provided" if § 402(a) was understood as an indication of Congressional intent to apply the Act retroactively. In the court's view, this interpretation was consistent with Congress' expressed desire to "undo the effects" of recent Supreme Court decisions.

The Court of Appeals for the District of Columbia reached a different conclusion in Gersman v. Group Health Association, Inc., 975 F.2d 886 (D.C.Cir.1992), cert. denied, 511 U.S. 1068 (1994). *Gersman* involved plaintiffs seeking remedies under 42 U.S.C. § 1981, a post civil war statute prohibiting discrimination in the "making and enforcement" of contracts. In 1989, in Patterson v. McLean Credit Union, 491 U.S. 164 (1989), the Supreme Court had limited the relief available under § 1981 to plaintiffs claiming discrimination in the *formation* of contracts, and therefore held that the statute did not apply to plaintiff's claim of discriminatory *breach* of contract. The 1991 Civil Rights Act returned the law to its pre–1989 state by explicitly defining the phrase "make and enforce contracts" so as to include contractual performance, modification and termination.

Concluding that the Act's statutory language did nothing more than reiterate the conflicting presumptions of *Bradley* and *Bowen,* the *Gersman* majority sought to reconcile the two decisions within the language of the *Bennett* decision: statutes affecting substantive rights should be applied prospectively, while those involving procedural changes should be presumed retroactive.

However, the dissent argued that at the time of the defendant's conduct (pre–1989), the law was identical to that set forth in the 1991 Civil Rights Act. Thus, no "settled expectations" or "vested rights" would be disturbed by the Act's retroactive application in this case. Absent "manifest injustice," the *Gersman* dissent believed that the *Bradley* presumption favoring retroactivity should be applied.

Finally, in the lower court's 1992 decision in Landgraf v. USI Film Products, 968 F.2d 427 (5th Cir.1992), the Fifth Circuit argued that even if the *Bradley* presumption in favor of retroactivity should prevail, the "manifest injustice" exception articulated in that case should control the outcome in *Landgraf*. The court ruled that the Act's provision for compensatory damages imposed on private parties "an additional or unforeseeable obligation" resulting in "manifest injustice."

## Landgraf v. USI Film Products

Supreme Court of the United States, 1994.
511 U.S. 244, 114 S.Ct. 1483, 128 L.Ed.2d 229.

■ STEVENS, J., delivered the opinion of the Court, in which REHNQUIST, C.J., and O'CONNOR, SOUTER, and GINSBURG, JJ., joined. SCALIA, J., filed an opinion concurring in the judgment, in which KENNEDY and THOMAS, JJ., joined. BLACKMUN, J., filed a dissenting opinion.

■ JUSTICE STEVENS delivered the opinion of the Court.

The Civil Rights Act of 1991 (1991 Act or Act) creates a right to recover compensatory and punitive damages for certain violations of Title VII of the Civil Rights Act of 1964. See Rev.Stat. § 1977A(a), 42 U.S.C. § 1981a(a), as added by § 102 of the 1991 Act, Pub.L. 102–166, 105 Stat. 1071. The Act further provides that any party may demand a trial by jury if such damages are sought. We granted certiorari to decide whether these provisions apply to a Title VII case that was pending on appeal when the statute was enacted. We hold that they do not.

### I

From September 4, 1984, through January 17, 1986, petitioner Barbara Landgraf was employed in the USI Film Products (USI) plant in Tyler, Texas. She worked the 11 p.m. to 7 a.m. shift operating a machine that produced plastic bags. A fellow employee named John Williams repeatedly harassed her with inappropriate remarks and physical contact. Petitioner's complaints to her immediate supervisor brought her no relief, but when she reported the incidents to the personnel manager, he conducted an investigation, reprimanded Williams, and transferred him to another department. Four days later petitioner quit her job.

Petitioner filed a timely charge with the Equal Employment Opportunity Commission (EEOC or Commission). The Commission determined that petitioner had likely been the victim of sexual harassment creating a hostile work environment in violation of Title VII of the Civil Rights Act of 1964, 42 U.S.C. § 2000e et seq., but concluded that her employer had adequately remedied the violation. Accordingly, the Commission dismissed the charge and issued a notice of right to sue.

On July 21, 1989, petitioner commenced this action against USI, its corporate owner, and that company's successor-in-interest. After a bench trial, the District Court found that Williams had sexually harassed petitioner causing her to suffer mental anguish. However, the court concluded that she had not been constructively discharged. The court said:

> "Although the harassment was serious enough to establish that a hostile work environment existed for Landgraf, it was not so severe that a reasonable person would have felt compelled to resign. This is particularly true in light of the fact that at the time Landgraf resigned from her job, USI had taken steps . . . to eliminate the hostile working environment arising from the sexual harassment. Landgraf voluntarily resigned from her employment with USI for reasons unrelated to the sexual harassment in question." App. to Pet. for Cert. B–3–4.

Because the court found that petitioner's employment was not terminated in violation of Title VII, she was not entitled to equitable relief, and because Title VII did not then authorize any other form of relief, the court dismissed her complaint.

On November 21, 1991, while petitioner's appeal was pending, the President signed into law the Civil Rights Act of 1991. The Court of Appeals rejected petitioner's argument that her case should be remanded for a jury trial on damages pursuant to the 1991 Act. Its decision not to remand rested on the premise that "a court must 'apply the law in effect at the time it renders its decision, unless doing so would result in manifest injustice or there is statutory direction or legislative history to the contrary.' Bradley [v. Richmond School Bd., 416 U.S. 696, 711, 94 S.Ct. 2006, 2016, 40 L.Ed.2d 476 (1974) ]." 968 F.2d 427, 432 (C.A.5 1992). Commenting first on the provision for a jury trial in § 102(c), the court stated that requiring the defendant "to retry this case because of a statutory change enacted after the trial was completed would be an injustice and a waste of judicial resources. We apply procedural rules to pending cases, but we do not invalidate procedures followed before the new rule was adopted." 968 F.2d, at 432–433. The court then characterized the provision for compensatory and punitive damages in § 102 as "a seachange in employer liability for Title VII violations" and concluded that it would be unjust to apply this kind of additional and unforeseeable obligation to conduct occurring before the effective date of the Act. Ibid. Finding no clear error in the District Court's factual findings, the Court of Appeals affirmed the judgment for respondents.

We granted certiorari and set the case for argument with Rivers v. Roadway Express, Inc., 507 U.S. 908, 113 S.Ct. 1250, 122 L.Ed.2d 649 (1993). Our order limited argument to the question whether § 102 of the 1991 Act applies to cases pending when it became law. 507 U.S. 908, 113 S.Ct. 1250, 122 L.Ed.2d 649 (1993). Accordingly, for purposes of our decision, we assume that the District Court and the Court of Appeals properly applied the law in effect at the time of the discriminatory conduct and that the relevant findings of fact were correct. We therefore assume that petitioner was the victim of sexual harassment violative of Title VII, but that the law did not then authorize any recovery of damages even though she was injured. We also assume, arguendo, that if the same conduct were to occur today, petitioner would be entitled to a jury trial and that the jury might find that she was constructively discharged, or that her mental anguish or other injuries would support an award of damages against her former employer. Thus, the controlling question is whether the Court of Appeals should have applied the law in effect at the time the discriminatory conduct occurred, or at the time of its decision in July 1992.

## II

Petitioner's primary submission is that the text of the 1991 Act requires that it be applied to cases pending on its enactment. Her argument, if accepted, would make the entire Act (with two narrow exceptions) applicable to conduct that occurred, and to cases that were filed, before the Act's effective date. Although only § 102 is at issue in this case, we therefore preface our analysis with a brief description of the scope of the 1991 Act.

The Civil Rights Act of 1991 is in large part a response to a series of decisions of this Court interpreting the Civil Rights Acts of 1866 and 1964. Section 3(4) expressly identifies as one of the Act's purposes "to respond to recent decisions of the Supreme Court by expanding the scope of relevant civil rights statutes in order to provide adequate protection to victims of discrimination." That section, as well as a specific finding in § 2(2), identifies Wards Cove Packing Co. v. Atonio, 490 U.S. 642, 109 S.Ct. 2115, 104 L.Ed.2d 733 (1989), as a decision that gave rise to special concerns.[3] Section 105 of the Act, entitled "Burden of Proof in Disparate Impact Cases," is a direct response to Wards Cove.

Other sections of the Act were obviously drafted with "recent decisions of the Supreme Court" in mind. [citations omitted]. A number of important provisions in the Act, however, were not responses to Supreme Court decisions. For example, § 106 enacts a new prohibition against adjusting test scores "on the basis of race, color, religion, sex, or national origin"; § 117 extends the coverage of Title VII to include the House of Representatives and certain employees of the Legislative Branch; and §§ 301–325 establish special procedures to protect Senate employees from discrimination. Among the provisions that did not directly respond to any Supreme Court decision is the one at issue in this case, § 102.

Entitled "Damages in Cases of Intentional Discrimination," § 102 provides in relevant part:

(a) Right of Recovery.—

(1) Civil Rights.—In an action brought by a complaining party under section 706 or 717 of the Civil Rights Act of 1964 (42 U.S.C. 2000e–5) against a respondent who engaged in unlawful intentional discrimina-

---

**3.** Section 2(2) finds that the Wards Cove decision "has weakened the scope and effectiveness of Federal civil rights protections," and § 3(2) expresses Congress' intent "to codify" certain concepts enunciated in "Supreme Court decisions prior to Wards Cove Packing Co. v. Atonio, 490 U.S. 642 [109 S.Ct. 2115, 104 L.Ed.2d 733] (1989)." We take note of the express references to that case because it is the focus of § 402(b), on which petitioner places particular reliance. See infra, at 1493–1496.

tion (not an employment practice that is unlawful because of its disparate impact) prohibited under section 703, 704, or 717 of the Act (42 U.S.C. 2000e–2 or 2000e–3), and provided that the complaining party cannot recover under section 1977 of the Revised Statutes (42 U.S.C.1981), the complaining party may recover compensatory and punitive damages . . . in addition to any relief authorized by section 706(g) of the Civil Rights Act of 1964, from the respondent.

. . .

(c) Jury Trial.—If a complaining party seeks compensatory or punitive damages under this section—

(1) any party may demand a trial by jury.

Before the enactment of the 1991 Act, Title VII afforded only "equitable" remedies. The primary form of monetary relief available was backpay. Title VII's back pay remedy, modeled on that of the National Labor Relations Act, 29 U.S.C. § 160(c), is a "make-whole" remedy that resembles compensatory damages in some respects. See Albemarle Paper Co. v. Moody, 422 U.S. 405, 418–422, 95 S.Ct. 2362, 2372–2374, 45 L.Ed.2d 280 (1975). However, the new compensatory damages provision of the 1991 Act is "in addition to," and does not replace or duplicate, the backpay remedy allowed under prior law. Indeed, to prevent double recovery, the 1991 Act provides that compensatory damages "shall not include backpay, interest on backpay, or any other type of relief authorized under section 706(g) of the Civil Rights Act of 1964." § 102(b)(2).

Section 102 significantly expands the monetary relief potentially available to plaintiffs who would have been entitled to backpay under prior law. . . .

Section 102 also allows monetary relief for some forms of workplace discrimination that would not previously have justified any relief under Title VII. As this case illustrates, even if unlawful discrimination was proved, under prior law a Title VII plaintiff could not recover monetary relief unless the discrimination was also found to have some concrete effect on the plaintiff's employment status, such as a denied promotion, a differential in compensation, or termination. Section 102, however, allows a plaintiff to recover in circumstances in which there has been unlawful discrimination in the "terms, conditions, or privileges of employment," 42 U.S.C. § 2000e–2(a)(1), even though the discrimination did not involve a discharge or a loss of pay. In short, to further Title VII's "central statutory purposes of eradicating discrimination throughout the economy and making persons whole for injuries suffered through past discrimination," Albemarle Paper Co., 422 U.S., at 421, 95 S.Ct., at 2373, § 102 of the 1991 Act effects a major expansion in the relief available to victims of employment discrimination.

In 1990, a comprehensive civil rights bill passed both Houses of Congress. Although similar to the 1991 Act in many other respects, the 1990 bill differed in that it contained language expressly calling for application of many of its provisions, including the section providing for damages in cases of intentional employment discrimination, to cases arising before its (expected) enactment.[4] The President vetoed the 1990 legislation, however, citing the bill's "unfair retroactivity rules" as one reason for his disapproval.[5] Congress narrowly failed to override the veto. See 136 Cong. Rec. S16589 (Oct. 24, 1990) (66–34 Senate vote in favor of override.)

The absence of comparable language in the 1991 Act cannot realistically be attributed to oversight or to unawareness of the retroactivity issue. Rather, it seems likely that one of the compromises that made it possible to enact the 1991 version was an agreement not to include the kind of explicit retroactivity command found in the 1990 bill.

**4.** The relevant section of the Civil Rights Act of 1990, S. 2104, 101st Cong., 1st Sess. (1990), provided:

"SEC. 15. APPLICATION OF AMENDMENTS AND TRANSITION RULES.

"(a) APPLICATION OF AMENDMENTS.—The amendments made by—

(1) section 4 shall apply to all proceedings pending on or commenced after June 5, 1989 [the date of Wards Cove Packing Co. v. Atonio, 490 U.S. 642, 109 S.Ct. 2115];

"(2) section 5 shall apply to all proceedings pending on or commenced after May 1, 1989 [the date of Price Waterhouse v. Hopkins, 490 U.S. 228, 109 S.Ct. 1775];

"(3) section 6 shall apply to all proceedings pending on or commenced after June 12, 1989 [the date of Martin v. Wilks, 490 U.S. 755, 109 S.Ct. 2180];

"(4) sections 7(a)(1), 7(a)(3) and 7(a)(4), 7(b), 8 [providing for compensatory and punitive damages for intentional discrimination], 9, 10, and 11 shall apply to all proceedings pending on or commenced after the date of enactment of this Act;

"(5) section 7(a)(2) shall apply to all proceedings pending on or after June 12, 1989 [the date of Lorance v. AT & T Technologies, Inc., 490 U.S. 900, 109 S.Ct. 2261]; and

"(6) section 12 shall apply to all proceedings pending on or commenced after June 15, 1989 [the date of Patterson v. McLean Credit Union, 491 U.S. 164, 109 S.Ct. 2363].

"(b) TRANSITION RULES.—

"(1) IN GENERAL.—Any orders entered by a court between the effective dates described in subsection (a) and the date of enactment of this Act that are inconsistent with the amendments made by sections 4, 5, 7(a)(2), or 12, shall be vacated if, not later than 1 year after such date of enactment, a request for such relief is made.

\* \* \*

"(3) FINAL JUDGMENTS.—Pursuant to paragraphs (1) and (2), any final judgment entered prior to the date of the enactment of this Act as to which the rights of any of the parties thereto have become fixed and vested, where the time for seeking further judicial review of such judgment has otherwise expired pursuant to title 28 of the United States Code, the Federal Rules of Civil Procedure, and the Federal Rules of Appellate Procedure, shall be vacated in whole or in part if justice requires pursuant to rule 60(b)(6) of the Federal Rules of Civil Procedure or other appropriate authority, and consistent with the constitutional requirements of due process of law."

**5.** See President's Message to the Senate Returning Without Approval the Civil Rights Act of 1990, 26 Weekly Comp.Pres. Doc. 1632–1634 (Oct. 22, 1990), reprinted in 136 Cong.Rec. S16418, 16419 (Oct. 22, 1990). The President's veto message referred to the bill's "retroactivity" only briefly; the Attorney General's Memorandum to which the President referred was no more expansive, and may be read to refer only to the bill's special provision for reopening final judgments, see n. 8, *supra*, rather than its provisions covering pending cases.

The omission of the elaborate retroactivity provision of the 1990 bill—which was by no means the only source of political controversy over that legislation—is not dispositive because it does not tell us precisely where the compromise was struck in the 1991 Act. . . . Our first question, then, is whether the statutory text on which petitioner relies manifests an intent that the 1991 Act should be applied to cases that arose and went to trial before its enactment.

## III

Petitioner's textual argument relies on three provisions of the 1991 Act: §§ 402(a), 402(b), and 109(c). Section 402(a), the only provision of the Act that speaks directly to the question before us, states:

> Except as otherwise specifically provided, this Act and the amendments made by this Act shall take effect upon enactment.

That language does not, by itself, resolve the question before us. A statement that a statute will become effective on a certain date does not even arguably suggest that it has any application to conduct that occurred at an earlier date.[6] Petitioner does not argue otherwise. Rather, she contends that the introductory clause of § 402(a) would be superfluous unless it refers to §§ 402(b) and 109(c), which provide for prospective application in limited contexts.

The parties agree that § 402(b) was intended to exempt a single disparate impact lawsuit against the Wards Cove Packing Company. Section 402(b) provides:

> (b) CERTAIN DISPARATE IMPACT CASES.—

> Notwithstanding any other provision of this Act, nothing in this Act shall apply to any disparate impact case for which a complaint was filed before March 1, 1975, and for which an initial decision was rendered after October 30, 1983.

Section 109(c), part of the section extending Title VII to overseas employers, states:

> (c) APPLICATION OF AMENDMENTS.—The amendments made by this section shall not apply with respect to conduct occurring before the date of the enactment of this Act.

---

**6.** The history of prior amendments to Title VII suggests that the "effective-upon-enactment" formula would have been an especially inapt way to reach pending cases. When it amended Title VII in the Equal Employment Opportunity Act of 1972, Congress explicitly provided:

"The amendments made by this Act to section 706 of the Civil Rights Act of 1964 shall be applicable with respect to charges pending with the Commission on the date of enactment of this Act and all charges filed thereafter." Pub.L. 92–261,

§ 14, 86 Stat. 113. In contrast, in amending Title VII to bar discrimination on the basis of pregnancy in 1978, Congress provided:

"Except as provided in subsection (b), the amendment made by this Act shall be effective on the date of enactment." § 2(a), 92 Stat. 2076.

The only Courts of Appeals to consider whether the 1978 amendments applied to pending cases concluded that they did not. [citations omitted].

According to petitioner, these two subsections are the "other provisions" contemplated in the first clause of § 402(a), and together create a strong negative inference that all sections of the Act not specifically declared prospective apply to pending cases that arose before November 21, 1991.

Before addressing the particulars of petitioner's argument, we observe that she places extraordinary weight on two comparatively minor and narrow provisions in a long and complex statute. Applying the entire Act to cases arising from preenactment conduct would have important consequences, including the possibility that trials completed before its enactment would need to be retried and the possibility that employers would be liable for punitive damages for conduct antedating the Act's enactment. Purely prospective application, on the other hand, would prolong the life of a remedial scheme, and of judicial constructions of civil rights statutes, that Congress obviously found wanting. Given the high stakes of the retroactivity question, the broad coverage of the statute, and the prominent and specific retroactivity provisions in the 1990 bill, it would be surprising for Congress to have chosen to resolve that question through negative inferences drawn from two provisions of quite limited effect.

Petitioner, however, invokes the canon that a court should give effect to every provision of a statute and thus avoid redundancy among different provisions. Unless the word "otherwise" in § 402(a) refers to either § 402(b) or § 109(c), she contends, the first five words in § 402(a) are entirely superfluous. Moreover, relying on the canon "[e]xpressio unius est exclusio alterius," petitioner argues that because Congress provided specifically for prospectivity in two places (§§ 109(c) and 402(b)), we should infer that it intended the opposite for the remainder of the statute. [citations omitted].

Petitioner emphasizes that § 402(a) begins: "Except as otherwise specifically provided." A scan of the statute for other "specific provisions" concerning effective dates reveals that §§ 402(b) and 109(c) are the most likely candidates. Since those provisions decree prospectivity, and since § 402(a) tells us that the specific provisions are exceptions, § 402(b) should be considered as prescribing a general rule of retroactivity. Petitioner's argument has some force, but we find it most unlikely that Congress intended the introductory clause to carry the critically important meaning petitioner assigns it. Had Congress wished § 402(a) to have such a determinate meaning, it surely would have used language comparable to its reference to the predecessor Title VII damages provisions in the 1990 legislation: that the new provisions "shall apply to all proceedings pending on or commenced after the date of enactment of this Act." S. 2104, 101st Cong., 1st Sess. § 15(a)(4) (1990).

It is entirely possible that Congress inserted the "otherwise specifically provided" language not because it understood the "takes effect" clause to establish a rule of retroactivity to which only two "other specific provisions" would be exceptions, but instead to assure that any specific timing provisions in the Act would prevail over the general "take effect on enactment" command. The drafters of a complicated piece of legislation containing more than 50 separate sections may well have inserted the "except as otherwise provided" language merely to avoid the risk of an inadvertent conflict in the statute.[7] If the introductory clause of § 402(a) was intended to refer specifically to §§ 402(b), 109(c), or both, it is difficult to understand why the drafters chose the word "otherwise" rather than either or both of the appropriate section numbers.

We are also unpersuaded by petitioner's argument that both §§ 402(b) and 109(c) merely duplicate the "take effect upon enactment" command of § 402(a) unless all other provisions, including the damages provisions of § 102, apply to pending cases. That argument depends on the assumption that all those other provisions must be treated uniformly for purposes of their application to pending cases based on preenactment conduct. That thesis, however, is by no means an inevitable one. It is entirely possible— indeed, highly probable—that, because it was unable to resolve the retroactivity issue with the clarity of the 1990 legislation, Congress viewed the matter as an open issue to be resolved by the courts. Our precedents on retroactivity left doubts about what default rule would apply in the absence of congressional guidance, and suggested that some provisions might apply to cases arising before enactment while others might not.[8] [citations omitted]. The only matters Congress did not leave to the courts were set out with specificity in §§ 109(c) and 402(b). Congressional doubt concerning judicial retroactivity doctrine, coupled with the likelihood that the routine "take effect upon enactment" language would require courts to fall back upon that doctrine, provide a plausible explanation for both §§ 402(b) and 109(c) that makes neither provision redundant.

Turning to the text of § 402(b), it seems unlikely that the introductory phrase ("Notwithstanding any other provision of this Act") was meant to refer to the immediately preceding subsection. Since petitioner does not contend that any other provision speaks to the general effective date issue, the logic of her argument requires us to interpret that phrase to mean nothing more than "Notwithstanding § 402(a)." Petitioner's textual argument assumes that the drafters selected the indefinite word "otherwise" in § 402(a) to identify two specific subsections and the even more indefinite term "any other provision" in § 402(b) to refer to nothing more than § 402(b)'s next-door neighbor—§ 402(a). Here again, petitioner's statutory argument would require us to assume that Congress chose a surprisingly

---

**7.** There is some evidence that the drafters of the 1991 Act did not devote particular attention to the interplay of the Act's "effective date" provisions. Section 110, which directs the EEOC to establish a "Technical Assistance Training Institute" to assist employers in complying with antidiscrimination laws and regulations, contains a subsection providing that it "shall take effect on the date of enactment of this Act." § 110(b). That provision and § 402(a) are unavoidably redundant.

**8.** This point also diminishes the force of petitioner's "expressio unius" argument. Once one abandons the unsupported assumption that Congress expected that all of the Act's provisions would be treated alike, and takes account of uncertainty about the applicable default rule, §§ 109(c) and 402(b) do not carry the negative implication petitioner draws from them. We do not read either provision as doing anything more than definitively rejecting retroactivity with respect to the specific matters covered by its plain language.

indirect route to convey an important and easily expressed message concerning the Act's effect on pending cases.

The relevant legislative history of the 1991 Act reinforces our conclusion that §§ 402(a), 109(c) and 402(b) cannot bear the weight petitioner places upon them. The 1991 bill as originally introduced in the House contained explicit retroactivity provisions similar to those found in the 1990 bill.[9] However, the Senate substitute that was agreed upon omitted those explicit retroactivity provisions. The legislative history discloses some frankly partisan statements about the meaning of the final effective date language, but those statements cannot plausibly be read as reflecting any general agreement. The history reveals no evidence that Members believed that an agreement had been tacitly struck on the controversial retroactivity issue, and little to suggest that Congress understood or intended the interplay of §§ 402(a), 402(b) and 109(c) to have the decisive effect petitioner assigns them. Instead, the history of the 1991 Act conveys the impression that legislators agreed to disagree about whether and to what extent the Act would apply to preenactment conduct.

Although the passage of the 1990 bill may indicate that a majority of the 1991 Congress also favored retroactive application, even the will of the majority does not become law unless it follows the path charted in Article I, § 7, cl. 2 of the Constitution. [citation omitted] In the absence of the kind of unambiguous directive found in § 15 of the 1990 bill, we must look elsewhere for guidance on whether § 102 applies to this case.

## IV

It is not uncommon to find "apparent tension" between different canons of statutory construction. As Professor Llewellyn famously illustrated, many of the traditional canons have equal opposites.[16] In order to resolve the question left open by the 1991 Act, federal courts have labored to reconcile two seemingly contradictory statements found in our decisions concerning the effect of intervening changes in the law. Each statement is framed as a generally applicable rule for interpreting statutes that do not specify their temporal reach. The first is the rule that "a court is to apply

**9.** See, e.g., H.R. 1, 102d Cong., 1st Sess. § 113 (1991), reprinted in 137 Cong. Rec. H3924–H3925 (Jan. 3, 1991). The prospectivity proviso to the section extending Title VII to overseas employers was first added to legislation that generally was to apply to pending cases. See H.R. 1, 102d Cong., 1st Sess. § 119(c) (1991), reprinted in 137 Cong. Rec. H3925–H3926 (June 5, 1991). Thus, at the time its language was introduced, the provision that became § 109(c) was surely not redundant.

**16.** See Llewellyn, Remarks on the Theory of Appellate Decision and the Rules or Canons about How Statutes are to be Construed, 3 Vand.L.Rev. 395 (1950). Llewellyn's article identified the apparent conflict between the canon that

> "[a] statute imposing a new penalty or forfeiture, or a new liability or disability, or creating a new right of action will not be construed as having a retroactive effect;"

and the countervailing rule that

> "[r]emedial statutes are to be liberally construed and if a retroactive interpretation will promote the ends of justice, they should receive such construction."

Id., at 402 (citations omitted).

the law in effect at the time it renders its decision," *Bradley*, 416 U.S., at 711, 94 S.Ct., at 2016. The second is the axiom that "[r]etroactivity is not favored in the law," and its interpretive corollary that "congressional enactments and administrative rules will not be construed to have retroactive effect unless their language requires this result." *Bowen*, 488 U.S., at 208, 109 S.Ct., at 471.

\* \* \*

[W]e turn to the "apparent tension" between the two canons mindful of another canon of unquestionable vitality, the "maxim not to be disregarded that general expressions, in every opinion, are to be taken in connection with the case in which those expressions are used." Cohens v. Virginia, 6 Wheat. 264, 399, 5 L.Ed. 257 (1821).

# A

As Justice Scalia has demonstrated, the presumption against retroactive legislation is deeply rooted in our jurisprudence, and embodies a legal doctrine centuries older than our Republic. Elementary considerations of fairness dictate that individuals should have an opportunity to know what the law is and to conform their conduct accordingly; settled expectations should not be lightly disrupted. For that reason, the "principle that the legal effect of conduct should ordinarily be assessed under the law that existed when the conduct took place has timeless and universal appeal." [citation omitted]. In a free, dynamic society, creativity in both commercial and artistic endeavors is fostered by a rule of law that gives people confidence about the legal consequences of their actions.

It is therefore not surprising that the antiretroactivity principle finds expression in several provisions of our Constitution [including the Ex Post Facto, Takings, and Due Process Clauses and the prohibition on Bills of Attainder].... The Constitution's restrictions, of course, are of limited scope. Absent a violation of one of those specific provisions, the potential unfairness of retroactive civil legislation is not a sufficient reason for a court to fail to give a statute its intended scope....

\* \* \*

A statute does not operate "retrospectively" merely because it is applied in a case arising from conduct antedating the statute's enactment, see Republic Nat. Bank of Miami v. United States, 506 U.S. 80, ___, 113 S.Ct. 554, 556–557, 121 L.Ed.2d 474 (1992) (Thomas, J., concurring in part and concurring in judgment), or upsets expectations based in prior law.[24]

---

**24.** Even uncontroversially prospective statutes may unsettle expectations and impose burdens on past conduct; a new property tax or zoning regulation may upset the reasonable expectations that prompted those affected to acquire property; a new law banning gambling harms the person who had begun to construct a casino before the law's enactment or spent his life learning to count cards. See Fuller 60 ("If every time a man relied on existing law in arranging his affairs, he were made secure against any change in legal rules, the whole body of our law would be ossified forever"). Moreover, a statute "is not made retroactive merely because it draws upon antecedent facts for its operation." [citations omitted].

Rather, the court must ask whether the new provision attaches new legal consequences to events completed before its enactment. The conclusion that a particular rule operates "retroactively" comes at the end of a process of judgment concerning the nature and extent of the change in the law and the degree of connection between the operation of the new rule and a relevant past event. Any test of retroactivity will leave room for disagreement in hard cases, and is unlikely to classify the enormous variety of legal changes with perfect philosophical clarity. However, retroactivity is a matter on which judges tend to have "sound ... instinct[s]," see Danforth v. Groton Water Co., 178 Mass. 472, 476, 59 N.E. 1033, 1034 (1901) (Holmes, J.), and familiar considerations of fair notice, reasonable reliance, and settled expectations offer sound guidance.

Since the early days of this Court, we have declined to give retroactive effect to statutes burdening private rights unless Congress had made clear its intent.... The presumption against statutory retroactivity has consistently been explained by reference to the unfairness of imposing new burdens on persons after the fact.

The largest category of cases in which we have applied the presumption against statutory retroactivity has involved new provisions affecting contractual or property rights, matters in which predictability and stability are of prime importance. The presumption has not, however, been limited to such cases. At issue in Chew Heong v. United States, 112 U.S. 536, 5 S.Ct. 255, 28 L.Ed. 770 (1884), for example, was a provision of the "Chinese Restriction Act" of 1882 barring Chinese laborers from reentering the United States without a certificate prepared when they exited this country. We held that the statute did not bar the reentry of a laborer who had left the United States before the certification requirement was promulgated. Justice Harlan's opinion for the Court observed that the law in effect before the 1882 enactment had accorded laborers a right to re-enter without a certificate, and invoked the "uniformly" accepted rule against "giv[ing] to statutes a retrospective operation, whereby rights previously vested are injuriously affected, unless compelled to do so by language so clear and positive as to leave no room to doubt that such was the intention of the legislature." Id., at 559, 5 S.Ct., at 266–267.

Our statement in *Bowen* that "congressional enactments and administrative rules will not be construed to have retroactive effect unless their language requires this result," 488 U.S., at 208, 109 S.Ct., at 471, was in step with this long line of cases. *Bowen* itself was a paradigmatic case of retroactivity in which a federal agency sought to recoup, under cost limit regulations issued in 1984, funds that had been paid to hospitals for services rendered earlier, see id., at 207, 109 S.Ct., at 471; our search for clear congressional intent authorizing retroactivity was consistent with the approach taken in decisions spanning two centuries.

... Requiring clear intent assures that Congress itself has affirmatively considered the potential unfairness of retroactive application and determined that it is an acceptable price to pay for the countervailing benefits. Such a requirement allocates to Congress responsibility for fundamental policy judgments concerning the proper temporal reach of statutes, and has the additional virtue of giving legislators a predictable background rule against which to legislate.

## B

Although we have long embraced a presumption against statutory retroactivity, for just as long we have recognized that, in many situations, a court should "apply the law in effect at the time it renders its decision," *Bradley*, 416 U.S., at 711, 94 S.Ct., at 2016, even though that law was enacted after the events that gave rise to the suit. There is, of course, no conflict between that principle and a presumption against retroactivity when the statute in question is unambiguous. . . .

Even absent specific legislative authorization, application of new statutes passed after the events in suit is unquestionably proper in many situations. When the intervening statute authorizes or affects the propriety of prospective relief, application of the new provision is not retroactive. Thus, in American Steel Foundries v. Tri–City Central Trades Council, 257 U.S. 184, 42 S.Ct. 72, 66 L.Ed. 189 (1921), we held that § 20 of the Clayton Act, enacted while the case was pending on appeal, governed the propriety of injunctive relief against labor picketing. In remanding the suit for application of the intervening statute, we observed that "relief by injunction operates in futuro," and that the plaintiff had no "vested right" in the decree entered by the trial court.

We have regularly applied intervening statutes conferring or ousting jurisdiction, whether or not jurisdiction lay when the underlying conduct occurred or when the suit was filed. . . . Changes in procedural rules may often be applied in suits arising before their enactment without raising concerns about retroactivity. . . .[29]

 . . . In *Thorpe*, we held that an agency circular requiring a local housing authority to give notice of reasons and opportunity to respond before evicting a tenant was applicable to an eviction proceeding commenced before the regulation issued. *Thorpe* shares much with both the "procedural" and "prospective-relief" cases. Thus, we noted in *Thorpe* that new hearing procedures did not affect either party's obligations under the lease agreement between the housing authority and the petitioner, 393

---

**29.** Of course, the mere fact that a new rule is procedural does not mean that it applies to every pending case. A new rule concerning the filing of complaints would not govern an action in which the complaint had already been properly filed under the old regime, and the promulgation of a new rule of evidence would not require an appellate remand for a new trial. Our orders approving amendments to federal procedural rules reflect the common-sense notion that the applicability of such provisions ordinarily depends on the posture of the particular case [citations omitted]. Contrary to Justice SCALIA's suggestion, we do not restrict the presumption against statutory retroactivity to cases involving "vested rights." (Neither is Justice Story's definition of retroactivity, so restricted.) Nor do we suggest that concerns about retroactivity have no application to procedural rules.

U.S., at 279, 89 S.Ct., at 524–525, and, because the tenant had "not yet vacated," we saw no significance in the fact that the housing authority had "decided to evict her before the circular was issued," id., at 283, 89 S.Ct., at 527. The Court in *Thorpe* viewed the new eviction procedures as "essential to remove a serious impediment to the successful protection of constitutional rights." [citations omitted].

Our holding in *Bradley* is similarly compatible with the line of decisions disfavoring "retroactive" application of statutes. In *Bradley*, the District Court had awarded attorney's fees and costs, upon general equitable principles, to parents who had prevailed in an action seeking to desegregate the public schools of Richmond, Virginia. While the case was pending before the Court of Appeals, Congress enacted § 718 of the Education Amendments of 1972, which authorized federal courts to award the prevailing parties in school desegregation cases a reasonable attorney's fee. The Court of Appeals held that the new fee provision did not authorize the award of fees for services rendered before the effective date of the amendments. This Court reversed. We concluded that the private parties could rely on § 718 to support their claim for attorney's fees, resting our decision "on the principle that a court is to apply the law in effect at the time it renders its decision, unless doing so would result in manifest injustice or there is statutory direction or legislative history to the contrary." 416 U.S., at 711, 94 S.Ct., at 2016.

Although that language suggests a categorical presumption in favor of application of all new rules of law, we now make it clear that *Bradley* did not alter the well-settled presumption against application of the class of new statutes that would have genuinely "retroactive" effect. Like the new hearing requirement in *Thorpe*, the attorney's fee provision at issue in *Bradley* did not resemble the cases in which we have invoked the presumption against statutory retroactivity. Attorney's fee determinations, we have observed, are "collateral to the main cause of action" and "uniquely separable from the cause of action to be proved at trial." [citations omitted]. Moreover, even before the enactment of § 718, federal courts had authority (which the District Court in *Bradley* had exercised) to award fees based upon equitable principles. As our opinion in *Bradley* made clear, it would be difficult to imagine a stronger equitable case for an attorney's fee award than a lawsuit in which the plaintiff parents would otherwise have to bear the costs of desegregating their children's public schools. See 416 U.S., at 718, 94 S.Ct., at 2019–2020 (noting that the plaintiffs had brought the school board "into compliance with its constitutional mandate") (citing Brown v. Board of Education, 347 U.S. 483, 494, 74 S.Ct. 686, 691, 98 L.Ed. 873 (1954)). In light of the prior availability of a fee award, and the likelihood that fees would be assessed under pre-existing theories, we concluded that the new fee statute simply "did not impose an additional or unforeseeable obligation" upon the school board. *Bradley*, 416 U.S., at 721, 94 S.Ct., at 2021.

In approving application of the new fee provision, *Bradley* did not take issue with the long line of decisions applying the presumption against retroactivity. Our opinion distinguished, but did not criticize, prior cases that had applied the anti-retroactivity canon [citations omitted]. The authorities we relied upon in *Bradley* lend further support to the conclusion that we did not intend to displace the traditional presumption against applying statutes affecting substantive rights, liabilities, or duties to conduct arising before their enactment. See *Kaiser*, 494 U.S., at 849–850, 110 S.Ct., at 1583–1584 (Scalia, J., concurring). *Bradley* relied on *Thorpe* and on other precedents that are consistent with a presumption against statutory retroactivity, including decisions involving explicitly retroactive statutes, the retroactive application of intervening judicial decisions,[32] statutes altering jurisdiction, and repeal of a criminal statute. [Citations omitted]. Moreover, in none of our decisions that have relied upon *Bradley* or *Thorpe* have we cast doubt on the traditional presumption against truly "retrospective" application of a statute.

When a case implicates a federal statute enacted after the events in suit, the court's first task is to determine whether Congress has expressly prescribed the statute's proper reach. If Congress has done so, of course, there is no need to resort to judicial default rules. When, however, the statute contains no such express command, the court must determine whether the new statute would have retroactive effect, i.e., whether it would impair rights a party possessed when he acted, increase a party's liability for past conduct, or impose new duties with respect to transactions already completed. If the statute would operate retroactively, our traditional presumption teaches that it does not govern absent clear congressional intent favoring such a result.

## V

We now ask whether, given the absence of guiding instructions from Congress, § 102 of the Civil Rights Act of 1991 is the type of provision that should govern cases arising before its enactment....

\* \* \*

[T]he new compensatory damages provision would operate "retrospectively" if it were applied to conduct occurring before November 21, 1991. Unlike certain other forms of relief, compensatory damages are quintessentially backward-looking. Compensatory damages may be intended less to sanction wrongdoers than to make victims whole, but they do so by a mechanism that affects the liabilities of defendants. They do not "compensate" by distributing funds from the public coffers, but by requiring particular employers to pay for harms they caused. The introduction of a

---

**32.** At the time *Bradley* was decided, it was by no means a truism to point out that rules announced in intervening judicial decisions should normally be applied to a case pending when the intervening decision came down. In 1974, our doctrine on judicial retroactivity involved a substantial measure of discretion, guided by equitable standards resembling the *Bradley* "manifest injustice" test itself. [citations omitted]. While it was accurate in 1974 to say that a new rule announced in a judicial decision was only presumptively applicable to pending cases, we have since established a firm rule of retroactivity. [citations omitted].

right to compensatory damages is also the type of legal change that would have an impact on private parties' planning.[35] In this case, the event to which the new damages provision relates is the discriminatory conduct of respondents' agent John Williams; if applied here, that provision would attach an important new legal burden to that conduct. The new damages remedy in § 102, we conclude, is the kind of provision that does not apply to events antedating its enactment in the absence of clear congressional intent.

In cases like this one, in which prior law afforded no relief, § 102 can be seen as creating a new cause of action, and its impact on parties' rights is especially pronounced. Section 102 confers a new right to monetary relief on persons like petitioner who were victims of a hostile work environment but were not constructively discharged, and the novel prospect of damages liability for their employers. Because Title VII previously authorized recovery of backpay in some cases, and because compensatory damages under § 102(a) are in addition to any backpay recoverable, the new provision also resembles a statute increasing the amount of damages available under a preestablished cause of action. Even under that view, however, the provision would, if applied in cases arising before the Act's effective date, undoubtedly impose on employers found liable a "new disability" in respect to past events. See *Society for Propagation of the Gospel*, 22 F.Cas., at 767. The extent of a party's liability, in the civil context as well as the criminal, is an important legal consequence that cannot be ignored.[36] Neither in

---

**35.** As petitioner and amici suggest, concerns of unfair surprise and upsetting expectations are attenuated in the case of intentional employment discrimination, which has been unlawful for more than a generation. However, fairness concerns would not be entirely absent if the damages provisions of § 102 were to apply to events preceding its enactment, as the facts of this case illustrate. Respondent USI's management, when apprised of the wrongful conduct of petitioner's coworker, took timely action to remedy the problem. The law then in effect imposed no liability on an employer who corrected discriminatory work conditions before the conditions became so severe as to result in the victim's constructive discharge. Assessing damages against respondents on a theory of *respondeat superior* would thus entail an element of surprise. Even when the conduct in question is morally reprehensible or illegal, a degree of unfairness is inherent whenever the law imposes additional burdens based on conduct that occurred in the past. Cf. Weaver, 450 U.S., at 28–30, 101 S.Ct., at 963–965 (Ex Post Facto Clause assures fair notice and governmental restraint, and does not turn on "an individual's right to less punishment").

The new damages provisions of § 102 can be expected to give managers an added incentive to take preventive measures to ward off discriminatory conduct by subordinates before it occurs, but that purpose is not served by applying the regime to preenactment conduct.

**36.** The state courts have consistently held that statutes changing or abolishing limits on the amount of damages available in wrongful death actions should not, in the absence of clear legislative intent, apply to actions arising before their enactment. See, e.g., Dempsey v. State, 451 A.2d 273 (R.I. 1982) ("Every court which has considered the issue . . . has found a subsequent change as to the amount or the elements of damage in the wrongful-death statute to be substantive rather than procedural or remedial, and thus any such change must be applied prospectively"); . . . Mihoy v. Proulx, 113 N.H 698, 701, 313 A.2d 723, 725 (1973) ("To apply the increased limit after the date of the accident would clearly enlarge the defendant's liability retrospectively. In the absence of an express provision, we cannot conclude that the legislature intended retrospective application"). [citations omitted].

*Bradley* itself, nor in any case before or since in which Congress had not clearly spoken, have we read a statute substantially increasing the monetary liability of a private party to apply to conduct occurring before the statute's enactment. [citations omitted].[37]

It will frequently be true, as petitioner and amici forcefully argue here, that retroactive application of a new statute would vindicate its purpose more fully. That consideration, however, is not sufficient to rebut the presumption against retroactivity. Statutes are seldom crafted to pursue a single goal, and compromises necessary to their enactment may require adopting means other than those that would most effectively pursue the main goal. A legislator who supported a prospective statute might reasonably oppose retroactive application of the same statute. Indeed, there is reason to believe that the omission of the 1990 version's express retroactivity provisions was a factor in the passage of the 1991 bill. Section 102 is plainly not the sort of provision that must be understood to operate retroactively because a contrary reading would render it ineffective.

The presumption against statutory retroactivity is founded upon sound considerations of general policy and practice, and accords with long held and widely shared expectations about the usual operation of legislation. We are satisfied that it applies to § 102. Because we have found no clear evidence of congressional intent that § 102 of the Civil Rights Act of 1991 should apply to cases arising before its enactment, we conclude that the judgment of the Court of Appeals must be affirmed.

It is so ordered.

■ JUSTICE SCALIA, with whom JUSTICE KENNEDY and JUSTICE THOMAS join, concurring in the judgments.

I

I of course agree with the Court that there exists a judicial presumption, of great antiquity, that a legislative enactment affecting substantive rights does not apply retroactively absent clear statement to the contrary. See generally Kaiser Aluminum & Chemical Corp. v. Bonjorno, 494 U.S. 827, 840 (1990) (Scalia, J., concurring). The Court, however, is willing to let that clear statement be supplied, not by the text of the law in question, but by individual legislators who participated in the enactment of the law, and even legislators in an earlier Congress which tried and failed to enact a

---

**37.** We have sometimes said that new "remedial" statutes, like new "procedural" ones, should presumptively apply to pending cases. See, e.g., Ex parte Collett, 337 U.S., at 71, and n. 38, 69 S.Ct., at 952–953, and n. 38 ("Clearly, § 1404(a) is a remedial provision applicable to pending actions"); Beazell, 269 U.S., at 171, 46 S.Ct., at 69 (Ex Post Facto Clause does not limit "legislative control of remedies and modes of procedure which do not affect matters of substance"). While that statement holds true for some kinds of remedies, we have not classified a statute introducing damages liability as the sort of "remedial" change that should presumptively apply in pending cases. "Retroactive modification" of damage remedies may "normally harbo[r] much less potential for mischief than retroactive changes in the principles of liability," Hastings v. Earth Satellite Corp., 628 F.2d 85, 93 (C.A.D.C.), cert. denied, 449 U.S. 905, 101 S.Ct. 281, 66 L.Ed.2d 137 (1980), but that potential is nevertheless still significant.

similar law. For the Court not only combs the floor debate and committee reports of the statute at issue, the Civil Rights Act of 1991, Pub.L. 102–166, 105 Stat. 1071, but also reviews the procedural history of an earlier, unsuccessful, attempt by a different Congress to enact similar legislation, the Civil Rights Act of 1990, S. 2104, 101st Cong., 1st Sess. (1990).

This effectively converts the "clear statement" rule into a "discernible legislative intent" rule—and even that understates the difference. The Court's rejection of the floor statements of certain Senators because they are "frankly partisan" and "cannot plausibly be read as reflecting any general agreement" reads like any other exercise in the soft science of legislative historicizing,[1] undisciplined by any distinctive "clear statement" requirement. If it is a "clear statement" we are seeking, surely it is not enough to insist that the statement can "plausibly be read as reflecting general agreement"; the statement must clearly reflect general agreement. No legislative history can do that, of course, but only the text of the statute itself. That has been the meaning of the "clear statement" retroactivity rule from the earliest times. [citations omitted]. I do not deem that clear rule to be changed by the Court's dicta regarding legislative history in the present case.

\* \* \*

## II

The Court's opinion begins with an evaluation of petitioner's argument that the text of the statute dictates its retroactive application. The Court's rejection of that argument cannot be as forceful as it ought, so long as it insists upon compromising the clarity of the ancient and constant assumption that legislation is prospective, by attributing a comparable pedigree to the nouveau *Bradley* presumption in favor of applying the law in effect at the time of decision. See Bradley v. Richmond School Bd., 416 U.S. 696, 711–716 (1974). As I have demonstrated elsewhere and need not repeat here, *Bradley* and Thorpe v. Housing Authority of Durham, 393 U.S. 268 (1969), simply misread our precedents and invented an utterly new and erroneous rule. See generally *Bonjorno*, 494 U.S., at 840 (Scalia, J., concurring).

Besides embellishing the pedigree of the *Bradley–Thorpe* presumption, the Court goes out of its way to reaffirm the holdings of those cases. I see nothing to be gained by overruling them, but neither do I think the indefensible should needlessly be defended. And *Thorpe*, at least, is really indefensible. The regulation at issue there required that "before *instituting an eviction proceeding* local housing authorities ... should inform the tenant ... of the reasons for the eviction.... " *Thorpe*, *supra*, at 272, and n. 8 (emphasis added). The Court imposed that requirement on an eviction proceeding instituted eighteen months before the regulation issued. That

---

**1.** In one respect, I must acknowledge, the Court's effort may be unique. There is novelty as well as irony in his supporting the judgment that the floor statements on the 1991 Act are unreliable by citing Senator Danforth's floor statement on the 1991 Act to the effect that floor statements on the 1991 Act are unreliable.

application was plainly retroactive and was wrong. The result in *Bradley* presents a closer question; application of an attorney's fees provision to ongoing litigation is arguably not retroactive. If it were retroactive, however, it would surely not be saved (as the Court suggests) by the existence of another theory under which attorney's fees might have been discretionarily awarded.

### III

My last, and most significant, disagreement with the Court's analysis of this case pertains to the meaning of retroactivity. The Court adopts as its own the definition crafted by Justice Story in a case involving a provision of the New Hampshire Constitution that prohibited "retrospective" laws: a law is retroactive only if it "takes away or impairs vested rights acquired under existing laws, or creates a new obligation, imposes a new duty, or attaches a new disability, in respect to transactions or considerations already past." Society for Propagation of the Gospel v. Wheeler, 22 F.Cas. 756, 767 (No. 13,516) (CCNH 1814) (Story, J.).

\* \* \*

The seemingly random exceptions to the Court's "vested rights" (substance-vs.-procedure) criterion must be made, I suggest, because that criterion is fundamentally wrong. It may well be that the upsetting of "vested substantive rights" was the proper touchstone for interpretation of New Hampshire's constitutional prohibition, as it is for interpretation of the United States Constitution's ex post facto Clauses. But I doubt that it has anything to do with the more mundane question before us here: absent clear statement to the contrary, what is the presumed temporal application of a statute? For purposes of that question, a procedural change should no more be presumed to be retroactive than a substantive one. The critical issue, I think, is not whether the rule affects "vested rights," or governs substance or procedure, but rather what is the relevant activity that the rule regulates. Absent clear statement otherwise, only such relevant activity which occurs after the effective date of the statute is covered. Most statutes are meant to regulate primary conduct, and hence will not be applied in trials involving conduct that occurred before their effective date. But other statutes have a different purpose and therefore a different relevant retroactivity event. A new rule of evidence governing expert testimony, for example, is aimed at regulating the conduct of trial, and the event relevant to retroactivity of the rule is introduction of the testimony. Even though it is a procedural rule, it would unquestionably not be applied to testimony already taken—reversing a case on appeal, for example, because the new rule had not been applied at a trial which antedated the statute.

The inadequacy of the Court's "vested rights" approach becomes apparent when a change in one of the incidents of trial alters substantive entitlements. The opinion classifies attorney's fees provisions as procedural and permits "retroactive" application (in the sense of application to cases involving pre-enactment conduct). It seems to me, however, that holding a person liable for attorney's fees affects a "substantive right" no less than holding him liable for compensatory or punitive damages, which the Court treats as affecting a vested right. If attorney's fees can be awarded in a suit involving conduct that antedated the fee-authorizing statute, it is because the purpose of the fee award is not to affect that conduct, but to encourage suit for the vindication of certain rights—so that the retroactivity event is the filing of suit, whereafter encouragement is no longer needed. Or perhaps because the purpose of the fee award is to facilitate suit—so that the retroactivity event is the termination of suit, whereafter facilitation can no longer be achieved.

\* \* \*

Finally, statutes eliminating previously available forms of prospective relief provide another challenge to the Court's approach. Courts traditionally withhold requested injunctions that are not authorized by then-current law, even if they were authorized at the time suit commenced and at the time the primary conduct sought to be enjoined was first engaged in [citations omitted]. The reason, which has nothing to do with whether it is possible to have a vested right to prospective relief, is that "obviously, this form of relief operates only in futuro," Deering, ibid. Since the purpose of prospective relief is to affect the future rather than remedy the past, the relevant time for judging its retroactivity is the very moment at which it is ordered.

I do not maintain that it will always be easy to determine, from the statute's purpose, the relevant event for assessing its retroactivity. As I have suggested, for example, a statutory provision for attorney's fees presents a difficult case. Ordinarily, however, the answer is clear—as it is in both *Landgraf* and *Rivers*. Unlike the Court, I do not think that any of the provisions at issue is "not easily classified." They are all directed at the regulation of primary conduct, and the occurrence of the primary conduct is the relevant event.

■ JUSTICE BLACKMUN, dissenting.

Perhaps from an eagerness to resolve the "apparent tension," between Bradley v. Richmond School Bd., 416 U.S. 696 (1974), and Bowen v. Georgetown University Hospital, 488 U.S. 204 (1988), the Court rejects the "most logical reading," of the Civil Rights Act of 1991, 105 Stat. 1071 (Act), and resorts to a presumption against retroactivity. This approach seems to me to pay insufficient fidelity to the settled principle that the "starting point for interpretation of a statute 'is the language of the statute itself,' " and extends the presumption against retroactive legislation beyond its historical reach and purpose. [citations omitted].

A straightforward textual analysis of the Act indicates that § 102's provision of compensatory damages and its attendant right to a jury trial apply to cases pending on appeal on the date of enactment. This analysis begins with § 402(a) of the Act, 105 Stat. 1099: "Except as otherwise specifically provided, this Act and the amendments made by this Act shall take effect upon enactment." Under the "settled rule that a statute must, if possible, be construed in such fashion that every word has operative effect," § 402(a)'s qualifying clause, "[e]xcept as otherwise specifically provided," cannot be dismissed as mere surplusage or an "insurance policy" against future judicial interpretation. Instead, it most logically refers to the Act's two sections "specifically providing" that the statute does not apply to cases pending on the date of enactment: (a) § 402(b), 105 Stat. 1099, which provides, in effect, that the Act did not apply to the then pending case of Wards Cove Packing Co. v. Atonio, 490 U.S. 642 (1989), and (b) § 109(c), 105 Stat. 1078, which states that the Act's protections of overseas employment "shall not apply with respect to conduct occurring before the date of the enactment of this Act." Self-evidently, if the entire Act were inapplicable to pending cases, §§ 402(b) and 109(c) would be "entirely redundant.". Thus, the clear implication is that, while § 402(b) and § 109(c) do not apply to pending cases, other provisions—including § 102—do. " 'Absent a clearly expressed legislative intention to the contrary, [this] language must . . . be regarded as conclusive.' " The legislative history of the Act, featuring a welter of conflicting and "some frankly partisan" floor statements, but no committee report, evinces no such contrary legislative intent.[2] Thus, I see no reason to dismiss as "unlikely," the most natural reading of the statute, in order to embrace some other reading that is also "possible[.]" [citations omitted].

Even if the language of the statute did not answer the retroactivity question, it would be appropriate under our precedents to apply § 102 to pending cases. The well-established presumption against retroactive legislation, which serves to protect settled expectations, is grounded in a respect for vested rights.[citation omitted]. This presumption need not be applied to remedial legislation, such as § 102, that does not proscribe any conduct that was previously legal [citations omitted].

At no time within the last generation has an employer had a vested right to engage in or to permit sexual harassment; " 'there is no such thing as a vested right to do wrong.' "[citations omitted]. Section 102 of the Act expands the remedies available for acts of intentional discrimination, but does not alter the scope of the employee's basic right to be free from discrimination or the employer's corresponding legal duty. There is nothing unjust about holding an employer responsible for injuries caused by conduct that has been illegal for almost 30 years. Accordingly, I respectfully dissent.

**2.** Virtually every Court of Appeals to consider the application of the 1991 Act to pending cases has concluded that the legislative history provides no reliable guidance. See, e.g., Gersman v. Group Health Ass'n, Inc., 975 F.2d 886 (C.A.D.C.1992); Mozee v. American Commercial Marine Service Co., 963 F.2d 929 (C.A.7 1992). The absence in the Act of the strong retroactivity language of the vetoed 1990 legislation, which would have applied the new law to final judgments as well as to pending cases, [citations omitted] is not instructive of Congress' intent with respect to pending cases alone. Significantly, Congress also rejected language that put pending claims beyond the reach of the 1990 or 1991 Act. See 136 Cong.Rec. H6747 (daily ed. Aug. 3, 1990) [citations omitted].

## Notes and Questions

**1.** The Supreme Court in *Landgraf* held that the "manifest injustice" exception of *Bradley* is controlling, absent clear Congressional intent.

> *Bradley* [does] not alter the well-settled presumption against application of the class of new statutes that would have genuinely "retroactive" effect ... [Section] 102 can be seen as creating a new cause of action, and its impact on parties' rights is especially pronounced.

The *Landgraf* test appears to ask "whether the new provision attaches new legal consequences to events completed before its enactment." Do you think this law has a "genuinely 'retroactive' effect"? Recall that in *Bradley,* the Court upheld a "retroactive" award of attorney's fees. How would you define retroactive effect?

**2.** What happens with restorative statutes, where the intent of the statute is to correct a wrong judicial interpretation? This question was addressed in Rivers v. Roadway Express, Inc., 511 U.S. 298 (1994).

In *Rivers,* the petitioners alleged they had been wrongfully dismissed from their jobs based on their race. They sued under 42 U.S.C. § 1981. Before the trial, the Supreme Court issued Patterson v. McLean, 491 U.S. 164 (1989), holding that 42 U.S.C. § 1981 prohibited discrimination only in the making and enforcement of contracts and therefore did not prohibit racial discrimination in the *termination* of the contract. This interpretation precluded the *Rivers* claim. The District Court therefore dismissed the case. While the petitioner's appeal was pending, Congress passed § 101 of the Civil Rights Act of 1991, "overruling" the Supreme Court's decision in *Patterson.* The Court of Appeals nonetheless ruled that the Civil Rights Act of 1964 as interpreted by *Patterson,* not new § 101, governed the *Rivers* case.

The Supreme Court affirmed. Applying its reasoning in *Landgraf,* the Court ruled that "Congress' decision to alter the rule of law established in one of our cases ... does not, by itself, reveal whether Congress intends the 'overruling' statute to apply retroactively to events." The Court noted that a proposed version of § 101 included explicitly retroactive language not contained in the enacted version. Its elimination from the final version strongly suggested that Congress did not intend for the amended statute to apply to pending cases.

How does this compare with *Newport News Shipbuilding and Dry Dock,* (*supra* p. 470), in which the restorative nature of the statute significantly influenced the Court?

**3.** Recall Justice Scalia's remark in *Bonjorno, supra,* that *Bradley* and *Bowen* "are not merely, as the Court confesses, in 'apparent tension' ... they are in irreconcilable contradiction." How, if at all, have *Rivers* and *Landgraf* helped to reconcile *Bradley* and *Bowen*?

**4.** For a discussion of these questions see, e.g., Jill E. Fisch, Retroactivity and Legal Change: An Equilibrium Approach, 110 Harv. L. Rev. 1055 (1997); Duncan B. Hollis, The Retroactivity of the Civil Rights Act of 1991 and 1981: Rivers v. Roadway Express, Survey: 1993–94 Annual Survey of Labor and Employment Law: Employment Discrimination Law, 36 B.C. L. Rev. 373 (1995); Daniel Patrick Tokaji, Note, The Persistence of Prejudice: Process–Based Theory and the Retroactivity of the Civil Rights Act of 1991, 103 Yale L.J. 567 (1993); and Scott M. Pearson, Canons, Presumptions and Manifest Injustice: Retroactivity of the Civil Rights Act of 1991, 3 S.Cal.Interdisc.L.J. 461 (1993).

### 3. POSTSCRIPT: WHAT IS "GENUINELY" RETROACTIVE?

## Martin v. Hadix

Supreme Court of the United States, 1999.
527 U.S. 343, 119 S.Ct. 1998, 144 L.Ed.2d 347.

O'CONNOR, J., delivered the opinion of the Court, in which REHNQUIST, C. J., and KENNEDY, SOUTER, THOMAS, and BREYER, JJ., joined, in which SCALIA, J., joined as to all but Part II–B, and in which STEVENS and GINSBURG, JJ., joined as to Parts I, II–A–1, and II–B–1. SCALIA, J., filed an opinion concurring in part and concurring in the judgment. GINSBURG, J., filed an opinion concurring in part and dissenting in part, in which STEVENS, J., joined.

■ JUSTICE O'CONNOR delivered the opinion of the Court.*

Section 803(d)(3) of the Prison Litigation Reform Act of 1995 (PLRA or Act), 110 Stat. 1321–66, 42 U.S.C. § 1997e(d)(3) (1994 ed., Supp. II), places limits on the fees that may be awarded to attorneys who litigate prisoner lawsuits. We are asked to decide how this section applies to cases that were pending when the PLRA became effective on April 26, 1996. We conclude that § 803(d)(3) limits attorney's fees with respect to postjudgment monitoring services performed after the PLRA's effective date but it does not so limit fees for postjudgment monitoring performed before the effective date.

I

The fee disputes before us arose out of two class action lawsuits challenging the conditions of confinement in the Michigan prison system. The first case, which we will call Glover, began in 1977 when a now-certified class of female prisoners filed suit under Rev. Stat. § 1979, 42 U.S.C. § 1983 (1994 ed., Supp. II), in the United States District Court for the Eastern District of Michigan. The Glover plaintiffs alleged that the defendant prison officials had violated their rights under the Equal Protection Clause of the Fourteenth Amendment by denying them access to vocational and educational opportunities that were available to male prisoners.... The second case at issue here, Hadix, began in 1980. At that time, male prisoners at the State Prison of Southern Michigan, Central Complex (SPSM–CC), filed suit under 42 U.S.C. § 1983 in the United

* For the reasons stated in his separate opinion, JUSTICE SCALIA joins Parts I, II–A, and II–C of this opinion. For the reasons stated in JUSTICE GINSBURG's separate opinion, she and JUSTICE STEVENS join Parts I, II–A–1, and II–B–1 of this opinion.

States District Court for the Eastern District of Michigan claiming that the conditions of their confinement at SPSM–CC violated the First, Eighth, and Fourteenth Amendments to the Constitution. . . .

In 1985, the parties agreed to, and the District Court entered, an order providing that the plaintiffs were entitled to attorney's fees for post-judgment monitoring of the defendants' compliance with the court's reme-dial decrees. This order also established the system for awarding monitor-ing fees that was in place when the present dispute arose. Under this system, the plaintiffs submit their fee requests on a semiannual basis, and the defendants then have 28 days to submit any objections to the requested award. The District Court resolves any disputes. In an appeal from a subsequent dispute over the meaning of this order, the Court of Appeals for the Sixth Circuit affirmed that the plaintiffs were entitled to attorney's fees, at the prevailing market rate, for postjudgment monitoring. The prevailing market rate has been adjusted over the years, but it is currently set at $150 per hour. [citations omitted].

\* \* \*

The fee landscape changed with the passage of the PLRA on April 26, 1996. The PLRA, as its name suggests, contains numerous provisions governing the course of prison litigation in the federal courts. It provides, for example, limits on the availability of certain types of relief in such suits, see 18 U.S.C. § 3626(a)(2) (1994 ed., Supp. III), and for the termination of prospective relief orders after a limited time, § 3626(b). The section of the PLRA at issue here, § 803(d)(3), places a cap on the size of attorney's fees that may be awarded in prison litigation suits:

"(d) Attorney's fees

"(1) In any action brought by a prisoner who is confined to any jail, prison, or other correctional facility, in which attorney's fees are authorized under [ 42 U.S.C. § 1988], such fees shall not be awarded, except to the extent [authorized here].

. . .

"(3) No award of attorney's fees in an action described in paragraph (1) shall be based on an hourly rate greater than 150 percent of the hourly rate established under [ 18 U.S.C. § 3006A (1994 ed. and Supp. III)], for payment of court-appointed counsel." § 803(d), 42 U.S.C. § 1997e(d) (1994 ed., Supp. II).

Court-appointed attorneys in the Eastern District of Michigan are compensated at a maximum rate of $75 per hour, and thus, under § 803(d)(3), the PLRA fee cap for attorneys working on prison litigation suits translates into a maximum hourly rate of $112.50.

Questions involving the PLRA first arose in both Glover and Hadix with respect to fee requests for postjudgment monitoring performed before the PLRA was enacted. In both cases, in early 1996, the plaintiffs submit-ted fee requests for work performed during the last half of 1995. These requests were still pending when the PLRA became effective on April 26,

1996. In both cases, the District Court concluded that the PLRA fee cap did not limit attorney's fees for services performed in these cases prior to the effective date of the Act. Fee requests next were filed in both Glover and Hadix for services performed between January 1, 1996, and June 30, 1996, a time period encompassing work performed both before and after the effective date of the PLRA. As relevant to this case, the defendant state prison officials argued that these fee requests were subject to the fee cap found in § 803(d)(3) of the PLRA, and the District Court accepted this argument in part. In nearly identical orders issued in the two cases, the court reiterated its earlier conclusion that the PLRA does not limit fees for work performed before April 26, 1996, but concluded that the PLRA fee cap does limit fees for services performed after the effective date.

* * *

In this Court, the Hadix and Glover plaintiffs are respondents, and the defendant prison officials from both cases are petitioners.

II

Petitioners contend that the PLRA applies to *Glover* and *Hadix,* cases that were pending when the PLRA was enacted. This fact pattern presents a recurring question in the law: When should a new federal statute be applied to pending cases? To answer this question, we ask first "whether Congress has expressly prescribed the statute's proper reach." Landgraf v. USI Film Products, 511 U.S. 244, 280 (1994). If there is no congressional directive on the temporal reach of a statute, we determine whether the application of the statute to the conduct at issue would result in a retroactive effect. Ibid. If so, then in keeping with our "traditional presumption" against retroactivity, we presume that the statute does not apply to that conduct. Ibid.

A

1

Congress has not expressly mandated the temporal reach of § 803(d)(3). Section 803(d)(1) provides that "in any action brought by a prisoner who is confined [to a correctional facility] ... attorney's fees ... shall not be awarded, except" as authorized by the statute. Section 803(d)(3) further provides that "no award of attorney's fees ... shall be based on an hourly rate greater than 150 percent of the hourly rate established under [ 18 U.S.C. § 3006A], for payment of court-appointed counsel." Petitioners contend that this language—particularly the phrase "in *any* action *brought* by a prisoner who *is* confined," § 803(d)(1) (emphasis added)—clearly expresses a congressional intent that § 803(d) apply to pending cases. They argue that "any" is a broad, encompassing word, and that its use with "brought," a past-tense verb, demonstrates congressional intent to apply the fees limitations to all fee awards entered after the PLRA became effective, even when those awards were for services performed before the PLRA was enacted. They also contend that § 803(d)(3), by its own terms, applies to all "awards"—understood as the actual court order directing the payment of fees—entered after the effective date of the PLRA, regardless of when the work was performed.

The fundamental problem with all of petitioners' statutory arguments is that they stretch the language of § 803(d) to find congressional intent on the temporal scope of that section when we believe that § 803(d) is better read as setting substantive limits on the award of attorney's fees. Section 803(d)(1), for example, prohibits fee awards unless those fees were "directly and reasonably incurred" in the suit, and unless those fees are "proportionately related" to or "directly and reasonably incurred in enforcing" the relief ordered. 42 U.S.C. § 1997e(d)(1). Similarly, § 803(d)(3) sets substantive limits by prohibiting the award of fees based on hourly rates greater than a specified rate. In other words, these sections define the substantive availability of attorney's fees; they do not purport to define the temporal reach of these substantive limitations. This language falls short of demonstrating a "clear congressional intent" favoring retroactive application of these fees limitations. *Landgraf*, 511 U.S. at 280. It falls short, in other words, of the "unambiguous directive" or "express command" that the statute is to be applied retroactively. Id., at 263, 280.

In any event, we note that "brought," as used in this section, is not a past-tense verb; rather, it is the participle in a participial phrase modifying the noun "action." And although the word "any" is broad, it stretches the imagination to suggest that Congress intended, through the use of this one word, to make the fee limitations applicable to all fee awards. Finally, we do not believe that the phrase "no award" in § 803(d)(3) demonstrates congressional intent to apply that section to all fee awards (i.e., fee payment orders) entered after the PLRA's effective date. Had Congress intended § 803(d)(3) to apply to all fee orders entered after the effective date, even when those awards compensate for work performed before the effective date, it could have used language more obviously targeted to addressing the temporal reach of that section. It could have stated, for example, that "No award entered after the effective date of this Act shall be based on an hourly rate greater than the ceiling rate."

The conclusion that § 803(d) does not clearly express congressional intent that it apply retroactively is strengthened by comparing § 803(d) to the language that we suggested in Landgraf might qualify as a clear statement that a statute was to apply retroactively: "The new provisions shall apply to all proceedings pending on or commenced after the date of enactment." Id., at 260 (internal quotation marks omitted). This provision, unlike the language of the PLRA, unambiguously addresses the temporal reach of the statute. With no such analogous language making explicit reference to the statute's temporal reach, it cannot be said that Congress has "expressly prescribed" § 803(d)'s temporal reach. Id., at 280.

* * *

According to respondents, a comparison of §§ 802 and 803 of the PLRA leads to the conclusion that § 803(d) should only apply to cases filed after its enactment. The attorney's fees provisions are found in § 803 of the PLRA, and, as described above, this section contains no explicit directive that it should apply to pending cases. By contrast, § 802—addressing "appropriate remedies" in prison litigation—explicitly provides that it applies to pending cases: "[This section] shall apply with respect to all prospective relief whether such relief was originally granted or approved before, on, or after the date of the enactment of this title." § 802(b)(1), note following 18 U.S.C. § 3626 (1994 ed., Supp. III)....

\* \* \*

Because §§ 802 and 803 address wholly distinct subject matters, [a] negative inference does not arise from the silence of § 803. Section 802 addresses "appropriate remedies" in prison litigation, prohibiting, for example, prospective relief unless it is "narrowly drawn" and is "the least intrusive means necessary to correct the violation." § 802(a),18 U.S.C. § 3626(a)(1)(A) (1994 ed., Supp. III). That section also creates new standards designed to encourage the prompt termination of prospective relief orders, providing, for example, for the "immediate termination of any prospective relief if the relief was approved or granted in the absence of a finding by the court that the relief is narrowly drawn, extends no further than necessary to correct the violation of the Federal right, and is the least intrusive means necessary to correct the violation of the Federal right." § 802(a), 18 U.S.C. § 3626(b)(2). Section 803(d), by contrast, does not address the propriety of various forms of relief and does not provide for the immediate termination of ongoing relief orders. Rather, it governs the award of attorney's fees. Thus, there is no reason to conclude that if Congress was concerned that § 802 apply to pending cases, it would "have been just as concerned" that § 803 apply to pending cases.

Finally, we note that respondents' reliance on the legislative history overstates the inferences that can be drawn from an ambiguous act of legislative drafting. Even if respondents are correct about the legislative history, the inference that respondents draw from this history is speculative. It rests on the assumption that the reason the fees provisions were moved was to move them away from the language applying § 802 to pending cases, when they may have been moved for a variety of other reasons. This weak inference provides a thin reed on which to rest the argument that the fees provisions, by negative implication, were intended to apply prospectively.

B

Because we conclude that Congress has not "expressly prescribed" the proper reach of § 803(d)(3), *Landgraf*, 511 U.S. at 280, we must determine whether application of this section in this case would have retroactive effects inconsistent with the usual rule that legislation is deemed to be prospective. The inquiry into whether a statute operates retroactively demands a common sense, functional judgment about "whether the new provision attaches new legal consequences to events completed before its enactment." *Id.* at 270. This judgment should be informed and guided by "familiar considerations of fair notice, reasonable reliance, and settled expectations." Ibid.

1

For postjudgment monitoring performed before the effective date of the PLRA, the PLRA's attorney's fees provisions, as construed by the respondents, would have a retroactive effect contrary to the usual assumption that congressional statutes are prospective in operation.... The PLRA, as applied to work performed before its effective date, would alter the fee arrangement post hoc by reducing the rate of compensation. To give effect to the PLRA's fees limitations, after the fact, would "attach new legal consequences" to completed conduct. *Landgraf*, supra, at 270.

... While it may be possible to generalize about types of rules that ordinarily will not raise retroactivity concerns, see, e.g., id. at 273–275, these generalizations do not end the inquiry. For example, in *Landgraf*, we acknowledged that procedural rules may often be applied to pending suits with no retroactivity problems, id. at 275, but we also cautioned that "the mere fact that a new rule is procedural does not mean that it applies to every pending case," id. at 275, n. 29. We took pains to dispel the "suggestion that concerns about retroactivity have no application to procedural rules." Ibid. When determining whether a new statute operates retroactively, it is not enough to attach a label (e.g., "procedural," "collateral") to the statute; we must ask whether the statute operates retroactively.

Moreover, petitioners' reliance on our decision in Bradley v. School Bd. of Richmond, 416 U.S. 696, 40 L. Ed. 2d 476, 94 S. Ct. 2006 (1974), to support their argument that attorney's fees provisions can be applied retroactively is misplaced. In *Bradley*, the District Court had awarded attorney's fees, based on general equitable principles, to a group of parents who had prevailed in their suit seeking the desegregation of the Richmond schools. While the case was pending on appeal, Congress passed a statute specifically authorizing the award of attorney's fees for prevailing parties in school desegregation cases. The Court of Appeals held that the new statute could not authorize fee awards for work performed before the effective date of the new law, but we reversed, holding that the fee award in that case was proper. Because attorney's fees were available, albeit under different principles, before passage of the statute, and because the District Court had in fact already awarded fees invoking these different principles, there was no manifest injustice in allowing the fee statute to apply in that case. Id., at 720–721. We held that the award of statutory attorney's fees did not upset any reasonable expectations of the parties. In this case, by contrast, from the beginning of these suits, the parties have proceeded on the assumption that 42 U.S.C. § 1988 would govern. The PLRA was not passed until well after respondents had been declared prevailing parties and thus entitled to attorney's fees. To impose the new standards now, for work performed before the PLRA became effective, would upset the reasonable expectations of the parties.

2

With respect to postjudgment monitoring performed after the effective date of the PLRA, by contrast, there is no retroactivity problem. On April

26, 1996, through the PLRA, the plaintiffs' attorneys were on notice that their hourly rate had been adjusted. From that point forward, they would be paid at a rate consistent with the dictates of the law. After April 26, 1996, any expectation of compensation at the pre-PLRA rates was unreasonable. There is no manifest injustice in telling an attorney performing postjudgment monitoring services that, going forward, she will earn a lower hourly rate than she had earned in the past. If the attorney does not wish to perform services at this new, lower, pay rate, she can choose not to work. In other words, as applied to work performed after the effective date of the PLRA, the PLRA has future effect on future work; this does not raise retroactivity concerns.

Respondents contend that the PLRA has retroactive effect in this context because it attaches new legal consequences (a lower pay rate) to conduct completed before enactment. The pre-enactment conduct that respondents contend is affected is the attorney's initial decision to file suit on behalf of the prisoner clients. . . . [R]espondents' argument assumes that once an attorney files suit, she must continue working on that case until the decree is terminated. Respondents provide no support for this assumption, however. They allude to ethical constraints on an attorney's ability to withdraw from a case midstream, see Brief for Respondents 29 ("And finally, it is at that time that plaintiffs' counsel commit themselves ethically to continued representation of their clients to ensure that the Constitution is honored, a course of conduct that cannot lightly be altered"), but they do not seriously contend that the attorneys here were prohibited from withdrawing from the case during the postjudgment monitoring stage. It cannot be said that the PLRA changes the legal consequences of the attorneys' pre-PLRA decision to file the case.

C

In sum, we conclude that the PLRA contains no express command about its temporal scope. Because we find that the PLRA, if applied to postjudgment monitoring services performed before the effective date of the Act, would have a retroactive effect inconsistent with our assumption that statutes are prospective, in the absence of an express command by Congress to apply the Act retroactively, we decline to do so. *Landgraf,* 511 U.S. at 280. With respect to postjudgment monitoring performed after the effective date, by contrast, there is no retroactive effect, and the PLRA fees cap applies to such work. Accordingly, the judgment of the Court of Appeals for the Sixth Circuit is affirmed in part and reversed in part.

It is so ordered.

■ JUSTICE SCALIA, concurring in part and concurring in the judgment.

* * *

I agree with the Court that the [PLRA's] intended temporal application is not set forth in the text of the statute, and that the outcome must therefore be governed by our interpretive principle that, in absence of contrary indication, a statute will not be construed to have retroactive application, see *Landgraf*. But that leaves open the key question: retroactive in reference to what? The various options in the present case include (1) the alleged violation upon which the fee-imposing suit is based (applying the new fee rule to any case involving an alleged violation that occurred before the PLRA became effective would be giving it "retroactive application"); (2) the lawyer's undertaking to prosecute the suit for which attorney's fees were provided (applying the new fee rule to any case in which the lawyer was retained before the PLRA became effective would be giving it "retroactive application"); (3) the filing of the suit in which the fees are imposed (applying the new fee rule to any suit brought before the PLRA became effective would be giving it "retroactive application"); (4) the doing of the legal work for which the fees are payable (applying the new fee rule to any work done before the PLRA became effective would be giving it "retroactive application"); and (5) the actual award of fees in a prisoner case (applying the new fee rule to an award rendered before the PLRA became effective would be giving it "retroactive application").

My disagreement with the Court's approach is that, in deciding which of the above five reference points for the retroactivity determination ought to be selected, it seems to me not much help to ask which of them would frustrate expectations. In varying degrees, they all would. As I explained in my concurrence in *Landgraf*, 511 U.S. at 286 (opinion concurring in judgments), I think the decision of which reference point (which "retroactivity event") to select should turn upon which activity the statute was intended to regulate. If it was intended to affect primary conduct, No. 1 should govern; if it was intended to induce lawyers to undertake representation, No. 2—and so forth.

In my view, the most precisely defined purpose of the provision at issue here was to reduce the previously established incentive for lawyers to work on prisoners' civil rights cases. If the PLRA is viewed in isolation, of course, its purpose could be regarded as being simply to prevent a judicial award of fees in excess of the referenced amount—in which case the relevant retroactivity event would be the award. In reality, however, the PLRA simply revises the fees provided for by § 1988, and it seems to me that the underlying purpose of that provision must govern its amendment as well—which purpose was to provide an appropriate incentive for lawyers to work on (among other civil rights cases) prisoner suits.[1] That being so, the relevant retroactivity event is the doing of the work for which the incentive was offered.[2] All work rendered in reliance upon the fee assurance contained in the former § 1988 will be reimbursed at those rates; all work

---

**1.** Although the fees awarded under § 1988 are payable to the party rather than to the lawyer, I think it clear that the purpose of the provision was to enable the civil rights plaintiffs to offer a rate of compensation that would attract attorneys.

**2.** I reject the dissent's contention that the retroactivity event should be the attorney's undertaking to represent the civil rights plaintiff. The fees are intended to induce not merely signing on (no time can be billed for that) but actually doing the legal work. Like the Court, I do not think it true that an attorney who has signed on cannot terminate his representation; he assuredly can if the client says that he will no longer pay the hourly fee agreed upon.

rendered after the revised fee assurance of the PLRA became effective will be limited to the new rates. The District Court's announcement that it would permit future work to be billed at a higher rate operated in futuro; it sought to regulate future conduct rather than adjudicate past. It was therefore no less subject to revision by statute than is an injunction. Pennsylvania v. Wheeling & Belmont Bridge Co., 59 U.S. 421, 18 HOW 421, 436 (1856).

For these reasons, I concur in the judgment of the Court and join all but Part II–B of its opinion.

■ JUSTICE GINSBURG, with whom JUSTICE STEVENS joins, concurring in part and dissenting in part.

I agree with the Court's determination that § 803(d) of the Prison Litigation Reform Act of 1995,(PLRA or Act), does not "limit fees for postjudgment monitoring performed before the [Act's] effective date," ante, at 1, and with much of the reasoning set out in Parts I, II–A–1, and II–B–1 of the Court's opinion. I disagree, however, with the holding that § 803(d) "limits attorney's fees with respect to postjudgment monitoring services performed after ... the effective date." Ibid. I do not find in the PLRA's text or history a satisfactory basis for concluding that Congress meant to order a midstream change, placing cases commenced before the PLRA became law under the new regime. I would therefore affirm in full the judgment of the Court of Appeals for the Sixth Circuit, which held § 803(d) inapplicable to cases brought to court prior to the enactment of the PLRA....

\* \* \*

## II

\* \* \*

As the Court recognizes ... § 803(d)'s "any action brought" language refers to the provision's substantive scope, not its temporal reach, see ante, at 8; "any" appears in the text only in proximity to provisions identifying the law's substantive dimensions. Had Congress intended that § 803(d) apply retroactively, it might easily have specified, as the Court suggests, that all post-enactment awards shall be subject to the limitation, see ante, at 9, or prescribed that the provision "shall apply in all proceedings pending on or commenced after the date of enactment of this Act." Congress instead left unaddressed § 803(d)'s temporal reach.

Comparison of § 803(d)'s text with that of a neighboring provision, § 802(b)(1) of the PLRA, is instructive for the retroactivity question we face. Section 802(b)(1), which governs "appropriate remedies" in prison litigation, applies expressly to "all prospective relief whether such relief was originally granted or approved before, on, or after the date of the enactment of this title." 110 Stat. 1321–70, note following 18 U.S.C. § 3626. "Congress [thus] saw fit to tell us which part of the Act was to be retroactively applied," i.e., § 802. Jensen v. Clarke, 94 F.3d 1191, 1203 (C.A.8 1996). While I agree with the Court that the negative implication created by these two provisions is not dispositive, see ante, at 12, Congress' silence nevertheless suggests that § 803(d) has no carryback thrust.

Absent an express statutory command respecting retroactivity, *Landgraf* teaches, the attorney's fees provision should not be applied to pending cases if doing so would "have retroactive effect." 511 U.S. at 280. As the Court recognizes, see ante, at 15, application of § 803(d) to work performed before the PLRA's effective date would be impermissibly retroactive. Instead of the court-approved market-based fee that attorneys anticipated for work performed under the old regime, counsel would be limited to the new statutory rate. We long ago recognized the injustice of interpreting a statute to reduce the level of compensation for work already performed.

**III**

In my view, § 803(d) is most soundly read to cover all and only representations undertaken after the PLRA's effective date. Application of § 803(d) to representations commenced before the PLRA became law would "attach new legal consequences to [an] event completed before [the statute's] enactment"; hence the application would be retroactive under *Landgraf* 511 U.S. at 270. The critical event effected before the PLRA's effective date is the lawyer's undertaking to prosecute the client's civil rights claim. Applying § 803(d) to pending matters significantly alters the consequences of the representation on which the lawyer has embarked.[2] Notably, attorneys engaged before passage of the PLRA have little leeway to alter their conduct in response to the new legal regime; an attorney who initiated a prisoner's rights suit before April 26, 1996 remains subject to a professional obligation to see the litigation through to final disposition. See American Bar Association Model Rules of Professional Conduct, Rule 1.3, and Comment [3] (1999) ("[A] lawyer should carry through to conclusion all matters undertaken for a client."). Counsel's actions before and after that date are thus "inextricably part of a course of conduct initiated prior to the law." Inmates of D. C. Jail v. Jackson, 332 U.S. App. D.C. 451, 158 F.3d 1357, 1362 (C.A.D.C.1998) (Wald, J., dissenting).

While the injustice in applying the fee limitations to pending actions may be more readily apparent regarding work performed before the PLRA's effective date, application of the statute to work performed thereafter in pending cases also frustrates reasonable reliance on prior law and court-approved market rates. Consider, for example, two attorneys who filed similar prison reform lawsuits at the same time, pre-PLRA. Both attorneys initiated their lawsuits in the expectation that, if they prevailed, they would earn the market rate anticipated by pre-PLRA law. In one case, the lawsuit progressed swiftly, and labor-intensive pretrial discovery was completed

---

**2.** An attorney's decision to invest time and energy in a civil rights suit necessarily involves a complex balance of factors, including the likelihood of success, the amount of labor necessary to prosecute the case to completion, and the potential recovery. Applying § 803(d) to PLRA representations ongoing before April 26, 1996 effectively reduces the value of the lawyer's prior investment in the litigation, and disappoints reasonable reliance on the law in place at the time of the lawyer's undertaking.

before April 26, 1996. In the other, the suit lagged through no fault of plaintiff's counsel, pending the court's disposition of threshold motions, and the attorney was unable to pursue discovery until after April 26, 1996.[3] Both attorneys have prosecuted their claims with due diligence; both were obliged, having accepted the representations, to perform the work for which they seek compensation. There is scarcely greater injustice in denying pre-PLRA compensation for pretrial discovery in the one case than the other. Nor is there any reason to think that Congress intended these similarly situated attorneys to be treated differently.

The Court avoids a conclusion of retroactivity by dismissing as an unsupported assumption the attorneys' assertion of an obligation to continue their representations through to final disposition. See ante, at 16. It seems to me, however, that the assertion has secure support.

Like the ABA's Model Rules, the Michigan Rules of Professional Conduct, which apply to counsel in both *Hadix* and *Glover*, see Rule 83.20(j) (1999), provide that absent good cause for terminating a representation, "a lawyer should carry through to conclusion all matters undertaken for a client." Mich. Rules of Prof. Conduct, Rule 1.3 Comment (1999) It is true that withdrawal may be permitted where "the representation will result in an unreasonable financial burden on the lawyer," Rule 1.16(b)(5), but explanatory comments suggest that this exception is designed for situations in which "the client refuses to abide by the terms of an agreement relating to the representation, such as an agreement concerning fees," Rule 1.16 Comment Consistent with the Michigan Rules, counsel for petitioners affirmed at oral argument their ethical obligation to continue these representations to a natural conclusion. See Tr. of Oral Arg. 43 ("[Continuing the representation] does involve ethical concerns certainly, especially in these circumstances."). There is no reason to think counsel ethically could have abandoned these representations in response to the PLRA fee limitation, nor any basis to believe the trial court would have permitted counsel to withdraw. See Rule 1.16(c) ("When ordered to do so by a tribunal, a lawyer shall continue representation."). As I see it, the attorneys' pre-PLRA pursuit of the civil rights claims thus created an obligation, enduring post-PLRA, to continue to provide effective representation.

Accordingly, I conclude that the Sixth Circuit soundly resisted the "sophisticated construction," 143 F.3d at 252, that would split apart, for fee award purposes, a constant course of representation. "The triggering event for retroactivity purposes," I am persuaded, "is when the lawyer undertakes to litigate the civil rights action on behalf of the client." *Inmates of D. C. Jail*, 158 F.3d at 1362 (Wald, J. dissenting).

*Landgraf*'s lesson is that Congress must speak clearly when it wants new rules to govern pending cases. Because § 803(d) contains no clear

---

**3.** If counsel's conduct caused delay or protraction, the court could properly exercise discretion to deny or reduce the attorney's fee. See 42 U.S.C. § 1988(b) (1994 ed., Supp. II) ("The court, in its discretion, may allow ... a reasonable attorney's fee.").

statement on its temporal reach, and because the provision would operate retroactively as applied to lawsuits pending on the Act's effective date, I would hold that the fee limitation applies only to cases commenced after April 26, 1996.

### Questions

**1.**   The history of the case and of the legislation suggests several "retroactivity events." What are they, and at what point would the legislation, if effective as of that event, have "genuinely retroactive" effect? What activity is the statute endeavoring to address and change?

**2.**   Was anything left of the *Bradley* presumption after *Landgraf* ? After *Martin v. Hadix*? Can you articulate a meaningful distinction between "substance" and "procedure"? One that will afford guidance in a future case?

# PART IV

# REVIEW PROBLEMS

## Problem 1[1]

Francine Odegaard was recently elected governor. She received 50.2 per cent of the vote, and her opponent received 49.8 per cent. A state legislative committee set up to monitor the effects of the Election Campaign Finance Act investigated the funding sources of the two candidates and learned that Odegaard's campaign committee received $41,995.00 from her grandfather after the election. This amount was precisely the debt with which her campaign committee ended the general election. Odegaard's natural parents died when she was very young. She was raised by her grandfather, although he never formally adopted her. Her grandfather made no other contributions to her campaign. The committee has drafted a report recommending that she be prosecuted for violating section 31 of the Act. The committee has hired you to review its recommendation.

The **Election Campaign Finance Act** provides in part:

> Sec. 2.   This Act is intended to regulate political activity, to regulate campaign financing, and to restrict campaign contributions and expenditures without jeopardizing the ability of candidates for state public office to conduct effective campaigns.

> Sec. 31.   (a) Except as provided in subsection (b), a person other than a campaign committee shall not make contributions on behalf of the winner of a primary election for the office of governor in excess of $600.00 for any purpose after the date of such primary election.

> (b) A contribution from a member of a candidate's immediate family to the campaign committee for that candidate is exempt from the limitation of subsection (a).

> (c) As used in subsection (b), "immediate family" means a spouse, parent, brother, sister, son, or daughter.

> Sec. 44.   A person who violates the provisions of this act is guilty of a misdemeanor and shall be fined not more than $1,000.00.

The highest appellate court in the state has decided the following cases:

### Alberts v. Election Commission (1977)

Per Curiam

> Section 31 of the Election Campaign Finance Act prohibits any person from making contributions "on behalf of the winner of a primary election for the office of governor in excess of $600.00 for any purpose after the date of such primary election." Appellant challenges the validity of a trial court determination that he violated section 31 by contributing $1,500.00 to the unsuccessful candidate for governor in

---

1.   This problem is adapted from John C. Dernbach & Richard V. Singleton II, A Practical Guide to Legal Writing and Legal Method (1981), used with permission.

the 1976 general election. He argues that he made the contribution to help retire that candidate's debt from the primary. We affirm.

Section 31 of the Election Campaign Act was designed to reduce, if not eliminate, the improper influence a contributor gains from a large contribution near the end of the campaign. More generally, the act was designed to help improve the integrity, and the appearance of integrity, of our election system. These policy considerations make it particularly important that the phrase, "for any purpose," be read for its full meaning. We hold that the phrase includes payments made for the purpose of reducing primary debts. Affirmed.

### Toland v. Election Commission (1976)

Per Curiam

Clyde Swanson lost the general election for governor after winning his party's primary election. His son Raymond handled the finances for Clyde's general election campaign. As treasurer, Raymond received funds from various sources, deposited them in his personal checking account, and then wrote checks from that account to pay for campaign expenses. Clyde's largest contribution, a $15,000 check from Alphonse Toland, was processed in this manner. Toland was convicted of a misdemeanor for violating section 31 of the Election Campaign Finance Act. We affirm that conviction.

Section 31 limits contributions to candidates for governor in a general election to $600.00 per person, unless the contributor is a member of the candidate's "immediate family." The immediate family exception is premised on a legislative desire to protect freedom of expression. In addition, the Act's purpose of reducing the corrupting influence of outside financial sources has much less force when the contributor is from the candidate's immediate family. Although Swanson's son was a conduit, rather than a source, of the funds. The important purposes of the Act should not be undermined by such transparent schemes.

Based on your analysis of the statute and the case law interpreting it, write a memo to the Committee giving your determination whether Odegaard has violated the Act, and fully articulating the reasons for your determination.

### Problem 2

Melody Harmony rents a nice home with a large lot which backs onto a public park in a residential area of Blissville in the state of New Hazard. Melody operates a catering business from her kitchen and sells baked products out of her garage. Business had been slow of late, and she canvassed friends and relatives about how to market her pies more aggressively. As a result of these consultations, she decided on the following scheme.

Melody parked her pick-up truck alongside her front yard. She mounted a cannon, which she leases from a circus, on the bed of the truck. The cannon operates using a small generator, which every forty-five minutes, must be recharged using the battery of the truck. At the back of her yard, just before the boundary of the public park, she placed a trampoline, building a concrete foundation around it to ensure its stability. Experimenting with her own durable two children, she discovered that a child shot out of the cannon would land exactly (more or less) in the center of the trampoline, bounce five to ten feet in the air, and then descend to earth gently on a mattress placed beside the trampoline. Her children confirmed it was a thrill to be remembered.

The kids spread word of this unique entertainment experience throughout the neighborhood. Melody advertised in the local paper. The use of the cannon was free to all those children whose parents bought either two cherry pies or a cheesecake. To Melody's delight, many Blissville parents showed up at her house to see their children propelled out of a cannon. She could barely keep up with the demand for her pies and cakes.

While no children were injured in flight or landing, the trampoline itself posed a hazard to people utilizing the park. It was positioned just outside the area used as the outfield to the baseball diamond in the park, and as no fence separated Melody's yard from the park, a number of wayward little-leaguers had crashed into it chasing fly balls. One such child had to be hospitalized.

Unfortunately for Melody, the parents of that child live in the same neighborhood and are alarmed at the traffic and carnival atmosphere that now characterizes their once serene residential street. They would like the town to initiate legal action against Melody. You are the Town Attorney, charged with enforcing compliance with the Blissville Town Code. Based on your analysis of the pertinent sections of the Town Code (below) and of the case law construing the Code (also below), explain whether and why (or why not), Melody has violated the Town Code.[1]

## BLISSVILLE TOWN CODE

**1.**   (a) Amusement. An amusement is any form of entertainment open to the public and generally conducted in the outdoors with the presence of tents, booths or temporary structures erected for such purpose or any combination of the foregoing, including but not limited to the following forms of entertainment commonly known as carnivals, circuses, fairs, bazaars, menageries, or sideshows. Such forms of entertainment are deemed to be generally characterized by the presence of any of the following activities or any combination of activities thereof: mechanical rides, exhibitions of skill, animal exhibitions, games of skill or games of chance where otherwise permitted by local regulation.

---

**1.**   The parents of the child have also   that claim is of no concern to you.
initiated a tort action against Melody but

(b) Amusement Device. An amusement device is any device whereby, upon the deposit therein of a coin or token, any apparatus is released or set in motion or put in a position where it may be set in motion for the purpose of playing any game including but not exclusively such devices as are commonly known as juke boxes, bowling games, pinball and video machines or pool tables.

**2.** Site Plan Review and Approval. A site plan review and approval is required in all zoning districts for all new buildings and structures or land use and/or for all alterations or changes in use thereto. The Town Board shall have the authority to impose such reasonable conditions and restrictions as are directly related and incidental to a proposed site plan.

**3.** (a) Special Use Permit. A special use permit is required for all amusements or amusement devices, where admission is charged, which occur on property zoned as a business district, or where a licensed restaurant, bar or eatery places on its property amusements or amusement devices for the enjoyment of customers.

(b) Certification. No amusement or amusement device may be used for purposes of amusement unless it possesses certification from the Blissville Amusement Devices Safety Board (BADSB) as to its safety, and is operated under the supervision of a qualified operator.

(c) Restrictions. Any amusement or amusement device operating within 200 yards of a public school which students 13 years old or younger attend, may only be used between the hours of 4:00 p.m.–9:00 p.m. on weekdays.

**4.** Public Safety or Welfare. Owners of property may not allow their premises to be used for purposes detrimental to public safety or welfare.

**5.** Stationary Motor Vehicles. No motor vehicle may operate for a period longer than three minutes in any hour while the vehicle is stationary, while the vehicle is parked on a public right-of-way, and while the vehicle is within 150 feet of a residential area, for reasons other than traffic congestion or emergency work.

## THE TOWN OF BLISSVILLE IN THE STATE OF NEW HAZARD v. DONALD SOSSIN

Supreme Court of New Hazard

Nov. 13, 1999

Radin, J.

The defendant is the owner of a bar/restaurant known as Avenues Night Club located in the town of Blissville, County of Pleasant, New Hazard. On June 26, 1988 the defendant was charged with four violations of the Blissville Town Code (hereinafter BTC). The alleged violations are all related to the activity of bungee jumping. The Superior Court found that Sossin had violated the BTC. The Court of Appeals affirmed.

The defendant had a crane brought onto the outdoor area of the property on which the night club was situated. Attached to the crane lift was a partially enclosed platform. A participant paid a fee to the operator, was secured to the platform by a bungee-type cord, then was lifted to a designated height from which a jump was made above a designated area. The defendant was charged with violating the BTC after several patrons had performed bungee jumps. The court shall now consider each of the charges.

Count one alleges that the defendant failed to obtain a site plan review and approval for the bungee jumping as mandated by BTC § 2. Said ordinance provides in pertinent part: "Site plan review and approval is required in all zoning districts for all new buildings and structures or land use and/or for all alterations or changes in use thereto." In the court's opinion the Town failed to prove that the mobile crane from which the bungee jumps were made is either a building, structure or land use as set out in BTC § 2, hence, a site plan review and approval was not necessary therefor.

Count two charges violations under BTC § 3(a) which sets out the requirements for obtaining a Special Use Permit for the operation of amusements. Section 3(a) prohibits the use of designated property as a place of amusement without a special permit. An amusement is defined in BTC § 1. In the court's opinion the instant activity of bungee jumping does not fall within the definition of an amusement. An amusement is generally characterized by the presence of multiple activities with more than one booth, tent or structure. Conversely, bungee jumping, as described herein, entails a singular activity. Therefore, the defendant was not mandated to obtain the Special Use Permit under BTC § 3(a) for which he is charged.

Count three alleges a violation of BTC § 4 in that the defendant allowed the premises to be used for purposes detrimental to public safety or welfare. It is the court's opinion that the Town failed to prove that the activity of bungee jumping, as described herein and conducted on defendant's property, was detrimental to the safety of the public. The Court's analysis might have been different had the Town shown that injuries resulted from the bungee jumps.

Finally, count four alleges a violation of BTC § 5 in that the defendant allowed a motor vehicle to operate for a period of longer than three minutes in any hour while the vehicle was stationary. The ordinance prohibits such operation of a vehicle on a public right-of-way, in a public space, and within 150 feet of a residential area for reasons other than traffic congestion or emergency work. The Town does not allege and did not prove that the crane as used for the bungee jumps was operated on a public right-of-way or public space within 150 feet of a residential area. Such are necessary elements of the offense charged.

Accordingly, the court reverses the decision below.

### THE TOWN OF BLISSVILLE IN THE STATE OF NEW HAZARD v. BARNEY'S PIZZERIA

Supreme Court of New Hazard

October 1, 2001

Ellis, J

This case comes before us on appeal from a judgment entered in the Superior Court, affirmed by the Court of Appeals, enjoining the defendant,

Barney's Pizzeria, from operating an amusement device on its property. Defendant is charged with four separate violations of the Blissville Town Code ("the Code") sections 3(a), (b), and (c) and 4.

Barney's Pizzeria is located in Blissville across the street from Serenity Junior High. In order to attract students from the school, the restaurant installed a "Bronco Barney" machine on the back patio. The machine was in the form of a giant purple dinosaur wearing a saddle. The owner of Barney's purchased the amusement device from Melron Amusements Corp. Customers who satisfied the minimum height requirement (4 feet) paid an additional dollar on top of the price of a slice of pizza to use the machine. The machine worked by jerking in all directions while the customer attempted to stay on. Mattresses were placed near the machine to soften the fall of those customers who were unsuccessful. Melron Amusements recommended the use of mattresses or similar cushioning devices but did not supply them to the restaurant. One of the waiters at the Pizzeria, recruited from the neighboring Blissville Community College, supervised the machine after receiving one day of training by Melron personnel.

It is alleged that Barney's Pizzeria violated § 3(a) of the Code, which provides that "[a] special use permit is required for all amusements or amusement devices, where admission is charged, which occur on property zoned as a business district, or where a licensed restaurant, bar or eatery places on its property, amusements or amusement devices for the enjoyment of customers." We find, as Barney's Pizzeria clearly falls within the category of an "eatery," a special use permit was required for the operation of the amusement device.

Section 3(b) of the Blissville Town Code stipulates that, "[n]o amusement or amusement device may be used for purposes of amusement unless it possesses certification from the Blissville Amusement Devices Safety Board (BADSB) as to its safety, and is operated under the supervision of a qualified operator." On these facts, Barney's Pizzeria adduced no evidence of certification of any kind. Further, one day of training by the manufacturer is not sufficient to qualify the employee as a "qualified operator."

Additionally, it is clear that the defendant has violated § 3(c) of the Code by allowing the Bronco Barney machine to be operated during the hours 12:00 p.m.–1:00 p.m. contrary to the clear language of this section.

Finally, § 4 of the Code provides that, "Owners of property may not allow their premises to be used for purposes detrimental to public safety or welfare." The evidence in the record establishes that the Town Board was concerned that the availability of these amusement devices to school-age children during school hours would encourage truancy and related problems. In addition, because children will tend to congregate where these devices are clustered, the Town Board was also concerned about traffic congestion and the possibility of accident. These legislative determinations are made in furtherance of the protection of the public health, safety, and general welfare. However, in view of the foregoing violations, it is not necessary to determine in addition whether the operation of the Bronco Barney machine was detrimental to the public safety or welfare.

We affirm the determination that the defendant has violated the Blissville Town Code and the "Bronco Barney" device shall be shut down until such time as the defendant is in full compliance with the provisions of the Code.

## Problem 3

Wilma Young and Donald Ryan always wanted to be medical school professors. After completing their third year of medical school at the State of New Hazard's Columbus University School of Medicine, both were accepted into a unique program known as "Med–Teach", which allows aspiring academics to complete their medical studies while gaining valuable teaching experience. Med–Teach participants are given two years to complete the course work ordinarily taken in the fourth year of medical school. During those two years, they are also required to teach a first year introductory anatomy course titled "Our Bodies Ourselves". Med–Teach participants are given a tuition waiver, are paid a salary $15,000 a semester, and are provided with offices in the Columbus University Hospital, which is adjacent to the medical school. Columbus University owns both the Hospital and the Medical School.

To assist Wilma and Donald in their teaching roles, the Medical School has assigned Professor Batalla to act as their faculty advisor. Last semester Professor Batalla taught a revolutionary new course called Medical Methods and gave Wilma and Donald the option of sitting in on that class. Both of them chose to do so.

Last summer, the Medical School, affectionately known as "the Blender" because of its unconventional design, began undergoing major renovations. Columbus University hired the Carbo Construction Company to be the general contractor for the construction project. At the beginning of the project, Columbus University provided hard hats to students and faculty, and instructed them to wear the hats during periods of heavy demolition.

During the initial phase of construction, several of the medical school professors complained to the New Hazard Occupational Safety and Health Commission about the burning odor produced by some of the engines of the heavy machinery involved in the construction. After investigating the incident, the Commission issued a citation to Columbus University for violating the New Hazard Occupational Safety and Health Act ("NHO-SHA"). The contractor and Columbus University thereafter corrected the odor problem, and construction proceeded smoothly.

However, more trouble surfaced last month when at the end of one Medical Methods class water and cardboard ceiling tile began falling in an unoccupied part of the classroom. After several hours, the debris stopped falling, and Columbus University custodians cordoned off the affected area.

The next day Wilma and Donald arrived late to Medical Methods. The only seats remaining were those adjacent to the area that had been cordoned off. Just as Wilma and Donald were taking two seats in that area, a heavy beam crashed through the ceiling and landed on Wilma, killing her instantly. Neither Wilma nor anyone else in the class was wearing a hard hat at the time of the incident. Donald, who was looking directly at Wilma at the time of the tragedy, was extremely traumatized and has spent the past month in the Hospital, where the Medical School's best psychiatrists have diagnosed and been treating him for "Post Accidental Distress Syndrome" ("PADS").

Donald has retained your firm to represent him in a potential action against Columbus University. Based on your analysis of the pertinent sections of NHOSHA, does Donald have a claim? Although no New Hazard courts have construed any provisions of NHOSHA (the statute is only a year old), courts from other jurisdictions, in the cases provided, have interpreted virtually identical statutes.

One of your fellow associates is looking into the various common law tort claims that Donald may have against Columbus University. Additionally, the New Hazard Occupational Safety and Health Commission is pursuing a separate claim against the school under section 5 of NHOSHA. You need not concern yourself with those matters.

### New Hazard Occupational Safety and Health Act

1. Short Title.

   This Act shall be known as the "New Hazard Occupational Safety and Health Act" and also may be referred to by abbreviations such as "NHOSHA".

2. Legislative Purpose.

   It is the policy of this state to assure so far as possible to every working person in the state safe and healthful working conditions and to preserve human resources.

3. Definitions.

   A) Employer.

   i) the State of New Hazard, any state agency, county, city, town, school district or other unit of local government; ii) any public or quasi-public corporation; iii) any person, firm, corporation, partnership or association; and iv) any officer or management official having direction or custody of any employment or employee.

   B) Employee.

   an individual who is employed by an employer, but does not include a domestic employee or a volunteer nonsalaried firefighter.

   C) Place of employment.

   any place, area or environment in or about which an employee is required or permitted to work.

D)  Occupational Safety and Health Hazard.

any practice or condition in a place of employment which may be deemed detrimental to the safety and health of employees.

E)  Occupational Injury or Illness.

any abnormal condition or disorder of an employee caused by exposure to factors associated with his/her employment.

**4.**   Duties of Employers and Employees.

A) Each employer has the duty to provide a place of employment that is safe, healthful, and free from recognized occupational safety and health hazards likely to cause death or serious harm.

B) Each employee has the duty to comply with reasonable safety requirements imposed by the employer to the extent that such requirements are applicable to the employee's own actions and conduct.

**5.**   Enforcement by Commission.

The New Hazard Occupational Safety and Health Commission shall issue a citation to any employer who violates any provision of this Act and may impose on such employer a fine of not more than $10,000 for each violation.

**6.**   Civil Action.

Any employee who suffers an occupational injury or illness as a result of his/her employer's violation of any provision of this Act may bring a civil action in the New Hazard Superior Court for compensatory damages. If such violation is willful or repeated, the employee may recover punitive damages in addition to compensatory damages.

## LYRIA'S CONSTRUCTION COMPANY v. SIMON MOUNT

Supreme Court of South Tranquility

October 1, 1985.

Learned Foote, J.:

This case comes before us on appeal from a judgment entered in the Superior Court, affirmed by the Court of Appeals, upholding the complaint by appellee Simon Mount against Lyria's Construction Co., appellant. The Superior Court and the Court of Appeals found that the appellant had violated the employment safety provisions of section 4(A) of the Connecticut Occupational Safety & Health Act (STOSHA) and awarded plaintiff compensatory and punitive damages in accordance with section 5 of the Act. We affirm.

Lyria's Construction Co. is a large general contractor that performs work at 20 to 30 worksites at any given time. For the past two years, Lyria's has been working on building a jail in Stamford Connecticut. Within the past year, a STOSHA compliance officer noted several violations for which Lyria's was given citations. The prior citations had been issued from 2½ months to a year prior to the accident at issue in this case, and had occurred at other projects within one to five miles from the jail worksite. Although all of the cited conditions were deemed to be a "health hazard" within section 3(D) of STOSHA, none involved the same conduct: one citation was for the failure to provide adequate scaffolding; another was for the failure to guard open manholes; another citation was issued as a result of the failure to keep passageways used by employees clear of hazardous obstructions.

The incident which leads to this appeal involves an accident in which one of Lyria's employees, Simon Mount was seriously injured when a trench that he was digging at the jail worksite caved in on him. In a separate action Lyria's has been charged by the Occupational Health and Safety Commission with violations under section 5 and fined accordingly. In this action, the plaintiff, Simon Mount claims damages for injuries he suffered as a result of the company's violation of section 6 of the Act which states:

> Any employee who suffers an occupational injury or illness as a result of his/her employer's violation of any provision of this Act may bring a civil action in the Connecticut Superior Court for compensatory damages. If such violation is willful or repeated, the employee may recover punitive in addition to compensatory damages.

Appellee concedes that its failure to shore, sheet, brace, slope, or otherwise support a trench of a depth greater than five feet, which permitted the collapse of the trench and the injury of an employee, constituted a "health hazard" under section 3(D) of STOSHA, but challenges the conclusion of the trial court that such failure was "willful" or "repeated" under section 5 of STOSHA.

We hold that the Superior Court's decision is fully warranted. Appellee was aware of the shoring requirements applicable in cases of trenches exceeding five feet in depth, and had been cited with several previous violations of the Act within a year. Appellee therefore willfully and repeatedly violated section 4(A) of STOSHA.

In the present case Lyria's foreman, Adrian Stone, himself measured the depth of the trench the afternoon before the accident, recording a distance of 4 ½ feet from the ground surface to the top of a transit water main just uncovered. At that point Stone knew that "[the workers] had quite a distance to go. To reach the depth that [they] needed, .... [they] would have to clear ... off (the pipe) and start digging in.... " The following morning Stone began that operation, instructing Mount to dig around and beneath the water main, which of necessity would result in passing the five foot safety mark. Yet, knowing this, and that the men were already beginning to dig, he left without giving any instructions as to shoring.

Under these circumstances the trial court could properly conclude that Stone did not expect that the men would install the shoring the moment five feet was reached, even though, in the past, there had been general instructions about shoring at the five-foot mark. Stone neither ordered shoring nor returned to the trench until the shouts of his men informed him that Mount had been trapped beneath the mud. Such indifference to the requirements of the law may alone represent a willful statutory violation. *See United States v. Illinois Central R.R.,* 303 U.S. 239 (1938). Stone's private determination that in this case there was no danger in failing to shore is not sufficient. STOSHA unambiguously forecloses such discretion. In addition, we believe the trial court was justified in taking Stone's testimony to mean that he had consciously decided not to shore the trench at that time because it would have been difficult, although not impossible, to do so in the presence of the transit pipe.

Willfulness implies that someone subject to the statutory provisions has knowingly acted in disregard of the legality of his actions. There is no need to show malicious intent. A conscious, intentional, deliberate, voluntary decision properly is described as willful, regardless of venial motive. *Brennan v. Heard,* 491 F.2d 1 (1974); *Coleman v. Jiffy Farms Inc.,* 499 Conn. 35 (1974); *Nabob Oil Co. v. United States,* 190 F.2d 478 (10th Cir.1951). Appellant, through its foreman, made its choice, a conscious, intentional, deliberate, voluntary decision, which, regardless of a venial motive, properly is described as willful. We hold that appellant's actions were "willful" and in so holding, we reject the appellant's argument that willfulness, requires an "obstinate refusal to comply." To require bad intent would place a severe restriction on the statutory authority of STOSHA to apply the stronger sanctions in enforcing the law, a result we do not feel was intended by the legislature.

We now come to the difficult issue of setting forth an acceptable and proper basis for determining what constitutes a "repeated" violation under section 6 of the Act. Several plausible suggestions have been proposed by the parties. There appears to be little agreement regarding the efficacy and acceptability of any one of the approaches.

The appellee Mount asserts that those violations which demonstrate that the employer has "flaunted" any requirement of the Act should be cited as repeated violations. The Company, on the other hand argues that only those violations that relate to the same or substantially similar violative conduct can be interpreted as constituting "repeated" violations. They cite to *Bethlehem Steel Corp. v. Leibman,* 540 N.Y. 157 (1980), which held that an employer cannot be cited for a repeated violation unless there have been at least two recurrences of the original violation. We reject this view.

Under the circumstances we think a more common usage of the term connotes only that a single prior infraction, regardless of its similarity to the present infraction need be proven to invoke the repeated violation sanction authorized by the Act. A strict interpretation of section 6 reveals that the Act applies even if the same standard is never violated twice, so long as the duty enunciated in section 4(A) is repeatedly violated in such a way as to demonstrate a flaunting disregard of the requirements of the Act. Among the factors that the court must consider when determining whether a course of conduct is flaunting the requirements of the Act are the number, proximity in time, nature and extent of violations, and the degree of care of the employer in her efforts to prevent violations of the type involved.

Intrinsic within the statutory scheme of enforcement is the overall policy of providing employers with incentive to comply with the safety requirements of the Act. The system of penalties contained in section 6 allows for punitive damages when the need arises to provide an employer with added incentive to comply.

After a review of the facts in the present case we are satisfied that the record is sufficient to sustain a finding of repeated violations under the Act. The actions of Lyria's are part of a more serious pattern of violations. Lyria's permitted the prior violations to occur three times during a period of less than a year and within a five-mile radius.

The judgment is affirmed with costs.

## JOHN B. REICH v. BEDLAM POLYTECHNIC INSTITUTE

Supreme Judicial Court of New Bedlam

August 20, 1994

Rugg IV, C.J.

John B. Reich ("Reich") appeals the trial court's entry of summary judgment against him on his claim under the New Bedlam Occupational Safety and Health Act ("NBOSHA"). We affirm.

### I.

Factual Background

We review the pertinent facts in the light most favorable to Reich. The events surrounding this litigation arise out of the construction of the Fuller Laboratories Building ("the project") at Bedlam Polytechnic Institute ("BPI"). Sometime in 1990, BPI, the owner of the project, hired Francis Harvey & Sons, Inc. ("Harvey") as the project's general contractor. With the consent of BPI's President John Walker ("President Walker"), Harvey engaged Johnson Sisters, Inc. ("Johnson Sisters") to be the project's design engineers.

The project got off to a rocky start in January 1991 when the heavy electrical equipment used by Harvey caused a severe power shortage across the BPI campus. As a result, lighting conditions in BPI classrooms were extremely poor. When BPI refused to take steps to improve the situation, several professors complained to the Massachusetts Occupational Safety and Health Commission (the "Commission"). After conducting a thorough investigation, the Commission issued a citation to BPI. Despite its efforts after receiving the citation, BPI was not able to significantly improve lighting conditions in the classrooms during the life of the project. From January 1991 to November 1992, BPI amassed a total of twelve citations from the commission due to the lighting problems.

More serious problems developed in late 1992, when Harvey began to pour the concrete which would serve as the ceiling for the project's first level and the floor for the project's second level. A reinforced temporary ceiling had already been constructed over the first level. On December 13, 1992, Harvey's superintendent, Mr. Dwight Mitchell, began pouring the first layer of concrete onto the temporary ceiling. After the first layer was poured, Mitchell noticed that a section of the temporary ceiling was beginning to sag.

Mitchell immediately attempted to telephone Johnson Sisters to inform them of the problem, but his call would not go through.[1] Mitchell next called President Walker, who decided to ask Reich, one of BPI's foremost engineering professors, to look into the problem. Reich agreed, and he and President Walker walked across campus to the project site and surveyed the temporary ceiling from a distance. As Reich moved nearer the structure, President Walker stated: "I can't see a thing; you're going to have to get a lot closer." Reich obliged, and just as he began to edge underneath the temporary ceiling, the whole structure collapsed, burying him. Remarkably, Reich survived. He is, however, paralyzed from the neck down.

Reich has brought the present action for compensatory and punitive damages alleging, *inter alia,* that BPI violated its duty under NBOSHA "to provide a place of employment that is safe, healthful, and free from recognized occupational safety and health hazards likely to cause death or serious harm." NBOSHA, § 4.[2] The trial court granted BPI's motion for summary judgment. This appeal followed.

## II.

### Discussion

Like the trial court, we believe that the dispositive question is whether the construction site was a "place of employment" which BPI had a duty under NBOSHA to protect. In light of the plain meaning of section 3 of NBOSHA, we find that BPI had no such duty. Reich is an engineering professor who conducted his classes and maintained his office in the engineering building at BPI. There is no indication that he was required, as a condition of his employment, to be on the construction site. Rather, the record reveals that he voluntarily accepted President Walker's invitation to inspect the sagging structure. Under these circumstances, we do not think that construction site is a "place of employment" which BPI had a duty under NBOSHA to protect.[3]

---

**1.** It was later discovered that the telephone company had accidently disconnected Johnson Sisters' telephone service that afternoon.

**2.** Section 6 of NBOSHA provides:

Any employee who suffers an occupational injury or illness as a result of his/her employer's violation of any provision of this Act may bring a civil action in the New Bedlam Superior Court for compensatory damages. If such violation is willful or repeated, the employee may recover punitive damages in addition to compensatory damages.

**3.** We should make perfectly clear that the only question now before us is BPI's liability under NBOSHA. We express no view on Reich's other New Bedlam-law claims against BPI.

Although we need go no further, we find it prudent to address certain questions with respect to punitive damages as well, since the trial courts of this state have come to different conclusions as to when such damages are appropriate. An employee is entitled to punitive damages if he or she is injured as a result of an employer's "willful or repeated" violation of NBOSHA. NBOSHA, § 6.

Willfulness connotes defiance or such reckless disregard of consequences as to be equivalent to a knowing, conscious, and deliberate flaunting of NBOSHA. Willful means more than merely voluntary action or omission—it involves an element of obstinate refusal to comply. Unless an employer engages in such deliberate behavior, it is not liable for punitive damages under the "willful" prong of section 6.

As for "repeated", we could construe that term to mean that an employer is liable for punitive damages if it merely violates the general duty to provide a work place free from recognized hazards more than once, no matter how unrelated the multiple infractions may be. Given the breadth of the general duty provision, such an interpretation would render nearly every employer liable for punitive damages in every case. It is clear that the punitive damages aspect of section 6 is directed at particularly flagrant conduct, such as an employer's failure to cure an identified safety hazard for which it has already been cited. Therefore, we conclude that a violation is "repeated" under section 6, only if the employer has previously been cited as having engaged in the same or substantially similar violative conduct.

The judgment of the Superior Court is affirmed. ORDER ACCORDINGLY.

## Problem 4

The Plaintiff, Henry Hurtz, worked as one of five waiters in the Caffe Violenti in the state of New Hazard. The Defendant, Bobbie Basher, also worked at the restaurant. On the evening of August 21, 1993, after closing, Hurtz was washing trays when Basher pointed a loaded handgun in the direction of Hurtz's feet and fired. Basher intended merely to frighten Hurtz, for she believed the gun was filled with blank cartridges. Needless to say, the cartridges were not blank and Hurtz suffered serious and permanent injuries when a bullet struck him in the left foot. After several other restaurants in the vicinity had been robbed, Basher began carrying the weapon to protect herself and the employer's money when making night bank deposits of the day's proceeds.

Having received workers compensation from his employer, Mr. Hurtz has filed a common law action in tort against Basher in the New Hazard trial court, alleging that the accident was proximately caused by Basher's wrongful conduct. Basher has moved to dismiss the action on the ground that the plaintiff's exclusive remedy is under the New Hazard Workers Compensation Act.

You are the law clerk to the judge who must decide the motion. She has asked you to prepare a draft opinion for her on the question of whether the case should be dismissed. Draft the analysis of the court's opinion (i.e. it is not necessary to repeat the facts in a "Facts" section) in the case of Hurtz v. Basher, taking into account the statute and other relevant authority.

The State of New Hazard enacted a Workers Compensation Act in 2000 which is set out in relevant part below. No New Hazard courts have yet ruled on the Workers Compensation Act.

The New Hazard Workers Compensation Act is identical to the workers compensation acts of South Tranquility, enacted in 1953, and New Bedlam, enacted in 1950. Decisions from the Supreme Courts in these jurisdictions follow.

## NEW HAZARD WORKERS COMPENSATION ACT, 2000

*Section 1.   Definitions*

When used in this Act:

(a) The term "employment" includes employment by the state and all political subdivisions thereof and all public and quasi-public corporations therein and all private employments in which three or more employees are employed in the same business or establishment.

(b) The term "employee" means every person engaged in an employment under appointment or contract of hire or apprenticeship, express or implied, oral or written.

(c) The term "employer" means the state and all political subdivisions thereof, and every person, firm or corporation carrying on any employment, or the legal representative of a deceased person or the receiver or trustees of any person.

(d) The term "injury" means personal injury or death arising out of and in the course of employment and such diseases or infections as naturally or unavoidably result from such injury.

*Section 2.   Coverage—Liability for Compensation*

(a) Compensation shall be payable under this Act in respect of disability or death of an employee if the disability or death results from an injury.

(b) Every employer, as defined in this Act, shall be liable for and shall secure the payment to his employees of the compensation payable under this Act.

(c) Compensation shall be payable irrespective of fault as a cause for the injury.

*Section 3.   Exclusiveness of Liability*

The liability of an employer prescribed in section 2 shall be exclusive and in place of all other liability of such employer to the employee, his or her legal representative, husband or wife, parents, dependents, next of kin, or anyone otherwise entitled to recover damages from such employer on account of injury to the employee.

*Section 4.  Compensation for Injuries Where Third Persons Are Liable*

If an employee is injured or killed in the course of his or her employment by the negligence or wrongful act of any person other than the employer, such injured employee, or in the case of his or her death his or her dependents, may accept compensation benefits under the provision of this law and, in addition, may pursue his or her remedy by action at law or otherwise against such third party tort-feasor.

## MAJORS v. MONEYMAKER

Supreme Court of New Bedlam

July 23, 1954.

Drumble, C. J.

The plaintiff, Elsie N. Majors, sued the defendant, Elizabeth Moneymaker, in the Circuit Court of Knox County for damages arising out of an automobile accident. Mrs. Majors was riding as an invited guest when the car, which was being operated by the defendant, came in violent collision with another automobile.

The defendant, Elizabeth Moneymaker, filed a motion to dismiss and averred therein that she and the plaintiff were fellow workers and employees of the American National Insurance Company, working out of the Knoxville office of said company; were acting in concert within the scope and course of their employment; that the Insurance Company and the parties had agreed to be bound by the terms of the Workers Compensation Law of New Bedlam, and that both the plaintiff and defendant were bound by the provisions of said statute. It is further alleged in the plea that both the plaintiff and the defendant were paid compensation by the Indemnity Insurance Company of North America for injuries resulting from the said accident; that the "defendant is not such other or third party or person within the meaning of the Workers Compensation Law of New Bedlam as would permit her to be sued for negligence at common law, the plaintiff's rights against her employer and/or its workers compensation insurance company being the only right and exclusive remedy of the plaintiff against either this defendant or her employer."

The plaintiff demurred to the motion to dismiss, as follows: "Defendant's motion to dismiss is not sufficient in law because: the injuries sustained by plaintiff for which she claims damages in a tort action were caused by the act or acts of the defendant under circumstances creating a legal liability against the defendant to pay damages, the defendant not being plaintiff's employer or such other person legally liable to pay workers compensation to her."

The trial judge sustained the motion to dismiss and dismissed the plaintiff's suit. The sole question made in the assignment of error is that it was error by the trial judge to sustain the motion to dismiss because the plaintiff's remedy is not exclusive as provided in the Statute; her right was to prosecute her common law action against the defendant, she being "any person other than the employer" as provided in Section 4.

Now in the case at bar the demurrer admits as true the averment in the motion to dismiss that the employer, American National Insurance Company, and both the plaintiff and the defendant are within the compensation system, i.e. all were subject to the provisions of the New Bedlam Workers' Compensation Act. Both Mrs. Majors and Mrs. Moneymaker were paid workers' compensation benefits by their employer's insurance carrier, Indemnity Insurance Company of North America.

In the case at bar it is clear that the alleged negligence of the defendant is chargeable to her principal, American National Insurance Company, who is also the common employer of both the plaintiff and the defendant. The negligence of the defendant, Elizabeth Moneymaker, created a legal liability against her employer. But, as forcibly and clearly argued by defendant's counsel, the language used in the quoted Statute specifically limits the action to circumstances creating a legal liability against 'any person other than the employer'.

If we should adopt the construction of the Act according to the plaintiff's contention it would create an unfair result.

One purpose of the Workers Compensation Act was to sweep within its provisions all claims for compensation flowing from personal injuries arising out of and in the course of employment by a common employer insured under the act, and not to preserve for the benefit of the insurer or of the insurer and those injured liabilities between those engaged in the common employment which but for the act would exist at common law.

The defendant, Moneymaker, being a co-employee of the plaintiff, is exempt from liability by the Workers' Compensation Law. As an employee acting within the scope of her employment, and not "on a frolic of her own," she was the agent of the employer. Her acts and conduct became the acts and conduct of the employer, and the exemption from damages at law extended to the employer by the Workers Compensation Law is also by that act extended to co-employees through whom the employer acts. Thus, the co-employee becomes merged in the employer and is not a third person, within the meaning of the compensation law, against whom a damage action may be maintained.

Another purpose of the workers compensation scheme is to place the cost of work related injuries on the employer. Suits against fellow employees shift the burden to the employees and circumvent the theory of workers compensation. The insurance company, who paid workers compensation benefits to both the plaintiff and the defendant, would in the case at bar recover, by means of subrogation, from the defendant all sums of money which it had paid the plaintiff, Elsie N. Majors. And while the defendant, Elizabeth Moneymaker, could recover only a limited amount under the Workers Compensation Act, the plaintiff, Mrs. Majors, and the insurance carrier could recover from the defendant unlimited damages under the common law. The foregoing is in substance the argument of the defendant's counsel in support of the latter's construction of the statute. We think it is logical and give it our unqualified approval.

We furthermore take notice of the fact that in many cases arising under the Workers Compensation Act the injury results from the negligence of some fellow employee. If the insurance carrier is subrogated to the rights of an employee against his fellow servant, the result would be a flood of litigation over claims that were never contemplated by the statute. The statute was never designed to permit the employer and his insurance carrier to sue employees for damages for negligent injuries arising out of and in the course of the employment. In all such cases the injured defendant employee sometimes suffering either death or total and permanent injuries would, by force of the statute, be required to surrender all his compensation benefits to the insurance carrier, and in many cases a sizable amount in addition thereto by way of damages. This is certainly contrary to the spirit, if not the letter of the statute, in that the right of every employee to compensation is made to depend upon whether or not he is free from some proximate negligent act committed during his employment.

The judgment of the trial court is affirmed.

## VICTOR HOCKETT v. J.E. CHAPMAN

Supreme Court of South Tranquility

Nov. 27, 1961.

Hanigsberg, C. J.

This is a personal injury action. The appeal results from the dismissal of appellant's complaint on the ground that appellant, having received workers compensation benefits, may not recover for the negligence of a coemployee where the damages sought are based on injuries received in an accident arising out of and in the course of employment and where such injuries were caused by the negligence of a coemployee.

Appellant and appellees were fellow employees. Appellant was injured as the result of a collision between a truck driven by appellee Chapman, in which he was a passenger, and a truck driven by appellee Bachus. The accident arose out of and in the course of their employment. Appellant received workers compensation benefits and thereafter brought a negligence action against the appellees. The employer's insurance carrier intervened as a plaintiff and appellant.

The sole question presented by this appeal is whether, under the South Tranquility Workers Compensation Act, a coemployee is a "person other than the employer" against whom a negligence action may be maintained, or whether a coemployee comes within the immunity from such an action which is granted to the employer.

The Workers Compensation Act provides that an employee, or someone claiming through him or on his behalf, is not denied his common-law right to recover damages caused by the negligence of a third person because he has received workers' compensation benefits for the same injury. The pertinent provision of the Act reads as follows:

*Section 4.   Compensation for Injuries Where Third Persons Are Liable*

If an employee is injured or killed in the course of his or her employment by the negligence or wrongful act of any person other than the employer, such injured employee, or in the case of his or her death his or her dependents, may accept compensation benefits under the provision of this law and, in addition, may pursue his or her remedy by action at law or otherwise against such third party tort-feasor.

It is clear, therefore, that our Workers Compensation Act was not intended to relieve one other than the employer, his insurer, guarantor or surety from liability imposed by statute or by common law, while providing against a double recovery by an employee.

Appellees urge upon this court that since they were employees of the same employer, and were admittedly within the scope of their employment, they were the agents or servants of the employer, and that as such their liability is limited, the same as that of an employer. We are unable to agree with appellees' analysis of the statute. Section 3 deals with the exclusiveness of the remedy between an employer and employee. We see nothing in this section of the Act which could be said to mean that a fellow employee shall be the same as the employer for the purpose of limiting his liability thereunder.

The appellees, Chapman and Bachus, have cited authorities supporting their position that an employee is immune from a negligence action by a coemployee. In these jurisdictions, the courts have held that a coemployee is not a "person other than the employer," either on the theory of agency, making the conduct of an employee the conduct of the employer, or on the broad ground that the Workers Compensation Act intended to cover by its terms all liability arising out of and in the course of employment by a common employer insured under the Act.

Despite appellees' arguments, in the states having workers' compensation laws similar to those of South Tranquility, in that they provide the Act shall not affect any cause of action an employee may have against "a person other than his employer," or against a third party, or a "third party tortfeasor", most, albeit not all, courts have held that a coemployee is a third person, or a person other than the employer, and that such an action may be maintained. The basic reasoning behind these holdings is that the workers compensation laws have predicated an employer's liability to his employee on the employer-employee relationship and not in tort; that consequently the right of an employee to receive benefits under workers compensation is not based on fault or negligence, but is contractual in nature; that a negligent employee is not liable for compensation and is, therefore, a stranger to the Act, being a person other than the employee entitled to receive compensation and the employer liable to pay it. Further, that coemployees are in no way subject to the provisions of the compensation act in their relationship with each other. Some of these courts have said that to hold otherwise would be to unjustly confer upon a worker freedom to neglect his duty towards a fellow employee and immunize him against all liability for damages proximately caused by his negligence.

Where it was the intention in other states, in enacting workers compensation laws, to include fellow employees within the limited liability of the employer, the acts have expressly restricted actions by an employee by providing that action may be maintained by an employee "provided such third person be not a fellow servant" or against "third persons who are not in the same employ," or they have provided that actions may not be so maintained against an employer "or any worker," or "his employees" or "persons in the same employ," or "those conducting his (the employer's) business." The judicial decisions in these jurisdictions have, therefore, by virtue of the express legislative intent, excluded suits against a coemployee.

In the absence of express language in the South Tranquility Workers Compensation Act denying an employee the right to maintain a negligence action against a coemployee, and in view of the sound reasoning upon which we consider the weight of authority to be based, we must conclude that a coemployee is "a person other than the employer" against whom such an action for damages may be maintained and that the court below erred in dismissing appellant's complaint.

This reasoning is consistent with the generally recognized rule that a co-employee who causes injury while acting outside the course of his employment is not protected from liability in common law actions arising out of the injury. Likewise, when an employee is injured by a coemployee who intentionally inflicts injuries upon him, the employee-victim may maintain a common law action against his co-employee. In accepting employment, a worker does not render himself vulnerable to every type of wrong, with the workers compensation laws being his sole remedy.

The judgment is reversed with directions to the trial court to proceed in a manner not inconsistent with the views expressed herein.

It is so ordered.

## Problem 5

Your client is Leinad Smith, a partner in the Cacophony, New Hazard branch of the well-known national accountancy firm Shady Anderson ("SA"). Mr. Smith wants to sue a business called Corporate Therapy, which is a slickly-marketed firm of registered naturopaths. Naturopaths treat illnesses and practice preventive medicine by using nutrition, herbalism, homoeopathy, iridology and other natural therapies to stimulate the body's own ability to heal itself without pharmaceutical drugs or surgery.

In New Hazard, naturopaths must register (according to the Alternative Medical Treatments Act) with the governing body of their practice, the N.H. Naturopathic Society (the "Society"). Naturopaths do not train as physicians. They must, however, complete two years of training in a certified institution to register with the Society. The Society takes a keen interest in the 'medical' activities of its members, often organizing training activities and requiring all members to undergo "buddy review" sessions in which, for three weeks each year, one naturopath closely monitors another's professional practice.

All of the naturopaths employed by Corporate Therapy are properly registered. Corporate Therapy caters to the top end of the business market and deals with commercial clients only. It offers package deals to large firms which are interested in reducing and/or managing the stress levels among their employees.

Mr. Smith wants to sue Corporate Therapy because of the way Corporate Therapy conducted a recent treatment course at SA. The pertinent facts are as follows. In June 2002 one of the marketing executives in SA saw an advertisement for Corporate Therapy. The executive had been noting extended sick leave and decreased productivity levels at SA and was on the lookout for possible solutions. The executive invited Corporate Therapy to give a presentation to the firm outlining its services.

Corporate Therapy gave a lunchtime presentation aided by sophisticated computer technology that outlined the many ways naturopathy could help relieve stress and illness. The presentation was convincing. It included relaxing music and many illustrations of naturopaths directly administering treatment to patients. At the close of the presentation a deal was struck, in which SA [CT] agreed in writing to provide the following services over the course of five sessions:

1. Examining the patients' health and eating habits;

2. Prescribing diets, foods, minerals and vitamins to help improve general health;

3. Stimulating the healing powers of the patient's body by using small, strengthened doses of herbal, mineral or animal substances;

4. Performing "pressure touching" on the patient to promote well-being; and

5. Examining the patient's iris (colored part of the eye) to analyze and treat illness in various organs of the body ("iridology").

SA wrote a check for $25,000 for the treatment course on the spot.

The treatment course was free for invited SA staff to attend. Mr. Smith attended. The course was not, however, a success. The main objections of Mr. Smith and SA generally were that the first four treatments did not offer hands-on service but were in the form of "holistic" power-point presentations outlining the background and the benefits of the specific naturopathy technique being illustrated. Corporate Therapy representatives, when asked by attendees whether hands-on service would be provided, said that the classes were too large but that Corporate Therapy "highly recommends advanced personal treatment sessions at our offices; only $100 for each half-hour. Please feel free to make an appointment."

As a partner of SA, Mr. Smith felt incensed that the firm had paid so much money for a series of lectures. It is his view that SA paid for personal treatment sessions and that is what Corporate Therapy should have delivered.

The last treatment session was different and, at least initially, more in line with Mr. Smith's expectations. The naturopath who attended that day, Ms. Danielle Yduj, claimed to be an expert iridologist and saw each attendee in turn to examine his or her eyes. To do so, Ms. Yduj used a device called a laser eye probe, which enabled her to clearly view the irises of each attendee. When Mr. Smith's turn came, Mr. Smith told the naturopath that he suffered from a congenital eye disease which made his eyes extremely sensitive.[1] Ms. Yduj listened to Mr. Smith, smiled indulgently, then told Mr. Smith that she was a professional, that his "disease" was exacerbated by Western medicine and that natural treatment was safe and would ease the symptoms.

Ms. Yduj then directed the laser to Mr. Smith's left pupil. As soon as the laser struck, Mr. Smith screamed due to a burning pain. Colleagues of Mr. Smith raced into the treatment room and helped Mr. Smith to the emergency room of the Cacophony Memorial Hospital. For the next two weeks Mr. Smith could not see out of his left eye at all. Mr. Smith's improvement has been gradual. His sight today is still considerably worse than it was before the treatment.

Mr. Smith would like to sue Corporate Therapy under the New Hazard Consumer Protection Act in two capacities:

> first, as an individual harmed by Ms. Yduj's eye treatment, seeking damages for his medical costs, pain and suffering and loss of capacity; and

> secondly, as a partner in SA on behalf of the firm, for recovery of the $25,000 spent on the five treatment courses.

Do not concern yourself with any other possible liability. You can assume that Corporate Therapy is liable for the actions of Ms. Yduj. Please advise Mr. Smith on his chances of success under each of the above claims.

## NEW HAZARD CONSUMER PROTECTION ACT

### 1. Short title

(1) This Act shall be known and may be cited as the "New Hazard Consumer Protection Act" of 1985.

### 2. Definitions

(1) As used in this Act:

[1]. Mr. Smith suffers from Bietti's crystalline dystrophy ("BCD"), which is an inherited eye disease. The symptoms of BCD include: crystals in the cornea (the clear covering of the eye); yellow, shiny deposits on the retina; and progressive atrophy of the retina, choriocapillaries and choroid (the back layers of the eye). This tends to lead to excessive sensitivity, progressive night blindness and visual field constriction.

(a) "Person" means a natural person, corporation, trust, partnership, incorporated or unincorporated association, or other legal entity.

(b) "Trade or commerce" means the conduct of a business providing goods, property, or service primarily for personal, family, or household purposes and includes the advertising, solicitation, offering for sale or rent, sale, lease, or distribution of a service or property, tangible or intangible, real, personal, or mixed, or any other article, or a business opportunity.

### 3.   Unfair trade practices

(1) Unfair, unconscionable, or deceptive methods, acts, or practices in the conduct of trade or commerce are unlawful and are defined as follows:

(a) Representing that goods or services are of a particular standard, quality, or grade, or that goods are of a particular style or model, if they are of another.

(b) Representing that a part, replacement, or service is needed when it is not.

(c) Failing to reveal a material fact, the omission of which tends to mislead or deceive the consumer, and which fact could not reasonably be known by the consumer.

(d) Failing to reveal facts that are material to the transaction in light of representations of fact made in a positive manner.

(e) Gross discrepancies between the oral representations of the seller and the written agreement covering the same transaction.

### 4.   Exemptions; burden of proof

(1) This Act does not apply to either of the following:

(a) A transaction or conduct specifically authorized under laws or rules administered by a regulatory board or officer acting under statutory authority of this state or the United States.

(2) The burden of proving an exemption from this Act is upon the person claiming the exemption.

### 5.   Actions

(1) Whether or not he seeks damages or has an adequate remedy at law, a person may bring an action to do either or both of the following:

(a) Obtain a declaratory judgment that a method, act, or practice is unlawful under section 3.

(b) Enjoin in accordance with the principles of equity a person who is engaging or is about to engage in a method, act, or practice which is unlawful under section 3.

(2) Except in a class action, a person who suffers loss as a result of a violation of this Act may bring an action to recover actual damages or $250.00, whichever is greater, together with reasonable attorneys' fees.

## NELSON v. HO

Supreme Court of New Hazard

February 25, 1997

Bronlee, C.J.

Plaintiff appeals as of right the trial court's grant of summary disposition for defendant. We affirm.

In April 1989, plaintiff visited defendant's office to seek treatment for a sinus problem. In June 1989, defendant performed nasal surgery on plaintiff. In the months following the surgery, plaintiff's nose became infected, and plaintiff began to feel what she believed to be a suture breaking through the skin at the tip of her nose. Plaintiff went to see defendant at least four times between October 1989 and January 1991 regarding infections and her belief that a suture was breaking through the skin of her nose. Plaintiff alleges that during these visits, although defendant recorded in his notes that plaintiff did have a suture breaking through the skin of her nose, defendant consistently and intentionally told plaintiff that it would be impossible for a suture to be breaking through the skin because he had used dissolvable sutures. Yet plaintiff continued to experience problems and hold onto her belief. In September 1993, plaintiff visited Dr. Frank Ritter. Ritter informed plaintiff that there was indeed a suture breaking through the skin of her nose and referred plaintiff to a plastic surgeon, who removed stitches from plaintiff's nose in October 1993. Plaintiff filed the instant action, alleging that defendant's conduct violated the New Hazard Consumer Protection Act ("NHCPA"). Defendant moved for partial summary disposition, arguing that the NHCPA does not apply to physicians. The trial court granted defendant's motion, dismissed plaintiff's complaint, and plaintiff appealed. The Court of Appeals affirmed.

The primary issue in this case is whether a suit brought under the NHCPA may be maintained against a physician. This issue is one of first impression in New Hazard.

The NHCPA prohibits, and defines, "unfair, unconscionable, or deceptive methods, acts or practices in the conduct of trade or commerce": § 3. The NHCPA contains no language expressly including or excluding physicians from its purview, but broadly defines "trade or commerce" in § 2(b) as follows:

> "Trade or commerce" means the conduct of a business providing goods, property, or service primarily for personal, family, or household purposes and includes the advertising, solicitation, offering for sale or rent, sale, lease, or distribution of a service or property, tangible or intangible, real, personal, or mixed, or any other article, or a business opportunity.

Plaintiff argues that because defendant performed a service primarily for personal purposes, his conduct falls within the definition of "trade or commerce". The trial court ruled, in part, that physicians are not engaged in "trade or commerce" and granted defendant's motion for summary disposition.

The trial court's ruling was based in part on the theory that there is a distinction between the practice of a trade and the practice of a "learned profession". It was stated in dictum in *The Schooner Nymph*, 16 N. Hz. 506, 507 (1834), that wherever any occupation, employment, or business is carried on for the purpose of profit, gain, or a livelihood, not in the liberal arts or in the learned professions, it is constantly called a trade. The trial court added that "[i]n contrast to practicing a trade or running a business, competition is inconsistent with the practice of a profession because enhancing profit is not the goal of professional activities; the goal is to provide services necessary to the community." We generally agree.

We agree also, however, with defendant's submission to this Court that "it would be a dangerous form of elitism, indeed, to dole out exemptions to our consumer protection laws merely on the basis of the educational level needed to practice a given profession, or for that matter, the impact which the profession has on society's health and welfare." Also, because the NHCPA broadly defines "trade or commerce", in part, as the "conduct of a business", and the practice of medicine clearly has a business aspect, a blanket exemption for the learned professions would be improper. However, we are also of the opinion that it would be improper to view the practice of medicine as interchangeable with other commercial endeavors and apply to it concepts that originated in other areas. Therefore, a blanket inclusion in the NHCPA for physicians would also be improper. Consequently, we hold that only allegations of unfair, unconscionable, or deceptive methods, acts, or practices in the conduct of the entrepreneurial, commercial, or business aspect of a physician's practice may be brought under the NHCPA. Allegations that concern misconduct in the actual performance of medical services or the actual practice of medicine would be improper. We do not consider the Legislature's use of "trade or commerce" in defining the application of the Act to exhibit an intent to include the actual performance of medical services or the actual practice of medicine. If we were to interpret the Act as such, the legislative enactments and well-developed body of law concerning medical malpractice could become obsolete.

In determining whether an action is proper under the NHCPA, courts must examine the nature of the conduct complained of case by case and determine whether it relates to the entrepreneurial, commercial, or business aspect of the practice of medicine. In this case, plaintiff alleges that defendant failed to tell her before operating on her that he would be using nondissolvable sutures in her nose and also failed to explain the risks involved. Plaintiff also alleges that defendant represented to her that she did not have a suture breaking through the skin at the tip of her nose when in fact she did. We do not consider either one of these allegations to charge defendant with misconduct in the entrepreneurial, commercial, or business aspect of his practice. Rather, we consider these to be principally attacks on the actual performance of defendant's medical services, which would be more appropriately addressed in the context of a timely filed medical malpractice claim. Therefore, the NHCPA does not apply, and plaintiff has failed to state a claim upon which relief can be granted.

Although it is not strictly necessary to address it, the trial court also ruled that even if defendant was engaged in "trade or commerce", he is exempt from application of the Act under § 4(1)(a) which states that the NHCPA does not apply to "[a] transaction or conduct specifically authorized under laws or rules administered by a regulatory board or officer acting under statutory authority of this state or the United States."

The defendant argues that his activities as a registered medical practitioner are exempt. He points out that the New Hazard Medical Council has statutory responsibility to govern the practice of medicine in this State and, in particular, to determine to whom a medical license should be granted and whose license should be taken or suspended.

We recall that, in his approach, the trial judge stated that:

[since] the defendant is under the auspices of the New Hazard Medical Council, it is apparent that the defendant is not subject to sanctions under the New Hazard Consumer Protection Act.

The defendant contends that this ruling was correct. The plaintiff, however, argues that § 4(1)(a) of the NHCPA exempts only "[a] transaction or conduct *specifically authorized*". She contends that a license to engage in an activity is not a basis for concluding that one is "specifically authorized" to employ deceptive practices in that activity. She argues:

If every person or business which engages in an activity authorized by some statute or regulation were exempt from the New Hazard Consumer Protection Act, pursuant to § 4(1)(a), then the New Hazard Consumer Protection Act would be a cruel hoax on the many legislators and others who sought to give New Hazard consumers protection in the marketplace. A consumer could sue an unlicensed optician for deception, but not a licensed optometrist. A consumer could sue a grocery store, but not a licensed car dealer or auto repair facility. A licensed hearing-aid dealer would be exempt from suit, but not the corner baker.

The defendant responds that to accept plaintiff's construction of § 4(1)(a) would be to render the exemption meaningless. He asserts:

Obviously, there is no statute which specifically authorizes misrepresentations or false promises. Yet under plaintiff's rationale, it is only where a statute which is administered by a regulatory agency specifically authorizes unscrupulous conduct that the statutory exemption would apply.

The defendant argues that such a result is absurd.

We agree with the plaintiff that the defendant's medical license does not exempt him from the NHCPA. While the license generally authorizes the defendant to engage in the activities of a physician, it does not specifically authorize the conduct that plaintiff alleges is violative of the Act. In so concluding, we disagree that the exemption of § 4(1)(a) becomes meaningless. While defendant is correct in stating that no statute or regulatory agency specifically authorizes misrepresentations or false promises, the exemption will nevertheless apply where a party seeks to attach such labels to "[a] transaction or conduct specifically authorized under laws or rules administered by a regulatory board or officer acting under statutory authority of this state or the United States". For this case, we need only decide that a medical license is not specific authority for all the conduct and transactions of the defendant's business.

Summary disposition with regard to the claim under the NHCPA was proper. Appeal dismissed.

## HAPPY HAZARD HOSTELS, INC., v. ARBOR DRUGS, INC.,

Court of Appeals of New Hazard

January 16, 2001, Decided

Carpet, J.

Plaintiff, Happy Hazard Hostels, Inc., appeals as of right from an order of the New Hazard Trial Court granting summary disposition for defendant, Arbor Drugs, Inc. We affirm.

Plaintiff's business is providing budget accommodation for youthful travelers to this fine state. Plaintiff now has 38 state-wide branches and 458 employees. Because of the constant contact plaintiff's employees have with travelers from distant shores, they are exposed to a constant range of cultures–and of diseases. Influenza has been a particular problem. Accordingly, in 1999, as part of its health benefits policy, plaintiff contracted with defendant for defendant to provide influenza immunization injections for each of plaintiff's employees. Plaintiff claims that defendant's general manager, Mr. Browne–Wilkinson, promised plaintiff by letter dated March 28, 1999, that defendant's influenza immunizations were "germ-proof" and that a properly immunized plaintiff employee would be "110% safe" from influenza. Plaintiff purchased 458 immunizations and administered them to all its employees. During the winter of 1999, some 35% of plaintiff's employees were stricken by the "Mongolian flu". Plaintiff now sues defendant alleging numerous breaches of the New Hazard Consumer Protection Act ("NHCPA").

Defendant filed a motion for summary disposition, which was granted by the trial court on the basis that the NHCPA did not apply due to defendant for two reasons. First, defendant falls within the § 4(1)(a) exemption of the NHCPA; secondly defendant is not engaged in "trade or commerce".

We treat the first ground as dispositive of this case and look to the exemption language of § 4(1)(a) to determine if plaintiff's complaint speaks to a transaction or conduct which would be the subject of regulatory control "under laws or rules administered by a regulatory board or officer acting under statutory authority of this state or the United States".

Plaintiff cites Nelson v. Ho, 414 N.Hz.2d 603 (1997), in support of its proposition that defendant is not exempt from the NHCPA under § 4(1)(a). In *Nelson*, the Supreme Court interpreted the exemption language of the section where the defendant claimed an exemption from the NHCPA because of his medical license. In that case, the Court rejected defendant's argument that § 4(1)(a) applied.

*Nelson* is distinguishable from the case at bar. The activities of the physician in *Nelson* were not subject to pervasive regulation under his medical license. The only genuine contact a physician has with the New Hazard Medical Council is in paying his or her yearly dues. That is not true for pharmacists in this state. Defendant is subject to all of the provisions of the Pharmaceutical Provisions Act. The pharmaceutical industry, which has been under the public spotlight for some years, is under the rigorous authority of the New Hazard Board of Pharmacy, which is a "regulatory board or officer acting under statutory authority of this state" and operates within an extensive statutory and regulatory scheme.

Given this conclusion, it is not necessary for us to discuss whether defendant was engaged in "trade or commerce", and in particular the vexed question of the scope of the "learned profession" exception. We do, however, wish to respond to a particular argument by defendant's attorney which we feel is contrary to the spirit of the Act. Defendant argued that the NHCPA does not apply to the transaction in question because plaintiff is an incorporated company which did not purchase the immunizations "primarily for personal, family, or household purposes". NHCPA § 2(1)(b). We disagree. The phrase just quoted modifies the words "goods, property, or service" so that the inquiry must be whether the goods, property, or services sold were sold primarily for personal, family, or household purposes. Accordingly, the question here is whether the immunizations were sold primarily for personal, family, or household purposes. We conclude that they were.

In its brief, defendant defines "personal" as "of or relating to a particular person". WEBSTER'S THIRD NEW INTERNATIONAL DICTIONARY (1976). However, "person" is defined by § 2(1)(a) of the NHCPA as:

> *a natural person, corporation, trust, partnership, incorporated or unincorporated association, or other legal entity.*

Thus, it is apparent that "personal", in the context of the Act, should be defined as "of or relating to a particular person, corporation, trust, partnership, incorporated or unincorporated association or other legal entity".

Since the drugs in this case were intended for the use of plaintiff's company, and since the incorporated company is a "person" under the Act, we conclude that the immunizations were primarily for personal use.

Due to § 4(1)(a), however, plaintiff has failed to state a claim upon which relief can be granted and we conclude that no factual development can possibly justify a right to recovery under the NHCPA. The Trial

Court's granting of the motion for summary judgment in favor of defendant was proper and the trial court is affirmed.

Briffault J., dissenting.

I respectfully dissent. I do not agree with defendant that it is exempt from the NHCPA because it is governed by a regulatory board, the New Hazard Board of Pharmacy. It is true that the NHCPA does not apply to a transaction or conduct specifically authorized under laws or rules administered by a regulatory board or officer. NHCPA § 4(1)(a). This exemption does not apply in this case because the alleged violative conduct falls outside the realm of the regulatory commission. *Nelson v. Ho,* 414 N.Hz.2d 603 (1997). Here, plaintiff is claiming that defendant's marketing of its influenza immunization violates the NHCPA. Marketing is not within the purview of the Pharmacy Board's regulatory powers. Therefore, plaintiff's claim that defendant's marketing of its immunizations violates the NHCPA falls outside the realm of the regulatory commission and § 4(1)(a) of the NHCPA does not apply.

### Problem 6

In the city of Cacophony, State of New Hazard, there is a ski area called Fluff Resort. Fluff Resort is owned and operated by Fluff Inc. The area has several thousand vertical feet of ski runs ranging from easy, to intermediate, to extreme. It has several ski lifts and a gondola. At the ski area's base, there are several shops, restaurants, video arcades, and hotels. Some of these are owned and operated by Fluff, while others are owned by the National Forest Service land on which the area sits.

The majority of the area's slopes are populated by people on skis and snowboards. However, the ski area will sell a ticket to all persons willing to pay the $55 dollar lift ticket price, and will allow them to ride the lifts. Daily, many people buy lift tickets and board the lift with snowshoes, sleds, bikes, or just hiking boots, taking the lift to the top of the mountain to enjoy the Forest Service land in the wintertime.

Three weeks ago, Joey Smith, age 12, paid the $55 ticket fare his mother had given him, and walked onto the lift. He did not have any skiing or snowboarding equipment with him. Instead, he was dressed in his new nylon ski suit. He was wearing tennis shoes.

About this same time, Judy Moss had descended from the lift at the mountain's top and started skiing to her destination halfway down the big, wide run named Mach Three, which was on the front face of the main mountain. The run was well known as one of the steeper slopes in the state. This slope was featured in Warbin Ziller's famous ski movie; in it, skiers who had lost their balance were seen comically sliding down the hill in their slippery ski clothes, unable to stop until they slowed to a stop down on the flatter part of the slope about 50 yards down the mountain. Fluff was proud of the run's reputation and kept it well groomed and free from debris or obstacles.

Halfway down this hill, about 15 feet off to one side of the slope, was a picnic deck overlooking Cacophony. It was owned and maintained by Fluff, Inc. Fluff had installed some wooden tables there, and sometimes it had an outdoor grill/restaurant set up where skiers could buy a cheeseburger and a soda. This day, though, while it was a beautiful sunny day, it was cold out, so the grill was not set up.

As she approached the picnic area, which was visible to her from the slope's top (about 100 feet), Ms. Moss saw that the picnic deck was empty. The deck was wooden and raised about three feet up from the snow. It was surrounded on three sides with a sturdy pine railing, but the side facing the uphill slope had no railing; instead, three steps running the entire length of the uphill side of the deck lead from the top of the snow to the platform.

Ms. Moss approached the deck from the slope. Because there was a five-foot wide bare spot in between the slope and the deck, however, Ms. Moss was able to ski only about 5 feet off the slope. There, she removed her skis and walked the remaining 10 feet up and onto the deck. Once settled at the table closest to the uphill side of the platform, Ms. Moss took out her grilled cheese sandwich to enjoy her lunch.

Right about this time, Joey was disembarking the ski lift. He had to run down the ski lift's off ramp. The lift operators gave him some strange looks but did not say anything to him. He looked determined.

Joey had seen Warbin Ziller's movies, and was set on conquering the steep face of Mach Three. He was ready for a wild ride down the hill, on his backside. From his vantage point at the top of the slope, he could see the picnic platform, and a pink figure sitting there. He was not concerned, however, for he was convinced that with his slippery pants and his trusty sneakers, he could safely navigate his descent.

Joey sat down on the slope, and began to scoot forward with his heels. He quickly gained speed and before he knew it, the trees were flying by him in a blur. The snow beneath him had turned icy, and he was unable to grip the firm snow with his hands or his rubber shoes. Next thing he knew he was airborne. He heard a scream, and felt a thud.

Joey had collided with the picnic table, and with Ms. Moss, after flying the full 15 feet from the slope's edge, to the platform. He'd hit a small rise on the edge of the slope that set him in flight. He suffered a fractured arm. Ms. Moss suffered a broken collar-bone.

You represent the Fluff. Both Ms. Moss and Joey's parents (who are the proper parties to bring suit on his behalf) have brought suit against Fluff alleging negligence in separate cases. While the two cases have not been consolidated into one, you have been asked to prepare a memo dealing with both cases as related. Fluff admits that it is the operator of Fluff ski area.

Other associates are researching other issues. The only issue presented to you is whether either party has a claim, or whether the Ski Area Liability Limitation Act bars their claims?

The cases have been heard at both the trial level and the Court of Appeals, both of which have granted summary judgment in favor of Fluff. The Plaintiffs have appealed both cases, certiorari has been granted, and you are now before the New Hazard Supreme Court.

## NEW HAZARD SKI AREA LIABILITY LIMITATION ACT

### 1. Legislative Declaration

**(a)** This article shall be known and may be cited as the "Ski Area Liability Limitation Act," (hereinafter "Act"). The Act shall be deemed an exercise of the state's power for the protection of the welfare, health, peace, morals, and safety of the people of the state. All its provisions shall be liberally construed for the accomplishment of those purposes.

**(b)** The ski industry and its economic success is important to the welfare of this state. The sport of skiing is inherently dangerous, regardless of any and all reasonable safety measures that a ski area can employ. The purpose of this Act is to define the rights and liabilities existing between the skier and the ski area. The general assembly hereby finds and declares that it is in the interest of the state of New Hazard to limit the liability of ski areas from suits brought against the skiers using them where the skier assumed the risk of these inherent dangers. However, the state of New Hazard also recognizes that there are dangers that are not inherent to skiing. The ski areas of this state have a responsibility to keep skiers safe from danger areas that do not present inherent dangers and risks of skiing.

### 2. Definitions

As used in this article, unless the context otherwise requires:

**(a)** "Inherent dangers and risks of skiing" means those dangers or conditions which are an integral part of the sport of skiing, including changing weather conditions; snow conditions as they exist or may change, such as ice, hard pack, powder, packed powder, wind pack, corn, crust, slush, cut-up snow, and machine-made snow; surface or subsurface conditions such as bare spots, forest growth, rocks, stumps, streambeds, and trees, or other natural objects, and collisions with such natural objects; impact with lift towers, signs, posts, fences or enclosures, hydrants, water pipes, other man-made structures and their components; variations in steepness or terrain, whether natural or as a result of slope design, snowmaking or grooming operations, including but not limited to roads and catwalks or other terrain modifications; collisions with other skiers; and the failure of skiers to ski within their own abilities. Nothing in this section shall be construed to limit the liability of the ski area operator for injury caused by the use or operation of ski lifts.

**(b)** "Ski area" means all ski slopes or trails and other places under the control of a ski area operator.

**(c)** "Ski area operator" means an area operator and any person, partnership, corporation, or other commercial entity having operational responsibility for any ski areas, including an agency of this state or a political subdivision thereof.

**(d)** "Skier" means any person using a ski area for the purpose of skiing; for the purpose of sliding downhill on snow or ice on skis, a toboggan, a sled, a tube, a ski-bob, a snowboard, or any other device; or for the purpose of using any of the facilities of the ski area, including but not limited to ski slopes and trails.

**(e)** "Ski slopes or trails" means those areas designated by the ski area operator to be used by skiers for any of the purposes enumerated in subsection (d) of this section. Such designation shall be set forth on trail maps, if provided, and designated by signs indicating to the skiing public the intent that such areas be used by skiers for the purpose of skiing.

**3. Limitation on actions for injury resulting from inherent dangers and risks of skiing**

**(a)** No skier may make any claim against or recover from any ski area operator for injury resulting on a ski area from any of the inherent dangers and risks of skiing.

**(b)** Nothing in this section shall limit a skier's claims against a ski area operator for injury resulting on a danger area of the ski area where the ski area operator failed to take reasonable precautions to protect skiers from the danger area. Danger areas do not include areas presenting inherent dangers and risks of skiing.

### ISAAC SAMAROFF v. SKY BLUE BASIN, INC.

Court of Appeals of New Hazard

June 16, 2001
Cert. denied, January 30, 2002

Carpet, C.J.

In this action to recover damages for injuries sustained in a skiing accident, plaintiff, Isaac Samaroff, appeals from a summary judgment entered in favor of defendant, Sky Blue Associates, Inc. ("Sky Blue"). We affirm.

In his complaint, plaintiff alleged that, while skiing at Sky Blue ski resort in New Hazard, on April 3, 1992, he was coming to a stop at the side of an intermediate ski run when he encountered "slushy snow and lost his edges, fell down, slipped several feet, then plunged forty-fifty feet down an unmarked steep ravine" next to the ski slope, and collided with a cluster of trees. Plaintiff claimed that Sky Blue, as operator of the ski area, had negligently failed to post signs warning skiers of the "ravine."

Sky Blue filed a motion for summary judgment in which it argued that plaintiff's claim was barred by the New Hazard Ski Area Liability Limitation Act, ("SALLA" or "Act") § 1, et seq. (New Hazard, 1990). The trial court granted the motion for summary judgment.

Plaintiff contends that the trial court erred in granting Sky Blue's motion for summary judgment. We disagree. The purpose of summary judgment is to permit the parties "to pierce the formal allegations of the pleadings and save the time and expense connected with trial when, as a matter of law, based on undisputed facts, one party could not prevail." *Peterson v. Halsted*, 829 N.Hz.2d 373, 375 (1992).

Summary judgment is a drastic remedy and should be granted only if there is no genuine issue as to any material fact and the moving party is entitled to judgment as a matter of law. N.Hz.R.C.P. 56(c). A material fact is a fact that will affect the outcome of the case. *Peterson v. Halsted*, 829 N.Hz.2d at 375.

In response to Sky Blue's motion for summary judgment here, plaintiff submitted his own affidavit, in which he stated that he had been skiing for twenty-two years, identified the run he was skiing on when he fell, and described the ravine as a precipice located next to the ski run. He also stated that, in his opinion, and in the opinion of others with whom he skied, falling down a 40–50 foot ravine is not an inherent risk of skiing. He concluded that the ravine was a dangerous area such that the Act did not limit his claims. The trial court accepted the factual allegations in plaintiff's affidavit as true for purposes of the summary judgment motion.

In its order granting summary judgment, the trial court concluded that there were no material factual issues in dispute, and that plaintiff's injuries were caused by inherent dangers and risks of skiing on the ski area.

In challenging the summary judgment, plaintiff first argues that the court erred in concluding that the ravine or drop-off was within the definition of "inherent dangers and risks of skiing" contained in SALLA § 2(a). We perceive no error.

At the outset, we note that the issue of whether the ravine was an "inherent risk" is a question of law to be resolved by the court. This issue can be resolved here through an interpretation of the Act.

Our goal in interpreting any statute is to determine and give effect to the intent of the General Assembly. A statute should not be interpreted in a piecemeal fashion. Rather, it should be "construed as a whole so as to give consistent, harmonious, and sensible effect to all of its parts." *Massey v. District Court*, 506 N.Hz.2d 128, 130 (1973). Thus, the meaning of any one section of a statute must be gleaned from a consideration of the overall legislative purpose. *People v. Alpert Corp.*, 660 N.Hz. App.2d 1295 (1982).

The SALLA was originally enacted in 1990. The New Hazard legislature, according to its declaration at the outset of SALLA, was particularly concerned to maintain the economic health of the ski industry, and, as part of that goal, to limit ski-related litigation. The Act does not immunize ski resort operators from all liability, however. The act provides that "nothing in this section shall limit a skier's claims against a ski area operator for injury resulting on a danger area of the ski area where the ski area operator failed to take reasonable precautions to protect skiers from the danger area. Danger areas do not include areas presenting inherent dangers and risks of skiing." SALLA § 3(b). Thus, an operator may be held liable in a negligence action where a skier is injured due to a ski area's failure to take reasonable precautions to protect the skier from the danger area, such as posting warning signs.

However, the General Assembly's clear intent was to limit, rather than expand, the liability of ski area operators. The trial court concluded that plaintiff's injuries were caused by inherent dangers and risks of skiing. Plaintiff does not dispute the court's conclusion that the slush he encountered and the trees with which he collided at the base of the drop-off were inherent dangers of skiing. However, he contends that a ravine is not within the statutory definition of inherent dangers of skiing. She argues that a ravine is a terrain change off the skiable area, and is not, therefore, a "variation in steepness or terrain" that is specifically mentioned in § 2(a) of SALLA. We disagree with this contention.

The statutory definition of inherent risks includes "variations in steepness or terrain, whether natural or as a result of slope design, snowmaking or grooming operations." SALLA § 2(a). The inclusion of natural terrain variations in this section demonstrates that, under the statute, inherent risks include terrain variations that might be encountered adjacent to ski runs, not solely those occurring within skiable areas. The ravine into which Samaroff fell was a natural unaltered part of the ski area. Virtually every trail at a ski resort is bounded by inherent risks such as trees, natural objects, and terrain variations. The Act does not restrict the definition of inherent risks to include only topographical conditions occurring within sites delineated as ski runs. The Act does not only apply to the skiable parts of a mountain. Here, the ravine is within the statutory definition of "inherent danger or risk of skiing." SALLA § 2(a).

Further, the statute's legislative history supports the conclusion that the definition of inherent risks was meant to include variations in steepness or terrain such as a ledge or a ravine that could cause injury. During the legislative debates on the bill, those opposed to the bill presented a document entitled "Reasons for Opposition to SALLA." Under a subheading entitled "Accident/Injuries which will not be covered if the Act passes," the following example appeared: "Skier injured when he/she strikes unmarked ledge. No recovery because variation in terrain (even man made) are inherent dangers." Legislative Summary on Hearings on S.B. 80 (Jan. 30, 1990). Despite this objection, the bill passed unchanged. Therefore, it is clear the legislature intended that a ravine is an inherent danger.

Nevertheless, relying on *Clover v. Snowbird Ski Resort*, 808 P.2d 1037 (Utah 1991), plaintiff argues that whether a particular risk is a danger that is inherent to the sport of skiing is a factual question that must be answered on a case-by-case basis. *Clover* involved a suit brought by a skier who was injured in a collision with an employee of the resort operator. Under Utah's Inherent Risk of Skiing Statute, inherent risks include, "but [are] not limited to" risks specifically defined in the statute. *Id.* As a result, Utah's Supreme Court held that because the list of inherent dangers in its act were "expressly nonexclusive," courts were to determine whether an inherent risk was an "integral part of skiing" on a case-by-case basis. *Id.* Unlike Utah's Act, however, SALLA does not contain express language of limitation. To the contrary, SALLA does not contain any language indicating that the statute contemplates inherent risks other than those specifically identified.

Also, were this Court to follow the example set in *Clover*, it would frustrate the Act's purpose in reducing costs caused by the escalating numbers of claims for skiers' personal injury. In introducing the Act as a bill, Senator Xavier stated: "This statute will allow ski area operators to get rid of frivolous claims very early in the legal process, hopefully." Floor Debate on S.B. 80 (Jan. 30, 1990). The case-by-case approach suggested in *Clover* would allow a skier who was injured by statutorily identified inherent risks to avoid summary judgment and to proceed to trial merely by alleging that the inherent risk encountered was not "an integral part of the sport of skiing." This is anathema to the Act's intent, and it is a result we will not sustain.

In conclusion, the slush, the trees, and the ravine, which were allegedly factors in plaintiff's injury, are all within SALLA's definition of "inherent dangers and risks of skiing," and the act expressly bars recovery for injuries resulting from such defined dangers and risks. SALLA § 2(a), 3(a).

Danger Area

Relying on § 3(b), plaintiff contends that the alleged ravine was a danger area and that Sky Blue was negligent because it failed to post a sign warning skiers of the danger. As discussed above, § 3(b) expressly provides that the term "danger area," as it relates to the reasonable precautions requirement, does not include "areas presenting inherent dangers and risks of skiing." An area presenting variations in steepness or terrain, such as the drop-off or ravine at issue here, is thus not a "danger area" within the meaning of the statute. Accordingly, Sky Blue cannot be held liable for failing to post such a warning sign.

We conclude that the trial court properly determined that plaintiff's injuries were caused by "inherent dangers and risks of skiing," as defined in SALLA. Thus, the trial court properly concluded, as a matter of law, that plaintiff's claim was barred under SALLA.

The judgment is affirmed.

Taylor, J. concurs.

Spera, J. dissenting:

I respectfully dissent.

I disagree with the Court's conclusion that the ravine in this case was an inherent risk rather than a danger area. I am of the opinion that this case should proceed past summary judgment to allow the trial court to determine the question as one of fact.

Under the Court of Appeals' interpretation, any type of terrain variation wherever located falls within the definition of "inherent dangers and risks of skiing." However, the definitional language of § 2(a) strongly suggests that the variations in steepness or terrain described are those occurring within skiable areas and do not necessarily include those that might be encountered adjacent to the runs. This construction derives from the legislature's references to the source of the variations as "a result of slope design" and of "snowmaking or grooming operations," situations to be encountered within the areas intended for skiing. The complaint and the plaintiff's affidavit in the present case indicate that he slid down a steep ravine or precipice immediately next to the ski run. The steep ravine or precipice, therefore, was a terrain feature outside the ski trail and was not as a matter of law included within the statutory description.

The prefatory language of the definition of "inherent dangers and risks of skiing" is also important in determining the nature of terrain variations included within that definition. This is so because when interpreting a statute, we must read and interpret the language "so as to give consistent, harmonious, and sensible effect to all of its parts." *People v. Andrews*, 871 N.Hz.2d 1199, 1201 (1994). The dangers and risks detailed in § 2(a) are intended to describe those "which are an integral part of the sport of skiing." The detailed listing of dangers and risks must be read with that intent and limitation in mind. *Clover v. Snowbird Ski Resort*, 808 P.2d 1037, 1044–45 (Utah 1991) (distinguishing between risks on the basis of whether they are an integral part of the sport of skiing).

The legislative history of the Act is also consistent with a more narrow construction of "inherent dangers and risks of skiing." The scope of the phrase "variations in steepness or terrain" was addressed in hearings before the House State Affairs Committee. George Ruff, representing the bill's proponents, Ski and Softball Country USA, explained "variations in steepness or terrain" as follows: "Skiers encounter terrain changes, a trail turning to the right or left, or a trail dipping, and a skier going too fast out of control will fall, and instead of looking to himself will sue the ski areas." Hearings on S.B. 80 (March 13, 1990). The Act was not presented as including precipices or ravines located outside skiable areas within the scope of the phrase "variations in steepness or terrain."

Skiing is a dangerous sport. Ordinary understanding tells us so, and the legislature has recognized that dangers inhere in the sport. Not all dangers that may be encountered on the ski slopes, however, are inherent and integral to the sport, and this determination cannot always be made as a matter of law. In the present case, the plaintiff describes the terrain that precipitated her injuries as a ravine immediately next to the ski run. This description conjures up an image of a highly dangerous situation created by locating a ski run at the very edge of a steep dropoff. If such a hazardous situation presents an inherent risk of skiing that need not be marked as a danger area, the ski area operator's duty to take reasonable precautions under § 3(b) is essentially meaningless. Therefore, I do not construe § 2(a) to include such a situation within the inherent dangers and risks of skiing as a matter of law. Instead, here, there are questions of material fact as to whether the ravine was an inherent risk, or a danger area. Consequently, I would reverse the judgment below, and would remand for further proceedings.

## ROBERTA SCOTT v. SNOW HEAVEN RECREATIONAL ASSOC.

Supreme Court of New Hazard

July 7, 2000

Bronlee, C.J.

Plaintiff, Roberta Scott, appeal the trial court's summary judgment. The trial court held in favor of Defendant on the grounds that the New Hazard Ski Area Liability Limitation Act, ("SALLA" or "Act") § 1, et seq. (New Hazard, 1990) applied to bar Plaintiff's claims of negligence against the Defendant, Snow Heaven Recreational Association ("Snow Heaven"). We reverse.

Plaintiff filed her complaint against Snow Heaven, alleging that on February 23, 1991, while she was in a parking lot owned by Snow Heaven, waiting for a shuttle bus operated by it, a sign affixed to a concrete block that was owned, maintained, and positioned by Snow Heaven fell on the plaintiff, causing her serious personal injuries. Snow Heaven's answer to the complaint admitted that it was the "operator" of the parking lot, but generally denied the remaining allegations of the complaint. In addition, its answer affirmatively asserted that plaintiff's claims were barred by the provisions of the Act.

Shortly thereafter, Snow Heaven filed a motion, requesting the entry of a judgment of dismissal, based upon the applicability of SALLA. This statute establishes that "no skier may make any claim against or recover from any ski area operator for injury resulting on a ski area from any of the inherent dangers and risks of skiing." SALLA § 3(a).

A "ski area" consists of "ski slopes or trails and other places under the control of a ski area operator and administered as a single enterprise within this state." SALLA § 2(b). Thus, the question before the trial court, and before us, is whether the parking lot in which the plaintiffs were waiting was an "other place" under this statute and, therefore, a part of a "ski area," as contemplated by the Act.

In entering judgment for Snow Heaven as requested in its motion, the trial court held that the parking lot involved was one of the "other places" referred to by the Act. Thus, it concluded that the Act applied and barred plaintiffs' action.

Plaintiffs argue, however, that the term "other places" refers only to places used in conjunction with the skiing activity itself, such as ski lifts and ticket areas, and does not refer to other areas, such as shops, restaurants, and parking lots, not directly devoted to skiing activities. Thus, they assert that the Act does not apply to bar their claim because the parking lot is not part of the "ski area." SALLA § 3(a). We agree.

The Act was adopted in 1990 in order to "define the rights and liabilities existing between the skier and the ski area." SALLA § 1(b). A "ski area operator" is an entity that has operational responsibility for any ski areas, including an agency of this state or a political subdivision thereof. SALLA § 2(c). A skier is deemed to assume the risk of "inherent dangers and risks of skiing," which means "those things which are an integral part of the sport of skiing." SALLA § 2(a).

As a result, the Act only discusses the ski area's limitation of liability with regard to skiing and the facilities directly devoted to skiing. It does not purport to regulate either the conditions under which a skier assumes other risks associated with other facilities (such as restaurants, shops, and parking lots), or the activities of persons making use of such facilities. Considering the purpose of the Act and the nature of the activities governed by it, therefore, we conclude that the term "ski area" was not intended to encompass any area that is not directly devoted to skiing activities.

The Act must be construed with a due regard for its underlying purposes. Since it is an enactment designed to declare principles of public policy, it need not be strictly or literally interpreted. See *Phillips v. Monarch Recreation Corp.*, 668 N.Hz. App.2d 982 (1983).

While it is unnecessary to determine the precise boundaries of Snow Heaven's "ski area" in this case, we conclude that the area here at issue, which is devoted to the parking of motor vehicles and the operation of shuttle buses, is not an area that is included within the statutory definition of that term. Thus, none of the provisions of the Act is applicable to this controversy, and the trial court erred in concluding otherwise.

The judgment of the district court is reversed and the cause is remanded for further proceedings consistent with the views contained herein.

Kernberg, J., dissenting.

The question is whether there is any genuine issue of material fact that the parking lot where plaintiff was injured was a "ski area" as defined by SALLA § 2(b). That section states that "ski area" means all ski slopes or trails and other places under the control of a ski area operator.

This language is plain, clear and unambiguous. As such our role is to apply the plain and ordinary meaning of its words and phrases as written. See *Sargent School District No. RE–33J v. Western Services, Inc.*, 751 N.Hz.2d 56 (1988). Application of this fundamental principle here leads me to conclude that the parking lot is an "other place." It was undisputedly managed and controlled by Snow Heaven, a ski area operator.

## Problem 7

You are a member of the Bar of the State of New Hazard, where, as a solo practitioner, you specialize in Legal Ethics. Your client, Clara Grubsnig, a fellow member of the Bar who is a partner in the leading Metropolis firm of Grubsnig & Areps, is concerned about her possible exposure to disciplinary action under the New Hazard Rules of Professional Conduct, and consults you regarding the following problem.

Grubsnig's client, Mega Industries Conglomerated, has asked her to draft a contract between Mega and Kiddie Kable TV, to place advertisements for its Choco–Cruncho Cereal during Kiddie's Saturday morning cartoon programs. Choco–Cruncho Cereal features the cuddly Cruncho character on its boxes and in the shape of the cereal morsels. Cruncho is a loveable, if toothy, reptilian figure, somewhat reminiscent of the wildly popular children's television purple dinosaur, Barney. The Choco–Cruncho advertisements would include animated versions of the Cruncho character. Grubsnig has just learned from Mega that Mega's TV ads contain subliminal messages promoting another Mega Product, WayCool Cigarettes. The ads depict Cruncho smoking WayCools with great pleasure. Kiddie Kable is unaware of the subliminal messages hidden in the ads.

Grubsnig has attempted to dissuade her client, Mega, from placing the advertisements, but Mega persists in its intent to air the ads containing the subliminal messages.

Based on the following New Hazard authorities (disregard any possibly relevant federal authorities), what would you advise Grubsnig to do?

## NEW HAZARD COMPILED STATUTES, COURT RULES NEW HAZARD SUPREME COURT RULES ARTICLE VIII. NEW HAZARD RULES OF PROFESSIONAL CONDUCT[1]

### PREAMBLE

The practice of law is a public trust. Lawyers are the trustees of the system by which citizens resolve disputes among themselves, punish and deter crime, and determine their relative rights and responsibilities toward each other and their government. Lawyers therefore are responsible for the character, competence and integrity of the persons whom they assist in joining their profession; for assuring access to that system through the availability of competent legal counsel; for maintaining public confidence in the system of justice by acting competently and with loyalty to the best interests of their clients; by working to improve that system to meet the challenges of a rapidly changing society; and by defending the integrity of the judicial system against those who would corrupt, abuse or defraud it.

To achieve these ends the practice of law is regulated by the following rules. Violation of these rules is grounds for discipline. No set of prohibitions, however, can adequately articulate the positive values or goals sought to be advanced by those prohibitions. Lawyers seeking to conform their conduct to the requirements of these rules should look to the values described in this preamble for guidance in interpreting the difficult issues which may arise under the rules.

The policies which underlie the various rules may, under certain circumstances, be in some tension with each other. Wherever feasible, the

---

**1.**   The following is based on the Illinois Rules of Professional Conduct.

rules themselves seek to resolve such conflicts with clear statements of duty. For example, a lawyer must disclose, even in breach of a client confidence, a client's intent to commit a crime involving a serious risk of bodily harm. In other cases, lawyers must carefully weigh conflicting values, and make decisions, at the peril of violating one or more of the following rules. Lawyers are trained to make just such decisions, however, and should not shrink from the task. To reach correct ethical decisions, lawyers must be sensitive to the duties imposed by these rules and, whenever practical, should discuss particularly difficult issues with their peers.

Lawyers also must assist in the policing of lawyer misconduct. The vigilance of the bar in preventing and, where required, reporting misconduct can be a formidable deterrent to such misconduct, and a key to maintaining public confidence in the integrity of the profession as a whole in the face of the egregious misconduct of a few.

Legal services are not a commodity. Rather, they are the result of the efforts, training, judgment and experience of the members of a learned profession. These rules reflect the sensitive task of striking a balance between making available useful information regarding the availability and merits of lawyers and the need to protect the public against deceptive or overreaching practices. All communications with clients and potential clients should be consistent with these values.

The lawyer-client relationship is one of trust and confidence. Such confidence only can be maintained if the lawyer acts competently and zealously pursues the client's interests within the bounds of the law. "Zealously" does not mean mindlessly or unfairly or oppressively. Rather, it is the duty of all lawyers to seek resolution of disputes at the least cost in time, expense and trauma to all parties and to the courts. . . .

## Rule 1.6. Confidentiality of Information

(a) Except when required under Rule 1.6(b) or permitted under Rule 1.6(c), a lawyer shall not, during or after termination of the professional relationship with the client, use or reveal a confidence or secret of the client known to the lawyer unless the client consents after disclosure.

(b) A lawyer shall reveal information about a client to the extent it appears necessary to prevent the client from committing an act that would result in death or serious bodily harm.

(c) A lawyer may use or reveal:

   (1) confidences or secrets when required by law or court order;

   (2) the intention of a client to commit a crime in circumstances other than those enumerated in Rule 1.6(b); or

   (3) confidences or secrets necessary to establish or collect the lawyer's fee or to defend the lawyer or the lawyer's employees or associates against an accusation of wrongful conduct.

### Rule 1.7.   Declining or Terminating Representation

(a) A lawyer representing a client before a tribunal shall withdraw from employment (with permission of the tribunal if such permission is required) if:

  (1) the lawyer knows or reasonably should know that the client is bringing the legal action, conducting the defense, or asserting a position in the litigation, or is otherwise having steps taken, merely for the purpose of harassing or maliciously injuring any person;

  (2) the lawyer knows or reasonably should know that such continued employment will result in violation of the law;

(b) Except as required in Rule 1.7(a), a lawyer shall not request permission to withdraw in matters pending before a tribunal, unless such request or such withdrawal is because:

  (1) the client:

   (A) insists upon presenting a claim or defense that is not warranted under existing law and cannot be supported by a reasonable argument for an extension, modification, or reversal of existing law;

   (B) seeks to pursue an illegal course of conduct;

   (C) insists that the lawyer pursue a course of conduct that is illegal or that is prohibited by these Rules;

  (2) the lawyer's inability to work with co-counsel indicates that the best interests of the client likely will be served by withdrawal;

  (3) the client consents to termination of the lawyer's employment after disclosure; or

  (4) the lawyer reasonably believes that a tribunal will, in a proceeding pending before the tribunal, find the existence of other good cause for withdrawal.

(c) A lawyer shall not withdraw from representing a client in a matter not pending before a tribunal, unless such withdrawal is because the client:

  (1) insists that the lawyer pursue a course of conduct that is illegal; or

  (2) insists that the lawyer engage in conduct that is contrary to the judgment and advice of the lawyer although not prohibited by these Rules.

### NEW HAZARD COMPILED STATUTES THE PUBLIC HEALTH CIGARETTE SALES ACT, 1992

WHEREAS the New Hazard State Legislature finds that cigarettes are potentially dangerous, lethal and addictive;

The New Hazard State Legislature enacts the Public Health Cigarette Sales Act of 1992, which provides:

### § 1234   sale of tobacco products to minors:

The sale of tobacco products to minors shall be considered unlawful and shall subject the seller, and all those acting in concert with him or her, to civil liability.

## BALLA v. GAMBRO, INC.*

### Supreme Court of New Hazard.

### Dec. 19, 1999.

Bell, J.,

The issue in this case is whether in-house counsel should be allowed the remedy of an action for retaliatory discharge.

Appellee, Roger Balla, formerly in-house counsel for Gambro, Inc. (Gambro), filed a retaliatory discharge action against Gambro. Appellee alleged that he was fired in contravention of New Hazard public policy and sought damages for the discharge. The trial court dismissed the action on appellants' motion for summary judgment. The appellate court reversed. We granted appellant's petition for leave to appeal.

Gambro is a distributor of kidney dialysis equipment manufactured by Gambro (Germany). The manufacture and sale of dialyzers is regulated by the federal government, including the United States Food and Drug Administration (FDA).

Appellee, Roger J. Balla, is and was at all times throughout this controversy an attorney licensed to practice law in the State of New Hazard. Appellee held the title of director of administration at Gambro. As director of administration, appellee's specific responsibilities included coordinating and overseeing corporate activities to assure compliance with applicable laws and regulations.

In July 1985 Gambro learned that certain dialyzers its affiliated company (Gambro Germany) had manufactured were about to be shipped to Gambro and that they did not comply with federal regulations. Appellee told the president of Gambro about the violations and told the president to reject the shipment. The president notified Gambro Germany of its decision to reject the shipment on July 12, 1985.

However, one week later the president informed Gambro Germany that Gambro would accept the dialyzers. Appellee contends that he was not informed by the president of the decision to accept the dialyzers but became aware of it through other Gambro employees. Appellee maintains that he spoke with the president in August regarding the company's decision to accept the dialyzers and told the president that he would do whatever necessary to stop the sale of the dialyzers.

On September 4, 1985, appellee was discharged from Gambro's employment by its president. The following day, appellee reported the shipment of the dialyzers to the FDA. The FDA seized the shipment.

---

* This opinion is based on *Balla v. Gambro, Inc.*, 584 N.E.2d 104 (Ill.1991).

On March 19, 1986, appellee filed a four-count complaint in tort for retaliatory discharge seeking $22 million in damages.

On July 28, 1987, Gambro filed a motion for summary judgment. Gambro argued that appellee, as an attorney, was precluded from filing a retaliatory discharge.

On November 30, 1988, the trial court granted appellants' motion for summary judgment. The trial court concluded that the duties appellee was performing which led to his discharge were conduct clearly within the attorney-client relationship and that Gambro had the absolute right to discharge its attorney. On appeal, the court below held that an attorney is not barred as a matter of law from bringing an action for retaliatory discharge.

We agree with the trial court that appellee does not have a cause of action against Gambro for retaliatory discharge under the facts of the case at bar. Generally, this court adheres to the proposition that an employer may discharge an employee-at-will for any reason or for no reason at all. However, this court has recognized the limited and narrow tort of retaliatory discharge. This court stressed that if employers could fire employees for filing workers' compensation claims, the public policy behind the enactment of the Workers' Compensation Act would be frustrated.

In this case it appears that Gambro discharged appellee, an employee of Gambro, in retaliation for his activities, and this discharge was in contravention of a clearly mandated public policy. Appellee allegedly told the president of Gambro that he would do whatever was necessary to stop the sale of the "misbranded and/or adulterated" dialyzers. In appellee's eyes, the use of these dialyzers could cause death or serious bodily harm to patients. There is no public policy more important or more fundamental than the one favoring the effective protection of the lives and property of citizens. However, in this case, appellee was not just an employee of Gambro, but also general counsel for Gambro.

In-house counsel do not have a claim under the tort of retaliatory discharge. We base our decision as much on the nature and purpose of the tort of retaliatory discharge, as on the effect on the attorney-client relationship that extending the tort would have. We caution that our holding is confined by the fact that appellee is and was at all times throughout this controversy an attorney licensed to practice law in the State of New Hazard. Appellee is and was subject to the New Hazard Code of Professional Responsibility adopted by this court.

In this case, the public policy to be protected, that of protecting the lives and property of citizens, is adequately safeguarded without extending the tort of retaliatory discharge to in-house counsel. Appellee was required under the Rules of Professional Conduct to report Gambro's intention to sell the "misbranded and/or adulterated" dialyzers. Rule 1.6(b) of the Rules of Professional Conduct reads: "A lawyer shall reveal information about a client to the extent it appears necessary to prevent the client from committing an act that would result in death or serious bodily injury." (N. Haz. Prof. Resp. R. 1.6(b).)

Appellee alleges, and the FDA's seizure of the dialyzers indicates, that the use of the dialyzers would cause death or serious bodily injury. Thus, under the above-cited rule, appellee was under the mandate of this court to report the sale of these dialyzers.

In his brief to this court, appellee argues that not extending the tort of retaliatory discharge to in-house counsel would present attorneys with a "Hobson's choice." According to appellee, in-house counsel would face two alternatives: either comply with the client/employer's wishes and risk both the loss of a professional license and exposure to criminal sanctions, or decline to comply with client/employer's wishes and risk the loss of a full-time job and the attendant benefits.

We disagree. In-house counsel do not have a choice of whether to follow their ethical obligations as attorneys licensed to practice law, or follow the illegal and unethical demands of their clients. In-house counsel must abide by the Rules of Professional Conduct. Appellee had no choice but to report to the FDA Gambro's intention to sell or distribute these dialyzers.

We recognize that under the New Hazard Rules of Professional Conduct, attorneys shall reveal client confidences or secrets in certain situations (see N. Haz. Prof. Resp. R. 1.6(a), (b), (c)), and thus one might expect employers/clients to be naturally hesitant to rely on in-house counsel for advice regarding this potentially questionable conduct. However, the danger exists that if in-house counsel are granted a right to sue their employers in tort for retaliatory discharge, employers might further limit their communication with their in-house counsel. The attorney-client privilege is supposed to encourage full and frank communication between attorneys and their clients and thereby promote broader public interests in the observance of law and administration of justice. The privilege recognizes that sound legal advice or advocacy serves public ends and that such advice or advocacy depends upon the lawyer being fully informed by the client. If extending the tort of retaliatory discharge might have a chilling effect on the communications between the employer/client and the in-house counsel, we believe that it is more wise to refrain from doing so.

However difficult economically and perhaps emotionally it is for in-house counsel to discontinue representing an employer/client, we refuse to allow in-house counsel to sue their employer/client for damages because they obeyed their ethical obligations. In this case, appellee, in addition to being an employee at Gambro, is first and foremost an attorney bound by the Rules of Professional Conduct. These Rules of Professional Conduct hope to articulate in a concrete fashion certain values and goals such as defending the integrity of the judicial system, promoting the administration of justice and protecting the integrity of the legal profession. (N. Haz. Prof. Resp. R., Preamble.) An attorney's obligation to follow these Rules of Professional Conduct should not be the foundation for a claim of retaliatory discharge.

For the foregoing reasons, the decision of the appellate court is reversed, and the decision of the trial court is affirmed.

## SPAULDING v. ZIMMERMAN*

Supreme Court of New Hazard.

Aug. 3, 1998

Ellis, J.

Appeal from an order of the trial vacating and setting aside a prior order of such court dated May 8, 1985, approving a settlement made on behalf of David Spaulding on March 5, 1985, at which time he was a minor of the age of 20 years.

The prior action was brought against defendants by Theodore Spaulding, as father and natural guardian of David Spaulding, for injuries sustained by David in an automobile accident, arising out of a collision which occurred August 24, 1984, between an automobile driven by John Zimmerman, in which David was a passenger, and one owned by John Ledermann and driven by Florian Ledermann.

After the accident, David's injuries were diagnosed by his family physician, Dr. James H. Cain, as a severe crushing injury of the chest with multiple rib fractures; a severe cerebral concussion, probably with petechial hemorrhages of the brain; and bilateral fractures of the clavicles. At Dr. Cain's suggestion, on January 3, 1985, David was examined by Dr. John F. Pohl, an orthopedic specialist, who made X-ray studies of his chest and found that his heart and aorta were normal.

In the meantime, on February 22, 1985, at defendants' request, David was examined by Dr. Hewitt Hannah, a neurologist. On February 26, 1985, the latter reported to Messrs. Field, Arveson, & Donoho, attorneys for defendant John Zimmerman, as follows:

> The one feature of the case which bothers me more than any other part of the case is the fact that this boy of 20 years of age has an aneurysm, which means a dilatation of the aorta and the arch of the aorta. Whether this came out of this accident I cannot say with any degree of certainty and I have discussed it with the Roentgenologist and a couple of Internists.... Of course an aneurysm or dilatation of the aorta in a boy of this age is a serious matter as far as his life. This aneurysm may dilate further and it might rupture with further dilatation and this would cause his death.

Prior to the negotiations for settlement, the contents of the above report were made known to counsel for defendants Florian and John Ledermann, but not to counsel for plaintiff.

The case was called for trial on March 4, 1985, at which time the respective parties and their counsel possessed such information as to David's physical condition as was revealed to them by their respective

---

* This case is based on *Spaulding v. Zimmerman*, 116 N.W.2d 704 (Minn.1962).

medical examiners as above described. It is thus apparent that neither David nor his father, the nominal plaintiff in the prior action, was then aware that David was suffering the aorta aneurysm but on the contrary believed that he was recovering from the injuries sustained in the accident.

On the following day an agreement for settlement was reached wherein, in consideration of the payment of $6,500, David and his father agreed to settle in full for all claims arising out of the accident.

Richard S. Roberts, counsel for David, thereafter presented to the court a petition for approval of the settlement, wherein David's injuries were described as: ' * * * severe crushing of the chest, with multiple rib fractures, severe cerebral concussion, with petechial hemorrhages of the brain, bilateral fractures of the clavicles.' At no time was there information disclosed to the court that David was then suffering from an aorta aneurysm which may have been the result of the accident. The court on May 8, 1985, made its order approving the settlement.

Early in 1987, David was required by the army reserve, of which he was a member, to have a physical checkup. For this, he again engaged the services of Dr. Cain. In this checkup, the latter discovered the aorta aneurysm. He then reexamined the X rays which had been taken shortly after the accident and at this time discovered that they disclosed the beginning of the process which produced the aneurysm. He promptly sent David to Dr. Jerome Grismer for an examination and opinion. The latter confirmed the finding of the aorta aneurysm and recommended immediate surgery therefor. This was performed by him at Mount Sinai Hospital in Metropolis on March 10, 1987.

Shortly thereafter, David, having attained his majority, instituted the present action for additional damages due to the more serious injuries including the aorta aneurysm which he alleges proximately resulted from the accident. As indicated above, the prior order for settlement was vacated. The trial court noted that, by reason of the failure of plaintiff's counsel to use available rules of discovery, plaintiff's doctor and all of plaintiff's representatives did not learn the seriousness of his plaintiff's injuries.

That defendants' counsel concealed the knowledge they had is not disputed. There is no doubt, however, of the good faith of both defendants' counsel. During the course of the negotiations, when the parties were in an adversary relationship, no rule required or duty rested upon defendants or their representatives to disclose this knowledge. Under Rule 1.6 of the New Hazard Rules of Professional Responsibility, a lawyer is required to disclose information about an act that would lead to death or serious bodily harm. The application of this rule often requires a delicate balance of competing interests. On the one hand, a lawyer must uphold the sanctity of the attorney-client relationship by strictly maintaining client confidences. At the same time, however, a lawyer has an obligation to society and to the physical well-being of the very people our system of justice is designed to protect. In considering these countervailing interests and the express language of Rule 1.6, we conclude that defense counsel's conduct in this case did not violate the New Hazard Rules of Professional Responsibility.

Despite the lack of any ethical obligation to disclose the life threatening condition, the concealment was of such character as to result in an unconscionable advantage over plaintiff's ignorance or mistake during settlement discussions. The court may vacate such a settlement for mistake.

From the foregoing it is clear that in the instant case the court did not abuse its discretion in setting aside the settlement which it had approved on plaintiff's behalf while he was still a minor. It is undisputed that neither he nor his counsel nor his medical attendants were aware that at the time settlement was made he was suffering from an aorta aneurysm which may have resulted from the accident. The seriousness of this disability is indicated by Dr. Hannah's report indicating the imminent danger of death therefrom. This was known by counsel for both defendants but was not disclosed to the court at the time it was petitioned to approve the settlement. While no canon of ethics or legal obligation may have required them to inform plaintiff or his counsel with respect thereto, or to advise the court therein, it did become obvious to them at the time, that the settlement then made did not contemplate or take into consideration the disability described. This fact opened the way for the court to later exercise its discretion in vacating the settlement.

Affirmed.

## Problem 8

Cameron Wandle is a well-known standup comedian who has recently signed a deal to write and star in a television show about his life. Under the terms of the contract, the XYZ network agreed to pay Cameron $10,000 for each script he writes, and $50,000 per episode for acting in the show. XYZ produced the first episode in the series—tentatively titled "Cameron!"—and invited him to attend the premiere screening of the show in Hollywood. XYZ, eager to make a good impression on Cameron, promises to send a corporate jet to pick up Cameron at the Teterboro, New Jersey, airport.

XYZ hires Brenda Nelwood to fly Cameron to California for the premiere of the television show. Brenda is the chief pilot of Charter–Jet Aviation, a company which offers charter flights in small but luxurious corporate jets. She obtained her flight training in the U.S. Marine Corps, where she also received a black belt in kung fu. Charter–Jet's services are available to the general public, although due to its $1000 per hour fee, most of its customers are corporate executives and show business personalities. XYZ is a frequent customer of Charter–Jet, and Brenda has flown many New York-based entertainers to the West Coast in her years of working for the company.

Cameron and Brenda take off in Brenda's jet, bound for California. As they are cruising along at 33,000 feet, the plane suddenly goes into a violent spin. Brenda manages to regain control, but as a precaution, she decides to land at the airport in Cacophony, a small city in the state of New Hazard, to have the flight control system inspected.

Brenda and Cameron rent a car at the Cacophony airport and drive into town to kill some time. As they walk around the quaint downtown area, Brenda asks whether she can film Cameron with her camcorder. "My kids are huge fans of yours," she says, "and they'll never believe I was actually hanging around in New Hazard with *Cameron Wandle*." Cameron agrees, and poses for a shot. As Brenda is filming Cameron, she notices through the viewfinder of the camera that a man across the street is getting mugged. "Cameron, come here!" she calls out. Cameron runs over to Brenda's side and watches the mugging, while Brenda continues to film the scene.

"What a dork," Cameron says.

"Yeah. Look at him. He looks so scared. Do you think we should do something, Cameron?"

"What do you mean, do something?"

"Like stop the mugging," says Brenda with an air of exasperation

"No way," replies Cameron, "I'm a performer. How would it look for me to give a show with a big black eye? Besides, that guy could be using or carrying a gun."

"He's not armed! Look, he's wearing shorts and a t-shirt. Besides, he's a wimp. I could take that guy with one arm tied behind my back."

"You?" asks Cameron incredulously.

"Yeah, me. What's so unbelievable about that? When I was in the Marines, I was a martial arts instructor. I taught pilots how to defend themselves in hand-to-hand combat behind enemy lines."

"Well, why don't you go stop this mugging then?"

"Nah. I'd rather film it—this is pretty funny. Maybe I can send the film in to America's Funniest Home Videos. If you're so concerned, why don't you call the cops? You always carry around a cell phone."

"I don't feel like it. I'll just watch."

The mugging ends when the victim, John Gansbeck, surrenders his wallet and the mugger flees. John staggers to his car in a daze and drives himself to the Cacophony City Hospital. There, he is admitted for observation after showing signs of post-traumatic stress disorder. He is discharged a week later, but is unable to return to work for three months due to his anxiety. John hires a lawyer and explains his story. "There's got to be a law against what Cameron and his friend did," he exclaims. "That's just not decent!"

You are John's lawyer. Your investigator learned, through a buddy who works at the airport, that Cameron Wandle arrived in town on a plane owned by Charter–Jet, flown by Brenda Nelwood. Your client wants to know, therefore, whether he can sue Cameron and Brenda for their role in his mugging. After some diligent research you have located a statute and two cases:

## THE NEW HAZARD CIVILITY AND DECENCY ACT

### N.Hz. Civil Code § 301—Emergency Assistance.

(a) Any person who reasonably believes that the life, health, or safety of a person or persons is under imminent threat of danger and could be aided by reasonable and accessible emergency procedures under the circumstances existing at the scene thereof shall render assistance or service in a manner reasonably calculated to lessen or remove the immediate threat to the life, health, or safety of such person or persons, but shall be obliged to provide such services only as set forth in subsection (b) of this section.

(b) The person rendering assistance shall provide only such emergency care or assistance as a reasonable and prudent person concerned for the immediate protection of the life, health, and safety of the person for whom the services were rendered would lend under the circumstances present at the scene at the time the services were rendered.

### § 302—Enforcement.

The New Hazard Civility and Decency Agency shall be empowered to issue summons to any person whose failure to provide assistance as set forth in Section 301 was the cause of injury to another person. The summons may require the recipient to appear in court and pay a fine of no more than $50.

### § 303—Good Samaritans.

No person who, in good faith, provides or obtains, or attempts to provide or obtain, assistance as defined in Section 301, shall be liable in a civil suit for damages as a result of any acts or omissions in providing or obtaining, or attempting to provide or obtain, such assistance unless such acts or omissions constitute willful, wanton or reckless conduct.

### JUDITH PECK v. NICHOLAS IAMMARINO, Dean, New Hazard School of Medicine*

Supreme Court of New Hazard

Decided May 10, 1997

Bronlee, C.J.

Appellant, Judith Peck ("Ms. Peck") alleges that her application for admission to the New Hazard School of Medicine ("the School") was denied by the appellees because she is a woman. Accepting the truth of those allegations for the purpose of its decision, the Superior Court held that Ms. Peck has no private right of action against the School. We now reverse the Court of Appeals.

---

* Based on *Cannon v. University of Chicago*, 441 U.S. 677 (1979).

Only two facts alleged in the complaint are relevant to our decision. First, Ms. Peck was excluded from participation in the School because of her sex. Second, the School was receiving financial assistance from the state of New Hazard at the time of her exclusion. These facts, admitted *arguendo* by the School's motion to dismiss the complaint, establish a violation of Section 901(a) of the New Hazard Right to Education Act. According to her complaint, Ms. Peck was qualified to attend the School based on both objective (i.e., grade-point average and test scores) and subjective criteria. In fact, the School admitted some male applicants despite the fact that those persons had less impressive objective qualifications than Ms. Peck did. Upon her rejection by the School, Ms. Peck sought reconsideration of the decision by way of written and telephonic communications with admissions officials. Finding these avenues of no avail, she filed a complaint in the New Hazard Superior Court.

## I.

The statute at issue in this case provides:

> No person in the State of New Hazard shall, on the basis of sex, be excluded from participation in, be denied the benefits of, or be subjected to discrimination under any education program or activity receiving financial assistance from the State of New Hazard.

N.Hz. Civil Code § 901. The statute does not, however, expressly provide a civil cause of action to a person injured by a violation of Section 901. For that reason, and because it concluded that no private remedy should be inferred, the Superior Court granted the School's motion to dismiss. As our recent cases demonstrate, the fact that a statute has been violated and some person harmed does not automatically give rise to a private cause of action in favor of that person. Instead, before concluding that the New Hazard Legislature intended to make a remedy available to a special class of litigants, a court must carefully analyze two factors. *See Ashe v. DeLaCort*, 422 N.Hz. 66 (1975). Our review of those factors persuades us, however, that the Superior Court reached the wrong conclusion and that Ms. Peck does have a statutory right to pursue a civil action based on her claim that the School rejected her application on the basis of her sex.

## A.

The first factor is whether the plaintiff is "one of the class for whose special benefit the statute was enacted." That question is answered by looking to the language of the statute itself. Thus, the statutory reference to "any employee of any such common carrier" in the 1893 New Hazard Railway Safety Act, which required railroads to equip their cars with secure "grab irons or handholds," *see* N.Hz. Civ. Code § 117(c), compelled the Court to infer a private right of action in favor of a railway employee who was injured when a grab iron gave way. *Cacophony & Harmony Railway Co. v. Rigsby*, 241 N.Hz. 33 (1922). The language in the Railway Safety Act, which expressly identifies the class the legislature intended to benefit, contrasts sharply with statutory language customarily found in laws enacted for the protection of the general public. The Court has been especially reluctant to imply causes of action under statutes that create duties on the part of persons for the benefit of the public at large. *See, e.g., Borak v. Air New Hazard*, 359 N.Hz. 464 (1954) (no private cause of action under price-fixing statute, in favor of airline passenger where statute provided "it is the duty of every common carrier ... to establish ... just and reasonable rates").

There would be far less reason to infer a private remedy in favor of individual persons in this case if the legislature, instead of drafting Section 901 with an unmistakable focus on the benefitted class, had written it simply as a prohibition against the disbursement of public funds to educational institutions engaged in discriminatory practices. Because the right to be free of discrimination is a personal one, a statute conferring such a right will almost have to be phrased in terms of the persons benefitted. Unquestionably, therefore, the first of the two factors favors the implication of a private cause of action. Section 901 explicitly confers a benefit on persons discriminated against on the basis of sex, and Ms. Peck is clearly a member of that class for whose special benefit the statute was enacted.

## B.

Second, a private remedy should not be implied if it would frustrate the underlying purpose of the legislative scheme. On the other hand, when that remedy is necessary or at least helpful to the accomplishment of the statutory purpose, this Court is decidedly receptive to its implication under the statute.

Based on the language of Section 901, we can infer that the Legislature sought to accomplish two related, but nevertheless somewhat different, objectives. First, it apparently wanted to avoid the use of public resources to support discriminatory practices; second, it wanted to provide individual citizens effective protection against those practices.

The New Hazard Civil Rights Agency does not have the resources necessary to enforce Section 901 in a substantial number of circumstances. As a practical matter, the N.Hz.C.R.A. cannot hope to police all state-funded education programs, and even if administrative enforcement were always feasible, it often might not redress individual injuries. An implied private right of action is necessary to ensure that the fundamental purpose of Section 901, the elimination of sex discrimination in state-funded education programs, is achieved. Thus, we conclude that the award of individual relief to a private litigant who has prosecuted her own suit is not only sensible but is also fully consistent with—and in some cases even necessary to—the orderly enforcement of the statute.

## II.

When the Legislature intends private litigants to have a cause of action to support their statutory rights, the far better course is for it to specify as much when it creates those rights. But the Court has long recognized that under certain limited circumstances the failure of the Legislature to do so is not inconsistent with an intent on its part to have such a remedy available to the persons benefitted by its legislation. Section 901 presents the situation in which the two circumstances that the Court has previously identified as supportive of an implied remedy are present. We therefore conclude that Ms. Peck may maintain her lawsuit, despite the absence of any express authorization for it in the statute. The judgment of the Superior Court is reversed, and the case is remanded for further proceedings consistent with this opinion.

## CELIS v. SHINER SECURITIES CO., INC.*

### Supreme Court of New Hazard

### Decided August 29, 2002

Bell, J.

Once again, we are called upon to decide whether a private remedy is implicit in a statute not expressly providing one. Here we decide whether customers of securities brokerage firms that are required to file certain financial reports with regulatory authorities by the New Hazard Securities Act ("the Act") have an implied cause of action for damages against the brokerage firms based on misstatements contained in the reports.

Shiner Securities Inc. ("Shiner") is a securities brokerage firm registered as a broker-dealer with the New Hazard Securities Commission ("the Commission"). This case arises out of a criminal investigation into fraudulent acts by Shiner. In 1993, the Commission learned of possible violations of the Act by Shiner and its officers. In May 1993, the Commission sought and was granted an injunction barring Shiner and five of its officers from conducting business in violation of the Act. Some months later, several of Shiner's officers were indicted for a conspiracy to violate and a number of substantive violations of the record keeping and reporting regulations adopted by the Commission under Section 17(a). Four of the defendants pleaded guilty to at least one offense.

Pearl Celis ("Ms. Celis") was a customer of Shiner, who had deposited nearly $50,000 in an investment account. After the criminal investigation became public, she sued Shiner, alleging that as a result of the acts of concealment by Shiner's officers, she did not learn that Shiner had consistently lost money for its customers during the period in which she was investing with the firm. Ms. Celis sought $40,000 in damages. The New Hazard Superior Court dismissed the complaint, holding that no claim for relief was stated because no private cause of action could be implied from Section 17(a).

### I.

The question of the existence of an implied private cause of action is, of course, one of statutory construction. *See Peck v. Iammarino*, 441 N.Hz. 677 (1987). As with any case involving the interpretation of a statute, our

---

* Based on *Touche Ross & Co. v. Redington*, 442 U.S. 560 (1979).

analysis must begin with the language of the statute itself. The statute provides:

> Every broker or dealer who transacts a business in securities shall make, keep, and preserve for such periods, such accounts, correspondence, memoranda, papers, books, and other records, and make such reports, as the New Hazard Securities Commission by its rules and regulations may prescribe as necessary or appropriate in the public interest or for the protection of investors.

N.Hz. Business & Commerce Code § 17(a). In addition to the statute, we must consider the two-factor test set forth in *Ashe v. DeLaCort*, 422 N.Hz. 66 (1975).

### A.   Is Ms. Celis Within the Class of Persons Protected by the Statute?

This statute simply requires broker-dealers and others to keep such records and file such reports as the Commission may prescribe. It does not, by its terms, purport to create a private cause of action in favor of anyone. It is true that in the past our cases have held that in certain circumstances a private right of action may be implied in a statute not expressly providing one. But in those cases finding such implied private remedies, the statute in question at least prohibited certain conduct or created legal rights in favor of private parties. *See, e.g., Peck; Cacophony & Harmony Railway Co. v. Rigsby*, 241 N.Hz. 33 (1922).

By contrast, Section 17(a) neither confers rights on private parties nor proscribes any conduct as unlawful. The intent of Section 17(a) is evident from its face. Section 17(a) is like provisions in countless other statutes that simply require certain regulated businesses to keep records and file periodic reports to enable the relevant governmental authorities to perform their regulatory functions. The reports and records provide the regulatory authorities with the necessary information to oversee compliance with and enforce the various statutes and regulations with which they are concerned. The information contained in the Section 17(a) reports is intended to provide the Commission and other authorities with a sufficiently early warning to enable them to take appropriate action to protect investors before the financial collapse of the particular broker-dealer involved. But Section 17(a) does not by any stretch of its language purport to confer private damages rights or, indeed, any remedy in the event the regulatory authorities are unsuccessful in achieving their objectives and the broker becomes insolvent before corrective steps can be taken. In short, there is no basis in the language of Section 17(a) for inferring that a civil cause of action for damages lay in favor of anyone.

### B.   Will the Purpose of Section 17(a) Be Frustrated by Not Implying a Private Right of Action?

Under *Ashe*, we must also must consider whether an implied private remedy is necessary to "effectuate the purpose of the statute." The mere fact that Section 17(a) was designed to provide protection for brokers' customers does not require the implication of a private damages action in their behalf. More importantly, implying a private right of action would interfere with enforcement of the statute by the Commission. Where there is an administrative agency charged with investigating and remedying violations of a statute, we are hesitant to imply a right of action in favor of private citizens. The Legislature intended to centralize enforcement authority with the Commission. This regulatory scheme provides the agency with discretion to determine appropriate levels of enforcement and punishment. Perhaps some violations of Section 17(a) are merely technical or inconsequential. The law does not concern itself with trifles. But a private citizen whose investments have lost money may nevertheless be tempted to sue a broker on the basis of a minor infraction in the Section 17(a) reporting requirements. Permitting a private right of action in this case would clearly invite litigation by aggrieved investors and would interfere with the regulatory discretion that enables the Commission to carry out the salutary goal of protecting investors from fraud.

## II.

Obviously, nothing we have said prevents the Legislature of this State from creating a private right of action on behalf of brokerage firm customers for losses arising from misstatements contained in Section 17(a) reports. But if the Legislature intends those customers to have such a private right of action, it is well aware of how it may effectuate that intent. The judgment of the Superior Court is affirmed.

## Problem 9

The Young Pathfinders is a nonprofit, volunteer-run organization located in the very small state of New Hazard. It describes itself as "an association dedicated to instilling values in young men and preparing them to make ethical choices over their lifetimes in achieving their full potential." *See* Pathfinder Charter ¶ 3. To this end the local Pathfinders organization plans a variety of activities for the boys of New Hazard. (Girls are not permitted to become Pathfinders.) Pathfinders help clean up the city streets, work at soup kitchens, and collect newspapers for recycling. As a reward for this hard work, and as a further means of teaching Pathfinder values to the boys, adult leaders periodically take the boys on hikes, canoe outings, and camping trips. The Pathfinders organization does not own or lease any building or other facility for meetings. Instead, adult Pathfinder leaders conduct meetings at their houses. The nature trips, of course, take place outdoors.

In order to become a Pathfinder according to the organization's by-laws, a boy must pay his membership dues, purchase a uniform, and swear the Pathfinder Oath. *See* Pathfinder By–Laws ¶ 1. The Oath is set forth in the by-laws, and reads as follows:

> I swear on the name of Almighty God that I will do my best to obey the Pathfinder Code, to help other people at all times, to keep myself physically strong, mentally awake, and morally straight.

*See* Pathfinder By–Laws ¶ 2. Adult Pathfinder leaders, who must be men, are required to comply with the same requirements, including taking the Oath. In addition, under the by-laws, each adult leader must certify that he is not a convicted felon, a homosexual, or an atheist. *See id.* ¶ 4. The Pathfinder Code, which the boys and adult leaders all promise to obey, states that a Pathfinder is "trustworthy, loyal, helpful, friendly, courteous, kind, obedient, cheerful, thrifty, brave, clean, and reverent." *See* Pathfinder Charter ¶ 2.

The Pathfinders are funded through membership dues paid by the boys and the adult leaders. Additionally, Pathfinders conduct door-to-door sales of candy and cookies, the proceeds of which help fund the organization.

Wendel Black, a schoolteacher, lives with his male partner in New Hazard. Wendel's sexual orientation is commonly known in town, but it has never adversely affected his standing in the community. Indeed, parents of the children he teaches at New Hazard Elementary School report that he is an excellent teacher who is well liked by his students. (When Wendel was a young boy he was a Pathfinder. He attained the rank of Bull Moose, the highest rank a boy can reach.) Because he enjoys working with children and has fond memories of his days as a Pathfinder, Wendel applied to be an adult Pathfinder leader. He paid his dues, bought his uniform, and swore the Pathfinder Oath. However, the organization rejected his application and returned his dues, citing a provision in the Pathfinder by-laws that prohibits accepting gay adults as volunteer leaders.

Bradley Adelle is a twelve year-old boy from New Hazard who has always wanted to become a Pathfinder. He paid his dues and purchased his uniform, but refused to take the Pathfinder oath. Bradley and his family are atheists, and Bradley believed he could not in good conscience swear "on the name of Almighty God." He was willing to affirm "on his honor" that he would follow the Pathfinder Code, but was unwilling to express belief in a supreme being, as required by the Oath. Because of his refusal to take the Oath, the Pathfinders declined his application and returned his dues.

You are a new associate at a prominent civil rights law firm in New Hazard. Wendel and Bradley have come to your firm seeking advice. Your boss, Senior Partner Ginsburg, has asked you to analyze whether one or both of your clients has a claim against the Pathfinders under the New Hazard Civil Rights Act. Please analyze only the claims that might arise under New Hazard Civil Code Chapter 51, and do not consider any federal or state constitutional claims against the Pathfinders or any federal or state constitutional defenses that the Pathfinders may assert.

**NEW HAZARD CODES**
**CIVIL CODE**
**DIVISION 1. PERSONS**
**PART 2. PERSONAL RIGHTS**

## Chapter 51: New Hazard Civil Rights Act

§ 1.   It is the purpose of this Act—

(a) to provide a clear and comprehensive mandate for the elimination of discrimination against individuals;

(b) to provide clear, strong, consistent, enforceable standards addressing discrimination against individuals;

(c) in particular to promote equality between men and women. [§ 1(c) amended on January 1, 1994].

§ 2.  This Chapter shall be known, and may be cited, as the New Hazard Civil Rights Act.

§ 3.  As used in this Chapter, unless the context otherwise requires:

(a) "Business establishment" includes any public library or educational institution, or schools of special instruction, or nursery schools, or day care centers or children's camps; provided that nothing contained in this definition shall be construed to include or apply to any institute, bona fide club, or place of accommodation or employment, which is by its nature distinctly private, including fraternal organizations, nor shall anything contained in this definition apply to any educational facility, columbarium, crematory, mausoleum, or cemetery operated or maintained by a bona fide religious or sectarian institution; and,

(b) "Sex" includes pregnancy.

§ 4.  All persons within the jurisdiction of this state are free and equal, and no matter what their sex, race, color, religion, creed, ancestry, national origin, marital status or disability are entitled to the full and equal accommodations, employment opportunities, advantages, facilities, privileges, or services in all business establishments.

§ 5.  Any person injured under this Chapter has a direct cause of action in the New Hazard Superior Court.

## GUTIERREZ v. BURNETT, DIRECTOR, NEW HAZARD DEPARTMENT OF PUBLIC TRANSPORTATION

Supreme Court of New Hazard

Decided May 10, 1998

Radin, J.

Alva Gutierrez, a Mexican–American citizen of New Hazard, brought an action challenging an English-only rule enacted by the New Hazard Department of Public Transportation. She alleged that the rule violated Chapter 51 of the New Hazard Civil Code, which prohibits discrimination on the basis of ancestry or national origin. The New Hazard Superior Court granted the Department's motion for summary judgment, and Gutierrez appealed. We reverse.

Facts

The New Hazard Department of Public Transportation employs Alva Gutierrez and a number of other Spanish-speaking employees as city bus drivers. Ms. Gutierrez has held her position since 1978. In March, 1984, the

Department promulgated a new personnel rule which forbade employees to speak any language other than English.

Ms. Gutierrez filed this action against John W. Burnett, the Director of the Department, seeking monetary damages, injunctive relief, and attorneys fees. In her Superior Court complaint, Ms. Gutierrez contends that the personnel rule constitutes national origin discrimination with respect to employment in violation of New Hazard Civil Code Chapter 51. The Superior Court granted the Department's motion for summary judgment, concluding that the English-only rule did not discriminate against Ms. Gutierrez on the basis of her national origin or ancestry.

Discussion

Section 4 of the New Hazard Civil Rights Act prohibits discrimination on the basis of national origin or ancestry in the enjoyment of "the full and equal accommodation, *employment*, advantages, facilities, privileges, or services in all *business establishments*." (Emphasis added.) Thus, the first question we must confront is whether the Department of Public Transportation is a "business establishment." We have no doubt that it is. The Department owns and maintains a fleet of buses that transport paying passengers in various cities in the State of New Hazard. The fact that the Department is not a profit-making venture is immaterial. The bus system is a "business establishment" within the meaning of Section 4 because it engages in substantially the same business as traditional profit-making enterprises, such as taxicab companies, shuttle services, and airport limousine operators. If the city buses were owned by a private company, it would be absolutely clear that the system would be a "business establishment." The mere fact of state ownership of the buses, and the Department's not-for-profit status, do not change this result.

The more difficult question we face is whether the Department restricted Ms. Gutierrez's employment on account of her national origin or ancestry. Ms. Gutierrez asserts that a regulation mandating the speaking only of English is discriminatory toward Mexican–Americans. She contends that the rule unfairly disadvantages her because her ethnic identity is linked to use of the Spanish language. The Department responds that the plain language of the statute refers only to "national origin" and not to broader concepts like "ethnic identity," so its English-only rule did not violate the statute. We reject the Department's narrow interpretation of the language in Chapter 51.

In the United States, persons of Spanish-speaking origin constitute large minorities. For many of these individuals Spanish is their primary tongue. Spanish-speaking Americans have made great contributions to the development of our diverse multicultural society and its tradition of encouraging the free exchange of ideas. The multicultural character of American society has a long and venerable history and is widely recognized as one of the United States' greatest strengths.

Language is an important aspect of national origin. The cultural identity of certain ethnic groups is tied to the use of their primary tongue.

The mere fact that an employee is bilingual does not eliminate the relationship between her primary language and the culture that is derived from his national origin. Although an individual may learn English, her primary language remains an important link to her ethnic culture and identity. The primary language not only conveys certain concepts, but is itself an affirmation of that culture.

The purpose of the New Hazard Civil Rights Act is to provide a "clear and comprehensive mandate for the elimination of discrimination." *See* N.H. Civ. Rts. Act § 1. It must be interpreted in light of this salutary purpose, which would be thwarted by a restrictive construction of the grounds of prohibited discrimination. Reading Section 4 strictly to exclude discrimination on the basis of language would allow an employer to interfere with a vital part of an individual's cultural identity—that is, her "national origin"—with impunity.

Therefore, we conclude that the Department's rule prohibiting use of languages other than English violates Chapter 51 of the New Hazard Civil Code. The district court's summary judgment in favor of the Department is REVERSED and the case is REMANDED for trial on Ms. Gutierrez's claims.

## WORTH v. DIAMOND GOLF & COUNTRY CLUB

Supreme Court of New Hazard

Decided July 15, 1993

Kernberg, J.

This case comes before us on appeal from the Superior Court. We are called upon to determine whether the New Hazard Civil Rights Act ("the Act") precludes the Appellee, Diamond Golf & Country Club, ("the club") from engaging in prohibited discrimination in its membership policies, and, in particular, whether this statute bars the Appellee from excluding women from individual membership.

Facts

The facts underlying this litigation are largely undisputed. The appellee is a nonprofit social and recreational club that is owned and operated by its membership. Appellant in the present proceeding, Chirelle Worth, an avid golfer, moved to New Hazard from New Hazard in May, 1987. She soon became interested in the appellee club after attending as a guest of several members. In New Hazard, she had found that membership in a golf club could not only be recreational but also an important source of contacts for pursuing her residential real estate business, so she was anxious to join. She asked her colleague, Farns Stein, to propose her for membership at the club. He did so, but the proposal was rejected by a vote of the board in July 1987. Mr. Stein was advised to propose Ms. Worth's husband, Jan Berg, instead. Mr. Berg would be eligible for family membership pursuant to the relevant provisions of the bylaws, to which Ms. Worth would have access. Mr. Stein and Ms. Worth angrily refused the board's offer of what—on the basis of her status as a woman—they considered second class citizenship in the club. Ms. Worth brought suit before the Superior Court.

Discussion

Section 4 of the Act provides that "[a]ll persons within the jurisdiction of this state are free and equal, and no matter what their sex, race, color, religion, creed, ancestry, national origin, marital status or disability, are entitled to the full and equal accommodations, employment opportunities, advantages, facilities, privileges, or services in all business establishments." The issue we must decide is whether the activities and operations of the club render it a "business establishment", so as to prohibit the club from excluding women from the "advantages" and "privileges" of membership.

We emphasize at the outset that our resolution of the legal issue before us does not turn upon our personal views as to the wisdom or morality of the exclusionary membership policy challenged in this case. Instead, our task involves a question of statutory interpretation.

As a remedial, civil rights statute, the Act is to be liberally construed to achieve its object and to promote justice. Although it has been broadly construed, the Act has its limits. The preamble places a premium not only on strong standards, but on clear, enforceable ones. The language of the Act, its historical background, and the past decisions of this court interpreting the statutory provisions establish that a distinctly private bona fide club would not constitute a "business establishment" within the meaning of the Act.

This does not mean that an entity is excluded from the ambit of the Act simply because it is private or non-profit, as the examples listed in Section 3 indicate. Similarly, an entity is not invariably immune from the nondiscrimination mandate of the Act simply because it exhibits some of the attributes of a bona fide club.

Rather, courts must consider a wide range of factors to determine whether the entity has sufficient businesslike attributes to be a "business establishment" within the broad meaning of the Act, or whether by its distinctly private nature it falls within the more narrow realm of a bona fide club.

In this case, there are not sufficient businesslike attributes. The appellant acknowledges that the club admits members only on a selective basis. They have to be proposed by existing members and are investigated and interviewed. The record indicates that appellee's financial support comes almost exclusively from dues and fees paid by its members. Further, only invited guests of members may be admitted onto the property.

It is true that the club derives revenue from the use of its facilities, notably the cafe on the premises, by members and invited guests. However, the cafe is clearly incidental, or complementary, to the central purpose and activities of the golf club. There is no suggestion that the cafe revenue, which is quite negligible, is intended to maintain the facilities or subsidize the activities of the club. Finally, although members enjoy the opportunity to obtain advantageous business contacts provided by club membership, on its own this attribute is insufficient to classify the club's activities as business-related.

For these reasons, the club cannot be said to be a "business establishment" within the meaning of this Act. It is unnecessary to consider whether the actions of the club constitute discrimination on the basis of sex or marital status.

The judgment of the Superior Court is AFFIRMED.

*

# INDEX

†